THE TEMPLE
IN ANCIENT EGYPT

THE TEMPLE
IN ANCIENT EGYPT

New discoveries and recent research

Edited by Stephen Quirke

Published for the Trustees of the British Museum
by British Museum Press

First published in 1997 by British Museum Press
A division of The British Museum Company Ltd
46 Bloomsbury Street, London WC1B 3QQ

A catalogue record for this book is available from the British Library

ISBN 0-7141-0993-2

Printed in Great Britain by Henry Ling Ltd,
The Dorset Press, Dorchester, Dorset

Jan Quaegebeur
in memoriam

Contents

Editorial foreword viii

Rainer Stadelmann 1
The development of the pyramid temple in the Fourth Dynasty

Paule Posener-Kriéger 17
News from Abusir

Stephen Quirke 24
Gods in the temple of the king: Anubis at Lahun

Christian Leblanc 49
Quelques reflexions sur le programme iconographique et la fonction des temples de "millions d'années"

Betsy Bryan 57
The statue program for the mortuary temple of Amenhotep III

Charles Bonnet and Dominique Valbelle 82
The Middle Kingdom temple of Hathor at Serabit el-Khadim

Jaromir Malek 90
The temples at Memphis. Problems highlighted by the EES survey

Christine Favard-Meeks 102
The temple of Behbeit el-Hagara

Sue Davies and H.S. Smith 112
Sacred Animal temples at Saqqara

Susanne Woodhouse 132
The sun god, his four Bas and the four winds in the sacred district at Sais: the fragment of an obelisk (BM EA 1512)

Dieter Kurth 152
The present state of research into Graeco-Roman temples

Jan Quaegebeur 159
Excavating the forgotten temple of Shenhur (Upper Egypt)

Claude Traunecker 168
Lessons from the Upper Egyptian temple of el-Qal'a

Penelope Wilson 179
Slaughtering the crocodile at Edfu and Dendera

Olaf E Kaper 204
A painting of the gods of Dakhla in the temple of Ismant el-Kharab

John Baines 216
Temples as symbols, guarantors, and participants in Egyptian civilization

Black and white plates

Colour plates

Editorial foreword

The title of this collection of papers is taken from the British Museum colloquium 'the Temple in Ancient Egypt', held by the Department of Egyptian Antiquities on 21-22 July 1994. On that occasion the speakers included Rainer Stadelmann, the late Paule Posener-Kriéger, Betsy Bryan, Charles Bonnet and Dominique Valbelle, Jaromir Malek, Dieter Kurth, the late Jan Quaegebeur, Claude Traunecker and Olaf Kaper. Speakers at the colloquium were invited to submit their contributions for publication. Invitation was also made to John Baines, who closed the colloquium with a summary of work, as well as to other colleagues working in the field. The additional papers received were from Christian Leblanc, Christine Favard-Meeks, Professor H.S. Smith and Sue Davies, Susanne Woodhouse and Penelope Wilson. Publication has been substantially aided by a generous grant from the Raymond and Beverly Sackler Foundation, for which the Museum offers its particular thanks.

The editor is deeply grateful to his colleagues at British Museum Press, in particular Joanna Champness, for unstinting assistance and practical suggestions. He also expresses his debt of gratitude to his colleagues in the Department of Egyptian Antiquities, above all Claire Thorne, without whose expertise and support this volume could not have been completed.

It is the particular wish of the Keeper and all colleagues in the Department to dedicate this volume to the memory of Jan Quaegebeur, whose contribution to the colloquium, published here, testifies once again to his profound insight and the range of his application in the epigraphic and philological branches of Egyptology. The cruel fate which has deprived us of his presence can do nothing to diminish our appreciation of all his many achievements, not least among them the project to rescue the forgotten temple of Shenhur, the object of his attention here. We wish also to remember Paule Posener-Kriéger, who to the last continued to move forward our understanding of the precious if fragmentary papyri of the Pyramid Age, a meticulous research in which none could rival her.

Rather than arranging the papers in one alphabetic sequence by name of contributor, I have grouped them into the three sections as they emerged from the discussions at the colloquium itself.

Temples for the royal cult

The first group addresses the temples to the cult of the king, beginning with the pyramid complexes of the Old and Middle Kingdoms. Rainer Stadelmann provides a direct and radical reinterpretation of the early development of the royal pyramid, by taking the pyramid complex as a whole and not as isolated elements of chambers inside and outside the pyramid. The late lamented Paule Posener-Kriéger presented at the colloquium some of her findings from the new Czech discoveries of papyrus archive debris at Abusir, source material complementing and completing the evidence of architecture and archaeology; her paper is reproduced here in homage to a great hieraticist, whose publication of the Abusir papyri has made an economic history of the pyramid complex possible and accessible to scholarship. The paper by the editor takes the Middle Kingdom equivalent to the Abusir papyri, the fragmentary mass of manuscript from Lahun, and seeks to place the pyramid complex of Senusret II there in its diachronic context within a monumental history of cult where the focus ostensibly shifts from king to gods.

Christian Leblanc carries the theme of royal cult into the New Kingdom with a review of the dominant motifs of the temples of millions of years, where king and local main deity fuse. His paper concentrates on Thebes, which is likewise the setting for the most extraordinary sculptural programme in Egyptian history, as revealed by Betsy Bryan in her contribution on the statuary from the temple for the cult of Amenhotep III on the Theban West Bank. Bryan returns the architecture and its sculpture to the rituals which demanded them; this enables us to understand and appreciate Egyptian art in a radically different setting, original to the civilization.

Temples for the cults of the gods

The following five papers concern temples with a different intended main occupant, those built for the cult of a god or goddess rather than primarily for the cult of the king. Dominique Valbelle and Charles Bonnet present one of the most unusual shrines of Egypt, on desert ground in Sinai, the temple of Hathor at Serabit el-Khadim. The full publication of their work has since appeared as a monograph; this shorter account is an important reminder, in this wider collection of papers, of the existence of Egyptian temples outside the Nile Valley already in the Middle Kingdom. From periphery to centre, Jaromir Malek demonstrates two unexpected solutions to the questions of the principal temple at Memphis, first that of Ptah, and then that of the Aten. Although Memphis has suffered extreme destruction and neglect, the scant evidence can be used to put forward and then test hypotheses, here in the expert knowledge of the site topography and the inscribed fragments scattered over the site and across collections. Christine Favard-Meeks discusses the more dramatic but equally neglected ruins of one of the greatest masterpieces of Pharaonic architecture, the temple of Isis at Behbeit el-Hagara. Her contribution is also an urgent appeal to the scholarly and wider community to rescue the temple from its undeserved oblivion. Recently she has found it impossible, not least for lack of adequate funding, to fulfil her wish to excavate and restore the temple, but it is planned to produce a CD-ROM publication on the site, a project also meriting the support of Egyptologists. Sue Davies and Professor Smith take the evidence for animal temples at the necropolis of Memphis in the Late Period, now virtually invisible on the rock face at Saqqara, but once a series of sanctuaries equal in scale and magnificence to the temple of Horus at Edfu. They investigate, too, the disputed question of the relation between animal cults and the local population, and suggest wide participation in the cults founded and promoted by the king. As a starting-point to studying another lost religious complex, the temples of Sais, Susanne Woodhouse takes a monument unique in the surviving record, a four-sided column with tapering summit, like an obelisk, but crowned with a falcon. From parallel inscriptions she is able to suggest an interpretation for the monument, relocating it in the history of similar monuments and in the geographical setting of the Osirian burial shrine at Sais evoked by the classical authors.

Temples of the Ptolemaic and Roman Periods

The last group of papers concerns the temples of the Ptolemaic and Roman Periods, including some of the best preserved examples of religious architecture and text from the ancient world. The field is dominated by the sandstone temples of Upper Egypt, in the first rank Dendera, Edfu, Esna, Kom Ombo and Philae, but numerous other survivals of the period are emerging for study as publication and excavation proceeds throughout the Nile Valley and in the oases of the western desert. By the accident of their material, the great southern Upper Egyptian temples, along with other smaller structures, escaped the burning of stone for lime in the fourth and fifth centuries AD. That late and devastating instance of the Egyptian practice of recycling building materials, in a destructive programme itself of monumental scale, removed from the landscape the vast majority of limestone sanctuaries at the time of the Christianisation of late Roman Egypt. As a result of being built in sandstone the originally more remote sanctuaries of the south now preserve a mass of architectural and inscriptional data. This colossal database remains largely at the primary stages of study - discovery and first publication.

The terrain is so extensive that it requires some introduction, here expertly provided by Dieter Kurth in his summary of this specialised branch of Egyptology as far as it has progressed by the early 1990s. Two fine case studies from this group are represented in this volume by Claude Traunecker and the late Jan Quaegebeur. For several years Claude Traunecker has worked with Laura Pantalucci on publication of the early Roman Period shrine at el-Qal'a, which gives another instance of a shrine preserved from destruction by the choice of building stone; it is constructed of a fossil-rich limestone which defeated the late Roman lime-burners, and all but defeated the sculptors charged with decorating the walls in relief. At the time of his death Jan Quaegebeur was working together with Traunecker on the publication of the substantial but curiously forgotten temple at Shenhur. As elsewhere, their work sets standards of historical discipline for scholarship of all periods; they do not exclude material outside the segment of history of most interest to them personally, but instead, whatever the century of the evidence they encounter, they have responded with exact recording of the detail and with wider interpretation. The study of temple inscriptions of Ptolemaic and Roman Period date is represented here by the article by Penelope Wilson on a curiously divisive Upper Egyptian phenomenon of the period, the crocodile cults and their opposite, crocodile-slaying, at Edfu and Dendera. Her detailed account of the texts and their vocabulary demonstrates the potential for research in this vast ancient database. Finally, Olaf Kaper transports us once more out of the Nile Valley to the western oases; he homes in on one recently discovered painting of the Roman Period and deploys it with other evidence from the area as a key to the cult topography of this region in its links with Nile towns and their deities.

The volume is brought to a close, as was the 1994 colloquium, by John Baines in an elegant and comprehensive review of the role of the temple across Egyptian history.

The development of the pyramid temple in the Fourth Dynasty

Rainer Stadelmann

During the Third Dynasty the pyramid evolved to become the monumental royal tomb in the form of a steep step pyramid surrounded by a rectangular precinct oriented north-south. To date only the pyramid complex of Netjerchet Djoser has been completely excavated (PM III[2] 399 - 415; Lauer 1936 and id. 1962; Ricke 1944; Kaiser 1969; Edwards 1985; Stadelmann 1985, 35-72; id. 1990, 54-74). Within its vast area a number of rather disconnected units of courts, chapels and altars are distributed. There are two large courts to the south and to the north of the step pyramid, each with a big altar overlooking the court and belonging respectively to the south tomb and to the pyramid tomb in the north extension of the precinct (fig.1). The long monumental entrance hall with its eastern gate and the vestibule at its western end forms an inner causeway (MRA III 52; rejected by Lauer 1967, 245-6). The eastern part of the precinct is occupied by a range of courts and chapels (fig.1).The so-called Heb-Sed Court is directly connected with the entrance hall through a narrow corridor and has a range of chapels to the east and west attributed and identified by their facades to the gods and numina of the two lands, north and south.

Then follow two large and spacious courts each with a voluminous solid building at its northern end and identified by the decoration of the facades of the courts and buildings as "maison du sud" and "maison du nord", the chapels of the king of Upper Egypt and the king of Lower Egypt.

The following large court with the so-called serdab-chapel lies to the north of the pyramid tomb (fig. 1). This may have been the purification place before entering the pyramid temple and the offering chapel for the entrance to the pyramid tomb.The fact that all these chapels are solid buildings has been highly overestimated in previous studies. On closer inspection these apparently solid chapels and "maisons" reveal a close resemblance to the chapels of the later pyramid temples. Like those they contain a deep niche in which a statue of a god or the king probably rested.The main difference is the fact that the chapels in the Djoser complex were free standing whereas the chapels of the later pyramid temples were incorporated into a building of solid masonry.

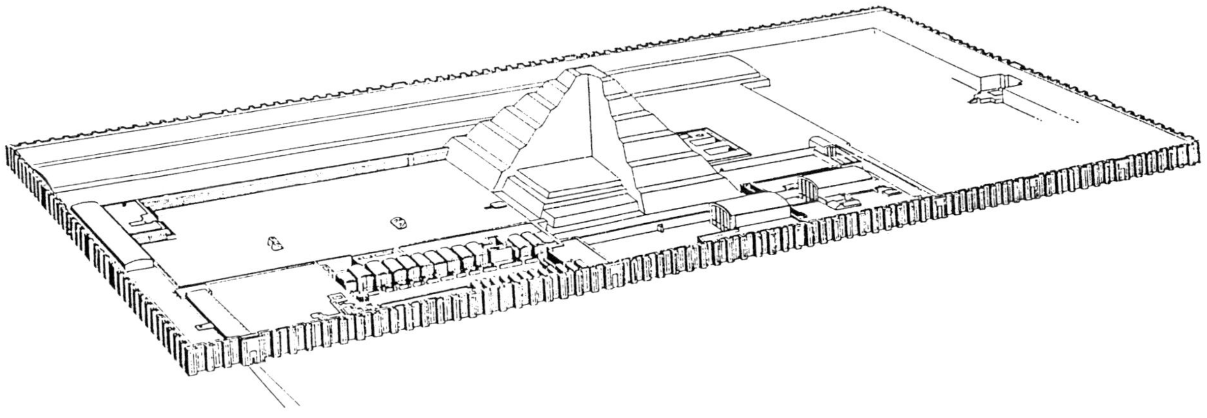

Fig. 1 Sakkara. Djoser Precinct. Reconstructed view (this, and all other figures in this article, by Nairi Hampikian).

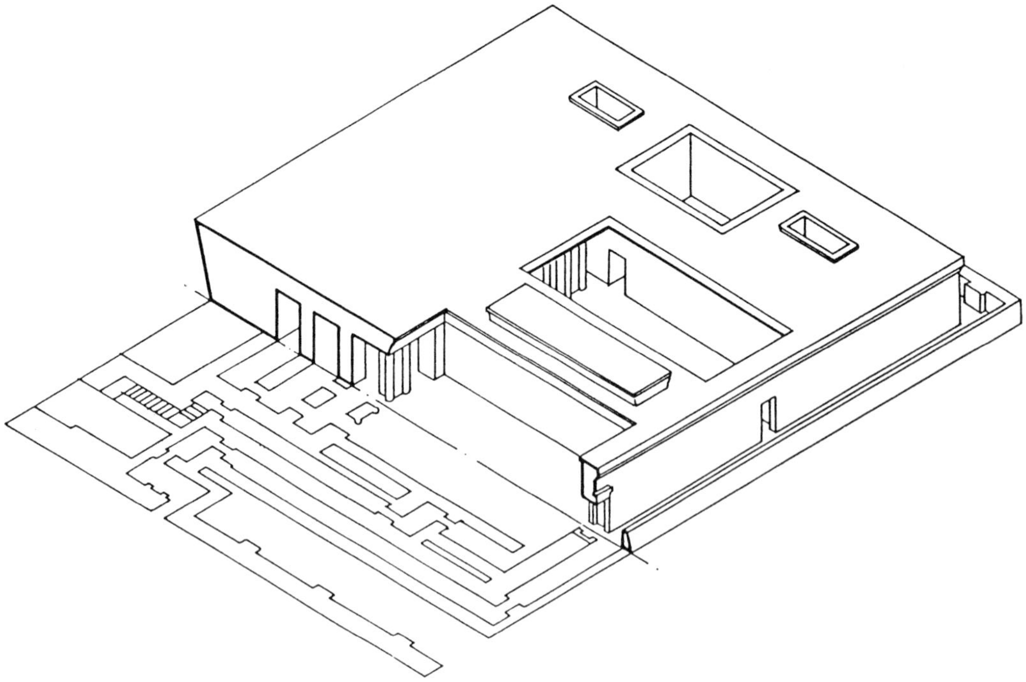

Fig. 2 Sakkara. Djoser Precinct . Mortuary Temple on the north of the pyramid.

The real funerary temple of Djoser lies on the north side of the pyramid (fig. 2). It shows already the partition into an inner temple section, the funerary temple proper, probably with two funerary chapels and most likely two false doors (Stadelmann 1991, 65), and a more open temple section, the "Verehrungstempel", with two entrances, two open courts, and also two slaughterhouses in accordance with the strict observance of the division of the cultic installations for Upper and Lower Egypt. These different cultic installations were surely not conceived and erected each according to a separate plan, but rather evolved and grew together within the development of the whole complex to become a unity, that is a sequence of cult installations and stations which were all necessary to function together for the eternal cult of the dead king (Kaiser 1969; Lauer 1988, 5-11; Stadelmann 1991).

The succeeding pyramid precincts of the Third Dynasty, those of Sechemchet at Sakkara (PM III [2] 415-17) and the Layer Pyramid at Zawiet el-Ariyan (PM III[2] 313) are not yet completely excavated and properly investigated.

A new development begins with the pyramids of Snofru, first king of the Fourth Dynasty. Whereas the great mastaba tombs of the First and Second Dynasty at Sakkara and the pyramid precincts of the Third Dynasty were strictly aligned north-south, the new pyramid complexes of the Fourth Dynasty, beginning with the step pyramid of Snofru and its precinct at Meidum, were oriented east-west in accordance with the course of the sun (Stadelmann 1985, 82). This new alignment from east to west in the form of a strict sequence of valley temple, causeway, pyramid temple and pyramid tomb is most perfectly established at Giza.

Where and how did the development take place from a more or less open and possibly random order in the complex of Djoser to the strict sequence of the Giza temples ?

At Meidum we find already the new east-west orientation, a long causeway leading from the cultivated land up to the pyramid, a pyramid town - not yet discovered but at least attested by textual evidence, and a kind of gateway or protovalley temple. The cult installation at the pyramid, however, does not fit into the anticipated or expected evolution (fig. 3).

Nor did the cult installations of the Bent Pyramid at Dahshur excavated by Ahmed Fakhry (Fakhry 1959-61) conform to the development proposed by Herbert Ricke (1950, 41ff.). This cult place proved to be an almost identical repetition of the small installation at Meidum: two enormous stelae - originally about nine metres high - in an open court, an offering altar covered or roofed over by large stone slabs resting on two stone walls and a small antechamber or vestibule (fig. 4).

An open causeway led down to a valley temple in a now sandy valley which might, however, have been a lake or lagoon in ancient times, flooded during the inundation season. Ahmed Fakhry remarked that the causeway had a kind of brick plastering or cover laid over the original limestone pavement (Fakhry 1959, 106 and figs. 59-61). I wonder if this brick plaster was not the remains of a brick filling which closed the causeway completely after its abandonment for the burial of Snofru in the Northern Pyramid. The causeway of Sahure was perhaps already blocked by a wall at the exit of the valley temple after the burial had passed the causeway. The observation that a causeway became obsolete and was closed after the burial procession had passed through it would also explain why and how Newosere could afford to divert the causeway of his venerated father Neferirkare for his own use.

Snofru's valley temple displays already the main features of the later valley temples of the Fourth Dynasty (pl. 1a and fig. 5). From the outside it is a rectangular, block-like structure with

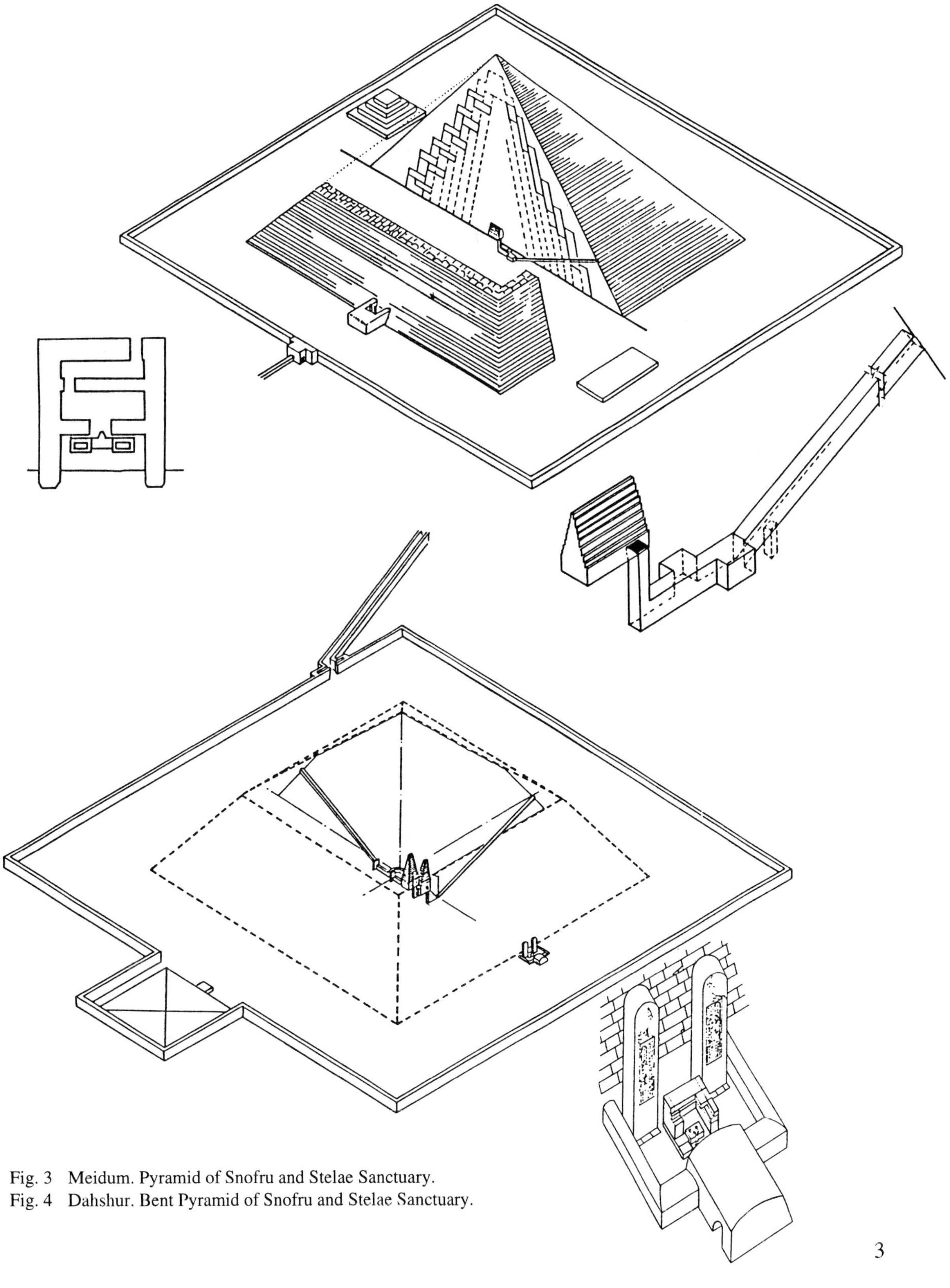

Fig. 3 Meidum. Pyramid of Snofru and Stelae Sanctuary.
Fig. 4 Dahshur. Bent Pyramid of Snofru and Stelae Sanctuary.

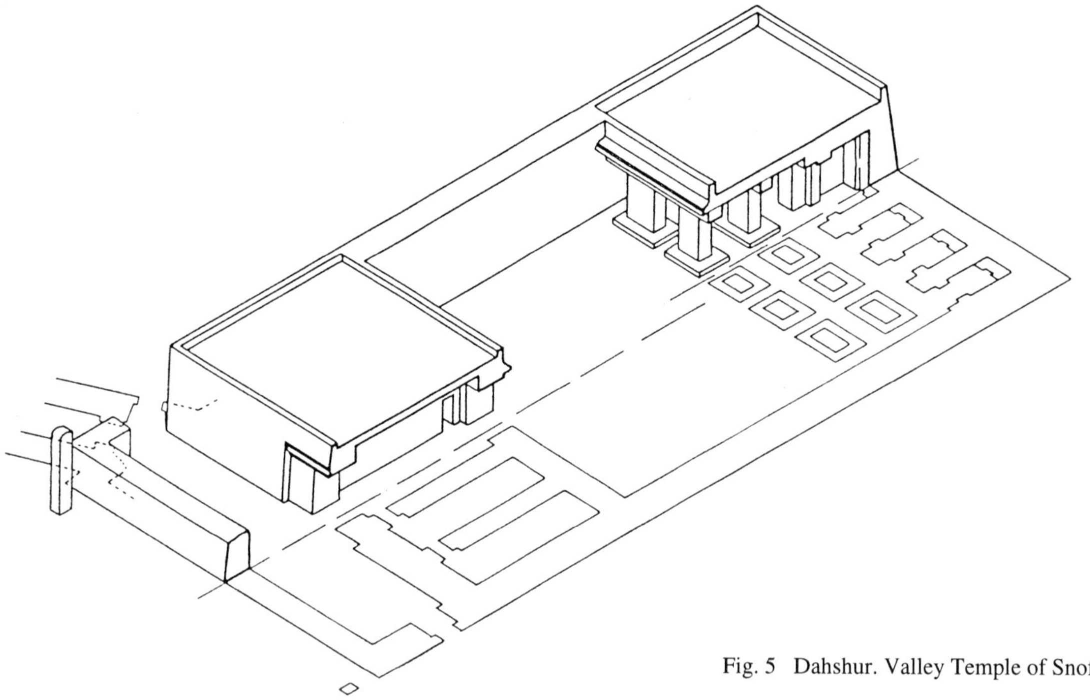

Fig. 5 Dahshur. Valley Temple of Snofru.

severe undecorated facades; two stelae on the south front identify the royal owner, and between them is a rather unobtrusive entrance. The causeway passes the temple lateral. On either side of the entrance vestibule, decorated with the figures representing the estates of Snofru in Upper and Lower Egypt, lie two large magazines. A wide, open court is faced on its northern side by a pillared portico, which leads into a row of six chapels. The pillars and the walls under the portico are decorated with relief scenes showing the king in the presence of various deities, among them a fragment of Snofru embracing Bastet. This reminds us that the two main goddesses of the valley temples of Giza were Bastet and Hathor (Hölscher 1912, 16-17). In the chapels stood over-lifesize figures of Snofru, most probably connected with the rear wall, which thus functioned as a back pillar plate. Two of the fragments bear the white crown; no other crown fragment was found.

Also remarkable is the orientation of the valley temple to the north in a direct line to the Northern Pyramid of Snofru, his final burial pyramid. I have no doubts that the valley temple was finally designed and built in this direction during the last two decades of Snofru's reign when the Northern Pyramid was under construction.

The expectations for finding the missing link in the evolution from the Djoser complex to the Giza temples rested thus on the Northern Pyramid of Snofru at Dahshur. In autumn 1980 the German Institute of Archaeology obtained the necessary permissions and began excavating at and around the Northern Pyramid, the so-called Red Pyramid of Snofru (Stadelmann 1982; id. 1983; id. 1993). The slopes of the pyramid were covered by enormous heaps of debris, up to seventeen metres high and twenty-five to thirty metres deep (pl. 1b). As we did not know what remains could be expected the excavation work was confined to manual labor. Every single stone was examined for its form, structure and remains of reliefs and inscriptions. This gave us for the first time the possibility to investigate the graffiti and control notes on the casing stones on the spot and partially *in situ*.

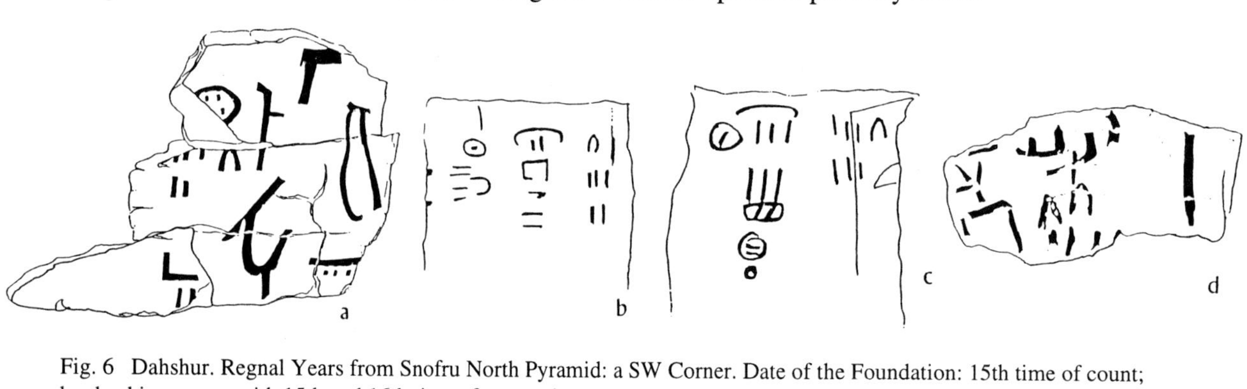

Fig. 6 Dahshur. Regnal Years from Snofru North Pyramid: a SW Corner. Date of the Foundation: 15th time of count; b-c backing stones with 15th and 16th time of count; d Fragment with a 24th time of count.

The fragments of the corner stone of the south west corner of the pyramid which we could collect and adjust provided us with the date of the placing of the corner stone (fig. 6a). It is the 15th time of counting, which, according to the system of counting in the Old Kingdom and specifically the reign of Snofru, would be his 29th year. At the east side we found further counting notes of the 15th, (fig. 6b) and the 16th time of counting (fig. 6c), i.e. the 29th and 31st years respectively, on backing stones still *in situ* in the 12th layer and the 16th layer of the casing respectively.

With these marks we can follow the progress of building (Stadelmann 1987). A fragment of a 24th time of counting (fig. 6d), i.e. the 46th year of his reign, found in the debris must have come from the top part of the pyramid (Stadelmann 1987). That the pyramid was finally completed is proved by the perfectly polished pyramidion, which we found in the debris, broken into big pieces by the stone robbers of the Middle Ages (pl. 3a). The activity of these stone robbers is also the main reason for the destruction of the cult lay-out in front of our pyramid and generally of all pyramid temples because these workmen took first the fine limestone blocks of the temples and then destroyed the rest when extracting the stones and causing them to tumble down.

When we finally reached the Old Kingdom level we realized that nothing but the foundations had been preserved. Only the front part of the temple had been finished in stone, the rear part was obviously hastily completed in brickwork perhaps even after Snofru's death (pl. 2a and b).

On the desert surface one can clearly recognize the peribolos wall of the temple area, the outer north and south walls of the temple proper, a limestone block marking the middle of the east wall, two solid limestone foundations in the north-east and south-east of the area and a foundation bed of limestone chips dividing the temple area into an eastern (front) part and a western (rear) part, where only brick walls remained.

The pyramidion in the middle has been reassembled and placed here temporarily on an existing large limestone slab. Several other limestone slabs have remained in this central part; we therefore suggest that there existed an open plastered peripheral pillared courtyard.

Among the blocks of the two limestone foundations we found fragments of relief scenes, some rather large and showing the king in a heb-sed cloak sitting on a throne (pl. 3b). These reliefs are definitely not finished, providing evidence for the uncompleted condition of the temple. Regrettably there were no graffiti with year dates surviving on the blocks of the temple. Around these stone

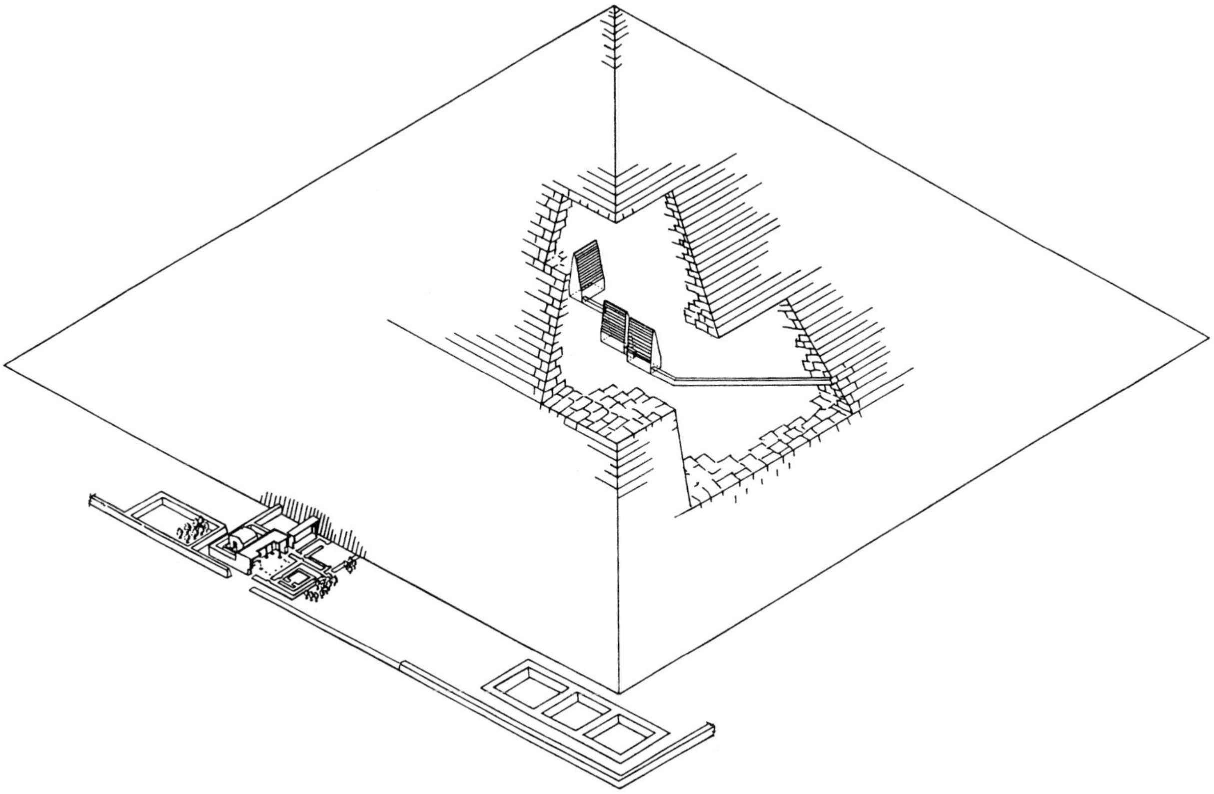

Fig. 7 Dahshur. Northern Pyramid. Isometric view and reconstruction of the Pyramid Temple.

foundations traces of brick walls are preserved. We have reinforced the existing brick walls with new bricks to protect the endangered remains from further erosion (pl. 2b).

In the centre, near the alignment of the pyramid, three thick brick walls define two rooms (pl. 2 and fig. 7). The central one is clearly the funerary chapel, the room beside a magazine which had two side entrances. The thickness of the walls indicates strongly that these rooms were covered by vaults. At the foot of the pyramid at the western end of the funerary chapel we came upon a deep excavation, not regularly done and surely modern. Inside this hole we found pieces of dark granite which may have belonged to a false door. To the south of the funerary chapel lies an open court with numerous holes still containing offering vases and bowls of stone and pottery.

At the beginning of our investigation we had expected an architectural feature such as those at Meidum or Dahshur-South at the Bent Pyramid (figs. 3 and 4), but no traces of big stelae or even their foundations were unearthed.

We therefore had to reconsider our ideas about the pyramid temple. On the basis of the findings in the royal cemetery at Abydos and at the pyramids of Meidum and Dahshur-South Reisner (1936, 307ff.), Lauer (1962, 46-50) and Ricke (1950, 14-22) had postulated a pair of stelae as the main cult place in pyramid temples of the Fourth Dynasty, neglecting the fact that from the end of the Fourth Dynasty at the Mastaba el-Faraun till to the end of the New Kingdom it was always and only a false door that marked the central cult place in the royal funerary temples. Stelae on the contrary determine tumuli or pyramids as cenotaphs or royal memorials (Stadelmann 1983, 237-41). This is evidently the case for the pyramid of Meidum and the Bent Pyramid as well as for the pyramid of Seila which had two stelae of Snofru (Swellim 1987 and Lesko 1988, 223-35), and for the so-called south pyramids, better regarded as cult pyramids for the *ka* of the king. This definition is, however, not applicable to the royal tombs at Abydos, where it is uncertain where the stelae stood. Furthermore, these tombs were definitely subterranean monuments, which, according to the new findings of Günter Dreyer, contained in their subterranean chambers several false doors leading to the west (Dreyer 1993, pl.5). The stelae may just have been indicators for the localization and identification of the flat and humble superstructures of the tombs.

The question of the false door in the early Fourth Dynasty funerary temples must be examined more closely and under different aspects (Stadelmann 1983, 237-41). The recent treatment of this subject by P. Jánosi neglects the fact that already the early dynastic royal tombs at Abydos had false doors (Jánosi 1994, 143-63).

I am convinced that a new and painstaking reinvestigation at the temples of Giza and Abu Rowash will support us with more archaeological evidence. Further evidence may be adduced from our understanding of the cultural function of the pyramid temple within the whole pyramid complex. There can be no doubt that the pyramid represents the eternal residence for the dead king. Even if his desire and hope is that his soul will be reunited with the sun-god or the stars of the northern sky, his body stays in his pyramid tomb and is in permanent need of provisions in the form of offerings. In the Third Dynasty pyramids these provisions were stored in subterranean galleries under the pyramid. In the Fourth Dynasty these provisions come in the form of daily deliveries and offerings from the different estates, the residence and other institutions. They are distributed and offered on the altar in the open court and in the funerary chapel. There is only one way for the dead king to come out from his eternal pyramid residence to participate in these offerings and this is to enter the offering/funerary chapel through the false door.

In our reconstruction of the pyramid temple of Snofru we have inserted the false door as the principal element for the transition and offering place. Of course this model of reconstruction is still open to criticism and modifications. The basic elements are more or less evident and certain but there is too much missing to be definitive. To the east of the funerary chapel we have the two stone foundations with relief blocks. They can be reassembled as two freestanding chapels for the statues of the king of Upper and Lower Egypt similar to the chapels/maisons in the precinct of Djoser. In between these chapels there was an open court with some limestone slabs for a pavement or the foundation of a pillared courtyard.

Outside the temple proper but still inside the temenos walls we found on both the north and south sides regular arrangements of deep holes, some still filled with earth. This must have been a sacred grove once attested in the Old Kingdom in a private necropolis (Fischer 1991, 130). The first certain examples around a royal tomb are the plantations at Deir el Bahari in front of Mentuhotep's tomb and much later at Kahun. I wonder, however, whether the strange holes around Khufu's and Khephren's pyramids at Giza could have contained temporary plantings (Goyon 1969, 71-7; MRA III 66-7; Lehner 1983, 8-9) .

These rather sporadic architectural elements show us, however, already the principal features of the normal pyramid temple: *the open court*, perhaps even a *pillared peristyle courtyard, two statue chapels* and the *offering chapel in the rear part.* There were no indications of a vestibule or even a more prominent entrance and we found no certain traces of a causeway if one was ever begun or accomplished.

If we now compare the remains and the plan of our temple with the pyramid temples at Giza it is extremely striking how much it resembles those of Khufu/Cheops and of Mycerinus (fig. 8). The temple of Khufu was about double the size of that of Snofru. It was entirely built in stone of different types, the walls of fine limestone, the pillared cloister of red granite, while black basalt was used for the pavement. The principal part of the temple is a large open court surrounded by a pillared cloister. There was no vestibule. The pillared cloister has a triple order in the western part. On the northern and southern sides of this deep recess lie two rooms, the equivalent to the statue chapels in the temple of

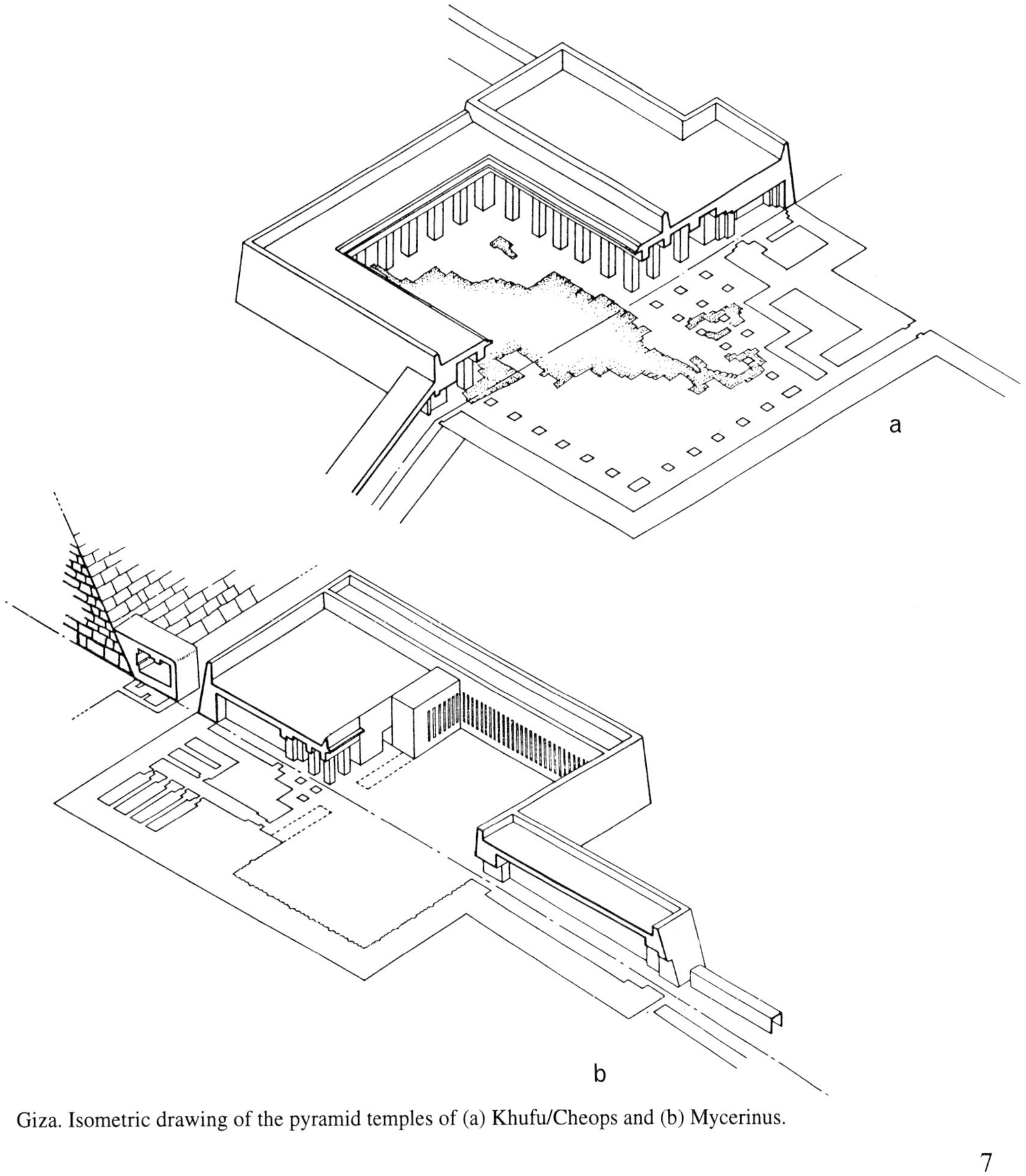

Fig. 8 Giza. Isometric drawing of the pyramid temples of (a) Khufu/Cheops and (b) Mycerinus.

Snofru. Unfortunately the western part of the temple was heavily destroyed by a large and deep shaft tomb of the Late Period. Traces on the pavement suggest that the triple portico ends in a large and deep recess which most probably contained the offering chapel with the false door and two magazines.

This kind of reconstruction is in accordance with the findings and the plan of the temple of Mycerinus. There we may also remark on the large and magnificent court decorated with carved panelling instead of a pillared cloister, and on a double portico which leads to a deep offering chapel flanked on both sides by magazines. As in Khufu's temple the statue chapels must have been located south and north to the offering chapel. The entrance to the temple is preceded by a vestibule.

Compared with the temples of Khufu and Mycerinus, the mortuary temple of Khephren seems to exhibit quite a different structure (fig. 9). Khephren has added to the above mentioned elements a massive reception building, a repetition of his valley temple. The cyclopean massive stonework of this front part conveys the impression that this temple is not constructed but cut into solid rock. The open court, with its pillared peristyle, is rectangular and seems to be hidden within the massive walls. For the first time there are five statue chapels, a number which becomes canonical later in the Fifth Dynasty. The offering room is again oblong and rather narrow. The recess in the centre of the west wall of this oblong room is clearly visible and quite impressive enough to quell all doubts about its existence.

Without the knowledge and the existence of the later temple of Mycerinus there would be no hesitation in explaining the differences between the temple of Khufu and that of Khephren as a logical evolution towards the canonical and formal funerary temple of the Fifth Dynasty. This is indeed the common explanation. The obvious dissimilarities in the Mycerinus temple are usually disregarded, being explained away as the consequence of irregularities in his reign which would have prevented completion of his temple according to a more contemporary plan.

Yet this does not seem a reasonable argument; at all events we do not know and have not the faintest trace of evidence of rivalries or family struggle for power in the Fourth Dynasty in general and specifically from the reign of Mycerinus. All such theories of strife are conjectural and lack any historical evidence.

We should therefore look carefully at the archaeological arguments. Although we archaeologists are commonly speaking about pyramid precincts, pyramid complex or pyramid ensemble, we have been constantly regarding only parts of it and investigating partial aspects: *the funerary apartments inside the pyramids* and their development or the *pyramid temples* and their evolution. Even Ricke and Schott in an ingenious but rather speculative essay on architecture and worship in royal funerary ensembles did not evaluate the correspondence of these two ensembles (Ricke and Schott 1956). They tried rather to impose a ritual observance which they intended to deduce from the pyramid texts on to the sequence of rooms in the pyramid temples and, by analogy, on to and into the funerary apartments; so also did Spiegel (1971) and finally Altenmüller (1972).

A critical reaction by Dieter Arnold to these sophistic and unsustained theories (1977) goes too far in denying any association between the pyramid temple and the funerary procession or rituals. His architectural reasoning that the procession could not have passed the mortuary temple must certainly be modified in the light of the new investigations of the pyramid precincts. It is evident that there was no other entrance into the temenos and the surrounding court but through an opening on the north side of the funerary temple at the cross point of the front temple and the rear temple. The possibility that the causeway was closed and walled up after the burial indicates that the funeral procession passed through it into the pyramid temple.

If, however, we look openmindedly and attentively at the ensemble of pyramid temples and pyramid apartments of the Fourth Dynasty, we become aware of an extraordinary fact which has until now clearly escaped the notice of archaeologists. This may be expressed succinctly in the following two complementary propositions, supported clearly by the comparison of the drawings of the funerary apartments and pyramid temples when juxtaposed, as on fig.10:

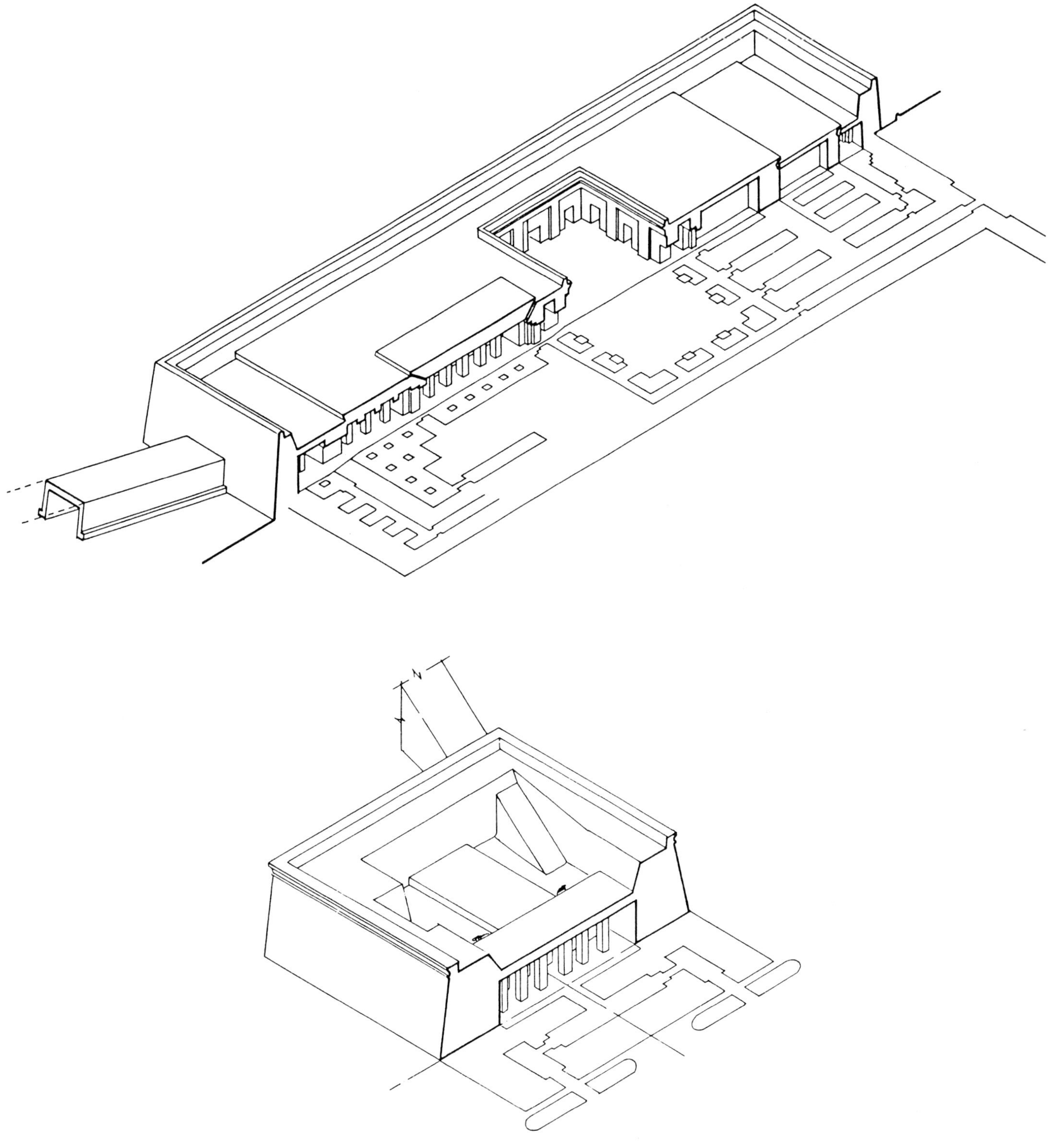

Fig. 9 Giza. Isometric drawing of the pyramid temple and the valley temple of Khephren.

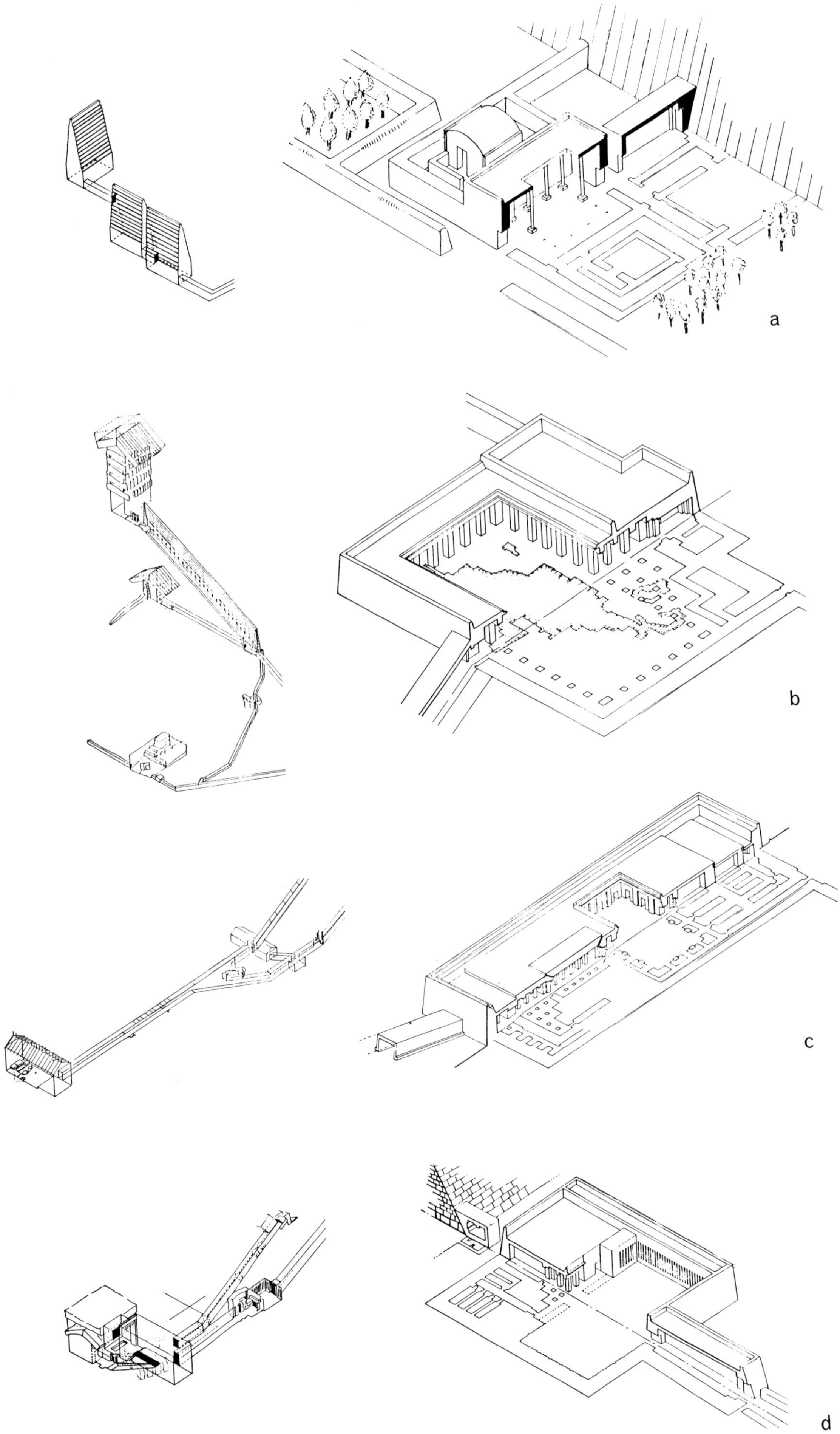

Fig. 10 Funerary apartments and pyramid temples of Snofru at Dahshur (a), and of Khufu (b), Khephren (c), Mycerinus (d) at Giza.

(1) pyramids with a sophisticated system of funerary apartments have a rather simple and distinct pyramid temple (fig. 10a-b,d);
(2) on the other hand, pyramids with a simple unsophisticated system of apartments have a rather sophisticated and complex funerary temple (fig. 10c).

These observations and reflections concern especially the front part of the funerary temple which is enlarged by a succession of rooms and halls, whereas the rear part with the offering chapel and the supposed false door remains unchanged. Yet this evidence even includes the valley temples which correspond closely to the pyramid temples both in their general appearance and in such details as the arrangement of pillars or columns in both temples.

This observation is already clear at Snofru's North Pyramid at Dahshur. The funerary apartments comprise a sequence of superb halls with high corbelled roofs. The first two apartments are only slightly different, the third one lies nearly nine metres higher. The pyramid temple is, as we have seen, very modest yet certainly also lucidly arranged and certainly planned according to an intended design (fig. 11).

The strongest evidence for this theory can be found at Giza. The funerary apartments inside

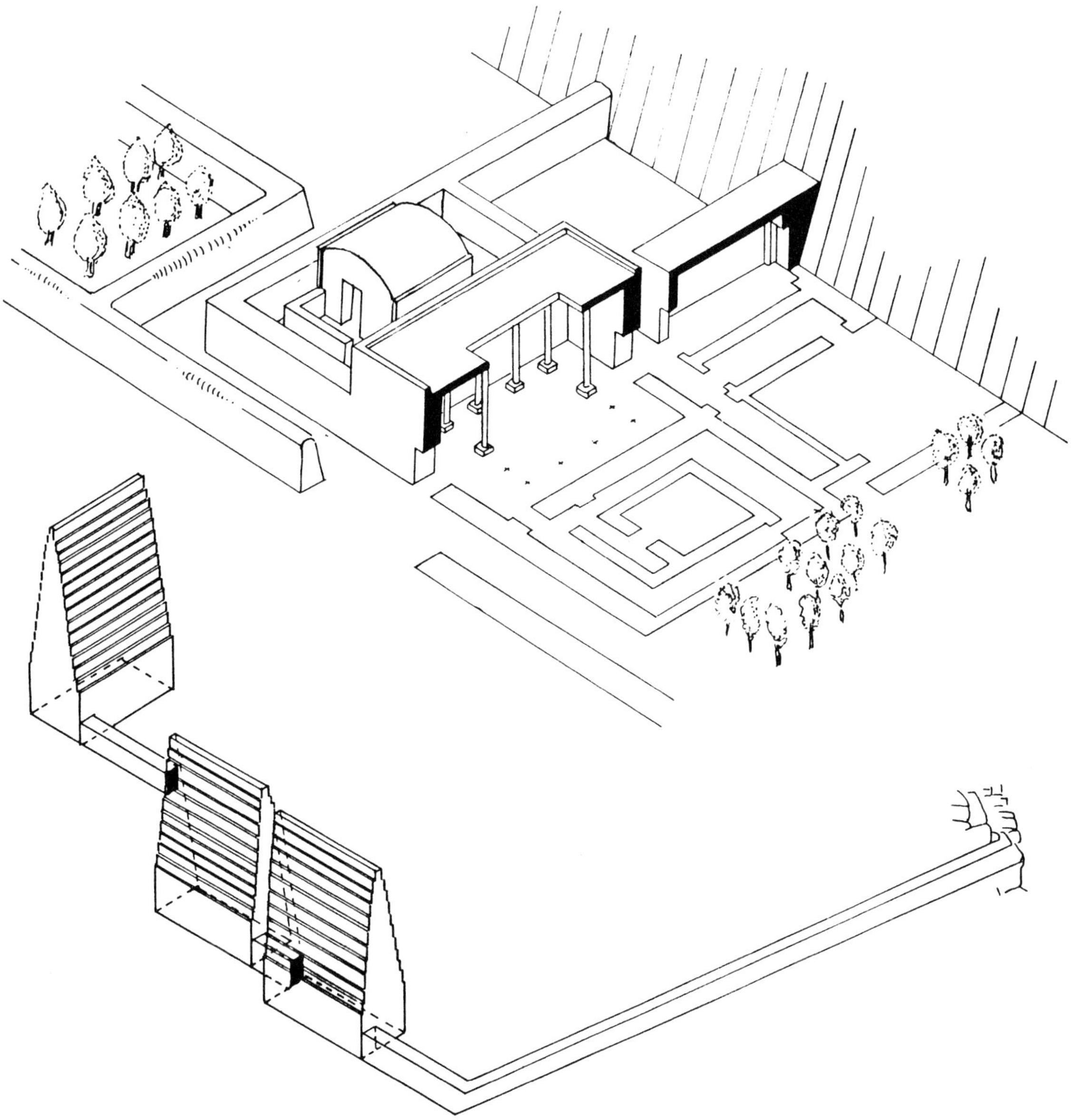

Fig. 11 Dahshur. Funerary apartments and pyramid temple of Snofru.

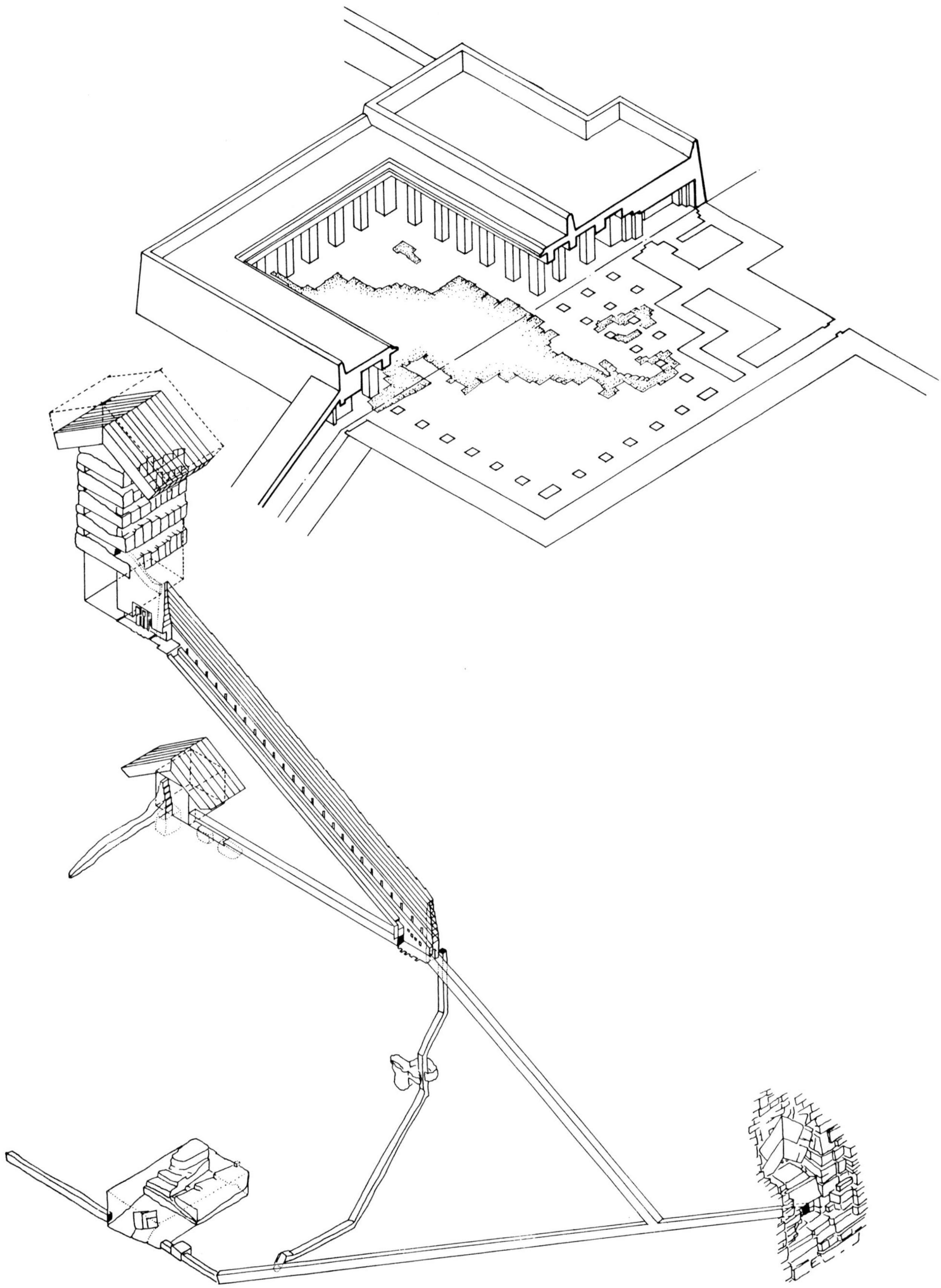

Fig. 12 Giza. Funerary apartments and pyramid temple of Khufu.

the pyramid of Khufu form a magnificent stage for the ascension of the king to the heavens (fig. 12). Their arrangement is certainly not the result of several changes in the construction of the pyramid, the building periods proposed by Borchardt (1937; see also Edwards 1994). These are pure invention and nowhere visible, nor do they take into consideration the natural condition of the rock foundation of the pyramid. The sequence of the rooms follows an ingenious and sublime plan according to which the dead king was to rest eternally in a high and splendid hall where he was incorporated into the sun-god.

As we do not know much about the royal burial ritual we cannot suppose correspondences between the open funerary temple and the funerary apartments inside the pyramid for the funerary rituals, the burial procession and the actual interment. However, if the pyramid tomb and the pyramid temple are conceived as a unity, and as the eternal residence in the hereafter, it becomes conceivable that the distribution of the necessary rooms could vary from time to time according to prevailing ideas which drew attention away from the localization of the eternal apartments within the pyramid in favour of other beliefs which dictated their location instead in the front part of the pyramid temple.

This is certainly the case in the Khephren complex (fig. 13). The funerary apartments inside the pyramid are very simple, the arrangement almost dull. The pyramid temple, however, is enlarged in its fore-part by a series of halls which are remarkable state rooms yet enclosed in a massive solid rock masonry as if it were intended to transfer part of the pyramid construction into the temple.

The Khephren complex might not have been the first example of this kind of arrangement. The

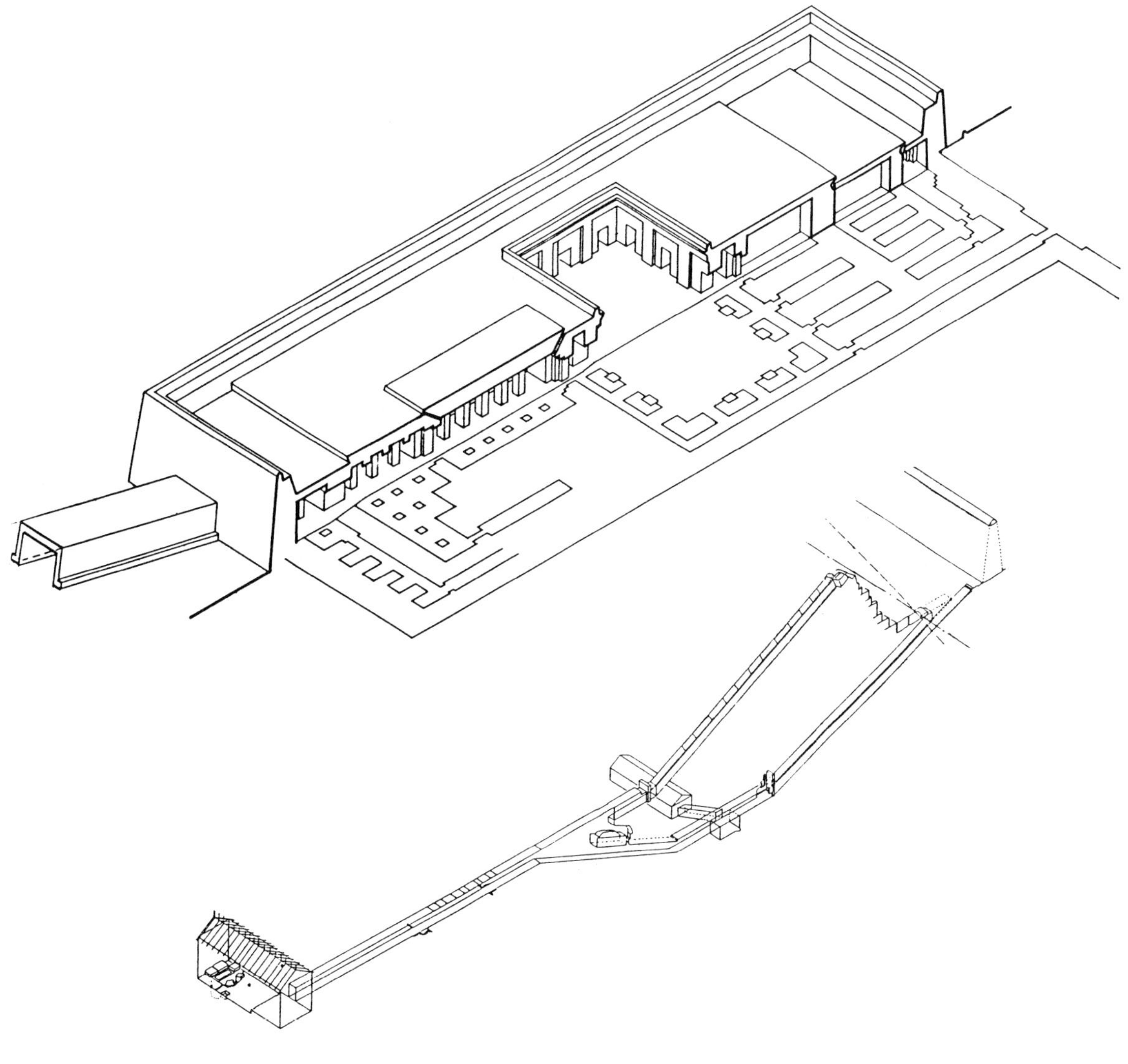

Fig. 13 Giza. Funerary apartments and pyramid temple of Khephren.

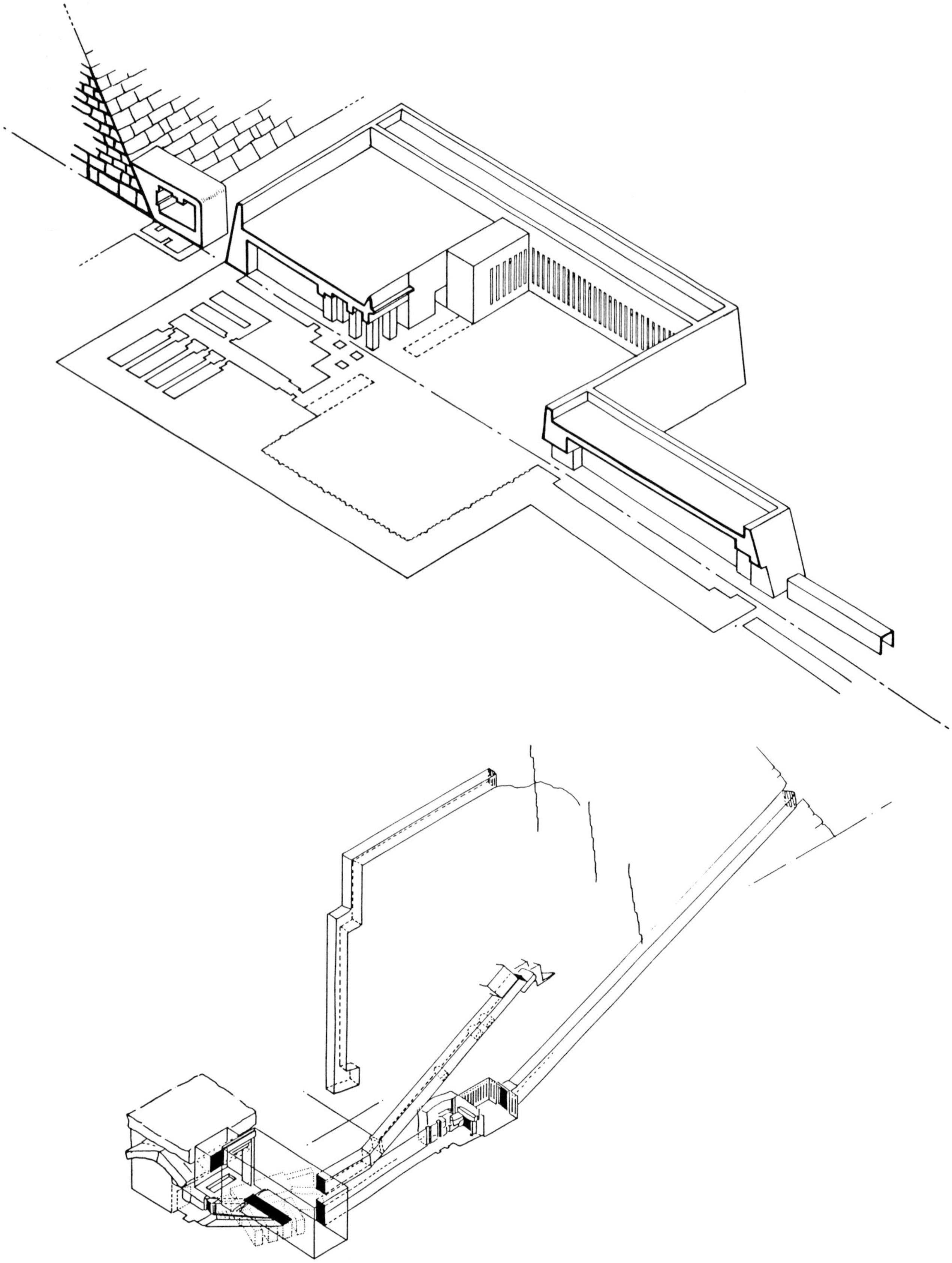

Fig. 14 Giza. Funerary apartments and pyramid temple of Mycerinus.

pyramid of Djedefra at Abu Rowash and its temple were not completed nor are they adequately excavated and recorded. The excavated shaft suggests that the funerary apartments must have been arranged in a rather simple T-form whereas the remains of the pyramid temple suggest a rather complex construction. We can only hope that this very important place will soon benefit from more detailed archaeological attention before it is completely destroyed by the activities of powerful contractors and mining companies.

In the Mycerinus pyramid complex we find a repetition of that of Khufu. The apartments inside the pyramid are very sophisticated and impressive rooms. Here too this is not the result of several changes during the construction of the pyramid. Rather, the pyramid temple resumes the simple arrangement of the Khufu pyramid temple. The Mycerinus valley temple follows the same plan (fig. 14).

This obvious correspondence between pyramid apartments and the design of the pyramid temples can be followed more or less indefinitely until the end of the New Kingdom. At the beginning of the Fifth Dynasty the evolution of the apartments inside the pyramid came to an end with the final and formal T- form of three rooms. At the same time the pyramid temple expanded and became more and more splendid until it had also reached a formal and standardized plan at the end of the Fifth Dynasty. Now further transformations, or perhaps better modifications, took place again inside the pyramid, with the pyramid texts written on the walls of the burial chamber, the antechamber and finally on the walls of the corridor. The temple remained unchanged.

In the pyramid complexes of the Middle Kingdom the pyramid temple was reduced to the funerary chapel, whereas inside the pyramid a dynamic development again took place, with rearrangements in the funerary apartments following the dominant requirements of the Osirian ritual.

In the New Kingdom the pyramid tomb was finally abandoned, being no longer appropriate to the new ideas of a stage in the night journey of the sun-god through the nether world. The pyramid temple too underwent great changes to reappear as the "house of millions of years" with very definite features derived from the old pyramid temples of the Fourth Dynasty.

Bibliography

Altenmüller, H 1972. *Die Texte zum Begräbnisritual in den Pyramiden des Alten Reiches.* Ägyptologische Abhandlungen 24. Wiesbaden, Otto Harrassowitz.

Arnold, D 1977. Rituale und Pyramidentempel. In *Mitteilungen des Deutschen Archäologischen Instituts Kairo* 33, 1-14.

Borchardt, L 1937. *Einiges zur dritten Bauperiode der großen Pyramide bei Giseh.* Beiträge zur Ägyptischen Bauforschung und Altertumskunde 1 [3], Cairo.

Edwards, I E S 1985. *The Pyramids of Egypt.* Viking.

Edwards, I E S 1994. Do the Pyramid Texts Suggest an Explanation for the Abandonment of the Subterranean Chamber of the Great Pyramid. In *Hommages à Jean Leclant*, Cairo, 159-67.

Fakhry, A 1959. *The Monuments of Sneferu at Dahshur I. The Bent Pyramid.* Cairo, Government Printing Offices.

Fakhry, A 1961. *The Monuments of Sneferu at Dahshur II. The Valley Temple.* Cairo, Govenment Printing Offices.

Goyon, G 1969. Quelques observations effectuées autour de la pyramide de Khéops. In *Bulletin de l'Institut Français d'Archéologie Orientale* 67, 49-70.

Jánosi, P 1994. Die Entwicklung und Deutung des Totenopferraumes in den Pyramidentempeln des Alten Reiches. In R Gundlach and M Rochholz, *Ägyptische Tempel - Struktur, Funktion und Programm (Akten der Ägyptologischen Tempeltagungen in Gosen 1990 und in Mainz 1992).* Hildesheimer Ägyptologische Beiträge 37, Gerstenberg Verlag, 143-63.

Hölscher, U 1912. *Das Grabdenkmal des Königs Chephren.* Leipzig, J C Hinrichs.

Kaiser, W 1969. *Zu den königlichen Talbezirken der 1. und 2. Dynastie in Abydos und zur*

Baugeschichte des Djoser-Grabmals. In *Mitteilungen des Deutschen Archäologischen Instituts Kairo* 25, 1-22.
Lauer, J-P 1936. *Fouilles à Saqqarah. La Pyramide à degrés. L'architecture.* Cairo, Institut Français d'Archéologie Orientale.
Lauer, J-P 1962. *Histoire Monumental des Pyramides d'Egypte I. Les pyramides à degrés (IIIe Dynastie).* Bibliothèque d'Etude 39. Cairo, Institut Français d'Archéologie Orientale.
Lauer, J-P 1967. In *Orientalia N.S.* 36,
Lauer, J-P 1988. Sur certaines modifications et extensions apportées au complexe funéraire de Djoser au cour de son règne. In A Lloyd (ed), *Pyramid Studies and other Essays Presented to I. E. S. Edwards,* London, Egypt Exploration Society, 5-11.
Lehner, M 1983. The Layout of the Khufu and Khafre Pyramids. In *Journal of the American Research Center in Egypt* 20, 7-25.
Lesko, L 1988. Seila. In *Journal of the American Research Center in Egypt* 25, 223-35.
MRA = V. Maragioglio and C. Rinaldi, *Architettura delle Pyramide Menfite,* Torino/Rapallo 1963-1975.
Reisner, G 1936. *The Development of the Egyptian Tomb down to the Ascension of Cheops.* Cambridge, Harvard University Press.
Ricke, H 1944. *Bemerkungen zur ägyptischen Baukunst des Alten Reiches I.* Beiträge zur Ägyptischen Bauforschung und Altertumskunde 4, Zurich, Borchardt-Institut für Ägyptiche Bauforschung und Altertumskunde.
Ricke, H and S Schott 1956. H Ricke, *Bemerkungen zur ägyptischen Baukunst des Alten Reiches II,* with S Schott, *Bemerkungen zum Âgyptischen Pyramidenkult.* Beiträge zur Ägyptischen Bauforschung und Altertumskunde 5, Cairo, Schweizerisches Institut für Ägyptiche Bauforschung und Altertumskunde.
Spiegel, J 1971. *Das Auferstehungsritual der Unas-Pyramide. Beschreibung und erläuterte Übersetzung.* Ägyptologische Abhandlungen 23. Wiesbaden, Otto Harrassowitz.
Stadelmann, R 1965. Snofru und die Pyramiden von Meidum und Dahschur. In *Mitteilungen des Deutschen Archäologischen Instituts Kairo* 36, 437-49.
Stadelmann, R 1982. Die Pyramiden des Snofru in Dahschur. Erster Bericht. In *Mitteilungen des Deutschen Archäologischen Instituts Kairo* 38, 379-93.
Stadelmann, R 1983. Die Pyramiden des Snofru in Dahschur. Zweiter Bericht. In *Mitteilungen des Deutschen Archäologischen Instituts Kairo* 39, 226-41.
Stadelmann, R 1985. *Die ägyptischen Pyramiden. Vom Ziegelbau zum Weltwunder.* Kulturgeschichte der Antiken Welt 30. Mainz, Philipp von Zabern.
Stadelmann, R 1987. *Beiträge zur Geschichte des Alten Reiches.* In *Mitteilungen des Deutschen Archäologischen Instituts Kairo* 43, 230-40.
Stadelmann, R 1990. *Die großen Pyramiden von Giza* Graz.
Swelim, N 1987. The BYU Expedition to Seila in the Fayum. In *Newsletter of the American Research Center in Egypt.*

News from Abusir

Paule Posener-Kriéger

Since the Deutsche Orientgesellschaft left the field of Abusir in 1907 (Borchardt 1907; id. 1909; id. 1910; id. 1913; Schäfer 1908) and since the publication of the Abusir papyri in 1968 (Posener-Kriéger and Cenival 1968), things have changed significantly on this site. The excavations undertaken by the Czechoslovak Institute of Egyptology under the direction of Miroslav Verner have brought to light new monuments, in which more papyri have been discovered, and I feel that a certain number of statements which had seemed to me perfectly reasonable when I published the commentary of the papyri from the temple of Neferirkara (Posener-Kriéger 1976) have to be reconsidered, given the discoveries of our Czech colleagues. I refer above all to the question of the king's mother Khentkaus.

In the Neferirkara papyri the king's mother Khentkaus is cited in duty-tables as well as in accounts, and it seemed natural to think that the king's mother named in the documents was the mother of Neferirkara, that is the queen who was buried at Giza (Hassan 1933, 1-62, pl.1-4). The evident conclusion was that this lady had a place of worship in the place of her son, since in one of the duty-tables of the staff of the Neferirkara temple a heading records "the one who applies the seal on the *ꜥfdt* box", and, after days of this duty carried out by a *ḥm nṯr* well known from other duty-tables, a red note reads "apply the seal in the *ḥwt-nṯr nt mwt-nswt ḫnt-k3w.s*" (Posener-Kriéger and Cenival 1968, pl.6A, col.d) which meant, I thought, that in the temple of Neferirkara there was a room or place which was regarded as the *ḥwt-nṯr* of the king's mother. Such a place was readily found, since, to the north of the five expected cult chapels there is a sixth room (see the plan in Posener-Kriéger 1976, 495, fig.32, room 6, also 502, 532-3) perfectly suited for the purpose - or so I thought - for another duty-table refers to "the one who receives the papyrus roll after performing the rites for the king's mother Khentkaus" (Posener-Kriéger and Cenival 1968, pl.3, col.c). This implied a cult in the temple, and the cult seemed in the hands of the staff of the Neferirkara temple. A circular calcite offering-table bearing the name of "Khentkaus, beloved of Neferirkara", as well as the title *mwt-nswt* (Borchardt 1907, 146; id. 1938, 213) showed that there really was a cult of Khentkaus in the temple, although the *Tagebuch* of the Borchardt expedition preserved in the departmental library of the Berlin Museum does not state exactly where the object was discovered. To these items of evidence one should add the accounts: a sheet of daily income shows that income from the estate of the king's mother as well as that of the king's son *Ỉrỉ-n-Rꜥ* reached the temple (Posener-Kriéger and Cenival 1968, pl.46A^{1}-A^{7}), and on various occasions pieces of meat are stated to be offered to the "king's mother Khentkaus" (Posener-Kriéger and Cenival 1968, pl.46B, 45B, 65,9 and 32). There was no reason then to doubt that the queen cited in the Neferirkara papyri was the mother of this king, the lady buried at Giza in a sarcophagus-shaped mastaba. The complete title of that woman is *nswt bỉty mwt nswt bỉty* or *mwt nswt bỉty nswt bỉty*, a very rare title which remains of uncertain interpretation: it may be "the king of Upper and Lower Egypt, the mother of the king of Upper and Lower Egypt", as Junker understood it (Junker 1932, 130-3), or the mother of two kings, as is more generally admitted, the two being Sahura and Neferirkara (Vikentiev, article in *La Bourse Egyptienne*, cited Junker 1932, 209, cf. Smith 1971, 178).

When the Czechoslovak Institute began to excavate on the south of the temple of Neferirkara and found practically adjoining it a very destroyed pyramid and a temple built to the east of this pyramid with the name of Khentkaus, we thought that it was the funerary monument of the wife of Neferirkara who is also called Khentkaus; but when on pillars of the portico leading to the court of the temple this very extraordinary title *nswt bỉty mwt nswt bỉty* appeared before the name of Khentkaus, we wondered if the temple was not a sort of cenotaph for the king's mother buried at Giza, the idea being to provide a link with the Fourth Dynasty at Abusir in order to make the new dynasty more legitimate.

During excavation small pieces of papyri were also found in the newly discovered temple (Verner 1979, 97-100; id. 1995, pl.80). The documents are largely destroyed but quite extraordinary. The script is very similar to the script of the Neferirkara papyri and they are probably contemporary; no date is quoted in the documents and the estimate of date is based on palaeographical considerations, leaving a margin of error of about twenty-five years either way. From seal impressions found in the temple we know that the building continued to function until the reign of Pepy I. The most interesting pieces show figures of a woman: she wears in general no dress, but is described as having the vulture headdress on her head, with her eyebrows, hair and headdress painted blue (*m sš m ḫsbḏ*); some of the figures have a *w3s* sceptre in one hand and an *ʿnḫ* sign in the other, others have the two arms hanging down, and one figure is even shown inside her chapel, which is called *tpḥt*. One image (pl.4a) is described as having eyes and eyebrows of onyx (*k33*). In all there should have been some sixteen different figures of the lady, certainly statuettes for the cult which should have been clad during the cult ceremonies with appropriate cloths, as shown by Berlin 10003A, a papyrus from a Middle Kingdom pyramid temple (Borchardt 1899, 95-6; Möller 1909, pl.5). One of the fragments describes a shrine which was decorated with figures of lapis lazuli and gold (pl.4b). Another shrine had two doors and three rings for a bolt of copper, as well as twenty-four pieces of imported acacia wood probably to carry it, implying that the object was of some size. Figures of priests (?) in action in front of a statue are also depicted, and on one fragment one can see that *ḫntyw-š* were employed in the cult. In the documentation the name of the person represented by the statues is nowhere written, but it would not be too bold to propose that it is the lady honoured in the temple.

One must add to this material faience pieces discovered near the small ritual pyramid of the temple. One of the pieces shows the queen enthroned holding a sceptre in the shape of a lotus flower in one hand, and an *ʿnḫ* sign in the other; she is clad in a tight fitting dress, with the vulture headdress on her head (pl.5). This faience image mirrors exactly the representation of Khentkaus to be seen on the north pillar of the portico leading to the court of the temple. On the parallel pillar of the portico the queen, also seated, holds a *w3s* sceptre in her hand as in the papyri, but, instead of having a vulture headdress, she wears an uraeus. Among the faience fragments we see also signs deriving from an inscription inlaid or fastened on an object: the bee, the *sw* of *nswt*, a *wr* bird, a *mwt* vulture, etc. These elements corroborate the very short descriptions of shrines or caskets which we can read on the papyrus fragments which are described as having decoration in electrum and lapis lazuli, although in fact blue faience was used in the surviving fragments (cf. Posener-Kriéger and Cenival 1968, pl.27G and J, and pl.28C and G; Borchardt 1909, frontispiece and pl.III-VIII). These objects are to be published with the other faience items found in the temple of Raneferef.

Now the question arises, who is this *nswt bỉty mwt nswt bỉty* Khentkaus ? One of the masons' marks of the extremely destroyed pyramid states that the monument was intended for a *ḥmt nswt*, and there were also found fragments of a granite sarcophagus as well as remains of mummy wrappings in or around the destroyed pyramid. So there was someone buried in the monument which had been intended for Khentkaus, wife of Neferirkara. The building work stopped probably at the death of Neferirkara, in year 10, as indicated by a masons' mark, and was finished by Niuserra of whom this Khentkaus was the mother as well as of Raneferef (Verner 1995). But did this lady bear the very curious, hitherto assumed unique, title held by the Khentkaus of Giza ? Or was the funerary monument converted into a cultplace for the mother of the dynasty ? Among the faience fragments two pieces show the sign *ḥm* of *ḥmt nswt* which the Giza Khentkaus did not hold: she was a *s3t nṯr* (Hassan 1933, 16, fig.2). So we have to suppose that the two Khentkaus bore the same unusual title with similar and very special status.

Then as regards the Neferirkara archives, how are we to understand the documentation ? Are the attendants supposed to go to the nearby temple of Khentkaus to perform the rites, taking the sacred objects out of the temple (this is a difficulty) ? And why, since the Khentkaus temple had its own staff, as stated by fragments of papyri found inside the building, and its own revenues, as demon-

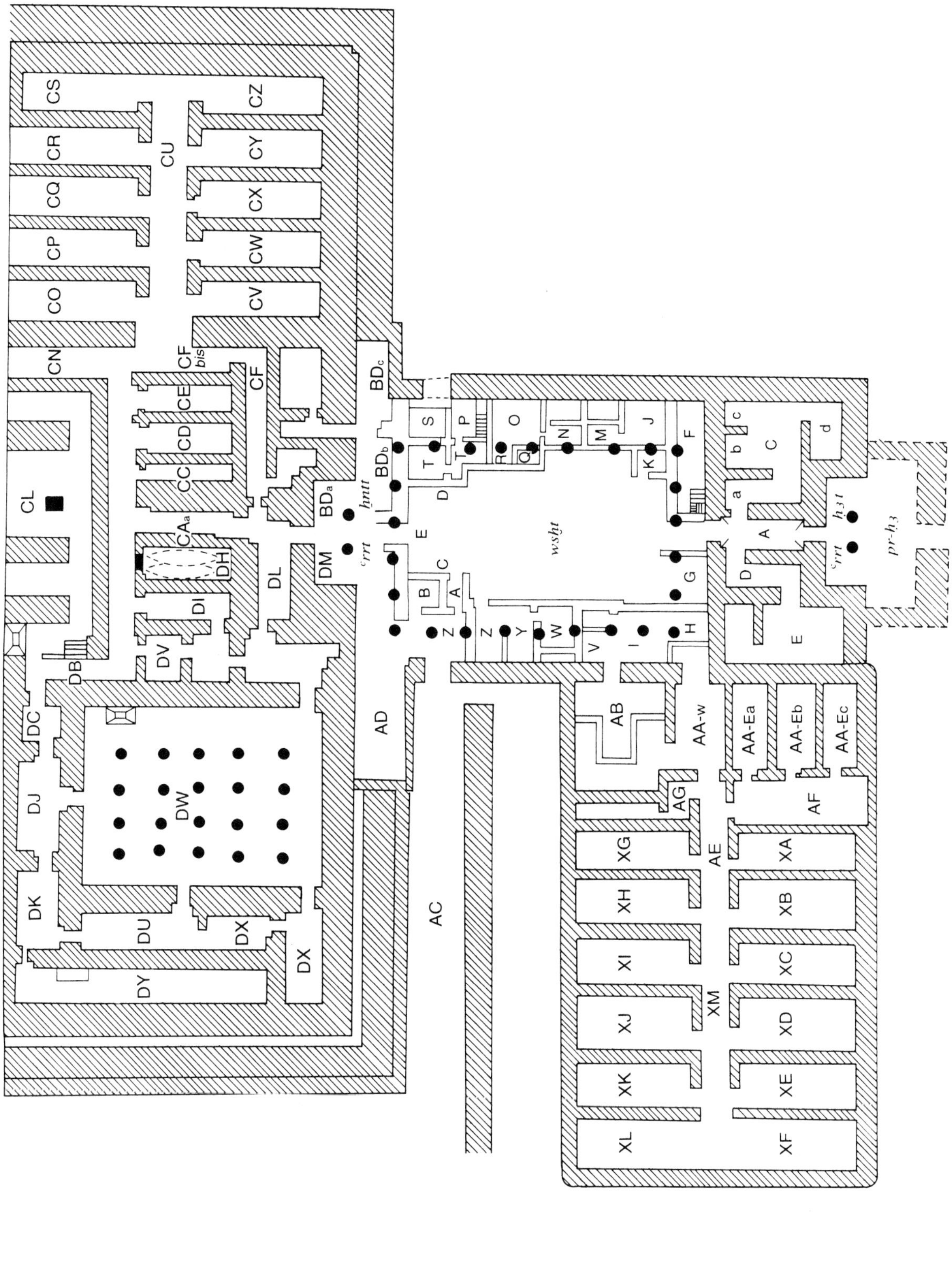

Fig.1 Plan of the temple of Raneferef at Abusir.

strated by fragments of accounts, should the Neferirkara temple receive income from the property (*pr*) of the queen mother and the king's son *Ỉri-n-Rˁ* (Posener-Kriéger and Cenival 1968, pl.46 A^1 - A^7) ? A king's son *Ỉri-n-Rˁ* the youngest (*nḏs*) is depicted on a relief fragment of the temple of Khentkaus making offerings (to be published in Verner, *Abusir* III), but in the Neferirkara archives the man does not seem to be "the youngest" and is probably a homonymous dead prince, son of Khentkaus - only, which Khentkaus ?

The most reasonable interpretation, I feel, would be to admit that, once the temple of the wife of Neferirkara had been completed by Niuserra for his mother (who, for some dynastic reason that we cannot understand, had taken up the title of mother of the dynasty, the Khentkaus of Giza), the economy as well as the cult in the two temples - the main temple of Neferirkara and the smaller temple of Khentkaus - functioned to a certain extent together, at least while the papyri were written under Isesi and Unas. I cannot see an adequate solution either by admitting that there was a cult for the mother of Neferirkara in the king's temple and another Khentkaus cult in the nearby temple of his wife, or by supposing that there was a mingling between the cult of the two ladies, a sort of assimilation of two personalities for which there is no evidence: people at that time knew who was who. Such an arrangement or compromise does not appear satisfactory.

Consequently I think that the monument in question was the funeral temple of the wife of Neferirkara and that it must be she who is mentioned in the Neferirkara archives and not the Khentkaus of Giza, as I believed when I wrote the commentary of the first set of Abusir papyri.

Shortly after the discovery of the monument of Khentkaus the Czechoslavak Institute undertook the excavation of the complex of Raneferef, in which more papyri were discovered. The documents refer to places and features of the temple and it is interesting - although not easy - to try to understand to which part of the temple the archives allude. The monument lies south west of the pyramid of Neferirkara; the pyramid of the king, never completed, was hastily finished off and cased in the shape of a mastaba, and only the middle of the western part of the temple, which is badly destroyed, was built in stone. Except for the limestone bases of wooden columns, the temple is essentially a mudbrick building. Originally the temple extended from north to south along the eastern side of the mastaba, but was entered from the east. The temple was completed towards the east probably by Niuserra, who added a pillared court and an entrance. I do not wish to analyse the different building stages and development of the temple, being only interested here by what the papyri found in the temple have to say about its architecture. The papyri were written during the second half of the reign of Isesi and the beginning of the reign of Unas when the temple was completed. The earliest certain date among the Isesi papyri is *rnpt sp 15* (Posener-Kriéger 1985, 202, fig.B2). A mutilated royal letter, in which the name of the king is not preserved (Isesi ?) states that the temple is in a poor state of preservation (*w3sj*) and has to be repaired, which is not surprising for a brick monument.

The temple differs greatly from the other mortuary temples of the dynasty (see plan, fig.1). The most striking feature is, in the south-west, a hypostyle hall with four rows of wooden lotiform columns, of which only the marks of the six stems remain on limestone bases. To the north-west of this hall, against its north wall, is a basin with outlet and a drainage system under the mud pavement of the hall. Another curious feature of the temple is the absence of the five cult chapels. To the north-west, almost against the royal mastaba, runs a series of five parallel storerooms oriented east-west, divided into two symmetrical series by a passage running north-south. It is in these storerooms that the papyri were discovered, more precisely mostly in the last storerooms to the north-west (CS/CZ). One should point out that the number of storerooms matches the number of sections of phyles of the temple, and this is certainly not fortuitous, since stones bearing the names of sections of a phyle were discovered in this area.

Another curious feature is a large rectangular structure originally quite detached from the temple, on the south-east of the original building. This structure was incorporated into the main building complex when the temple was extended to the east; a slaughterblock and flint knives were found there, and Miroslav Verner identified the place as the *ḥwt-nmt* of the temple (Verner 1986, 182-9). This building also has various storerooms and other features such as a room in which a wooden fence provided some degree of isolation and which reminds one of the wooden fence which isolated the scribes seated on a low podium in the pillared hall of the town of Balat (Posener-Kriéger 1989, 294-

5). The archives of the temple, though much damaged, mention a certain number of rooms in the temple which one can try to identify, regardless of the time of their construction, since at all events the documents refer to the temple after completion by Niuserra.

A document dated to *rnpt ḥt sp 4,* that is to say year 8 or 9 of an unnamed king (Unas ?) records that the two sections of the phyle *sṯt* of the temple were to bring bricks and build at the north wall of the temple on two occasions. The number of bricks is given: more than thirty-two thousand bricks; five persons are listed for each section of the phyle under the supervision of the chief of each section. The document can be compared with a papyrus of the Neferirkara archives in which officials are registered under the heading "income of bricks brought to the *pr-šnʿ* " (Posener-Kriéger and Cenival 1968, pl.62, and cf. pl.63 for other objects given to the temple by officials attached to the cult of Neferirkara). Thus it is clear that the men attached to a funerary temple also had to look after the building and attend to its maintenance. The western section of the north wall of the temple appears to have been doubled, which may correspond to the work of the sections of the *sṯt* phyle, but it may be somewhere else on this north wall of the temple that the men have been busy, since, as in many mudbrick buildings, changes and repairs were easy and numerous.

Various rooms of the temple are named in the archive, such as the *ʿrrt ḥ3t* and the *ʿrrt ḫntt,* which can be easily located. As in the Neferirkara archive the duty of the persons employed in the temple is to keep watch there. The pillared court is naturally the *wsḫt* which had palmiform wooden columns. Another place in which people had to keep watch is said to be *mḥt r wsḫt* "at the north of the opening of the *wsḫt* court", which may be in the *wsḫt* court proper or just to the east of it, and the *pr-ḥ3* "out-house" could be the building which stands in front of the temple (?). All this is quite in keeping with what we know from the Neferirkara archives and does not bring any great surprises (Posener-Kriéger 1976, 493-518).

A document of the type of the inventories in layout records the checking of seals applied on places in the temple. We see first something north and something south, with one seal for both: this can only be the north and south leaf of a double-leaf door which should be oriented east-west, and a second double-leaf door with the same orientation is alluded to in the following column of the document. Then comes probably a door which leads to two places, and has only one leaf. The two places reached through this door are first *i3t* and then *pḫr*. If we keep in mind the heading of a duty table among the Neferirkara papyri naming "those who have to walk around the pyramid" (*pḫrw m-ḥ3 mr*), and another heading referring to "the route of the *ḥm-nṯr* when he walks around the pyramid", it seems logical to see in *pḫr* the path around the mastaba. Thus I think that we have here one door, with one leaf, leading to the mastaba and to the route used to walk around it. There is only one such door on the south-west side of the *wsḫt*. Then the two double-leaf doors named just before this have to be on the east/west axis at each end of the entrance passage (?) since there are no other double-leaf doors in the building on this axis, as far as the excavators record. The interesting point, I feel, is the designation of the mastaba as "the mound", which indeed it is, and which could be the architectural name for a mastaba. The more general term *is* does not specify whether a monument is a mastaba or a rock-cut tomb. The inventory records in addition a door, *rwt*, a single-leaf door, probably the entrance door to the inner part of the building. Farther to the left, after a major division of the papyrus sheet, the document continues with a check on imported wood marked with the name of *Rʿ-nfr.f.* There are five of those and I cannot see, for the time being, anything five in number in the temple which could explain the data of the document.

Now we come to more difficult statements. In a duty table a heading names "the door which is under the staircase of the *ʿt* (room, bureau) of the *ḥm-nṯr*". Five people are on duty there, but only three seem to have been present. As we know there was a *tp-ḥwt*, a terrace, where four people had to stay during the night in order to observe the stars, and thus there should be a stairway leading to the terrace and the *ʿt* of the *ḥm-nṯr* should be either on the ground floor or on the first floor somewhere on the way leading to this terrace. The staircases existing in the storerooms, in the south building (*ḥwt-nmt*) or in the north wing of the temple were probably used for ascending to a second floor of the magazines, and thus I feel that the staircase leading to the terrace *tp-ḥwt* has yet to be discovered.

On the verso of the document the checking of the building (*pr*) is registered when one phyle goes out of duty and the next enters into its month of service. The seals on the doors of the various rooms are checked. The following are identified in the document: *pr-ḥḏ ꜥ3* (the great treasury), *pr-ꜥnḏ* (house of fat), then three pillars or columns (?), further the *pr-mnḫt* (house of linen), the *ꜥt* of some official (no reading yet available), the *wsḫt* court, the *pr-twt* (house of the statue), the *r3 pr-šnꜥ* (set of storerooms), and finally four pillars or columns. Apart from the *wsḫt* court these features are difficult to locate on the plan of the temple. The only thing we know, thanks to another document, is that the *pr-ḥḏ* and the *r3 pr-šnꜥ* seem to have a common door; all effort to find a logical order in the enumeration of the rooms in the document defeats me, but there must be some principle of organization. Two documents tell us that the cult material was stored in the *pr-mnḫt,* but where this place is remains for the time being quite uncertain. Another question is the *pr-twt* (the house of the statue). As mentioned above, the five cult rooms for statues which exist in the other royal temples at the time do not exist in our building, and while we know for sure that in the temple of Neferirkara there were at least three statues that were brought from the *pr-ḥḏ* of the Residence, in the temple of Raneferef twenty packages of linen were brought for <u>the</u> statue while sixty were brought for the temple in general and two hundred for the *ḫry-ḥbt*. Now where is the *pr-twt*? There is no evident place outside the hypostyle hall in which we find a basin with outlet certainly meant for cult practices. It is in this hall that the well-known wooden images of captives were found; those figures came probably from a throne, and there were also discovered in the hypostyle a beard and foot from a statue larger than lifesize. For the time being, and without real certainty, I would like to place the *pr-twt* in the hypostyle hall but remain at a loss as regards the position of the *pr-ꜥnḏ*, the *pr-ḥḏ ꜥ3* and above all the *pr-mnḫt*. Faience fragments from vases, boxes or shrines, as well as a *psš kf* and two *ḥnwt* cups, one white and the other grey, together with various stone vases, complete or not, were found in the central and northern part of the temple. Two damaged wooden boats were placed in a room adjoining on the south the ten storerooms of the north wing; I would like to locate the *pr-mnḫt* in this part of the temple. The place has to be rather large since a minimum of one hundred and forty-two boxes and various objects (totalling two hundred and six items) had to be stored there for one phyle alone. The north wing of the temple with its ten rooms - one for each section of the five phyles - could very well be the *pr-mnḫt*.

I would like to state also that in the thirty-sixth year of Isesi the *wsḫt* was probably already partly occupied by buildings, since the head of a section of a phyle comes on the fourteenth day of the third month of *šmw* to protest about probably the door of "his house in the temple" which had been opened; therefore, in the time of Isesi, the aspect of the *wsḫt* must have been already a little disturbed by small houses and the colonnades absorbed into mudbrick buildings.

Such are the principal questions and problems concerning the architecture of the temple of Raneferef as mirrored by the archives of the building. I hope, with the help of our Czech colleagues, to go a little further in the understanding of the documents they generously gave me to read and to study for my greatest pleasure.

Bibliography

Borchardt, L 1899. Der Zweite Papyrusfund von Kahun und die zeitliche Festlegung des mittleren Reiches der ägyptischen Geschichte. In *Zeitschrift für Ägyptische Sprache und Altertumskunde* 37, 89-103.

Borchardt, L 1907. *Ausgrabungen des Deutschen Orient-Gesellschaft in Abusir 1902-1904. I Das Grabdenkmal des Königs Ne-user-Reʻ*. Leipzig, J C Hinrichs.

Borchardt, L 1909. *Ausgrabungen des Deutschen Orient-Gesellschaft in Abusir 1902-1908. V Das Grabdenkmal des Königs Nefer-ir-ke3-Reʻ*. Leipzig, J C Hinrichs.

Borchardt, L 1910. *Ausgrabungen des Deutschen Orient-Gesellschaft in Abusir 1902-1908. VI Das Grabdenkmal des Königs S'a3hu-Reʻ I. Der Bau.* Leipzig, J C Hinrichs.

Borchardt, L 1913. *Ausgrabungen des Deutschen Orient-Gesellschaft in Abusir 1902-1908. VI Das Grabdenkmal des Königs S'a3hu-Reʻ II. Die Wandbilder.* Leipzig, J C Hinrichs.

Borchardt, L 1938. *Hnt-k3w.s*, die Stammutter der 5ten Dynastie. In *Annales du Service des Antiquités de l'Egypte* 38, 209-15

Hassan, S 1943. *Excavations at Gîza IV 1932-1933*. Cairo, Government Press, Bulâq.
Junker, H 1932. Die Grabungen der Universität Kairo auf dem Pyramidenfeld von Gîza. In *Mitteilungen des Deutschen Archäologischen Instituts Abteilung Kairo* 3, 123-49.
Möller, G 1909. *Hieratische Paläographie. Die aegyptische Buchschrift in ihrer Entwicklung von der Fünften Dynastie bis zur römischen Kaiserzeit* I. *bis zum Beginn der Achtzehnten Dynastie*. Leipzig, J C Hinrichs.
Posener-Kriéger, P 1976. *Les archives du temple funéraire de Néferirkare Kakaï. Traduction et commentaire* (2 volumes). Bibliothèque d'Etude 65. Cairo, Institut Français d'Archéologie Orientale du Caire.
Posener-Kriéger, P 1985. Décrets envoyés au temple funéraire de Rêneferef. In id. (ed.), *Mélanges Gamal Eddin Mokhtar* II, Cairo, Institut Français d'Archéologie Orientale, 195-210 with 6 pl.
Posener-Kriéger, P 1989. Travaux de l'IFAO au cours de l'année 1988-1989. In *Bulletin de l'Institut Français d'Archéologie Orientale* 89, 291-341.
Posener-Kriéger, P and J-L de Cenival 1968. *The Abu-Sir Papyri.* Hieratic Papyri in the British Museum, Fifth Series. London, British Museum Publications.
Schäfer, H. 1908. *Priestergräber und andere Grabfunde vom Ende des Alten Reiches bis zur griechischen Zeit vom Totentempel des Ne-User-Re'*. Deutsche Orient-Gesellschaft, Wissenschaftliche Veröffentlichungen 8. Leipzig, J C Hinrichs.
Smith, W S 1971. The Old Kingdom in Egypt and the beginning of the First Intermediate Period. Chapter 14 in I E S Edwards, C J Gadd and N Hammond (eds.), *The Cambridge Ancient History,* 3rd edition, I, part 2, Cambridge University Press, 145-207.
Verner, M 1979. Neue Papyrusfunde in Abusir. In *Revue d'Egyptologie* 31, 97-100.
Verner, M 1986. A slaughterhouse from the Old Kingdom. In *Mitteilungen des Deutschen Archäologischen Instituts Abteilung Kairo* 42, 181-9, pl.27.
Verner, M 1995. *Abusir III. The Pyramid Complex of Khentkaus.* Prague, Universitas Pragensis Academia.

Gods in the temple of the King: Anubis at Lahun

Stephen Quirke

In general the evidence for identifying the deity and rituals of a particular religious building or complex consists of hieroglyphic inscriptions on monuments either from the site or referring to it. In the case of the pyramid complex of Senusret II at Lahun, the hieroglyphic sources are outnumbered by a mass of fragmented hieratic papyri. These contain numerous references not only to the cult of the king and his family but also to the god Anubis. In this paper I review the evidence for deities at Lahun in the Middle Kingdom, and compare the position of the most prominent among them, Anubis, with that of deities in other royal cult temples of the Middle Kingdom and at other periods.

1 The site of Lahun

On the north side of the entrance to the Fayum, near the modern village called Lahun, are two major Middle Kingdom sites: the pyramid complex of Senusret II, fourth king of the Twelfth Dynasty, and a large late Middle Kingdom town with rectangular enclosure wall and orthogonal street plan (fig.1). The plan of neither is known in detail; already in antiquity almost one half of the settlement site had eroded away, and the temples of the pyramid complex had been robbed of their stone. Excavations by

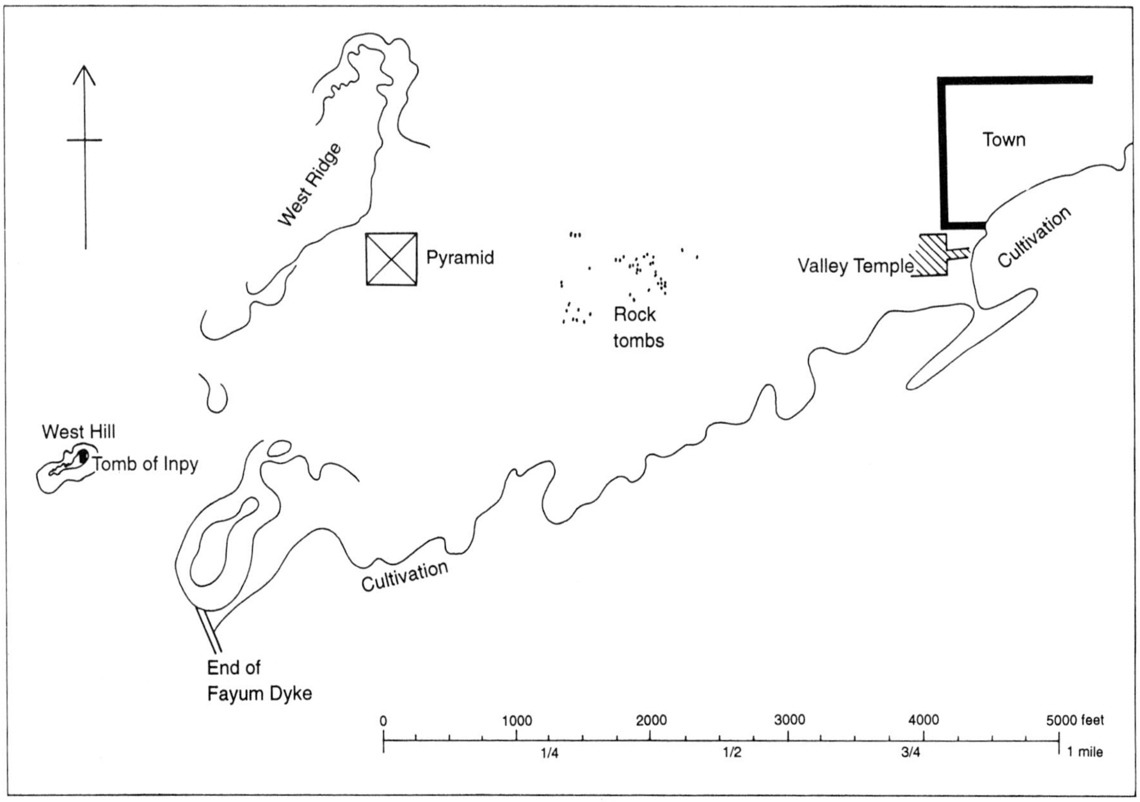

Fig.1 The area north of the Fayum gap at Lahun, showing the pyramid complex and adjacent "new town".

Flinders Petrie in the spring and winter of 1889, without stratigraphic record, enabled him to publish a basic street map of the town in 1891, refined in later seasons of work, particularly regarding the valley temple of the pyramid complex, immediately adjacent to the town (Gallorini 1997). During 1889 Petrie retrieved a number of both isolated examples and groups of papyri from various parts of the settlement site, in most cases without record of the findspot. These date predominantly to the end of the reign of Amenemhat III and to the reigns of his successors in the early Thirteenth Dynasty, and are now in the Petrie Museum, University College London; the more complete fragments were published by Griffith in 1898, and a new edition of the entire corpus is being prepared by Dr Mark Collier and myself at present. In early 1899 large numbers of late Middle Kingdom hieratic business papyri appeared on the market, and Ludwig Borchardt succeeded in collecting virtually all of these and in pinpointing the findspot through trial excavations at one of the mounds on the western side of the town enclosure wall, immediately to the north of the site of the valley temple. From their contents the 1899 papyri can be identified as a homogeneous group comprising the business papers of a temple scribe named Horemsaf working mainly in the early reign of Amenemhat III (Borchardt 1899, 89 plan, and calculation of contents as 41 glass frames of temple journal fragments, 63 of temple accounts, 53 of letters on temple business, 5 of festival lists, 5 of priests lists, 32 then unidentified, totalling 199 frames). They are now in the Egyptian Museum, Berlin, frames P10001-10130, 10132-10161, 10201-10450, of which some early numbers have been renumbered (e.g. old P10057 is now 10163, old 10075 is now 10164), apart from four exchanged with the Egyptian Museum, Cairo, in the 1930s for other objects, Berlin P10005A and B, 10017, 10020, 10022 > Cairo J.71580-71583 (Kaplony-Heckel 1971); in pioneering work never fully appreciated by Egyptology, Eugène Dévaud completed transcriptions of virtually every item in Berlin before the First World War. A full publication of the Berlin papyri has now been launched by Dr Ulrich Luft. Both groups of papyri contain references to deities other than the deceased Senusret II, and these are the starting-point for my enquiry into the role of gods in the cult of the king. I wish to express at the outset my gratitude to Dr Ingeborg Müller and her colleagues in Berlin for access to this material, to her and the directors of the museum for permission to cite these largely unpublished sources, and to Dr Luft for his constant encouragement during my research on the Lahun papyri.

2 Mentions of deities in Lahun papyri

The London Lahun papyri

The papyri published by Griffith in 1898 include references to deities and temple titleholders in ten legal and accounts documents:

wpwt "household listing" of the ordinary lector-priest in Sekhem-Senusret justified (*ẖry-ḥbt ꜥš3 n sḫm-snwsrt m3ꜥ-ḫrw*) Senusretseneb Khakaurasneferu called Sneferu, as owner of a household: his wife was daughter of a *mty n s3 r-pr pn,* implying perhaps that *r-pr* is a term for Sekhem-Senusret (UC 32166, Petrie lot IV.1: Griffith 1898, pl.10-11);

ỉmt-pr "deed of conveyance" of the phyle-controller (*mty n s3*) Mery, in favour of his son Intef (UC 32037, Petrie lot VII.1: Griffith 1898, pl.11);

ỉmt-pr "deed of conveyance" of the pure-priest over the phyle of Sepdu lord of the east (*wꜥb ḥry s3 n spdw nb ỉ3btt*) Wah, in favour of his wife *st nt gs-ỉ3b* Sheftu (UC 32058, Petrie lot I.1: Griffith 1898, pl.12-13);

a petition concerning the *ỉmt-pr* conveying the position of *wꜥb ḥry s3 n spdw nb ỉ3btt* to a scribe in charge of the seal of Gesiab (*sẖ ḥry ḫtm n gs-ỉ3b*) Iyemiatib (UC 32055, Petrie lot II.1: Griffith 1898, pl.13);

a works list including the titles ka-servant of the king's documents scribe, phyle-controller, and general lector-priest (*ḥm-k3 n sẖ ꜥ n nswt, mty n s3*, and *ẖry-ḥbt ꜥš3*) (UC 32170, Petrie lot VI.14vso: Griffith 1898, pl.14);

an account of cattle herds citing the "stalls of divine offerings of Sobek (of Shedyet which are in the charge of this town)" and "cattle of the Dual King Sehetepibra [= Amenemhat I] justified which are in the charge of this town" (*mḏt nt [ḥtpw]-nṯr sbk* and *mḏt nt [ḥtpw]-nṯr sbk-šdty ntt r-ḫt n nỉwt tn* and

mnmnt nt nswt-bîty sḥtpîbrᶜ m3ᶜ-ḫrw ntt r-ḫt n nîwt tn) (UC 32179, Petrie lot VI.10: Griffith 1898, pl.16-17);
a land account citing a pure-priest over the phyle (*wᶜb ḥry s3*) Khuinpu (? or Inpunakht ?) as land-owner (UC 32186, Petrie lot XIII.1: Griffith 1898, pl.21);
a grain account summary including the titles pure-priest over the phyle, district overseer, temple (or domain ?) overseer and man of the god's pavilion (*wᶜb ḥry s3, îmy-r w, îmy-r ḥwt, sḥy-nṯr*) (UC 32189, Petrie lot XVI.1: Griffith 1898, pl.21);
the record of attendance of *ḫbw* "dancers" and *ḥsw* "singers" in *s3w* "phylae", mainly *ᶜ3m* "Asiatics" and *mḏ3y* "Medjay", for festivals which include *mnḫt* of Khakheperra, sailing of Hathor lady of Henennesut (*ḫnt ḥwtḥr nbt ḥnnnswt*) and sailing of Hathor (*ḫnt ḥwtḥr*), as well as the Sokar festivals *ḥb skry* and *sṯ3 skry*; (UC 32191, Petrie lot XLI.1: Griffith 1898, pl.24);
a list of *înw b3kw* revenue including the titles stolist of Horus, pure-priest of the king, adorer, libationer, embalmer, acolyte (*sm3 ḥr, wᶜb nswt, dw3w, w3ḥ-ḫt, wtw, îmy-st-ᶜ*) (UC 32194, Petrie lot LV.8: Griffith 1898, pl.26).

The cult of Senusret II, the king buried in the pyramid complex at Lahun, is attested here directly only in the festivals calendar, which also provides the references to both Sokar and Hathor lady of Henennesut (Ihnasya el-Medina); the Sokar festivals are probably part of annual ceremonies not restricted to particular cult places. In the cattle account Sobek is identified as 'he of Shedyet' (Medinet el-Fayum), but neither this nor the Hathor cult is located by the placename at that town, rather than at Lahun; a cult of Hathor lady of Atfih is attested for the pyramid complex of Senusret I at Lisht (see below, section 6). If Lahun might have housed cults of Sobek and Hathor, it seems less likely for the cult of Amenemhat I, attested here only by reference to its estate in the cattle account. The town Gesiab, literally meaning "the left side", houses a cult of Sepdu, but has not been located; control marks on stone blocks at the pyramid of Senusret I, published by Felix Arnold, indicate that this is a separate settlement already existing in that reign (F Arnold 1990, 25), rather than a name for one part of the town at Lahun, as I had previously interpreted the name. The depiction of Senusret II with Sepdu on the Wadi Gasus stela, at the eastern end of the Wadi Hammamat road to the Red Sea, presumably reflects his importance as the lord of the east, rather than as a deity of a town founded or favoured by Senusret II. The title 'stolist of Horus' may refer to a role within pyramid complex cult, rather than to a separate cult for that deity at Lahun.

The letters published by Griffith contain the following mentions of deities (Griffith 1898, pl.27-37):
Amenemhat IV and all gods; Sokar *m tp-sḏmw* and Anubis *nb mîw* (?); Amenemhat I; Amenemhat IV (? - partly lost); Sekhmet ...; Sobek *nb ḫny*; Hathor *rst mḥtt* (?); and Sobek *nb nîwt* .. in the model letters UC 32196, Petrie lot III.2 (Griffith 1898, pl.27-8);
Sobek *nb [ ]-yt/w*, Senusret II and all gods in letter UC 32197, Petrie lot IV.4 (Griffith 1898, pl.28);
Atum *nb îwnw ḥnᶜ psḏt.f*, Rahorakhty, Sepdu *nb î3btt ḥnᶜ psḏt.f* and *nṯr.k nîwty* in letter UC 32198, Petrie lot I.7 (Griffith 1898, pl.29);
Sepdu *nb î3btt ḥnᶜ psḏt.f* and all gods in letter UC 32199, Petrie lot II.2 (Griffith 1898, pl.29);
Sobek and Horus as *sbk-šdty [ḥr ḥr]-îb šdyt*, Khentkhety *nb Kmwy*, Amenemhat III *ᶜnḫ ḏt r nḥḥ* and all gods in letter UC 32202, Petrie lot VI.6 (Griffith 1898, pl.31);
reference to *îmy-r ḥwt-nṯr n ḥkt ppî* and formula with Sobek *nb r-sḥwy* in rubric note letter UC 32204, Petrie lot VI.8 (Griffith 1898, pl.32);
Sobek *nb r-sḥwy*, Amenemhat IV *ᶜnḫ ḏt r nḥḥ* and all gods in letter UC 32205, Petrie lot III.4 (Griffith 1898, pl.33);
Heryshef *nb ḥnnnswt* in different formula between 'brothers' in UC 32205;
Sobek and Horus as *[sbk-šdty] ḥr ḥr-îb šdyt*, Sobek *nb r-sḥwy ḥnᶜ psḏt.f*, Senusret [II] and all gods in letter UC 32210, Petrie lot VIII.1 (Griffith 1898, pl.35);
in letter UC 32212, Petrie lot V.1 (Griffith 1898, pl.35) no formula at start but mention of grain *nty m w pn îr m înw šnwt tn* for three places: Hetep-Senusret (*ḥtp-snwsrt m3ᶜ-ḫrw*), the "domain of the king's daughter Neferuptah justified" (*ḥwt nt s3t nswt nfrw-ptḥ m3ᶜ-ḫrw*), and Atfih (*tp-îḥw*); at the end is a formula invoking the Theban Mont and Amun (*mnṯw nb w3st, îmn nb nswt t3wy*) and all gods;

Sobek and Horus as *sbk-šdty ḥr ḥr-ib šdyt*, Senusret II and all gods in letter UC 32214, Petrie lot LVI.1 (Griffith 1898, pl.36);
Khentkhety [..], Senusret II and the gods of [Upper and ?] Lower Egypt in letter UC 32213, Petrie lot VI.5 (Griffith 1898, pl.36).
(Note also the following instances: in UC 32201 = Petrie lot VI.4 [..] *ḥnᶜ psḏt.f*; in letters to or from women the formulae are absent, UC 32200 = Petrie lot XV.1 and UC 32203 = Petrie lot III.3, probably also UC 32209 = Petrie lot XII.1 although there not preserved; there are no mentions in UC 32216 = Petrie lot LVII.1, or in the short notes UC 32207-8 = Petrie lot XIV.3-4, UC 32212 = Petrie lot VI.9, UC 32215 = Petrie lot LXV.1).
This series of attestations can be expanded from the fragments not published by Griffith:
UC 32115C letter with formula invoking Senusret II *m3ᶜ-ḫrw*
UC 32126 letter with formula invoking Sepdu *nb i3btt*.

The placenames in the model letters might include inventions for didactic or literary effect, and ought not to be treated as secure attestations of existing towns and cults without corroboratory evidence. The references to Atum and Ra-Horakhty of Heliopolis, and Amun and Mont of Thebes seem to establish not the presence of particular cults at Lahun, so much as the geographical scope of the letters; the same may be true of references to Heryshef of Henennesut, Khentkhety of Kemwer (Athribis) and the paired Sobek and Horus of Shedyet. It is less clear where the cults of Sobek lord of Resehwy and of Heqet are to be placed. The kings cited are Senusret II and the reigning king (Amenemhat III and IV). The *ḥwt* of Nefruptah seems a separate establishment, mentioned with Hetep-Senusret and Atfih in the letter invoking Theban deities, perhaps sent from Upper Egypt (UC 32212). In invocations the adjunct 'and his ennead' may identify specifically the principal deity of a separate cult-centre; it is applied to Atum of Heliopolis, Sepdu lord of the east, and the paired Sobek and Horus of Shedyet. If this were the case, it could be taken as evidence that Sepdu received worship not at Lahun but elsewhere, the likely site in this context being the unlocated town Gesiab.

The unpublished University College papyri also include fragments of texts so close in format and content to the Berlin papyri that they may provisionally be ascribed to the same source, the discarded files of the temple scribe Horemsaf:

UC 32094B	journal entries of *ḥtpw-nṯr* and *ḥbyt nt hrw pn*
UC 32097A	temple phyle transfer formula
UC 32101E	namelist headed *wnwt ḥwt-nṯr* and fragments including *ḥtpw-nṯr m ḥbyt* [
UC 32111E	account of *ḥbyt*
UC 32133A	account headed *inw ḥbyt nt* [
(UC 32135B	fragments including note of festival *h3w mnḫt*)
UC 32137B	fragment with *t-ḥḏ bnbn*[as in temple journal notes
UC 32137J	note of *hrw n ḥb sm3y*[and below *šnᶜ n ḥtpw-nṯr* [
(UC 32142C	notes including *di r m3ᶜ ḥtpw-nṯr,* not necessarily temple)
UC 32143B	list of statues (only determinatives and priests survive)
(UC 32145D	journal notes, not necessarily temple)
UC 32147(?)	namelist of *wᶜbw* to serve [at pyramid] for a fixed period.

If these fragments were acquired at the same time as the others in the Petrie Museum, in 1889, they indicate that the men working for Petrie discovered the temple files as much as ten years before they began to appear on the market. This seems more likely than a later acquisition via Petrie, Griffith, or another person, because (a) the Petrie fragments seem to have been sorted by Griffith and Newberry before 1894, with no evidence for subsequent treatment until the unpacking of the Petrie Museum after the Second World War, and (b) Borchardt was clearly under the impression that he had secured all fragments available in 1899 for the Berlin Museum, and among the scholars from whom he obtained fragments was Griffith himself. Whatever the date of acquisition, these fragments of temple files introduce us to the substantial corpus of data in the Berlin Lahun papyri.

The Berlin Lahun papyri

In these documents, information on deities at the temple may be divided into four sets of references:
(a) to buildings or institutions identified by names for types of building (pyramid, temple, granary, food-production area);
(b) to offerings to particular deities;
(c) to statues of particular deities;
(d) to priests of particular deities.

(a) References to buildings

(i) *The pyramid*

About a dozen journal entries record the names of one or two staff at a time appointed for fixed periods of time to look after the pyramid. This is a kilometre from the Valley Temple, and the distance presumably made such appointments necessary: this raises the question of function of the Pyramid Temple as opposed to the Valley Temple, and, specifically, what relation existed between the rites at the two temples. The identification of *mr* as the Pyramid Temple (perhaps specifically the raised level of Totenopfertempel in contrast to causeway and Verehrungstempel) may be supported by the phrase *ḥwt mr* (standard in the Pyramid Texts) which occurs in these files at P10003A vso.

The references to the pyramid of Senusret II show that the files are concerned with the running of the pyramid complex of the king, and do not derive from another religious institution on the site; this already seems clear from the reported findspot, confirmed in test excavation by Borchardt in 1899 at the rubbish mounds west of the town wall and north of the Valley Temple.

Sources

P10001B fragments 3-4, 10002B col.2, 10012A, 10012A vso, 10091, 10092b col.2, 10092 vso, 10137, 10201a, 10232b (? broken), 10280, 10338a
= namelists of *wꜥbw* to keep vigil at the *mr* for a fixed period
P10128Bb namelist including a double heading for one set of at least five names of *rsw mr* and *dw3w mr* (respectively "vigil" and "adorers", presumably the hymn-singers, at the pyramid)
P10003A vso reference to the pyramid complex of Senusret II, the temple of Anubis in Sekhem-Senusret, and another temple (?) in Sekhem-Senusret

[ ]*ḥwt mr n nswt-bỉty ḫꜥḫprrꜥ* [
[*ḥw*]*t*-[*nṯr*] *nt ỉnpw tpy-ḏw.f m sḫm-snwsrt m3ꜥ-ḫrw*
[*ḥw*]*t (?) m sḫm-snwsrt m3ꜥ-ḫrw*

P10096 letter copy concerning walls of *ḥwt*-[*nṯr*] *nt sḫm-snwsrt m3ꜥ-ḫrw mr*
P10116Ac letter fragment with *mr*] (pyramid determinative) *n nswt-bỉty ḫꜥḫprrꜥ m3ꜥ-ḫrw* [
P10322 vso account of revenue expended at the pyramid at the arrival of an unknown entity (lacuna), given at the procession of a statue placed in an unknown position (lacuna)

sšm ḫnt n[*n*
dỉ r mr ḫft ỉwt .. [
ntt dỉt ḫft wḏ3 twt [
twt dỉ r .. [

(ii) *The temple (ḥwt-nṯr)*

The files include sheets or rolls (*šfdw*) from a temple of Sobek lord of Resehwy, an unlocated cult-centre presumed to lie within the cultivation in the general area of the Fayum gap. Offerings for the cult of Senusret II are brought from the temples of Sobek of Shedyet (Medinet el-Fayum) and Hathor lady of Atfih; these are two of the towns closest to Lahun, but it is possible that the two deities with these epithets received cult elsewhere. It is also unclear, for example, whether or not the shrine of Hathor lady of Atfih at Khenemsut the pyramid complex of Senusret I (see below) would fall within the main estate of Hathor lady of Atfih, rather than lying at the heart of a separate economic unit. Therefore the toponym in an epithet of a deity in a Lahun account may not in fact directly identify the location of the estate funding the Lahun cults.

Of these attestations the most important source for the relation between gods and royal cult temple is P10003B, which involves the statue of Anubis and may best be discussed with the other references to statues under (c).

P10003B col.1 *ỉrt mỉ* [ ] *wḏ3 sḫm ỉnpw* (?) *r snsn m ḥwt-nṯr* [

nswt bỉty [*m3*ʿ]-*ḫrw m sḫm-snswrt m3*ʿ-*ḫrw ḫft ḫnt-nt-t3*

the inventory for this statue procession lists *sšm n ỉnpw* and its *st* (image of Anubis and its throne), an ivory statue of Senusret III *ʿnḫ ḏt r ḥḥ*, an ebony statue of Senusret II *m3*ʿ-*ḫrw*, and the apparatus of cult (one *sḥtpy* "censer", one *ḥst*-vase).

P10056A col.1 letter-copy referring in column 1 to *ḥtpw-nṯr* for Senusret II from the temple of Sobek of Shedet (*ḥwt-nṯr nt sbk šdt*) and in column 2 to the same from the temple of Hathor lady of Atfih (*ḥwt-nṯr nt ḥwtḥr nbt tp-ỉḥw*)

P10062B vso unclear context, *ḥwt-nṯr nt ḥwtḥr nbt tp-ỉḥw*

P10069 col.1, [extract from] *šfdw n hryt nt ḥwt-nṯr nt sbk nb r-sḥwy* "a roll of the journal of the temple of Sobek lord of Resehwy"

P10161b *šfdw n hryt nt ḥwt-nṯr* [

P10237a linen and metal as items entered into the treasury of the temple of [..] (*sʿkt r pr-ḥḏ [n] ḥwt-nṯr nt* [..)

P10300b [ ] *n ḥwt-nṯr nt sbk nb r-sḥwy*

P10304f uncertain, possibly reading *ḥwt (?)-nṯr nt nswt-bỉty ḫʿḫprr*ʿ ʿ*.w.s. (?)*

P10314 *ỉnnw m* [temple of] *ḥwtḥr nbt* [

(iii) *The granaries and processing areas of offerings*

P10048+10319 namelist of *mrt* 'estate-workers' of *šn*ʿ *ḥtpw-nṯr sḫm-snwsrt* [ ] "the food-production area of offerings of Sekhem-Senusret"; the unqualified reference to a single food-production area could be taken to imply that a single group of workers prepared offerings for all cults there

P10055 vso *šnwt nt ḥtpw-nṯr* "granary of divine offerings"; this again seems to imply a single granary, but the lost context may have supplied the separate identity of this offerings granary as opposed to others for other cults

P10203 vso note of deficit *ntt ʿḥ*ʿ *m šnwt ntt m sḫm-[sn]wsrt*[ ] "which is outstanding in the granary which is in Sekhem-[Sen]usret"; again this reference to one granary, qualified only by the statement of location "which is in Sekhem-Senusret" might be taken to imply a single granary there

P10307b *šnwt nt ḥtpw-nṯr nt[*

sbk nb r-sḥwy

perhaps a heading in a journal note, or a column heading in a table of accounts ?

P10414b [*šnwt nt*] *ḥtpw-*[*nṯr*] *nt ỉnpw ḫnty ỉmnty* "[granary of divine] offerings of Anubis foremost of the West"; the restoration is uncertain, and it must be noted that the epithet is not otherwise attested for Anubis in Lahun papyri, although it might perhaps be restored in the offerings to a deity in fragment 10354d (see below)

Here too mention should be made of the *mḏt nt ḥtpw-nṯr*, although this is not attested for Sekhem-Senusret: instead, the cattle for offerings there are brought from other temple estates, as the following references show.

P10203 *ḥtpw-nṯr* of *ỉnpw tpy-ḏw.f m sḫm-snwsrt m3*ʿ-*ḫrw*, four items, all from the *mḏt nt ḥtpw-nṯr sbk-šdty ḫrp ḥr ḥtp-snwsrt m3*ʿ-*ḫrw*

P10254b cattle *km m mḏt nt ḥtpw-nṯr ḥr-š.f nb* [

cf. P10233d delivery of two oxen

Note too the account of *ḥtpw-nṯr* P10233d, cited below under offerings, with division into two estates implied at least at the level of delivery, one of Senusret II and the other of Anubis

(b) **References to offerings to deities**

(i) *Offerings to more than one deity or person*

P10011 col 3 *ḥsb* [ ] *ḥtpw-nṯr* with five items:

1-2 daily and festival offerings to Senusret II
3-4 daily and festival offerings to Anubis
item 5 month and halfmonth festival offerings to Sobek *nb r-sḥwy*
P10112Bc *m3ʿt n* *nswt bỉty [*
ỉnpw [
ḥwtḥr nbt [
P10233d delivery of two oxen for *ỉnpw tpy-ḏw.f m sḫm-*[*sn*]*wsr*[*t*]
sḫm-snwsrt m3ʿ-ḫrw
P10328a summary of offerings with five items:
1-2 daily and festival offerings (deity not stated, presumably Senusret II)
3-4 daily and festival offerings to Anubis
5 *ỉmnyt nt ʿt šps*t (perhaps the offerings at the falsedoor at the pyramid)
P10415b an account of daily and festival offerings to Senusret II (lines 1-3) and Anubis (lines 4-5) on the epagomenal days

ʿḳw nswt bỉty ḫʿḫprrʿ n 3bd 4 šmw 5 ḥryw rnpt
ỉmnyt nt ʿt špst nt 3bd 4 šmw 5 ḥryw rnpt
[*ḥb*]*yt nt 3bd 4 šmw 5 ḥryw rnpt*
[*ʿḳw..*] *ỉnpw tpy-ḏw.f n 3bd 4* [
[*ḥb*]*yt nt ỉ*[*np*]*w nt* [*3bd 4* (trace)

From these references it seems clear that Anubis received offerings at Sekhem-Senusret on a level comparable only with the cult of Senusret II himself. It is also interesting that the delivery of oxen in P0233d places Anubis first; this could be taken to imply that the Anubis cult could on at least some occasions (particular festivals ?) take first place over the main cult (that of Senusret II).

(ii) *Offerings to the king or a member of his family*
P10009 col.2 *m3ʿt n nswt bỉty* [ ] *m3ʿ-ḫrw m ḥbyt nt sỉnt*
P10039 forecast of festival *mnḫt ḫʿḫprrʿ*
P10041 offerings at Sokar festival to Senusret II
P10053 offerings of fowl at Sokar festival (and other occasions ?) to Senusret II and *s3t nswt Ỉ.*[
P10056A copy of letter with mention of *ḥtpw-nṯr m3ʿ n nswt-bỉty ḫʿḫprrʿ m3ʿ-ḫrw ỉnnw m ḥwt-nṯr nt sbk šdt*
P10092a+b vso *m3ʿt n nswt-bỉty ḫʿ*[*ḫpr*]*rʿ*
P10095 *n nswt-bỉty ḫʿḫprrʿ m3ʿ-ḫrw m sḫm-snwsrt m3ʿ-ḫrw m ḥwt-nṯr* [..] *ḥwtḥr nbt tp-ỉḥw mỉtt ỉry n ḥmt nswt mwt nswt ẖnmt nfrt ḥḏt* [ ] *m sḫm-snwsrt m3ʿ-ḫrw*
similarly below *m3ʿt* [*n*] *nswt-bỉty ḫʿḫprrʿ m3ʿ-ḫrw m sḫm-snwsr*[*t*] *ḥmt nswt mwt nswt ẖnmt nfrt ḥdt m3ʿt-ḫrw* [
P10127B [*m3*]*ʿt n nswt-bỉty ḫʿḫprrʿ m3ʿ-ḫrw* [ ] .. *ḥb skr* [*ḥr] tp ʿ.w.s. nswt bỉty nm3ʿtrʿ ʿnḫ ḏt r nḥḥ*
P10128Ab loaves and beer *m3ʿt n s3t nswt Ỉ.t [*
P10202 day-note of items *m3ʿt n nswt* [(twice) and *m3ʿt n nswt-bỉty ḫʿḫprrʿ m3ʿ-ḫrw..*[
P10222a [ ] *⌜ḳw twt n nswt bỉty ḫʿ*[ ]*rʿ*[
[*rp*]*yt nt s3t nswt Ỉ.t-k3yt* [
ḫft wḏ3.n.sn m ḫntyt [
P10223 ox (*ỉw3*) *m3ʿt n nswt-bỉty ḫʿḫprrʿ*
P10255 [offerings] for Senusret II
P10321a day-note of items *m3ʿt n nswt* [
P10322a day-note of items *m3ʿt n nswt* [
P10322c day-note of items [offered to] *nswt bỉty* (?) *ḫʿḫprrʿ m3ʿ-ḫrw*
P10377f vso offerings for *s3t nswt nfrt m3<ʿ>t*[*-ḫrw* ?]
P10397d day-note of items [*m3*]*ʿt n s3*[*t*?] *nswt* [
P10410 *ḥbyt nt sm3-t3 nt snt nswt ʿnḫt* (?) *m3ʿt-ḫrw* (the item is *swt*)
P10416g reference to offerings for queen (?)
P10417]*4 3bd 4 šmw hrw 5 ḥryw rnpt* [ ] *m3ʿ n nswt-bỉty ḫʿḫprrʿ m3ʿ-ḫrw* [

P10418a day-note of items offered to Senusret II (? broken)
P10443 day-note of items *m3ʿt n nswt [bìty ḫʿ]ḫpr[rʿ] m3ʿ-ḫrw* for Sokar festival
Perhaps also here belongs the reference of P10300c vso to *] nswt-bìty ḫʿḫprrʿ m3ʿ-ḫrw m sḫm-snwsrt m3ʿ-ḫrw*

These sources confirm that the main cult at Sekhem-Senusret was that of Senusret II; some offerings are supplied from the temple of Hathor lady of Atfih (if P10095 is so to be understood), and others from the temple of Sobek of Shedyet (P10056A). Several of the offerings for the king are for the Sokar festival. Named members of the royal family are the king's daughter Itekayt, the king's daughter Nefret (?), and the king's sister Ankhet (??), in addition to the king's wife and king's mother Khenmetnefrethedjet.

(iii) *Offerings to a deity*
The only deity to receive offerings in isolation from the king or another deity is Anubis:
P10044 *ḫt ìnpw tpy-ḏw.f m sḫm-snwsrt m3ʿ-ḫrw*
P10044 vso *ḥtpw-nṯr* (?) of *ìnpw tpy-ḏw.f m sḫm-snwsrt m3ʿ-ḫrw*
P10046 .. of *ìnpw tpy-ḏw.f m sḫm-snwsrt m3ʿ-ḫrw*
P10055 offerings of fowl throughout the year to *ìnpw tpy-ḏw.f m sḫm-snwsrt m3ʿ-ḫrw*
P10118Ac offerings of fowl to *ìnpw tpy-ḏw.f*
P10203 *ḥtpw-nṯr* of *ìnpw tpy-ḏw.f m sḫm-snwsrt m3ʿ-ḫrw*, four items, all from *mḏt nt ḥtpw-nṯr sbk-šdty ḫrp ḥr ḥtp-snwsrt m3ʿ-ḫrw*
P10207a *ḥtpw-nṯr ḥr rnpt m3ʿ n ìnpw tpy-ḏw.f*
P10209a *ḥtpw-nṯr m3ʿ n ìnpw* [
P10256 in cursive hieroglyphs].. *ʿkw ḥbyt* .. [ ] *ìnpw tpy-ḏw.f m sḫm-*[*ḥr-tp*] *ʿ.w.s. nswt-bìty ḫʿk3wrʿ*[
P10354d day-note of items *m3ʿt n ìnpw tpy-ḏw.f*
with *dbḥt-ḥtpw nt ìnp[w*
ḫnt[
the last line could be an epithet of Anubis (cf. the uncertain *ìnpw ḫnty ìmnty* of 10414b), or, perhaps less likely, a second deity, e.g. Khentkhety
P10401 *m3ʿt n ìnpw tpy-ḏw.f m ḫnm* (?) [
this could refer to Khenemsut, the cult temple of Senusret I at Lisht: the Memphis inscription of Amenemhat II refers to a cult of Anubis in Khenemsut, see below
P10414b [*šnwt nt*] *ḥtpw-*[*nṯr*] *nt ìnpw ḫnty ìmnty* (?), cf. 10354d
P10424b day-note of items *m3ʿt n ìnpw*..[
P10424b day-note of items .. *n ìnpw*..[
Perhaps also here belongs the reference of P10080 to *ìnpw tpy-ḏw.f m sḫm-*[ ].

(c) **References to statues**

P10003A col.2-3 statues of Senusret II, Senusret III, two queens, all of wood or hard stone, none of precious metals
P10003B col.1 *ìrt mì* [ ] *wḏ3 sḫm ìnpw r snsn m ḥwt-nṯr* [
nswt bìty [*m3ʿ*]*-ḫrw m sḫm-snwsrt m3ʿ-ḫrw ḫft ḫnt-nt-t3*
the inventory for this statue procession lists *sšm n ìnpw*, its *st*, an ivory statue of Senusret III *ʿnḫ ḏt r ḥḥ*, an ebony statue of Senusret II *m3ʿ-ḫrw*, and the rite apparatus (one *sḥtpy*, one *ḥst*). The entry documents the passage of an Anubis image to *snsn* "fraternize" in the temple of [Senusret II] in Sekhem-Senusret on the occasion of the festival Sailing of the Land, possibly an annual celebration on the day of the burial of the king.
At the 1994 British Museum colloquium Rainer Stadelmann drew attention to the importance of this passage for the understanding of the role of Anubis in the cult of the king, noting the special significance of the word *snsn* in this context.
P10003C col.2 statues of Senusret II, Senusret III, two queens
P10112Bd *rpyt nt sḫm-snwsrt m3ʿ-ḫrw*, with references to Heryshef, Sobek of Shedyet, and Ra-Horakhty, in unclear context

P10222a [ ] ⌜*kw twt n nswt bity ḫ*⌜[ ]*r*ʿ[
[*rp*]*yt nt s3t nswt ỉ.t-k3yt* [
ḫft wḏ3.n.sn m ḫntyt [

P10237d statues of queens (fragment of longer list)

P10239d wooden statues of officials

P10248 statues of Senusret III (ivory) and II (ebony) in copies of letters about dates for *mnḫt ỉnpw tpy-ḏw.f m sḫm-snwsrt m3ʿ-ḫrw* and *ḫnp-šʿ n ỉnpw tpy-ḏw.f m sḫm-snwsrt m3ʿ-ḫrw*

This suggests that Anubis may have had his own festivals of *mnḫt t* and *ḫnp-šʿ*, but it is possible that the Sekhem-Senusret festivals of those names, elsewhere expressed as being of the king, were identified as festivals of Anubis in letters.

P10307f *snh dw3yw (?)* [ ] *r šms sḫm ỉnpw*

P10311 vso account *sšm ḫnt n*[*n*]
dỉ r mr ḫft ỉwt ..
ntt dỉt ḫft wḏ3 twt [
twt dỉ r .. [

This is the full extent of the account: *dmḏ* and *wḏ3t* lines follow.

P10312 statues of officials and royals

P10312 vso (materials lost) statue of Senusret III, statue of Senusret II, *sḫm ỉnpw*, its *st*, and the rite apparatus (one *sḥtpy*, one *ḥst*).

P10381c royal statue list fragment

P10388d royal statue list fragment

P10411c royal statue list fragment

In this section Anubis again occupies an exceptional position in the surviving record, being the only deity with a statue, and linked to the king by the phrase *snsn* ,"to fraternize" (to meet on the ritual and divine plane).

(d) **References to priests of particular deities**

The mayor of Lahun adds to his main title that of temple overseer, *ḥ3ty-ʿ ỉmy-r ḥwt-nṯr*, in contrast to the other common late Middle Kingdom title combination of mayor with overseer of god's servants, *ḥ3ty-ʿ ỉmy-r ḥmw-nṯr*. The contrast could be taken to imply that one covered several cults at a single centre, and the other several centres of cult: however, it must be stressed that the differentiation of these two title pairings remains to be studied.

The recurrent titles temple scribe (*sḫ ḥwt-nṯr*) and temple doorkeepers (*ỉry-ʿ3 n ḥwt-nṯr*) could be taken to imply that no ambiguity arose from referring to "the temple" and thus suggesting that only one *ḥwt-nṯr* existed in the town. This would accord with the excavation plan of the site from the 1889 and later seasons. However, it must be remembered that the manuscripts themselves form a homogeneous group from one temple site. Moreover the substantial proportion of the site now under the fields would have been closest to any access canal of the Senusret II Valley Temple, and would therefore perhaps have been the most likely location for another shrine in the town.

A key title with frequent attestations is pure-priest of the king (*wʿb nswt*), to be compared with the namelists of *wʿbw* appointed to keep vigil at the *mr*. The letter copy P10385c, from year 23 of an unnamed king (probably Amenemhat III), contains the more explicit reference *wʿbw nswt bỉty ḫʿḫprr*[..].

Another indication of local cults is the phrase *ḥm-k3 n* + title; such designations are more common in the town papyri, suggesting, as perhaps is to be expected, that the provision for the funerary cult of even the highest officials depended in large part on their own measures, and were not primarily the concern of the king. The presence of statues of high officials in the lists among the temple files need not imply more than a responsibility for safekeeping: the cult may have been entirely the responsibility of the privately appointed *ḥm-k3*. The only *ḥm-k3* in the accounts, as opposed to the letters, among the temple files, is one of the queen in P10050 col.2, cf. an apparent reference to offerings for the queen in P10416g.

The other title of especial note is embalmer of Anubis (*wtw ỉnpw*); this is the only title, among the staff on the Berlin papyri, to refer to a deity. It is prominent in the records of staff, e.g. in the day-note of P10046 after the record of *ḫnt (?) ỉnpw tpy-ḏw.f m sḫm-snwsrt m3ʿ-ḫrw*. This exceptional feature confirms the presence and importance of the Anubis cult at Lahun.

Other titles with particular affinity to a part of the pyramid complex and its cults may be libationer (*ỉbḥ*), and 'he of the god's booth' (*sḥy-nṯr*), the latter evoking the epithet of Anubis "foremost of the god's booth".

Summary of the evidence from the papyri

The papyri contain evidence for an unrivalled prominence of Anubis alongside Senusret II at Sekhem-Senusret. Two possible interpretations can be offered; according to the first, the cults would be housed within the same building or complex, and according to the second, a separate temple of Anubis would have to be envisaged elsewhere in the vicinity. Proponents of a lost temple of Anubis must account for the discovery of the temple files on the far side of the town alongside the site of the pyramid complex valley temple: the temple files suggest that a single institution maintained the cults of both Senusret II and Anubis in Sekhem-Senusret. In contrast to other researchers, I identify only the pyramid-complex as Sekhem-Senusret, and the orthogonally planned town as Hetep-Senusret, from a combination of the indications of the papyri (here there is a great difference in the attestations of the temple files and those from the diverse town fragments and groups of documents) and the evidence of unbroken and broken sealings from the site (for the most recent summary, concluding in favour of the opposing view, see Luft 1997). Therefore I interpret the attestations in the papyri as evidence for a single temple complex housing two cults, a main cult of Senusret II and a secondary cult of Anubis. This might be supported by the lack of qualifying epithets to *ḥwt-nṯr* "temple" in these sources; the only temples to be identified as those of a particular deity are those at some distance, those of Hathor lady of Atfih, Sobek of Shedyet, and Heryshef lord of Henennesut. It is striking that no other Twelfth Dynasty royal cult complex appears to be woven into the economic structure of the temple estates supporting the cults of Senusret II and Anubis at Lahun; possibly the marginally greater distance to Lisht, as compared with Atfih, might explain this, but there may be an institutional principle behind this feature of the accounts. It is not possible to determine the scale of the estates for the cult of Senusret II, but, given the importance of meat offerings, it is significant that Sekhem-Senusret housed no stalls of its own for cattle. Officials of Hetep-Senusret seem to have administered cattle herds and provided for meat offerings at Sekhem-Senusret, and elsewhere from these, as implied in the great cattle account UC 32179 (Petrie lot VI.10: Griffith 1898, pl.16-17).

3 Hieroglyphic evidence for Anubis in Sekhem-Senusret

(1) The Abydos stela of Dedusobek (Petrie 1925, pl.12, 7)

At the site of First Dynasty royal cult enclosures on the edge of the cultivation at north Abydos, Petrie uncovered a number of Middle Kingdom stelae, one of which depicts a man named Dedusobek with an unusual combination of titles:

ḫry-ḥbt ʿš3 m sḫm-snwsrt m3ʿ-ḫrw m3 bs m ḥwt-nṯr nt ỉnpw tpy-ḏw.f m sḫm-snwsrt m3ʿ-ḫrw (pyramid-determinative) *nty m srt m ḥtp-snwsrt m3ʿ-ḫrw*

"ordinary lector-priest in Sekhem-Senusret, he who sees the initiate in the temple of Anubis who is upon his mountain in Sekhem-Senusret, he who is among the officialdom in Hetep-Senusret".

In this stela the cult centre of Anubis appears to be treated as a separate entity but still within the place Sekhem-Senusret; this placename is given without a determinative at one point, but with the pyramid-determinative at the second attestation, and thus may be taken to refer to the pyramid-complex of Senusret II at Lahun.

(2) The Haraga stela of Nebipu (Ny Carlsberg 1540: Engelbach 1923, pl.71)

The cemeteries of Haraga lie on the sand island within the fields to the east of Lahun, and seem to have provided the ground for burials for the late Middle Kingdom inhabitants of Lahun. Tomb 41

yielded a stela with an extraordinary repeated offering formula invoking five different deities for the same man but on each occasion with a title appropriate to the patronage of that deity:
Hedjhotep - *ỉry-ʿt n pr-ḥḏ* "store keeper of the treasury"
Ptah - *ỉry ḥbsw* "keeper of clothing"
Anubis lord of Shespet - *sḥy-nṯr* "man of the god's pavilion"
Khentkhety lord of Kemwy (Athribis in the Delta) - *ỉmy-r ḫtmtyw* "overseer of sealers"
Khakheperra (= Senusret II) - *ỉbḥ* "libationer"
Berlev has drawn attention to this stela (Berlev 1978, 242-3) and in particular to the relation between titles and deities; I would suggest that the five titles form a description of a single local position at the temple, combining the role of *sḥy-nṯr* with service in the cult of the king as *ỉbḥ*. The common theme of the first four titles is cloth, and it is possible that the *sḥy-nṯr* was responsible for providing the linen to be placed around the cult statue(s) daily; he would then need to have access to (*ỉry-ʿt n pr-ḥḏ*) and custodianship of (*ỉry ḥbsw*) cloth, and some authority over the officials who sealed stores of such valuable material (*ḫtmtyw*). The fivefold titulary of this official may even be using the model of the royal fivefold titulary in order to explain this local duty of provider of statue-wrappings. At all events the case confirms the special role of Anubis in the cult-place of Senusret II at Lahun.

4 Lahun and Heracleopolis: isolating differences between temples of gods and royal cult complexes in the Middle Kingdom

On the evidence of the papyri and these two stelae, I propose as a working hypothesis to ascribe the cult of Anubis in Sekhem-Senusret to the pyramid complex of Senusret II. The site itself has been too efficiently quarried of its stone to permit any reconstruction of its plan, and the relief fragments as retrieved do not permit an attribution of function to any part of the site. An Anubis chapel or sector may not be locateable any longer on the ground at Lahun. However, fragments from other sites might derive from Lahun, and these ought to be taken into consideration in assessing the role of the gods in the pyramid complex.

The destruction of the Lahun temples was ascribed by Petrie to the reign of Ramses II on the basis of graffiti on blocks, and the presence of the name of Senusret II on a column of Ramses II at Heracleopolis (Petrie 1890, 22; id., 1891, 1). From the archaeological evidence Barry Kemp has drawn attention to the small scale of temples to local deities, as opposed to centres of the royal cult, prior to the New Kingdom (Kemp 1983, 103-4). This difference in scale might be expected to dictate a differential use of materials, especially large and hard stone elements. Accordingly the Middle Kingdom stone, and particularly the hard stone, at Heracleopolis could be taken to represent the most substantial surviving architectural elements of the Senusret II pyramid complex. However, Naville argued that blocks with the name of Senusret II unearthed by him at Heracleopolis belonged to an original Middle Kingdom temple to Heryshef there (Naville 1894, 2-3 with pl.I, D-E); he drew attention to an inscription of an official named Khuy sent to the Wadi Hammamat in year 14 of Senusret III to procure stone for monuments for Heryshef (Couyat and Montet, 1912, pl.14, no.47: *ỉs wḏ ḥm.f sbt r r-hnw r ỉnt mnw wḏ.n ḥm.f ỉrt.f n ḥr-š.f nb ḥnnnswt ḥr tp ʿnḫ nswt bỉty ḫʿk3wrʿ ʿnḫ ḏt r nḥḥ m ỉnrw nfr n bḫnw* "indeed His Person ordered an expedition to Rehenu to bring monuments ordered by His Person to be made for Heryshef lord of Henennesut on behalf of the life of the Dual King Khakaura living for ever and eternity as good stone of greywacke"). It should be noted that the scale and form of the monument are not recorded; nor does Khuy specify the destination of this monument, even if Heracleopolis seems to us the most likely. Thus the text does not of itself demonstrate the existence of extensive hard stone architectural elements in a local Middle Kingdom temple; indeed in that case one might perhaps have expected some reference to "temple" as well as or instead of "monument". Petrie subsequently carried out a more systematic excavation of the temple site at Heracleopolis, and recorded stone and brick walls of a substantial building below the level of the New Kingdom structure, the stone foundation wall measuring over two and a half metres in width and lying beneath a sand bed (Petrie 1905, 3-7 and pl.5); though surviving only as a fragment, the scale of the structure seemed comparable to that of the Ramesside portico, and therefore the Twelfth Dynasty elements on the site might be argued to derive after all from a Middle Kingdom Heracleopolitan temple, as argued recently by Mokhtar (1983, 78-9 n.1). However, the lower level of the stone wall beneath a sand layer can only be dated relatively, thus to any point before the final Ramesside portico, including Eighteenth or early Nineteenth Dynasty. Burials beneath the temple included scarabs and other seals with grouped hieroglyphs of late Middle Kingdom or even Second Intermediate Period type (Petrie 1905, pl.9a, nos.4, 15, 20). It is also striking that the finds echo the sequence of monumental building-programmes outlined by Kemp from the Upper Egyptian sites of Elephantine, Hieraconpolis, Medamud and Abydos; in this sequence non-orthogonal shrines are replaced over the course of the late Old and Middle Kingdoms by 'Early Formal' temples with a rectilinear plan but with limited use of stone, succeeded in turn by 'Mature Formal' temples of the New Kingdom with more extensive use of stone, and finally by the 'Late Formal' structures on uniformly massive scale, familiar to modern visitors to Ptolemaic and Roman Period sandstone temple sites from Philae to Dendera (Kemp 1989, 65-79). The difference between non-formal and formal is not simply a matter of the scale; 'Early Formal' shrines may not greatly exceed the area of the non-formal structures which they replace. The reason for difference would seem to lie rather in the degree of royal, we might say 'central state' or 'national', involvement; orthogonal-plan building programmes imply extended access to non-local materials, transport, workshops and planners. This schematic history of architecture may not apply to all shrines, particularly those of special status in the Middle Kingdom. The temple of Heryshef at Heracleopolis may have ranked as one of those 'first class' temples. Nevertheless, grounded in observation of the known scale and layout of temple plans, the Kemp schematic sequence provides a useful model with which to assess the original intended location of the Twelfth Dynasty architectural elements and sculpture at the site.

The Middle Kingdom elements at Heracleopolis are the following (with page and plate references to Petrie 1905):

the monolithic red granite columns of the portico, ascribed to the Middle Kingdom (12-15 and pl.8 and 10);
two quartzite statues ascribed to Senusret II or Senusret III (15);
quartzite statue fragment with nemes and uraeus, ascribed to the Twelfth Dynasty (20, pl.12)
a course of quartzite blocks ascribed to the Middle Kingdom temple (15 with plan pl.5);
block (material not specified) with cartouches of Senusret III facing words of a deity (20 and pl.11 centre);
granite lintel with Horus name of Senusret III at either end of scene with deities (20, pl.13);
granite jamb with Two Ladies name of Senusret II (20, pl.13);
granite block with "Behedet", ascribed to the Twelfth Dynasty (20, pl.13);
granite block with "words spoken by Sekhmet the great beloved of Ptah" (20, pl.13);
block (material not specified) with royal epithet "[living] like Ra eternally" (20, pl.13);
limestone blocks with name of Senusret III in a rectangle, and Horus name of Amenemhat III, before the title of a rite and the tip of the Red Crown (20, pl.14);
block (material not specified) with cartouche Senusret (20, pl.14);
two blocks (material not specified) with queenly epithets (20, pl.14);
block (material not specified) with offering jar (20, pl.14);
two blocks (material not specified) with Golden Horus name of Senusret III (20, pl.14)
block (material not specified) with royal titles facing Wadjyt and royal epithets (20, pl.15).
block (material not specified) with oil jars and natron bags, undated (20, pl.15)

The larger jamb blocks include the names of Senusret II and the goddess Sekhmet. The latter seems more closely associated with royal cult complexes (cf. section 6, below) than with the temple of Heryshef; in the Ramesside period the goddess appears on Heracleopolitan monuments, but only in the context of the Memphite triad (e.g. Mokhtar 1983, pl.5 statue Cairo [no no.], and pl.20, relief of Pahemnetjer Cairo J 47001).

The columns were again ascribed to Lahun, with due caution, by Dieter Arnold in the entry for the *Lexikon der Ägyptologie* (1986, 705-6 n.22), although more recently he has revised this view in favour of a large-scale pre-New Kingdom temple for the local deity at Heracleopolis.

In order to assess whether these and elements at other sites may have been moved from Lahun or not, it is necessary to reconsider possible differences between types of monuments and their materials in royal cult complexes and those in other cult-centres during the Middle Kingdom. The moving roadshow of quarried blocks is particularly striking in the embellishment of Delta cities from the founding of Per-Ramses in the thirteenth century BC (Uphill 1984) to that of Alexandria almost a millennium later. Despite this complicating factor, the surviving record may indicate programmatic differences between the commissions from the relief/sculpture workshops for royal cult centres and those for the temples of the gods.

Statues found in temples of gods

Mention of a deity is insufficient of itself to provenance a statue; Cairo CG 405 (Borchardt 1925, 17-8, pl.66), the statue of the official Sasobek from the town site at Lahun bears an invocation of Ptah-Sokar and Sobek lord of Sumenu, a cult-centre southwest of Thebes. Similarly, the granite statue of the mayor and god's sealer Hor (Cairo CG 520: Borchardt 1925, 79, pl.88) might be ascribed to either Hawara or Dahshur, because it invokes Amenemhat III (*ḥr ꜥ3-b3w nswt bỉty nym3ꜥtrꜥ m3ꜥ-ḫrw*), but it is said by Borchardt to have been acquired in Upper Egypt. Accordingly, for example, the epithet "beloved of Hathor lady of Atfih" on a 'black granite' maned sphinx of Khaneferra Sobekhotep (Cairo CG 421: Borchardt 1925, 29, pl.68) is insufficient evidence to ascribe the piece to that site.

The following statues of Twelfth Dynasty kings have been found at, and from their posture or inscriptions were probably made for, temple sites where the principal cult is of not the king but a deity:

Cairo CG 429 (Borchardt 1925, 33-4, pl.70), red granite Osiride statue of Senusret I, retrieved from the cult complex at Kom es-Sultan, on the edge of the cultivation at Abydos by Mariette in 1859.

Cairo CG 387 (Borchardt 1925, 6-7, pl.61), Memphis statue in 'brown sandstone' (presumably quartzite) of the kneeling and offering Senusret II with the epithet *sḥb ḥwt ptḥ-skr* "he who makes festive the temple of Ptah-Sokar", according to Borchardt acquired from Mitrahina in 1887. In scale and material this is the most important Twelfth Dynasty statue which can be ascribed to the shrine of a deity on the strength of the inscription. Its posture is appropriate to the context of a temple of a god rather than of the royal cult.

Medamud sculpture of Senusret III, e.g. 'grey granite' head Cairo CG 486 (Borchardt 1925, 65, pl.81), acquired 1896.

Cairo CG 422, 423, 425 (Borchardt 1925, 30-2, pl.68-9), small 'dark granite' statues of Senusret III, Amenemhat III and Senusret II acquired in 1888 at Kom el-Ahmar and bearing epithets 'beloved of Horus (of Nekhen) in Nekhen' or 'of Hathor lady of Inerty (Gebelein)'.

Cairo CG 391 (Borchardt 1925, 9, pl.62), limestone late Middle Kingdom maned sphinx, acquired in Elkab in 1891 (possibly Thirteenth Dynasty).

These statues include a new type, the standing worshipping king, and a new scale and material for the type of the kneeling king. It might be argued that these were devised precisely to meet a new architectural space, the orthogonal-plan (Kemp 'Early Formal') temple to a deity rather than to a king. They represent the Twelfth Dynasty development of a Sixth Dynasty innovation, the kneeling offering king, as in the small image of Pepy I, just as their architectural space too was introduced in Sixth Dynasty royal shrines such as those to the 'national' or 'dynastic' goddess Hathor at Dendera and Gebelein.

In contrast to such monuments linked by inscription or type to their place of discovery, other Twelfth Dynasty sculpture from temples to deities seems more likely to have been moved from royal cult complexes:

BM EA 1069, quartzite statue of Senusret III from Nebesha (Petrie 1888, 13, pl.9, 2a-b)

BM EA 1145 and 1146, quartzite statues of Senusret III from Tell Moqdam (Naville 1894, pl.4, A and C)

Cairo CG 538, Middle Kingdom 'black granite' royal statue from Tell Moqdam (Borchardt 1925, 87-8, pl.89)

Cairo CG 381, 382, 'dark granite' statues of queen Nefret from Tanis (Borchardt 1925, 1-2, pl.60)

Cairo CG 383, (Borchardt 1925, 3, pl.60) and BM EA 1063, 'dark granite' colossal statue heads of

Amenemhat III from Bubastis
Cairo CG 389, Middle Kingdom 'dark granite' royal statue from Bubastis (Borchardt 1925, 7-8, pl.62)
Cairo CG 392, 531, late Middle Kingdom 'dark/grey granite' offering-statues from Tanis (Borchardt 1925, 9-11, pl.63, and 83, pl.89)
Cairo CG 430, 432, Middle Kingdom 'dark granite' statues from Tanis (Borchardt 1925, 34-9, pl.70-71)
Cairo CG 424, 'dark granite' statue of *ḥmt nswt mwt nswt* Senet from Kom el-Fulus (Borchardt 1925, 31, pl.69)
Cairo CG 393, 394, 530, late Middle Kingdom 'dark/black granite' maned sphinxes from Tanis (Borchardt 1925, 11-3, pl.63-4, and 83, pl.89)

Of these, the statues from Bubastis are the most likely to have been intended for that site originally, although as a national cult focus its monumental history peaks under the Twenty-second Dynasty. The three quartzite statues of Senusret III from Nebesha and Tell Moqdam seem more likely to have been moved from a royal cult complex, given the parallels in the cult complex of that king at Abydos; the same argument could be applied to the quartzite statues of Senusret II or III discovered at Heracleopolis. The statues of queen Nefret bearing the cartouche of Senusret II might be ascribed to his pyramid complex at Lahun (in passing it may be noted that stela Cairo CG 20394 gives the family of a queen Nefret and is cited in *LdR,* 295-301 as a third source for the Nefret of the mid-Twelfth Dynasty, but it is dated to the Thirteenth Dynasty by its style and by the titles, e.g.*3ṯw n ṯt ḥḳ3* son of a *ʿnḫ n ṯt ḥḳ3*).

Sculpture from Karnak is more likely to have been intended for the temple, because, unlike the moves from one Lower Egyptian site to another, there is not the same quantity of evidence for large scale transport of sculpture between temple sites in Upper Egypt, other than the Amenhotep III sed statuary (see Bryan in this volume). The following items may be noted:

statue-groups of Amenemhat I with Amun, and of Senusret I with Amun (PM II^{2}, 107), found near the granite sanctuary
statue of Amenemhat I kneeling with two jars, from Karnak North
British Museum EA 44 (PM II^{2}, 276) standing 'black granite' statue of Senusret I, unearthed in the Karnak South area
Cairo CG 42007 (PM II^{2}, 93) head from a 'granite' sphinx of Senusret I, from the north court
Cairo CG 42008 (PM II^{2}, 108) statue-group of Senusret I standing with Hathor seated, from the central court area
Cairo CG 42011-2 (PM II^{2}, 136) two colossi of Senusret III found buried in front of the eighth pylon
Cairo CG 42013 (PM II^{2}, 136) statue of Senusret III kneeling with jars, from the cachette
Cairo CG 42014-20 (PM II^{2}, 136) seven 'granite' statues of Amenemhat III from the cachette
Cairo J.38386-7 (PM II^{2}, 173) two colossi of Senusret I, in Court II, located between the seventh and eighth pylons
Cairo J.41472 (PM II^{2}, 281) headless 'granite' sphinx of Amenemhat III
Cairo J.43598 (PM II^{2}, 281) part of a statue of Senusret II enthroned
Cairo J.48851 (PM II^{2}, 89) Osiride colossus of Senusret I, found in the foundations of the sixth pylon

In addition to the monuments set up by Twelfth and Thirteenth Dynasty kings at the temple for the cult of Nebhepetra Mentuhotep at Deir el-Bahri (e.g. PM II^{2}, 394-5), there may have been a cult for him at Karnak, where a sandstone Osiride statue found at the seventh pylon bears the dedication *nswt bỉty ḫʿnfrrʿ dỉ ʿnḫ ỉr.f m mnw.f n nswt bỉty nbḥptrʿ m3ʿ-ḫrw m sm3 ỉrt.n nswt bỉty ḫʿk3wrʿ m3ʿ-ḫrw nswt bỉty ḫʿḫprrʿ m3ʿ-ḫrw ỉt.f dỉ ʿnḫ mỉ rʿ ḏt* "the dual king Khaneferra (= Sobekhotep 'IV' of the mid-Thirteenth Dynasty) granted life: he made (it) as a monument to the dual king Nebhepetra true of voice as a renewal of what was made by the dual king Khakaura (Senusret III) true of voice and the dual king Khakheperra (Senusret II) true of voice, his father, granted life like Ra eternally" (Cairo J.38579: Legrain 1906). The cult of the deified reunifier of Egypt would to some extent bridge the gap between temples of gods and those of kings.

Also from the Theban nome, and one of the most curious innovations of the early Twelfth Dynasty, is the hexad of Amenemhat I from Armant, a pillar of rectangular section with two figures each of the king, a god, and the goddess Hathor (Mond and Myers 1940, pl.20, find S.35, pp.51, 190 noting the absence of the double plume and therefore rejecting identification of the god as Montu despite the findspot, a cult-centre of that deity).

These finds suffice to demonstrate the presence of soft and hard stone royal statuary in Middle Kingdom temples to deities as well as in royal cult complexes, but include differences in type such as the kneeling and worshipping king and the hexad. Allowing for the gaps in the record, there remains a clear need to specify type, material and scale of surviving elements when studying the differences or similarities between the two kinds of institution.

Inscribed blocks in temples of gods

The different form and scale of cult centres as noted by Kemp might be expected to affect selection of stone for walls, columns and gateways, and the extent to which these were inscribed. Again, the record is broken, but may be examined for any differential pattern.

The monolithic granite naos of Senusret I found at Karnak is one of the most important and substantial survivals from Middle Kingdom temples to gods (Daressy 1927); recently it has been argued that, as this naos could not have stood on the calcite naos stand of Senusret I in the sanctuary area, already under Senusret I two cults of Amun operated, one for the fixed and most precious image, the other for a less precious processional statue (Gabolde 1995).

The White Chapel and other blocks of Senusret I at Karnak (notably the wall-block with niche, Maarouf and Zimmer 1993, 227-32, 236-7; and the bark chapel, Traunecker 1982) and Coptos (Lyon MBA E501: Durey et al. 1988, 40-3), the gateways of Senusret III and Sekhemrakhutawy Amenemhat Sobekhotep at Medamud (Janosi 1994, 24-5, no.4), and the doorway of Amenemhat II at Ashmunein indicate the use of inscribed limestone blocks at temples of deities at this period. An extended inscription in a local temple is the wall of Senusret I at Tod, partly obliterated by Ptolemaic reuse (Barbotin and Clère 1991). Limestone blocks inscribed with the accession text of Amenemhat III, the text redeployed in the mid-Eighteenth Dynasty by Hatshepsut at Deir el-Bahri, are said to come from Medinet el-Fayum. If this is the correct provenance, it might indicate an exceptional role for the Sobek temple in kingship ritual at the end of the Twelfth Dynasty.

Among the doorway elements, two blocks stand out, being of quartzite and mentioning the deities of Heliopolis with Senusret III (Quirke 1995):

BM EA 145 quartzite lintel of Senusret III (not Senusret II despite loss of lower cartouche, from parallel of lintel BM EA 74753) from Alexandria, with Rahorakhty and *nṯr b3w ỉwnw* "the god the Souls of Heliopolis" (pl.Ia)

BM EA 74753 quartzite lintel of Senusret III probably from Alexandria, with Rahorakhty and Atum (pl.Ib).

These are not broad enough to stand over a doorway accommodating more than a single person at a time; BM EA 74753 measures 1.425 metres across, and BM EA 145 is of the same scale. They might derive originally either from Dahshur or from Heliopolis itself, and therefore do not clarify differences in deployment of stone in temples of gods and those of kings.

The Heliopolitan connection reminds us that we do not know the scale of the Middle Kingdom 'national' temples of Ra at Heliopolis, Ptah at Memphis, and, for the late Middle Kingdom, Sobek, and that this may be expected to qualify the picture of smaller scale temples to the gods as observed by Kemp from the archaeological record. One striking indicator of larger scale is the obelisk of Senusret I at Heliopolis (PM IV, 60); this is still standing but there has been no excavation or survey to provide evidence for its original architectural setting. For the reconstruction of the cults at Lahun, it is difficult to know where within the spectrum of monumental architecture the Heryshef temple might fall, and this is crucial for determining the original provenance of hard stone elements found at Heracleopolis.

The original provenance of the Memphis annals of Amenemhat II is equally uncertain (Petrie 1909, pl.5 with Farag 1980). The annals appear to have been inscribed on a series of blocks reused in the temple of Ramses II in the domain of Ptah; most were eroded, but the principal surviving text on one red granite block includes after the name of Amenemhat II the epithet "beloved of Atum lord of

Heliopolis". Three possible original sites for the monument may be proposed: (i) the temple of Ptah at Memphis, (ii) that of Atum at Heliopolis, (iii) the Dahshur pyramid complex of Amenemhat II.

On the original location of the long lintel of Senusret III at Heracleopolis (Petrie 1905, pl.13) and the other granite doorway blocks of the Twelfth Dynasty cited above, including the item bearing the name of Sekhmet, the following parallels for granite doorway elements in temples of the gods can be cited:

lintel showing Nebhepetra Mentuhotep between Horus and Wadjyt, and Seth and Nekhbet, from Karnak, possibly part of a Twelfth Dynasty monument for the cult of Nebhepetra, implied in the statue dedication by Khaneferra Sobekhotep cited above (Luxor J.18, Romano 1979, 22);

gateway of Amenemhat I at Qasr el-Dahr, Western Delta (Janosi 1994, 24-5, no.2);

gateway of Amenemhat I at Khatana, renewed by Senusret III and Amenemhat III (Janosi 1994, 20-7, with pl.1);

lintel of Amenemhat I at Dendera (PM VI, 110).

two gateways of Senusret I at Tod (Janosi 1994, 24-5, no.3);

blocks of Senusret I reused as ram embalming tables on Elephantine (*PSBA* 30 (1908), 72);

gateway of Senusret III at Medamud.

These gateways are most plausibly interpreted as being at or near their original location. The Elephantine blocks alone would not demonstrate general use of red granite in temples of gods away from centres dedicated primarily to the royal cult, because the stone was quarried locally and blocks would have been more available for monuments at the local level; the spectacular classical monuments of the Ptolemaic and Roman periods at Ashmunein reflect similar difference in use and scale of stoneworking at local level in those instances where monuments stood close to quarries or loading embankments. The Khatana temple seems to be related to the royal cult; the dedication of one statue from the site refers to the cult of the 'national' deity of the late Middle Kingdom, Sobek-Horus of Shedyet, in the *š n pr-ꜥ3* "estate of the palace". Similarly the Theban lintel showing Nebhepetra concerns the royal cult. This leaves the Medamud complex of Senusret III as the sole surviving Middle Kingdom instance of a granite doorway connected more with the cult of a deity than with that of a king; the name of the local god Mont does not appear on the part that survives, and it is built into the later Ptolemaic temple, but statues of Senusret III from the same site include the epithet "beloved of Mont", placing the focus of the cult on the relation between king and local deity rather than reserving it for the king and the goddesses of the crowns.

Although not of hard stone, note should also be made of the larger limestone gateway of Senusret III at Medamud (Janosi 1994, 24-5, no.4), and its copy by Amenemhat-Sobekhotep of the Thirteenth Dynasty. Janosi relates these monuments to the sed festival, and it is possible that all the granite doorways mentioned may have been created as part of a sed programme. In this context the structure to which and from which the gateway led can be classified as religious, whether it was a palace hall or a temple court. The selection of the stone in these monuments in the Delta and southern Upper Egypt would remain tied to the rites, processions and appearances of kingship festivals, rather than to the local daily cult. The few historical sed festivals, notably for Senusret I, would have been the occasion for the 'formalisation' (or nationalisation), of the city temples and their cults. Of the Twelfth Dynasty hard stone blocks at Heracleopolis, at least the granite elements might then belong to a kingship gateway in the Heryshef temple, and the Hammamat inscription might be cited as evidence for interest in such development of the site under Senusret III.

Hard stone columns in temples of gods

The few hard stone columns securely dated to the Middle Kingdom are of uncertain original provenance. As cited above, the red granite columns at Heracleopolis could have come either from a large temple of Heryshef on that site, or from the pyramid complex of Senusret II at Lahun. A column of red granite at Medinet el-Fayum bears the cartouche of an Amenemhat, identified by Golenischev as Amenemhat I but perhaps more likely to be Amenemhat III in view of the other surviving Middle Kingdom Fayum monuments (PM IV, 98). The god invoked is Sobek-Horus of Shedyet, but there is a possibility that the column stood originally at Hawara. The Egypt Exploration Fund expedition to Bubastis recorded reused Middle Kingdom columns (PM IV, 29), including a red granite palmleafcapital monolithic column now in the British Museum (EA 1065). At some stage this latter column stood at Avaris, judging by the mention of Seth great in strength, lord of heaven; it might be an Old Kingdom valley temple column, removed to the Eastern Delta first in the late Middle Kingdom or Second Intermediate Period, and then moved again in the New Kingdom.

There is also the indirect evidence of the scale of hard stone statues from temple to the gods. If the colossi of Amenemhat III were commissioned for a Middle Kingdom temple at Bubastis, the combined evidence would indicate a substantial Middle Kingdom local temple large enough to contain a hall with monolithic hard stone columns. For a slightly later and still innovatory period, the same might be said of the Thirteenth Dynasty sculpture from Karnak. Yet even at Karnak no monolithic hard stone columns seem to have been included in the Middle Kingdom temple. For Bubastis, as at Heracleopolis and Medinet el-Fayum, archaeological evidence of an extensive and formal ground plan would be required to demonstrate the existence of such extensive Middle Kingdom temples other than at centres for the royal cult. Without such evidence of emplacement, moveable monoliths cannot be ascribed with any certainty to their modern location.

Summary of the evidence from monument distribution

Centres of both the royal and other cults might house statues of the king, and contain limestone blocks with relief. Hard stone architectural blocks and columns may have been more restricted in distribution. Quartzite lies at the most restricted end of the scope of deployment, both in sculpture in the round and in architectural elements; it seems tightly allied to the royal focus of cult, and perhaps simultaneously to Heliopolis as centre of the solar cult. Red granite seems less restricted in architecture at first sight, but this too may have a specific field of reference in the original projects of the Middle Kingdom. Temples at pyramid complexes may have had granite columns, on the model of the Old Kingdom examples, whereas granite columns are not securely attested in cult centres for deities before the New Kingdom, and granite doorways are rare and perhaps always associated with the architectural sed programme. From this the scant surviving record, I would argue that the Heracleopolis Twelfth Dynasty hard stone elements are more likely to derive from one or more pyramid complexes, the closest being Lahun; the limestone blocks find parallels from temples to deities, as do the granite blocks under more restricted conditions, whereas the massive columns with palm capitals seem appropriate more to pyramid complexes. The Nefret statues from Tanis are other candidates for original location at the pyramid complex of Senusret II. This broken assemblage of granite and quartzite blocks with quartzite and 'dark granite' statues cannot easily be fitted into particular parts of the temples in that complex, so extensive is their destruction. There is the danger of circularity in assigning material of certain type to royal as opposed to local cult centres; nevertheless, under the rubric 'destination', future research may be directed at identifying specific workshops and the timing of their commissions in the building programmes of the Twelfth Dynasty. At present it may be noted that the evidence points to more extensive monumental architecture, especially in the use of hard stone, in pyramid complexes, as compared with temples of the gods; together with the evidence of Ramesside quarrying at the Lahun Valley Temple, this makes it more probable that the Heracleopolitan granite blocks of Senusret II, with the mention of Sekhmet, and in particular the columns of the great portico derive from Lahun.

5 Cults of gods in other Middle Kingdom royal cult complexes

The parallels for cults of gods from the other six royal cult complexes of the Twelfth Dynasty would be instructive, but they have fared little better than Lahun. Those of Amenemhat I at Lisht and Amenemhat III at Hawara lie close to the cultivation, and have accordingly suffered greatest destruction; the cult complexes of Amenemhat II, Senusret III and Amenemhat III at Dahshur have also been largely destroyed, and are less accessible to study under present conditions. The pyramid temple of Senusret I is best preserved and known, thanks largely to the recent years of excavation, study and publication by the expedition for the Metropolitan Museum of Art, New York, under the direction of Dieter Arnold. Its groundplan survives, and substantial fragments of relief were recovered in the excavations for the same museum in the first half of this century. However, even the pyramid complex of Senusret I was quarried of its stone, in part before the reign of Akhenaten, and in part perhaps after the Amarna period.

This leaves a highly broken record, in which different parts of each pyramid complex have suffered more or less extensively from ancient and more recent destruction. Each complex includes a pyramid, a temple at the pyramid, and probably every single one included also a valley temple and a causeway from it to the pyramid temple. Interpreting the function of each part is difficult, and it is equally difficult to assign a particular statue or cult to a particular place in the complex; thus it is not at present possible to locate the original intended position for the ten unfinished seated statues of Senusret I found in a cache north of the court of his pyramid temple. The functions of particular parts of the Twelfth Dynasty pyramid complexes are also concealed by the differences between them; even in their fragmentary condition their ground plans show considerable variation, and this makes it difficult to establish consistent functions.

Amenemhat I

At the pyramid temple of Amenemhat I Gautier and Jéquier found fragments mentioning Nekhbet and Wadjyt, but also Montu lord of the Two Lands and Atum lord of Heliopolis (Gautier and Jéquier 1902, 94-7 figs.108-14). Less importance may be attached to the invocation of Amenemhat I and Anubis who is upon his mountain in the case of two fragmentary non-royal offering-tables from the same pyramid complex (Gautier and Jéquier 1902, 103 figs.125-6); the north cemetery finds included one block with the names of Amenemhat III and [Hathor lady of Atf]ih (Gautier and Jéquier 1902, 106 fig.131). The Metropolitan Museum of Art, New York, brought back from its seasons before the First World War a long rectangular block, said to be the upper part of a lintel, from the early temple of Amenemhat I at the north pyramid (MMA 08.200.5: Hayes 1953, 172, fig.103, 173). It shows the ritual race of the king between, to the left (Horus) of Behdet (falcon-headed) and Nekhbet, and, to the right, (Anubis) who is upon his mountain, who is in the embalming-place (jackal-headed), and Wadjyt.

Senusret I

At Lisht South, Gautier and Jequier recorded a relief block in the pyramid temple of Senusret I on which the king is "beloved of Osiris lord of the [Sacred ?] Land " on one side, and "beloved of Nekhbet" and "beloved of Anubis who is upon his mountain" on the other side (1902, 20 fig.13); another fragment depicts the king, Amun-Ra and Ptah, and the great offering-table gives the king on each of four instances the epithet "beloved of Ra-Horakhty" (1902, 23 fig.16: for the nome-deities on the sides see figs. 17-20). A fragment of an offering-table from the temple by the pyramid invokes Kheperkara (= Senusret I) and Hathor amid Khenemsut. Relief fragments from the entrance-chapel on the north face of the Senusret I pyramid show Anubis (fragments aa and bb = Cairo J.63946 part, Arnold 1988, 79, pl.51). Among the most important finds of the Metropolitan Museum of Art expedition before the Second World War are the two painted wooden statues of the king found with a wooden shrine containing the *imiut* emblem of Anubis (Hayes 1953, 194). Although this does not help to identify an Anubis shrine with a particular building or sector, it reinforces the presence of that god within the royal cult complex. Dieter Arnold has suggested that there was a sanctuary of Hathor in front of the *ka* pyramid at the southeastern corner of the main pyramid, noting the extensive limestone subfoundations in the outer court east of the *ka* pyramid (1988, 17 and n.33); he compares this with the Old Kingdom *mrt* and New Kingdom Hathor shrines in royal cult temples, and the dedication to Hathor on the southern entranceway of the Khafra valley temple (Stadelmann 1985, 276 n.406).

Amenemhat III

At the temple by the pyramid of Amenemhat III at Dahshur, J de Morgan, in 1894-5, discovered fragments of limestone relief bearing part of the companion text to the offering formula (PT 210, the relevant section occurring also in CT 173 and 216); a fragment of a block with hieroglyphs facing in the opposite direction and bearing the same part of that text were retrieved from the sanctuary by the

German Institute excavations in 1975 (Morgan 1903, 98 fig.142; Arnold and Stadelmann 1975, pl.111b).

Monuments of Amenemhat III from Medinet el-Fayum and Hawara present a particular difficulty in disentangling royal cult complex from local temple in Middle Kingdom material. The Fayum area has yielded fragments of limestone architectural elements and wall blocks with hieroglyphic texts associated with Amenemhat III and Sobek of Shedyet:

Berlin fragments of the accession text of Amenemhat III, a composition of sufficient importance to be adapted as the installation text of Hatshepsut at Deir el-Bahri (Berlin 1913, 138, 268)

BM EA 1072 limestone lintel with the name of a king Amenemhat, presumably III, and of the double deity Sobek of Shedyet Horus amid Shedyet.

There is also a 'dark granite' statue of Amenemhat III in leopard-skin Cairo CG 395 (Borchardt 1925, 13, pl.64), from Mit Faris in the Fayum (acquired 1862).

These could be from the temple of Sobek at Medinet el-Fayum, but might instead come from the pyramid complex of Amenemhat III at Hawara; two statues of the king with the epithet "beloved of Sobek of Shedyet" are recorded at Hawara, one *in situ* and the second of limestone now in the Egyptian Museum, Cairo (CG 385: Borchardt 1925, 4-5, pl.61). The same ambiguity extends to the group of late Middle Kingdom bronze statues of officials (Louvre E27153: Delange 1987, 211-13), kings, a queen or goddess (Ortiz 1994, nos.33-7) and a crocodile (Munich ÄS6080: Schoske and Wildung 1987, 38-9), among which both Amenemhat III and the god Sobek seem prominent.

Senusret III at Abydos

Another complex for the cult of a Twelfth Dynasty king is that of Senusret III at Abydos. Little of the stonework from this survives, and the site has been insufficiently explored and recorded to allow any assessment of its internal divisions or the identity of its cults. Two seated quartzite statues of the king enthroned were discovered by Randall-Maciver in the 1899-1900 work on the site, and these and further fragments including part of a calcite statue of the king have now been retrieved in the recent excavations by Joe Wegner of the Pennsylvania-Yale Expedition to Abydos (Wegner 1995).

Thirteenth Dynasty evidence

After Amenemhat III, royal cult complexes are sparsely attested on the ground; there are few indications of groundplan and cults for the two Mazghuna pyramid sites, probably of early Thirteenth Dynasty date, or of the complexes at Saqqara for the early Thirteenth Dynasty king Khendjer and a pyramid nearby, of the same date, and at Dahshur for another early Thirteenth Dynasty king Ameny Qemau son of (or inverse filiation ?) Hornedjitef. At south Abydos a second great cult complex is thought to have existed between the partly excavated cult complexes of Senusret III and Ahmose I, because it yielded a sealing of one of the Thirteenth Dynasty viziers named Iymeru. It would be tempting to link this structure to the statue of the vizier Iymeru Neferkara (Louvre A 125) which bears the first attestation of the phrase later used for centres of royal cult, *ḥwt nt ḥḥ n rnpwt* "domain of millions of years", itself an indication that the relation between institutions of kings and those of gods may have changed; however, the statue was discovered at Karnak, and the royal cult place in question, Hetepka-Sobekhotep, was therefore presumably a Theban rather than an Abydene focus for worship of the king whom Iymeru served, Khaneferra Sobekhotep (Delange 1987, 66-8). Whether at Abydos or Thebes, this Upper Egyptian cult complex operated for a king who probably ruled all Egypt from Itjtawy; it seems most likely that he was buried in the Memphis Fayum area, and therefore that he received, like Senusret III and Amenemhat III, more than one cult centre.

Temple staff titles in the hieroglyphic evidence for the location of cults

Among the most important sources are, beside blocks and statues from the pyramid complexes themselves, monuments of individuals who held office at those sites and recorded the cults which they served there.

A scarab seal names the *wꜥb ꜥ3* of Hathor "lady of Atfih amid Khenmetsut" (Martin 1971, no.1125). This shows that Hathor of Atfih received worship at Khenemsut, name of all or part of the pyramid-complex of Senusret I. This is confirmed by the statue of the official Senusret, from the Northumberland collection, of unknown provenance, now in the Gulbenkian Oriental Museum of Durham University, inv.no.501 (Gomaà 1984). It presents Senusret seated, and may be an offering-chapel rather than a temple or tomb statue; the titles of the man show that he served at Lisht, for he is "mayor in Kha-Senusret", "overseer of priests in the house of Hathor lady of Atfih amid Khenemsut", "priest of Anubis who is upon his mountain", "overseer of priests of Wadjyt lady of Weptawy", "stolist of Min", "priest of Khnum lord of Semenuhor". The Amenemhat II annals on blocks now at Memphis include references to offerings for Anubis who is upon his mountain in Khenemsut (Petrie 1909, 18, pl.5, line 3), and Senusret I in Khenemsut (Farag 1980, 77 line 6). From the White Chapel the full name of Khenemsut is known as Khenemsut-Kheperkara, confirming that the primary cult at that place was that of Senusret I. Therefore the cults of Anubis and Hathor ought to be sited within the same complex, but secondary to the royal cult. The other titles of the mayor Senusret on the Durham statue raise the further possibility that Khenemsut may have housed in addition cult places for the goddess Wadjyt lady of Weptawy, Min and Khnum lord of Semenuhor. However, without the qualification "amid/foremost of/in Khenemsut", Lisht cult places for those deities are not securely attested; it is possible that Senusret may have held positions at their sanctuaries outside Lisht in Weptawy, Semenuhor or other towns of the vicinity.

Summary of the Middle Kingdom evidence

Discussion of Lahun is hindered by the extremely broken nature of the architectural record, which makes it difficult to ascribe the Twelfth Dynasty blocks at Heracleopolis with hieroglyphic inscriptions to one or the other site. This is partly a problem of scale and orthogonal as against non-orthogonal groundplan. The red granite columns seem appropriate to a royal pyramid complex rather than the temple of a god, and this might be taken to indicate wholesale move of the hard stone elements at Lahun to the New Kingdom building programme at Heracleopolis. However, the use of scale and orthogonal groundplan as criteria for differentiating Middle Kingdom temples to gods and temples to kings has not gone undisputed (see Baines in this volume). A rare opportunity to compare scale in temple-building for the royal cult and that for the gods arises in the architecture from the reign of Senusret I, respectively at Lisht and Thebes. Thebes is not at the centre of royal building programmes in the Twelfth Dynasty, but the monuments of Senusret I provide a partial exception to this attitude, and this may account in part for the specific reference to Senusret I in a late Middle Kingdom ritual book from Thebes, the Ramesseum Dramatic Papyrus (Sethe 1928). The area of the Amun temple laid out, or at least populated with hard stone and inscribed limestone, in the reign of Senusret I may be estimated at 80 x 55 m, if it covered only the area of the Middle Kingdom court and the bark-hall to its west, or up to 150 x 100 m if it included as well the area of the Tuthmosside Akhmenu and other spaces behind the Fifth Pylon and its enclosure wall (figures from plan Brunner-Traut 1988, 609). The outer enclosure wall of the upper part of the pyramid complex of the same king at Lisht measures 254.625 x 231 m (Arnold 1992, 15); this excludes the causeway and the valley temple, but already gives an indication of the instant difference in scale dictated by pyramid size. While the core of the royal tomb remained a solid pyramid on that scale, no building project could ever compete with the royal tomb and its associated cult complexes. As regards the inscriptional evidence, there is one reference to the feminine complement to solar kingship, the attestation of Sekhmet on one Heracleopolitan block. However, even if the Heracleopolitan columns are ascribed to the Lahun pyramid complex, it remains possible that other Middle Kingdom granite elements at Heracleopolis were originally intended for the Heryshef temple. The Heracleopolitan blocks cannot therefore be used as primary evidence in the discussion of the Lahun cults, but nor can they be altogether omitted from that discussion.

The presence of both Hathor and Anubis at the pyramid complex of Senusret I at Lisht provides a parallel for the role of Anubis at Lahun, although it makes it no easier to identify a particular part of the complex as the focus for the cult of either deity. Further indirect evidence for the cults in the pyramid complex of Senusret II may be gained from a closer look at the role of gods in royal cult complexes of the Old and New Kingdoms.

6 Parallels from other periods

Old Kingdom evidence

The Old Kingdom provides parallels for the inclusion of goddesses in reliefs and inscriptions. Hathor and Bast are present at the entranceways on the east side of the Valley Temple of Khafra (Hölscher 1912, figs.7-8), and the triads of Menkaura with a nome personification and the goddess Hathor were placed in his Valley Temple, while the preserved relief fragments include, beside papyrus marsh hunts and the king as a sphinx destroying his enemies, scenes of the king suckled by the goddess Sekhmet (Stadelmann 1986, 191). Such scenes also occur at the *Totenopfertempel* or upper level of the temple at the pyramid face; thus the functions and rites of the two spaces may have overlapped in part.

Altenmüller would locate the divine booth of Anubis near the entrance of the Valley Temple (Altenmüller 1972), and the association of that god with the lower part of the pyramid complex is borne out by fragments of a basalt Anubis figure found in room III.2 of the Valley Temple of Menkaura (Holden 1981). However, Arnold notes that, with Nekhbet and Wadjyt, Anubis who is upon his mountain is the most commonly attested deity in the raised level of the pyramid temple, the *Totenopfertempel* of Ricke, e.g. five times in the temple of Pepy II (of which three times in doorways), as if he is the protecting deity of the *Totenopfertempels* (Arnold 1977, 12-13 with n.68). Arnold stresses instead the role of Hathor in the Valley Temple, but it is possible that both deities are involved with the royal cult complex at more than one point. Anubis in particular may have been central to the rites in both upper and lower levels of a pyramid complex. Interpretation is complicated by the evident differences between the various complexes even within the same period.

New Kingdom evidence

The cult centres of the late Thirteenth and Seventeenth Dynasties have not survived, and that of Ahmose at Abydos has been extensively destroyed (Harvey 1994). The next royal cult complex to survive in good condition is that for Hatshepsut at Deir el-Bahri, protected from late Roman, medieval and modern limestone quarrying by the rubble and debris of successive layers of occupation and use down to the Roman period. The complex includes sanctuaries to the goddess Hathor and the god Anubis, echoing the prominence of those two deities in the Old and Middle Kingdom record. Anubis seems firmly asssociated with the northern side of the complex. The Anubis shrine at the northern end of the Middle Colonnade is identified as a "temple of Anubis" in the inscription at the east end of the south wall, where the steps from the Middle Colonnade lead to its outer, columned, hall: *bs m ḥwt-nṯr nt ỉnpw tpy-ḏw.f [ ] ẖnt ḏsr-ḏsrw*. This text may not be part of the original decoration, but indicates that the Anubis shrine could be considered a separate *ḥwt-nṯr* in the Deir el-Bahri complex (Naville 1896, pl.33). The god himself is identified on the east wall of the second inner chamber of the shrine as *tpy-ḏw.f sp3 ẖnty sḥ-nṯr ḥr-ỉb ḏsr-ḏsrw* and *ỉmy-wt nb t3-ḏsr tpy ḏw.f ẖnty ḏsr-ḏsrw* (Naville 1896, pl.43). In addition to the main, separate Anubis chapel at the northern end of the Middle Colonnade (PM II^2, 353-6; Naville 1896, pl.30-43; Werbrouck 1949, 113-18), there is an Anubis shrine on the northern side of the open court with sun altar on the upper level of the temple. The reliefs on the walls of that upper chapel appear to be the same as those on the walls of the inner part of the main Anubis shrine (Naville 1895, pl.9-12 for the end and east walls, and the niche: on pp.10-11 Naville describes the figure of Anubis at the west end of the north wall, which is not reproduced, as a completely destroyed figure of Anubis, the rest of this wall and the south wall being reporduced on pl.13-16). Werbrouck noted that the two shrines suffered different degrees of damage in the reign of Akhenaten (1949, 118): in the main shrine only Amun is affected, whereas in the shrine on the solar court the figures of the gods Anubis, Osiris, Sokar, and Ptah, as well as the central *imiut* emblem have also been erased, although their names were spared, as if the names were not offensive to the sun cult, but the images were too close to a place of solar worship.

Despite the difference in date, the Hatshepsut chapels of Anubis at Deir el-Bahri indicate, first, that the same relief programme could be repeated at two points in the temple complex, and, secondly, that the main reason for including Anubis was as a funerary god, since he stands in the company of Osiris, Ptah and Sokar. Specifically he may be the embalmer who brought the king to life eternally, counterpart to the goddess Hathor who could ensure the eternal birth and youthfulness of the king. Outside these two chapels, the god Anubis occurs in two scenes of the Hathor shrine, where he follows the cow-goddess as she licks the hand of the king (PM II², 350-1; Naville 1901, pl.87; Werbrouck 1949, pl.44). He is also present in the cycle of scenes on the divine birth of the king, where he accompanies the god Khnum; the scene is included in the second version of the cycle for Amenhotep III at Luxor Temple (PM II², 326, Luxor, and 349, Deir el-Bahri). It may be noted that a lintel of Thutmes III over the doorway to a shrine alongside the 'Botanical Chamber' of the Akhmenu at Karnak bears a scene of the king embraced by Hathor and then another of the king before Anubis (PM II², 119).

The analogy cannot be drawn directly with the evidence from Lahun, where the papyri seem to mention Hathor only in the context of sailings, as if as a visitor rather than a resident at the cult complex. Yet the destruction of the site may distort the record. There is the one block at Heracleopolis inscribed with "words spoken by Sekhmet the great beloved of Ptah"; it would be interesting to examine the original, if still extant, to see whether it belonged stylistically with the Senusret II and III blocks, as Petrie placed it (1905, pl.13, centre right). At all events there remains the evidence of the pyramid complex of Senusret I at Lisht, where the position is the opposite to that at Lahun: the goddess Hathor received a place of cult second only in the sources to that of the king, with Anubis only sparsely, if securely, attested. At Deir el-Bahri the Anubis chapel lies on the northern side, that of Hathor on the southern side. Although we know that the main New Kingdom temple of Hathor lay to the south of Memphis from the Great Harris Papyrus, it is possible that the adjective "southern" in her epithet "lady of the southern sycamore" refers not so much to the position of her temple in relation to that of Ptah at Memphis, as to the location of a cult centre of the goddess within the royal pyramid complex (however, see Malek in this volume for the Memphite epithets). This speculation rests solely on the evidence of Lisht and Deir el-Bahri, but might give the reason for the inclusion in at least those two sites of a counterbalancing cult of the embalming god Anubis. At all events, the Lahun royal cult too seems to embrace the goddess, whether Hathor, Sekhmet or Bast, or all of these as faces of the same divinity, and Anubis.

The greater prominence accorded Anubis in the papyri may reflect an emphasis on the dead body, its mummification and subsequent resurrection as Osiris; this could be reflected also in the layout of the subterranean chambers of the pyramid, which Erik Hornung has compared with the Osiris tomb of Sety I behind his temple for the royal cult at Abydos. It should not be forgotten that Senusret III, son and successor of Senusret II, constructed a great cult complex, and possibly his burial place, at Abydos South. Major changes in belief or at least in burial custom emerge in the late Twelfth Dynasty, with the replacement of tomb models by apotropaic 'wands' and figurines (Bourriau 1991); these changes may be heralded by the special emphasis on Anubis at Lahun.

The role of Sobek in the Fayum seems to contrast with this scheme; here the temple of the god becomes a setting for recognizing the divine essence of kingship, instead of the god playing a role within the temple for the cult of the king. It is true that any change in the relation of king to gods is complicated by the question of the original location of monuments found at Medinet el-Fayum; these may have been part of temple constructions by Amenemhat III on the site, or may have been moved from Hawara when the great Ptolemaic temple to Sobek was constructed at Medinet el-Fayum. Moreover, the Fayum programme of Amenemhat III locates Medinet el-Fayum within a web of royal cult temples from the colossi at Biahmu, and whatever lay behind them, to the pyramid complexes of the king and his daughter near Hawara. The reign of Amenemhat III would then mark not an abrupt change, so much as a shift toward the 'Mature Formal' focus on the many temples of the gods, instead of the one or few temples of the reigning king.

Conclusion: the history of a difference

When I began to look for reasons for the offerings to Anubis in the Lahun temple accounts, I compared it at first with the role of Sobek at the Hawara pyramid complex of Amenemhat III, and through this with the role of major deities in New Kingdom temples for the royal cult: Amun in those at Thebes, Osiris at Abydos, Ptah for the Memphite temple of Amenhotep III absorbed by Ramses II and III. The identity of the god at each focus of the royal cult depends in these cases on the locality, and each of these temples seems to merge the royal cult temple and the temple of a deity. In the Egypt of the New Kingdom and later the expansion in scale of temples for deities perhaps obscures the central role of kingship in cult, with mutual support of king and deities in a single world of the gods. The pyramid complexes indicate another relationship, within which the main cult of the king is supported by one or more other cults of gods, selected not by geographical location of the temple within Egypt but by role in the royal cult itself. The difference is between the temples in which the principal recipient is a king, and those in which the principal recipient is a deity; in more concrete terms, it is a difference in cult statue and priesthood, and this difference possesses its own history. The turning-point may come after the reign of Senusret II, in the Abydos complex of his son Senusret III, the inspiration for New Kingdom Abydene royal cult complexes, and in the Hawara complex of Amenemhat III which left its impact both on Amenhotep III and, as the Labyrinth, on the Greek-speaking world. The priests and cult statue of Anubis at Lahun belong on the earlier side of the division. They may also be considered part of the evidence on both sides tending to attenuate the differences and to remind us that at all periods all royal cult involves the gods, but equally that all cult of the gods involves the king -in Egypt all cult is royal cult.

Bibliography

Altenmüller, H 1972. Die Bedeutung der "Gotteshalle des Anubis" im Begräbnisritual. In *Jaarbericht van het vooraziatisch-egyptisch Genootschap Ex Orient Lux* 22, 307-17.

Arnold, D 1977. Rituale und Pyramidentempel. In *Mitteilungen des Deutschen Archäologischen Instituts Abteilung Kairo* 33, 1-14.

Arnold, D 1986. Totentempel II. In W Helck and W Westendorf (eds.), *Lexikon der Agyptologie* VI, Wiesbaden, 699-706.

Arnold, D 1988. *The South Cemeteries at Lisht I The Pyramid of Senwosret I.* New York, Metropolitan Museum of Art Egyptian Expedition 22.

Arnold, D 1992. *The South Cemeteries at Lisht III The Pyramid Complex of Senwosret I.* New York, Metropolitan Museum of Art Egyptian Expedition 25.

Arnold, D and R Stadelmann 1975. Dahchur, erster Grabungsbericht. In *Mitteilungen des Deutschen Archäologischen Instituts Abteilung Kairo* 31, 169-74, pl.110-12.

Arnold, F 1990. *The South Cemeteries at Lisht II. The Control Notes and Team Marks.* New York, Metropolitan Museum of Art Egyptian Expedition 23.

Barbotin, C and J-J Clère 1991. L'inscription de Sésostris Ier à Tôd. In *Bulletin de l'Institut Français d'Archéologie Orientale du Caire* 91, 1-32, pl.1-29 with foldout after pl.29.

Berlev, O D 1978. *Obshchestvenniye Otnosheniya v Egipte epokhu Srednego Tsarstva.* Moscow, Nauka.

Berlin 1913. *Aegyptische Inschriften aus den Königlichen Museen zu Berlin. I Inschriften von der ältesten Zeit bis zum Ende der Hyksoszeit.* Leipzig, J C Hinrichs.

Borchardt, L 1899. Der zweite Papyrusfund von Kahun und die zeitliche Festlegung des mittleren Reiches der ägyptischen Geschichte. In *Zeitschrift für Ägyptische Sprache und Altertumskunde* 37, 89-103.

Borchardt, L 1925. *Catalogue Général des Antiquités Egyptiennes du Musée du Caire Nos 1-1294.*

Statuen und Statuetten von Königen und Privatleuten 2. Berlin, Reichsdrückerei.
Bourriau, J 1991. Patterns of change in burial customs during the Middle Kingdom. In S Quirke (ed.), *Middle Kingdom Studies*, New Malden, SIA Publishing, 3-20.
Brunner-Traut, E 1988. *Ägypten. Kunst- und Reiseführer mit Landeskunde.* 6th edition, revised. Stuttgart, Berlin, Cologne and Mainz am Rhein, W Kohlhammer.
Couyat, J and P Montet, 1912. *Les Inscriptions hiéroglyphiques et hiératiques du Ouâdi Hammâmât.* Mémoires publiés par les membres de l'Institut Français d'Archéologie Orientale du Caire 34. Cairo, Institut Français d'Archéologie Orientale du Caire.
Daressy, G 1927. Sur le naos de Senusret Ier trouvé à Karnak. In *Revue de l'Egypte Ancienne* I. 203-11.
Delange, E 1987. *Musee du Louvre. Statues egyptiennes du Moyen Empire.* Paris, Réunion des Musées Nationaux.
Durey, P et al. 1988. *Les Reserves de Pharaon. L'Egypte dans les collections du Musée des Beaux-Arts de Lyon.* Lyon, Musée des Beaux-Arts.
Engelbach, R 1923. *Harageh.* London, British School of Archaeology in Egypt, and Bernard Quaritch.
Farag, S 1980. Une inscription memphite de la XIIe Dynastie. In *Revue d'Egyptologie* 32, 75-82, pl.3-5.
Gabolde, L 1995. Le problème de l'emplacement primitif du socle de calcite de Sésostris Ier. In *Cahiers de Karnak* 10, 253-6.
Gallorini, C 1997. Reconstructing the course of the Petrie excavations at the Middle Kingdom townsite near Lahun. In Stephen Quirke (ed.), *Lahun Studies.* New Malden, SIA Publishing.
Gautier, J-E and G Jéquier, 1902. *Mémoire sur les fouilles de Licht.* Mémoires publiés par les membres de l'Institut Français d'Archéologie Orientale du Caire 6. Cairo, Institut Français d'Archéologie Orientale du Caire.
Gomaà, F 1984. Die Statue Durham Nr.501. In *Studien zur Altägyptischen Kultur* 11, 107-12, pl.2-3.
Griffith, F Ll 1898. *The Petrie Papyri. Hieratic Papyri from Kahun and Gurob (principally of the Middle Kingdom).* London, Bernard Quaritch.
Harvey, S 1994. Monuments of Ahmose at Abydos. In *Egyptian Archaeology. The Bulletin of the Egypt Exploration Society* 4, 3-5.
Hayes, W C 1953. *The Scepter of Egypt. A background for the study of the Egyptian antiquities in The Metropolitan Museum of Art. Part I: from the earliest times to the end of the Middle Kingdom.* New York, Harper & Brothers, with The Metropolitan Museum of Art, New York.
Hölscher, U 1912. *Das Grabdenkmal des Königs Chephren.* Leipzig, J C Hinrichs.
Holden, L 1981. An Anubis figure in the Boston Museum of Fine Arts. In W K Simpson and W M Davis (eds.), *Studies in Ancient Egypt, the Aegean, and the Sudan. Essays in honor of Dows Dunham on the occasion of his 90th birthday, June I, 1980.* Boston, Museum of Fine Arts.
Janosi, P 1994. IV. Tell el-Dab'a - 'Ezbet Helmi. Vorbericht über den Grabungsplatz H/I (1982-1992). In *Ägypten und Levante* 4, 20-38.
Kaplony-Heckel, U 1971. *Ägyptische Handschriften. Teil 1.* Verzeichnis der Orientalischen Handschriften in Deutschland XIX,1. Wiesbaden, Franz Steiner.
Kemp, B 1983. In B Trigger et al., *Ancient Egypt. A social history.* Cambridge University Press.
Kemp, B 1989. *Ancient Egypt. Anatomy of a civilization.* London and New York, Routledge.
Legrain, G 1906. Notes d'inspection XXX: Une statue de Montouhotpou Nibhepetrî. In *Annales du service des Antiquités d'Egypte* 7, 33-34.
Luft, U 1997. Ancient placenames at Lahun. In Stephen Quirke (ed.), *Lahun Studies.* New Malden, SIA Publishing.
Maarouf, Abd el-Hamid, and T Zimmer 1993. Le Moyen Empire à Karnak: Varia 2. In *Cahiers de Karnak* 9, 223-37.
Martin, G T 1971. *Egyptian Administrative and Private-name Seals principally of the Middle Kingdom and Second Intermediate Period.* Oxford, Griffith Institute.
Mokhtar, M Gamal el-Din 1983. *Ihnasya el-Medina (Herakleopolis Magna) Its importance and its role in Pharaonic history.* Bibliotheque d'Etude 40. Cairo, Institut Français d'Archéologie Orientale du Caire.

Mond, R and O Myers 1940. *Temples of Armant. A preliminary survey.* London, Egypt Exploration Society.
Morgan, J de 1903. *Fouilles à Dahchour en 1894-1895.* Vienna, Adolphe Holzhausen.
Naville, E 1894. *Ahnas el Medineh (Heracleopolis Magna).* London, Egypt Exploration Fund.
Naville, E 1895. *The Temple of Deir el Bahari.* I. London, Egypt Exploration Fund.
Naville, E 1896. *The Temple of Deir el Bahari.* II. London, Egypt Exploration Fund.
Naville, E 1901. *The Temple of Deir el Bahari.* IV. London, Egypt Exploration Fund.
Ortiz, G 1994. *In Pursuit of the Absolute. Art of the Ancient World from the George Ortiz collection.* London, Royal Academy of Arts.
Petrie, W M F 1888. *Nebesheh (Am) and Defenneh (Tahpanhes).* London, Egypt Exploration Fund.

Quelques reflexions sur le programme iconographique et la fonction des temples de "millions d'années"

Christian Leblanc

Les temples de "millions d'années" édifiés au Nouvel Empire ont au moins un point commun qui permet de les définir. Construits pour rendre hommage à Pharaon et concrétiser son union avec le divin, ils sont, avant tout, destinés au culte royal (Haeny 1982, 113-5; Leblanc 1993, 64-9). On a longtemps dit que ce culte était célébré à titre posthume - et on l'écrit encore (Badawy 1968, 321-64; Stadelmann 1978, 171-80; *id.* 1979, 303-21) -, que certains de ces monuments, ceux de la rive occidentale thébaine en particulier, étaient des temples funéraires. Il semble pourtant clairement établi, maintenant, que si le culte funéraire prenait vraiment effet à la mort physique du roi, il n'en demeurait pas moins que, de son vivant, le temple de "millions d'années" fonctionnait déjà pour glorifier les actions du souverain constructeur et de son géniteur divin (Nelson 1942, 127-55; *id.* 1944, 44-53). L'iconographie nous le rappelle au besoin, en ce sens qu'elle se rattache à un répertoire qui, dans son ensemble, n'a d'autre but que d'immortaliser la conformité du roi avec la Maât ou le concept que celle-ci pouvait représenter.

Par ailleurs, il convient de prendre en considération, pour mieux entrevoir ou saisir la fonction de ces édifices, un autre facteur important. On a, en effet, trop souvent voulu limiter leur aire géographique d'implantation à Thèbes-Ouest, ce qui pouvait, naturellement, renforcer l'hypothèse que leur destination était "funéraire". Or, de tels temples existent également sur la rive orientale : dans l'enceinte même du grand temple d'Amon (Thoutmosis III, Séthi II, Ramsès III: Barguet, 1962, 51-2, 284, 295-6, 329-30), en Abydos (ceux de Séthi Ier et de Ramsès II), dans le Delta (ceux de Ramsès II et de Taousert, à Qantir: Hamza 1930, 38; Uphill 1984, 105-7), et même en Nubie ou au Soudan, puisque c'est sous cette désignation de *ḥwt n ḥḥ rnpwt* que nous sont connus les temples d'Amada (Thoutmosis III-Aménophis II-Thoutmosis IV) et de Soleb (Aménophis III: Haeny 1982, 115, n. 18). On serait tout aussi tenté de classer dans cette même catégorie les *hémi-speos* d'Abou-Simbel, de Gerf-Hussein, de Ouadi es-Seboua et de Derr qui ne semblent pas avoir eu, fondamentalement, une fonction très différente (Leblanc 1980, 69-89; Haeny 1982, 115-6 et n. 19).

Attendait-on que l'architecture et la décoration de ces temples soient achevées pour que le culte auquel était, à Thèbes, associé Amon, puisse commencer ? C'est peu probable, car des étiquettes de jarres retrouvées dans le contexte de ces monuments et datées dès le début du règne du pharaon constructeur (pour Ramsès II/Ramesseum: Spiegelberg 1898: an 3 nos.174, 177, 253, 313; an 4 nos.178, 219, 227, 254, 279, 303; an 5 nos.127a, 148, 152, 155, 160, 180, 204, 239, 248, 262), suggèrent, non seulement que le chantier était mis en oeuvre dès l'avènement ou, au plus tard, dans les premières années du règne, mais encore, que l'on devait y officier très tôt, puisque le produit de ces jarres était destiné au service quotidien du culte. La construction du sanctuaire, lieu sacré par excellence, constituait une priorité dans le programme architectural et tout porte à croire que l'on y célébrait le rituel avant même que le reste de l'édifice soit achevé : en effet, le saint-des-saints résumait, à lui seul, tout le contenu spirituel. A ce propos, le grand temple de Karnak, dont le chantier n'a cessé de se développer pendant des millénaires, en donne un exemple suffisamment éloquent (Barguet 1962; Goyon et Golvin 1989).

L'étude du décor, gravé sur les parois, piliers et colonnes des temples de "millions d'années", se réfère à quatre grands thèmes dont la présence, dans le contexte de ces monuments est loin d'être forfuite. Le choix porte sur des actions royales précises et complémentaires qui concourent à retracer et à immortaliser la geste de pharaon, à travers ses principales fonctions. Or, n'analyser que certaines séquences de ce décor, comme celles se référant, par exemple, au jubilé royal, pour en déduire que ces monuments avaient une signification ou fonction jubilaire, ne peut pleinement nous satisfaire. Sans nier pour autant la place non négligeable réservée à ce thème dans plusieurs temples de "millions d'années", force est de constater que nous ne trouvons jamais mention, pour les désigner, de l'appellation qui aurait dû, en l'occurrence, leur être donnée : celle de *ḥwt ḥb-sd*, "temple jubilaire". D'ailleurs, d'autres sujets couvrent des espaces parfois bien plus importants, ne serait-ce que celui de la guerre, glorifiant les hauts faits militaires du souverain régnant.

En revanche, le "rituel de la fondation du temple", habituellement à l'honneur dans les temples dits de culte divin (Edfou et Tôd, par exemple), et par lequel Pharaon consacrait la "demeure à son père", n'y apparaît qu'une seule fois, dans le sanctuaire nubien d'Amada (séquences figurées sur la paroi sud de la première chambre latérale nord du sanctuaire). Faut-il en déduire que les scènes relatives à ce rituel n'avaient pas vraiment leur place dans les châteaux de "millions d'années", ou bien tout simplement considérer que les autres exemples qui pouvaient exister dans leur contexte ont été perdus? La question mérite d'être posée, car si les séquences qui apparaissent à Amada, relèvent du programme iconographique de Thoutmosis III, ce n'est apparemment pas avant le règne de Thoutmosis IV que ce monument devient un *ḥwt n ḥḥ rnpwt.* Aurions-nous, dès lors, l'exemple d'un temple divin (consacré à Rê-Horakhty et à Amon-Rê) transformé en un temple de culte royal (c'est-à-dire consacré à ces deux mêmes divinités, auxquelles était associé désormais Thoutmosis IV) ? L'hypothèse n'est peut-être pas à écarter.

Aussi, nous paraît-il illogique — et ce dernier exemple le prouve — d'isoler un ensemble de tableaux relatifs à un thème particulier, pour tenter de démontrer la raison d'être des *ḥwt n ḥḥ rnpwt.* Nous nous attacherons donc à étudier les thèmes reconnus, pour déterminer quels sont leurs points communs ou, éventuellement, le chaînon qui les relie les uns aux autres dans le programme iconographique de ces grands livres de pierre. La présente communication n'a pas la prétention de résoudre tous les problèmes d'un débat qui demeure toujours très actuel. Son but est simplement d'exposer certaines remarques et réflexions qui, souhaitons-le, serviront à l'enrichir.

Le thème à caractère politique

Les tableaux qui y sont consacrés, ne retracent que les principales séquences du sacre royal et de son aboutissement : le choix divin qui fait que tel ou tel pharaon a été désigné légalement par les dieux, mais aussi par les hommes, pour accéder au trône et garantir la stabilité du royaume. D'une façon concrète, cette consécration officielle de la reconnaissance de l'essence divine du pharaon prend la forme d'un cérémonial organisé par le clergé et fait appel à toute une série de modalités rituelles (Bonhême-Forgeau 1988, 266-85). Là encore, scribes et décorateurs ont, soit par les textes, soit par l'iconographie, enregistré ou immortalisé la scénographie. Acte politique autant que religieux, le sacre royal mérite, dès lors, une place particulière dans l'iconographie et c'est la raison pour laquelle plusieurs scènes en illustrent le thème. Les images évoquant la montée royale (ex. = Ramesseum: mur du vestibule), celles de l'imposition des couronnes (ex. = Deir el-Bahari: paroi nord du second portique, moitié nord ; Ramesseum: mur du vestibule) ou de la remise des sceptres (ex. = Ramesseum: salle hypostyle, moitié sud du mur ouest), celles encore de la proclamation et de l'enregistrement, par Thoth, de la titulature du nouveau souverain (ex. = Ramesseum: mur du vestibule) constituent quelques-unes des phases essentielles du couronnement. Reconnu comme une personnalité démiurgique et historique, dépositaire de l'énergie divine (ex. = Amada : paroi nord du vestibule ; Ramesseum: salle hypostyle, moitié nord du mur ouest, scène où Amon insuffle à son fils Ramsès II, la vie et la vigueur émanant de lui-même), le roi doit, par l'investiture de cette suprême charge, oeuvrer pour le bien-être de son peuple, maintenir l'harmonie et l'équilibre du monde. Dans cette perspective, l'ordre apparaît comme la seule condition de toute existence, et le couronnement royal est perçu comme un véritable hymne à la vie.

Sous forme de développements (ex. = Karnak: Akhmenou de Thoutmosis III) ou d'extraits iconographiques, voire de textes allusifs, le *ḥb-sd* prend place, au même titre que le sacre royal, dans ce contexte. En effet, pour le roi, ce cérémonial réaffirme sa capacité d'assumer la charge divine qui lui a été confiée, et démontre qu'il en est le perpétuel garant (Leblanc 1980, 69-89). Ce n'est donc pas sans raison que la course rituelle avec la rame et le gouvernail (ex. = Amada, Thoutmosis IV: linteau de la porte latérale sud de la première salle ; Ramesseum : linteau de la porte menant de la salle des barques à la salle des litanies ; linteau de la porte du premier pylône) et l'évocation du roi assis, sous le double dais jubilaire de Haute et de Basse Egypte (ex. = Ramesseum: linteau de la porte du premier pylône) sont introduits dans la décoration qui orne certaines portes de ces temples, avec des textes de circonstance sur les montants (ex. = Ramesseum : porte du premier pylône) ou gravés sur les faces des piliers "osiriaques" (ex. = Deir el-Bahari: piliers des portiques sud et nord de la troisième terrasse; Ramesseum: piliers du portique nord-ouest de la seconde cour du temple; Medinet Habou: textes universalistes des piliers des portiques nord-ouest et sud-ouest de la seconde cour). Comme le couronnement, le renouvellement royal constitue un moyen de lutter contre l'interruption du cycle : celui de la vie, mais aussi de l'ordre établi. Sous cet aspect, le *ḥb-sd* apparaît comme la répétition nécessaire d'une lutte et finalement d'une victoire contre *isft*.

Le thème à caractère militaire

Pharaon, en tant que commandant des forces armées, se doit de maintenir la stabilité et la paix en Egypte. Sans cette stabilité et sans cette paix, le pays est voué au désordre, voire au chaos. Neutraliser le danger ou le mal, qu'il vienne de l'intérieur - troubles économiques et sociaux, révoltes et famines qui ont marqué certaines périodes historiques et dont le souvenir nous est conservé aussi bien par les textes que par les images - ou de l'extérieur - guerres, tentatives d'invasions ou d'infiltrations -, constitue donc l'une des tâches prioritaires du roi (Derchain 1966, 17-24; Bonhême et Forgeau 1988, 200-35). Dans cette perspective, le thème de la guerre, des épopées héroïques, où pharaon apparaît en défenseur et sauveur du pays, a tout à fait sa place dans le décor des temples et, en particulier, dans ceux de "millions d'années".

Les conflits, - qu'il s'agisse de la campagne menée par Ramsès II en l'an 5, contre les Hittites à Qadech (ex. = Ramesseum: façade occidentale du premier pylône; face ouest du montant nord du second pylône; Abydos: parois du mur extérieur du temple de Ramsès II), ou de celles conduites contre plusieurs cités asiatiques, en l'an 8 du règne (ex. = Ramesseum : extrémité de la face ouest du montant nord du premier pylône ; bataille contre Dapour, sur la moitié sud du mur est de la salle hypostyle), ou bien encore des opérations dirigées par Ramsès III, contre les Libyens (ex. = Medinet Habou, mur extérieur côté nord : campagne de l'an 5) ou les Peuples de la Mer (ex. = Medinet Habou : mur extérieur côté nord : campagne de l'an 8) - se réfèrent à des faits qui ont eu réellement lieu et qui ne se sont d'ailleurs pas toujours terminés par une victoire aussi éclatante qu'on veut bien parfois le laisser croire, mais l'essentiel n'est pas là. Ce qui est fondamental c'est que l'image, tout comme le texte, servent de témoignages, qu'ils attestent, l'un et l'autre, que le roi s'est conduit en digne défenseur de son peuple, en conjurant les forces du mal et en anéantissant tout ce qui était considéré comme pouvant déclencher l'imminence d'une fin du monde.

Les listes faisant état de la soumission des pays conquis, les frises de prisonniers ligotés, ou encore le massacre des ennemis de l'Egypte qui orne si magistralement la façade des pylônes (ex. = Medinet Habou: façade orientale du premier pylône; Karnak, pylône du temple-reposoir de Ramsès III), sont autant de sujets, qui, bien qu'appartenant à un répertoire d'événements le plus souvent fictifs (Derchain 1966, 21-2), traduisent un même concept, une même idée : celle du roi triomphateur qui a maîtrisé les forces négatives susceptibles de remettre en question l'ordre, c'est-à-dire la Maât. A ce titre, pharaon incarne, sur terre, un rôle similaire à celui de son père, dans le ciel. A l'instar de Rê qui est responsable de l'ordre cosmique et qui doit affronter régulièrement les pièges tendus par Apophis (personnification du Mal et des ténèbres), le roi est responsable de l'harmonie et de l'équilibre terrestres et doit, pour cela, combattre le danger omniprésent qui menace tout simplement la vie.

Le thème à caractère cultuel

Si l'harmonie du monde terrestre, et par conséquent la vie de l'Egypte, dépend de l'existence d'un souverain puissant, elle dépend tout autant d'un roi juste, qui se comporte en digne successeur d'Horus, en digne héritier de Rê. Au nombre des principales missions monarchiques, figure celle du culte sacrificiel et, en la circonstance, Pharaon doit apparaître comme un modèle pour les humains puisque, de sa conduite envers les dieux, de son respect envers la Maât, dépendront la paix, le renouveau de la crue, l'abondance des récoltes : en somme, le bien-être, la joie de vivre.

En tant que premier pontife du royaume, il lui revient d'assumer sa fonction sacerdotale et de présider aux grandes cérémonies religieuses. Honorer les dieux, c'est d'abord glorifier leurs noms par la récitation de prières ou de litanies, c'est aussi les pourvoir de multiples offrandes, bref, c'est leur assurer un service quotidien dans le but de maintenir cette solidarité mutuelle et nécessaire entre la vie cosmique et la vie sociale d'ici-bas. Le verbe a donc, dans le cas présent, une particulière importance, puisque c'est par son intermédiaire qu'il y a communication ou communion possible entre le monde terrestre et l'univers qui l'entoure (Assmann 1989, 108-10). Honorer les dieux, c'est encore les réjouir par toute une série de manifestations liturgiques, pour les remercier de leurs actions généreuses envers l'humanité. A ce titre, l'organisation de fêtes ou de panégyries que préside le souverain en personne, est un moyen de rappeler, une fois de plus, son intime relation avec la Maât, puisque, en tant que grand pontife, c'est à lui que revient, en ces occasions solennelles, de célébrer le rituel et de "rendre à dieu ce qu'il donne" (Assmann 1989, 107).

Fête des moissons consacrée en l'honneur de Min (ex. = Ramesseum: registre supérieur de la face occidentale du montant nord du second pylône; Medinet Habou: registre supérieur du mur nord de la seconde cour; Karnak, temple-reposoir de Ramsès III, paroi ouest de la cour à piliers osiriaques), fête d'Opet pendant laquelle Amon régénérait son pouvoir créateur (ex. = Karnak: sanctuaire-reposoir de Ramsès III, mur extérieur, côté ouest), pélerinage de la Belle Fête de la Vallée, en hommage aux dieux primordiaux et au cours de laquelle Amon rendait visite aux temples de "millions d'années" (ex. = Deir el-Bahari: paroi nord de la cour supérieure; Ramesseum: parois est et moitié sud-ouest de la salle des barques), sortie processionnelle de Sokaris, à l'occasion de la restauration des pouvoirs du dieu et de la réaffirmation de ceux du roi (ex. = Medinet Habou: registre supérieur du mur sud et du mur est, moitié sud, de la seconde cour), glorification des sanctuaires canoniques de Haute et de Basse Egypte (ex. = Ramesseum: paroi est de la salle des litanies), célébration de culte pour les ancêtres dynastiques (ex. = Deir el-Bahari : chapelle de Thoutmosis Ier; Gournah, temple de Séthi Ier: chapelle latérale sud dédiée à Ramsès Ier; Medinet Habou: chapelle latérale sud de la salle hypostyle, consacrée à Ramsès II déifié), sont autant de facettes iconographiques qui, prenant place dans le contexte des temples de "millions d'années", présentent, de manière tangible, Pharaon dans sa fonction de ritualiste par excellence, et démontrent, en l'occurrence, sa parfaite symbiose avec la Maât.

Le thème à caractère familial

Le roi est, par essence, une création du dieu et sa naissance est, à ce titre, considérée comme une oeuvre divine. A la XVIIIème dynastie, voire à l'époque ramesside, certaines scènes figurées dans les temples nous le rappellent: que ce soient les tableaux représentés sur la paroi ouest du second portique (moitié nord) du temple de Deir el-Bahari, évoquant l'hyménée de la reine Ahmès et du dieu-démiurge, la conception, puis la mise au monde de l'enfant-roi (Hatshepsout) résultant de cette union sacrée, ou encore les fragments d'une autre composition théogamique, provenant originellement du Ramesseum et retrouvés dans le contexte d'une construction tardive de Medinet Habou. Ceux-ci immortalisent la rencontre de Touy et du géniteur divin de Ramsès II, Amon, qui n'est autre que la forme encore cachée ou léthargique du démiurge, avant son émergence du Noun primordial (à ce titre: "maître de l'eau"). Au rituel de la naissance royale, est venu s'ajouter un certain nombre de développements. L'allaitement royal (Deir el-Bahari, chapelle d'Hathor; Amada, Thoutmosis IV: paroi nord de la première salle) qui témoigne de la filiation divine de Pharaon, et sert à perpétuer l'éternelle jeunesse du souverain (Bonhême et Forgeau 1988, 85-92) en constitue l'un d'eux. Rite de passage, comme le sont aussi les épisodes qui célèbrent l'éducation du jeune roi, ces images ont une signification évidente et traduisent, à leur manière, l'idée d'une force ou d'une puissance en permanence régénérée, à savoir celle de l'institution pharaonique.

Mais, pour bien marquer le caractère perpétuel de l'institution monarchique, l'iconographie va encore s'enrichir de tableaux complémentaires. C'est ce qui explique, sans le moindre doute, la place privilégiée qu'occupe, dans le contexte des temples de "millions d'années", à partir du Nouvel Empire, la famille royale. Statuaire, mais aussi reliefs n'ont d'autre motif de s'y trouver, sinon pour participer au renforcement du concept. La mère du roi (ex. = Ramesseum: montant intérieur sud de la porte de la salle hypostyle), la grande épouse (ex. = Ramesseum: registre supérieur de la face occidentale du montant nord du second pylône; montant intérieur sud de la porte de la salle hypostyle; Medinet Habou: registre supérieur du mur nord de la seconde cour; mur est, moitiés nord et sud, de la salle hypostyle; première chambre latérale de la salle hypostyle, côté nord), sans oublier les princes et les princesses qui, en longues théories, défilent sur les parois des portiques ou des salles (ex. = Abydos, temple de Séthi Ier: seconde cour, parois nord et sud; Ramesseum: registre inférieur du mur sud du vestibule; registre inférieur du mur ouest de la salle hypostyle, moitiés nord et sud; Medinet Habou: registre inférieur du mur ouest du portique de la seconde cour) sont garants, par leur simple présence, de ce renouveau, de cette continuité sans laquelle la vie de l'Egypte se trouverait menacée. Le thème ne se limite donc pas à proclamer exclusivement l'origine divine de Pharaon, mais il a encore pour vocation d'attester que le cycle ne peut s'interrompre puisque la progéniture royale est suffisamment nombreuse pour assurer, le moment venu, la relève. Pour Pharaon, c'est, une fois de plus, se trouver en pleine conformité avec la Maât, en ce sens que, par son action procréatrice, il oeuvre pour les générations futures, non seulement en maintenant l'Institution qu'il représente, mais encore en défendant, par ce processus, l'équilibre et la stabilité de l'Egypte. Dans cet esprit, la descendance du roi est perçue comme une nouvelle victoire sur les forces du chaos, puisqu'elle est censée continuer à générer harmonieusement le cycle.

Reflexions

Si, à l'époque ramesside, l'on revient à une vision plus traditionnelle, plus "anthropomorphique", des relations entre le monde céleste et le monde terrestre, il est intéressant de constater que la réforme amarnienne y est pour quelque chose. C'est dans ce creuset que va puiser la monarchie nouvelle et récupérer un certain nombre d'idées qui auront pour résultat essentiel de renforcer l'institution pharaonique, mais aussi de sublimer l'image du roi-dieu. Rétablie à sa place, la Maât devient, désormais, la "clef de voûte" sur laquelle s'appuie tout le système monarchique. Cette réaction va conduire à un développement du concept. C'est ainsi que Ramsès II en fait le "symbole-phare" de sa royauté et de sa divinité, un programme que résume admirablement l'image qui prend place dans la niche qui domine l'entrée du grand temple d'Abou-Simbel (Frandsen 1989, 95-6). Le roi présente la Maât à Rê-Horakhty, mais c'est aussi son nom de couronnement (Ouser-Maât-Rê) qu'il lui offre : la Maât devient ainsi, par le verbe, synonyme du roi, ce qui revient à dire que la Maât et Pharaon se confondent en une identité commune, se fondent en seul corps. Bien plus encore, car à y regarder de près, c'est aussi à sa propre image que Ramsès II présente la Maât (ce que met en évidence le rébus composé des sceptres divins et de la figuration de Rê) : un moyen de proclamer qu'il en vit lui-même comme le dieu et qu'il est, comme lui, le seul à pouvoir instaurer et maintenir l'équilibre du monde. La relation entre le dieu et le roi s'en trouve renforcée, ou mieux, sublimée, puisqu'à l'image de Rê qui illumine l'univers par l'intermédiaire de Maât, se superpose celle, toute aussi tangible, de Ramsès II, image transcendantale du "soleil" qui éclaire l'humanité. Il y a, ici, volonté de transposition de la formule "on rend à Dieu ce qu'il donne" par "Ramsès (entité terrestre/osirienne ou lunaire) rend ce que lui donne Ramsès (hypostase céleste/solaire)": [Dieu=Maât—Roi=Maât] — [Roi=Maât—Maât=Dieu].

Cette communion du roi avec la Maât va trouver encore bien d'autres moyens d'expression. Et le temple de "millions d'années", monument érigé à la gloire du roi, mais aussi à celle de son géniteur divin, en est — nous l'avons vu — la mémorisation la plus magistrale, la plus spectaculaire. Alors que les temples divins traduisent, comme on le sait, un microcosme de la création originelle (Nelson

1944, 47-8; Goyon 1987, 28-31), les châteaux de "millions d'années" nous semblent, en revanche, tout en perpétuant cette idée initiale, insister sur un autre concept. Nous avons cru reconnaître dans ces ensembles architecturaux, des temples où se régénéraient, où se revitalisaient le pouvoir royal et le caractère divin de pharaon (Leblanc 1993, 67-9). Sans remettre en question cette interprétation, nous pensons, aujourd'hui, pouvoir la développer, car tous les thèmes iconographiques qui constituent le support décoratif de ces temples, ne s'arrêtent pas à glorifier les actions historiques du roi, à magnifier l'institution pharaonique. En effet, les scènes qui en recouvrent les parois, en disent long sur la double lecture qu'il convient de faire de l'"imagerie" pharaonique. Tableaux politiques, séquences militaires, actes cultuels, tableaux familiaux, asseoient, assurément, l'autorité du roi et, d'une façon plus générale encore, celle de la monarchie. Ils rendent compte également de la gloire d'un pharaon, qui a su guider son peuple, qui a su juguler les invasions étrangères, qui a honoré le monde divin par le service du culte, enfin qui a assuré, par son action procréatrice, la continuité de la vie, puisque, par sa progéniture, l'institution qui en est garante, pourra se perpétuer. Mais, ce que l'on ne doit pas perdre de vue, c'est que tous ces thèmes donnent avant tout la plus belle illustration de l'intime symbiose qui existe entre le roi et la Maât. Dans cette perspective, les actes du sacre et des jubilés successifs, les victoires guerrières, les actes sacrificiels, la descendance dynastique résument, sans la moindre ambiguité, cette conformité de Pharaon avec la Maât, et le temple de "millions d'années" en devient la mémoire à la fois matérielle et spirituelle. Il symbolise une victoire totale et globale contre les forces destructrices, — ce qui signifie que le fils a dûment accompli sur terre, l'oeuvre de son père, au ciel — et constitue, en quelque sorte, le monument-témoin, pour l'éternité, d'une "ligne de conduite" qui vaudra, au roi, son immortalité. A l'instar des temples divins consacrés au dieu, les temples de "millions d'années" fonctionnent donc pour assurer un culte au roi, puisque, confirmé désormais dans son pouvoir non seulement royal mais divin, Pharaon apparaît, déjà sur terre, tel un dieu, auquel on peut assurer un office quotidien, à l'égal de celui de son géniteur céleste.

Le Nouvel Empire marque un important tournant, une métamorphose progressive dans les rapports entre l'homme et le cosmos, qui va finalement déboucher sur la conquête du divin. On pourrait ainsi en résumer brièvement les étapes :

— Le règne d'Hatshepsout semble constituer une première tentative dans cette voie de la confirmation tangible du pouvoir divin du roi. La Chapelle Rouge de Karnak nous donne, à ce propos, une bonne idée. Sur plusieurs blocs, la reine fait offrande à son image divinisée, mais cette image est encore osirienne (Leblanc 1982, 299-306 et pl. 50-3). Le rituel anticipe sur l'état, en ce sens que la reine accomplit un acte sacrificiel devant un personnage qu'elle n'est pas encore, mais qu'elle deviendra à sa mort. Ce n'est que par ce passage de la vie au trépas qu'elle sera reconnue comme dieu, mais il y a déjà là, par le dédoublement de l'image, l'attestation d'un culte qui s'adresse à une partie de sa nature divine : celle qui la confirme en tant qu'entité osirienne et lunaire et, à ce titre, détentrice de l'éternité-ḏt. Cette affirmation sera renforcée par la construction du temple de Deir el-Bahari où Hatshepsout recevra un culte, de son vivant, mais un culte osirien.

— Avec Aménophis III, le pas est franchi : il sera Osiris, mais il est déjà Rê. Le culte rendu par lui-même à son image n'anticipe plus sur l'état. A Soleb ou à Thèbes, c'est bien à son effigie vivante que Pharaon fait offrande. Dans son temple de "millions d'années", le service du culte n'est plus seulement osirien, mais aussi solaire. Aménophis III, "roi des rois" comme le vantent les textes des deux célèbres colosses du Kôm El-Heitan, est "Celui qui illumine le Double-Pays", "Le Globe des humains, qui écarte les ténèbres de l'Egypte", le pharaon-soleil. L'iconographie, la statuaire, mais également la présence, au sein des temples de "millions d'années", de complexes osirien/sokarien et solaire, inaugurés par Thoutmosis III à Karnak (Barguet 1962, 182-205) et repris à Thèbes-Ouest dans le contexte de l'Aménophium (complexes bien attestés également à l'époque ramesside, que ce soit au Ramesseum ou dans les temples de Merenptah et de Ramsès III), met clairement en évidence cette double nature de la personnalité royale.

— La doctrine d'Aménophis IV va conforter, sinon renforcer cet état, par une exaltation magistrale du pouvoir royal (Barguet 1968, 31-4) qui sera synonyme d'exaltation du pouvoir divin. Ce sera l'épisode amarnien, une sorte d'"hérésie", où le roi n'aura plus besoin d'intermédiaire pour communiquer, pour communier avec le cosmos (anthropocentrisme conduisant à la caducité de Maât qui ne joue plus aucun rôle dans le processus cosmique) (Assmann 1989, 110-1). Roi et dieu deviennent responsables au même titre. Il se produit une symbiose si forte que le pharaon se reconnaît comme étant le démiurge lui-même. Il est "le père et la mère de l'humanité", ce que traduisent ces colosses mi-homme/mi-femme, retrouvés à Karnak-Est, par lesquels il exprime qu'il est, à la fois, Atoum, Osiris, Shou, Hâpy, en somme, qu'il est l'Unité terrestre (et dieu, à ce titre), comme Aton est l'Unité céleste (et dieu, à ce même titre).

— Pour asseoir la légitimité de sa dynastie et de sa personne, Ramsès II devra composer : certes, il faudra bien revenir, du moins en apparence, à une conception plus traditionnelle du Monde, ne serait-ce que pour satisfaire des pouvoirs spirituels trop puissants. Il sera le "fils d'Amon" et à ce titre, s'incorporera à la triade thébaine, comme nous le montrent les représentations retouchées du grand temple d'Abou-Simbel. Mais il ne se contentera pas de demeurer exclusivement le rejeton d'une force "cachée", il voudra lui aussi proclamer sa divinité tangible. Pour y parvenir, il va non seulement restaurer la Maât, mais il en sera lui-même le principe ou le concept, c'est-à-dire Rê, idée —rappelons-le — qu'il fait traduire en haut-relief en façade du grand temple d'Abou-Simbel. Il s'agit là, à n'en pas douter, d'un superbe exemple de syncrétisme, par lequel Ramsès II s'approprie, par sa naissance théogamique, la qualité d'Amon (forme cachée, léthargique, du soleil) et, par le bon exercice de son pouvoir terrestre, celle de Rê (forme triomphante de l'astre). En associant Amon (le "Caché") à son propre culte au Ramesseum, c'était pour lui une manière éclatante de proclamer qu'il était Rê (le "Visible") et, désormais, possesseur de l'éternité-*nḥḥ*.

Au Nouvel Empire, la dissociation entre tombeaux et temples de culte royal a certainement là son origine.

— ANCIEN EMPIRE : pyramide et temple funéraire ne sont pas dissociés. Ils constituent un ensemble homogène, où le temple est bien destiné au culte divin du roi, mais du roi mort.

— AU NOUVEL EMPIRE : tombe royale et temple de culte royal sont dissociés. On veut manifestement souligner une différence. Hatshepsout inaugure le principe pour marquer une justification de sa divinité. Mais les colosses "osiriaques" sont encore à l'image d'une divinisation qui ne peut être obtenue que par le passage à l'état d'Osiris. Avec Aménophis III, apparaissent les piliers "osiriaques" du roi vivant (Leblanc 1980, 78-9): le temple de culte royal prend alors toute sa dimension. Il confirme la reconnaissance de cette nature divine du roi en tant qu'Osiris, mais aussi, voire surtout, en tant que Rê: c'est la sublimation de la divinité terrestre et céleste du roi. Le culte est célébré en son l'honneur, en l'honneur de son image vivante, et sera perpétué, au-delà de sa mort. Ce culte se maintiendra activement jusqu'à la fin de l'époque ramesside.

Pour Pharaon, la mort n'apparaîtra donc plus que comme un avatar, puisque confirmé dans son pouvoir divin, il aura déjà de son vivant, - du moins à partir du Nouvel Empire - gagné son immortalité. Son entité terrestre ira se fondre en Osiris (= la tombe royale), son hypostase céleste s'absorbera en Rê dans le cosmos (= temple de culte royal) : il sera "Osiris lorsqu'il se repose en Rê - Rê lorsqu'il se repose en Osiris", c'est-à-dire Osiris-Rê ou *ḏt-nḥḥ*, les deux principes unifiés de l'Eternité, de l'Unité divine.

Bibliographie

Assmann, J 1989. *Maât, l'Egypte pharaonique et l'idée de justice sociale.* Conférences, essais et leçons du Collège de France. Paris, Julliard.
Badawy, A 1968. *A History of Egyptian Architecture. The Empire (the New Kingdom). From the Eighteenth Dynasty to the End of the Twentieth Dynasty 1580-1085 B.C.* Berkeley et Los Angeles, University of California Press.
Barguet, P 1962. *Le temple d'Amon-Rê à Karnak.* Recherches d'Archéologie, de Philiologie et d'Histoire 21. Le Caire, Institut Français d'Archéologie Orientale.
Barguet, P 1968. Le pharaon Aménophis IV-Akhenaton et l'exaltation du pouvoir royal, dans *Cahiers d'Histoire*, Clermont-Lyon-Grenoble, 31-4.

Bonhème, M-A et A Forgeau, 1988. *Pharaon. Les secrets du pouvoir.* Paris, Armand Colin.
Derchain, P 1966. Réflexions sur la décoration des pylônes. Dans *Bulletin de la Société Française d'Egyptologie* 46, Paris, 17-24.
Frandsen, P 1989. Trade and Cult. Dans G Englund (ed.), *The Religion of the Ancient Egyptians. Cognitive structures and Popular expressions. Proceedings of Symposia in Uppsala and Bergen 1987 and 1988.* Acta Universitatis Upsaliensis, Boreas 20. University of Uppsala.
Goyon, J-C et J-C Golvin 1987. *Les bâtisseurs de Karnak.* Paris, Presses du Centre National de la Recherche Scientifique.
Haeny, G 1982. La fonction religieuse des 'châteaux de millions d'années'. Dans *L'Egyptologie en 1979*, tome 1, Colloques internationaux du Centre National de la Recherche Scientifique, n° 595, Paris, 111-6.
Hamza, M 1930. Excavations of the Department of Antiquities at Qantîr (Faqûs District). Dans *Annales du Service des Antiquités de l'Egypte* 30, 31-68.
Leblanc, C 1980. Piliers et colosses osiriaques dans le contexte des temples de culte royal. Dans *Bulletin de l'Institut Français d'Archéologie Orientale* 80, 69-89.
Leblanc, C 1982. Le culte rendu aux colosses osiriaques durant le Nouvel Empire. Dans *Bulletin de l'Institut Français d'Archéologie Orientale* 82, 295-311.
Leblanc, C 1993. Le temple de millions d'années de Ramsès II à Thèbes-Ouest. Histoire et sauvegarde du Ramesseum. Dans *Bulletin du Cercle Lyonnais d'Egytologie Victor Loret.* N° 7 [Lyon], 63-76.
Nelson, H 1942. The identity of Amon-Re of United-with-Eternity. Dans *Journal of Near Eastern Studies* 1, 127-55.
Nelson, H 1944. The significance of the temple in the ancient Near East. I.- The Egyptian temple with particular reference to the Theban temples of the Empire period. Dans *The Biblical Archaeologist* 7, fasc. 3, 44-53.
Spiegelberg, W 1898. *Hieratic Ostraka and Papyri found by J.E. Quibell in the Ramesseum, 1895-1896.* London, Bernard Quaritch.
Stadelmann, R 1978. Tempel und Tempelnamen in Theben-Ost und -West. Dans *Mitteilungen des Deutschen Archäologischen Instituts Abteilung Kairo* 34, 171-80.
Stadelmann, R 1979. Totentempel und Millionenjahrhaus in Theben. Dans *Mitteilungen des Deutschen Archäologischen Instituts Abteilung Kairo* 35, 303-21.
Uphill, E 1984. *The Temples of Per Ramesses.* Warminster, Aris and Phillips.

The statue program for the mortuary temple of Amenhotep III

Betsy M Bryan

One of the alluring aspects of Amenhotep III's ruined mortuary temple at Kom el Heitan (pl.IIa-b) concerns the vast amount of statuary and statue framents that lie *in situ*, have been found there, or can plausibly be attributed to the temple. It would be impossible to give an estimated number, but certainly there were once set up hundreds, and quite possibly as many as a thousand, life sized or larger stone images. The king himself boasted of the statuary on a number of monuments: on a stela (CG 34025) later carved on the back into Merenptah's "Israel Stela", Amenhotep described his temple for Amun-Re as "magnified (*sʿš3w*) with statues for my lord out of Aswan granite (*m3ṯ 3bw*), quartzite (*ʿ3t bi͗3t*) and every valuable stone." (Urk. IV 1648). On the large stela behind the colossus of Memnon, the king stated that he "filled it [the temple] with monuments from what I brought from Gebel Ahmar (*ḏw n bi͗3t*)... It is because of their numerousness that one rejoices greatly, I having done the like with *i͗b ḥr sd* [an unknown stone ?]. This is calcite, granite, and black granodiorite." (Urk. IV 1673). The four named stones: quartzite, calcite, granite, and granodiorite are exactly those found throughout the temple (pl.IIc , and see the catalogue at the end of this article), although *i͗nr km*, "black stone", meaning granodiorite, is far and away the most common material employed, represented by approximately eight hundred statues.

It is not only the numbers of these statues that are unusual, but their forms as well. Much of the sculpture from the temple is in the form of deities, both theriomorphic and anthropomorphic. Their original emplacements are often lost, and it remains difficult to reconstruct their original functions. The following discussion will focus on the question of how the statuary may have been conceived to participate in temple rituals, specifically those related to the first *Sed* festival. Most statues of the king are not included in the discussion, largely because of their primary association with architecture, either pylons or columned courts. (endnote 1) In addition none of the sculpture, much of it limestone, found in the temple of Merenptah is considered, because it is felt that it largely derives from a later phase of Amenhotep III's constructions at Kom el Heitan (Jaritz and Bickel 1994).

No complete published list of the deity statuary from the temple exists as yet, but a catalogue of god statuary, not including the Sakhmets, follows at the end of the article (for Sakhmet, Germond 1981; Haeny 1981; for other statues Vandier 1958, 378-89; Kozloff and Bryan 1992). Many of the statues in the catalogue do not have a certain provenance in the mortuary temple, and a number were found at other sites. A couple have added inscriptions that identify the site where they were found, and thereby inform us of their probable ancient transport. Those without inscriptions are identified on the basis of the stones used (see above), the technical finishes of the statues, the size and proportions of the statues, the iconography, and, of course, the style. (For these criteria, see Bryan in Kozloff and Bryan 1992; on the basis of size, the granodiorite statuary from Soleb has been removed from consideration. It is generally smaller in scale.)

A number of scholars have noted that that there is a great emphasis on the *Sed* festival in the preserved inscriptions (Vandier 1958; Habachi 1971). Most of the inscribed non-Sakhmet granodiorite statues that can be connected to the temple have an epithet related to the jubilee, and at least one calcite statue does. This in itself is unusual, because not since the Step Pyramid do we have indications of three-dimensional production of gods for the jubilee. The gods represented in inscriptions are sometimes traditional to the jubilee and sometimes not. Examples of statue inscriptions mentioning gods of the festival include the following:

Osiris the great saw, lord of the Sed within the per nes
Khnum lord of Kebeh, great god within the Sed
Ptah Lord of truth, great god lord of the Sed within the booth of annals
Soul of Nekhen, lord of the Sed
Redju lord of the Sed
Satis mistress of the Sed, goddess within the per wer
Hemen, lord of the Sed
Nepthys, foremost of the Sed within the booth of annals (later changed into Herakleopolis)
Horus maat kheru, lord of the Sed who is within the per nes
Maat, lady of the Sed, foremost of the booth of annals
Seshet foremost of Hut-Nebmaatre, mistress of Sed within the booth of annals

Some of these statues are unique to this temple, at least as is so far known, and most are rare, particularly on this scale and in stone. For example, there is no other statue of the snake headed Asbet (Cat. 29), with or without a king, as here. Nor is there another example of a statue of Osiris, the Great Saw (Cat. 7). And the crocodile-lion sphinx (Cat. 54) is, to my knowledge, entirely unknown three dimensionally. Up to this time, indeed, statues of falcon headed gods, jackal headed ones, and cow headed deities were rare, if not unknown, in life sized stone. Nor do they appear to belong to the traditional jubilee rituals as they appear at Soleb and Bubastis. Some of the statuary of Amenemhet III, such as the crocodile sculpture from his Hawara complex, suggests earlier parallels, although the ritual context for these is no more certain than is that at Kom el Heitan. And, of course, there were examples of some unusual god statues on a far smaller scale and in wood, found in royal tombs of the mid 18th Dynasty. Tutankhamun's tomb provides us a rather complete example of what the earlier ones might have once had. Again, however, the ritual uses for those statuettes are unclear, though it seems likely that they were funerary in aspect.

It appears that much of the statuary, as proposed in an earlier publication (Bryan in Kozloff and Bryan 1992), was placed for commemoration of the *Sed* rites, in booths or in interaction with other images, to recreate three dimensionally the scenes of the jubilee. However, many of the statues associated with Kom el Heitan cannot be directly linked to known rituals. Barry Kemp has pointed out that Amenhotep III's jubilee certainly was not traditional, despite apparent assertions, as by Kheruef, to the contrary (Kemp 1989), and it is probable that much of the statuary was made intentionally for multiple cult uses and was moved about for that purpose.

Let me then move to the proposed explanations I believe are possible. This paper proposes to identify all the mortuary temple statuary within ritual contexts well known in the time of Amenhotep III, earlier, and later. It requires suggesting that **the statuary was produced to perform two or more cultic and liturgical functions, associated, but not necessarily continuous, in time. These rituals were linked particularly to the king's first jubilee but need not have been exclusive to it. The function of these rituals was to invoke the protection of the gods throughout Amenhotep's jubilee year and to link the king's rejuvenation through the *Sed* with his rebirth as the sun god for millions of years to come. The statues may have functioned as different gods for different rituals: for examples, one snake headed deity may have served as both Renenutet and Asbet.**

A major premise of the argument below can be neither proven nor disproven. It is that the temple, as it existed in the last few years of Amenhotep III's reign (post years 30/31), was not standing at the time of the celebration of the first *Sed*. In part this is based on the fact that relief fragments illustrating the festival are both dated and inscribed with the names of actual officiants at the ritual. As with Soleb, the temple of Amenhotep son of Hapu, and the tomb of Kheruef, such reliefs could not have been designed until the actual celebrations had taken place. Whether this was a matter of months or years is immaterial to the discussion below, but the article does presume that, during the months prior to the *Sed* and throughout the jubilee celebrations, Kom el Heitan was generally uncluttered by stone buildings or sphinx alleys, although its brick enclosures and pylons may well have been standing. A recent article has already eliminated the sphinx alley of sandstone rams between pylons two and three, and this was the largest stumbling block to the design offered here (Cabrol 1995). In addition, archaeological soundings in this century and the last have offered strong indications that the temple went through changes during Amenhotep III's reign, and that statuary was buried beneath the pavement of the present peristyle court and in front of it as well. (endnote 2) I will return to this point below, but wish the reader from here to see the grand site of Kom el Heitan in year 28 of Amenhotep III as an enclosure some 700 by 700 meters, surrounded by brick walls, with gates on all four sides. Inside there may have been already three mudbrick pylons with large courts between, and ceremonial ways laid out on the east-west and north-south axes (fig.1).

Rituals to appease the Eye

I will begin with the Sakhmet statuary (pl.IIIa) which represents the largest, by many hundreds, group of deity sculpture. The ritual role of this statuary has been studied by others, and this allows me to use the work of Yoyotte and Germond, in particular, to support the notion of statues designed for festival rituals. Many Sakhmet statues may be seen in the sculpture galleries of the British Museum, and although those were collected in the temple of Mut at Karnak on the east bank at Luxor, they once graced the courts of Amenhotep III's mortuary temple where the fragmentary remains of many like them may still be seen and continue to be excavated. Although the number of Sakhmets cannot be

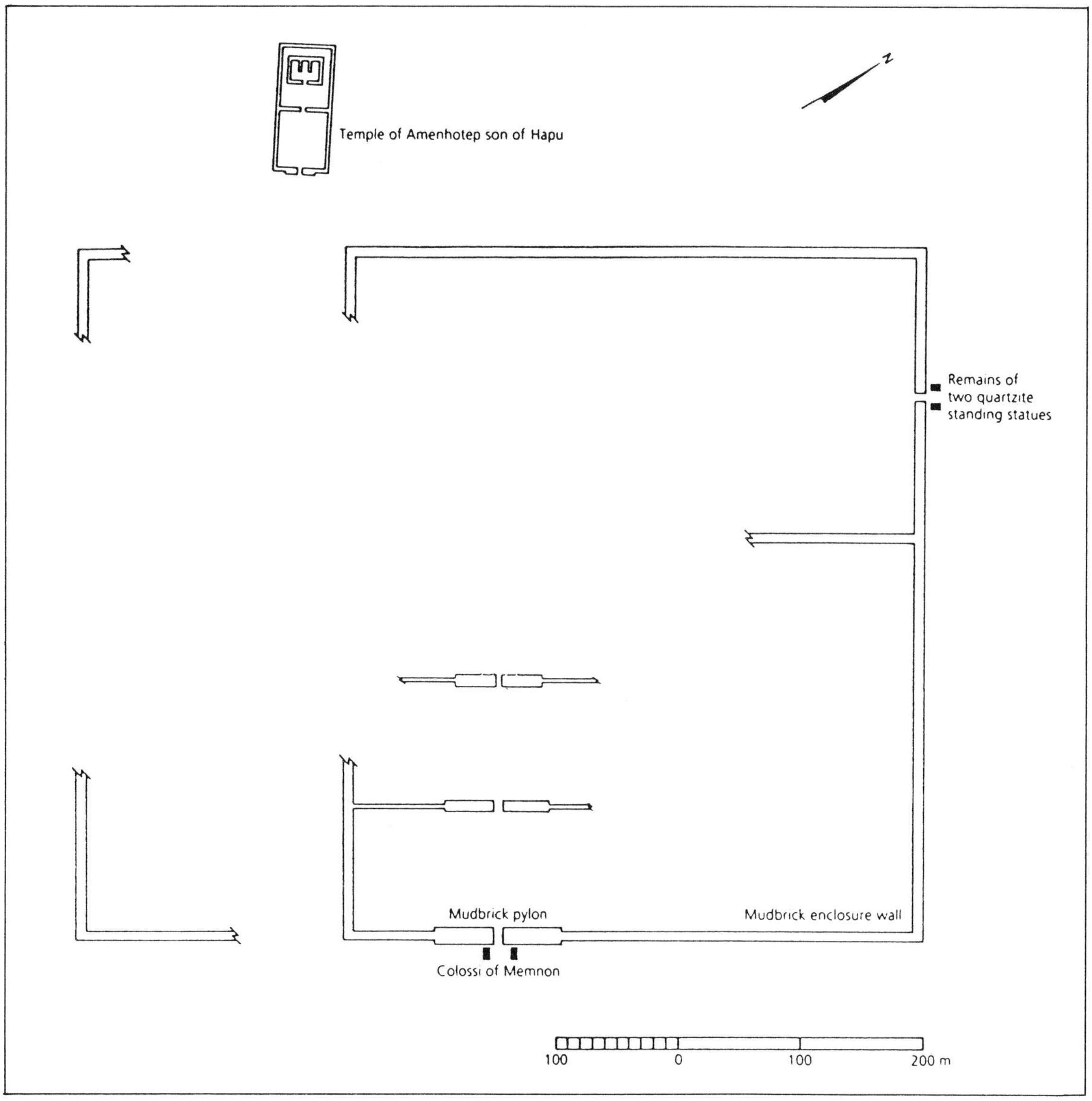

Fig.1 Plan of the mortuary temple of Amenhotep III, showing its probable incomplete state before the first *Sed* festival (after Haeny 1981, pl.1).

given precisely, Yoyotte in 1980 estimated that the number should have been twice 365, or 730. (Yoyotte 1980, 64) He noted that Benson and Gourlay believed the Mut precinct alone may have housed four or five hundred of the statues. Mariette had counted 498 and guessed 572 as a total. A few more have surfaced since then (Yoyotte 1980, 72 nn 15-16).

Yoyotte linked the Sakhmet statues directly to the Litany to Sakhmet. He noticed that at least sixty of the epithets found on Amenhotep III's Sakhmet statue inscriptions are the same as those on various recensions of late Sakhmet litanies from Edfu, Dendera, Kom Ombo and Tod. As Yoyotte pointed out, the purpose of Sakhmet litanies at these temples was to invoke the goddess not to act against the king with the negative power of which she was capable. Rather the litany appeased Sakhmet by and on behalf of the king and thereby assured a favorable cast for the year: that is, it prevented the dread of "Sakhmet being in a year of her pestilence," a possibility that Egypt ran each year. Each strophe of the litany appealed to the goddess to protect the king and deliver him from all illnesses and evils for the present year. Such a role for Sakhmet is already old in the 18th Dynasty. The association of Sakhmet-Bastet and Hathor with control of the year's fortune is present in the Coffin Texts and can be traced back as far as the 11th Dynasty (Yoyotte 1980, 64; Weigall 1911, 170 = Mentuhotep II "Nebhepetre beloved of Hathor, mistress of the year"; CT VI 171m; CT VII, Spell 955 = "Sakhmet-Bastet who guards the seasons... mistress of all years").

The Sakhmet litanies coupled with 730 Sakhmet statues invoke the protection of the king for the year and also assure a propitious outcome for each day of the year. The litanies have been most commonly associated with the Festival of the New Year, a celebration recently discussed by Germond (Yoyotte 1980; Germond 1981). However, in his 1981 discussion of Sakhmet, Germond noted that the litanies were also commonly linked to any period in the year when great change was imminent, such as both beginning and end of year, coronation time, because a new king was about to take over, or jubilee time, because the king was to be renewed. Although Yoyotte linked the litany only to the New Year for Amenhotep, the placement in this particular temple suggests a connection to his jubilee - and also to his cult of eternity. Given that Amenhotep III's mortuary temple relief program contained numerous *Sed* festival scenes, and given that much of the statuary from the temple explicitly refers to the *Sed,* it seems not presumptuous to suggest that a litany to Sakhmet might have been associated with that festival as it approached in Year 30.

A second aspect of Sakhmet's litanies as they are preserved in Third Intermediate Period to Roman sources demonstrates that the decans of the southern heavens were linked to Sakhmet. Due to their role as time keepers, like Sakhmet they had the potential of bringing evils during the year, but might conversely be forced to assist the king in his appeasement of Sakhmet's negative power. The decans appear not only following the king in his litanies to the goddess on temple walls, but in opposite role on the sides of Sakhmet's thrones on late period bronze votive statuettes. In those instances it was Sakhmet who was called upon to protect the offerer from the pitfalls of the coming year. Yoyotte cites late magical protective objects that used the litany to protect or heal people: "We will protect her at midnight (decree the gods), we will guard over her at night, we will take care of her night and day, at every moment. We will preserve her from the decans, we will preserve her from all errant mischief" (Edwards 1960, 7-8, pl. 2).

Although Yoyotte noted Sakhmet's connection to the decans, his interest in them was only to demonstrate the completeness of Sakhmet's power over the days of the year. He wished most particularly to show that the goddess could represent the possibility for either good or evil on any single day and as such was connected to the calendars for lucky and unlucky days known from the late New Kingdom through the Greco-Roman period. In those examples a set of 365 Sakhmets was doubled by a set of 365 deities for the days, but as Yoyotte pointed out, at Kom Ombo a hymn invoking Isis-Sothis and Sakhmet speaks of "She whom his Majesty follows, in the number of 730, lady of years, sovereignness of months and of days" (Yoyotte 1980, 63, 73 n. 43). He thus argued that given Amenhotep's large number of statues, there must have been a total of 730, half seated, half standing. We can neither confirm nor deny this last conclusion of Yoyotte's, but his connection of Sakhmet to the litany appears to be well established.

What remains to be explained is first, when Amenhotep III might have conducted the Sakhmet litanies in his temple and, second, how the Sakhmet statuary may have been connected with other temple statues and their cultic associations.

For a date of celebration we turn to Amenhotep III's favorite inspiration, Hatshepsut, from whom he appears also to have borrowed the Divine Birth cycle, the Opet festival generally, and the arrangement of east bank processional routes in Karnak and Luxor. On the quartzite Red Chapel of Hatshepsut from Karnak, among the festivals noted in regard to the Feast of the Valley, is the *sḥtp sḫmt*, celebrated on the 29th of Mechir, which is the 29th day of the IInd month of *peret*. Given the variable observed length of the lunar month, we may point out that the next day could be II *peret* 30 or III *peret* 1, so that II 29 may or may not have been the last day of the month. As it turns out it is specifically the last day that finds a suitable need for the litany of Sakhmet, in specific preparation for III *peret* 1. Chapter 125 of the Book of the Dead (Naville, Totenbuch, Tafel 133, line 22 = stela BM 155, HTES VIII, 48, pl. 39) refers to "that day of the completion of the Wedjat eye in Heliopolis on II *peret* 30" (*hrw pwy n mḥ[t] wḏ3t m iwnw m 2 prt ʿrḳy*). That is, it is the day when the solar eye, which may, of course, be Sakhmet (Germond 1981, 8-11), is appeased and reconstituted in Heliopolis. Likewise the Late Period Book of the Dead Chapter 140: "Roll to be used when the Wedjat Eye becomes full on the last day of month 2 of *peret*". The same day is likewise referred to negatively (all days having good or bad contingencies) as when Seth is identified as "he who has damaged the Eye in Heliopolis on the Festival of the Faces, on the last day of the second month of *peret*." This negative assessment of the day occurs in a mythological text (Urk VI, 138, ll. 19-22; Leitz, 1989, 87f.). Clearly the role of the king in performing the litanies to Sakhmet effected the "completion of the eye". It is possible that the litanies were begun on II *peret* 29 not only for Hatshepsut but also for Amenhotep III, because of that day's position as propitious for completing the Eye.

The next day being, quite possibly, III *peret* 1 was also of great concern, for it was the traditional, not actual, day of mid-winter, half way through the year, when the sun was at its weakest point (Leitz 1989, 21; Spalinger 1991, 212-213). On the Dendera Roman mammisi the day gods are lined up above and framing the arbor where Hathor holds her new-born son (pl.5a). The gods heading the two lines represent I *akhet* 1 who faces III *peret 1*. As Leitz notes, Sauneron, in discussing the great festival of Esna on III *peret* 1, stated that on that day in Esna all the same rites were performed as were done in Edfu on New Year's Day, I *Akhet* 1, that is, the celebration of the *ḫnm itn* and the birth of the king (Leitz 1989, 19-21;Sauneron 1962, 3-8). So these two days were times for first preparing for and then celebrating the rebirth of the sun. Such preparations would have been viewed as particularly precarious on the day seen as the sun's least powerful. The litany to Sakhmet must therefore have been efficacious as prologue to III *peret* 1, a festival for the sun's rebirth. The date of III *peret* 1 provides us with a further link to the second usage of statuary in Amenhotep III's temple - the formation of a calendrical sky map whose year began on exactly that date.

Rituals to guarantee a propitious year

The form this sky map may have taken is that on Amenhotep III's clepsydra (pl.5b-e: Neugebauer and Parker 1969 Text, 12-14; Plates, pl. 2). On that clock Amenhotep III himself appears offering to the gods of the sky, and is so designated as "beloved of the gods of the sky". In addition to the constellations, decans, and lunar gods, the solar deities of the day and night are summarized in the forms of Re-Horakhty and Iah before whom Amenhotep III offers. This combination of solar and stellar cycles is entirely within the scope of 18th Dynasty funerary temples. Hatshepsut appeared in Deir el Bahri in the offering room south of the upper colonnade performing a similar ritual. In a tympanum set in the west wall of the room the queen adores the goddess of the day sky and the goddess of the night sky (PM II^2 360-61; Naville 1906, pl.104,106,115M; Barwik 1995). Between is the solar bark with the queen backed by Nepthys riding with the sun god. On the ceiling are the deities of the day and night hours. Hymns to the hours of the day are known from here and are the earliest examples of such liturgy. Likewise Thutmose III appeared in his funerary temple in the same ritual performance, again with the liturgies and the solar boat (pl.6a). The preservation is much poorer, but in both cases the rulers are shown adoring the gods governing the day and night hours (PM II^2 427; H. Ricke, 1939, 11, pls. 1, 9 and 10).

The action of Amenhotep III in creating a sky map in his mortuary temple, therefore, was not as revolutionary as it might first seem. The map he used was similar to that employed by Hatshepsut's steward Senenmut on his tomb ceiling, but the activity of the sky chart, i.e., the king appeasing the deities who govern the movements of the heavens, was exactly that practiced already by his great-grandfather and great-great aunt. Amenhotep III, however, adapted the forms of heavenly time keeping for his own purposes. It is well known that he personally appeared in the night bark towed like the sun god through the body of Nut during one of the rituals of his first *Sed* (pl.6b: Epigraphic Survey 1980, TT 192 of Kheruef). Taking for himself the role that Hatshepsut pictured for herself and the sun god together, the king produced a three dimensional image of the Stundenhymnik, marking the movement of the sun god through the hours of the night and day. Barta has pointed out the direct descendance of the Day Book from the Hour Hymns found in Hatshepsut's and Thutmose III's funerary temples (Barta 1985, 133-34). When the Day Book is first found in 20th Dynasty royal tombs, a large scale representation of the solar boat moving through the sky appears with the hours marked, but the king still appears in the corners of the ceiling kneeling and adoring the hour goddesses, just as in the mid-18th Dynasty.

As we proceed to the statues that may have been used to create a form of sky map in Amenhotep III's mortuary temple, it might be asked why, if the texts tell us specifically only of the king's solar boat journey in connection with his jubilee, must we postulate a map including the northern sky, month deities, and decans? The response must be that Amenhotep III was, despite his innovation, a product of the 18th Dynasty, and the sky maps of that time were derived from Middle Kingdom sources. As Hornung points out, this was not altered during the 18th Dynasty but was only begun to be so in the reign of Seti I, who however, still showed the northern sky in his tomb, while placing the Book of Nut on his cenotaph (Hornung 1982, 126-27). His son Ramesses II, who often used Amenhotep III as a model, found it appropriate to place the entire sky on the ceiling of his own Ramesseum mortuary temple (pl.7a). Indeed, Parker and Neugebauer noted that his ceiling is a nearly exact copy, including mistakes, of Amenhotep's clepsydra! (Neugebauer and Parker 1969, Text, 13-14.) If the king had a form of the heavens in his temple, therefore, it must have been the entire sky as seen on Senenmut's ceiling or Amenhotep's own clepsydra.

A sky map enacted with statues

1. The single most suggestive piece is the crocodile-lion sphinx (Cat. 54) which is found, as far as I know, only in the northern sky on the sky maps of the New Kingdom. Habachi had suggested it was a local god of the Delta associated with magic and medicine (Haeny 1981, 60-61). However, that god Horus *ỉmy snwt* was never shown with a crocodile tail but rather was a crocodile or falcon headed sphinx. The crocodile-lion sphinx as we have it here is first seen on the map of Senenmut from his lower tomb 353 at Deir el Bahri (pl.7b: Bryan in Kozloff and Bryan 1992, 216, figs. VII 2-3). It also occurs on the water clock of Amenhotep III himself, the ceilings of Ramesses II at the Ramesseum and other maps derived from Senenmut's as described by Parker and Neugebauer. This particular constellation appears as a normal lion on maps from other sources. If one notes the placement of the "divine lion who is among them", the crocodile-lion sphinx's name, it will be seen that it lies west of the meridian or transit line that bisects the northern sky constellations. Were we to consider the possibility that the sphinx is now in approximately its original position, it will be found that it sits, facing east (for the temple, not actually) and south of the central axis of the temple, within the second court. Making the crocodile-lion part of a central section for the map, would then presuppose, following the clepsydra, three bands, of statues, each running east-west, with the southern sky band showing the king and decan stars in boats, to the south; the northern sky and followers gods (lunar days ?) in the center; and the month gods on the north. To complete a northern sky map, a statue of Hippo in a far larger scale should have stood opposite it to the east, and the harpooner, Meskhetyu, Selket and the crocodile Sak must all be accommodated. Two calcite colossi (Cat. 6), one definitely of the seated king, do sit to the east, and there are calcite masses unidentified in and under the precinct that could have represented some of these heavenly deities. Certainly out of granodiorite, there are statues of a god referred to as a falcon headed harpooner (Cat. 37 Hemen), and there are unidentified female deity statues who might be Selket. A single bull statue is known from the statuary (*msḫtyw* ?) (Cat. 52, 37, 26).

2. If one reads the quoted liturgies and, even more relevant here, the cross bands on the ceiling, Senenmut's astronomical ceiling emerges again as an aid to the understanding of Amenhotep III's

statuary. One liturgy, Number 7, Section 21 is addressed to Osiris in your name of "Great knife". The cross bands contain four spells addressed to Osiris, and spell two, representing Pyramid Text sections 774 and 626-27, invokes the enemies of that god to "lift up the one who is greater than you", and speaks to Osiris in his name of "Osiris the Great Saw" (*itf3 wr*) (Dorman 1991, 107, 139). This altogether unlikely deity was one of the granodiorite images in life size form left in Amenhotep III's temple (Cat.7). For what reason other than to locate the action of the statue in the heavens could this particular image have been produced?

3. Another group of deities whom Parker believed to represent days of the lunar month stand behind both sides of the northern sky constellations. These appear in forms often attested by statues from the temple, i.e., falcon headed, human headed and jackal headed gods.

4. If we move to the portion of sky map representing the names of the months (northern side), there are even more correspondences. For example, on contemporary and Ramesseum examples (those considered the most reliable comparisons) the king appears before the god of each month. There are statues that could account for at least 10 out of 12, with specific names for several: Ptah, Sakhmet, Khentykhety, Rekeh (wer or nedjes), Hathor, Renenutet, Thoth, Re-Horakhty, Khonsu, Tekhy (Cats. 21, a standing Sakhmet, 30 or 38, 56, 27, 29, 32 or 57, 40, 41 or 39, 28). The most unusual figure that may represent one of the months is a 2 meter long hippopotamus standing on four legs (Cat. 56). Made of calcite and now headless, this unusual piece was found during the digging of a series of test trenches in and around the north east sides of the peristyle court in 1970. The sondage discovered a packed earth layer and beneath it a calcite mass that eventually was recognized to be the hippopotamus. It has not been possible to free it from the ground due to the inability to introduce a crane at that point, and the ground water has since risen dramatically. Haeny pointed out that stories of complete and partial statues being found at greatly deeper levels than the temple floors are sufficiently believable to suggest that a crane would free "a zoo" from the mud (Haeny 1981, 104). (2)

Haeny believed that the hippopotamus possibly belonged to a three-dimensional version of the "white Hippopotamus ritual" known from 5th Dynasty and from Karnak under Thutmose III. This is possible, for although the meaning of the ritual is uncertain, it is associated with the jubilee in Niuserre's sun temple. Like some of the statuary may have done, however, this hippopotamus may have served in more than one capacity during the festival of the 30th/31st year, and there were likely to have been two hippopotami: on the clepsydra of Amenhotep III the months of Rekeh wer and Rekeh nedjes were illustrated by hippos on standards - just like this. The correspondence would not be very convincing were it not nearly unique: the only other time the Rekeh months were shown as hippos is on a Ptolemaic representation in Edfu temple. Otherwise they are shown as jackals. This last was attested among Amenhotep III's temples statuary, but the presence of hippos on Amenhotep's clepsydra sky map certainly would make conceivable their use to illustrate the months on a statuary map. The Rekeh hippopotami would have formed the ends of the northern east-west band of statuary, and the one found beneath the northeast portion of the peristyle court should represent the western, or Rekeh wer month god.

With regard to the southern sky, which in a mortuary temple map would have been located to the south and proceeding from east to west, the temple statuary as known at present could represent several of the decanal constellations shown as heavenly deities in boats: falcon-headed gods (2 in barks) (Cats. 42-44), Isis-Sepdet/Sothis as female in a bark (Cat. 24), and Sahu/Orion as male god in a bark (Cat. 15). No ram, turtle, or *bnw* bird statue has turned up, but as said earlier there is some reason to believe that there is a considerable amount of buried statuary in the temple. During the ritual enactment, the southern sky deities would have occupied actual boats that may have travelled along the Birket Habu, or a canal therefrom. (See further below.) On Amenhotep III's clepsydra, there are only two boats with falcon-headed gods, while there are three on the Ramesseum ceiling. However, Amenhotep III appears along with the planet gods and Orion as a heavenly body himself (he wears a star on his head). The missing falcon god was Re-Horakhty, and it seems quite possible that Amenhotep III should be understood to have assumed the role of the sun god, travelling in the heavenly barks (pl.6b).

As said above, the king, wearing the khepresh, rides in the boat with the two planet constellations (and with Sahu-Orion, as one can reconstruct from his inscription above the boat). The goddess Isis-Sepdet rides alone, but is followed by the king's Ka name. We could expect slightly smaller images to have been made for placement in the boats, and it is interesting to note that deity statues, as well as royal ones, vary from over life size to just under: this can mean as much as 30 centimetres overall, enough to account for the height of a boat: the figure of Nepthys (Cat. 24) is a good example of this, being of a scale 20-30 centimetres shorter than the goddess figure from Marseille (Cat. 28), though of the same type. Compare also the head of the king in the Louvre (A 25) with the head in Cleveland (52.513), both in the khepresh and representing smaller and larger statues proportioned exactly as with Nephthys and the Marseille goddess (Bryan in Kozloff and Bryan 1992, Nos. 10-11, 18). Nephthys may have stood in a boat representing both the realm of Isis-Sepdet and the sun bark, as is seen in the Deir el Bahri tympanum representation of Hatshepsut.

The month statues on the north side of the temple were perhaps set in booths with accompanying royal statues to represent the king offering before each set of two-month deities, as on the water clock. These we might expect to have been of larger scale than the decanal figure statues, as they were illustrated as cult statues approached by the ruler and are shown comparatively large on maps. The statues mentioned above as corresponding to the month gods are, like the Cleveland royal statue, of the larger scale similar to the standing Sakhmet figures.

As to the remainder of the decan stars, the Sakhmet statues may well have represented these, placed to enclose the sky map. On Senmut's ceiling, four circles representing the *sẖntyw,* or four pillars of heaven, appear forming corners for the bands of stars (pl.IId). (Two such circles occur on the west corners of the Ramesseum ceiling.) Sakhmet statues might have been placed in rows around the temple perimeter to create such bands (pl.IIIa-b). Although the earliest attestation of decans in leonine or Sakhmet forms is otherwise 22nd Dynasty, the existence of the Sakhmet statues recreating the litany to the goddess is itself a forceful argument to make equation with the days of the year.

A summation of the solar liturgical books in statue form exists in two pair statues of red granite, now in the rear court of Ramesses III's Medinet Habu temple (Cats. 1, 31). On the clepsydra this is found in a panel that represents the middle of the year. On one statue the king, wearing a sun disc on his head, with the nemes headdress, sits next to an ibis-headed god, while on the other he sits, wearing the same headgear, next to a goddess, face lost. The solar color of the stone used underlines the association of these statues with the king-as-sun-god's journey through the sky and further makes of it the transition piece between the starry sky and the solar orbit. As on the clepsydra, where Re-Horakhty and Iah represent the day and night gods, probably Maat and either Thoth or Iah here form the same reference. The placement of these two significant dyads was likely to have been at opposite east and west ends of the temple, but south of the present processional way. The statues, like the panel on the clepsydra, form an addition and a transition from the traditional star map to the Day and Night books of the later New Kingdom, concentrating as they do on the king's worship of the gods of day and night. This combination of the heavenly map with the solar cycle is the link, also, between the king as Re-Horakhty in the Orion and planet boats, and the king as sun god in the solar barks.

The solar rituals

In the tomb of Kheruef, Amenhotep III is towed in the day and night barks during a ritual that took place on an unspecific date in III *shemu,* the latest known event in the jubilee (pl.6b). An inscription of particular importance there states that "Amenhotep Ruler of Thebes... will *occupy the dais of the one who begat him* (my emphasis) in the jubilee which he celebrated on the west of the City. Beginning of the journey by a great Hapy in order to transport the gods of the jubilee by water... Making the water procession of 'those of Pe [and those of Nekhen in] the evening bark and the morning bark" (Epigraphic Survey 1980, 53) (Cats. 36, 46). The chosen representation in the tomb was of the king heading to shore in the night bark, because he was to be reborn at the end of night. Queen Tiye, probably substituting for Nephthys who appeared on Hatshepsut's solar boat illustration, stands behind the king in Kheruef's tomb. In statue form Nephthys and the king, as well as Maat, are spoken for, and the numerous figures of jackal and falcon headed gods, as seen in the solar boats in royal tombs, are also abundant. Of course the statuary may only have been used in a stone tableau ritual enactment that followed a ceremony. From the waters of the Birket Habu, and eventually transported to Kom el Heitan, such a procession must have been striking even in the flashy times of Amenhotep

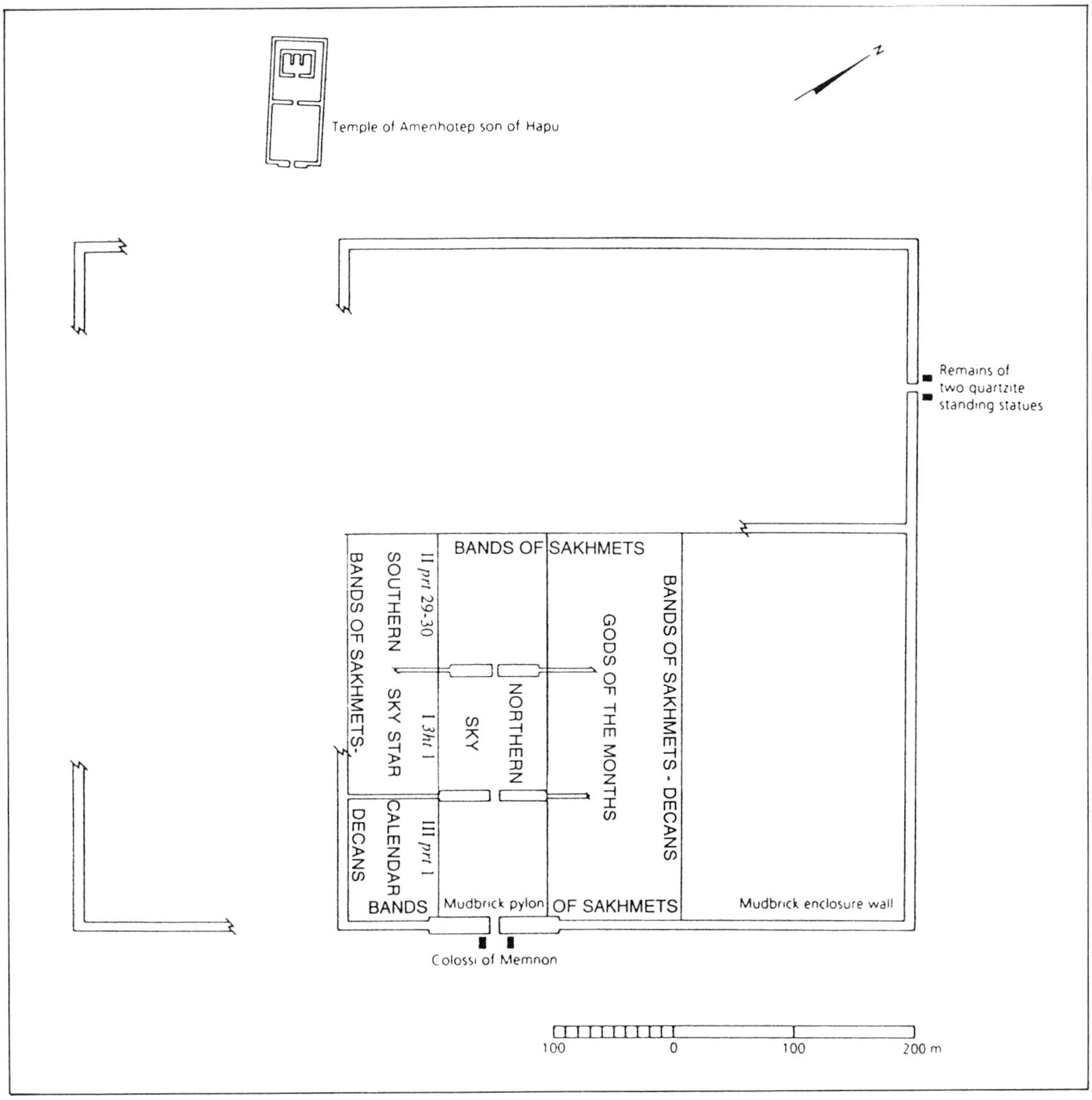

Fig.2 Plan of the mortuary temple of Amenhotep III indicating where statuary may have been placed to create a three-dimensional map of the heavens for use during the rituals for the first *Sed* festival.

III. Whether these same statues, or persons dressed as the gods, were used in a live enactment and once stood at Kom el Samak is of course unknown. But given the unusual things we often discover in Egypt, it should not be ruled out.

Accompanying such a procession must have been, as with Hatshepsut and Thutmose III, the recitation of hymns to the hours of the day and night. The stars, who were female but ruled by a deity either male or female, were charged to keep the king as sun god on course and on time through the heavens, particularly at the precarious time of the approaching jubilee. And the gods of the hours of the day and night were met by the ruler for their accompaniment, before he solicited the protection of the sun god on his journey. For example, as Hatshepsut greets the god of the twelfth hour of the day, the hymn goes as follows: "The twelfth hour of the day, "she who is united with life" is her name. She (the hour) raises herself for the god "He who gives protection by the inundation" (the name of the twelfth hour god). Following this recognition format is a recitation to the sun god: "To be recited: Praise to you O Re-Atum, May you go to rest in the holy fields in western Lightland..." And at the end an invocation to the sun to unite with the ruler (Assmann 1969, 139-140).

Each hour of the day and night had a deity ruling it, and of the day hours several have statues that might represent them (Maat, Hu, Sia, Thoth, Horus, Isis, etc.), but none is more prominent than Asbet (Cat. 29). This snake-headed goddess is known from the Pyramid Texts and the New Kingdom funerary texts only. Her name is etymologically associated with burning the enemies of the sun. As an hour goddess she ruled the fourth hour of the day (Assmann 1969, 123). It is noteworthy that on the fragmentary inscription on the back of Amenhotep III's statue with the hour goddess, the sun god Khepri is also mentioned, underlining the connection to the sun liturgies and to the ultimate purpose of these rituals: the rebirth of the sun in the form of Amenhotep III. A statue for that god is of course known in the form of the great red granite scarab now set in Karnak (Cat. 54). The text on it, however, mentioned the mortuary temple, and it must have formed part of the sun god's rebirth at the docking of the night bark.

This completes the pieces of a three dimensional celestial puzzle that I can place at present. We must now consider the question of why such rituals would have been considered so important to the royal jubilee. Barta has noted that the sun god repeatedly gives commands to the hours as their lord, sets them in motion and orders their risings (Barta 1985, 185-86). Like all created things, the lifetimes *(ʿḥʿw)* of the heavenly bodies were fixed in years and measured by the calendar alongside the lifetime of Re, which was eternity. The king's lifetime, it was hoped, could by means of the *Sed* become that of Re - that is, then, eternity. The existence of a representation of cosmic movements with attendant hymns to invoke efficacy, assured that the fixed movement of the sun with attendant stars took place, thereby guaranteeing the king's and Re's lifetimes.

The sky map as ritual calendar

The sky map's role within Amenhotep III's festival becomes even better understood in the light of an important time keeping instrument intimately associated with the jubilee: the clepsydra. It appears, for example, in scenes at Soleb Temple for Amenhotep III and at Bubastis for Osorkon II. It is also associated with the New Year's ritual which, it has been pointed out, has many points of contact with Amenhotep's *Sed* (Germond 1981, 270-72). The clepsydra, the *wensheb*, was presented in rituals at the moment of the appeasement of the solar Eye, and never before from what Germond has been able to determine. Germond pointed to the scene on the lowest band of the water clock where Amenhotep III offers to the month gods. He stands before Hathor offering wine of appeasement and behind him stands "Sakhmet the great lady of heaven" who promises him 100s of 1000s of years like Re (pl.5e). Obviously she is already appeased and in his following, just as she is on a statue (Cat. 4) from the temple. This is because the rituals of the *sḥtp sḫmt* had started and concluded already before those represented on the clepsydra were to begin in Year 30. For the calendar used by Senenmut, Amenhotep III, and Ramesses II and III begins with none other than III *peret* 1, a date already discussed as one when the solar eye was reborn after a precarious period and in direct link with the beginning of the litany to propitiate Sakhmet. The date may be found on the Ramesseum ceiling above the southern sky band on the east end.

A possible chronology for the rituals, arranged to guarantee the most propitious circumstances for each hour of each day of each month of Amenhotep III's 30th/31st years, would thus have run as follows:

II *peret* 29 or 30: beginning of the *sḥtp sḫmt* to appease the goddess on behalf of the king for the entirety of the year. This would have gone on at length one might assume from the enormity of effort put into the production of statuary for the purpose. This constitutes the solar half of the appeasement of the Eyes.

III *peret* 1: the beginning of counting time following the liturgical appeasement of Sakhmet, according to an idealized calendar that identified III *peret* 1 as a mid-year rebirth of the sun. This must have continued to be seen as the guarantee of Re's lifetime for the king, as a statue of Sakhmet and the time gods of the map, were addressed day by day up to and perhaps through the jubilee itself.

IV *peret* 27: the beginning of the festival of Illumination at Soleb to propitiate the lunar eye in preparation for the jubilee. This festival, which I discussed at the Turin Congress, lasted until the day before the official beginning of the *Sed* festival, II *shemu* 1 (Bryan in Kozloff and Bryan, 108-109, 115 nn. 93-95). This constitutes the lunar half of the appeasement of the Eyes (see fig.3 overleaf).

II *shemu* 1 - III *shemu*: the festivals and associated activities of the jubilee in Thebes. Renewal of the king at Malqata, and presentation to gods, taking place in an unknown location (Van Siclen 1973, 290-300 for dates).

III *shemu* 1or 2: towing of the morning and night barks with king and gods in a water procession.

They were, according to the inscription, "set in their stations" (Epigraphic Survey 1980, 53).
III *shemu* X: creation of tableaux of the jubilee rituals to commemorate the *Sed* (see fig.2).
Unknown date: redistribution of some of the temple statuary to major temples of Egypt: Coptos (Cats. 27, 54), Herakleopolis (Cat. 24); Athribis (Cat. 30), Elephantine (Cats. 8,22), Dendera (Cat. 38), Armant (Cat. 43), Middle Egypt [Hermopolis ?] (Cats. 9,10,32,39), Memphis (Cats. 2,3,57), Karnak (Cats. 19,21,35,36,44,46,54), Luxor (Cat. 47).

At the close of this carefully orchestrated time period, Amenhotep III had achieved more than his Thutmoside precedessors had hoped for: they asked to be included in the solar bark and to be united with the sun god at the end of the journeys, but Amenhotep "occupied the dais of the one who begat him in the jubilee", (Epigraphic Survey 1980, 53) thereby becoming the newly born and living deity of the heavens.

Fig.3 Falcon-head emblem of the lunar deity at Soleb, shown in a kiosk at the time of the festival of illuminating the eye (IV *peret* 27 to II *shemu* 1). After an unpublished line-drawing by the author.

Notes

1. For example, the colossus of Memnon and its twin. Likewise the standing colossi from the peristyle court. These last royal images of Amenhotep III are also taken to represent a later form of the temple (see further below). The limestone colossi reused at the Merneptah temple are also not included because of their apparent connection to a northern possibly Ptah-Sokar-Osiris wing of the temple. The granite and quartzite colossi at the north gate of the temple are excluded too, again for reasons of processional placement. Naturally architectural employment would not exclude the association of a statue with ritual function too, but the reader may find a cosmological explanation of all these colossal statues, commonly found before or behind gateways, to be rather too convenient.
2. Haeny's description of his own sondage is convincing as to the position of the hippopotamus statue beneath the paving of the court. It is important to note, however, that given the site's damp mud consistency, some pieces could have settled deep into the mud.

CATALOGUE OF STATUARY

Anthropomorphic statues

1. King with sun disc with a female goddess
Provenance: main portion at present in Medinet Habu, Third Inner Hall (pl.IIIb). Apparently brought there by Ramesses III who placed an inscribed sandstone socle atop column bases for the statues' emplacement. Head in Cairo (pl.8a).
Material: Red granite.
Size: Ht. 2.7 m.
Inscription: Recarved inscription on back slab; inscriptions naming Ramesses III beside legs on seat.
Condition: Headless king; head in Cairo, JE 54477; goddess faceless. Otherwise lower legs damaged.
Bibliography: Habachi in Haeny 1981, plate 31, pp. 117-19; Bryan 1994, with photo of king's head; PM II^2 512 [157]; Epigraphic Survey, 1964: pls. 483-484.

2.*King with Ptah Tatenen*
Provenance: Memphis; Cairo, CG 554 = JE 30167 (pl.8b).
Material: Red granite.
Size: Ht. 1.7 m. (Incomplete.)
Inscription: Inscribed for Ramesses II.
Bibliography: PM III^2, 835; Borchardt 1925, 101-02, pl. 93; Vandier 1958, pl. 128, 4, pp. 396, 408, 410, 418; identified by Habachi as belonging to this group, Haeny 1981, 118; Bryan 1994.
Comment: Size and proportions nearly identical to two Medinet Habu red granite dyads. Recarved.

3. *Bust from Khepri and king dyad*
Provenance: Memphis, near Ptah temple enclosure; Cairo, CG 38104 = JE 27856.
Material: Red granite.
Size: Ht. .85 m.
Bibliography: PM III^2, 835; Daressy 1906, 35.
Comment: Statue wears the *khat*, a uraeus, and a scarab atop the head.

4.Sakhmet, Amenhotep III, Amen, Amenet
Provenance: *in situ*, Kom el Heitan (pl.IVa).
Material: probably quartzite. Heavily eroded.
Size: From Wilkinson: Ht. 8'3", including base (heads lacking); 3'6" wd. shoulder; 3'8" ht. knee; 1'10.5" length of foot.
Condition: Amen and Amenet have been mutilated such that only the eroded image of their lower halves remains. The lion-headed Sakhmet has lost her head, as has the king.
Inscription (left to right):
1. The good god lord of the cult act, Nebmaatre, beloved of Sakhmet, given life forever.
The son of Re Amenhotep, ruler of Thebes, beloved of Sakhmet, the Great, mistress of the sky, forever (no *'nh* before *dt*).
2. The King of Upper and Lower Egypt, lord of appearances, Nebmaatre, beloved of Amen, king of the gods, forever.
The son of Re of his body Amenhotep ruler of Thebes, beloved of Amen Re, lord of the thrones of the two lands, forever.
3. The good god lord of the cult act, Nebmaatre, beloved of Amen Re lord of the sky, given life.
The King of Upper and Lower Egypt, lord of appearances Nebmaatre, beloved of Amen Re, lord of the thrones of the two lands, given life.
4. The son of Re, his beloved, Amenhotep, ruler of Thebes, beloved of Amen Re lord of the sky, forever.

The good god lord of the two lands, lord of the cult act, the King of Upper and Lower Egypt Nebmaatre, beloved of Amenet, given life.
Bibliography: Haeny 1981, 56-57, pl. 12
Comment: Whether the inscriptions are contemporary to the original production of the statue is impossible to say with certainty. They are in better condition than the figures themselves and show no hacking. The omission of "living" before "forever" in the inscriptions occurs three times and implies that all the texts were carved at the same time, but not necessarily before the statue was already mutilated.

5. Ptah
Provenance: Medinet Habu; found in the second court of the temple. Now in the fourth shrine north of the hypostyle hall (pl.9).
Material: Calcite.
Size: Ht. 2.3 m. with base.
Inscriptions: The Good God Nebmaatre, the Son of Re [Amenhotep ruler of Thebes], given life, stability, dominion like Re, beloved of Ptah lord of truth, foremost of the *Sed*.
Bibliography: Habachi in Haeny 1981, plate 32 b, pp. 119-120; PM II^2 506 [122]; Hölscher 1941, pl. 21[A].
Comment: Headless, holding combined *ankh* and *was* scepter. Otherwise good condition.

6. Two colossal seated royal figures
Provenance: Kom el Heitan *in situ* (pl.10a). Possibly the bases now in the second court of Medinet Habu, one with nome god procession remaining (pl.10b), belonged to these colossi. Those bases appear to be very hard limestone and accommodated seated statues of some 10-11 meters according to Hölscher, whose estimate was based on the size of the socle. Based on the measurements, it is estimated the Kom el Heitan statues would have been approximately 7-8 m. in height.
Material: Calcite.
Size: Northern one: Ht. 3.5 m; 2.7 m. from shoulder to above waist. Ht. of back pillar preserved 1.65 m. Width of shoulders 2.77 m.
Inscriptions: Southern one: ... as king ... the son of Re Amenhotep ... Nebmaatre, lord of the *khepesh*, the great image of the lord of the gods. It is as heir upon his throne that he places him, the lord of virility Nebmaatre, [living] forever.
Condition: Northern: poor; eroded with little surface remaining. Southern: poor condition.
Bibliography: Habachi in Haeny 1981: pl. 10, pp. 57-58; Wilkinson 1835, p. 39; Belzoni Researches, p. 15; Hölscher 1941, 9, pl. 17b.

7. Osiris the Great Saw
Provenance: Medinet Habu storeroom (pl.10c).
Material: Granodiorite.
Size: Statue base only preserved. Length approximately .55 m; width approximately .33 m. Length of feet approximately .26 m.
Inscriptions: The good god, lord of the two lands Nebmaatre, the son of Re, his beloved, Amenhotep, ruler of Thebes, given life forever, beloved of Osiris the Great Saw, lord of the *Sed* who is in the midst of the *Per-Nes*.
Bibliography: Habachi in Haeny 1981, p. 120, pl. 33c.

8. Redju
Provenance: Elephantine.
Material: Granodiorite.
Size: Not recorded.
Inscriptions: The good god Nebmaatre, son of Re Amenhotep, ruler of Thebes, given life forever, beloved of Redju, lord of the *Sed*.
Bibliography: Weigall, 1907, 10; Helck 1955, 1757.

9. Seated mummiform god: anthropomorphic, headdress and lappets
Provenance: Sheikh Abada (Middle Egypt). At present in Egyptian Museum garden. Temp. No. 7/3/45/2 (pl.IVb).
Material: Granodiorite.
Size: Ht. 1.65 m.
Inscriptions: Inscribed for Ramesses II, beloved of Osiris (no epithet).
Bibliography: None.
Comment: Retrieved from soundings at Sheikh Abada, 1943, and transferred to Cairo 1945. Condition excellent. No evidence of recarving other than inscription.

10. Seated mummiform god: anthropomorphic, headdress and lappets
Provenance: Sheikh Abada. Cairo JE 89616 (pl.12).
Material: Granodiorite.
Size: Ht. 1.79 m.; wd. .44 at shoulder.
Inscriptions: Inscribed for Ramesses II, beloved of Isis (no epithet).
Condition: Excellent. No evidence of recarving other than inscription.
Bibliography: None.

11. Statue base of Djeser
Provenance: Unknown. National Museum Dublin, 1896.19.
Material: Granodiorite.
Size: Ht. .30 m.; wd. .16; d. .16.
Inscriptions: The King of Upper and Lower Egypt, lord of the two lands, Nebmaatre, given life, beloved of Djeser and all the gods of the *Sed* festival. Variant interpretation: ... beloved of Djeser-Netjeru, lord of the *Sed* festival.
Bibliography: None.
Comment: Wildung 1969, 15, 73, on deification of Djeser intended when, as here, name not written in cartouche. Also, p. 77ff. for Djeser's ancient associations with the *Sed*. If this is a reference to Djeser as a god, it would slightly predate Wildung's earliest attestation in the 19th Dynasty. See Helck, 1955 1869-70 for mentions of the *ntrw ḥbw-sd.*
Condition: Statue base was cut down into block, original surfaces in good condition.

12. Unidentified god: anthropomorphic, archaic beard.
Provenance: Purchased Cairo, 1920. University of Chicago Oriental Institute 10607 (pl.IVc).
Material: Granodiorite.
Size: Ht. .627 m.; wd. .407 m.
Inscriptions: None.
Bibliography: Kozloff and Bryan 1992, 178-81; Vandier 1958, 384, pl. 123, 6.
Comment: Complete upper torso to waist.

13. Unidentified god: anthropomorphic, archaic beard.
Provenance: Unknown. DeYoung Museum, San Francisco CA 5466. Gift of M. H. De Young Endowment Fund, 1935 (pl.IVd).
Material: Granodiorite.
Size: Ht. .95 m.; wd. .37 m.
Inscriptions: None.
Condition: Torso preserved from neck to knee; left arm absent.
Bibliography: Kozloff-Bryan 1992, 182.

14. Head of unidentified god: anthropomorphic, archaic beard.
Provenance: Purchased Luxor 1919. Metropolitan Museum of Art 19.2.15.
Material: Granodiorite.

Size: Ht. .315 m.; wd. .227.
Inscriptions: None.
Condition: Head only; excellent condition. Identified by R. Johnson as the head to no.18 below.
Bibliography: Hayes, 1959, 239, fig. 145 on p. 240.; Kozloff-Bryan 1992, fig. 17a, p. 179.

15. Head of unidentified god: anthropomorphic, archaic beard
Provenance: Unknown. Boston Museum of Fine Arts 1979.42, formerly Peabody Museum 44.28.
Material: Granodiorite.
Size: Ht. .224 m.; wd. .214.
Inscriptions: None.
Condition: Head only; in two parts.
Bibliography: None.

16. Face of an unknown god
Provenance: Thebes, Temple of Merenptah. British Museum 69053, originally Victoria and Albert Museum 917.1896 (pl.13a).
Material: Granodiorite.
Size: Ht. .23 m.; wd. .18.5 m.
Inscriptions: None.
Bibliography: Barbara Adams 1977, 3-4, figs. 4 and 5.

17. Unknown male deity
Provenance: Kom el Heitan (pl.13b). Excavated by G. Haeny in the area of the west hall of the peristyle court.
Material: Granodiorite.
Size: Not reported.
Inscriptions: None.
Condition: Lower torso, from below breast to knee. Right arm absent.
Bibliography: Haeny, 1981, 99-100, plate 21c.

18. Unknown male deity
Provenance: Royal Athena Gallery. Drouot sale, December 1995. Ex-Georges Halphen Collection. Acquired in 1996 by the Metropolitan Museum of Art, New York.
Material: Granodiorite.
Size: Ht. .64 m.
Inscriptions: None.
Condition: Intact knee to chin line. Arms absent.
Bibliography: J. Eisenberg 1996, 27. Sale Catalog, Hotel Druot, December 1995.
Comment: Excellent modelling, holds *w3s* scepter. See no.17 for kilt type. Head now identified by R. Johnson as no.14 above.

19. Seated statue of Ptah in two parts
Provenance: Karnak Ptah Temple; head from cachette (apparently). Cairo Egyptian Museum, no number.
Material: Granodiorite.
Size: Headless statue in Ptah Temple, slightly less than life size. Head ht. .135 m.; wd. .35.
Inscriptions: None.
Bibliography: Schwaller de Lubicz 1982, pl. 311. Head unpublished.
Comment: Joined here for the first time. Half of the head remains with features resembling those of Luxor J.137. Original statue did not have a king kneeling before the god. Lower legs and feet have been reshaped, along with whatever offering table or other object originally before the god. God holds combined *ankh-djed-was* scepter. Original design on sides of throne.

20. Two Ptah torsos

1. Provenance: Louvre Museum.
Size: Ht. 1 m.
Inscriptions: Inscribed for Ramesses II.
Condition: Preserved above waist to lower legs.
2. Provenance: Memphis, palace area. University Museum, Philadelphia E 13653.
Size: Ht. .75 m.
Inscriptions: None.
Condition: Headless. Preserved from necklace (broad collar) to hips. Unfortunately the number was not available on my files at the time of preparation for this publication.
Bibliography: PM III[2] 858.

21. Ptah
Provenance: Thebes. Turin 86, Drovetti Collection, almost certainly found by Rifaud in Karnak.
Material: Granodiorite.
Size: Ht. 2.06 m.
Inscription: Live, the good god Nebmaatre, son of Re Amenhotep, ruler of Thebes, beloved of Ptah, lord of Truth, great god, lord of the *Sed*, who is in the midst of the Booth of Annals.
Condition: Good.
Bibliography: Curto 1984, 121, 344; Helck 1955, 1755; Redford 1986, 80-82.
Comment: Holding combined *ankh* and *was* scepter.

22. Satis
Provenance: Elephantine.
Material: Granodiorite.
Size: Ht. 1.5 m.
Inscriptions: The King of Upper and Lower Egypt Nebmaatre, given life, beloved of Satis, mistress of the *Sed*. Outside the rectangle is added, "Goddess who is in the midst of the *Per-Wer*".
Condition: Preserved to height of breast.
Bibliography: Weigall, 1907, 9-10; Helck 1955, 1757 .

23. Seshet
Provenance: Formerly seen at Medinet Habu by Golenischeff. Now lost.
Material: Unknown, presumably granodiorite.
Size: Unknown.
Inscriptions: The good god Nebmaatre, beloved of Seshat, foremost of Hut-Nesyu (var. Hut-Nebmaatre), mistress of the *Sed*, who is in the midst of the Booth of Annals.
Bibliography: Haeny, 1981, p. 120-121, Abb. 18; Redford 1986, 80-82.

24. Nepthys
Provenance: Herakleopolis; Louvre E25389 (pl.14).
Material: Granodiorite.
Size: Ht. 1.65 m; wd. .235 m. Length of base .66 m.
Inscriptions:The good god lord of performing the cult act, Nebmaatre, the son of Re, his beloved, [Amenhotep, ruler of Thebes], given life forever, beloved of Nephthys, foremost of the *Sed*, who is in the midst of the Booth of Annals. "Annals" was later changed into "Herakleopolis".
Bibliography: Vandier 1958, 384-7, pl. 123, 5; Kozloff and Bryan 1992, 183-4; Redford 1986, 80-2.

25. Maat
Provenance: Thebes. (Salt Collection) British Museum 91 (pl.15a). Almost certainly from Kom el Heitan.
Material: Granodiorite.
Size: Base only: Length .75 m; wd. .36 m.
Inscriptions: The good god, lord of the two lands, Nebmaatre, son of Re, his beloved, Amenhotep,

ruler of Thebes, given life forever, beloved of Maat, lady of the *Sed* amid the Booth of Annals.
Bibliography: James 1970, 6-7, pl. III; Redford 1986, 80-82.

26. Statue base of Weret-Hekaw
Provenance: Unknown. Cairo Egyptian Museum N127 (not in registers: pl.15b).
Material: Granodiorite.
Size: Base depth .58 m.; wd. .37 m.; ht. .17 m.; length of foot .26 m.
Inscriptions: The good god, lord of the cult act [Neb]maatre, the son of re of his body [Amenhotep ruler of Thebes], given life forever, beloved of Weret-Hekaw, mistress of the *Sed*.
Bibliography: None.

27. Goddess, perhaps Isis.
Provenance: Coptos. Turin Egyptian Museum 694 (pl.16a). Acquired in Coptos by Vitaliano Donati for King Carlo Emmanuele, 1753.
Material: Granodiorite.
Size: Ht. 1.53 m.
Inscriptions: None.
Condition: Excellent, but lacking lower legs and base.
Bibliography: Curto 1980, 15-20 pl. 3; Curto 1984, 123, 344; Vandier 1958, 384-85, pl. 123, 3.

28. Unidentified goddess
Provenance: Marseilles, Musée d'Archéologie 206 (pl.16b).
Material: Granodiorite.
Size: Ht. 1.15 m.
Inscriptions: None.
Bibliography: Vandier 1958, 385, pl. 123, 1; Kozloff and Bryan, fig. 19a; no headdress (similar to Nepthys but larger scale).

Theriomorphic deities
Snake-headed deities

29. King with snake-headed Asbet
Provenance: Probably now in a magazine near Medinet Habu (see bibliography: pl.17a-b). Formerly seen by Napoleonic expedition (*Description* II, 1821[2], Texte p. 182), Wilkinson (1835, p. 32, note 2), and Burton (unpub., British Library, Collectanea Aegyptiaca, Add.MS. 25639, p. 4) north of the western ruins of Kom el Heitan. One of two groups, according to all sources. Perhaps the triad of a snake goddess, the king, and an unknown deity, now in a shrine north of the hypostyle hall at Medinet Habu, is meant. The Napoleonic expedition also noted numerous granitic chips in region.
Material: Red granite.
Size: Back slab preserved ht. approx. .95 m.; wd. approx. .90 m.
Inscription: Horus, victorious bull, appearing in truth, the King of Upper and Lower Egypt [breaks off], He of the Two Ladies, the one who establishes laws, who quiets the two lands, the son of Re [breaks off].
Utterance by Asbet, the great, of [breaks off]. Khepri, his effective image (*tit*) *di n.f* [breaks off].
Condition: Upper half of dyad, preserved to king's waist and goddess' thorax. Faces of both battered.
Bibliography: Bruyère 1930, 219, fig. 112. Haeny, pp. 113-117, Tafel 30; Helck 1955, 1753.
Comment: Perhaps broken up for reuse.

30. Snake of Hor-Khenty-khety
Provenance: Athribis. Cairo Temp. No. 30/10/26/9, S.R. 11441 (pl.18).
Material: Dark granodiorite. May have darkened resin or pigment on surface.
Size: Ht. 1.5 m.; wd. .37 at base, .21 at top.

Inscriptions: The good god Nebmaatre, the son of Re of his body, Amenhotep, ruler of Thebes, beloved of the good (lucky?) guardian snake of the house of Hor-Khenty-khety.
Condition: Snake head lacking; slot indicates repaired anciently; otherwise excellent.
Bibliography: Vernus 1978, 30-31; PM IV, 65; Varille 1968, fig. 31, p. 134.
Comment: The snake of Athribis is represented in the *Sed* festival scenes of Osorkon II at Bubastis. Osorkon's scenes and texts are based on the Soleb temple of Amenhotep III.

Ibis headed gods

31. King with sundisc with a moon god
Provenance: At present in Medinet Habu, Third Inner Hall (pl.Va). Apparently brought there by Ramesses III who placed an inscribed sandstone socle atop column bases for the statues' emplacement.
Material: Red granite.
Size: Ht. 2.7 m.
Inscription: Recarved inscription on back slabs; newly incised inscriptions naming Ramesses III beside legs on seat.
Condition: Moon god faceless; king now headless but had head when published in 1964. Otherwise lower bodies damaged somewhat.
Bibliography: Daressy 1896, p. 148; Habachi in Haeny 1981, plate 31, pp.117-19; Kozloff and Bryan 1992, fig. V.24; Bryan 1994; PM II^2 512 [158]; Epigraphic Survey, 1964, pls. 483-484.

32. Thoth
Provenance: Sheikh Abada, Cairo, temp. 7/3/45/1 (pl.19).
Material: Calcite.
Size: Ht. 1.94 m., of base .305; wd. .61 (shoulders).
Inscriptions: Inscribed for Ramesses II with dedication to Thoth, lord of Hermopolis and lord of hieroglyphs.
Bibliography: None.
Comment: Carefully sculpted, but no details carved. Touches of pigment visible.

Ram headed deities

33. Statue base of Khnum
Provenance: Medinet Habu (pl.20a).
Material: Granodiorite.
Size: Statue base only. Length approximately .55 m; width approximately .33 m.
Inscriptions: The good god, lord of the two lands, Nebmaatre, the son of re, his beloved, Amenhotep ruler of Thebes, given life forever, beloved of Khnum, lord of Kebeh, great god in the midst of the *Sed*.
Bibliography: Habachi in Haeny, 1981, p. 120, pl. 33b.

34. Statue base of Khnum
Provenance: Berlin 15133.
Material: Granodiorite.
Size: Not recorded.
Inscriptions: The good god lord of the cult act, Nebmaatre, son of Re of his body Amenhotep ruler of Thebes, given life forever, beloved of Khnum lord of Herwer, great god lord of the *Sed* festival.
Bibliography: Helck 1955, 1757.

35. Standing statue of ram headed god
Provenance: Karnak. Cairo CG 38500 (pl.20b).
Material: Granite.

Size: Ht. 1.27 m.; wd. shoulder .43;
Inscriptions: None.
Bibliography: Daressy 1906 134-35; pl. 29.
Comment: Preserved to knee; sundisc on head is better worked than remainder of present state. If this is original to Amenhotep III, it was reworked extensively later, with addition of kilt hem decoration, new belt, armlets, and facial features. Kilt pleating, wig lappets, and sundisc may be original. Proportions are consistent with standing statuary of Amenhotep III. (Shoulders 5.51 grid squares; breast 3.4; waist 2.7. See Kozloff and Bryan 1992, Appendix p. 464).

Falcon headed or falcon shaped statues

36. Soul of Nekhen (Uncertain whether there is anything of a falcon head original to the figure. May have been a jackal head)
Provenance: Karnak. Cairo JE 41211, formerly Temp. 8/6/24/1 (pl.21a-b). In Beni Suef Museum as of 9/95.
Material: Granodiorite (red inclusions).
Size: Ht. 1.1 m.
Inscriptions: The good god Nebmaatre, given life, beloved [sic] of the Souls of Nekhen, lord of the *Sed*. [*mry* is written before *di͗ ꜥnḫ*]
Condition: Falcon head heavily restored and incorrectly, apparently using CG 64735, the Ramesses II and Hauron colossus as model. Falcons do not have the large bulging eyes and short hooked beak seen here in the reign of Amenhotep III. Also restored are parts of right arm, legs, and small portion of base.
Bibliography: *Urk.* IV 1755.

37. Statue base of Hemen
Provenance: Unknown. Purchased 1836. Musée Calvet, Avignon A38.
Material: Granodiorite.
Size: Length .688 m.; wd. .32; ht. .17. Overall ht. .252.
Inscriptons: The good god Nebmaatre, given life, beloved of Hemen, lord of the *Sed* festival.
Bibliography: *RT* 35 (1913) 196-197; Sydney Aufrère 1985; R. Stadelmann 1977.
Comment: Hemen was the god of Mo'alla, ancient Hefat, some 30 km south of Thebes. He was honored with the gods of Elephantine at the time of inundation; he had the role of hippopotamus harpooner (PT 236, Utterance 231), and in the Book of the Dead (Spell 99 Introduction) appears to control the rigging of the ferryboat in the sky.

38. Statue base of Horus Maa-kheru
Provenance: Dendera (pl.22a).
Material: Granodiorite.
Size: Length .65 m.; wd. .33; ht. .17.
Inscriptions: The good god Nebmaatre, given life, beloved of Horus Maat-kheru, lord of the *Sed* festival who is in the midst of the *Per Nes*.
Bibliography: None.
Comment: Horus Maa-kheru is known in the Middle Kingdom and appears much later at Dendera in a temple inscription (cited by *Wb.* II, 17, note 13: the *Wb. Belegst.* gives *LD Text* II, 185 with determinative of a falcon wearing the red crown.). In the "Hymn to the Egyptian Crown" one finds: "Horus, whose voice is just in the presence of the ennead of gods, in his name of Maat-kheru" (Hymn. Diad. 11,1).
I am grateful to Robert Morkot for providing me with slides of this statue base. It now lies in the court before the temple, along with a number of earlier blocks from the temple.

39. Falcon god
Provenance: Sheikh Abada. Cairo Museum JE 89615, in garden (pl.Vb and 22b)
Material: Granodiorite; red inclusions.
Size: Ht. 1.42 m. (from ankle to shoulder).
Inscriptions: None.
Condition: Feet and base lacking. Otherwise excellent.
Bibliography: None.

40. Seated solar falcon god
Provenance: Tanis, July 1904. Cairo JE 37485 (pl.23).
Material: Granodiorite; red inclusions, high polish.
Size: Ht. 1.03 m; wd. .445 at shoulder.
Inscriptions: Inscribed for Ramesses II.
Condition: Excellent. Lacking lower legs and throne with base; also had sun disc on head originally. Highly polished. Inscription and frame design on throne sides appears to have been added on the original surface.
Bibliography: None.
Comment: compare the different proportions and details on JE 89723, ht. 1.41., an original Ramesses II statue. Ex-Eid collection.

41. Mummiform falcon
Provenance: Unknown. Egyptian Museum Cairo, no register number (pl.24a).
Material: Granodiorite; red inclusions.
Size: Ht. .51 m; wd. .29 m.; dp. .28 m.
Inscriptions: None.
Condition: lacking feet and base. Excellent otherwise.
Bibliography: None.
Comment: May have been on a base shaped like a god's standard. Highly polished finish, except eyes and broad collar area. May have been retouched in those regions. Probably was set forward at an angle. Back has outline of a large *menat* (?) broken away, extending 34 cm. in length.

42. Falcon headed god
Provenance: Found in Rome. Munich Staatlichen Sammlung WAF 22 (pl.24b).
Material: Granodiorite.
Size: 1.63 m.
Inscriptions: None.
Bibliography: Schoske and Wildung 1985, 84, fig. 58, 152.
Comment: Roman period restorations for feet and base, as well as possibly reshaping of right hand. For the kilt, see no.17 above.

43. Faces of falcon god
Provenance: Found at Armant by Mond Expedition, 1937. Cairo, JE 67376.
Material: Granodiorite.
Size: The larger is Ht. .147m.; wd. .147; dp. .6.; smaller ht. .095; wd. .10.
Inscriptions: None.
Condition: face sheared off from statue; nose (beak) broken.
Bibliography: Mond 1940, pl. 20.

44. Soul of Pe Adoring
Provenance: Karnak. Cairo CG 38593.
Material: Granodiorite.
Size: Ht. .62 m.
Inscriptions: Utterance by [name lost]. ...Utterance.... in his name of ... Backpillar: Utterance by the souls of Pe. Adoration of Re-Horakhty rejoicing in the horizon in his name of Shu [which is in the

Aten]. May he rest in the western horizon of the sky upon the noble pure high building of Re [//].
Bibliography: Mond 1940, pl. 20.
Comment: Same facial characteristics as no.43, with heavy relief circles around eyes.

45. Sokar
Provenance: Unknown. Musée Calvet, Avignon, A39. Formerly Sallier Collection (?). Purchased 1833.
Material: Granodiorite.
Size: Ht. .75 m.; wd. .28; dp. .26.
Inscriptions: Words spoken by Sokar: I have given all joy to the lord of the two lands, [////]re.
Bibliography: *RT* 35 (1913) 202-03, pl. xli; Meeks in Aufrère and Meeks 1985, 141, 269, fig. 66bis.
Comment: Eyes possibly recarved. Original polish on wig and head. Shown as anthropomorphized falcon god, standing and mummified. Name of the king on the inscription is unknown.

Jackal headed or jackal shaped statues

46. Soul of Nekhen
Provenance: Karnak. Cairo JE 41210, formerly 8/6/24/2 (pl.25a-b). In Beni Suef Museum since September 1995.
Material: Granodiorite.
Size: Ht. 1.0 m.
Inscriptions: None.
Bibliography: *Urk.* IV 1755.
Comment: Parts of jackal head and base restored. No inscription remains: the jackal head indicates that this is a soul of Nekhen, rather than of Pe.

47. Seated statue of Anubis
Provenance: Copenhagen Ny Carlsberg Glyptothek AEIN 33, A 89 (pl.26a). Ex-Sabattier Collection.
Material: Granodiorite.
Size: Ht. 1.6 m.
Inscriptions: The good god Nebmaatre, beloved of Anubis in Ipet-Resy (Luxor Temple), given life. The son of Re [Amenhotep, ruler of Thebes], beloved of Anubis in Ipet-resy, given life.
Bibliography: Koefoed-Petersen 1950, 24, pl. 39; Koefoed-Petersen 1962, pl. 27; Helck 1955, 1758, no.604.
Comment: By size and pose, this could be the pendant to no. 40 above, the seated solar falcon god found at Tanis. The inscription, if the statue was transported from Kom el Heitan, was added later. The reference to an Anubis of Luxor Temple is exceptional, as far as I know.

48. Striding jackal
Provenance: Tanis. Cairo CG 38517 (pl.26b).
Material: Granodiorite.
Size: Ht. 1.0 m.
Inscriptions: None.
Condition: Preserved from knee to top.
Bibliography: Daressy 1906, 138, pl. 30.
Comment: Original size approximately that of the smaller standing god figures (1.5 m. without base).

49. Recumbent jackal on shrine
Provenance: Deir el Medina. Cairo Temp. No. 3/4/53/1. Head in British Museum EA 64400 (pl.27).
Material: Granodiorite.
Size: Overall approximately ht. 1.0 m.; depth 1.5 m.; ht. head .11.
Inscriptions: None.
Bibliography: PM II^2 478; Bruyère 1926, 26, fig. 17. Head unpublished.

50. Jackal head
Provenance: Smith College 1970.19 (pl.28).
Material: Granodiorite.
Size: Ht. .298 m.; wd. .242.
Inscriptions: None.
Bibliography: To be published by Ms. Kara Sullivan of Smith College. I am grateful to her for the photographs.
Comment: This head derives from a free standing statue like CG 38517, No. 49 above. Its eyes are carved exactly like that statue's, as "buttonholes". The soul of Pe, JE 41210, No. 46 above, has this same eye treatment. All three also have similar ear detailing, with horizontal striations to indicate ear fur. Nos. 47 and 50 have almond-shaped eyes with cosmetic lines; they also lack indications of ear fur.

Cow/bull headed or cow/bull shaped statues

51. Cow goddess
Provenance: Purchased in Luxor. Metropolitan Museum of Art 19.2.5 (pl.29a).
Material: Granodiorite.
Size: Ht. .51 m.
Inscriptions: None.
Bibliography: PM II^2 534; Hayes 1959, fig. 144; Vandier 1958 385, pl. 124.2.

52. Bull headed god
Provenance: Unknown. Vatican Museum 22808 (pl.29b).
Material; Granodiorite.
Size: Ht. .76 m.
Inscriptions: None.
Bibliography: Botti and Romanelli 1951, 104-5, pl. 71 #156; Grenier 1993, 53, pl. 16.
Comment: Holds *was* scepter. Dated much later in publications, but the kilt type, necklace, size and features are entirely consistent with this group.

Cat headed or cat shaped statues (other than Sakhmet)
53. Bastet
Provenance: Coptos. Cairo Egyptian Museum N109 (not in the registers: pl.29c).
Material: Granodiorite.
Size: Base depth .55 m.; wd. .29 m.; ht. .16 m. Length of foot .225 m.
Inscriptions: King of Upper and Lower Egypt Nebmaatre, given life, beloved of Bastet, mistress of the *Sed*. (Apparently added): Beloved of Sakhmet, mistress of Coptos-*Sty*.
Bibliography: None.

Other animal forms

54. Khepri as a scarab
Provenance: Now in Karnak at northwest corner of sacred lake (pl.Vc).
Material: Red granite.
Size: Ht. 1.5 m.
Inscription (mentions mortuary temple): The king of upper and lower Egypt Nebmaatre, the son of Re Amenhotep ruler of Thebes, beloved of Khepri, who has come into being in the land. Giving [wine]. Utterance by Atum lord of the two lands and of Heliopolis: Take for yourself life for your nose, O lord of the two lands Nebmaatre. I have given to you millions of years as king and chief of the living. Horus enduring eternally, may you live, may you be young forever.

Utterance by Khepri who has come into being in the land: O my son, Nebmaatre. I have given to you life, stability [and dominion] to your nose, that you might perform millions of *Sed* festivals. You are lord of what the *aten* illumines, the Nine Bows being destroyed beneath your sandals, in exchange for these things which you have done for me. *I am pleased because you made for me my temple on the west (imy-wrt) of Thebes. Your Majesty fashioned my ennead, each one in his bodily form, after I had made him.* (Italics my emphasis.)
Condition: Excellent.
Bibliography: PM II^2 221; Schwaller de Lubicz 1982, pls. 338-340; Helck 1955, 1753-54,

55. Crocodile-lion sphinx
Provenance: Kom el Heitan *in situ* (pl.Vd).
Material: Calcite.
Size: Base length 5.3 m.; length of statue 4.87 m; wd. 1.03 m.; ht. of base .29 m; ht. above base at shoulder .83 m.; wd. of shoulders .87 m.; wd. across lappets .60 m.
Inscriptions: None.
Condition: Headless but otherwise well preserved. Since 1996 placed on pedestal at original find spot.
Bibliography: Habachi in Haeny 1981, plate 11a, pp. 59-61; Bryan in Kozloff and Bryan, figure VII.3, pp. 216-217.

56. Hippopotamus
Provenance: Kom el Heitan *in situ.* Still embedded in the ground.
Material: Calcite.
Size: Approximately 2 m. in length.
Inscriptions: None seen.
Condition: Apparently headless, standing on four legs. Base has not been freed from the mud.
Bibliography: Haeny 1981, pp. 102-104; Behrmann 1989, Dokumente 163.

57. Baboon
Provenance: Memphis. Cairo JE 13858.
Material: Brown quartzite.
Size: Ht. .70 m.; wd. .58; dp. .50. (Feet lacking.)
Inscriptions: Name of Ramesses II.
Bibliography: None.
Comment: Pectoral carved in raised relief shows lunar disc on the solar bark. Behind squatting child on the prow is an incised set of cartouches of Ramesses II. Unusual place for the name.

Bibliography

Adams, B 1977. *Egyptian Objects in the Victoria and Albert Museum.* Egyptology Today No. 3. Warminster, Aris and Phillips.

Assmann, J 1969. *Liturgische Lieder an den Sonnengott Untersuchungen zur altägyptischen Hymnik,* I. Münchner Ägyptologische Studien 19. Berlin, Bruno Hessling.

Aufrère, S and D Meeks, 1985. *Egypte et Provence: Civilisation survivances et "Cabinetz de Curiositez".* Avignon, Fondation du Muséum Calvet.

Barta, W 1985. *Die Bedeutung der Jenseitstexte für den verstorbenen König.* Münchner Ägyptologische Studien 42. Munich and Berlin, Deutscher Kunstverlag.

Barwik, M 1995. The so called 'Ritual of Hours' from Hatshepsut's Temple at Deir el-Bahari, In C Eyre (ed.), *Abstracts of Papers, Seventh International Congress of Egyptologists, Cambridge, 3-9 September 1995.* Oxford, Oxbow Books for the International Association of Egyptologists, 12.

Behrmann, A 1989. *Das Nilpferd in der Vorstellungswelt der Alten Ägypter Teil 1. Katalog.* Europäische Hochschulschriften, Reihe 38 Archäologie, 22. Frankfurt am Main, Peter Lang.

Borchardt, L 1925. *Catalogue Général des antiquités égyptiennes du Musée du Caire, Nos.1-1294. Statuen und Statuetten von Königen und Privatleuten* II. Berlin, Reichsdruckerei.

Botti, G and P Romanelli 1951. *Le sculture del Museo gregoriano Egizio.* Vatican.
Bruyère, B 1926. *Rapport sur les fouilles de Deir el Médineh (1924-1925).* Fouilles de l'Institut Français d'Archéologie Orientale au Caire. Cairo, Institut Français d'Archéologie Orientale au Caire.
Bruyère, B 1930. *Mert-Seger à Deir el-Médineh, Mémoires publiés par les membres de l'Institut Français d'Archéologie Orientale au Caire* 58. Cairo, Institut Français d'Archéologie Orientale au Caire.
Bryan, B 1994. Amenhotep III United in Eternity: A Join for Two Statue Parts from Medinet Habu. In B Bryan and D Lorton (eds.), *Essays in Egyptology in honor of Hans Goedicke.* San Antonio, Van Siclen Books, 25-30.
Cabrol, A 1995. Une représentation de la tombe de Khâbekhenet et les dromos de Karnak-sud: nouvelles hypothèses. In *Cahiers de Karnak* X, 33-57.
Curto, S 1984. *L'antico Egitto nel Museo Egizio di Torino.* Turin, Tipografia Torinese Editrice.
Curto, S 1980. Una statua di dea con diadema di Hathor nel Museo Egizio di Torino. In *Studi di archeologia dedicati a Pietro Barocelli,* Turin, Ministerio per i beni culturali e ambientali, Soprintendenza Archeologica del Piemonte, 15-20, pl. 3.
Dorman, P 1991. *The Tombs of Senenmut: the architecture and decoration of tombs 71 and 353.* New York, Metropolitan Museum of Art.
Edwards, I E S 1960. Oracular Amuletic Decrees in the Late New Kingdom. Hieratic Papyri in the British Museum. Series 4. London, British Museum Publications.
Epigraphic Survey, 1964. *Medinet Habu VII: The Temple Proper Part III,* University of Chicago Oriental Institute. Chicago, Oriental Institute.
Epigraphic Survey, 1980. *The Tomb of Kheruef: Theban tomb 192,* University of Chicago Oriental Institute. Chicago, Oriental Institute.
Germond, P 1981. *Sekhmet et la protection du monde.* Aegyptiaca Helvetica 9. Basel and Geneva, Ägyptologisches Seminar der Universität Basel and Faculté des Lettres de l'Université de Genève.
Grenier, J-C 1993. *Museo Gregoriano Egizio.* Guidi Cataloghi Musei Vaticani 2. Rome, "L'Erma" di Bretschneider.
Habachi, L 1971. Jubilees of Ramesses II and Amenophis III. In *Zeitschrift für Ägyptologie Sprache und Altertumskunde* 97, 64-72.
Haeny, G (ed.), 1981. *Untersuchungen im Totentemple Amenophis' III.* Beiträge zur Ägyptischen Bauforschung und Altertumskunde 11. Wiesbaden, Franz Steiner.
Hölscher, U 1941. *Medinet Habu III: The Mortuary Temple of Ramesses III Part I,* University of Chicago Institute Publications Volume LIV. Chicago, Oriental Institute.
Hornung, E 1982. *Tal der Könige. Die Ruhestätte der Pharaonen.* Zurich and Munich, Artemis.
James, T G H 1970. *Hieroglyphic Texts from Egyptian Stelae, etc., in the British Museum,* Pt. 9. London, British Museum Publications.
Jaritz, H and S Bickel, 1994. Une porte monumentale d'Amenhotep III. Second rapport préliminaire sur les blocs réemployés dans le temple de Merenptah à Gourna. In *Bulletin de l'Institut Français d'Archéologie Orientale au Caire* 94, 227-86.
Kemp, B 1989. *Ancient Egypt. Anatomy of a Civilization.* London and New York, Routledge.
Koefoed-Petersen, O 1962. *Egyptian Sculpture in the Ny Carlsberg Glyptothek.* Copenhagen, Bianco Luno.
Koefoed-Petersen, O 1950. *Catalogue des statues et statuettes égyptiennes.* Publications de la Glyptothèque Ny Carlsberg 3. Copenhagen, E Munksgaard.
Kozloff, A and B Bryan 1992. *Egypt's Dazzling Sun. Amenhotep III and his World.* Cleveland, Cleveland Museum of Art.
Leitz, C 1989. *Studien zur ägyptischen Astronomie.* Ägyptologische Abhandlungen 49. Wiesbaden, Otto Harrassowtiz.
Mond, R 1940. *Temples of Armant. A Preliminary Survey.* Egypt Exploration Society Memoir 43. London, Egypt Exploratin Society.
Naville, E 1906. *The Temple of Deir el Bahari* IV. London, Egypt Exploration Fund.
PM II^2 = B Porter and R Moss, *Topographical Bibliography of Ancient Egyptian Hieroglyphic Texts, Reliefs, and Paintings. II, Theban Temples.* 2nd edition, 1972. Oxford, Clarendon Press.

PM III^2 = B Porter and R Moss, *Topographical Bibliography of Ancient Egyptian Hieroglyphic Texts, Reliefs, and Paintings. III. Memphis.* 2nd edition, 1974-81. Oxford, Griffith Institute.
PM IV = B Porter and R Moss, *Topographical Bibliography of Ancient Egyptian Hieroglyphic Texts, Reliefs, and Paintings. IV, Lower and Middle Egypt (Delta and Cairo to Asyût).* 1934. Oxford, Clarendon Press.
Ricke, H 1939. *Der Totentempel Tuthmoses' III. Baugeschichtliche Untersuchung.* Beiträge zur Ägyptischen Bauforschung und Altertumskunde 3.1. Glückstadt, J J Augustin.
Sauneron, S 1962. *Les fêtes religieuses d'Esna aux derniers siècles du paganisme.* Esna V. Cairo, Institut Français d'Archéologie Orientale au Caire.
Schwaller de Lubicz, R A 1982. *Les Temples de Karnak. Contribution à l'étude de la pensée pharaonique.* Paris, Dervy-Livres.
Spalinger, A 1991. An unexpected source in a festival calendar. In *Revue d'Egyptologie* 42, 209-222.
Stadelmann, R 1977. Hemen. In *Lexikon der Ägyptologie* II, 1117.
Vandier, J 1958. *Manuel d'archéologie égyptienne* III *Les grandes époques: La Statuaire.* Paris, A et J Picard & Cie.
Van Siclen, C 1973. The Accession Date of Amenhotep III and the Jubilee. In *Journal of Near Eastern Studies* 32, 290-300.
Varille, A 1968. *Inscriptions concernant l'architecte Amenhotep fils de Hapou.* Bibliothèque d'Etude 44. Cairo, Institut Français d'Archéologie Orientale.
Vernus, P 1978. *Athribis: Textes et documents relatifs à la géograpie, aux cultes, et à l'histoire d'une ville du delta égyptien à l'époque pharaonique,* Bibliothèque d'Etude 74. Cairo, Institut Français d'Archéologie Orientale.
Weigall, A 1911. Miscellaneous notes: 2. A royal cylinder of the Middle Kingdom. In *Annales du Service des Antiquités d'Egypte* 11, 170-176.
Weigall, A 1907. A Report on Some Objects Recently Found in Sebakh and Other Diggings. In *Annales du Service des Antiquités d'Egypte* 8, 39-50.
Wildung, D 1969. *Die Rolle ägyptischer Könige im Bewusstsein ihrer Nachwelt.* Münchner Ägyptologische Studien 17. Berlin, Bruno Hessling.

The Middle Kingdom temple of Hathor at Serabit el-Khadim

Charles Bonnet and Dominique Valbelle

1.Archaeological study

The increase in the number of visitors to Serabit el-Khadim has prompted the Egyptian Antiquities Organization to plan the rehabilitation of the site. In order to prepare this intervention, we were asked by the authorities to make suggestions regarding the preservation and the enhancement of the remains. Since the project would require the removal of a few blocks, as well as some alterations in the outline of the enclosure wall, it was evident that inscriptions and other fragile archaeological materials would have to be moved during the consolidation works. This made a reinterpretation of the site highly desirable. At the time of the British Museum colloquium we had carried out a brief survey to be completed for 15-30 days in the following season (Bonnet, Le Saout and Valbelle 1994). The completed work has now been published (Valbelle and Bonnet 1996); the following account, from that given at the colloquium, provides a summary of the project in the context of this volume on research projects on Egyptian temples.

The numbers of stelae refer to Gardiner and Peet 1917, and Gardiner, Peet and Cerny 1955.

The site of Serabit el-Khadim

Two drawings by Ricci give a first picture of Serabit-el-Khadim, in the temple of which Sir Flinders Petrie undertook rather important excavations in 1904-1905. The publication which Petrie made one year later has remained famous. In 1935, a new survey conducted by R. Starr from Harvard University was less successful. The lack of stratification was perceived as a discouraging factor by a majority of the team, with the notable exception of Jaroslav Cerny, in charge of collating the inscriptions, who thought that the research should continue. From 1968 to 1978, an Israeli team led by R. Giveon carried out excavations on the site. To the present day, its results have not been published in detail.

A short survey rapidly convinced us that in spite of the regrettable lack of stratification in the temple, a topographical study linked to the inscribed and dated monuments would be of value, and would help to refine the general chronology. Moreover, for obvious reasons (unstable blocks, worn pathway, etc.) a circuit had to be proposed quickly. Hence it would be useful to reinvestigate the outline of the ancient paths across the sacred area in order to possibly follow them. As the remains of the New Kingdom were rather well documented, due to a better state of conservation, we focused on the remains of the Middle Kingdom. Many questions remained unresolved, and indeed Petrie had even expressed the view that the presence of a real temple in the Middle Kingdom was less than certain.

On Conservation

It should be emphasized that the inscriptions and the decoration of the temple are in a very poor condition. A comparison with the earlier documentation is highly instructive in this respect. Erosion and salts whose efflorescences can be seen after the rains seem to have been the main factors of destruction. Moreover, the rock of Hathor Speos shows dangerous cracks, which may have been caused by an earthquake. Man has also contributed to damage in various ways, such as the collapse of walls, scattering of enclosure stones, digging of unfortunate trenches, etc. In our view, the first step should be the creation for visitors of a circuit linked to the liturgy of the temple. A partial restoration of the outline of the enclosure wall would also be feasible and would make the archaeological features more intelligible to visitors. Only materials found on the spot should be used. Of course, the archaeological investigations will help to define the priorities of this rehabilitation project.

The archaeological data

There seem to have been two approach paths leading to the Hathor and Soped sanctuaries. The northern one was dotted by groups of two stelae, defining a passage which occasionally might have been closed by a door. In front of the "shrine of the kings", the pathway runs along a fairly thick wall.

The second approach, situated in the middle of the sacred area, was gradually modified during the New Kingdom as the successive chapels were established. However, four stelae and a lintel of Sesostris I allow us to reconstruct a former path, probably also with a series of rooms and courtyards.

These two main axes of the religious complex joined in a courtyard leading up to the Speos' porticos. The two sanctuaries were oriented askew, a feature perhaps related to the quality of the sandstone layers or to a more ancient layout.

The processional approach

A surface clearance of the northern path has exposed a certain number of sockets cut for some now missing stelae. The door-jamb foundations of an entrance pierced through the enclosure wall, near its north end, have also been exposed. This entrance-way, hitherto not recorded, is related to the axis defined by the pairs of stelae above mentioned. Shortly after the entrance, the approach path seems to become twofold, with several groups of stelae. The "shrine of the kings" was certainly a major station on the way to the sanctuary.

This monument, built on a bank of rock that juts out to the north, displays some unusual features. For instance, the south wall of around 8 metres long has a marked batter as if in an attempt to create something like a pylon along the path. The wall and its returns were carved with relief scenes and inscriptions. In front of the south wall there is a colonnade between pilasters. A new clearance of the area has revealed that the bases of the four columns were set in shallow cavities directly cut into the rock. The prints of two bases of smaller diameter were also noticed, indicating the presence of an earlier colonnade. The scattered drums of fluted columns may derive from both building stages.

One stela (n° 136), still *in situ*, stands in front of the colonnade, almost in the middle, sunk in a level of earth and stone chippings set to compensate for the slope downward of the rock in this place. The bottom of the stela is surrounded by a stone pavement in which, facing the Speos, an offering-table was embedded. Two small square sockets cut into the stela and cuts on the surface of the rock enable us to reconstruct a slight dividing wall which cut the "shrine of the kings" into two.

An entrance and several stelae bounded the shrine towards the east. Many alterations have been noticed in this sector. For instance, the setting up of a new stela with a pavement around it, possibly indicating the presence of another thin dividing wall. The northern wall was rebuilt on the orientation of these lesser structures and this seems to imply that during the Middle Kingdom already different areas were gradually arranged as the successive expeditions took place. A little farther on, there was yet another stela with an offering table facing the Speos.

The access to the large court preceding the Speos was through the entrance of the New Kingdom. Clearing the surface beneath, we exposed the sockets of a more ancient entrance which might belong to the works undertaken under Amenemhat III. Three small circular cavities outline a curb running towards a second entrance to the west, where two square sockets cut for the door-jambs were uncovered. All of these features differed markedly from the New Kingdom chapels established on a higher level.

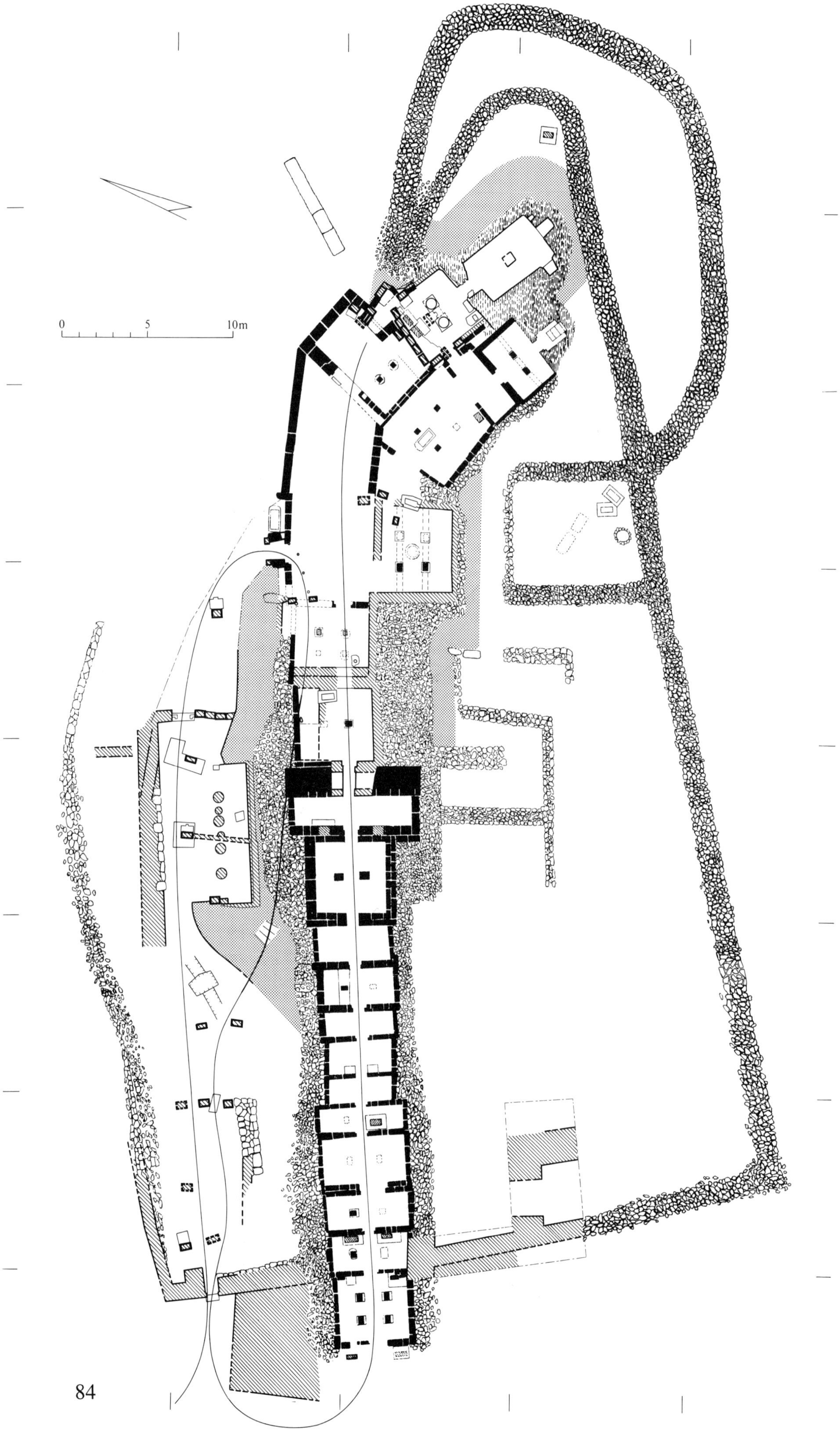

Fig.1 Plan of the Hathor temple at Serabit el-Khadim, showing in grey the excavated areas of the Middle Kingdom temple.

Thus, after the first entrance, the path turned back towards the second entrance. The circular cavities might have been used to set up poles which would have blocked the way to the sanctuary. This new axis enabled one to pass along the rear of the "shrine of the kings". Large foundation blocks discovered underneath the New Kingdom walls seem to indicate that during this stage the main central path was turned southwards, leaving enough space for the intermediary way. To proceed to the groups of stelae and the western entrance, one has to go down the sandstone bedrock, where some clearance has revealed the traces of what seems to be a staircase.

All these observations seem to confirm the curious outline of the processional path, which first ran eastwards towards the Speos, then turned backwards towards the western entrance. To proceed to the sanctuaries, one had to pass through the main central axis.

The main entrance to the temple

A massive foundation stonework leaning against the enclosure wall on the north of the main entrance has been fully excavated. Stones of various sizes covered a quadrilateral surface, with sides of approximately six metres long. Originally, the stones were bound with a yellowish mud mortar, identical to the mortar used in the enclosure wall. A sounding undertaken along the enclosure wall seems to indicate the presence of a similar feature towards the south. Unfortunately, the structure has been almost completely destroyed by a trench cut some years ago. Though it is difficult to date this massive structure precisely, we may assume that it belonged to one of the Middle Kingdom phases.

These two massive stone constructions flanking the main entrance are reminiscent of the mounds of a pylon. In this case, the front part would have been quite prominent, compared to the pylon of the New Kingdom set in the middle of the sacred area. Curiously, the latter is not facing the Speos and, though it is posterior to the "shrine of the kings", it could nevertheless have been somehow associated with it.

The portico of the Hathor Speos

It is again the presence of sockets cut in the sandstone floor of the Hathor portico that testifies to an ancient building stage. About two metres in front of the hewn room, at a time when the portico did not yet exist, a stela was set in with an offering table facing the sanctuary. This is probably the stela of the year 8 of Amenemhat III (n° 91), which had to be removed later during the construction of the portico. Its size fits with the size of the sockets exposed in front of the portico. The inscription carved on the stela confirms the displacement (see *infra*). It is certain that the two column bases were set at a later date, hence the stela could not have been left *in situ*. Traces of several other alterations to the floor and to the portico have also been revealed. There is no doubt that the stelae that today close off the axial passage have often been displaced. One may even assume that the way was not axial from the beginning but rather wound around several stelae before reaching the entrance.

The Soped sanctuary

The preliminary study of the Soped complex and of the chapel situated on the west has shown that these structures belong to a later phase than Hathor portico. However, the nature of the masonry as well as the general outline suggest a dating rather close to the neighbouring structures. This assumption remains to be confirmed by future clearance work.

The structures of the southern sector

To the south, a large area inside the enclosure wall of the temple remains to be studied. A short superficial survey and a restricted sounding have been performed. In the western part, a large building can be reconstructed through the discovery of a thick wall and an entrance. Within a few metres, a large quantity of fragments of lime mortar has been collected. Their analysis has shown the presence on the surface of a blue and perhaps also white coating. Slightly farther on, many bread-moulds have been collected from some lower levels. There were also numerous fragments of faience. Although these findings may seem modest, they indicate the presence of a residential building in this remote area. The presence of bakeries is less surprising. The study of the type of bread-moulds will help in the dating of these structures.

C.B.

2.Epigraphic study

When I was asked by the EAO to organize a mission in Serabit el-Khadim in order to prepare a project of restoration for the temple of Hathor, I began to consider at the same time the opportunity of undertaking a new scientific work on this monument. A careful re-reading of Gardiner, Peet and Cerny's *Inscriptions of Sinai*, of Petrie's *Researches in Sinai* and of recent articles by Giveon and Ventura showed clearly that a comprehensive study of this extraodinary religious complex remained to be done. While the archaeologists of our team were coming to the evidence showing that study of the Middle Kingdom temple would provide the clues to solve many important questions, the epigraphers were coming to the same conclusion by a different way, without any concertation between the two sides.

The peculiarity noticeable in the general plan of this first temple is paralleled in its iconographic epigraphic programme. This can be traced back to the lintel of Sesostris I (n° 64), and followed until the last monuments of Amenemhat IV or even to the inscriptions of the Speos of Soped engraved under Hatshepsut and Thutmosis III, which are inspired by those of the Middle Kingdom. Egyptologists were astonished by the unusual presence of commemorative texts apparently non-religious in content (such as the composition of staff) and private representations accompanied by inscriptions including members of the family of the expedition leaders (n° 94).

Nevertheless, it appeared clear to us that several important problems underlined by Giveon and Ventura concerning the interpretation of the New Kingdom temple could not be solved without a previous study of the Middle Kingdom complex, problems such as the age and meaning of the Speos of Soped or the abnormal position of the pylon built by Thutmosis III and the change of direction in the circulation after his reign. Our discovery of architectural elements, from the beginning, the reign of Sesostris I, was giving to the whole a new aspect and a greater consistency. It strengthened our conviction that a real temple was intended from the first expeditions organized in the Twelfth Dynasty, and it helped us greatly in our research.

The situation of the epigraphy was intricate. An incredible amount of work had been already conducted by Petrie, Peet, Cerny and others. When we consider the monuments themselves, the photographs used for the facsimiles and the squeezes kept in the British Museum, the result published in the *Inscriptions of Sinai* appears of unexpectedly high quality. However, the difficult conditions of work at Serabit el-Khadim and especially the crude light, the originality of several texts and their poor state of preservation often prevented Cerny from giving us a definitive, if not a complete, copy of some of the most important inscriptions of the site. He was of course conscious of the limits assigned then to his efforts and wrote a few words about the subject in the introduction of his revised second edition. He was also convinced that the place was full of yet unknown blocs and various fragments of inscribed monuments, as was later demonstrated by the Israeli teams and, more recently, by ours.

The dissatisfaction of Cerny, owing to his perfectionism, did not mean that it could have been possible to go further and produce better copies of the texts, particularly because many of the most important ones from the historical point of view, or for the liturgical interpretation of the temple, are now in a hopeless condition, when they have not partly (e.g. n° 71 / n° 109) or completely disappeared. Our chances of improving older copies being slight, we tried to use every available possibility in order to progress: first, since Cerny's work, our general knowledge of Middle Egyptian vocabulary has advanced, thus permitting us to read a few new signs or to correct other ones here and there. Moreover, we could copy some unpublished parts of already known monuments: for instance, the pillar in the Speos of Hathor (n° 93), or the unpublished back of the architrave n° 415 b which bears the name of Amenemhat III or IV.

It is a very patient, rough and modest, but useful work, conducted hour after hour according to the changes of the sunlight and, by night, with the help of electric light. Besides, the alternating study of the texts in the library and their reexamination on the monuments themselves proved to be very fruitful.We must remember that all the first corrections made by Cerny are only noted in the volume of texts of the second edition; the volume of facsimiles remained unchanged except for the addition of new inscriptions at the end. Moreover, we have now been able to visit several museums in Cairo, London, Brussels and Toronto, where a number stelae, offering tables and statues from Petrie's excavation are kept. Some very pleasant surprises awaited us there, such as unknown fragments of already published monuments, or even completely unknown monuments.

Of course, our principal interest concerned the understanding of the temple itself in connection with the new excavation: the evolution of the building, the specificity of the monument, the function of its different parts, the kind of worship paid to its gods, the priests, the offerings, and so on. To be able to assist usefully the archaeologists, we tried to analyse and keep in mind by frequent readings every inscription linked to any of these aspects, and to classify them according to their precise date when we know it. The first season was devoted to the study of each group of Middle Kingdom scenes and inscriptions in its proper context, in order to get a precise idea of each corresponding part of the monument as a whole. Few Middle Kingdom temples are known at present, and fewer are decorated with well preserved scenes and inscriptions. Therefore we cannot expect much help from direct comparisons.

The Shrine of Kings is however characteristic of the contemporaneous cult of dead kings attested at Dahshur. That of Snefru is well known in both sites, but the situation of Middle Kingdom kings, on the Slab of Kings (n° 71) as well as on the wall of the chapel, is still more important for the understanding of the official conventions in use during these expeditions in Sinai. The king who ordered the expedition and his predecessors are present through their statues which are treated as those of gods. Hathor, the lady of Turquoise, as the producer of gemstones , usually plays an active part. The leaders of expeditions are exceptionally represented in the midst of gods and kings - as representatives of the last. The complete interpretation of the Shrine of Kings is difficult as only the lower row of decoration and few blocks of the second one are preserved, but its political function seems quite clear: to commemorate the action of the kings, delegated to their divine chancellors, at Serabit el-Khadim.

The Portico of Hathor, in its latest stage, under Amenemhat IV, needs considerable effort and imagination to be reconstructed by drawing. The blocks of its walls are no longer in their proper place and are in very bad condition (n° 149) where they are still complete. The facsimiles were reproduced without any scale and the outline of the blocks is often missing in the publication. The preserved scenes seem to reproduce the offerings made there and the texts allow a large place for the identity and titles of the chiefs of the corresponding expeditions.

The Speos of Hathor (the "Sacred Cave" of Petrie) requires special attention. The examination of its architecture reveals a strong closing device for the external door, and a lighter one for the three niches excavated on the rear and right walls. These security dispositions imply that the Speos contained precious goods, such as offerings to the goddess, her statues, and maybe the turquoise production during the expedition. A cleaning of the floor, next season, will certainly give us some precision on the specificity of the cults celebrated in the Speos in the Middle Kingdom and may hold in store other welcome surprises.

The different monuments placed inside the Speos under the reign of Amenemhat III by the chiefs of expeditions present a particular interest. Like the representations and texts in the Shrine of Kings, Hathor Portico and in the Speos itself, they are half official (with the image of the reigning king and that of Hathor), half private (with personal claims, especially *ḥtp dỉ nsw* prayers, and association of various members of their family). One of them is rather unusual: it is described by its dedication text as a staircase (n° 89). The monument, already broken in four pieces in 1935, has now lost another fragment. Yet the remaining pieces are still enough to show that, in spite of the sketch accompanying the description of the monument in the publication, it did indeed look like a staircase or temporary altar of the type usually called *ḫtyw* (*ALex* I, 77.3203; II, 78.3158; III, 79.2291), as those of Karnak, Medinet Habu, etc. Testimonies of private cults in temples are not so frequent in the Middle Kingdom, except for the funerary chapels on the terrace of the temple in Abydos. And it is also a funerary form that these devotions take here in Serabit el-Khadim, either in the Speos, or on stelae standing near the Speos in the temple, or even outside the temple.

Last spring, we concentrated our efforts on the study of the stelae. We tried to analyze the inscriptions and to classify the principal items enclosed, in order to find a link, if it were to exist, between them and the temple. We took into account the rock stelae near the mines as well as the standing ones in and near the temple. Of course, many of them were commemorating the expeditions and gave various details on them: composition of the staff, date and circumstances of the expeditions, opening of the galleries, etc. But some of them bear texts, unfortunately often incomplete, placing the mining of turquoise on a mythic level: for instance they compare the fields of turquoise on the plateau of Serabit el-Khadim with the "garment of Geb" (n° 110).

The stelae also bore information concerning the building of parts of the temple and the religious practices connected with those. The oldest text related to this subject is stela n° 91 engraved in the 8th year of Amenemhat III, now in the Stonehenge-like fence, erected in front of the Speos. The external face of the stela gives a list of offerings according to a weekly calendar, while the inner face contains this much eroded passage : "[...] in gold and sistra of (?) [...] offerings of oxen and geese, incense [upon] the flame. I [made] for her a festival courtyard (*[ỉr.n].ỉ n.s wsḫt ḥbyt)* and provided [her altars...] I [doubled] any movement to this place (*ḳ3b.n.ỉ ỉy nb r st tn).*"

The second text on the same subject is the rock stela n° 53, probably copied from the first one. It was engraved in the 44th year of Amenemhat III. It seems to parallel stela n° 91 and gives a more complete version of it : "I brought to her (Hathor) an altar of faience, fine linen, white linen, various [...] together with *ỉns*-cloth. I presented to her offerings of bread and beer, oxen and geese, incense upon the flame. I made for her a festival place (*ỉr.n.ỉ n.s ḥbyt*) and I doubled any movement to this place (*ḳ3b.n.ỉ ỉy nb r st tn).*"

The disposition of the space in front of the Speos in the time of Amenemhat III - before the building of the Amenemhat IV's portico - is clearly described in these two texts. It is called once *wsḫt ḥbyt* and the second time simply *ḥbyt*, well known designations of offering courtyards or halls. The arrangement found this season in the natural rock in front of the door of the Speos fitted the bottom of stela n° 91 and an associated offering table behind it, as has already been discovered elsewhere, inside and outside the temple.

Concerning the doubling of the processional way to this place, the second text is the only reliable one, considering its state of preservation. It presents the arrangement which has been observed this season by the archaeologists in the centre of the temple as the result of a change in the liturgy. The new circulation affects the general form of the sign *ḳ3b*. The determinative used on the rock stela n° 53 is also remarkable. It resembles a staircase rather more than the sign *st*. The monument already quoted (n° 89) was in existence at that time and this sign may have refered to it.

The two quoted mentions *(wsḫt ḥbyt/ ḥbyt)* were not understood as real places of the temple by J. Cerny. The first one was translated by him as a plural,"festival courtyards", with a general meaning, and the second one as "festival gifts". It is probably the reason why Paul Barguet, Patricia Spencer, and, more recently, Christine Favard-Meeks (Barguet 1962, 309, n.2; Spencer 1984, 80-1; Favard-Meeks 1991, 436) did not know any example of *wsḫt ḥbyt* earlier than a Seventeenth Dynasty monument in Abydos. Several architraves of the temple describe other parts of the monument, for instance n° 415a *(ḫ3 ḥḏ).*

An inscription engraved on the western wall of the Shrines of Kings, enumerates "the rations of the temple of Hathor, lady of the turquoise" (*ḥt-nṯr nt ḥt-ḥr nbt mfk3t).* It is the definitive proof, if necessary, that a fully operational temple existed already in the Middle Kingdom. This monument requires of course a careful scientific study but, in view of its exceptional interest and its harmonious ruin in this wild landscape, it deserves also a beautiful publication which may be appreciated by a broader public. Other more specialized studies (lexicographical, prosopographical, new translations of some historical texts, etc.) will follow.

D.V

Bibliography

Barguet, P 1962. *Le Temple d'Amon-Rê à Karnak.* Recherches d'Archéologie, de Philologie et d'Histoire 21. Cairo, Institut Français d'Archéologie Orientale.

Bonnet, C, F Le Saout and D Valbelle 1994. Le temple de la déesse Hathor, maîtresse de la turquoise, à Sérabit el-Khadim. Reprise de l'étude épigraphique. In *Cahier de Recherches de l'Institut de Papyrologie et d'Egyptologie de Lille* 16, 15-29.

Favard-Meeks, C 1991. *Le temple de Behbeit el-Hagara. Essai de reconstitution et d'interprétation.* Studien zur Altägyptischen Kultur Beiheft 6. Hamburg, Helmut Buske.

Gardiner, A H and T E Peet 1917. *The Inscriptions of Sinai* I. London, Egypt Exploration Fund.

Gardiner, A H, T E Peet and J Cerny 1955. *The Inscriptions of Sinai* II. London, Egypt Exploration Society.

Spencer, P 1984. *The Egyptian temple. A lexicographical study.* London, Kegan Paul International.

Valbelle, D and C Bonnet 1996. *Le Sanctuaire d'Hathor, maîtresse de la turquoise. Sérabit el-Khadim au Moyen Empire.* Lille.

The temples at Memphis. Problems highlighted by the EES survey

Jaromir Malek

It is arguable to what extent a convincing proof in history or archaeology is a subjective matter, and how much of it can be defined objectively. The difficulty lies in recognizing at which point the facts which have been marshalled, and the theories which have been evolved from them, produce the critical mass which turns a hypothesis into the generally valid scholarly truth. This is well illustrated by the two problems discussed below: the relationship between the city of Memphis and its temple of Ptah, and the location of the Memphite temple of the Aten.

I wish to thank the Keeper of Egyptian Antiquities, Vivian Davies, for inviting me to take part in the colloquium on *The Temple in Ancient Egypt* in the British Museum in July 1994. This is a revised version of the paper, and I am grateful to Mrs M E Cox for drawing the maps for figs. 1 and 2.

1. The city of Memphis and its temple of Ptah. Fig.1.

Egyptian sources are silent about the founding of Memphis. The opinions generally voiced are much dependent on Herodotus (Book II, chapter 99), but his account may have been heavily coloured by the situation in the mid-5th c. BC and the bias of his priestly informants: '... Min was the first king of Egypt, and ... he separated Memphis from the Nile by a dam. All the river had flowed close under the sandy mountains on the Libyan side, but Min made the southern bend of it which begins about an hundred furlows above Memphis, by damming the stream; thereby he dried up the ancient course, and carried the river by a channel so that it flowed midway between the hills. ... Then, when this first king Min had made what he thus cut off to be dry land, he first founded in it that city which is now called Memphis ... and outside of it he dug a lake to its north and west, from the river (the Nile itself being the eastern boundary of the place); and secondly, he built in it the great and most noteworthy temple of Hephaestus' (Godley 1926; Egyptological commentary by Lloyd 1988, 10-13).
For us, the most important information gleaned from this account is as follows:
1. King Min founded the city of Memphis on land which had been reclaimed from the river.
2. Canals protected Memphis to the north and west, while the Nile formed its eastern boundary.
3. The temple of Hephaestus was built in the city.

For the purpose of this discussion it makes little difference which of the rulers at the beginning of the First Dynasty was meant by Min=Menes. In the surviving fragments of an *Epitome* of Manetho's *Egyptian History*, the building of the palace at Memphis is ascribed to Menes's son Athothis (Waddell 1940, 28-33). Modern chronologies start the First Dynasty, and so date the founding of Memphis, between *c.*3100 and 2925 BC.

Contemporary evidence to support the account given by Herodotus is far from overwhelming, although not entirely contradictory. During the Early Dynastic period, Memphite cemeteries stretched from Saqqara as far north as Abu Rawash (Jeffreys and Tavares 1994). Predynastic remains have so far been conspicuous by their absence but this may be due to topographical or technical factors, such as the closeness of the water-table below the modern surface, and so for the time being this had better be merely noted rather than used as an argument. The appearance of the large mastabas at Saqqara, the most important part of the necropolis, coincided with the beginning of the First Dynasty. Tomb S 3357 dates to the reign of Aha (Emery 1939), and Narmer's name was found on a porphyry bowl under the Step Pyramid of Djoser (Lacau and Lauer 1961, 1-2 [1] pl. 1 [1]; Emery 1961 provides a good survey of the situation at Saqqara). The purpose of the new foundation probably was to establish an administrative, commercial and defensive centre conveniently situated between the Delta and the valley. Such a move was to be imitated, though not in an identical fashion, by the other great state-builders of the Egyptian history. Amenemhet I at the beginning of the Twelfth Dynasty, the early kings of the Eighteenth Dynasty, and then again the rulers of the Twenty-sixth Dynasty. The foundation almost certainly incorporated a royal palace and became the focal point of the main settlement in the area. In the 'circumambulation of the wall' (*pḫr ḥ3 ỉnb*), a ceremony associated with the coronation of king Djer on the Palermo Stone (Schäfer 1902, 15), *ỉnb* almost certainly refers to this foundation.

Two variants of its name existed side by side. The plural form *ỉnbw ḥḏ*, 'White Walls', is first attested on an impression of the seal of the Memphite vineyard under Khasekhemui, found at Abydos (Petrie 1901, pl. xxiii [193]). The earliest example of the singular form *ỉnb ḥḏ*, ''White Wall', is on an impression of an administrative seal from a tomb dated to Djoser at Beit Khallaf (Garstang 1903, pl. x [11]; for the vase inscription published by Kaplony 1962, 16 [16], Abb. 16, claimed to be an even earlier instance of *ỉnb ḥḏ*, see Kaiser 1969, 20 n. 4 at end). Despite the delay of some 250 years or more in our documentation, the name was probably given to the foundation already at its creation and there was no other designation for the city, or its parts, before the appearance of the pyramid towns of the early Sixth Dynasty.

A better translation of *ỉnb ḥḏ* may be 'White Fort' (Montet 1957, 27). I am not going to digress by speculating on the reason for the plural form *ỉnbw ḥḏ*, although the problem is not without interest. Why 'White'? Sethe (1905, 125-9) tried to connect the name with the colour symbolism of the pharaonic period which associates Upper Egypt with white and Lower Egypt with red. 'White Wall' would have been Upper Egypt's bastion against the recently conquered Lower Egyptian kingdom. This, however, no longer fully fits our ideas concerning the process of political unification at the end of the Predynastic period and so the more pedestrian explanation, based on the external appearance of the brick-built walls covered with white gypsum plaster, is more likely to be correct. Such a building technique is known from an Early Dynastic town structure, perhaps a palace, at Hierakonpolis (Weeks 1971-2, 30; I am grateful to Barbara Adams for pointing this out).

The new foundation lent its name to the whole district (Helck 1974, 147-9). In the hieroglyphic writing, unless the name is followed by the 'land marked out with irrigation runnels' sign (N 24), or later the 'standard' sign (R 12), it is not always easy to establish which of the two terms was meant. It is a different way of forming a name as compared with the other, more traditional, Egyptian districts (Sethe 1905, 123-4). Although the situation is complicated by the fact that the 'White Wall' district contained Egypt's capital, this strongly supports the view that both the city and the district were, indeed, created artificially. Geographically, however, the situation is less clear, and it is a moot point precisely where the foundation of *ỉnb ḥḏ* took place. One of the many epithets of the god Ptah (the Hephaestus of Herodotus) at Memphis was *rsy ỉnb.f* 'south of his wall' (Sandman Holmberg 1946, 206-8), to be understood as 'Ptah (whose sanctuary is situated to the) south of his wall'. Ptah was the chief Memphite deity, so it is logical to connect 'his wall' in the epithet with 'White Wall', and to place the temple of Ptah *rsy ỉnb.f* to the south of the new foundation. Other examples of the abbreviation *ỉnb* for *ỉnb ḥḏ* are known from the Old Kingdom (Sethe 1905, 131-3). However, according to Herodotus, the temple of Ptah was founded in the new city, not outside. Sethe (1905, 129), as always, suggested an ingenious solution. According to him, the city was enclosed by walls only on three sides and remained open to the south, the home territory of the Upper Egyptian conqueror from where no danger threatened. The temple of Ptah was then situated as if inside a horseshoe-shaped perimeter of a defensive wall, enclosed by it, yet to the south of it. This, however, is an uneasy explanation, and other possibilities should be considered.

The number of Old Kingdom examples of the epithet *rsy ỉnb.f* is surprisingly small and none of them is very helpful. An inscription in the tomb of Persen at Saqqara accompanies representations of offering-bearers (Mariette 1889, 300; Sethe 1933, 37 [25]) and talks about reversion offerings *ḫppt m ḥwt-nṯr nt Ptḥ rsy ỉnb.f*, 'sent from the temple of Ptah south of his wall', for the king's mother Neferhetpes. By an act issued *m rk s3ḥw-Rʿ*, 'in the time of Sahure', Persen received them from her funerary establishment in another phase of redistribution. The temple of Ptah south of his wall, as the main temple in the area and the chief beneficiary of royal largesse, acted as a re-distribution point for funerary offerings in Sahure's reign. This is confirmed by the Palermo Stone which records a land donation made to Ptah south of his wall in an unknown year of king Neferirkare (Schäfer 1902, 41). A letter in Brooklyn, dated to the reign of Pepy II (Posener-Kriéger 1976, 454 n.4), contains a series of wishes for the addressee, including *snḏm Ptḥ rsy inb.f ib.k m ʿnḫ*, 'may Ptah south of his wall cheer you with life'. This is an early example of the 'Memphite formula' which became common in the Middle Kingdom (James 1962, 123).

Old-Kingdom references to Ptah or his temple were usually not accompanied by more precise indications of which Ptah was meant. Later sources leave little doubt that the temple of Ptah 'south of his wall' was the main Memphite temple of Ptah, so the lack of epithets in the Old Kingdom suggests that there was only one temple of Ptah at Memphis at that time, a situation which probably persisted until the late Eighteenth Dynasty. The earlier kings modified or enlarged the existing temple (see the material collected by Helck 1961, 130-44). Tuthmosis IV may have been the first king of the Eighteenth Dynasty whose contribution was meant to be an autonomous structure within the traditional precinct, as indicated by his foundation deposits found at Kom el-Fakhry (Daressy 1902, 25; Petrie 1909, 8 pls. xix [upper left], xx [top]).

Following the work of the Egypt Exploration Society at Memphis (Jeffreys and Malek 1988; Giddy, Jeffreys and Malek 1990; Giddy and Jeffreys 1993), there is no doubt that the early temple of Ptah is different from the large structure in the birka to the east of Mit Rahina. Although the definitive proof can only be obtained by excavation, it seems almost certain that the early temple lies further to the west, under the houses of Kom el-Fakhry. 'White Wall' has always been sought in the same area as the temple of Ptah or, at least, in its close vicinity further to the north, though not beyond Kom Tuman. In ancient Egypt, the town and the temple of the main local deity usually formed a contiguous unit which developed spontaneously. 'White Wall', however, was an artificial foundation and such rules need not apply. Let us now review the main candidate areas for the location of the Early Dynastic foundation.

The traditional options have not a great deal in their favour. 'White Wall' might be sought at Kom el-Fakhry itself, with the temple adjoining it immediately to the south. The area has not been systematically explored, but the cemetery and an adjoining settlement excavated there by El Hitta (1955; Lilyquist 1974; Jeffreys 1985, 29, 68 figs. 19-20) and Mohammed Ashari in the mid-1950s and the early 1980s can hardly represent Memphis of the First Intermediate Period or the Middle Kingdom, impoverished though the city may have been. At present, there is no archaeological evidence to suggest that 'White Wall' is situated at Kom el-Mit Rahina which adjoins Kom el-Fakhry to the north, but, again, no controlled excavation in the area has ever been undertaken. There is even less cause to look for it at Kom Tuman, Petrie's Kom el-Kelb, with the palace mound of the Twenty-sixth Dynasty (Jeffreys 1985, 40-3), an area which has been at least to some extent explored.

The following observations can be cited in support of a rather different location of *inb-ḥḏ*:

1. The relationship between a city and its necropolis is never simple or obvious, and it would be wrong to reduce it to the shortest line of approach. Nevertheless, large mastabas of the Early Dynastic period at Saqqara, the main necropolis in the area, start at the northern tip of the plateau, close to the Abusir wadi which approaches Saqqara from the north-east (PM III², Part 2, plan xlvi). The tombs then continue, in an almost regular chronological fashion, southwards, as far as the area of the future pyramid of Teti. More humble Early Dynastic burials are found below the northern tip of the gebel plateau (Bonnet 1928) and to the north-west of the Serapeum (Macramallah 1940). The Abusir wadi probably was the main approach to the royal tombs of the Second, and perhaps even the early Third, Dynasties, as suggested by the results of the survey conducted by I. Mathieson on behalf of the National Museums of Scotland (Mathieson 1993). All this indicates strongly that the city of *inb-ḥḏ* of the Early Dynastic period and the early Old Kingdom might be in the valley to the east or south-east of the Abusir wadi, below the escarpment of the gebel with the Early Dynastic tombs.
2. The drill core survey undertaken by D. G. Jeffreys on behalf of the Egypt Exploration Society is one of the most important projects carried out at Memphis at present (Jeffreys and Malek 1988, 19-

23; Jeffreys and Giddy 1989, 8-9; Giddy, Jeffreys and Malek 1990, 12-13; Giddy and Jeffreys 1991, 5-6; 1992, 2-8; 1993, 12-14). Its provisional conclusions are strongly in favour of the existence of an important Early Dynastic settlement in the valley to the east of North Saqqara, in the approximate area of the modern town of Abusir or its environs (Jeffreys and Tavares 1994, 159).

3. Only the Abusir area fits well into the later pattern of the development of the whole Memphite area. *ḏd-ỉswt*, known from the Teaching for Merykare (Golénischeff 1913, pl. xii, line 101) to have been an important part of Memphis during the First Intermediate Period, was, as the name suggests, to the east of the pyramid of Teti, and thus to the south of the presumed Early Dynastic town. Moving on again, *mn-nfr* was, by definition, to the east of the pyramid of Pepy I, still farther south. It appears, therefore, that the centre of gravity of the Memphite settlements in the valley to the east of Saqqara shows a tendency to move southward (Giddy 1994, 195), and in this perspective, 'White Wall' somewhere in the Abusir area would have been the obvious starting point.

4. In the Royal Canon of Turin (Gardiner 1959), our most important ancient source on Egyptian chronology, kings are arranged not by 'dynasties' (these were introduced much later, sometimes on dubious grounds, by Manetho), but according to the place of their residence. When the royal residence (or 'capital') changed, a new line of kings was begun in the Turin Canon. The first group of kings starts with Meni (and thus the legendary founder of Memphis) and ends with Unis, the last ruler of the Fifth Dynasty, and is followed by a total giving the length of this period. The second group begins with Teti, the first ruler of the Sixth Dynasty, and ends with the last king of what we nowadays conventionally describe as the Eighth Dynasty. It is followed, as expected, by a total for this second group, and then by a grand total for the two periods. The next kings are the Heracleopolitans. There is no reason to doubt that the capital of Egypt, and the residence, of the kings listed as two different groups was in the Memphite area. How to explain this curious historical view and strange accounting procedure?

The Turin Canon clearly suggests that the location of the royal residence changed between the reigns of Meni and the last king of the Eighth Dynasty. The kings of the first group (the First to Fifth Dynasties) resided at *ỉnb-ḥḏ* or an area immediately adjacent, while the second group of kings transferred their residence to what was perceived as a distinct place in the same general area (hence the grand total for both groups). The pyramids of the Sixth Dynasty are, with the exception of that of Teti, at South Saqqara. It is, therefore, logical to assume that the new royal residence of the Sixth Dynasty was in the valley to the east of South Saqqara. We may read too much into the wording of Herodotus who refers to the city 'which is now called Memphis' (Book II, chapter 99; Godley 1926).

5. The term 'White Wall' would have probably lost some of its precision as a toponym once it started to be applied to the whole Memphite district, and the terms *ỉnb-ḥḏ* and *mn-nfr* may have become interchangeable. Nevertheless, it would not be surprising if in some specialized contexts they retained their original meaning. On Piankhy's stela (Grimal 1981, *mryt nt ỉnb-ḥḏ* in line 87, pl. 30* facing p. 96, and *mryt nt mn-nfr* in lines 90, probably, and 94, twice, pls. 31* facing p. 98 and 33* facing p. 102; in Grimal's opinion, 115 n. 335, the terms were used indiscriminately), a distinction seems to be made between the harbours of *ỉnb-ḥḏ*, to the north, and *mn-nfr* further south (Jeffreys and Smith 1988, 60-1). However, in the Twenty-fifth Dynasty the term *mn-nfr* certainly included the main Ptah temple at Kom el-Fakhry. Unless this is purely a matter of literary style, it seems likely that *mn-nfr* and *ỉnb-ḥḏ* were at some distance apart, perhaps quite considerable, because they were served by two different harbours.

6. It is improbable that the founder of 'White Wall' would have introduced the cult of the god Ptah to Memphis. There would have been a primitive shrine of Ptah and the Apis-bull, his avatar, in the area already at the end of the Predynastic period and this would not have ceased to exist when the new foundation was created (for Apis in the reign of Aha see Simpson 1957, 139-42, although a scientific re-examination of such stone vessels is now in order). Yet, as it has been suggested above, it appears that there was only one temple of Ptah at Memphis during the Old Kingdom, so it is likely that this was identical with the original sanctuary. 'White Wall' would hardly have been built on land reclaimed from the Nile, as stated by Herodotus, if it had been situated next to the traditional sanctuary of Ptah.

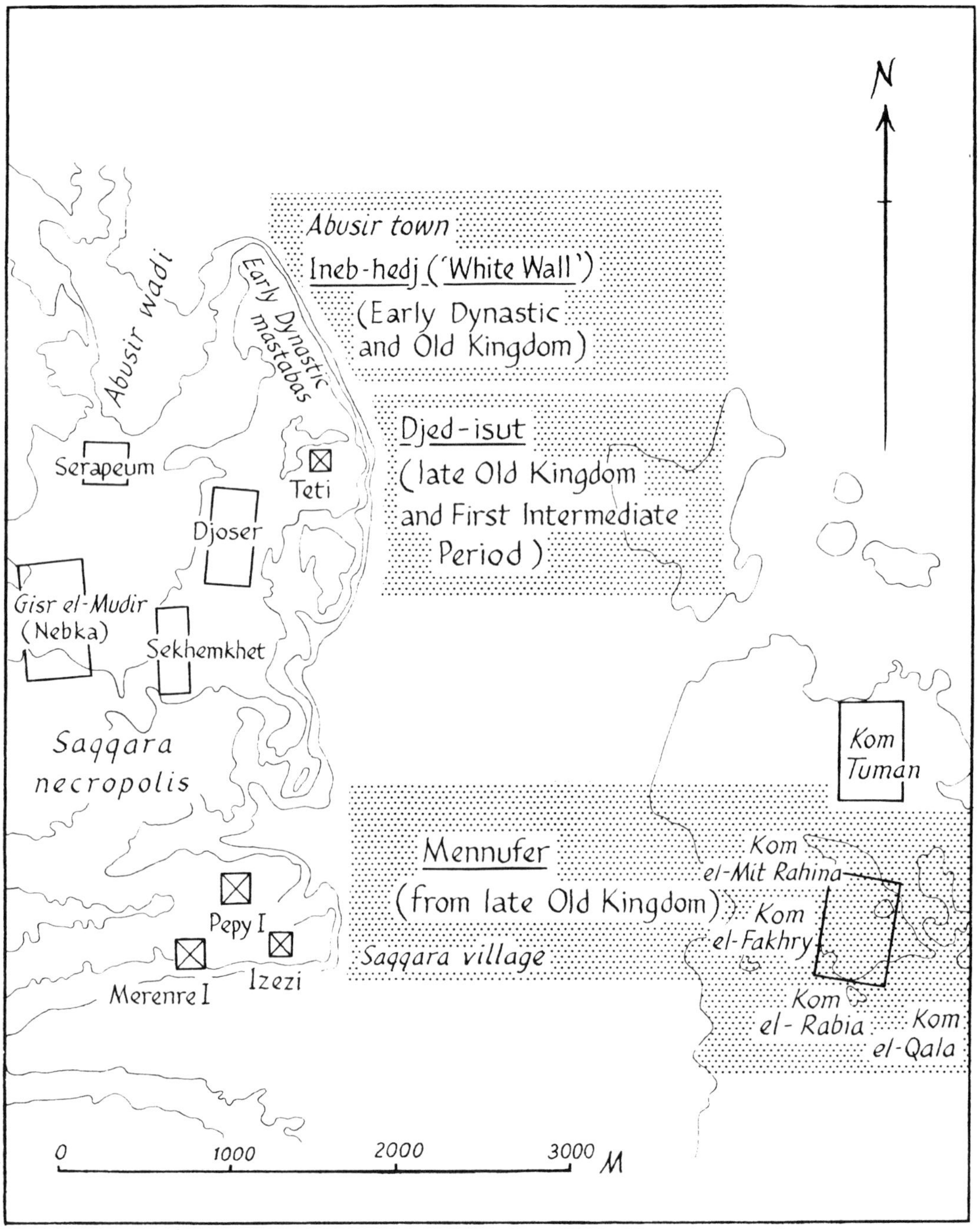

Fig.1 The city of Memphis and its temple of Ptah.

To sum up, I wish to propose a new theoretical model for the founding and the subsequent development of the city of Memphis, and especially its relationship with the temple of Ptah. This model is different from that of other Egyptian cities and their temples. The changes were dictated by environmental and topographical, rather than political, factors (Giddy 1994, 198). The original 'White Wall' was somewhere at the geographical latitude of the modern town of Abusir, most probably to the east of it, on the western bank of the river Nile (the precise location of the river at that time is not known). The selection of the site was dictated by local topography, and the foundation was probably surrounded by canals and dykes in order to protect it from inundation. It was fortified and its appearance gave it its name, 'White Wall'. The city which grew around the original foundation remained the capital of Egypt for some six hundred years, and so we must expect that it eventually occupied much of the space available between the Nile and the western gebel.

A modest sanctuary of the god Ptah which had existed further south, in the area of Kom el-

Fakhry, was gradually transformed into the new city's main temple by the building activities of successive kings. A corollary of the new location of *inb-ḥḏ* is that the location of the Memphite shrine of Neith 'north of the/her wall', *mḥtt inb* or *mḥtt inb.s*, must now be sought in the Abusir area or farther north. The city and Ptah's temple precinct remained separate physical entities for much of the third millennium BC, and possibly even later. A settlement of priests and employees of the temple grew up in its vicinity. It is this settlement, rather than a quarter of the city itself, which the Egypt Exploration Society's expedition to Memphis has been excavating at Kom el-Rabia, at least as far as its early strata are concerned (Jeffreys, Malek and Smith 1986, 2-10; 1987, 15-18; Jeffreys and Malek 1988, 17-19; Jeffreys and Giddy 1989, 1-8; Giddy and Jeffreys 1991, 1-4). This has serious implications for the evaluation of the material found at the site.

Throughout the rest of Egyptian history, the city was drawn farther and farther to the south and south-east, mainly because of environmental factors, in particular the fluctuation in the conditions favouring the existence of a sophisticated city (singled out as a decisive factor for the period from the late Old Kingdom until the Middle Kingdom by Giddy 1994, 197-9), the continuing eastward retreat of the river (Jeffreys 1985, 48-55 fig.2; Jeffreys and Smith 1988: 58-9; Jeffreys and Tavares 1994, fig. 15), and possibly even progressive sand deposition (Giddy and Jeffreys 1992, 2). Artificially created stimuli, such as the location of the pyramid-towns farther to the south (for the question of the distribution of pyramids in the Memphite area, see Malek 1994, 111-13), the lines of communication between the settlement and its main sanctuary, and the location of the temple of Ptah itself, also played a part. It is unlikely that the older quarters of the city were abandoned completely, but they would have been marginalized and, if modern experience is anything to go by, deteriorated into slums.

ḏd-iswt, at the geographical latitude of the pyramid of Teti and probably just a natural extension of *inb-ḥḏ* in the southern direction, became a thriving part of the city at the end of the Old Kingdom and during the First Intermediate Period. A second population centre, however, gained in importance in the Memphite area during the Sixth Dynasty. This was in the valley to the east of southern Saqqara, at the geographical latitude of the temple of Ptah at Kom el-Fakhry, and may have been separated from its northern counterpart by a lake (Jeffreys and Tavares 1994, 156). At present, nothing is known about its beginnings. The royal residence was transferred there, a move reflected by the distribution of the pyramids of the late Old Kingdom at South Saqqara. The city came to be known as *mn-nfr*, after the pyramid-town of Pepy I, and quickly took over as the centre of the Memphite area from its northern counterpart. Our records concerning the city are still sparse. Its earliest *ḥ3ty-ᶜ* is known from the late Middle Kingdom (Martin 1971, no. 182). We cannot be certain when, at last, this city physically joined up with the temple precinct at Kom el-Fakhry, but there is no doubt that this was a *fait accompli* by the reign of Amosis at the beginning of the Eighteenth Dynasty (Sethe 1906, 3, line 9).

2. The location of the Memphite temple of the Aten. Fig.2.

There is only one dated document known from Memphis during the reign of Akhenaten. This is a letter (Griffith 1898, 91-2, pl. xxxviii) written by the steward Ipy, the son of the steward Amenhotpe Huy, in year 5, the 3rd month of *prt*, day 19. It states, in a typically ancient Egyptian fashion, that nothing is happening: among other things, the temple of the god Ptah south of his wall is in good order and offerings to all the gods and goddesses are maintained. Early in his reign Amenophis IV ordered that offerings to the sun-god be presented on the sun-altars of the temples in the Delta (Saad and Manniche 1971, 70-2; Helck 1973). This does not seem to have initially involved the building of new temples for the sun-god. At Memphis, the offerings would have been presented in the traditional temple of Ptah at Kom el-Fakhry, the easternmost part of which may have now been located (Jeffreys and Malek 1988, 29, fig. 7; Jeffreys and Smith 1988, 62-3).

The evidence for the temple of the Aten at Memphis is threefold. A fundamental study of it, by B. Löhr (1975), exists, and so I shall summarize it only briefly and review it in the light of new information. Löhr's perceptive conjectures (1975, 163) concerning the location of the temple of the Aten can be further strengthened.

a. Textual evidence.
t3 ḥwt p3 ỉtn is mentioned in P. Rollin 1882 (Paris, Bibliothèque Nationale, 213, fragment a, *recto* 4, Spiegelberg 1896, 29, 73-4, pls. xvi, xvia). This is a list of deliveries of wood to various Memphite buildings, probably early in the reign of Sethos I.

b. Prosopographic evidence.
Three officials associated with the temple are known from their tombs at Saqqara and Nazlet el-Batran, but none of them has a title which would describe him as a priest of the Aten.
b1. *mryty-nt* (changed to *mryty-rʿ/mryty-ỉtn*), *ỉmy-r n pr-ỉtn*, 'steward of the temple of the Aten' (PM III^2, Part 2, 666; the titles of the *ḥry-ḥbt* and *stm*-priest are not those of Merytyneit, *pace* Löhr 1975, 172). The occurrence of the name of the goddess Neith in Merytyneit's name suggests that the tomb dates to the first half of the reign of Akhenaten.
b2. *ḥy, ḥry šwtyw n t3 ḥwt p3 ỉtn.* 'overseer of traders of the temple of the Aten' (Cairo CG 34182 = JE 10174, PM III^2, Part 2, 737). The later form of the names of the Aten indicates that he died in the second half of the reign of Akhenaten.
b3. *ptḥ-my, ḥry ỉryw nbw p3ḳ n pr ỉtn,* 'overseer of the makers of gold foil in the temple of the Aten' (C.M. Zivie 1975; date, Löhr 1975, 180-6; PM III^2, Part 1, 303). Ptahmay's name and the names of his sons, *ptḥ-ms* and *ptḥ-ʿnḫ*, confirm iconographic indications that his tomb is later than the Amarna period proper, perhaps from the reigns of Tutankhamun, Aye or Haremhab.

c. Monumental evidence (Löhr's numbering in brackets).
Limestone blocks decorated in sunk relief and fragments of quartzite sculptures dating to the Amarna period have been found at Memphis, but may come from more than one structure. Altogether seventeen of these can be listed.

Blocks re-used in the eastern part of the Ptah enclosure (J. Hekekyan, July 1854):
c1 [II 8]. A libation-jar and rays of the Aten, in Sydney, Nicholson Mus. R.1143 (Nicholson 1870, pls. 1 [Nos. 2a, 7], 2; Hekekyan MSS. 37452, 288 [lower], 37454, 58 [lower]; PM III^2, Part 2, 839). The inscription gives the early names of the Aten 'in the temple *3ḫ-n- ỉtn*', and those of Akhenaten and Nefertiti.
c2 [II 7]. The early names of the Aten 'engraved on the leg of a human figure of which this square block contains about a third' (Nicholson 1870, pl. 1 [No. 2 (middle) and 3 (Nicholson's captions are confused)]; Hekekyan MSS. 37452, 288 [upper], 37454, 58 [upper]).
c3 [-]. The lower part of the figure of a courtier (Nicholson 1870, pl. 1 [No. 2 (the 8th block from the left)]).

Blocks found nearby (J. Hekekyan, July 1854):
c4 [II 9]. A king and a fan-bearer (Nicholson 1870, pl. 1 [No. 5]; Hekekyan MSS. 37452, 289; Malek 1996).
c5 [II 10]. Cartouches with the names of the Aten, faced by probably those of Smenkhkare and a queen, and the rays of the Aten (Nicholson 1870, pl. 1 [No. 4]; Newberry 1928, 9, fig. 4 [lower]; Hekekyan MSS. 37454, 58 verso).
c6 [II 5]. The later form of the name of the Aten (Hekekyan MSS. 37452, 261, 37454, 59; Mariette 1872, pl. 27 [e]; PM III^2, Part 2, 850). The text probably mentions a 'sun-shade' temple.
Another small fragment found by Hekekyan is British Museum EA 66023. It bears the fingers of a hand in Amarna style, and therefore may come from a talatat. An old label still affixed to the stone identifies the findspot as 'The Palms', a little to the south-east of the hypostyle hall of the large Ptah temple.

Blocks found in the Ptah enclosure (F. Petrie, 1913):

c7 [II 12]. A chariot and men before altars, formerly in F. W. von Bissing collection (Petrie 1915, 32, pl. liv [10]; PM III^2, Part 2, 850).
c8 [II 11]. The upper part of a queen, probably Nefertiti, in London, UC 73 (Petrie 1915, 32, pl. liv [9]; PM III^2, Part 2, 850).
c9 [II 14]. Boat-scene, in Cambridge, Fitzw. E.19.1913 (Petrie 1915, 32, pl. liv [7]; PM III^2, Part 2, 850).
c10 [II 13]. Offerings, oxen and two attendants, in Brussels, Mus. Roy. E.7636 (Petrie 1915, 32, pl. liv [8]; PM III^2, Part 2, 850).
The fragment of a rewarding scene in raised relief (Petrie 1915, 32 pl. liv [6]), now in Brussels, Mus. Roy. E.4494, is a re-used block, presumably from Saqqara, which probably dates from the Fifth to Sixth Dynasties rather than the reign of Akhenaten (*pace* Löhr 1975, 161 [II, 15] Taf. v [2]; Delvaux et al. 1993, 141 [1]).

Block re-used in the pylon of the large Ptah temple (EES, 1989):
c11 [-]. The middle part of the body of a man, removed to a magazine of the SCA (Giddy, Jeffreys and Malek 1990, 4).

Block re-used in the pylon of the small Ptah temple at Kom el-Rabia (Anthes, 1956):
c12 [II 16]. A bowing courtier (Habachi 1965, 65 pl. 23 [c, left]; PM III^2, Part 2, 844).

Block, find-spot uncertain:
c13 [II 6]. The later form of the name of the Aten, in Brussels, Mus. Roy. E.4491 (Speleers 1923, 100 [410]; PM III^2, Part 2, 872).

'Stela' from Kom el-Qala (Mariette, 1870s):
c14 [II 4]. The early names of the Aten and Akhenaten, supposedly in Cairo (Mariette 1872, 10, pl. 34 [e]; PM III^2, Part 2, 862).

Sculptures from Kom el-Qala (Fisher, 1915):
c15 [II 1]. The head of a quartzite statue, probably of Nefertiti, in Cairo JE 45547 (*Penn. Mus. Journ.* vi, 1915, fig. 62 on p. 82; PM III^2, Part 2, 857).
c16 [II 3]. A fragment of the back pillar of a quartzite statue of Akhenaten, with a late cartouche of the Aten, in Philadelphia E 13644 (Löhr 1975, 149-50 fig.; PM III^2, Part 2, 858).

Sculpture, find-spot uncertain (F. Petrie, 1910):
c17 [II 2]. A fragment of the back pillar of a quartzite statue with the early Aten cartouches, in Copenhagen, Ny Carlsb. Glypt. AE.I.N. 1144 (Mogensen 1930, 6, pl. III [A 7]; PM III^2, Part 2, 863).

It may be significant that Ipy's letter does not refer to the temple of the Aten in the year 5. Merytyneit retained the name of the goddess Neith in his own while holding the post of steward of the Aten temple's estate. This would have been difficult when exclusivist tendencies became more pronounced. The beginning of thc construction of the temple can then be tentatively placed some time between years 5 and about 9 of Akhenaten, and it continued for some time after that. The text on one of the reliefs refers to 'the temple Akhenaten'; this makes its name identical with that of the king. The possibility that we should understand this as 'the temple (or precinct) of (king) Akhenaten' is less likely. The temple still functioned during the reign of Sethos I, but fell victim to the building enterprises inaugurated around the first jubilee of Ramesses II.

Tens of thousands of wall-blocks and similar monuments of Akhenaten have been recovered at Karnak, Luxor and el-Ashmunein, yet only seventeen pieces (including statues) are known from Memphis. One reason may have been the modest size of the Memphite temple of the Aten. More important, however, seems to have been the later architectural history of Memphis. During the reign of Ramesses II Memphis witnessed building activities on an unprecedented scale. Large amounts of building material were required and earlier monuments in the city and its necropolis were being

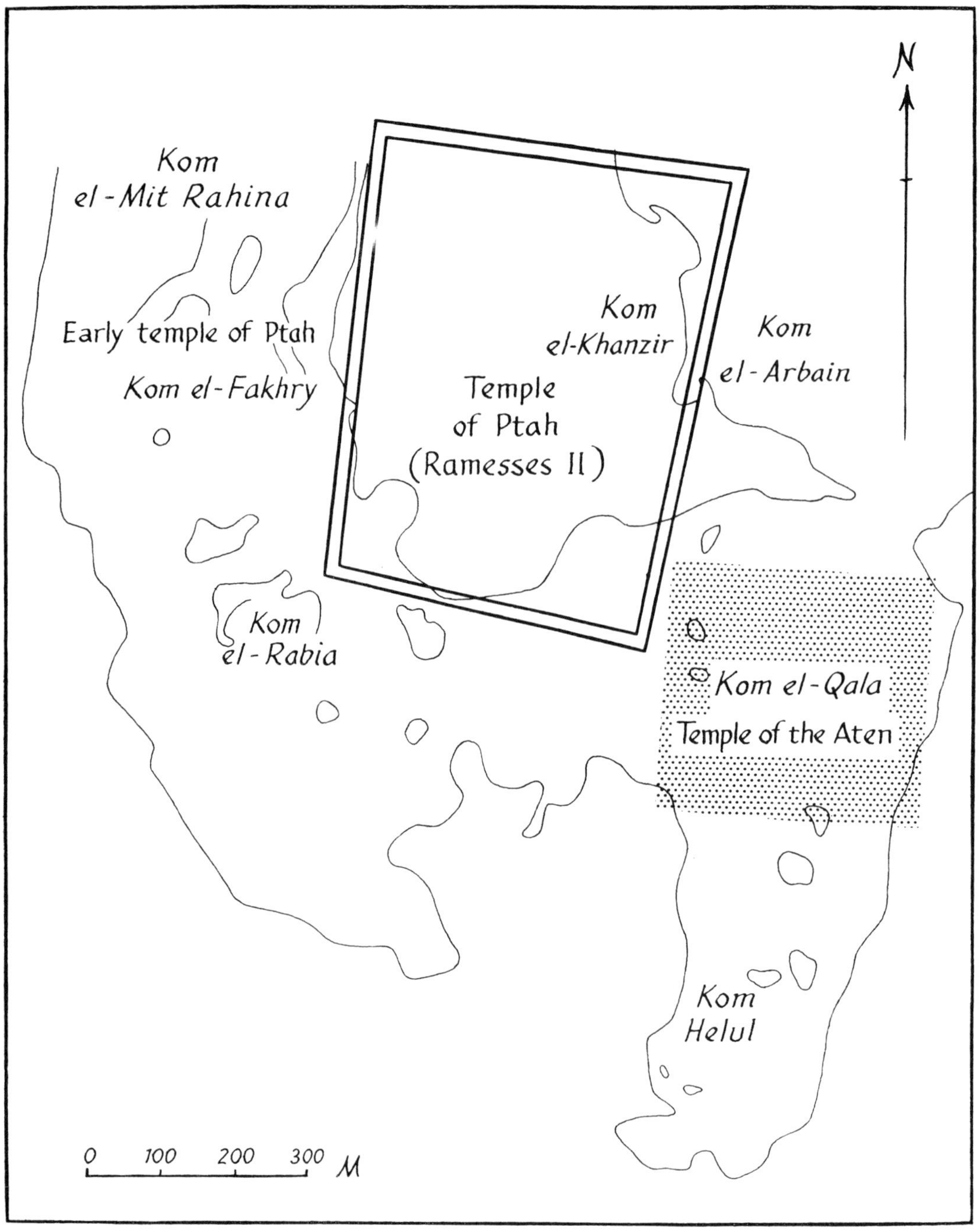

Fig.2 The location of the Memphite temple of the Aten.

exploited as quarries. Akhenaten's talatat would have been ideally suited for such a purpose. At least two blocks were found in what is left of the pylons of the temples erected by Ramesses II at Memphis, and this suggests that practices at Memphis were not dissimilar from those elsewhere. It is not impossible that the pylons of the new temples at Memphis were packed with talatat from the dismantled local structure(s) of Akhenaten, just like their counterparts at Thebes and el-Ashmunein. An EES team, consisting of L. L. Giddy, K. Eriksson, and J. Malek, investigated one section of the southern wing of the pylon of the large Ramessid temple of Ptah in the autumn of 1994. Fragments of re-used Old Kingdom and Eighteenth Dynasty reliefs were found, but no talatat. This does not vitiate the theory: only a very small part of the pylon could be investigated and only exceptionally large blocks were still found *in situ* (this excludes talatat), or those which were difficult to extract. Unfortunately, this was not the end of the matter at Memphis, as it was at the other sites. In the thirteenth and fourteenth centuries AD, Memphite pharaonic monuments provided building material for the new mosques, madrasas and houses of Cairo. Indeed, the study of the way pharaonic material was re-used in the buildings of Islamic Cairo by J. Jakeman (1993) suggests that at least in some cases a high degree of ideological emphasis placed on them put them beyond mere re-use as building material. Until now, all the talatat found in Cairo have been assigned to Heliopolis but at least some of them will have originated at Memphis. Of limestone only the massive foundation blocks and pieces of awkward shapes, such as columns, remained in the large temple of Ptah at Memphis. The rest consists of hard stone such as granite, basalt, alabaster, and quartzite of which only a limited amount would have been required by Islamic builders.

Memphis has shown us that material from earlier structures was recycled in different ways. Some was highly re-usable and travelled long distances. Other was of limited interest and so was mostly left behind near the place where it had been originally used.

The find-spot of fifteen of the seventeen monuments of Akhenaten found at Memphis is known at least in a general way. Twelve of them are limestone blocks, ideal for re-use, found in the temples built by Ramesses II: eleven in the large Ramessid enclosure of the temple of Ptah and one at Kom el-Rabia. The re-use value of the remaining three provenanced pieces is small: a stela with the early names of the Aten found by Mariette, and the head of a quartzite statue of Nefertiti and a fragment of the back pillar of a quartzite statue of Akhenaten with a late cartouche of the Aten, both found by Fisher. All three come from Kom el-Qala and because of their shape and material it is difficult to see them being taken there for re-use.

A statistician would dismiss such a small sample (one fifth out of fifteen) of material as insignificant. Some support can, however, be gleaned from elsewhere. Kom el-Qala lies to the south-east of Kom el-Fakhry and the old Ptah temple there. This area would have been available for development in the second half of the Eighteenth Dynasty following an eastward retreat of the Nile, and would have been uncontaminated by earlier temple structures. In his boundary stelae at El-Amarna, Akhenaten places an emphasis on the fact that the site did not belong to any of the earlier gods. Clarence Fisher reported 'virgin soil' under the palace of Merneptah at Kom el-Qala, and this has been confirmed by the recent drill core survey (Jeffreys and Giddy 1989, 8). This, however, need not preclude the possibility that the temple of the Aten may have been situated nearby. Interestingly, the temple of the Aten at Karnak was situated to the east of the old temple of Amun. Kom el-Qala is similarly placed.

To sum up, Kom el-Qala, to the south-east of Kom el-Fakhry with its old temple of Ptah, is the likeliest location of the Memphite temple of the Aten.

Bibliography

Bonnet, H 1928. *Ein frühgeschichtliches Gräberfeld bei Abusir.* Leipzig, J C Hinrichs.

Daressy, G 1902. Le temple de Mit Rahineh. In *Annales du Service des Antiquités d'Egypte* 3, 22-31.

Delvaux, L et al. 1993. Collection d'antiques. In Dierkens, A and J-M Duvosquel (eds.), *Henri-Joseph Redouté et l'Expédition de Bonaparte en Égypte*, Brussels, 141-9.

Emery, W B 1939. *Hor-Aha.* Cairo, Government Press, Bulâq.

Emery, W B 1961. *Archaic Egypt.* Harmondsworth, Penguin Books.

Gardiner, A H 1959. *The Royal Canon of Turin.* Oxford, Griffith Institute.

Garstang, J 1903. *Mahâsna and Bêt Khallâf.* London, Bernard Quaritch.

Giddy, L L 1994. Memphis and Saqqara during the Late Old Kingdom: some topographical considerations. In: Berger, C, G Clerc, and N Grimal (eds.), *Hommages à Jean Leclant*, Bibliothèque d'Etude 106 (4 vols.), Cairo, Institut Français d'Archéologie Orientale, I, 189-200.

Giddy, L and D Jeffreys, 1991. Memphis, 1990. In *Journal of Egyptian Archaeology* 77, 1-6.

Giddy, L and D Jeffreys, 1992. Memphis, 1991. In *Journal of Egyptian Archaeology* 78, 1-11.

Giddy, L and D Jeffreys, 1993. Memphis, 1992. In *Journal of Egyptian Archaeology* 79, 11-16.

Giddy, L L, D G Jeffreys, and J Malek, 1990. Memphis, 1989. In *Journal of Egyptian Archaeology* 76, 1-15.
Godley, A D 1926. *Herodotus, i. Books I and II.* London, William Heinemann, and New York, G P Putnam's Sons.
Golénischeff, W 1913. *Les Papyrus hiératiques NoNo. 1115, 1116A et 1116B de l'Ermitage Impériale à St. Pétersbourg.* Manufacture des Papiers de l'Etat.
Griffith, F Ll 1898. *The Petrie Papyri. Hieratic Papyri from Kahun and Gurob.* London, Bernard Quaritch.
Grimal, N-C 1981. *La Stèle triomphale de Pi('ankh)y au Musée du Caire JE 48862 et 47086-47089.* Cairo, Institut Français d'Archéologie Orientale.
Habachi, L 1965. The discovery of the northern tower of the pylon and its inscriptions. In R. Anthes, *Mit Rahineh 1956.* Philadelphia, Pa., The University Museum, 60-5.
Hekekyan MSS. In the British Library, London.
Helck, W 1961. *Materialien zur Wirtschaftsgeschichte des Neuen Reiches,* I. Akademie der Wissenschaften und der Literatur, Abhandlungen der Geistes- und Sozialwissenschaftlichen Klasse Jahrgang 1960, Nr.10. Mainz, Verlag der Akademie der Wissenschaften und der Literatur in Mainz.
Helck, W 1973. Zur Opferliste Amenophis' IV. (JEA 57, 70 ff.). In *Journal of Egyptian Archaeology* 59, 95-9.
Helck, W 1974. *Die altägyptischen Gaue.* Wiesbaden, Dr. Ludwig Reichert Verlag.
Hitta, M A T El 1955. Fouilles de Memphis à Kom el Fakhri. In *La Revue du Caire* XXXIII [175], 50-51.
Jakeman, J 1993. *Abstract Art and Communication in 'Mamluk' Architecture.* D.Phil. Thesis, Faculty of Oriental Studies, Oxford. Not published.
James, T G H 1962. *The Hekanakhte Papers and Other Early Middle Kingdom Documents.* New York, Metropolitan Museum of Art.
Jeffreys, D G 1985. *The Survey of Memphis, I. The Archaeological Report.* London, Egypt Exploration Society.
Jeffreys, D G and L L Giddy, 1989. Memphis, 1988. In *Journal of Egyptian Archaeology* 75, 1-12.
Jeffreys, D G and J Malek, 1988. Memphis, 1986, 1987. In *Journal of Egyptian Archaeology* 74, 15-29.
Jeffreys, D G, J Malek and H S Smith, 1986. Memphis 1984. In *Journal of Egyptian Archaeology* 72, 1-14.
Jeffreys, D G, J Malek and H S Smith, 1987. Memphis 1985. In *Journal of Egyptian Archaeology* 73, 11-20.
Jeffreys, D G and H S Smith, 1988. Memphis and the Nile in the New Kingdom: a preliminary attempt at a historical perspective. In A-P Zivie (ed.), *Memphis et ses nécropoles au Nouvel Empire. Nouvelles données, Nouvelles questions. Actes du colloque international CNRS, Paris, 9 au 11 octobre 1986,* Paris, Editions du Centre National de la Recherche Scientifique, 55-66.
Jeffreys, D and A Tavares, 1994. The historic landscape of Early Dynastic Memphis. In *Mitteiliungen des Deutschen Archäologischen Instituts Abteilung Kairo* 50, 143-73.
Kaiser, W 1969. Zu den königlichen Talbezirken der 1. und 2. Dynastie in Abydos und zur Baugeschichte des Djoser-Grabmals. In *Mitteilungen des Deutschen Archäologischen Instituts Abteilung Kairo* 25, 1-21.
Kaplony, P 1962. Gottespalast und Götterfestungen in der ägyptischen Frühzeit. In *Zeitschrift für Ägyptische Sprache und Altertumskunde* 88, 5-16.
Lacau, P and J-P Lauer, 1961. *Fouilles à Saqqarah. La Pyramide à Degrés, IV. Inscriptions gravées sur les vases.* Cairo, Institut Français d'Archéologie Orientale.
Lilyquist, C 1974. Early Middle Kingdom tombs at Mitrahina. In *Journal of the American Research Center in Egypt* 11, 27-30.
Lloyd, A B 1988. *Herodotus Book II. Commentary 99-182.* Leiden, E J Brill.
Löhr, B 1975. Aḫanjāti in Memphis. In *Studien zur Altägyptischen Kultur* 2, 139-87.
Macramallah, R 1940. *Un Cimetière archaïque de la classe moyenne du peuple à Saqqarah.* Cairo, Imprimerie Nationale, Boulâq.

Malek, J 1994. Orion and the Giza pyramids. In *Discussions in Egyptology* 30, 101-14.
Malek, J 1996. The "coregency relief" of Akhenaten and Smenkhkare from Memphis. In *Studies in Honor of William Kelly Simpson*, forthcoming.
Mariette, A 1872. *Monuments divers recueillis en Egypte et en Nubie.* Paris, Librairie A Franck.
Mariette, A 1889. *Les Mastabas de l'Ancien Empire.* Paris, F. Vieweg, Libraire-éditeur.
Martin, G T 1971. *Egyptian Administrative and Private-Name Seals, principally of the Middle Kingdom and Second Intermediate Period.* Oxford, Griffith Institute.
Mathieson, I 1993. *Saqqara Project 1993.* Edinburgh, National Museums of Scotland.
Mogensen, M 1930. *La Glyptothèque Ny Carlsberg. La Collection Egyptienne.* Copenhagen, Levin & Munksgaard éditeurs.
Montet, P 1957. *Géographie de l'Egypte ancienne, I.* Paris, Imprimerie Nationale and Librairie C Klincksieck.
Newberry, P E 1928. Akhenaten's eldest son-in-law 'Ankhkheprure'. In *Journal of Egyptian Archaeology* 14, 3-9.
Nicholson, C 1870. On some remains of the disk worshippers discovered at Memphis. In *Transcriptions of the Royal Society Literature*, 2nd Series 9, 197-214 (reprinted in *Aegyptiaca*, London, Harrison and Sons, 1891, 117-34, pls.1-2 after p.134).
Petrie, W M F 1901. *The Royal Tombs of the Earliest Dynasties II.* London, Egypt Exploration Fund.
Petrie, W M F 1909. *Memphis I.* London, School of Archaeology in Egypt and Bernard Quaritch.
Petrie, W M F 1915. Memphis VI. In R. Engelbach, *Riqqeh and Memphis VI.* London, School of Archaeology in Egypt and Bernard Quaritch.
PM III^2, Part 1. Porter, B, R L B Moss, E W Burney, and J Malek (eds.), *Topographical Bibliography, etc.*, III^2, Part 1. Oxford, Griffith Institute. 1974.
PM III^2, Part 2. Porter, B, R L B Moss, E W Burney, and J Malek (eds.), *Topographical Bibliography, etc.*, III^2, Part 2. Oxford, Griffith Institute. 1981.
Posener-Kriéger, P 1976. *Les Archives du temple funéraire de Néferirkarê-Kakaï* ii. Cairo, Institut Français d'Archéologie Orientale.
Saad, R and L Manniche, L 1971. A unique offering list of Amenophis IV recently found at Karnak. In *Journal of Egyptian Archaeology* 57, 70-2.
Sandman Holmberg, M 1946. *The God Ptah.* Lund, C W K Gleerup.
Schäfer, H 1902. *Ein Bruchstück altägyptischer Annalen.* Berlin, Verlag der königlichen Akademie der Wissenschaften.
Sethe, K 1905. Menes und die Gründung von Memphis. In *Untersuchungen zur Geschichte und Altertumskunde Aegyptens* III. Leipzig, J C Hinrichs.
Sethe, K 1906. *Urkunden der 18. Dynastie* I. Leipzig, J C Hinrichs.
Sethe, K 1933. *Urkunden des Alten Reichs* I. Leipzig, J C Hinrichs.
Simpson, W K 1957. A running of the Apis in the reign of 'Aha and passages in Manetho and Aelian. In *Orientalia N.S.* 26, 139-42.
Speleers, L 1923. *Recueil des inscriptions Egyptiennes des Musées Royaux du Cinquantenaire à Bruxelles.* Printed by I Vanderpoorten of Ghent.
Spiegelberg, W 1896. *Rechnungen aus der Zeit Setis I.* Strassburg, Karl J Trübner.
Waddell, W G 1940. *Manetho.* London, William Heinemann Ltd., and Cambridge, Mass., Harvard University Press.
Weeks, K R 1971-2. Preliminary report on the first two seasons at Hierakonpolis. Part II. The Early Dynastic Palace. In *Journal of the American Research Center in Egypt* 9, 29-33.
Zivie, C M 1975. À propos de quelques reliefs du Nouvel Empire au Musée du Caire. I. La tombe de Ptahmay à Giza. In *Bulletin de l'Institut Français d'Archéologie Orientale* 75, 285-310.

The temple of Behbeit el-Hagara

Christine Favard-Meeks

By the village of Behbeit el-Hagara (Province of Gharbia, district of Talkha), lie the ruins of a temple dedicated to the Osirian family. This village is located in the Central Delta, a few kilometres south of Mansurah (markaz of Dakahlia), where St Louis, king of France, was held captive, and north of Samannûd (markaz of Mehalla el Kubra), the ancient Sebennytos, capital of the XIIth nome of Lower Egypt to which territory the site belongs (Baines and Malek 1981, 171; PM IV, 40-2).

The site and the temple

The Arabic name of Behbeit derives from the ancient toponym *Per-hebite(t)* which means the 'Domain of the Festive (goddess)' (Favard-Meeks 1991, 434). The site has been linked with the *Iseion* described by the classical writers. This tradition was born when European travellers in the early Eighteenth Century discovered the site. Their knowledge of classical texts soon led them to equate these ruins with the Isis temple described by Herodotus in Busiris. This explains why the ruins of Behbeit have been considered for some time as those of Busiris. It has also been identified with *Isiospolis*. Without methodical excavation of the site, the problem is difficult to resolve since we have to deal, according to the sources, either with various sanctuaries named *Iseion* (and they are quite numerous in Egypt) or the name of a city named after Isis. In Demotic Demi-n-Aset/Temenesi obviously corresponds in the *Archive of Hor* to the Greek *Isiospolis* (Ray 1976, 19) and is probably identical to the Latin *Isidis oppidum* (Calderini 1978, 34).

The temple itself is named *Hebit* (Favard-Meeks 1991, 435-8) and thus describes the type of monument it is: the Festival Hall or Festival Pavilion. The name survived into Coptic. It has been demonstrated that the Coptic word *hbw* derives from *hebit*, which is an abbreviated form of *wesekhet hebit* the 'Festival hall' of divine temples from the New Kingdom onwards (Osing 1976, 143; 632 n.654). This throws some light on a fundamental aspect of the cults and rites of the sanctuary, since the 'Festival hall', in general, is the place where, more especially at the time of holy feasts, the funerary world meets the divine. It is in this hall, for instance, that some Egyptians had the privilege to place their private statues hoping thus to benefit in the feast offerings made to the gods. In fact, the *hebit* as a cultual space (whether a permanent building or a temporary pavilion) has been described as being any type of dwelling-place for funerary or divine statues where they benefit in festal offerings (Bruyère 1952, 28).

In the case of the temple of Behbeit el-Hagara, as it is dedicated to funerary gods within the sphere of Busirite cults, it is in essence a place where the Osirian family is worshipped but also a place where the respective cultual activities of Isis the wife and Horus the son are dedicated to Osiris-Andjety. They are described as the ritualists of Osiris, their specific function being to 'set offerings down'. This explains the other name of the site, 'The-place-where-offerings-are-set-down', information already provided by the Mythological Delta Papyrus of the Third Intermediate Period (Meeks 1985). Through this sacred name, we thus know that the main cultual activities of the temple concern the fabrication of a clay statue of Osiris Khenty-imentet, support of his rebirth guaranteed by the rite of 'setting offerings down'.

Before the late temple

As is the case for many Delta sites, the history of the place is poorly known. Although the site has been identified since the early eighteenth century, and although some Egyptologists copied the inscriptions of the surface blocks, at the end of the nineteenth century (PM IV, 40-2; Steindorff 1944-5), the site, as far as digging is concerned, has never been given any special attention. Only the Mission Montet, in the late forties and early fifties, dug out blocks in the south-east corner of the temple (Lezine 1949). As a consequence, the historical background is difficult to reconstruct: on the one hand, immediate information is given by the names of the builders of the temple (Nectanebo II, Ptolemy II, Ptolemy III), and on the other, from the New Kingdom onwards, external sources mention *Per-hebite(t)* the name of the site, or *Hebit*, the name of the temple. Both names being recurrent in other parts of Egypt, the equation of all these attestations with this single site remains to be confirmed. At all events, the first mention of *Per-hebite(t)* is no earlier than the reign of Amenophis III and that of *Hebit* also dates from the New Kingdom. The presence on the site of an isolated granite block of the Ramesside Period (Naville 1930, pl. I.A; Favard-Meeks 1991, 443) does not give proof of a building during that period, since reused blocks were regularly brought from nearby places at other Delta sites (the case of Tanis is well known). Nevertheless, according to textual sources, it is fairly certain that an earlier construction was undertaken by the last kings of the Saite Dynasty, the cult of their statues being attested in Behbeit (Yoyotte 1958). As the site lies within the sphere of influence of a major and ancient cult place of the order of Busiris, it may only have been, before the construction of the Nectanebos' permanent foundation, a place for festival offerings dedicated to the annual clay statue of Osiris guaranteeing the king's rebirth. The determinative used in the writing of *Per-hebite(t)* in the Mythological Delta Papyrus already mentioned (Meeks 1985) would suggest a temporary construction.

Another important fact should be underlined which could eventually confirm the rather late and ephemeral existence of the temple: this religious foundation, unless not identified as such, has not well survived in the archives of the late Ptolemaic and Roman temples, and in particular in the geographical inscriptions (Naville 1930, 42) as if these archives had been elaborated before the temple was founded.

The builders of the temple

The temple today is a late and quite ephemeral foundation. According to the inscriptions, the construction of the temple started under Nectanebo II (360-43 BC), the last Egyptian pharaoh. The name of Nectanebo I does not appear on the walls of the sanctuary, but the inscriptions of a statue of Harsiesis, the future vizir of Nectanebo II, indicates that some work was carried out to create a watery link between Behbeit and the Busirite nome by the first ruler of the Thirtieth Dynasty (De Meulenaere 1958; Gallo 1987). This probably means that the building of the temple was then planned but not started. It seems at least that this foundation owes much to Nectanebo II himself, for the temple name *Hebit* is included in his nomen (Barguet 1954).

It should also be noted that Nectanebo I, on Harsiesis' statue, is said to be 'beloved of Osiris-Hemag, the great god which lives in Behbeit' and that the only chapel of the temple which has been partly decorated and inscribed by Nectanebo II is precisely the 'Chapel of Osiris-Hemag'. This could suggest that this aspect of Osiris was particularly favoured by the Nectanebos. The site shows no trace of the Persian and Macedonian kings, though the nearby Sebennytos (capital of the Nectanebos) benefited in the building activities of Philip Arrhidaeus and Alexander IV when Ptolemy I was only Satrap. Subsequently the most important part of the temple was completed by Ptolemy II (284-46 BC). As long as an anastylosis programme has not been carried out, it will be difficult to determine whether Ptolemy II modified the architecture of the Thirtieth Dynasty temple or whether he only had the existing walls decorated and inscribed. One point is fairly certain: Ptolemy III (246-22 BC) probably enlarged the sanctuary by adding a columned hall and a façade. Finally, the temple collapsed into ruins, at the latest before the end of Domitian's reign, as we shall see below.

Description of the site

The temple is completely isolated within cultivated land. There are apparently no other archaeological vestiges in the surrounding country.

The enclosure brick wall has survived on three sides, South, West and North. The entire eastern part as well as the south and north east has been destroyed to the level of site gates (see fig.1). This observation is made possible thanks to the map to the *Description de l'Egypte* (Favard-Meeks 1991, pl.3) which shows that, at the end of the eigtheenth century, the site was much larger than now and that its enclosure was complete. One fact has to be pointed out: even then, between the ruins of the temple and the enclosure wall, we see a large empty space, without any ruins of buildings. Now, on both the western and the eastern side, the land is under cultivation, and the northern and southern sides appear empty, apart from broken pieces of granite spread on the ground, as if unfinished or totally destroyed. These empty spaces seem, perhaps wrongly, to confirm the impression of a monument unfinished, ephemeral, and early abandoned. Finally, outside the enclosure, as is shown well on the map by Wilkinson, ran a canal on the south and west sides of the site leading to a lake which has now disappeared (Favard-Meeks 1991, pl.26). One should like to determine if it could correspond to the ancient waterway which Nectanebo I seems to have constructed. This supposition is made possible since the Organization of Egyptian Antiquities found in this canal, a few years ago, a sphinx probably coming from the dromos.

The sanctuary itself is made of huge and smaller granite blocks, here and there forming heaps of stone so thoroughly entangled that a plan is difficult to propose and will remain hypothetical pending future excavation. This disarray is the result of a collapse which took place in ancient times: earthquake and subsidence of the whole building under its own weight are among many possible reasons for its destruction; the ruination of the site could not have taken place later than the end of the first century AD, a date established by the reuse of a Behbeit block in a temple dedicated to Isis and Serapis in Rome, either at the time of its first foundation in 43 BC or when renovated under Domitian (AD 81-96). With the early Christians, religious opposition may have added to the destruction, and from then on the temple was obviously used as a quarry by the inhabitants of the region (pl.33a).

Tentative reconstruction

The reconstruction I propose, considering it is based on the study of inscriptions and of old and recent photographs, is bound to be imperfect since it only takes into account the surface blocks. It is not possible to evaluate the percentage of blocks either completely hidden by other huge blocks or simply buried. The plan of the site presented here (fig.1) is only a location sketch of the various courts and chapels identified so far.

The dromos

According to the reconstruction, a dromos was edged with the sphinxes of Nectanebo II (pl.33b). It led to the sector now occupied by monuments of Ptolemy III.

The main entrance

Ptolemy III added to the main temple what appears today to be the main entrance façade and a columned hall. The left wing of the façade seems to lie more or less on the ground (pl.33c) having fallen back on itself. The elevation shows from the ground to the top, one Nile procession, a line of dedicatory inscription, two or maybe three registers of seated gods, another dedicatory inscription and a Hathor head frieze alternating with the two cartouches of Ptolemy III and the one of Berenice II.

Of the right wing (pl.33d) little has survived and it is impossible to know whether the blocks are still buried or scattered away. Nevertheless, a few broken pieces showing the top of the third register with the upper dedicatory inscription and the Hathor frieze confirm that the decoration of the right wing was identical to the left one. From the upper dedicatory inscription, we learn that the left wing was built at the request of Ptolemy III for his father Osiris-Andjety. The same dedicatory inscription on the right side indicates that Berenice, the wife and sister of Ptolemy III had this monument built for Isis. Under Ptolemy II, the cartouche of Isis replaces the one of Berenice. This modification is nevertheless difficult to analyze. The cartouche of Berenice II could be considered as a first step to the assimilation of the queen with 'Isis the divine mother' in the sanctuary which must have been, at that time, one of the Egyptian dynastic temples *par excellence*. It must be remembered that

Berenice II, according to the reliefs, does not accompany the king in any offering scenes. She is only present in the temple through her cartouche of the upper frieze and in the dedicatory inscription of the right wing of the façade where she is said, as spouse and sister of the Son of Rê Ptolemy III, to have made a large monument for her mother Isis (Favard-Meeks 1991, 13). From this it is possible to deduce that the building and decoration of that part of the temple was carried out before the Decree of Canopus was issued, in 238 BC, when the priests of Egypt decided on behalf of Ptolemy III and Berenice II to establish a cult for the 'Gods Euergetes' (Préaux 1978, 259-61).

The iconography of the façade gives Osiris a preeminent place. On each register, the king makes offering to three aspects of this god, while Isis, on the left wing, is sitting behind him. From the remnants of the right wing, the king again makes offerings to three aspects of Osiris who is followed on this side instead by Harsiesis. The inscriptions recall the various cults in which Osiris benefits beyond that limit, Isis and Horus having the important function of protecting him (Roeder 1909) and as a consequence, being the main actors of the rites.

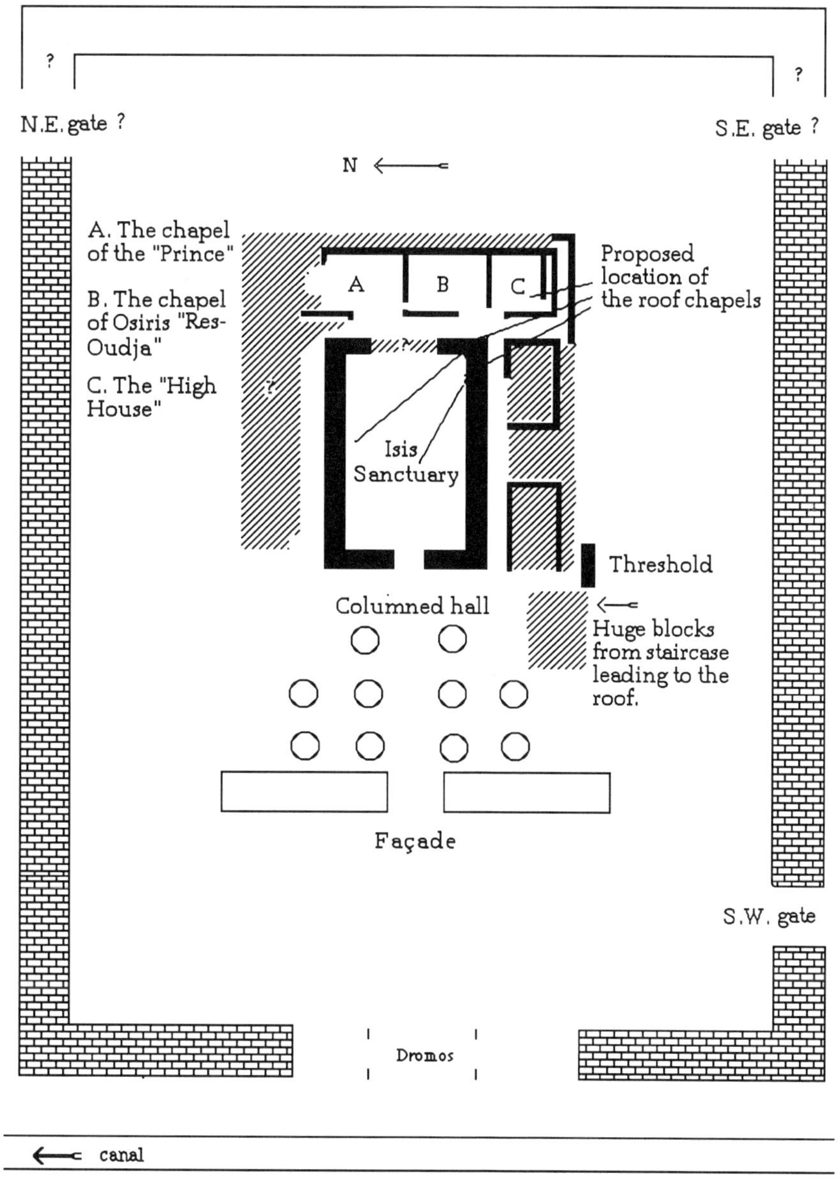

Fig.1 Plan of the temple of Isis at Behbeit el-Hagara.

The surrounding stone wall

From the western façade running eastward, an exterior wall made of huge blocks surrounded the whole building. Its thickness must have been considerable since it is made of one outside and one inside layer. The blocks are fastened together with the help of enormous tenons and mortises (Lezine 1949). This surrounding wall remained uninscribed.

The columned hall

It is difficult to describe the columned hall (pl.34a). Many fragments of red granite columns, which probably belong to the hall, were found scattered all over the ground between the brick enclosure and the temple proper. But, as the travellers of the eighteenth century already record, these columns were sawn to make millstones by the inhabitants of the region and the fragments left will hardly permit a reconstruction. It seems impossible to determine now if lateral rooms opened onto the hall. However, this must have been the case on the southern side, where huge blocks of black granite belong to a staircase which led to chapels on the roof of the main sanctuary (pl.34b).

The façade of the sanctuary of Isis

To the east of the hall are to be found the remains of the façade of the sanctuary of Isis (pl.34c). From that point on, the different sectors of the temple were inscribed under Ptolemy II with the exception of the Chapel of Osiris-*Hemag* (see below). The various scenes of the two wings display Isis and kingship. The lower register, above a Nile procession and a dedicatory inscription, shows the king being introduced to the goddess Isis by Horus of Behedet, Nekhbet and possibly Râyt. There, Isis warrants inheritance of the throne of Egypt, while on the upper register she guarantees domination over foreign countries. Both wings are here dedicated to Isis. Ptolemy II has chosen, for the decoration of the cornice, that each of his cartouches be associated with one dedicated to 'Isis the great, the divine mother'. It seems as if the queen, under that reign, is still kept out of the cult (see Entrance façade). Between the two wings, a huge lintel (pl.34d) decorated with the winged disc, though partly hidden, still shows the entrance to the sacred place of Isis, which is thus described in the dedication of the façade: 'This is the *akhet*-horizon of the queen of the gods, the venerable *djerit*-sanctuary of the Lady of Inheritance, the *heret*-sky of the [divine] female falcon' (Favard-Meeks 1991, 27-8).

The sanctuary of Isis

The sanctuary of Isis is the most spectacular part of the temple. It is highly regrettable that it has been so extensively destroyed, but the huge blocks of dark grey granite remaining on the site still demonstrate the magnificence the builders intended to give to the place (pl.35a). When European travellers began to visit the site in the eighteenth century, they all admired this part of the temple. The blocks copied by Lucas (Favard-Meeks 1991, pl.27), for instance, come from this place and the English traveller, R. Pococke, was well inspired when he wrote : '[...] *but what commanded our attention still more, was the exquisite sculpture of the hieroglyphics; and tho' the figures, about four feet high, are in the Egyptian taste, yet there is something so fine, so divine, in a manner, in the mein of the deities and priests, that it far exceeds any thing I ever saw in this way*' (Pococke 1743, 21). Before hieroglyphs were deciphered, Pococke uses the term 'divine' to qualify the reliefs and, as we shall see later on, 'the Divine (place)' is either the name of a major chapel on the roof of the sanctuary, or another name of the temple itself.

According to the reconstruction proposed from the surface blocks only, the elevation of the walls is composed of four registers (see fig.2). Over the Nile procession and the dedication, there are two registers of standing and one of seated deities. This elevation is found in most of the other chapels of the temple. The scenes in high relief (pl.32a) are principally devoted to the cult of the statue of Isis. A hymn to Isis, extremely fragmentary but the earliest known so far, belongs to the eastern axial wall. Praises and jubilations are addressed to her while her worshippers bow to the ground for her 'ka in peace like Atum when he sets (in the horizon)'. Here, as in the bark inscription of the south wall, where she is also described as the 'image of Atum', her action is compared to the prerogatives of this god: 'Isis the great, the divine mother, the mistress of Hebyt rests inside her bark as Atum when he sets in the Western horizon' (Favard-Meeks 1991, 42-4).

According to the reconstruction presently possible, the goddess only shares this sacred space

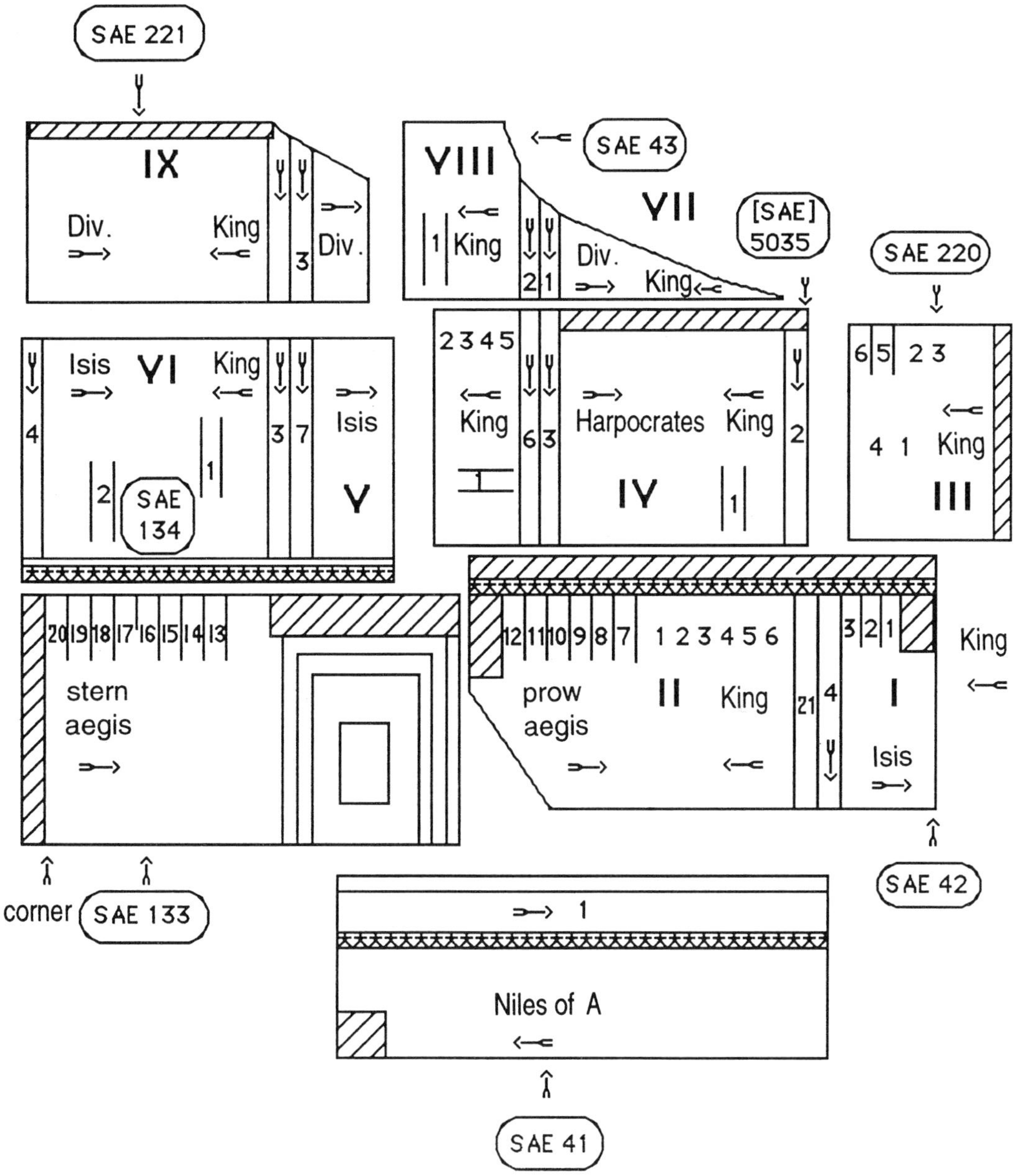

Fig.2 Reconstructed alignment of blocks showing the elevation of the south wall of the Isis sanctuary

with her son Horus who receives the crowns of Upper and Lower Egypt. Through this scene, she fully justifies the title of Isis the Great, the Divine mother. As such, she gives her son Horus-Ptolemy II legitimacy over Egypt (compare Colin 1994). However, in the main scene of the south wall, the bark scene, she is described as being the protectress of the major aspect of Osiris in the temple: 'the Great Prince, Osiris-*Onnophris* triumphant'. This introduces an important architectural problem which remains to be solved. This part of the sanctuary being so destroyed, it has not been possible to determine whether the sanctuary of Isis, to the East, opens on the Osirian chapels or if it is a closed space, her own cult being an end in itself. In the latter case, the Osirian chapels would then be only accessible by the south and north corridors running along the Isis sanctuary, whose entrances are in the columned hall.

The lateral chapels on the north and south sides of the Isis sanctuary

Chapels opened off the north (pl.35b) and south corridors. On the north side, so few blocks remain that it is not possible to determine how many chapels there could have been and to which gods they were dedicated. One block from a very small chapel shows, 'Amun, Lord of the orchards', while another depicts a falcon-headed god. This scene seems to establish a parallel with the gods of a southern chapel on the opposite side.

The chapels on the southern side are as difficult to identify but for quite the opposite reason. Many huge blocks of granite cover the whole southern side,and they are mixed up with those of the enclosure wall and of the exterior and interior walls of the Isis sanctuary. Two, perhaps three chapels were built.

In the south-east chapel are gathered together the falcon-headed gods Harsiesis and Khonsu-Neferhotep and Osiris-Alive (*Ankhy*), which, as we are going to see below, signifies that Osiris, through all the transformations he enjoys in Behbeit, has achieved his renewal and lives again through his son.

The south-west chapel must have had a very special status. In contrast to the other lateral chapels, the decoration is in high relief as in the Isis sanctuary and it is obviously dedicated to this goddess where she is described as 'shining like Rê, the [divine] falcon illuminating [.....]'. This room seems to be connected with the huge staircase nearby and the rites may be in relation with those of the roof chapels.

The eastern chapels and the chapels on the roof

All these chapels are devoted either to the rebirth of Osiris-Andjety into a young child or to his transformation into a falcon.

The chapel of the 'Prince'

The chapel of the 'Prince' (fig.1, room marked A) and the adjacent room lie at the north-east. corner of the temple. One can hardly speak of reconstruction for these two rooms since it is based only on the lower register of the axial walls (pl.35c). Nevertheless, we know that this sacred chapel carries great importance from the point of view of the cult. The name of the chapel is announced on the entrance façade along with the other cults dedicated to Osiris. As said before, it is also this aspect of Osiris that Isis protects in her own sanctuary. The armed geniuses, represented at the entrance of most of the Osirian chapels, are advised to grant their protection to this form of Osiris. The Mythological Delta Papyrus (Favard-Meeks 1991, 346) tells us that the 'great Prince from Andjet becomes a divine falcon' in Behbeit, and it could be supposed that the famous base of the falcon statue of Nectanebo II was located in that chapel (Barguet 1954, 88, fig.3; Yoyotte 1959) and, also, that it was the place where the Osiris-Nectanebo II achieved his transformation into a falcon. At all events, the importance of the chapel of the Prince is confirmed by the fact that the name of this sanctuary is mentioned in the nebty-name of Nectanebo II. Osiris in this context is called *Wenen-nefer*-justified and his name is inscribed in a cartouche. On a block seen at the end of the last century outside Behbeit (Edgar and Roeder 1913) and which seems to be one of the few blocks not dedicated to Osiris-*Hemag*, Nectanebo II receives from 'Horus, the protector of his father' the sign of life and is said to be 'the living image of the- Protector-of-his-father'. Osiris is reborn through his son, Horus-king.

The chapel of Osiris-*Res-wedja*

The chapel of Osiris-*Res-wedja* and the High House lie in the South-East corner of the temple. There, the blocks, more numerous, allow a reconstruction which remains, nevertheless, to be completed.

This chapel (fig.1, room marked B) shows the same elevation as that in the sanctuary of Isis. Above a Nile procession, without inscriptions, are a dedicatory inscription, two registers of standing deities and one of seated gods.

The place is representative, through its gods, of the major Delta religious centres such as Memphis, Heliopolis, Sais, Busiris and Mendes. Ptah, Nut, Hor-Akhty, Geb, Neith, Hat-Mehyt and Isis naturally are all devoted to the protection of Osiris. Through the epithet *Res-wedja*, the triumphant aspect of Osiris is evidenced and the gods of the dynastic centres of the Delta have served this purpose.

The parallelism existing beween this aspect of Osiris and the king is demonstrated on a half-buried block marking the axis of the chapel and showing the Nile procession reaching an inscribed panel made of four columns of text (pl.35d). On each side of the axis, a column is dedicated to the serekh-name of Ptolemy II while in the other, as an equivalence, the serekh is inscribed with the name of Osiris-*Res-wedja*. While in the other parts of the temple, he is always the benefactor of the offerings, giving in return power on earth and beyond, here he is described as the one who guarantees prosperity to humanity and the gods, a part usually assumed by Isis.

The High House

The 'High House' (fig.1, room marked C) is a kind of sanctuary well attested in Abydos and Thebes, from the Middle Kingdom onward, in relation with Hathor the funerary cow. In Behbeit it shows most of the gods assuring the protection of Osiris (Anubis, Sobek, Thoth and Isis-Akhet as a cow-headed goddess) under their zoomorphic aspect (pl.36a). The other divinities such as Onuris, Isis, Nephthys, Seshat and Hathor are anthropomorphic.

In the temple of Behbeit, Hathor is not depicted under her aspect as cow, a role played instead by Isis as Akhet, mistress of the chapel. Whereas in Abydos or Thebes, Hathor apparently enables the night sun to start his regenerating travel on mythological grounds, in Behbeit, this mythical function is transposed to the ritual plane. There Hathor acts as singer in the High House in an offering scene where Harpocrates receives the 'crowns of justification' which give him legitimacy over the Double Kingdom.

In addition, this chapel is more particularly described as a 'Place where offerings are set down' (the other name of Behbeit which is also mentioned in the sanctuary of Isis). As such it sheltered the annual clay statue of Osiris and we know, according to the Mythological Delta Papyrus, that in this document Hathor is there the goddess who 'sets down the offerings'. Though Isis and Horus have replaced Hathor in this function in the late temple, the older tradition can survive but in an ambiguous way.

This chapel raises the delicate problem of chapels supposedly existing on the roof. As has been observed before, some of the surface blocks obviously come from roof constructions (Lezine 1949) to which the staircase in the columned hall once led. The name of the place itself supposes a difference in height with respect to the other parts of the temple. As the main room is apparently on the same ground level as the other Osirian chapels, it may be supposed that another structure could be located on the roof. As stated before, great importance has been granted in this work of reconstruction to inscriptions. It must be emphasised that had the dedication of the entrance to the 'High House' not mentioned the name of the place as 'the High Chapel in the Upper Place' or 'the High Chapel as an Upper Place' (Favard-Meeks 1991, 167-8), we would not have supposed that part of it could be located on the roof.

Let us consider now two other chapels which could also be located on the roof: the chapel of Osiris-*Hemag* and the so-called 'Divine (Place)'.

The chapel of Osiris-*Hemag*

Some of the blocks lying along the northern wall of the Isis sanctuary are inscribed with the name of Nectanebo II. These scenes - all unfinished - are dedicated to a series of Osiris-*Hemag* crowned with the *atef*. Apparently, no other gods are associated with the cults of this chapel. It is of modest dimensions and its location on the ground floor does not seem possible. This is the reason why it has been supposed that it could have been built either within the thickness of the north wall of the Isis sanctuary or on the roof itself (pl.36b,c). The latter suggestion seems preferable since a comparison can be made with the Osiris rooms built on the roof of the Isis temple in Philae (PM VI, [248]-9; Benedite 1893, 126 l.5,7; pl.41). At the least, if this analysis is correct, it indicates, as said before, that all architectural features were constructed under Nectanebo II.

The study of the term *hemag* isolates two traditions, the one of the embalmer and the other of the goldsmith. The first tradition concerns the external protection of corpses and concerns more especially the funerary activities. Considering that there is no reference to the death of Osiris in Behbeit and that it would not suit the iconography of the temple where Osiris is always depicted as alive and reborn (a relief in Dendara confirms the analysis), the second tradition might be favoured. *Hemag,* in Behbeit, could describe the activity of the goldsmith's workshop of divine temples (Derchain 1990) and the covering in this context would be made of amulets of precious or semi-precious materials. In fact, this term in Behbeit may be the synthesis of the funerary and divine traditions elaborated around the cult of the annual clay Osiris figure.

It may be added that if the *hemag*-operation on the statue of Osiris took place on the north-west part of the roof of the temple, it was probably, afterwards, carried to the roof structure of the High House in the south-east corner, where it was kept during a whole year (compare Cauville 1988).

The 'Divine (Place)' or another name of the temple

It has already been proposed that the High House and the chapel of Osiris-Hemag could have been located partly or entirely on the roof. We have seen the importance at the site of the cult of Osiris, and the chapels just described, located on the roof of the temple, could justify the existence of this monumental staircase.

However, other traditions are present in the temple built by Nectanebo II, traditions evoked by the sacred name 'Divine (Place)'. Before this royal foundation took place, toponyms based on the root *-netjer* occur in various circumstances and places. In the Old Kingdom, *Netjeru* concerns royal funerary rites and the transformation of the dead king into a god, while *Netjery* might be another name for Coptos or might qualify spaces related to the cult of the living king or of his statues where commemoration and justification feasts take place (Favard-Meeks 1991, 375-9).

Through the inscriptions of the temple, the 'Divine (Place)' appears as the other sacred name of the sanctuary. However, we noted among the grey granite blocks of the sanctuary some red granite fragments which come from a huge granite naos or from broken walls (pl.36d). It does not seem possible that these red granite elements can find a place in the Isis sanctuary and we are bound to conclude that it constitutes a third chapel on the roof. This would then be evidence for a major aspect of cult, but the reconstruction is so tentative that it must be treated with great caution. On these red granite blocks the mention of the 'Divine (Place)' recurs several times, and we should like to suppose that instead of being just another name of the temple, it was that of a roof chapel where important rites must have taken place.

It is evident that the hypothesis remains fragile, since the protocol on the falcon statue of Nectanebo II is so established that the 'Divine (Place)' appears as the other name of Hebit. In the left inscription, the king is said to be the 'heir of the master of Egypt', while in the right inscription, it is indicated that he 'founded the "Divine (Place)" in its true aspect' (Barguet 1954). This expression, at least, underlines the will of the king to add the cults and rites of the 'Divine (Place)' to the liturgy of the Behbeit temple. One might wonder whether the same intention had not been transposed in the religious texts of the so-called 'Divine (Place)' when they indicate that 'Osiris-*Wenen-nefer* [...] installed the gods inside the 'Divine (Place)' (Favard-Meeks 1991, 264-5).

In conclusion: an accumulation of rites, a complementarity

The rites of the 'Divine (Place)' added to those of the 'Place-where-offerings-are-set-down' thus offer Pharaoh - Osiris reborn in his own child Horus - under the patronage of Isis, the Lady of the place, the optimum in ritual. As such, Osiris-Andjety reborn is the king in the same way that Neferhotep could be Amenophis III, the son-god but also Osiris (Vandersleyen 1975-6; Limme 1993), and as Onuris is Nectanebo II on a naos in the Cairo Museum (Favard-Meeks 1991, 461). The cult of Osiris-Andjety, in the guise of a living person, makes no allusion to his death, but only to his rebirth through the many rites from which he benefits in the temple of Behbeit el-Hagara.

This divinity is ambiguous having subsumed within himself the major aspects of several gods. Osiris came from Busiris to receive in Behbeit, thanks to his annual clay statue, his regeneration and the cultic means to transform himself into a divine falcon or into a young god whose personality can then be compared to Onuris-Shu, the main god of Sebennytos, and Khonsu-Neferhotep whose lunar aspects warrant his perpetual renewal as the moon. In the 'Place-where-offerings-are-set-down', Isis assumes the necessary duties to be accomplished at the time of funerary feasts, while through the rites of the 'Divine (Place)' she is associated, as in Coptos for instance, at the time of divine feasts, with the justification of the king and of the statue of the completely regenerated god. The main actress of this achievement is Isis and the cultic complementarity is made possible thanks to her own activity at the time of the feasts.

Bibliography

Baines, J and J Malek, 1981 *Atlas of Ancient Egypt*. Oxford, Phaidon.

Barguet, P 1954. Quelques fragments nouveaux au nom de Nekhethorheb. In *Kêmi* 13, 89-91, II, fig.3.

Bénédite, G 1893. *Le Temple de Philæ* I. Mémoires publiés par les membres de la Mission Archéologique Française au Caire 13. Paris, Ernest Leroux.

Bruyère, B 1952. *Rapport sur les Fouilles de Deir el-Medineh 1935-1940.* Fouilles de l'Institut Français d'Archéologie Orientale XX/3. Cairo, Institut Français d'Archéologie Orientale au Caire.

Calderini, A 1978. *Dizionario dei nomi geografici e topografici dell'egitto greco-romano* III/1. Milan.

Cauville, S 1988. Les Mystères d'Osiris à Dendara. Interprétation des chapelles osiriennes, In *Bulletin de la Société Française d'Egyptologie* 112, juin, 31.

Colin, F 1994. L'Isis "dynastique" et la Mère des dieux phrygienne. Essai d'analyse d'un processus d'interaction culturelle, In *Zeitschrift für Papyrologie und Epigraphik* 102, 271-95.

De Meulenaere, H 1958. Le vizir Harsiêsis de la 30e Dynastie. In *Mitteilungen des Deutschen Archäologischen Instituts Abteilung Kairo* 16, 230-6.

Derchain, P 1990. L'Atelier des Orfèvres à Dendara et les Origines de l'Alchimie. In *Chronique d'Egypte* 65/ 130, 219-42.

Edgar, C and G Roeder 1913. Der Isistempel von Behbêt. In *Recueil de Travaux* 35, 89-116.

Favard-Meeks, C 1990. Un temple d'Isis à reconstruire. In *Archeologia* 263, Paris, 26-33.

Favard-Meeks, C 1991. *Le temple de Behbeit el-Hagara.* Studien zur Altägyptischen Kultur Beiheft 6. Hamburg, Helmut Buske.

Gallo, P 1987. Nectanebo ed il ramo del Nilo di Busiri e Perhebit, *Egitto e Vicino Oriente* 10/1, 43-9.

LÄ I = Lexikon der Ägyptologie I, Wiesbaden 1975, Otto Harrassowitz, cols. 682-3.

Lézine, A 1949. Etat présent du temple de Behbeit el Hagar. In *Kêmi* 10, 49-57, pl. 4-5.

Limme, L 1993. Un "Prince ramesside" fantôme. In *Miscellanea De Meulenaere*, Brussels 112-7.

Meeks, D 1985. Un manuel de géographie religieuse du delta. In S Schoske (ed.), *Akten des vierten Ägyptologen Kongresse 1985* 3, Studien zur Altägyptischen Kultur Beihefte, Hamburg, Helmut Buske, 297-304. [Papyrus Brooklyn n° 47.218.84]

Montet, O 1949. Les divinités du temple de Behbeit el-Hagar. In *Kêmi* 10, 43-8.

Naville, E 1930. *Détails relevés dans les ruines de quelques temples égyptiens,* 2e Partie; Behbeit el-Hagar. Paris.

Osing, J 1976. *Die Nominalbildung des Ägyptischen*, Phillip von Zabern, 143; 632 n. 654.

Pococke, R 1743. *A description of the East and Some other Countries.* Volume the first. Observations on Egypt. London 1743.

PM IV = B Porter and R Moss, *Topographical Bibliography of Ancient Egyptian Hieroglyphic Texts, Reliefs and Paintings* IV. Lower and Middle Egypt, Oxford 1934.

PM VI = B Porter and R Moss, *Topographical Bibliography of Ancient Egyptian Hieroglyphic Texts, Reliefs and Paintings* VI. Upper Egypt: Chief Temples, Oxford 1939.

Préaux, C 1978, *Le Monde hellénistique. La Grèce et l'Orient* (323-146 av. J.C.) Tome I, PUF.

Ray, J 1976. *The Archive of Hor.* London, Egypt Exploration Society.

Roeder, G 1909. Der Isistempel von Behbêt. In *Zeitschrift für Ägyptische Sprache und Altertumskunde* 46, 62-73.

Steindorff, G 1944-5. Reliefs from the temples of Sebennytos and Iseion in American Collections. In *Journal of the Walters Art Gallery* 7-8, 39-59 [n° 1 (Metropolitan Museum New York), 2 (Montreal), 3 (Walters Art Gallery, Baltimore), 5 (Walters Art Gallery, Baltimore), 12 (Seattle Art Museum), 13 (Cranbrook Academy Michigan), 14 (Pennsylvania University), 15 (Virginia Museum), 16 (Metropolitan Museum of Art), 17 (Rhode Island School of Design), 18 (Brooklyn Museum)].

Yoyotte, J 1958. Néchao. In *Supplément au Dictionnaire de la Bible* VI, 363-93.

Yoyotte, J 1959. Nectanebo II comme faucon divin. In *Kêmi* 15, 70-4.

Sacred Animal Temples at Saqqara

Sue Davies and H S Smith

A: Introduction

To complement the papers delivered at the British Museum Colloquium in July 1994, we were invited to contribute to this volume an article upon temples connected with the cults of Sacred Animals.

There were temples in Egypt where a single Sacred Animal acted as the living incarnation of the god; examples are the 'Apis House' in the precinct of Ptah at Memphis (Jones and Milward Jones 1982-3, 1985, 1987-8), the temple of Mnevis at Heliopolis and that of the ram Banebdjed at Mendes. Both the latter have disappeared, like many others, while of the first only foundations survive. In other major temples, like those of Horus at Edfu and of Haroêris and Suchos at Kom Ombo, living species were certainly kept within the precincts and had individual cults in the Late Period, but were not necessarily the only or principal focus of worship. Finally, there were the sanctuaries attached to the burial places of Sacred Animals; many of these also have been substantially destroyed, even where the burials have been preserved.[1]

In this paper, we discuss only this last type of temple, and for practical reasons of space confine ourselves to those in the necropolis of Memphis at Saqqara. These sites have the advantage that several of the precincts have recently been the object of archaeological survey and excavation,[2] and the cults they served the subject of major studies.[3] The complex evidence which can be derived from Greek and demotic Egyptian documents of the Ptolemaic Period for the organization of the temple communities and their daily life has been evocatively set forth by Ray (1972b, 1976, 1978) and Thompson (1988). This article is confined to an attempt to give the reader a general impression of what the temple-precincts may have looked like and to comment upon the life which went on within and around them, focusing as far as is possible on the lesser known period of the sixth to fourth centuries BC.

B: Temples on the western escarpment of the Nile valley

There were three ways of reaching the necropolis from central Memphis in the Late Period. All three eventually reached Sarapieion, two via the western escarpment, one via the desert valley from Abusir. The first two led through the temple-towns of Bubastieion and Anubieion, which are discussed in this section.

The former route reached the desert edge near the Unas valley-temple and ran northwards below the cliff through the south gate of a large mud-brick enclosure (about 350 metres N-S by 250 metres E-W) (Jeffreys and Smith 1988, 78-9). This has been identified from the presence of cat burials as the site of Bubastieion, the Greek name for the precinct of the goddess Bastet (Thompson 1988, 21-4; Kessler 1989, 105-6; Zivie 1990, 31-5).[4] Few structures survive within the enclosure, but it seems clear that the main temple stood on a central bluff of rock within an inner precinct wall (fig.1). On the analogy of Anubieion, the remainder of the upper part of the enclosure may have housed further temple-complexes, while the low-lying area between the edge of the cultivation and the cliff was occupied by the mud-brick buildings of a town (fig.1). The road from the south gate led

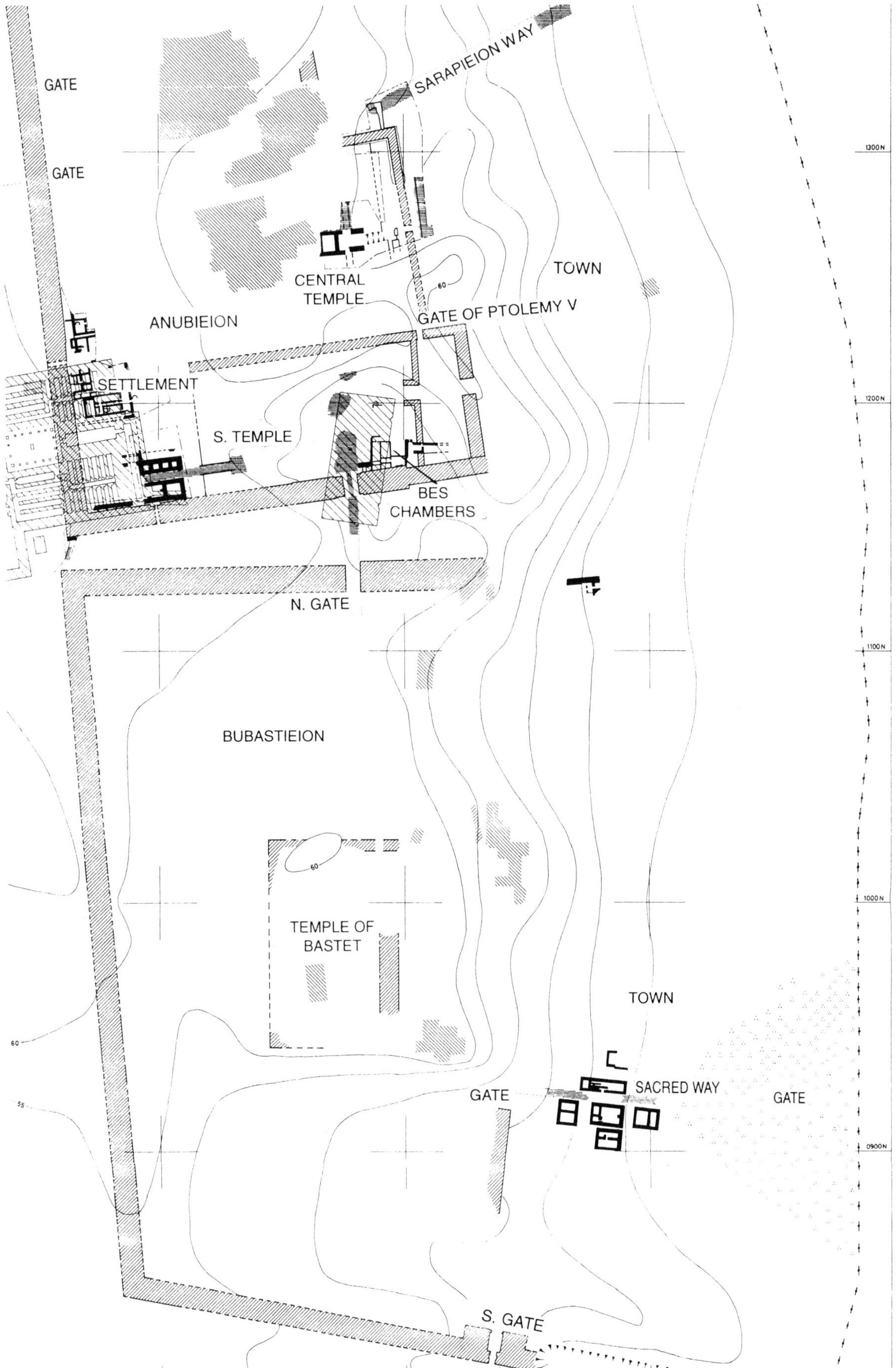

Fig.1 Plan of Bubastieion (below), showing sites of gates, town, sacred way and temple; with Anubieion (above), showing sites of town, settlement, south temple with 'Bes-chambers', central temple and Sarapieion Way. After the original by David Jeffreys.

northwards through this town area and eventually joined a sacred way which ran E-W across the main enclosure. This was lined with mud-brick buildings, perhaps of an administrative character.[5] Turning eastwards, one reached a gate in the main enclosure wall, which perhaps served a quay at the valley edge.[6] Turning westwards, one ascended a slope through a gate on the south side of the central bluff (fig.1).[7] To reach the temple of Bastet from the sacred way one would have had to turn northwards at this point and climb a ramp or stairway. Nothing now remains of the temple itself except some brick foundations concealed beneath a modern car-park.[8] The south and east faces of the bluff on which the temple stood had been utilized in the New Kingdom for rock-tombs on several levels. Their labyrinthine chambers and shafts were re-used in the Late and Ptolemaic Periods for the burial of mummified cats (Zivie 1990, 31-5, 67, 185-6 for bibliography), and were so extensive that there seems never to have been a need to construct a purpose-built catacomb, as was done for other Sacred Animals at Saqqara.

The enclosure of Anubieion lay immediately to the north of Bubastieion, whence it could be reached by a N-S road (fig.1) (Jeffreys and Smith 1988, 43, 52ff.). It could however also be reached from Memphis by the Sarapieion Way, and the two routes joined within the enclosure (Smith 1981, 331-4). Anubieion is the Greek name for the precinct of Anubis, where, according to Greek and demotic sources, the work-place of the embalmers and the centre of the necropolis administration lay.[9] Arriving from Memphis on the Sarapieion Way, one passed through the eastern enclosure wall into an area of mud-brick buildings between the edge of the cultivation and the cliff. The name *pr-grg-ỉnpw* (de Cenival 1972, 14) may refer to this town, while the temple-precinct is probably to be identified with *pr-hn-ỉnpw tpy ḏw=f* (de Meulenaere 1960; Yoyotte 1972).

Though the mud-brick enclosure of Anubieion (250 metres square) was smaller than Bubastieion, it provided space for three sizeable temples built on terraces up the escarpment;[10] each probably had its individual sacred way leading up from the valley edge, where, presumably, temple quays existed. Of the southern temple complex, only the foundation terraces and the 'Bes-chambers' survive (fig.1). These rough stone chambers were built on the lower terrace against the south wall of the main enclosure. They contained painted mud-statue groups of Bes flanked by nude female figures, set against the walls (pl.37a).[11]

From the southern complex, a gateway of Ptolemy V led through to the central temple (fig.1). This seems likely to have been the main temple of Anubis, since a block showing the same king worshipping this god was found within it (Jeffreys and Smith 1988, 3, 61, no. 76/26). A limestone fragment and a set of foundation plaques show that the central temple was founded in the reign of Amasis (Jeffreys and Smith 1988, 62, no. 77/u331; 64, no. 77/142). It must have been a building of considerable size and splendour to judge from the massive terraced foundations, which allow a partial reconstruction (fig.2). Through it led a central sacred way mounting the terraces by stairs to a granite gateway in front of the sanctuaries on the cliff top.[12] Behind the temple, but still within the enclosure wall, was a small settlement, possibly used by priests and suppliants (Jeffreys and Smith 1988, 25-30, 38-9; see below).

Of the northern temple, little subsists except foundations, but its existence is confirmed inferentially by the presence of a recently exposed gateway in the west enclosure wall upon its axis.[13] Some 250 metres to the north of the north enclosure wall of Anubieion are the entrances in the cliff face leading to the galleries where the mummified dogs were buried (fig.3).[14] Dogs were also buried, like the cats, in tomb-shafts and tomb-chambers within the temple enclosure and outside it to the north-west.[15]

The Sarapieion Way ascended the cliff between the central and northern temples of Anubieion by a series of stairways mounting from terrace to terrace, then crossed the level sanctuary area on the cliff top to a gate in the west enclosure wall (Smith 1981). From here, it ran westwards across the necropolis to Sarapieion. Within the Anubieion enclosure, the Sarapieion Way was apparently unadorned, but beyond the west gate of the precinct, it was lined with sphinxes, probably representing Nakhtnebof (Nectanebo I) (Lauer and Picard 1955, 24).

Thus in the Late Period, the Saqqara escarpment approximately opposite the 'Palace of Apries' in Memphis was occupied by two great Sacred Animal precincts, comprising at least four terraced temples, which would probably have presented a visual effect similar in essence to the New Kingdom

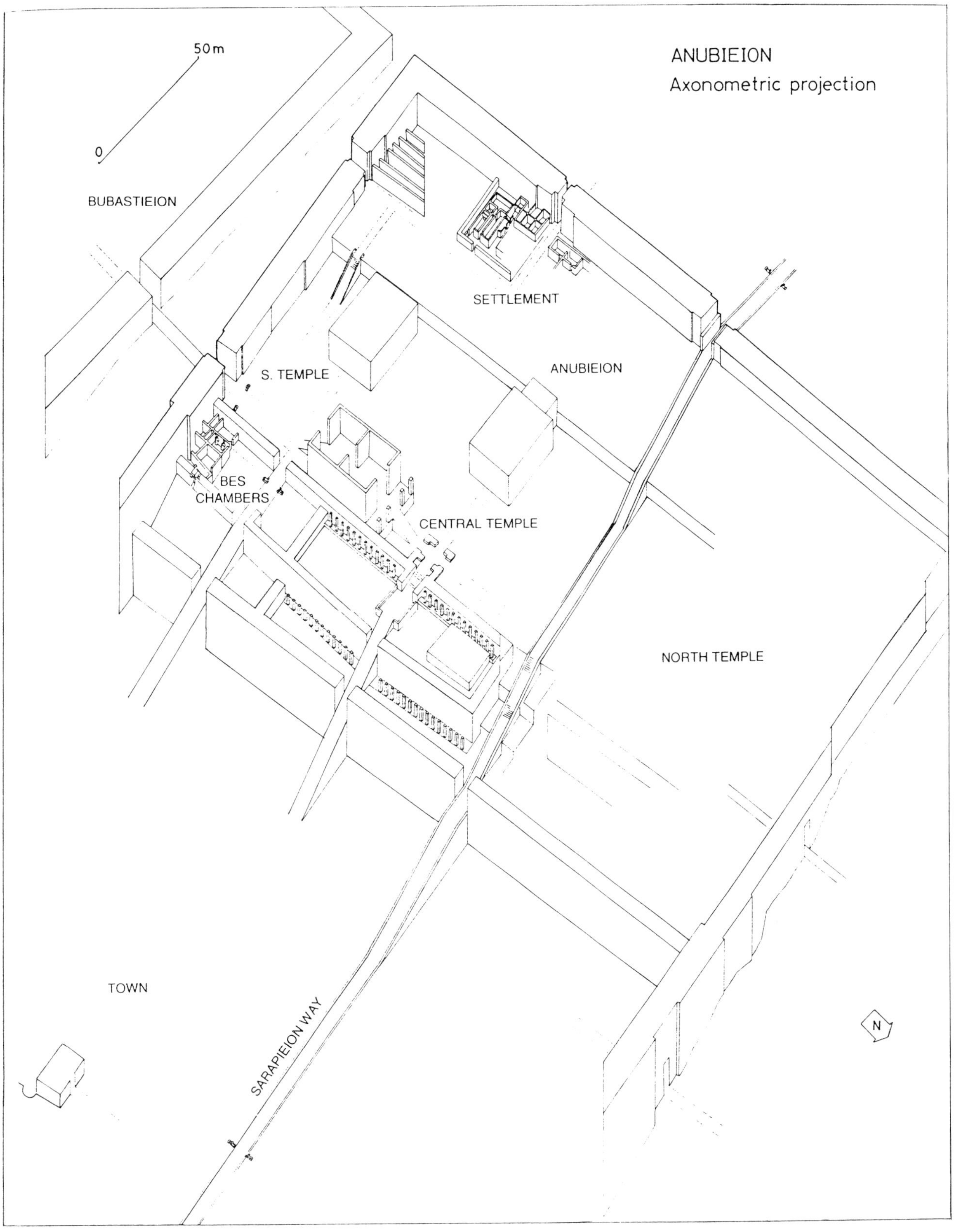

Fig.2 Axonometric projection of the Anubieion precinct restored, showing entrance from Bubastieion, south temple with 'Bes-chambers', central temple with settlement behind, and the Sarapieion Way. After the original by David Jeffreys.

temple of Hatshepsut at Deir el-Bahri, though with more monumental gates.[16]

C: Temples along the Abusir-Sarapieion route

A gently sloping desert valley running to the west of the bluff of North Saqqara from the modern village of Abusir to Sarapieion afforded another means of access to the necropolis (fig.3). The importance of this route in Archaic times has recently been emphasized (Jeffreys and Tavares 1994; Mathieson and Tavares 1993); in the Late Period it was no different. Indeed, now that it is established that the Sarapieion Way and other temple causeways ascended the escarpment by stairways, it is virtually certain that the immensely weighty Apis and Mother of Apis sarcophagi of granite and basalt must always have been dragged up via this valley (Smith 1981, 338-9). That there was a road up the centre of the valley to the north gate of Sarapieion was shown by Mariette, who traced its course for a considerable distance outside that gate from finds of bronzes.[17]

Along the escarpment on the east side of the desert valley were ranged the temples, shrines and catacombs of the Sacred Animal cults of Hepnebes (fig.3),[18] which appears to have been the sacred name of the area north of Sarapieion.[19] Sacred ways ran from the main axial valley road up to these cult complexes, the northernmost of which, as far as is known, was that attached to the North Ibis catacomb. The entrance to this catacomb is on the north side of the Abusir promontory (fig.3). Fronting the vaulted *dromos* was a rectangular courtyard ornamented with trees and shrubs, against the east wall of which stood two mud-statues of Bes, similar to those in Anubieion.[20] Analogy with the South Ibis complex (see below) suggests that at least a chapel was also present.

South of the Abusir promontory, a sacred way led off the axial valley road eastwards to a temple enclosure built on a terrace against the cliff-face and approached by a sloping brick ramp (fig.4; pl.37b). Although modest in size (95 x 56m.) compared with the Bubastieion and Anubieion enclosures, this precinct nevertheless comprised three major animal catacombs and the several shrines that served them. In the centre of the precinct was a temple which appears to have been dedicated jointly to Osiris-Apis and Isis, Mother of Apis.[21] It comprised an entrance pylon and a courtyard, from which a miniature double-stairway led through a kiosk and a second pylon to the sanctuary (pl.37c). In the rear wall of the sanctuary there was a statue niche and in the south wall there was provision for a central naos (pl.37d). A blind corridor allowed access to the rear of the latter (fig.4), which perhaps contained a divine image. The temple was constructed of brick and lined with limestone, probably bearing reliefs of Nakhthorheb.[22]

Immediately to the north of this central temple, a paved way and a broad limestone double stairway (pl.38a) led to a stone gateway, behind which was a simple rectangular brick shrine, perhaps also dedicated to the Mother of Apis. The catacomb of the cows was situated immediately north of the temple precinct, and was in use from 393-41 BC (Smith 1972); for at least the latter part of this period, it was surrounded by its own enclosure (fig.4).[23]

South of the central temple, a second broad paved way and double stairway (pl.38b) led via a monumental stone gateway to another rectangular brick chapel (pl.38c). Immediately to the south of this, a parallel sacred way led through a gate and walled *dromos* to the cavetto gate of the Baboon catacomb in the rock escarpment (pl.38c). Between these two sacred ways was a tiny chapel with ornamental façade (pls.38c-d) constructed within the thickness of the east precinct wall; internally it was lined with masonry and provided with a central dais, on which one of the two fine limestone baboon statues found in the catacomb may have sat (Emery 1970, pl.XIV, 2-3). Adjoining it was a cavity, also in the thickness of the wall, with access at the rear for a priest. In front of this, a large columned kiosk bearing cornice blocks of Nakhthorheb[24] has been conjecturally restored. The whole of this complex to the south of the central temple was probably dedicated to Osiris the Baboon.[25]

From the southern Baboon sacred way, a narrow paved path led off southwards to a small double stairway in the south-east corner of the main precinct. This gave access to a chapel, now lost, which presumably served the Falcon catacomb. The winding rock-cut stairs to the latter led down immediately to the west of this chapel. West of these again, a courtyard and light stone screen wall completed the Falcon complex.[26]

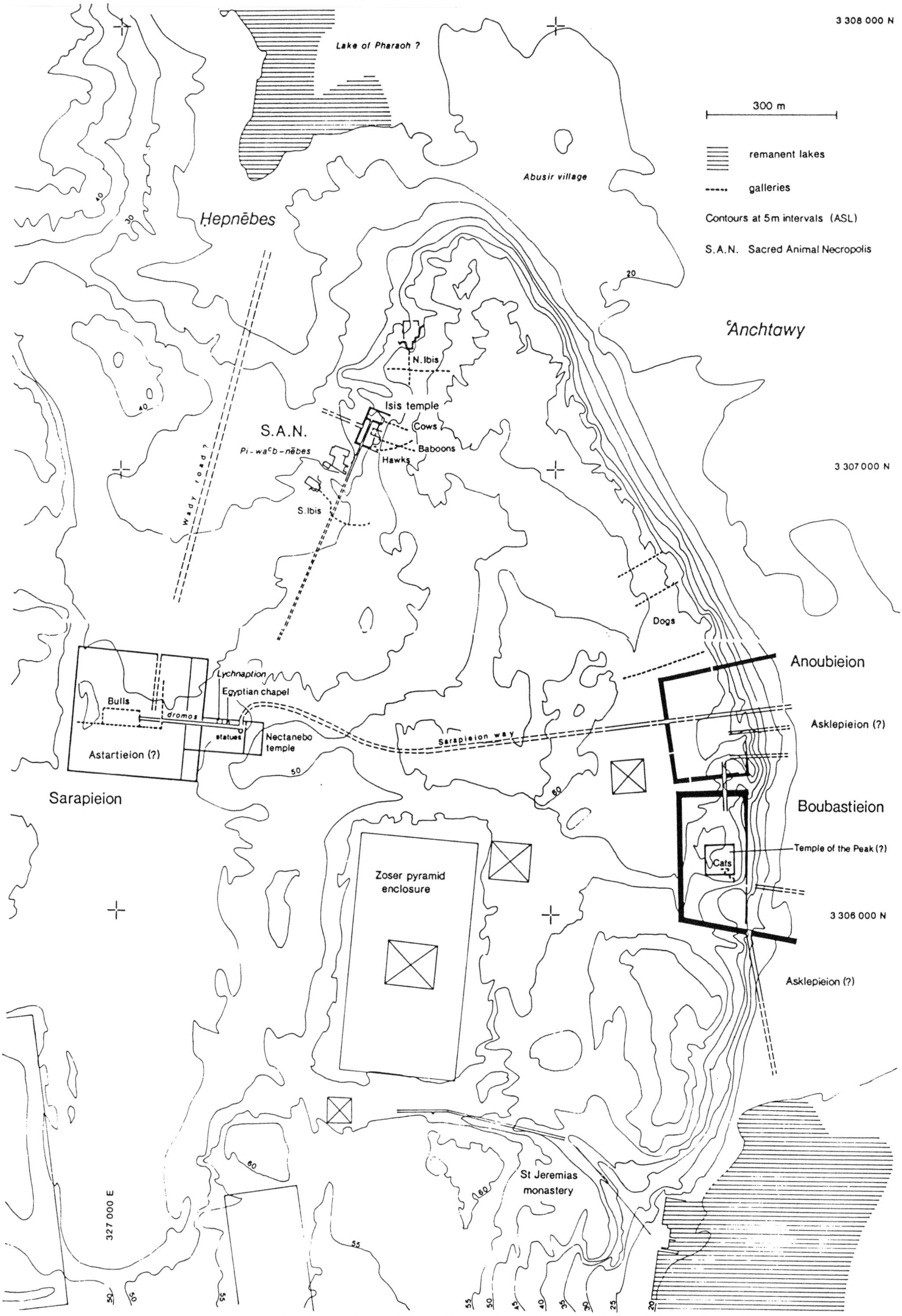

Fig.3 Map of North Saqqâra showing the precincts of Bubastieion, Anubieion, Hepnebes and Sarapieion, with the probable routes between them (courtesy Dorothy Thompson).

Across the middle of the main temple precinct, in front of the shrines described above, led a broad N-S sacred way, west of which was a large terrace, perhaps intended for further courts or structures apparently never completed (fig.4 and pl.39a). This sacred way left the precinct by a major gate in the south wall. Immediately west of this sacred way and south of the main temple precinct described above is the area shown on fig.4 as Sector 7. This area was surrounded by a stone enclosure wall and comprises several foundations of buildings, which were accessible from the sacred way.[27]

The northern portion of Sector 7 was perhaps occupied by a temple consisting of a courtyard, pylon and sanctuary. In view of the large quantities of birds' eggs found in the courtyard, Ray suggested that it be identified as 'the courtyard of the Ibis and the Falcon', mentioned in several of the ostraca from the archive of the scribe Hor.[28] This hypothetical temple may therefore have been a joint shrine of Osiris the Ibis and Osiris the Falcon, as the cults are known to have been closely associated.[29] In the centre of Sector 7 is a brick platform, which probably also bore a shrine; in debris apparently tipped from it into the aforementioned courtyard was found a range of phallic figurines and Bes figures.[30] The south-west corner of Sector 7 was occupied by a rectangular building, which appears to combine both cultic and domestic features and may have been used in connection with temple incubation.[31] Exceptionally, it was entered from the east down a sloping causeway and stairs. These were flanked on the north by domestic buildings on a higher terrace, some of which were overbuilt by a brick foundation platform, perhaps for a shrine.

The above precincts thus comprised at least eight temples, shrines and chapels of various sizes, with all their associated pylons, kiosks and monumental stone gateways. Seen from the main axial way in the desert valley below, the entire complex must have had an appearance which can now perhaps best be visualized in terms of the shrines on the island of Philae, different as the terrain and location is. Below the precincts, on the east slope of the valley, fragmentary evidence was recovered of domestic brick buildings, probably reflecting the existence of a community of priests, workmen, embalmers and craftsmen.[32]

Immediately to the south of Sector 7, a further stone paved sacred way led off to the south-east from the main axial way in the valley through a courtyard planted with trees, to a brick-vaulted, stepped *dromos* leading down to the South Ibis catacomb (Martin 1981, 7-16). Adjoining the *dromos* was a chapel, from the vicinity of which was recovered the 2nd century BC archive of the scribe Hor, which proves this to have been the focal point of the funerary cult of the ibises at that time (Ray 1976, 117-24, 136-46).[33]

South of this point, the eastern scarp of the desert valley falls away. At a distance of about 250m. south-west of the South Ibis entrance there exists a rectilinear stone structure, conceivably to be interpreted as the foundation or enclosure for a shrine complex.[34] This building and certain of those in Sector 7 may be connected with animal cults which are attested in texts but not yet located. One is that of *ḏdt b3 ʿnpt*, the Ram of Mendes, who is mentioned in a Mother of Apis stela as having a cult in the necropolis.[35] Ram-horns have been found in Sector 7, and in the valley, suggesting the presence of a nearby catacomb.[36] The second is that of *p3 gm,* shown by Ray to have been a young male bovid (Ray 1972a, 308-10). The 'House of Rest' (i.e. the burial-place) of this animal was 'in the House-of-Osiris-Apis (*pr-wsỉr-ḥp* i.e. Sarapieion) on the north side of the *ḫft-ḥr* (*dromos*) of Osiris-Apis the great god'. In the reign of Ptolemy V it belonged, with all its appurtenances and income, to a family of priests, who bore the titles 'priest of the children of the Apis' and 'priest of the *sbt(t)* of Isis'.[37] From the first of these titles it has been very tentatively inferred that the 'Gem' was a calf of the Apis bull. The burial-place, whether a single vault or a catacomb,[38] could have been anywhere north of the Sarapieion *dromos*, for the term *pr-wsỉr-ḥp* refers not only to the Sarapieion temple, but to the surrounding area of the temple estate. If 'the *sbt(t)*- compound of Isis' is to be identified with the precinct of Isis, Mother of Apis, the linkage of the two priesthoods in the hands of one family may suggest that the resting-place of the 'Gem' was in the same vicinity. It is further stated that human burial-places cut in the western mountain lay to its west,[39] which implies that it lay on the west side of the road up the centre of the Abusir valley; thus it was, perhaps, in the area marked 'Tombe des boeufs' on de Morgan's map.[40] The third is speculative; 'the burial and nourishment of the lions' are mentioned in a broken context in a Greek papyrus found near Sarapieion.[41] The lioness goddess Sakhmet, consort of Ptah, is known to have had a compound in the Sarapieion area,[42] but whether the

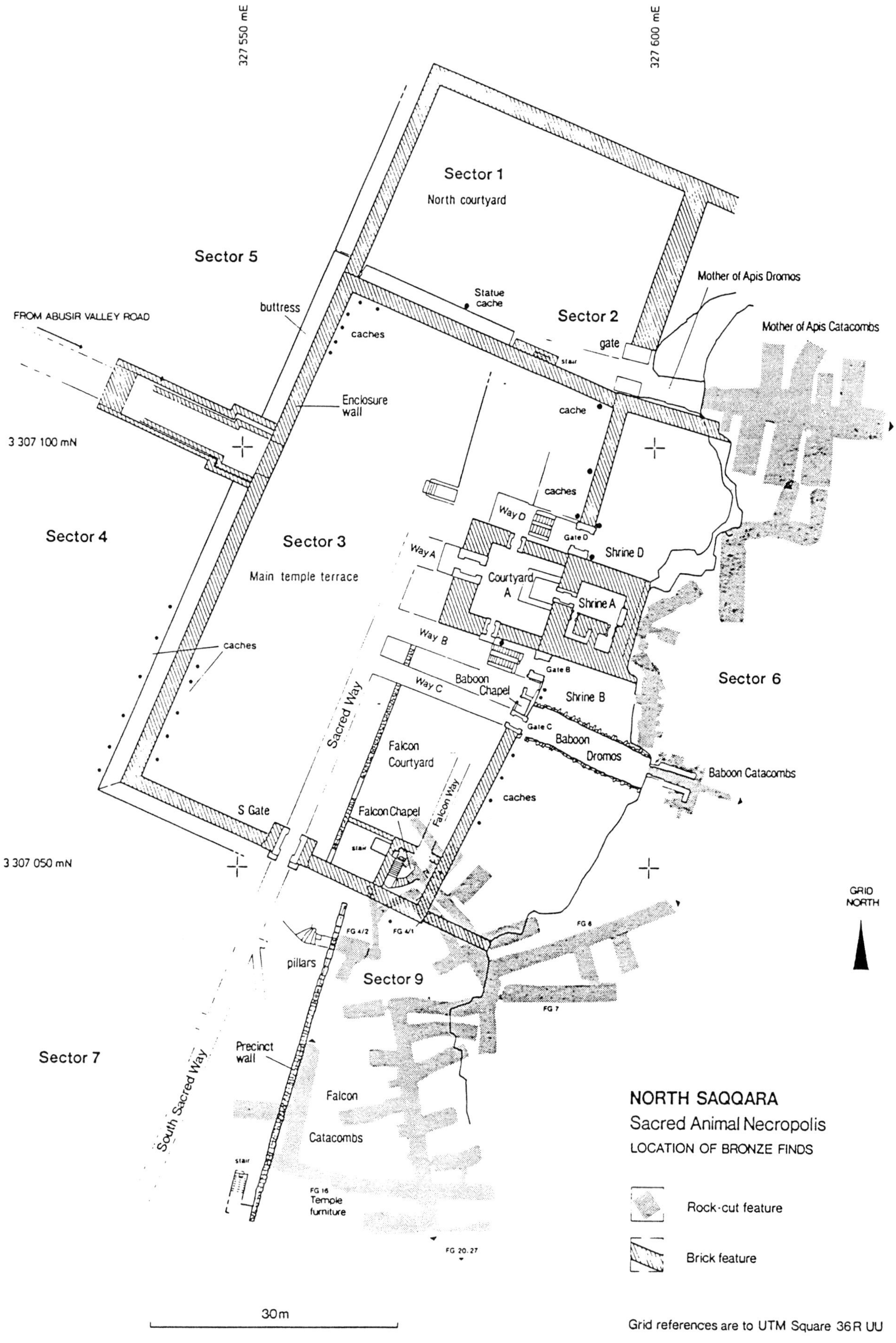

Fig.4 The Sacred Animal Necropolis precinct at Hepnebes, showing the relationship of the Mother of Apis, Baboon and Falcon catacombs with the temple-shrines, gates and sacred ways (site-numbers and caches also shown). After the original by David Jeffreys.

existence of a catacomb for the burial of lions and a cult at Saqqara should be assumed on such frail evidence is uncertain. An unsolved problem is presented by a reference in the same document to buildings in the 'House of Osiris-[ ]' on the south side of the *dromos* of the same deity, whose name has not been securely read;[43] this precinct, possibly also belonging to some Sacred Animal, must have been close to Sarapieion.

Modern sub-surface sensing and field observation tend to confirm the plans by Mariette and de Rhoné of the Sarapieion temple area.[44] The main temple, probably a structure rivalling Edfu in size, was surrounded on its north, east and south sides by a structure of stone pillars bearing an entablature, which enclosed an area of c.300m.sq., with pylon gates approximately at the centre of the north and east sides.[45] The axial way up the Abusir valley led to the north gate, through which the bull sarcophagi would have been dragged to the top of the sloping ramp down to the catacomb. Through the east pylon, which was flanked by the lions of Nakhtnebof, led the Sarapieion *dromos*, at the eastern end of which was the temple built by Nakhthorheb (fig.3). In the Ptolemaic Period, this *dromos* was lined with chapels and decorated with statuary reflecting Greek mythology. At the Nakhthorheb temple, the Sarapieion Way entered the *dromos* from the north, after curving round a bluff of rock on its course from the west gate of Anubieion (see above). A hemicycle of statues of philosophers was placed on the south side of the *dromos* opposite this point at the beginning of the Ptolemaic Period (fig.3).[46] The sacred way leading southwards from the Sacred Animal precincts at Hepnebes (see above) may also have terminated here.[47]

Thus, by the Thirtieth Dynasty at latest, the 'House-of-Osiris-Apis' (Sarapieion) was not simply a name for the catacomb of the Apis bulls and the *dromos* and temple that served it. Like Anubieion and Bubastieion, it comprised a large variety of temple-shrines, some of them probably of considerable size and beauty, together with the catacombs which they served, and these were spread the length of the valley from the Sarapieion main temple enclosure almost to the modern village of Abusir. To certain of these complexes were attached their own village settlements, comprising administrative quarters, workshops and the houses of the resident priests, embalmers and temple servants, together perhaps with accommodation for suppliants and visitors.[48] Indeed, it may be suspected that by the time of Nakhthorheb these were aggregating into the populous town of Sarapieion which the Ptolemaic documents attest.[49] This was indeed a change in the utilization and appearance of the Memphite necropolis from New Kingdom times.

D: The administration and organization of the Sacred Animal cults

The summary descriptions given above of Bubastieion, Anubieion, Sarapieion and the Sacred Animal precincts at Hepnebes highlight the fact that by the Thirtieth Dynasty at the latest these temple towns were not isolated cult centres, but important and integral parts of the city of Memphis. As the nuclei of the thriving necropolis district, they displayed many facets of life and supported large and varied populations. Thompson (1988, 190-265) has presented the Ptolemaic evidence for Sarapieion, Bubastieion and Anubieion, and given a succinct but vivid description of life in these temple towns during that period. Here we review summarily the evidence for the Sacred Animal precincts at Hepnebes, the large bodies of inscriptions and objects from which belong in part to the preceding period. Much of the material remains unpublished, but should eventually throw a flood of light on the demography, character and usage of this unusual site.[50]

The earliest dated inscription that we have from the site pertaining to its use as a necropolis and cult centre for Sacred Animals is a stela (72/1 + N; Smith 1992, 205-7, 221) recording a series of Mother of Apis burials, the earliest of them in year 37 of Amasis (533 BC). The last recorded Mother of Apis burial dates to 41 BC (70/52 and 70/19; Smith 1992, 216, 224), and though usage of the catacombs and temples may have continued into the Roman era, it is clear that by the time a Christian community occupied the site not earlier than the fourth century AD, the temple buildings had already been fairly comprehensively destroyed. The usage of the Sacred Animal precincts at Hepnebes thus covers the period at least from the late Twenty-sixth Dynasty to the end of the Ptolemaic era. However, the main development and expansion of the site took place during the last interval of independent rule that separated the First and Second Persian Periods (404-343 BC). This is confirmed by building history and by cartouches of Nakhthorheb on architectural elements from the sanctuaries (see above). The documents found also support this. The Aramaic papyri belong to the fifth to fourth centuries BC (Segal 1983, 3-4); the demotic papyri probably range over a wider time span from the late sixth or early fifth centuries to the third century BC, the bulk of them being likely to be of fourth century BC date. Although the objects are more difficult to date precisely, some sculptures found in various deposits date to the Saite-Persian Period (Hastings, in press), while a good proportion of the many bronze and wood figures of deities seem likely to belong to the pre-Ptolemaic Period.

Over seven hundred demotic papyrus documents and fragments of a very varied nature were recovered from the Sacred Animal precincts at Hepnebes, together with over one hundred miscellaneous ostraca. Most remain unpublished, and only a small proportion of them have so far been fully deciphered and analysed. Of these, however, several appear to have some bearing on the organization and operation of the cults at the site in the fourth century BC. This group includes oracle questions and pleas addressed to deities, letters, accounts, receipts and ration-lists. The oracle-questions and pleas are discussed further in Section E below. The evidence of the letters and administrative documents, together with that of the Mother of Apis stelae, is summarized here, but only in a preliminary and very tentative fashion, both because of the frustrating ambiguity of some of the texts, and because no integrated study of the material can be made prior to full publication.

The presence of a *lesonis (mr-šn)* , prophets *(ḥm.w-nṯr)* , priests *(wᶜb.w)* and *pastophoroi (wn.w)* in these papyrus documents, and of 'divine fathers' *(ỉt.w-nṯr)* in the Mother of Apis stelae (Smith 1992, 209-13) suggests that the organization of the Sacred Animal cults at Hepnebes (and probably, by extension, of the entire Saqqara necropolis), was no different from that of Late Period temples in general, except in so far as their structure had to allow, in addition, for the mummification and burial of the Sacred Animals. This last fact accounts for the presence of such titles as the 'servants of the Ibises' and the 'servants of the Falcons'. These titles recur in the second century BC archive of the scribe Hor (Ray 1976, 182, no. 24, see also n.51 below). This, together with the fact that the titles of the masons who excavated the vaults of the Mother of Apis cows continued in use from the fourth century BC to the end of the Ptolemaic Period, indicates that the organization of the Sacred Animal cults in the 2nd century BC probably differed little from what it had been two centuries earlier. Ray's account of the administration of the Ibis cult in the time of the scribe Hor (1976, 136-46) may, therefore, reasonably be applied to both periods.

The Mother of Apis stelae make it clear that during the fourth century BC the Mother of Apis cows lived within the Ptah temple precinct at Memphis in a 'House' next to that of the Apis bull, just as they did in Ptolemaic times, and that senior priests of Ptah were in charge of the obsequies of both animals (Smith 1992, 212; cf. Vercoutter 1962, 127-8). Evidence from the archive of Hor shows that in the second century BC authority over the Ibis cult at Hepnebes was vested in the priests of Ptah at Memphis (Ray 1976, 136-46). It is not unreasonable then to conclude that all the Sacred Animal cults of Sarapieion came under their authority (Kessler 1989, 93-6).

More problematic is the question of whether the Sacred Animal cults had differentiated rituals, or whether there was a unified body of cult practice which applied to them all. Kessler (1989, 253-90) regards all these cults as linked to the divine apotheosis of the King, and would see them as essentially unified. It is too early to judge whether the documentary evidence from Hepnebes confirms this. There was certainly a close association between the Ibis and Falcon cults at the site,[51] and some priests may have been attached to more than one cult.[52] But neither of these facts can necessarily be taken to indicate that the cults concerned shared common ritual or cult practices.

Although they are at present speculative, there are grounds for suggesting that there may have been a distinction, with regard to the organization and administration of the Sacred Animal cults, between the cultic and civil authorities, each body having its own spheres of responsibility and duties. The documents also provide grounds for suspecting that administrative divisions did not necessarily correspond to cultic ones, and that, for certain purposes at least, the Sacred Animal cults of Saqqara were treated by the civil authorities as an entity (cf. Yoyotte 1972, 6-10; Kessler 1989, 149-50).

E: The role of the temples within the community

In the Late Period, the whole phenomenon of Sacred Animal cults burgeoned in terms of patronage and popularity. Why this proliferation and growth in importance occurred under the Saite and fourth century BC Pharaohs is uncertain, but a plausible and widely accepted suggestion links the expansion to the history of Egypt during this time and sees it as a manifestation of resurgent Egyptian national pride and cultural consciousness after periods of foreign government. There can be little doubt that the expansion of Sacred Animal cults as a focus for such feelings was consciously and deliberately undertaken by the state, as Kessler (1989, *passim*) has argued. But causation in history is rarely simple, and the evidence outlined below suggests that, in addition to the premeditated state element, a spontaneous outflow of personal devotion, at every level of society, was also involved.

Dedicatory inscriptions have been discovered at Hepnebes, both in the catacombs and in the temple precinct. In the Mother of Apis catacomb, most of the inscriptions of the priests who authorized the burials are lost, but many of the stelae of the masons survive.[53] The principal purpose of both classes was to ensure that the names of the owners and those of their families should endure for ever before Apis-Osiris and Isis, Mother of Apis. The masons regularly call down the blessing of the gods of Hepnebes upon anyone who reads the stelae, and the destruction at their hand of anyone who breaks or defaces them. In stela 70/12 the mason Kha'ef recounts that he searched for the stelae of the masons belonging to his family, and, when he did not find them, had a new stela installed 'so as not to allow their names to perish from the earth' (Smith 1992, 218-19). This emphasizes the fact that in the Late Period the Egyptians believed their salvation to depend, not on grave-goods or mortuary cults, but upon the personal favour of the deity to whom they were devoted; they therefore sought to be buried and to have a memorial as close as possible to the god. The same desire is evident in the inscriptions in the Baboon and Falcon catacombs. A typical example from the entrance to Gallery 14 in the Falcon catacomb reads: 'May the gods who rest here give life to Paptah, son of Djeho'. In these graffiti too the names of members of the dedicator's family are often listed.

Some of the bronze temple furniture used in the cults at the sanctuaries was buried in the Falcon catacomb, mainly in Cache 9 in Gallery 16 (Emery 1971, 6-8), presumably because, once dedicated, it was considered sanctified (pl.39b). A number of these items also bore dedications by private individuals, of which a typical example is: 'Thoth, the great god, and Horus the Falcon, the great god, who are in Hepnebes, give life to Hor, son of Petenefertum, whose mother is Tawa' (Insley Green 1987, 56-7, No.129, a bronze jar). The offering-tables bearing hieroglyphic or demotic dedications to Osiris-Apis and Isis, Mother of Apis, likewise ask these deities to give life to or preserve the names of those who donated them.

The salient point about all these dedications, as with those upon the bronze, wood and faience statuettes of deities discussed below, is that in the majority of instances the dedicators do not appear to have held any public or priestly office of importance. Quite often they give no title at all, and where they do give one, it usually relates to the Sacred Animal deities, e.g. 'the mason of Apis-Osiris and the Mother of Apis, the servant of the living Apis' (Mother of Apis stela 70/30, Nakhtnebof, year 7), 'the servant of Osiris the Baboon' or 'the servant of Osiris the Ibis'. Thus Kessler's idea that cult offerings were made to the Sacred Animals principally by highly placed persons at festivals to show their loyalty to the royal cult (Kessler 1989, 143-9, 299-303) does not appear to be borne out by an important proportion of the available evidence.

Written evidence from Hepnebes attests the practices of incubation and dream invocation.[54] As Ray (1976, 130) observes, there is no reason to suppose for earlier periods that dreams were deliberately provoked in this way, and while accepting that this may be due to the inadequacy of early material, he concludes that the appearance of such practices could correspond to changes in Egyptian thought processes. Such changes, which can be identified as taking place from the New Kingdom onwards, resulted in new definitions for the concept of Ma'at and new strains of religious expression, such as the appearance of the movement often referred to as "Personal Piety".[55] This movement was characterized by direct appeals from individuals to gods in times of sickness, uncertainty, trouble, anguish, legal jeopardy etc. Sacred Animal cults were, it seems, totally suited to such a direct approach on the part of the worshipper. The great gods, immanent in their Sacred Animals, could be approached via the latter, and sentiments analogous to those found in the "Personal Piety" texts recur again and again in the documents from Hepnebes. In addition to dream texts, invocations and spells, there are oracle questions, pleas, requests and complaints addressed to deities.[56] These appeals are often touchingly simple and direct. For example, Osiris-Apis and 'the goddess' are asked whether Ahtefnakhte should sell an ass and its mother (S.71/2.DP.20); Isis, Mother of Apis, is asked by the woman Tiatenese whether 'the wrath of the god is in him?' (S.H5.DP.372); an unnamed deity, probably Osiris-Apis, is requested by an unnamed person to give a decision on whether a Syrian lady should make a journey to Syria (S.H5.DP.43). A man calling himself 'the servant Pshenese' prays for Isis, Mother of Apis, to bring down curses upon a woman before various named persons and 'all her neighbours and companions' (S.H5.DP.195+256+276); another amuletic document is designed to ensure the benevolence of the same goddess to a particular individual (S.H5.DP.130). A plea dated in the reign of Teos of the Thirtieth Dynasty asks Osiris-Apis to intervene because the servants of the divine Imhotep, son of Ptah, are being wrongfully seized (S.71/2.DP.146).

These appeals show the Sacred Animal cults to have been a focus of popular belief, with a popular input and usage without which they could not have functioned as they did. Kessler's thesis that these cults were founded by the state and that they were closely linked to the cult of the divinized king may well be correct. He further infers, however, that popular belief and usage had no significant role to play (Kessler 1989, 291-8); the oracle questions and pleas to the gods from Hepnebes seem to require a more balanced view.

If we allow that the nature of some of the written material from Hepnebes may reflect changes in Egyptian thought processes and religious expression, the millions of mummified ibises and falcons stacked in the catacombs there may, perhaps, be interpreted in similar terms.[57] If Sacred Animals were a natural medium for direct appeals to, and personal interaction with the divine, such a direct approach might have involved a desire, or need, on the part of the worshipper to express the personal relationship between himself and his god in a tangible way. The dedication of a mummified ibis or falcon would have given palpable, concrete expression to the bond between man and god[58]

The same reasoning can perhaps be applied to other categories of 'votive' material recovered from the site. These include figures of deities of bronze, wood and faience,[59] and occasionally the shrines that contained them; amulets and amuletic figurines; *erotica* and 'anatomical donaria'. Such objects were found both lying scattered in surface debris, and, more frequently, deliberately buried in numerous caches. While the contexts of the scattered material preclude any deductions about its original function,[60] many of the caches, because of their physical location, obviously have a direct link with the Sacred Animal precincts;[61] in a few cases, their relation to site structures suggests that they are foundation or dedication deposits.[62]

The statuettes of deities,[63] in particular the bronzes, frequently bear the name of a dedicator in a votive inscription on the base (pl.39c). As with the inscribed offering tables and temple furniture from Falcon Gallery 16 mentioned above, the donors named in these inscriptions do not appear to include any high-ranking civil or military officials. Unless it is argued that these figures were all originally used in other contexts, and simply brought to the Sacred Animal precincts for safe deposition,[64] the presence of such inscribed pieces should indicate that they were offered by ordinary citizens to the gods of Hepnebes.[65] The wooden and bronze statuettes with internal cavities or hollow bases (pl.39d), of which there are a number, seem peculiarly suitable for the conveyance of pleas to the gods.

Popular use of the Sacred Animal sanctuaries is also implied by the presence at the site of the alleged 'anatomical donaria'.[66] These groups of plaster casts, of Ptolemaic date, representing various parts of the human anatomy,[67] were, in Emery's view, medical votive offerings left by pilgrims, either to induce the gods to grant cures, or as tokens of gratitude for healing (Emery 1970, 10-1). It should be noted here that Emery always remained convinced that the area of the Sacred Animal precincts at Hepnebes was connected with Imhotep, and that it was, in all probability, the long-lost Asklepieion. Although this identification now seems very unlikely (Smith 1984, 424 and nn.101-2), there are, nevertheless, other indications that the cults at the site were used by people seeking cures and medical help. Ray (1976, 134) points out that an extended use of divine visitations, well attested from the Ptolemaic Period in Greek sources, is that found in the healing of the sick. The archive of Hor gives confirmation in demotic that such practices were observed at North Saqqara. Moreover, papyri recovered from Sector 7 include sections and fragments of books of spells and medical recipes (Smith in Martin 1981, 57, 62), and an accounts list recovered from the site makes frequent mention of "the sick". Their inclusion in such a document implies the existence of a sanatorium or of incubation chambers wherein such people might stay, waiting for a cure or for divine instruction. It also suggests that, in some cases at least, the stay may have been a prolonged one.

The phallic figurines and Bes figures recovered from Sector 7 (see above) clearly had important religious significance,[68] and prompt comparison with similar figures found at Anubieion (Quibell 1907, 12-14; Jeffreys and Smith 1988, 33-5, 41, 63). The Anubieion figures came both from an area behind the central temple, which the excavators suggest may have constituted the quarters used by suppliants incubating in the temples in order to receive divinely inspired dreams (Jeffreys and Smith 1988, 38), and from the 'Bes-chambers' (see above). Various suggestions about the exact nature of these rooms have been made (Stricker 1943, 101-37; de Meulenaere 1960, 105-7; Thompson 1988, 25-6), but they too may have been incubation chambers where pilgrims came to dream divinely inspired dreams prophesying fecundity. Whether similar rooms once existed at other Sacred Animal sites is unknown, but it is not improbable when we consider that clay wall reliefs of Bes were present also in the courtyard fronting the North Ibis catacomb at Hepnebes (see above) and at Sarapieion (Mariette and Maspero 1882, 17; Lauer and Picard 1955, 8-9).

When the Pharaohs of the Twenty-sixth and Thirtieth Dynasties endowed the Sacred Animal cults at Memphis and Saqqara, they certainly had reasons of state for doing so. These may well have included, as Kessler (1989) has argued, an association with the cults of divinized rulers. The evidence outlined above does, however, suggest that, from their inception, the temple precincts and associated towns at Saqqara played an important role in the daily lives of the people of Memphis.[69]

Notes

1. For a full list of Sacred Animal cemeteries, see Kessler 1989, 17-29.
2. For reports of the principal projects see Emery 1965-67, 1969-71; Martin 1973, 1974, 1981; Smith 1976; Smith and Jeffreys 1977, 1978, 1979-81; Jeffreys and Smith 1988; Zivie 1990; Mathieson and Tavares 1993.
3. Ray 1976, 117-66 is specific to the Ibis-cult; Thompson 1988, 21-31, 155-265, 284-96 and Kessler 1989, 56-150 cover all the Saqqara Sacred Animal cults.
4. The Bubastieion precinct has been identified, almost certainly correctly, as that of 'Bastet, Lady of Ankh-tawy' (Kessler 1989, 105-6), known to have existed from the New Kingdom at least (Sandman-Holmberg 1946, 214-15). A priest named Amasis bore the titles 'prophet of the statues of the son of Re` Amasis at the temple of Bastet, Lady of Ankh-tawy, prophet of "the Peak" of Ankh-tawy, prophet of Bastet, mistress of Ankh-tawy' (Berlin 14765; de Meulenaere 1960, 103-4), thus associating the temple of Bastet, Lady of Ankh-tawy, with "the Peak" (see below, note 16).
5. No reference to the excavation of these buildings has been identified.
6. Personal communication, D G Jeffreys.
7. Personal communication, A Tavares and A-P Zivie.
8. Personal communication, D G Jeffreys.
9. For discussion of the complex evidence from documents see Wilcken 1927, 9-18; Stricker 1943, 101-37; de Meulenaere 1960, 92-107; Pierce 1972, 40-1 (cf. Pestman 1977, I, 39, n.27); de Cenival 1972, 11-15; Kessler 1989, 106-7; Thompson 1988, 26-7, who also gives a full list of the documents forming the archives of the undertakers and choachytes, 280-2.
10. Titles of 'priests of the statues of King Nakhthorheb' associate *pr-hn-inpw* with *pr-wsir-m-rwḏ-iswt* 'the domain of Osiris at Rud-isut' and *pr-wsir-ḥp* 'the domain of Osiris-Apis' (de Meulenaere 1960, 94-5 and 103-4). Possibly therefore one of the temples in the enclosure was that of Osiris at Rud-isut, as de Meulenaere argues (note also Insley Green 1987, 30-1, no. 58); but 'the domain of Osiris-Apis' must surely refer to Sarapieion, so that the priesthoods seem more likely to have been held in three separate temple complexes at Saqqara.
11. Quibell 1907, 12-14, 28-9; see also Derchain in Martin 1981, 166-70. Stricker (1943, 101-37)

argued for these being part of Asklepieion, the temple precinct of Imhotep-Asklepios, which he suggested on grounds of Arabic sources concerning the prison of Joseph had occupied this enclosure. The location of Asklepieion is bound up with that of the temple of "the Peak", see note 16 below.
12. The form of these sanctuaries, now buried under a modern village, was shown slightly differently in the plans of Mariette (1882), de Morgan (1897), and de Rhoné (reproduced in Lauer and Picard 1955, pl.25), but seems to indicate, rather exceptionally, a temple oriented N-S with sanctuaries at the southern end; there was, however, also room for lesser shrines (see Jeffreys and Smith 1988, 52-8).
13. Excavated by Dr. Zahie Hawass, information from Prof. Naguib Kanawati.
14. Unfortunately, this catacomb was completely cleared, apparently in the late nineteenth century, without any published record (for plan see de Morgan 1897, pl.10).
15. Mariette and Maspero 1882, 75 with n.1; Sa'id el-Fikey, personal communication.
16. From Late Period documents, it is clear that Asklepieion, the temple complex of Imhotep-Asklepios, the god of healing, was associated closely with Bubastieion and Anubieion, and also with 'the temple of "the Peak"'. Whether the temple of "the Peak" was identical either with Bubastieion or Anubieion must remain rather uncertain on present evidence; but it formed part of Ankh-tawy, and had its own enclosure; de Meulenaere 1960, 104, document z (reign of Amasis) refers to a courtyard situated 'on "the Peak" of Ankh-tawy, outside (?) the enclosure of "the Peak", on the south side of the *dromos* of Imhotep'. De Meulenaere argued that the enclosure of "the Peak" should be identified with Anubieion, and on the basis of the passage quoted above suggested that Asklepieion should be placed north of Anubieion rather than south of Bubastieion, where Wilcken (1927, 38-41) placed it. The fact that the temple of Bastet lay on the bluff at the highest part of the escarpment might suggest that "the Peak" was within or lay close to Bubastieion, as Thompson (1988, 24) has concluded. Certainly it contained a treasury and windows of appearances, together with cults and sanctuaries, not only of Hathor, and of 'King Nakhthorheb the Falcon', but also of Horus the Falcon and Thoth the Ibis (de Meulenaere 1960, 94-5). The presence of the latter deities, whose catacombs are in the Abusir valley (see below), has probably influenced Ray (1976, 150-1) in regarding "the Peak" as the name for the whole of the North Saqqara plateau. However, Kessler (1989,126) identifies "the Peak" with the temple of Nakhthorheb at the east end of the Sarapieion *dromos* (1989, 126). In view of the uncertainty of the location of these two temples, it may be noted that there are massive mud-brick walls of the Late Period immediately north of the pyramid of Userkaf, suggesting the presence of a temple complex immediately west of Bubastieion (excavated by Dr Aly El-Khouly, to whom this information is due).
17. Mariette and Maspero 1882, 79: 'Des bronzes ont été trouvés dans les fondations du pylône du nord [of the Sarapieion enclosure]. D'autres bronzes ont été recueillis ça et là, non plus dans les fondations mais dans le sable, aux environs de ce même pylône, à l'intérieur de l'enceinte aussi bien qu'à l'extérieur. Il semblerait que les bronzes trouvés à l'extérieur marquent l'emplacement d'une sorte de voie qui se dirige en serpentant vers le nord-est. Nous avons suivi cette voie sur un assez longue parcours, et nous avons constaté qu'elle traverse toute une zône de la nécropole consacrée à des sépultures d'animaux. La voie n'est pas dallée; aucun mur ne la limite sur ces côtés; c'est par les bronzes seuls que nous avons reconnu la direction'. As Mariette also discovered large quantities of bronze statuettes of deities under the pavement of the main Sarapieion *dromos* (Mariette and Maspero 1882, 32, 77), his inference that the bronzes he found north of the north gate marked the course of a road was surely correct. The fact that it was not paved is probably to be explained by its use for dragging sarcophagi, where a surface of liquid mud would have been most advantageous, cf. the slipway for ships round the second cataract at Mirgissa (Vercoutter 1970, 204-14). Its serpentine course, if correctly observed, might also be explained by the need to drag sarcophagi across, not directly up, the slope of the valley, and this factor might also have rendered side-walls lining the road impracticable. Recent efforts by the National Museums of Scotland Survey to relocate and pursue the course of this road by sub-surface sensing have not yet met with success (Mathieson and Tavares 1993).
18. An account of the whole site for the general reader was given in Smith 1974, 21-63, and an excellent summary in Thompson 1988, 29-31. Only the 'Southern Dependencies' (Sector 7, see fig.4) have so far been fully published (Martin 1981); for the central temple precinct and the catacombs which it served reference must be made to the preliminary reports (Emery 1965-71; Smith 1976;

Smith and Jeffreys 1977). The hieroglyphic inscriptions from the site have been published (Martin 1979), also the demotic archive of the scribe Hor of the second century BC (Ray 1976), which provides much fascinating evidence for the interpretation of the site. Kessler (1989, 96-101, 107-22) has discussed the cults in detail, but his account of the actual disposition of the extant buildings is not wholly accurate.

19. Fully discussed in Ray 1976, 147-9.

20. No preliminary report available; see Martin 1971, 1-2.

21. The proximity of the shrine to the Mother of Apis catacomb, together with the large number of inscriptions mentioning Isis, Mother of Apis, found in its immediate vicinity adequately confirm the identity of its principal deity. For joint pleas to Osiris-Apis and Isis, Mother of Apis, see below.

22. A relief block which almost certainly came from this shrine bore a scene of Nakhthorheb worshipping Osiris-Apis and another damaged deity (Emery 1969, pl.IX.2 facing p.33).

23. This 'north courtyard' was excavated first (Emery 1967, Sectors 1-2), and its function as the enclosure of the Mother of Apis catacomb was not initially recognized. It is structurally later than the main temple precinct (Sector 3). In three Brooklyn contracts (Pestman 1977, I, 3-30 = Reich 1933, 9-129) the first party bears a title *wʿb n t3 sbt n is.t ḫnt -..... t3 nṯr.t ʿ3.t nti n pr-wsir-ḥp ḥr p3 ʿt mḥt n ḫftḥ wsir-ḥp* 'priest of the "hill-shrine"(?) of Isis of Khent-...., the great goddess, who is in the House of Osiris-Apis on the northern side of the *dromos* of Osiris-Apis'. Reich, the original editor, followed by Guilmot (1962, 380-1, map II), placed this 'hill-shrine'(?) within the Sarapieion enclosure itself, but Thompson (1988, 31, n.128, by implication) and Kessler (1989, 96-7, overtly) have placed it at the Mother of Apis complex, since they believe, correctly in our view, that 'the House of Osiris-Apis' included the area of Hepnebes. In this they follow Ray (1976, 152-3, figs.3-4), who identified the *sbt n ist* with the 'north courtyard'. Unfortunately, the reading of the title of Isis is still uncertain, the alternative readings suggested being *ḫnt-nṯr.wy* and *ḫnt-ʿb.wy* (Reich 1933, 64-70; Pestman 1977, I, 10, n.10). A reference in P. Leid. 379.3 to 'Isis upon the necropolis' probably also refers to this complex (Thompson 1988, 31, n.128). On the Isis-cult in the necropolis generally, see Bergman 1968, 251-6; Kessler 1989, 96-101.

24. Emery 1969, pl.IX, 3-4 opp. p.33. These cornice blocks seem too large to belong in the central sanctuary of Isis, Mother of Apis.

25. The inscriptions within the catacomb always name the deity as 'Osiris the Baboon', not as Thoth, and inform us that in life the baboons lived in 'the temple of Ptah under his moringa tree' in Memphis (Smith 1974, 42-3). Kessler (1989, 121-2) considers the sanctuary of Osiris the Baboon to have been unimportant. This view seems to rest on the small size of the chapel with ornamental façade and on his belief that the precinct included only one main temple, that decorated by Nakhthorheb, which included a sanctuary of Thoth ('Hermaion') to which the Baboon-cult was attached. In fact, the Baboon complex almost certainly comprised two chapels as described above, and seems, if correctly restored, to have been almost as impressive as that of the Mother of Apis.

26. In papyrus BM EA 10236, 2-3 *t3 sbt (n) ḥr ḫnt-...... p3 nṯr ʿ3 nti n pr-wsir-ḥp 'the "hill-*shrine"(?) of Horus of Khent- ...., the great god, who is in the House of Osiris-Apis' is mentioned (Reich 1933, 65); presumably this should refer to this complex if the identification in n.23 above is adopted.

27. For comprehensive description and plans of this area, see Martin 1981, 17-68 with pls.1 and 1A.

28. Texts 19, Ro.11; 21, Vo.9; 23, Vo.11; see Ray 1976, 139. See also n.33 below.

29. Ray 1976, 136-44. See also n.51 below.

30. See Derchain in Martin 1981, 166-70 with pl.23.

31. Martin 1981, 34-51, especially 34-7, where various suggestions are made concerning the purpose of this building.

32. This area is now mainly buried under dumps, but resistivity survey results suggest that it may have comprised a considerable area of buildings. For graphic accounts of the priests, embalmers and workers involved, see Ray 1976, especially 136-46; Ray 1972b; Thompson 1988, 29-31 and 155-211.

33. The area in which the burial and cult of the ibises was carried on was called *pr-wʿb-nb=s* in the Ptolemaic Period (Ray 1976, 148-9); this must therefore include the South Ibis galleries and the

shrines attached. Text 23 of the Hor Archive refers to 'the House-of-Thoth, which is upon the southern mountain of the Sarapieion which is (in) Memphis' and says: 'I spend (my) days (in) the House-of-Thoth, petitioning upon the (things) which the great god Thoth has said'. As the ostraca were found in the vicinity of the South Ibis courtyard, 'the southern mountain' should refer to this area in contradistinction to 'Hepnebes (in) the desert (of) the House of Osiris which is upon the mountain (of) the north of the necropolis of Ankhtawy' mentioned in the same passage, as Ray (1976, 148-9), has justly concluded (otherwise Kessler (1989, 113), who suggests that the 'House-of-Thoth' was on "the Peak"). The Ibis complex also included a temple and 'upper chapel', and a 'courtyard of the Ibis and the Falcon', all of which are likely to have been at the South Ibis catacomb or in the nearby Sector 7. The precinct described as *t3 sbt(t) n ḏḥwty nb ḫmnw r3 inhy rs pr-wsir-ḥp* 'the compound of Thoth, lord of Hermopolis (at?) the gate/entrance (of) the southern courtyard' (or 'south (of) the courtyard') 'of the Sarapieion' may not be the same (Ray 1976, 151-4). There was also a 'birth-chapel' which was 'in the lake of Pharaoh' (Ray 1976, 138-40). Kessler (1989, 107-17), who identifies the 'House-of-Thoth' as 'Hermaion', discusses these and other buildings and the cults practised in them in great detail, but does not always relate them convincingly to the topographical facts revealed by excavation.

34. This was partially cleared by Edel when searching for the Fifth Dynasty tomb of Weshptah; it is not to our knowledge published.

35. Mother of Apis stela 1970/66, unpublished.

36. Identified by J Boessneck in Martin 1981, 139; Kessler 1989, 119-20.

37. See n.23 above. The documents concerned (P. Brooklyn 37.1839A and B, and 37.1781, originally P. New York Historical Society 373a and b, and 388 respectively) have been extensively treated (Reich 1933, 9-129; Pestman 1977, I, 3-30; Zauzich 1968, 107-8, 111-12; Guilmot 1962, 359-81; Kessler 1989, 101-4).

38. In P. Brooklyn 37.1781.3 and P. Brooklyn 37.1839A.2 the expression 'House of Rest' is in the singular, whereas when it refers to a 'catacomb' containing many burials it is normally in the plural.

39. Reich 1933, 120-21, ll.3-4; cf. Pestman 1977, I, 6, ll.3-4; for other evidence of priestly burials north of Sarapieion, see Mariette 1856, 14; cf. Thompson 1988, 31.

40. De Morgan 1897, pl.10; it should be noted that the promontory south-west of the village of Abusir is not correctly positioned on this map, leading to distortion and uncertainty about the true locations of features named upon it.

41. El-Khouly 1973, 153, Pap. 59,13; Ray 1976, 154; Kessler 1989, 122-3.

42. P. Brooklyn 37.1839B.3; discussed in Kessler 1989, 122-3.

43. P. Brooklyn 37.1839B.3, see Pestman 1977, I, 28, n.15.

44. Mathieson and Tavares 1993. The topography and cults of Sarapieion have been very fully discussed, see especially Wilcken 1927, 7-18; Reich 1933, 1-44; Otto 1938, 11-23; Lauer and Picard 1955, 1-27; Guilmot 1962; Ray 1972b; Crawford, Quaegebeur and Clarysse 1980, 5-42; Thompson 1988, 27-31; Kessler 1989, 57-96, with conclusions which vary considerably.

45. Mariette and Maspero 1882, 28. Writing of the pylon at the west end of the *dromos,* Mariette states: 'À droite et à gauche du pylone commencent à se montrer les gros piliers carrés surmontés d'architraves monolithes qui forment l'enceinte.' This statement is explicit, and the pillars appear to be shown in Mariette's own plan (Mariette and Maspero 1882, between pp. 198-9); the north gate is shown as two rectangular outlines, apparently with internal pillars, suggesting that it did not follow the normal model of solid brick pylon-towers. Mariette refers to this enclosure again on p.78: 'Sur les trois côtés nord, est et sud, la grande enceinte a pour limite la muraille à claire-voie dont nous avons parlé; aucun mur n'existe du côté ouest, c'est à dire du côté du désert, et le temple n'est défendu dans cette partie que par la colline rocheuse qui lui sert d'horizon.' The matter is, however, complicated by de Rhoné's plan (Lauer and Picard 1955, pl.25), where the enclosure is shown with a solid line on all four sides, as if it were a mud-brick enclosure. It is of course conceivable that both existed. That this was in fact the case seems to be clearly indicated by an early plan of Mariette's (Arch. Zeit. 1851, 127, reproduced by Lauer and Picard 1955, 28, fig.15), which shows the pillars inside a solid masonry wall on three sides of the enclosure (albeit on the east, north and west sides, in contradistinction to the statement quoted above). This plan is also notable for showing what looks like a towered brick

barbican of the type known from Egyptian forts outside the north gateway on the line of the road down the Abusir valley. That there was a major structure outside the north enclosure wall at this point seems clear also from de Rhoné's plan, where, however, it is differently represented. Surface mounds marking the presence of this structure are clearly visible today.

46. The history, topography and purpose of the *dromos*, the statuary and shrines upon it and of the hemicycle have been discussed and illustrated with clarity and mastery by Lauer and Picard 1955, and the reader must be referred to their account. Unpublished photographs of Macramallah's excavations in 1938 in the Egyptian Antiquities Organization archive at Saqqara demonstrate even more clearly than those published by Lauer and Picard the existence of a pre-Ptolemaic phase of the *dromos* built in brick, which Lauer for good reasons ascribes to the Thirtieth Dynasty (1955, 24-6; cf. Smith 1981, 334-36).

47. This is suggested by projection on the plan (fig.3). In P. Brooklyn 37.1839B a property which is 'in the "House of Osiris-....." on the south side of the *dromos* of Osiris-...... the great god' is sold; its western boundary was 'the great street' (Pestman 1977, I, 25-30; Reich 1933, 114-16 with plan). This 'great street' must therefore have run north-south, but, as Pestman (1977, II, 33, note n) points out, its location is very uncertain, as Reich's reading 'Osiris-Apis' cannot be upheld. Thompson (1988, 30) regards this 'great street' as being identical with the road leading from the north gate of Sarapieion down the Abusir valley.

48. An area of brick domestic and storage buildings north of the north gate of the Sarapieion main temple enclosure excavated by Macramallah (1940, 77-84 with pls.II, LII-III) probably constituted only a small portion of these quarters. See note 32 for the Hepnebes village.

49. See the secondary sources quoted in note 44. The hypothetical map in Guilmot (1962, 381), published before the EES excavations, crowds all the shrines and their appendages within the enclosure and *dromos* area of Sarapieion itself; this now seems very unlikely to reflect the true position (Ray 1976, 147, 151-4; Thompson 1988, 27-31).

50. The published material is discussed by Kessler 1989, 96-101, 107-18.

51. This is attested by a stela mentioning Imhotep datable to 89 BC (Smith 1974, 48, pl.III.D), by graffiti in the Falcon catacomb, and by such joint phrases as 'the servants of the Ibis and the servants of the Falcon' (Ray 1976, texts 19,21,22 and 23).

52. See Insley-Green 1987, 47, No. 104; Smith 1992, 208, No. 70/2.

53. The blockings of the vaults upon which the priests' inscriptions were written have been destroyed, but the masons' stelae were set in niches in the rock-walls near the entrance of the catacomb and, though mostly fallen, have survived.

54. See Ray 1976, 7-20, 38-73 for the texts, 130-6 for comment; cf. Martin 1981, 35 for a building perhaps used for these purposes.

55. General accounts may be found in Assmann 1989, Brunner 1988, Smith 1994.

56. For the cults of Sacred Animals as oracle cults, see Quaegebeur 1973 and 1975.

57. For very approximate estimates of the numbers of ibis and falcon mummies involved, see Martin 1981, 8 with note 3; Ray 1976, 138; Smith 1974, 13; for the burial of large numbers of birds at other sites, see Kessler 1989, 17-43.

58. Falcons and ibises were buried in groups, since receipts for these gods and documents mentioning their burial are preserved (S.72/3.DP.44; S.71/2.DP.67; S.71/2.DP.135). Whether the mummies were dedicated at individual shrines by donors before being stored at 'the house-of-waiting of the god' (Ray 1976, 140) is not known for certain; the variation in the decorative quality of the ibis and falcon mummies renders attractive the notion that they may have been placed on display in embalmers' shops for purchase by offerers. For current investigations of the falcon and ibis mummies, see Nicholson 1994, 1-10.

59. For a list of the deities represented among the statuettes of bronze, wood and faience found in Sector 7, see Martin 1981, 121.

60. During the use of the site as a quarry for stone during the early Roman Period and its clearance when the Christian monastic settlement was founded, much material was disturbed and redeposited, destroying its original archaeological context.

61. The caches were mainly located immediately inside or outside the west enclosure wall. They

were mostly made in accumulating drift-sand and their archaeological stratigraphy and date of deposition is therefore very uncertain. Much of the material found in them seems likely to have been dedicated at the sanctuaries and then buried when no longer required because of its sanctified character. If this interpretation is correct, the date of deposition of the caches has no necessary relation to the date of manufacture of the objects in them.

62. An example of such a foundation deposit is illustrated in Emery 1970, 8, pl.IV.

63. Similar bronze statuettes of deities were found in large numbers by Mariette both under the Sarapieion *dromos* and under the road leading down the Abusir valley from the north gate of the Sarapieion main temple (Mariette and Maspero 1882, 32, 79).

64. In the case of the material from the 'statue cache' in the 'north courtyard', there are features which differentiate it from other caches and strongly suggest that this may have been done (Hastings, in press, Appendix A), but it is, in our view, exceptional.

65. For a different view see Kessler 1989, 143-9.

66. The main group of these were found in surface sand outside the east face of Mastaba 3518, the south shaft of which is directly over the Baboon catacomb; others were found within the catacomb.

67. Certain of these objects, representing human heads, are not dissimilar from those termed 'sculptors' models', but differ in some deliberate deformation, e.g. the eye being filled with plaster or a cicatrice across the skull. Others represent single limbs without much detail, and would hardly have been useful as 'sculptors' models'. For similar material from the Anubieion settlement, see Jeffreys and Smith 1988, 63, n.3 with fig.74 and pl.43a (78/u275).

68. On the identity and significance of these figurines and their association with the procession of the Pamyles, see Derchain in Martin 1981, 166-70.

69. Whether the factors we have stressed also applied to the temples in the cities in which living Sacred Animals were installed is a debatable matter, which would require separate discussion.

Bibliography

Assmann, J 1989. *Maat, l'Égypte Pharaonique et l'idée de justice sociale. Conférences, essais et leçons du Collège de France.* Paris, Julliard.

Bergman, J 1968. *Ich bin Isis. Studien zum memphitischen Hintergrund der griechischen Isisaretalogien.* Acta Universitatis Upsaliensis, Historia Religionum 3. Uppsala University.

Brunner, H 1988. *Das Hörende Herz: Kleine Schriften zur Religions- und Geistesgeschichte Ägyptens.* Freiburg and Göttingen.

de Cenival, F 1972. Un acte de renonciation consécutif à un partage de revenus liturgiques Memphites (P.Louvre E.3266). In *Bulletin de l'Institut Français d'Archéologie Orientale* 71, 11-65.

Crawford, D, J Quaegebeur and W Clarysse, 1980. *Studies on Ptolemaic Memphis.* Studia Hellenistica 24. Louvain.

El-Khouly, A 1973. Excavations east of the Serapeum at Saqqâra. In *Journal of Egyptian Archaeology* 59, 151-5.

Emery, W B 1965-7, 1969-71. Preliminary Reports on the Excavations at North Saqqâra. In *Journal of Egyptian Archaeology* 51 (1965), 3-8; 52 (1966), 3-8; 53 (1967), 141-5; 55 (1969), 31-5; 56 (1970), 5-11; 57 (1971), 3-13.

Guilmot, M 1962. Le Sarapieion de Memphis: Étude Topographique. In *Chronique d'Égypte* 37, 359-81.

Hastings, E A, in press. *The Sculpture from the Sacred Animal Necropolis at North Saqqâra 1964-1976.* London, Egypt Exploration Society.

Insley Green, C 1987. *The Temple Furniture from the Sacred Animal Necropolis at North Saqqâra 1964-76.* London, Egypt Exploration Society.

Jeffreys, D G and H S Smith 1988. *The Anubieion at Saqqâra I: The Settlement and the Temple Precinct.* London, Egypt Exploration Society.

Jeffreys, D G and A Tavares 1994. The Historic Landscape of Early Dynastic Memphis. In *Mitteilungen des Deutschen Archäologischen Instituts Abteilung Kairo* 50, 143-73.

Jones, M and A Milward Jones 1982. The Apis House Project at Mit Rahinah. First Season. In *Journal*

of the American Research Center in Egypt 19, 51-8.
Jones, M and A Milward Jones 1983. The Apis House Project at Mit Rahinah: Preliminary Report of the Second and Third Seasons, 1982-1983. In *Journal of the American Research Center in Egypt* 20, 33-45.
Jones, M and A Milward Jones 1985. Apis Expedition at Mit Rahinah. Preliminary Report of the Fourth Season, 1984. In *Journal of the American Research Center in Egypt* 22, 17-28.
Jones, M and A Milward Jones 1987. The Apis House Project at Mit Rahinah: Preliminary Report of the Fifth Season, 1984-1985. In *Journal of the American Research Center in Egypt* 24, 35-46.
Jones, M and A Milward Jones 1988. The Apis House Project at Mit Rahinah, Preliminary Report of the Sixth Season, 1986. In *Journal of the American Research Center in Egypt* 25, 105-16.
Kessler, D 1989. *Die Heiligen Tieren und der König: Teil I: Beiträge zu Organisation, Kult und Theologie der spätzeitlichen Tierfriedhöfe.* Ägypten und Altes Testament 16. Wiesbaden, Otto Harrassowitz.
Lauer, J-Ph and C Picard 1955. *Les Statues Ptolémaïques du Sarapieion de Memphis.* Publications de l'Institut d'Art et d'Archéologie de l'Université de Paris 3. Paris, Presses Universitaires de France.
Macramallah, R 1940. *Fouilles à Saqqarah: Un Cimetière Archaique de la Classe Moyenne du Peuple à Saqqarah.* Cairo, Institut Français d'Archéologie Orientale.
Mariette, A 1856. *Mémoire sur la mère d'Apis.* Paris, Gide & J Baudry.
Mariette, A and G Maspero, 1882. *Le Sérapeum de Memphis, publié d'après le manuscrit de l'auteur par G. Maspero.* Paris, F Vieweg.
Martin, G T 1971. Note in Editorial, *Journal of Egyptian Archaeology* 57, 1-2.
Martin, G T 1973. Excavations in the Sacred Animal Necropolis at North Saqqâra, 1971-2: Preliminary Report. In *Journal of Egyptian Archaeology* 59, 5-15.
Martin, G T 1974. Excavations in the Sacred Animal Necropolis at North Saqqâra, 1972-3: Preliminary Report. In *Journal of Egyptian Archaeology* 60, 15-29.
Martin, G T 1979. *The Tomb of Hetepka and other reliefs and inscriptions from the Sacred Animal Necropolis, North Saqqâra 1964-73.* London, Egypt Exploration Society.
Martin, G T 1981. *The Sacred Animal Necropolis at North Saqqâra; The Southern Dependencies of the Main Temple Complex.* London, Egypt Exploration Society.
Mathieson, I J and A Tavares 1983. Preliminary Report of the National Museums of Scotland Saqqara Survey Project, 1990-91. In *Journal of Egyptian Archaeology* 79,17-32.
Meulenaere, H de 1960. Les Monuments du culte des rois Nectanébo. In *Chronique d'Égypte* 35, 92-107.
de Morgan, J 1897. *Carte de la Nécropole Memphite: Dahchour, Sakkarah, Abou-Sir.* Cairo, Institut Français d'Archéologie Orientale.
Nicholson, P T 1994. Preliminary Report on Work at the Sacred Animal Necropolis, North Saqqara, 1992. In *Journal of Egyptian Archaeology* 80, 1-10.
Otto, E 1938. *Beiträge zur Geschichte der Stierkulte in Aegypten.* Untersuchungen zur Geschichte und Altertumskunde Aegyptens 13. Leipzig, J C Hinrichs.
Pestman, P W 1977. *Recueil de Textes Démotiques et Bilingues*, 3 vols. Leiden.
Pierce, R H 1972. *Three Demotic Papyri in the Brooklyn Museum. A Contribution to the Study of Contracts and their Instruments in Ptolemaic Egypt.* Symbolae Osloenses Fasc. Supplet. 24. Oslo, Universitetsforlag.
Quaegebeur, J 1973. Considérations sur le nom propre égyptien Teëphthaphônukhos. In *Orientalia Lovaniensia Periodica* 4, 85-100.
Quaegebeur, J 1975. Teëphibis, dieu oraculaire? In *Enchoria* 5, 19-24.
Quibell, J E 1907. *Excavations at Saqqara, 1905-1906.* Cairo, Institut Français d'Archéologie Orientale.
Ray, J D 1972a. The *Gm* of Memphis. In *Journal of Egyptian Archaeology* 58, 308-10.
Ray, J D 1972b. The House of Osorapis. In P J Ucko, R Tringham and G W Dimbleby (eds.), *Man, Settlement and Urbanism*, 699-704. London.
Ray, J D 1976. *The Archive of Hor.* London, Egypt Exploration Society.
Ray, J D 1978. Observations on the Archive of Hor. In *Journal of Egyptian Archaeology* 64, 113-20.
Reich, N J 1933. New Documents from the Serapeum of Memphis. In *Mizraim* 1, 9-129.

Sandman Holmberg, M 1946. *The God Ptah*. Lund, C W K Gleerup.
Segal, J B 1983. *Aramaic Texts from North Saqqâra with some fragments in Phoenician.* London, Egypt Exploration Society.
Smith, H S 1972. The Obsequies of the Mother of Apis. In *Revue d'Égyptologie* 24, 176-9 with tables 1-8.
Smith, H S 1974. *A Visit to Ancient Egypt: Life at Memphis and Saqqara (c. 500-30 B.C.).* Warminster, Aris & Phillips.
Smith, H S 1976. Preliminary Reports on Excavations in the Sacred Animal Necropolis: Season 1974-5. In *Journal of Egyptian Archaeology* 62, 14-7.
Smith, H S and D G Jeffreys, 1977. The Sacred Animal Necropolis, North Saqqâra: 1975/6. In *Journal of Egyptian Archaeology* 63, 20-8.
Smith, H S and D G Jeffreys, 1978. The North Saqqâra Temple-town Survey: Preliminary Report for 1976/77. In *Journal of Egyptian Archaeology* 64, 10-21.
Smith, H S and D G Jeffreys, 1979-81. The Anubieion, North Saqqâra: Preliminary Reports. In *Journal of Egyptian Archaeology* 65 (1979), 17-29; 66 (1980), 17-27; 67 (1981), 21-3.
Smith, H S 1981. À l'ombre d'Auguste Mariette. In *Supplément au Bulletin de l'Institut Français d'Archéologie Orientale 81*, Cairo, 331-9.
Smith, H S 1984. Saqqâra - Late Period. In *Lexikon der Ägyptologie* V, 412-28.
Smith, H S 1992. The Death and Life of the Mother of Apis. In A Lloyd (ed.), *Studies in Pharaonic Religion and Society in honour of J. Gwyn Griffiths*, London, Egypt Exploration Society, 201-25.
Smith, H S 1994. M3't and Isfet. In *Bulletin of the Australian Centre for Egyptology* 5, 67-88.
Stricker, B H 1943. La Prison de Joseph. In *Acta Orientalia* 19, 101-37.
Thompson, D J 1988. *Memphis under the Ptolemies*. Princeton University Press.
Vercoutter, J 1962. *Textes biographiques du Sérapéum de Memphis. Contribution à l'étude des stèles votives du Sérapéum.* Bibliothèque de l'Ecole des Hautes Etudes IVe Section (Sciences Historiques et Philologiques) 306. Paris, Librairie Ancienne Honoré Champion.
Vercoutter, J 1970. *Mirgissa I.* Paris, Ministère des Affaires Etrangères and Centre National de la Recherche Scientifique.
Wilcken, U 1927. *Urkunden der Ptolemäerzeit. Ältere Funden* I. Berlin and Leipzig.
Yoyotte, J 1972. La Localisation de Ouenkhem. In *Bulletin de l'Institut Français d'Archéologie Orientale* 71, 1-10.
Zauzich, K-T 1968. *Die Ägyptische Schreibertradition in Aufbau/Sprache und Schrift der demotischen Kaufverträge aus ptolemäischer Zeit.* Ägyptologische Abhandlungen 19, Wiesbaden, Otto Harrassowitz.
Zivie, A 1990. *Découverte à Saqqarah; Le vizir oublié.* Paris, Seuil.

The sun god, his four bas and the four winds in the sacred district at Saïs: the fragment of an Obelisk (BM EA 1512)

Susanne Woodhouse

The object BM EA 1512 was presented to the British Museum by E Meyer in 1910.[1] Meyer bought the piece in Alexandria for his own private collection. The object was said to have been found at Sais (Nash 1910, 194). Previously only Nash had offered an interpretation of this object, in a two page article (Nash 1910, 193-4: "Probably the whole obelisk and its inscriptions had a magical purpose"). BM EA 1512 has only been mentioned occasionally in Egyptological literature,[2] but it has never been studied scientifically, which may partly be attributed to its fragmentary condition.

Description

On a square base of 29.5 cm, rises the upper part of an obelisk to the max. height of 67.5 cm. It is made from Tura limestone.[3] The shaft is tapering slightly to the top, a fact that warrants the object's qualification as obelisk. The lower part of the shaft is broken away irregularly and has been complemented in modern times in order to gain a horizontal base. The original height of the former monument cannot be reconstructed.[4] The edges of the shaft had been chipped and were also restored in modern times. Each of the four sides of the shaft is divided by two sky hieroglyphs into a section for the depiction (height of each picture panel: 12.7 cm) and another one for the inscription (pl. 40-42). The upper edge of the sky hieroglyph that covers the picture panel is the dividing line between the shaft and the top. The east and west sides (each side is designated according to the wind god named upon it) rise vertically, while the north and south sides slant to the inside, so that the top of the obelisk is shaped like a gabled-roof. The "top ridge" develops into a long rectangle, measuring 29.5 cm in length and 7.4 cm in height. It served as a pedestal for the squatting falcon sculpture of which only the tips of the tail feathers remain (pl.39); the photographs in Nash 1910 show the object in the same condition. The bird of prey looked to the west side (side with the text of the west wind) of the obelisk (fig.1).

This singularly unique top to the obelisk was the reason why the artist relinquished the usual pyramidion for the benefit of the gabled-roof-shape.[5] The upper part has been chipped and parts were restored early in the twentieth century, presumably for display in the museum.

The panel for the inscription is bordered by two vertical lines. Another line runs down between the two columns of text on each side. The hieroglyphs are simply sunk into the surface without any inner structures and look towards this middle line.

In each picture panel on the east, north, and south sides the shape of two winged beings are worked into the surface without any differentiation of the parts of the body. On the contrary, the west side shows a sunk relief of high quality (see pl.40a). One of the beings is a falcon stretching out its wings and holding a shen-ring in each claw. The solar disc on its head relates it to the sun god. The other animal is the representation of one of the four wind gods. The gods face each other the same way as the two columns of inscriptions below them (fig.1).

The sky hieroglyph, the lines for delimiting text fields, the hieroglyphs and the depictions of the gods in the picture panel are painted red.[6] Their contours are lined quite often with red paint. This must have led the restorer to the misinterpretation that the whole surfaces had at one time been painted red. This is the only way to explain the red paint which remains in the modern tool marks. These traces are the only remains of paint on the surface, and it may safely be deduced that the surface of the obelisk was never painted.

The surfaces of the west and north sides are totally smooth, whilst on the east side the shaft and gabled-roof are covered with deep chisel marks (pl. 40b). The south side is smoothed to a large extent with a few slight chisel marks visible on the shaft (pl. 41a).

As already mentioned above the depiction of the gods in the western picture panel differs in quality from the other three sides: face, wig, solar disc, and body are executed in a very fine sunk relief (pl. 40a).

In addition to the last two observations the falcon sculpture, which looked towards the west (fig.1), indicates the priority of this side. It was clearly intended as the front. On the other hand, the east side which is covered with deep chisel marks and which was at the back of the falcon has to be qualified as the rear.

Dating the monument

Only the depictions of the wind gods in the picture panels provide a basis for assigning BM EA 1512 to a particular period in Egyptian history. Personifications of the four wind gods are depicted exclusively during Graeco-Roman times.[7] Since no stylistic development can be traced in the depictions of

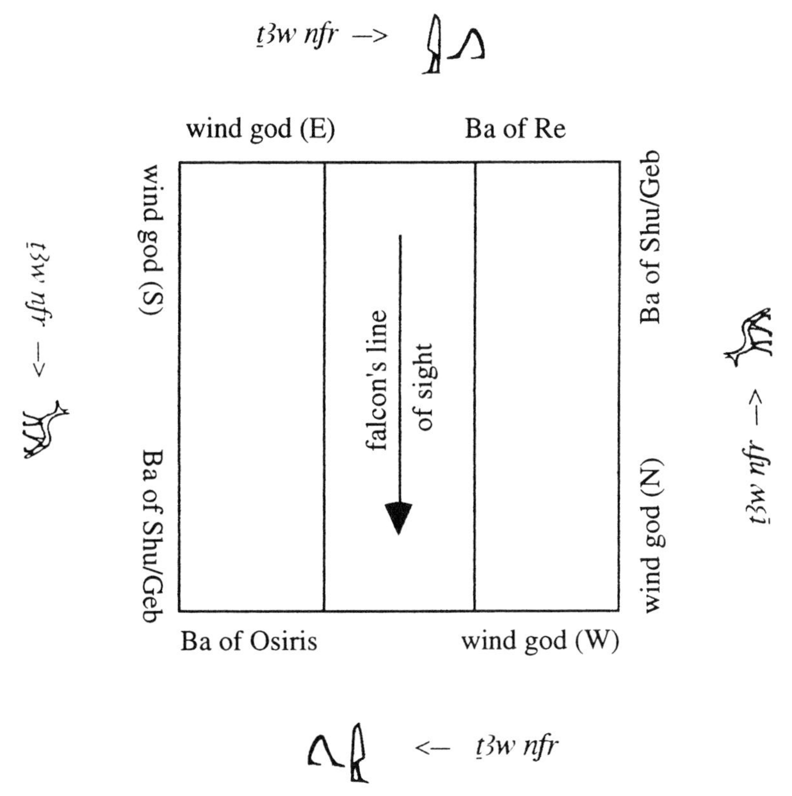

Fig.1 Alignment to the cardinal points of the deities in the vignettes and inscription of BM EA 1512.

the wind gods, it is impossible to describe a more specific date to BM EA 1512.

At maximum three squares of each text have survived, just enough to support the date deduced from the depictions of the wind gods on the grounds of phonetic rules and spellings, but not sufficient for a closer limitation.

Single obelisks

Studies on the orientation of the inscriptions on obelisks have shown that the hieroglyphs always look towards the sanctuary, the axis of which the obelisks flank.[8] Exceptions to this rule may be an indication of a single obelisk (Leclant and Yoyotte 1950, 82).

In both columns on each side of the shaft of BM EA 1512 the hieroglyphs are directed to the middle line. They face each other in the same way as the gods in the picture panel. The orientation of its decoration can be compared with the one of the inscriptions on the Lateran obelisk,[9] the only single obelisk that has survived from antiquity.[10] After the completion by Tuthmosis IV its inscriptions represent a system closed in itself: the two columns of Tuthmosis IV flank the inscription of Tuthmosis III on each side of the shaft and their hieroglyphs are orientated towards the column of Tuthmosis III.[11] Only by the addition of the two flanking columns on each side by Tuthmosis IV can the monument gain its inner centring and its consistency (cf. Martin 1977, 166 n.3). The decoration of BM EA 1512 reveals the same consistency as the decoration of the Lateran obelisk.

Aspects of the Ba and the wind theologies, which we will analyse below, support our identification of BM EA 1512 as a fragment of a single obelisk.

Single obelisks or monuments with the same function can be traced through all phases of Egyptian history.

Each Sun Temple from the 5th Dynasty possessed a monument constructed of bricks and limestone in the shape of an obelisk. To the solar character of the temple a funerary one is added, since the sun god, who was worshipped here, was at the same time the dead king, who after his death merged with his father Re (see Rochholz 1994, 271-80). Since we know neither the Egyptian denotation for these monuments nor their exact function, they can only be used as a limited reference for single obelisks and for the question of their function.

An obelisk stela of 75.5 cm height made from limestone dates from the late 13th Dynasty (Bourriau 1988, 66f.). It was dedicated by a certain Amenemhat and erected at Abydos. A funerary formula invokes among others Osiris, Upuaut, Min-Hornekhet, and other gods from Abydos. Thus this object is of a funerary character.

During the 18th Dynasty Tuthmosis IV completed the already mentioned *tḫn wꜥtj* of his grandfather Tuthmosis III and had it erected on the axis of the Karnak temple behind the jubilee temple, so that the statues in the counter temple of Tuthmosis III and Hatshepsut looked directly towards it (Barguet 1950; id. 1962, 241). Later Akhenaten changed the single obelisk into a benben-stone by having the obelisk walled in with sandstone from Gebel el-Silsila (Loeben 1994), and a *ḥwt-bnbn* was built around it (see the drawings in Redford 1989, 72-8). Under Ramesses II the benben-stone became an obelisk again: without changing its location, the *tḫn wꜥtj* of Tuthmosis III was a cult object in a temple, that was built around by Ramesses II (Barguet 1950, 274f., fig.1; id. 1962, 241). Ptolemy VIII Euergetes II altered the structure of this temple: the worshipper was enabled to approach the single obelisk in a straight line (Barguet 1950, 278f.; id. 1962, 241). Thus the *tḫn wꜥtj* was worshipped at Karnak as a symbol of the Sun from the 18th Dynasty till Ptolemaic times.

For the Ramesside Period we have several items of evidence for single obelisks. At Heliopolis Petrie found the upper part of a stela that depicts a single obelisk, which is flanked by Atum and Re-Harakhti (Petrie and Mackay 1915, 7 § 16, pl. 8.6). The obelisk is inscribed with the name of Ramesses II. This object illustrates for Heliopolis a single obelisk, that was dedicated by Ramesses II, and was worshipped like Atum and Re-Harakhti (Yoyotte 1957, 90f.). Predecessors of this Heliopolitan single obelisk have to be regarded as model for the *tḫn wꜥtj* of Tuthmosis III, who emphasizes the novelty of a single obelisk for Karnak.

A graffito from Gebel Ahmar dating to the Ramesside Period shows baboons adoring a single obelisk erected on a base (Daressy 1914, 45, 46 no.1; Yoyotte 1957, 91; Habachi 1977, 9 fig.2); this is another reference for a single obelisk as cult object within the frame of the sun cult.

As far as obelisks from Tanis feature a singular orientation of their inscriptions, Leclant and Yoyotte (1950, 82) assume that they might have been single obelisks.

For the Late Period two scenes from the temple of Hibis provide information about the cult of single obelisks (LÄ IV, 542 and n. 12, s.v. "Obelisk").

The cult of the *tḫn wꜥtj* at Karnak was continued during the Graeco-Roman Period (see above). Further examples of single obelisks can be added.

Pliny records the displacement of a single, undecorated obelisk of Nectanebo (II ? - Roullet 1972, 67f.) from Heliopolis to Alexandria, where Ptolemy II Philadelphos had it erected in the

Arsinoeion (Nat.hist. XXXVI, 67-9; Alföldy 1990, 51f. n.98; Roullet 1972, 67-9; Hölbl 1994, 97). If we cannot determine from this reference whether Ptolemy II Philadelphos had carried off from Heliopolis one obelisk of a pair, or the single erected cult object of the Sun, we can deduce that at this time according to Egyptian tradition a single obelisk was erected within a temenos for a deity, Arsinoë II, for whose cult see Hölbl 1994, 94-8.

Alföldy pointed out that the (uninscribed) obelisk on Saint Peter's square originally formed part of a building project of Cleopatra VII; it was intended to be erected on the square of the heroon of Anthony at Alexandria (1990, 38-54). When the Romans occupied Alexandria, C. Cornelius Gallus, who later became the first Prefect of Egypt, took over Cleopatra's monumental project. The heroon of Anthony was completed as the Forum Augusti, and in its middle the uninscribed single obelisk was erected on a base (Alföldy 1990, fig.12).[12] Caligula had this obelisk transferred to Rome, where it was set up on the spina of the Vatican circus on the western bank of the Tiber.[13]

In addition, single obelisks at Rome could decorate tombs (Roullet 1972, 81 (nos.81-82), 82 (no.86); Loeben 1992, 21).

Thus during all periods of Egyptian history single obelisks have in the first instance been cult objects within the scope of the sun cult. Beyond this they might be ascribed a funerary character.

Egyptian stone monuments crowned by an animal or other emblem

In order to clarify whether there is a reference between the falcon sculpture that crowned BM EA 1512 and its substructure, the obelisk proper, or whether the obelisk in this case served merely as a base for the falcon sculpture, we have to examine the Egyptian stone monuments, crowned by animals or emblems.[14]

Senusret I set up a pink granite stela of 12.9 m height at Abgîg.[15] It stood on a square base (3.6 m length) made from limestone on an artificial hill and raised above the surrounding landscape. The front shows the king in relations with Egyptian gods and an inscription, of which regrettably large parts are destroyed, comprising 14 columns. In the rounded top is a square recess of 40 cm depth, in which a statue or emblem might once have been fixed. Because it is a royal monument which had been set up in the scope of the development of the Fayoum, presumably commenced under Senusret I (*LÄ* I, 680, s.v. "Begig"), the crowning object should have belonged to royal iconography. Sourouzian (1989, 59, 218) likens the stela to Merneptah's commemoration monuments. In connection with these columns of Merneptah it becomes quite possible, that the stela at Abgîg was crowned by a falcon statue which was made from a different material to that of the stela itself.

Amenhotep III's monumental scarab at the NW corner of the Sacred Lake at Karnak is a monolith of pink granite.[16] The scarab squats on a pedestal as tall as a man. The inscription identifies the monument as Khepri, who "emerges from earth".[17] Thus the scarab is Khepri, and the substructure represents the earth from which the new born sun god emerges. The scarab looks towards a levelled part of the pedestal. This tableau shows the king offering wine to Atum, the night form of the sun god. As in BM EA 1512 the line of sight of the crowning animal defines the front of the object.

The monumental scarab near the Sacred Lake at Karnak belongs to the cult of the sun: first, the pink granite is of strong solar symbolism, and secondly, the night form of the sun god is addressed in the offering-scene, while the whole monument itself is dedicated to the morning form of the sun god. In the clearest possible manner this last mentioned form manifests the desired continuity of the passage of the sun. Thus the scarab refers to the decoration of the pedestal and to the pedestal itself since this represents the earth from which the young sun god emerges.

In front of the first pylon of the Uto temple at Nebesheh Petrie found a column measuring 3.66 m in height and made from pink granite (Petrie 1888, 9-10, 31, pl.14; Sourouzian 1989, 59f., 101f.). It is crowned by a falcon that shelters the kneeling Merneptah between its legs (see Sourouzian 1989, pl. 18c). Again column, falcon and king form a monolith. Sourouzian interprets this monument and the column from Heliopolis (see below) as a commemorative column. The shaft is decorated with the Horus-name of the king and several offering scenes. The crown in the shape of a falcon protecting the king echoes the Horus-names depicted on the shaft below it and classifies the monuments as royal. Again we could make evident the reference between substructure and crowning object.

Another commemorative column of Merneptah was found at Heliopolis (Sourouzian 1989, 55-

60, 91, 218). It is 5.42 m high and made from pink granite. The texts deal with the victory of Merneptah over the Libyan coalition in the 5th year. The "colonne du Caire" is the lower part of its pendant (most recently Sourouzian 1989, 50-60, pl. 10, 16). In the abacus of the Heliopolitan column is an 8 cm deep cavity, measuring 56 cm x 32 cm. According to Sourouzian this hollow did not fulfil any architectural purpose, but was intended to receive the base of a statue or emblem (Sourouzian 1989, 59f., 218). As a royal monument his column of victory could well have been crowned by a Horus falcon.

In the cachette of the Luxor temple, a falcon statue made from calcite depicted as squatting on a papyrus has recently been found. El-Saghir assumes that the total height of the falcon and the now lost column, which represented the stem of the papyrus umbel, would have been approximately 2.3 m (El-Saghir 1991, 50f.). The relation between the falcon statue and the papyrus plant upon which it sits, is based on the myth of Horus: Isis gives birth to her son in the swamps of Chemmis, which is covered with papyrus plants. Thus the young Horus is often depicted sitting on a lotus plant in the marshlands of Chemmis.

These examples demonstrate that the crowning object, whether forming a monolith with the base or made separately, always refers thematically to its base. Monuments glorifying the king were topped with a Horus falcon or a royal emblem, while a monument dedicated to a god bears a sacred animal, which belongs to the specific god or one of his emanations. Below we will indicate that the same holds true for BM EA 1512.

The inscriptions and depictions on BM EA 1512

At maximum the first three squares of the text columns are preserved, the rest of the inscriptions being lost with the lower part of the original obelisk. Textual parallels from Graeco-Roman temples will help us to disclose the contents of the lost inscriptions as well as their structure, but not to reconstruct the exact wording. This also means that we cannot calculate the exact height of the complete monument. Using the length of the wind and Ba texts as parallels we can only deduce that when intact it stood less than three metres high.

Besides the orientation of the hieroglyphs and of the depictions discussed above, the wind and Ba texts of BM EA 1512 point to a single obelisk as well. During all phases of Egyptian history there is evidence for a constant number of four wind gods. A hypothetical repetition of the same wind gods on the four sides of a pendant to the obelisk has to be rejected for the lack of variation. Moreover, in the case of a pair of obelisks, there would have been eight sides which would then have had to be related to eight Bas of the sun god (for the sun god see below). Such a number of Bas is not attested for the sun god. He owns four or seven Bas (Quaegebeur 1991, 261; RÄRG 74; LÄ V, 160, s. v. "Re"). Thus a pendant to the former obelisk BM EA 1512 seems highly unlikely.

A: The winds

Each side of the object is classed with a direction of the wind. In the picture panel right above the column with the wind text the corresponding wind god is depicted as an animal.

1) The west side (pl.40a):

ṯ3w nfr m[18] *jmntt ḥḏ3* [*rn.f ntf*[19] ... (lacuna of unknown length)]

The perfect west wind, Hedja[20] [is its name, who ... (lacuna of unknown length)].

The accompanying personification shows a being with a ram's head and the body of a falcon. It has spread its wings horizontally, and the ostrich feather of Shu stands between its horns.[21]

The text in the temple of Hathor at Deir el-Medineh states that the west wind receives the Bas of the gods in the horizon, and that this wind creates the vegetation.[22] The corresponding inscription from the temple of Apet at Karnak (Ptolemy VIII Euergetes II) attributes to the west wind the role of bringer of the inundation in order to cause the flora to grow.[23] Thus the attribute sentence here, introduced by *ntf*, will have comprised similar statements.

2) The east side (pl.40b):

ṯ3w nfr m[24] *j3btt* [*hnw šss rn.f ntf wṯs ḥ3jtj r pt*[25] ... (lacuna of unknown length)]
The perfect east wind, [Henusheses[26] is its name, who raises up the two lights (sun and moon) to the sky[27] ... (lacuna of unknown length)].

The accompanying wind god in the picture panel is a being with the body of a scarab and a ram's head, having just emerged from earth.[28] The forelegs are lifted up, the wings are spread horizontally and the ostrich feather decorates the horns.[29]

The east wind usually lifts the Sun and the moon up to the sky, in order to provide Egypt with light (Esna II, no.128, 2-3). It carries the Ba of Osiris up to heaven.[30] According to CT II, 389f. (see Kurth 1994d) it opens heaven and prepares the path for Re. The *ntf*-attribute-sentence might have mentioned some of these qualities in addition to the restoration given above.

3) The north side (pl.41a):
ṯ3w nfr m[31] *mḥtj ḳb* [*rn.f ntf* ... (lacuna of unknown length)]
The perfect north wind, the cold one[32] [is its name, who ... (lacuna of unknown length)].

The wind god is a four-headed ram with two wings. The ostrich feather is situated between the horns.[33]

The north wind brings the cool and moist air from the Mediterranean Sea to Egypt and thus refreshes and animates the Creation; in its function as bringer of the inundation it is responsible for the support of the plants, and is assigned to the qualification of preserving life.[34] Corresponding qualities are expected in the attribute-sentence introduced by *ntf*.

4) The south side (pl.41b):
ṯ3w nfr n[35] *rsj šhb* [*rn.f ntf wṯs b3w n nṯrw r pt* ... (lacuna of unknown length)]
The perfect south wind, the desiccating one[36] [is its name, who raises the Bas of the gods up to heaven[37] ... (lacuna of unknown length)].

The wind god in the picture panel is a ram with two wings, wearing the ostrich feather of Shu between his horns.[38]

The south wind is said to bring the Nile from its caverns, in order to supply Egypt and its gods with food,[39] it gives air to the embryo in the womb and it kills Apophis for Re.[40] The attribute-sentence might have continued with similar qualifications.

B: The Bas
Except for the column on the west side, the inscriptions on the remaining three sides break where the name of the god is mentioned.

In each of the four picture panels a falcon is depicted directly above the Ba text. The bird of prey spreads out its wings and the solar disc is placed on its head. The identification of the falcons becomes possible on the grounds of the texts on the shaft: the wind gods help the divine Bas ascending to the sky. Since both beings under the top sky-hieroglyph have spread out their wings and their feet are not in contact with the ground,[41] we can assume that they are shown here flying in the airspace below the firmament. So the picture panels illustrate the texts displayed directly below them. The falcon is the Ba[42] of the corresponding god mentioned in the text below him and is lifted up to heaven by one of the four wind gods in the aforementioned text. The solar disc on the falcon's head shows the bird to be part of the sun god.

1) The west side (pl.40a):
jj.n b3 n wsjr ꜥnḫj [... ... *ꜥḥj.f r pt* ... (lacuna of unknown length)]
The Ba of Osiris, the living one (?)[43] [... ...][44] has come [and flies (now)[45] up to the sky[46] ... (lacuna of unknown length)].

In order to understand this fragmentary text we need to reexamine the more or less complete Ba texts from Kom Ombo (Gutbub 1973, 387-94). The structure of these texts, dealing with the Bas of 14 different gods entering the lunar eye, can be described as follows:

Part **A**: *jj.n b3 n* god NN	The Ba of god NN has come
Part **B**: *ꜥḥj (šm, ꜥpj).f r pt*	and flies up to the sky (now)
Part **C**: *ꜥḳ.f m jtn (wḏ3t)*	in order to enter the disc (the moon).
Part **D**: *rdj.f* Egypt *n* king	May he give Egypt to the king.

The 14 Bas ascending to heaven, entering — i. e. filling — the moon, stand for the phase of the waxing moon. This skywards orientated text is displayed on an architrave in the immediate vicinity of the hypostyle ceiling,[47] which on the cosmic level is the firmament. So subject and place of display are co-ordinated with each other.

The transfer (mutatis mutandis) of contents and structure of this text Kom Ombo no. 327 onto BM EA 1512, which is a monument dedicated to the Sun, is justified by the following considerations:

1.) The beginning of the Ba texts is the same in both cases: *jj (jw).n b3 n* god NN.

2.) The divine beings in the picture panels of BM EA 1512 hover below the firmament. In the four scenes they are facing each other, by which the close relationship between both of them is expressed. Examining the wind texts we stated that the east and the south winds carry the divine Bas up to heaven, where they turn into stars. Translating this theological statement onto the picture panels on the east and south sides of BM EA 1512, it appears that the panels depict the moment when the wind god lifts the Ba of a god up to heaven. Since the arrangement in the picture panels on the west and north sides is identical to that on the east and south sides, it is obvious that they represent exactly the same subject, even though there is as yet no textual evidence for the west and north winds lifting divine Bas up to heaven.

3.) An obelisk as symbol of the Sun is an ideal monument for displaying the ascent of four Bas, which are related to the sun god by a solar disc on their heads.

4.) We noted above that the Ba texts from Kom Ombo were displayed on an architrave, thus in a very meaningful place with regard to the subject of these texts. The same holds true for BM EA 1512, on which the theological statement is orientated towards heaven: the inscriptions on the shaft described the ascent from the beginning to the end of the movement and the former obelisk, towering up from the ground, lifted up its decoration. High above the ground, the wind gods, who fill the airspace between earth and sky, and the Bas, ascending to the firmament, are represented in the picture panel.

Therefore to a limited extent the four sections of Kom Ombo no. 327 can be transferred to the Ba texts of BM EA 1512:

Part **A** is identical. The Ba of god NN has arrived in a place, in order to fulfil a special action.

Part **B** can be accepted on the base of the exemplified function of the winds to lift the divine Bas up to heaven, as it is shown in the picture panels.

Part **C**, the expression "entering the disc", is not attested in solar theology. However, entering the lunar disc can be described as a unification of 14 gods during the phase of the waxing moon: after 14 days they form the full moon. Thus in the case of BM EA 1512 one could expect the statement that the Ba has arrived in the firmament, where he joins the other three Bas. Together they traverse the sky in their new shape of stars. Below we will show that the unification of these four Bas is represented by one single god, the sun god, squatting on the top of the object.

Part **D** could have provided the close of the Ba texts of BM EA 1512. The contents of this section round off the text very well. However, since the object itself contains no indication as to the contents of the final part of the texts, the question must be left open.

The statement that the Ba of a god or king rises to heaven is a paraphrase, which describes the death of his owner.[48] While the corpse rests in its burial, its Ba flies up to the sky, where it turns into a star, in order to traverse the firmament for eternity together with the other stars (Zabkar 1968, 44f.). The inscriptions and the decoration of the former obelisk thus record what would occur directly after the death of the four gods mentioned in the four Ba texts.

2) The other sides (pl.40b, 41a-b):

Each Ba text starts with a verb in the sense of "to come". On the west and east sides the texts begin with  (*jj*), on the north and south sides they start with  (*jw/jj*), as shown in Fig. 1. Thus the opposite sides are marked to belong together and both, a west-east-axis and a north-south-axis are made obvious. The west-east-axis is emphasized by the crowning falcon who was orientated west-east. His tail feathers still remain on the rectangular base above the east side (pl.42), so he once looked out to the west side. On the theological level this means that the sun god is depicted during his daily course from East (sunrise) to West (sunset).[49] The manifestation of this concept in stone, i. e. an obelisk, which is the symbol of the Sun, fits well in the observation made above, that there is always a reference between the monument and its crowning object. Furthermore this statement will help us to identify the three missing gods. There must have existed a narrow relationship between the sun god on the top of the gabled-roof and the four gods mentioned in the Ba texts, as indicated by the depiction of a Sun-disc on the head of each Ba-falcon in the picture panel. Therefore we could trace the now lost names of the three gods on the east, north and south sides, if there was evidence for a relation between four Bas and the sun god. According to the Ba text on the west side one of the Bas is the one of Osiris.

In Egyptian texts the division of the sun god into four *b3 n* god NN is well attested. They are the Ba of Re, sometimes as Khepri,[50] the Ba of Shu, the Ba of Geb, and the Ba of Osiris.[51] Before the Ptolemaic Period they are given in the sequence Ba of Osiris - Ba of Shu - Ba of Geb - Ba of Khepri, while from the beginning of the Ptolemaic Period Re takes the place of Khepri and the succession then is Ba of Re - Ba of Shu - Ba of Geb - Ba of Osiris.[52] The favoured spellings for *b3* are and . The spellings , , and are rarely used.[53]

Together these four Bas form Re, Re-Harakhti,[54] Amun(-Re),[55] Amun-Re-Harakhti,[56] Horus(-Re),[57] and other forms of the sun god (Banebded, Herishef, Khnum, Month and Min-Re).[58] This god, comprising four Bas, is depicted and described as a ram with four ram's heads on a single neck or as an anthropomorphic god with four ram's heads on his neck (Quaegebeur 1991). Thus the most usual spelling of *b3* = Ba- "soul" with the hieroglyph of a ram is derived from the outer appearance of the god.[59] This spelling is based on the homonymy of *b3* = ram, and *b3* = Ba- "soul".[60] However, the underlying significance is not necessarily expressed in the depiction and the inscription at the same time as may be demonstrated by the two following examples.

In room G (*štjt*) of the temple at Edfu we find a list of those gods, who are to be offered incence in room F (*ḫnw-n-štjt*). Among others the Ba of Re, of Osiris, of Shu, and of Khepri[61] are named. The word *b3* is spelled each time (Edfou I, 182, 28-9). The list in the hypostyle hall gives the same sequence for these Bas, but this time the spelling is (Edfou II, 23, 84-5). These four Bas from the lists are depicted as anthropomorphic beings each with a ram's head[62] and in the accompanying inscriptions *b3* is written with the ram hieroglyph (Edfou I, 164, 7-10; 171, 7-10).

In the central sanctuary of the temple at Qal'a four anthropomorphic gods each with a ram's head are depicted in scenes 10, 11, 15 and 16. The inscriptions identify the Ba of Geb (scene 10) and the Ba of Shu (scene 11). The accompanying inscriptions are mostly destroyed, and therefore the Bas in the other two scenes can only be identified by their crowns and the inscription of no.31 as the Ba of Osiris-Wennefer and the Ba of Amun-Re (Quaegebeur 1991, 264f.). In scenes 10 and 11, in contrast to the depiction, for *b3* a spelling with was chosen (Pantalacci and Traunecker 1990, scenes 10, 11, 15, 16).

The nature of this sun god in the shape of a four headed ram is revealed in a passage from Edfu: Banebded, the fourheaded ram from Mendes is the god, who "unites four gods in one god, who is Re together with his children" (Edfou III, 258. 6-7; Kurth 1983, 152f.). Thus the ram embodies the first four generations of the divine reigning dynasty (Barta 1973, 195, n. 1; Kurth 1983, 154, n. 19).

Each of these four Bas is related to one of the four elements: Re/Khepri gives light (Fire), Shu provides the beings with breath (Air), Geb provides mankind with that which grows on him (Earth), and Osiris causes the Nile to come out of its caverns (Water).[63] So the sun god, comprising his four Bas, embodies his creatures and at the same time his Creation (cf. Kurth 1983, 154f., n. 26). On the other hand as Demiurge he is omnipresent in his creation (Goyon 1985, 186). He is the principal creative power (Chassinat 1916-1917, 41) and his outer appearance of a ram alludes to his procreative capacity.

The three missing names of the gods can now be restored as the Ba of Re,[64] the Ba of Shu, and the Ba of Geb. However, their assignment to a specific side of BM EA 1512 remains problematic, because none of the sources relates these Bas to special cardinal points. The text on the west side still preserves *b3 n wsir*, which is very striking. The name of Re would have been meaningful in the Ba text on the east side (sunrise). On the other hand there is no evidence for a relation between (the Ba of) Shu or (the Ba of) Geb either to the north or to the south. In this respect the completion of the Ba texts on the north and south side must be left open.

Summary:

1) The east side (pl. 40b):

jj.n b3 n [*rˁ* ... ... *ˁẖj.f r pt* ... (lacuna of unknown length)]

The Ba of [Re ... ...][65] has come [and flies (now) up to the sky ... (lacuna of unknown length)].

2) The north and south sides (pl. 41a-b):

jw/jj.n b3 [*n šw/gb* ... ... *ˁẖj.f r pt* ... (lacuna of unknown length)]

The Ba [of Shu/Geb ... ...][66] has come [and flies (now) up to the sky ... (lacuna of unknown length)].

Contents and structure of these three Ba texts are identical with those on the west side.

The subject of the inscriptions of BM EA 1512 determined even the spelling of *b3*. The artist chose the spelling [hieroglyph] which in the context with the four Bas of the sun god is rarely used, as shown above. The sun god's outer appearance of a ram was in most cases responsible for the spelling of *b3* with the ram-hieroglyph. In the case of BM EA 1512 it influenced the choice of hieroglyphs: the best shape for accomplishing the ascent to the sky is the one of a bird. So from all the spellings for *b3* = Ba-"soul" the most obvious was chosen.[67]

We may here recapitulate in brief the religious ideas conveyed by BM EA 1512 in its former shape of an obelisk:

1) The falcon, that once crowned the obelisk, represented the sun god during his daily sun course. The bird of prey looked towards the west side of the obelisk (fig.1), towards the spot where it ends the day journey and leaves the world of the living, where it mounts the nightbark and starts its night journey through the Underworld. The concept of the sun god embodying his four emanations, was also visualized in the former obelisk: immediately below their Creator (the squatting falcon on the top of the obelisk) the four Bas are shown ascending to heaven.

2) Its texts and decoration deal with the death of Re, Shu, Geb, and Osiris and the (unified) manifestation of their Bas in the sky as sun god. It thus combined aspects of the sun cult as well as of the funerary cult. But with regard to the fact, that the west side is designed as front and that the crowning falcon was directed to the West, the domination of the funerary character becomes evident.

This prevailing otherworldly character of the object will help identify the obelisk's former place of erection as at a specific religious complex.

The original site of erection of BM EA 1512 in its former shape of an obelisk

The object originates from Saïs.[68] Indeed there is evidence for obelisks erected in the enclosure of the temple of Neith at Saïs.

Herodotus and other sources give us a rough idea of the appearance of the Osirian district during Late Period and Ptolemaic times. It was situated in the northern part of the enclosure behind the temple of Neith (El-Sayed 1975: 207f., n. 50) and comprised a lake, on which the Osirian mysteries took place.[69] Next to this lake was the temple of Osiris, the so-called *ḥwt-bjt* (El-Sayed 1975, 199-208). This sanctuary housed the *ḥwt-ḥm3g*,[70] which in general is identified with the tomb of Osiris (El-Sayed 1975, 208-13), and chapels of gods worshipped beside Osiris (id. 207). According to Herodotus obelisks were erected in this complex (Hist. II, 170), a statement which can be supported by the two following pieces of evidence, both dating to the 26th Dynasty.

Inscriptions of the statue of Neferibre-Nefer record the building projects executed by Psametik I at Saïs (El-Sayed 1975, 102-8). Among others he had set up obelisks in the temples of Neith and raised a related monument, a benben-stone, in the *ḥwt-bjt* in *mḥ-nt* (El-Sayed 1975: 207f., n. 50).

The obelisk at Urbino and the one decorating the Piazza della Minerva in Rome today once formed a pair, erected by Apries at Saïs.[71] Each was about five metres high. The inscriptions name Osiris, the great god in *ḥwt-bjt*, Neith of Saïs in *ḥwt-bjt*, Neith of Saïs in *t3-ˁnḫ* (the necropolis),[72]

Neith of the *ḥwt-bjt* in *mḥ-nt* (El-Sayed 1975: 207f., n. 5[o]), Atum, the great god in Saïs and Atum, the great god in *t3-ʿnḫ*. All the toponyms indicate that this pair of obelisks was intended to be set up in the Osirian complex of the Neith temple at Saïs. Since they formed a pair we may assume that they once flanked a monument.

BM EA 1512 in its former shape of an obelisk was not only dedicated to the death and transformation of Osiris but also to that one of Re, Shu and Geb. No source known to me connects the three last named gods either with the *ḥwt-bjt* or with the Osirian complex in the northern temenos of the temple of Neith. Furthermore a text from Edfu assures us that the divine Bas ascend to heaven in the place where their corpses are buried in the Sacred District, which among others comprises the tombs of the Demiurge, the primeval gods and Osiris:[73] "The rise of (their) Bas to the sky takes place in (the Sacred District of) Behedet. They (the Bas) live together with the stars, their corpses are hidden in the divine mound and their burials are concealed in the necropolis."[74]

Thus the crucial point now is whether the *real* burial of Osiris can be located in the Osirian complex behind the temple of Neith at Saïs, as reported by Herodotus[75] and as taken for granted in Egyptology.[76] If this was the case, then that area comprised as well the burials of the deceased gods, which are with one exception associated with the last resting-place of Osiris.[77] Then it becomes likely that BM EA 1512 in its former shape once was erected in this complex, even though no source has yet been found which associates Re, Shu and Geb with the Osirian complex at Saïs.

However, whereas Herodotus reports that the tomb of Osiris is built directly behind the temple of Neith and extends along the whole length of this temple (Hist. II, 170), Strabo states that "a little above (ὑπερ) Saïs is the asylum of Osiris, in which the body of Osiris is said to lay" (Geogr. XVII, 803; translation Jones 1982, 73). ὑπερ in this context means "up the river Nile".[78] The tomb of Osiris then has to be located somewhere to the south of Saïs. A contradiction to Herodotus becomes obvious. To date only Lloyd has pointed out the incompability of the assertions by Herodotus and Strabo.[79]

Yet another aspect makes it doubtful that the *real* burial of Osiris can be identified with that described by Herodotus. The Sacred District, with its sanctuaries[80] and the burial of Osiris, is never part of the enclosure of the main temple,[81] as attested at Philae (Junker 1913), Kom Ombo,[82] Edfu (Kurth 1994a; id., 1994b; id. 1994c, 156-79), Esna,[83] Thebes (Traunecker, Le Saout, Masson 1981, 104f.; Lecuyot 1992; Lecuyot and Gabolde 1995), Coptos (Traunecker 1992, 36f., 358-63, 391), Dendera (Daumas 1969, 12-14), Abydos (Chassinat 1966, 253-60), Hermopolis (Chassinat 1966, 291-6), *ḥwt-nswt* in the 18th Upper Egyptian nome (Vandier 1961, 126, 139), and Heliopolis (Chassinat 1966, 282f., n. 8). On the contrary it formed a separate enclosure at a relatively short distance from the temple. Thus the location of the tomb given by Strabo suddenly makes sense when we take his statement for an indication of the Sacred District situated to the south of Saïs.

Is it possible that the classical historians refer to two different tombs of Osiris, one situated in the northern temenos of the temple of Neith, the other one situated somewhere to the south of Saïs? The question arises, whether the deceased Osiris can have two tombs in one and the same place of worship.

The positive answer to this question is provided by the mysteries of Osiris which took place in the month of Khoiak (Chassinat 1966; 1968). In the course of this festival three statues related to Osiris were produced and then kept in a special room of the temple for one year. This depository in general is called *štjt* (*ḥrjt*).[84] In the following year on the 30th Khoiak the statues produced during the mysteries of the previous year were transferred to the neighbouring divine necropolis (Chassinat 1966, 73) in order to be buried: they found their last resting-place in a mound (*j3t*) planted with trees (Chassinat 1966, 277-97; Hugonot 1989, 207-15). Thus in one and the same place of worship Osiris has a temporary tomb and an eternal burial-place.[85]

With reference to Saïs this means that Herodotus reports on the transitional depository, where one of the statues was kept and taken care of for one year. This temporary tomb could have been the *ḥwt-ḥm3g*, the main chapel of the *ḥwt-bjt* in the northern part of the temenos of the temple of Neith.

Strabo points out the last resting-place of Osiris in the Sacred District, situated a little south of Saïs. There the statue from the *ḥwt-ḥm3g* and the other two statues[86] produced during the festival of Khoiak of the previous year were transported on the 30th Khoiak in order to be buried for eternity in a sacred mound[87] in the vicinity of the Demiurge, the primeval and other gods.

The seclusion of this special complex becomes evident from Esna no.196, 2 where it is said that the Sacred District to the north of Esna should not be seen by man.[88] Furthermore, in order to prevent profanation of the Abaton at Philae, trespassing was prohibited (Junker 1913, 22, 31). According to these sources neither Herodotus nor Strabo could ever have seen the last resting-place of Osiris. This would explain the discrepancy between the two accounts, if Herodotus was shown the temporary tomb of Osiris in the *ḥwt-ḥm3g*, and also why Stabo only reports on the burial from hearsay ("... in which the body of Osiris *is said to lay*" (my italics), Geogr. XVII, 803; translation Jones 1982, 73).

We have no evidence for the structure of the Sacred District at Saïs, but texts from Edfu and Esna inform us about the different architectural components of their neighbouring Sacred Districts, which thus occupied a large area.[89] It is possible that the Napoleonic expedition came across the remains of the Sacred District at Saïs. The authors of the "Description de l'Egypte" mention large accumulations of antique brick constructions near the villages Asdymeh and el-Nahâriyeh to the South of Saïs and they identified those architectural remains with the tomb of Osiris mentioned by Strabo (Mallet 1888, 58f., 70f.).

The texts and decoration of BM EA 1512, conveying the concept of the death and transformation of gods, confine the place of erection of the former obelisk to the Sacred District. There it would have been linked to the cult of the deceased gods and as a single obelisk it would have received offerings.[90] The site of erection of the former obelisk in this complex at Saïs cannot be specified because we have no evidence for the groundplan. However, the object BM EA 1512 itself supplies us with three criteria for its original place of erection. Since the decoration of the object is executed in sunk relief and its hieroglyphs are cut into the surface of the shaft, we may assume that BM EA 1512 in its original place of erection was exposed to the sunlight. Thus, like the *tḫn wꜥtj* at Karnak[91] and the Benben-stone, BM EA 1512 in its former shape of an obelisk could have been worshipped in a part of a sanctuary that was open to the sky. In the second place, the deep chisel marks on the east side[92] give grounds for believing that this side was totally hidden from sight; perhaps the east side was next to a wall. Furthermore the four sides had been aligned according to the four cardinal points so that the sun god on the top of the obelisk was facing due West.

Summary

The object BM EA 1512 is the top of a single obelisk dating from the Graeco-Roman Period. With regard to its appearance, its texts and depictions, and its function, this former obelisk remains unique among known Egyptian obelisks. It manifests several Egyptian religious conceptions, each attested separately in other sources, but here combined in a single object. It was less than three metres in height. A crowning falcon sculpture squatted on an oblong base which cannot be conceived as the apex of a pyramidion; the top was shaped like a gabled-roof.

On the base of text parallels from Graeco-Roman temples it has proven possible to reconstruct the contents of the texts, which are largely lost together with the main part of the shaft: after the burial of the deceased gods Re, Shu, Geb and Osiris in the divine necropolis, their Bas ascend to heaven with the help of the four wind gods. In the sky the four Bas are transfigured and made manifest as stars.

The picture panels illustrate the crucial moment from the texts which are displayed on the shaft below them: in each panel a Ba in the appearance of a falcon is lifted up to the firmament by one of the four wind gods. The summit showed the god who embodies his children, the Bas of Re, of Shu, of Geb and of Osiris and thus his Creation. He is the sun god, represented on his diurnal course. His line of sight was directed to the Western horizon, where he ends his day trip and descends to the Underworld. The subject of the inscriptions covers the whole monument in chronological succession and influenced the spelling of the central term *b3*.

Having pointed out the correctness of both the tomb of Osiris described by Herodotus and that cited by Strabo, a location of the latter tomb was suggested. We advanced the hypothesis that Strabo reports on the last resting-place of Osiris in the Sacred District to the south of Saïs. In this enclosure dedicated to the deceased Demiurge, the primeval gods, and Osiris, BM EA 1512 in its former shape of an obelisk would originally have been erected. It would have been a cult object, in which the Sun god and the deceased gods Re, Shu, Geb and Osiris were worshipped. At its place of erection it was exposed to the sunlight and orientated alongside to the cardinal points so that the front was directed to the West, with its rear perhaps adjacent to a limiting wall.

Notes

1 Here the author would like to thank Vivian Davies, Keeper of Egyptian Antiquities at the British Museum, for permission to publish this object. The author is also indebted to Prof. Dr. Gert Audring, Dr. Morris Bierbrier, Muriel Elsholz, Prof. Dr. Manfred Kudlek, Prof. Dr. Dieter Kurth, Christian Loeben, Dr. Marion Meyer, Dr. Stephen Quirke, Prof. Dr. Helmut Satzinger, Dr. Claude Traunecker, and Dr. Hans-Dietrich Zimmermann for their helpful support and advice.

2 PM IV, 49 (reference); Wild 1960: 60, n. 2 (mentioning the object in connection with depictions of the personifications of the north wind); Iversen 1972, 152, No. 1512 (reference).

3 White and the light coloured limestone symbolize the Sun, cf. Kees 1943, 442; Schenkel 1963, 143; Martin 1977, 61. The obelisk of Teti I is made from yellow quartzite, see Martin 1977, 42ff., Abb. 3. For the different stones from which obelisks were made apart from pink granite, see Martin 1977, 59-62, 196-9.

4 However see the parallels to the inscriptions, offering a possible guide to original height.

5 This shape implies the same symbolism as the pyramidion. This can be demonstrated by the following two examples: an Apis stela from Saqqara shows three gabled-roofs instead of three pyramidia, see Mariette 1857, pl. 32 (left fig.); and the singular stela, also from Saqqara, of "the scribe of the cattle of Amun, Seti" (Jéquier 1935, 29, pl. 17, 10). The pyramidion on the top has the shape of a gabled-roof, as can be seen on a photo from the catalogue "Le règne du soleil. Akhenaton et Néfertiti" (Exposition organisé par le Ministère de la Culture aux Musées Royaux et d'Histoire, Brussels 1975, 143, no.71).

6 Red symbolizes the Sun, cf. Kees 1943, 448-52; Griffiths 1972, 85-90.

7 Gutbub 1977, 328-43. Two groups have to be distinguished: animal-like and anthropomorphic gods with animal heads. The wind gods depicted on BM EA 1512 belong to the first group.

8 Engelbach 1929b; Montet and Goyon 1935-1937; Leclant and Yoyotte 1950; Leclant and Yoyotte 1957; Yoyotte 1957, 81 and fig. 6 ("disposition normale des textes"); the direction of the inscription on a fragment from an obelisk found at Tanis was corrected by the Egyptian artist, see Engelbach 1929a, 20, Pl. I.

9 Urk. IV, 584-5 (inscriptions of Tuthmosis III); ibidem, 1548-1552 (inscriptions of Tuthmosis IV).

10 The inscriptions of the Lateran obelisk designate the obelisk as *tḫn wꜥtj*. Lefebvre (1948) recognized in this expression the qualification of Tuthmosis' III obelisk as an "obélisque unique". Further the king emphasizes that this was the first time that a single obelisk had been erected at Thebes (Urk. IV, 584, 11: *sꜥḥꜥ.n.f tḫn wꜥtj m sb3 ḥrj ḥwt-nṯr r h3w jpt-swt m š3ꜥ tpj sꜥḥꜥ tḫn wꜥtj m w3st*), which may be taken to imply that at the time of Tuthmosis III other temples had already been equipped with a *tḫn wꜥtj*. Lefebvre (1948, 592-3) traces this obelisk back to similar cult objects from Heliopolis.

11 For the orientation of the hieroglyphs on the Lateran obelisk see Yoyotte 1957, fig. 2. For the orientation of hieroglyphs on a pair of obelisks see Yoyotte 1957, 81, fig. 1.

12 The author further states (1990, 55-67), that the obelisk functioned already on the Forum Augusti as gnomon. As yet no archaeological evidence has been found which would support the existence of a monumental sundial in Ancient Egypt. Klein (1992, 275) has also expressed reservations concerning this hypothesis of Alföldy.

13 In Rome obelisks were connected with the sun god: on the top of the pyramidion a golden ball was fixed (Roullet 1972, 43; Loeben 1992, 21; Alföldy 1990, pl.11, 1), the obelisk from the Monte Citorio was the gnomon of Augustus' monumental sundial on the Campus Martius (Alföldy 1990, 55-67) and by the erection on the spina of a circus the obelisk became part of a Roman institution that was connected with the cult of the Sun; for obelisks in circi see Roullet 1972, 43ff., 67-71 (nos. 68-70), 72-3 (no. 72, secondary), 82 (no. 86, secondary); Loeben 1992, 20-1. For other functions of obelisks at Rome see Roullet 1972, *passim*; Loeben 1992, 21-3.

14 Since the question whether the columns of the Taharqa colonnade at the Karnak temple once

supported statues is not yet settled, we do not take them into account here. Most recently this subject has been discussed by Sourouzian (1989, 59f.).

A private stela from the mid-New Kingdom was found at Abydos (Mariette 1880, 460; Ranke 1935, 419, Nr. 4; id. no year, 279, Nr. 15; Martin 1977, 72). An explanation for the falcon and cobra that crown the rounded top of the stela cannot be given.

15 LÄ I, 680 (s. v. "Begig"); Chaaban 1926; El-Hamid Zayed 1964; Martin 1977, 72-75; Sourouzian 1989, 59, 218, Pl. 11b.

16 PM II^2, 221. BM EA 74 (Ptolemaic ?) represents another monumental scarab that forms a monolith with the now largely destroyed substructure. BM EA 1231 is a smaller scarab squatting on a slab which is only 15 cm high. It dates to the reign of Ramesses II, cf. Bierbrier 1993, pl. 12-3.

17 Urk. IV, 1753. 13, 1754. 2. In the Amduat the birth of Khepri takes place during the 11th hour.

18 In the wind texts on the west, east, and north sides the genitive *-n* is written *m*. However in the wind text on the south side it is written *n*. The phonetic requirements for this assimilation in the texts from the temple at Edfu are demonstrated by Kurth 1990, 60, e). The assimilation of the genitive *-n* can be found in the materials of the Edfu-Project (long-term project directed by Dieter Kurth and financed by the DFG), e. g. Edfou V, 96. 7 (*jwꜥw mnḫ m bḥdtj*), Edfou VI, 14. 14 (*ḫf ndb m dbnbnj*), Edfou VII, 196. 1 = 271. 11 (*sr m m3ꜥt*).

19 The construction of the preserved beginning of the wind texts of BM EA 1512 is similar to the structure of the wind texts in the temple at Deir el-Medineh (Piehl 1888: pl.162-3; date under Ptolemy VI Philometor) and in the temple at Esna (Esna II, nos. 105 and 128; date probably under Domitian): *ṯ3w nfr* + cardinal point + epithet of the wind. Therefore the wind texts of BM EA 1512 may be completed from those at Deir el-Medineh and Esna. While all four of these texts are preserved in the Hathor temple at Deir el-Medineh, in the temple at Esna only texts of the east and south winds have survived. Since the parallels from Deir el-Medineh and Esna can be varied in the section introduced by *ntf*, we will only complete those wind texts of BM EA 1512 that have survived in both temples. In Kom Ombo no.217 the text of the north wind starts with an identical structure. The construction of the beginning of the other three wind texts is less similar: the cardinal point is not followed by an epithet of the wind but directly by the attribute-sentence *ṯ3w nfr* + cardinal point + *ntf*.

20 The meaning of *ḥḏ3* is not clear, cf. Gutbub 1977: 340; LÄ VI, 1267 with n. 66 (s. v. "Wind"). It is the name of the west wind among others in the temple of Hathor at Deir el-Medineh. Piehl translates "the cold wind" (1888, 128, pl.163).

21 Cf. the other depictions of the god of the west wind in Gutbub 1977, 330f., 334-6 (the object BM EA 1512 was unknown to the author).

22 Piehl 1888, pl.163.

23 De Wit 1957; id. 1958-1962, no 101. The south wind also was regarded as the bringer of the inundation, cf. Gutbub 1977, 343.

24 See n. 18.

25 The text parallel Esna II, no.128 uses the term *ḥrt*.

26 For this unexplained name of the east wind cf. LÄ VI, 1267 with n. 62 (s. v. "Wind"); Meeks 1980, 77.2509.

27 Completed from the parallels in the temple of Hathor at Deir el-Medineh (Piehl 1888, 128, pl. 162) and in the temple at Esna (Esna II, no.128). The parallels diverge after*pt*/*ḥrt*; for the legitimation of this completion see n.19.

28 The depiction reflects the birth of the Sun in the earth.

29 For the iconography of the wind gods see Gutbub 1977, 330f., 334-43.

30 For this quality see Piehl 1888, pl. 162. In the corresponding text in the temple of Apet at Karnak it is said, that the east wind raises the Ba of Osiris together with the other gods (i.e. the stars) up to heaven, De Wit 1957; id. 1958-1962, no.101.

31 See n. 18.

32 The same designation for the north wind can be found in Deir el-Medineh (Piehl 1888, pl. 162) and in the temple of Apet at Karnak (De Wit 1957; id. 1958-1962, no 101); cf. *Wb* V, 24. 13-14; Meeks 1980, 77.4380.

33 See n. 29.

34 The temple of Hathor (Piehl 1888, pl. 162) and the temple of Apet (De Wit 1957; id. 1958-1962, no.101); in general cf. Gutbub 1977, 343 and LÄ VI, 1267 with n. 46 (s. v. "Wind").
35 See n. 18.
36 Name of the south wind among others in the temple of Hathor at Deir el-Medineh (Piehl 1888, pl.162) and in the temple at Esna (Esna II, no.105, 1), which derives from the heat this wind brings to Egypt, blowing from inner Africa, cf. LÄ VI, 1267 with n. 56 (s. v. "Wind"); Meeks 1980, 77.4270.
37 Completed on the grounds of the parallels from the temple of Hathor at Deir el-Medineh (Piehl 1888, pl.162) and the temple at Esna (Esna II, no.105); see n. 19.
38 See n. 29.
39 CT II, 389ff.; Piehl 1888, pl.162; De Wit 1957; id. 1958-1962, no 101; Esna II, no.105, 4. A similar passage can be found in Kom Ombo no.217.
40 Gutbub 1977, 349.
41 Mostly the wind gods are depicted on a baseline, except for the east wind in the shape of a scarab, cf. Gutbub 1977, 330f., 334-6.
42 The Ba (Wb I, 411. 6 - 412. 10) in the pure shape of a falcon (i. e. both body and head are that of a falcon) is exemplified by Spiegelberg 1927; Desroches-Noblecourt 1963, pl. 54 (facing p. 259); Zabkar 1968, 73; Esna III, n° 197, 24; Edfou I, 87. 13; Horapollo I, 7; in the materials of the Edfu-Project (see n. 18) the spellings with lamp and falcon (e.g. Edfou VI, 11.7; Edfou VII, 122.14; Edfou VIII, 20.10) and lamp, falcon and flail (e.g. Edfou V, 46.15; Edfou VII, 20.12; Edfou VIII, 47.9) are well attested for the designation of the Ba-soul.
43 The hieroglyph is broken away in the lower half. The remains of the sign are nearly round (Pl. I). Unlike the other hieroglyphs the inner part of the sign is not chiselled out but left intact, so that the remains go best with the loop of the *ʿnḫ*-sign. For this epithet of Osiris cf. Wb I, 201. 8. An inscription in the edifice of Taharqa characterizes Amun as *ʿnḫ* (Parker, Leclant, Goyon 1979, pl. 41, version B, col. 20). Further cf. Winter 1968, 85f.
44 Perhaps we have to add epithets of Osiris in the lacuna.
45 Cf. Kurth 1989 (with previous literature).
46 Completed on the grounds of the Ba texts from Kom Ombo, cf. Gutbub 1973, 387-394. This text no.327 once formed a unit together with a depiction of the filling of the lunar eye; cf. Herbin 1982.
47 Cf. Gutbub 1973, plan facing p. 546.
48 LÄ II, 1206f. (s. v. "Himmelsaufstieg"); Zabkar 1968, 44f., 73-5. For aging and death of the gods see Hornung 1971, 143-59.
49 For the sun god resting on the top of an obelisk see Kurth 1983, 271-3 and n. 605; cf. the determinative in the name of the Sun Temple Nekhen-Ra in Kaiser 1956. Further the frieze of the south wall of the pylon of the temple at Edfu comprises a similar decoration element: on the top of an obelisk the *ḥḥ*-hieroglyph is placed, above the arms of which the winged scarab hovers (inadequately published in Edfou XIV, pl.667, recorded during the collation campaign in spring 1995 by the Edfu-Project, photographs 2523-34).
50 Khepri can take the place of Re for example on the statue of Basa (Wild 1960); the base of a statue of Nisuweseret (Burchardt 1910); Medinet Habu VI, pl. 420 top left (only the last two Bas have remained, they are the Ba of Shu and the Ba of Khepri) and Wild 1960, 64; two lists from the temple at Edfu name for the *ḥnw-n-štjt* the Ba of Re, the Ba of Osiris, the Ba of Shu, and the Ba of Khepri (Edfou I, 182, (29); Edfou II, 23, (84) - (88)). In contrast to this list, in the room *ḥnw-n-štjt* itself (room F) not the Ba of Khepri, but the Ba of Geb is depicted (Edfou I, 171. 9-10).
51 Brugsch 1871; id. 1968, 736f.; Chassinat 1916-1917, 41; Wild 1960; Zandee 1966, 26-9; Kurth 1983, 152-4; Quaegebeur 1991; Bács 1992.
52 Cf. the lists given by Brugsch 1968, 736f. and Wild 1960, 61-4. Only at Esna is this sequence broken, in two instances: Esna II, nos.17, 47-8 (Re-Shu-Osiris-Geb); no.140 (Shu-Re-Geb-Osiris).
53 For these three spellings see Edfou I, 182, (28)-(29); Grenier 1980, nos.31,155; Pantalacci and Traunecker 1990: scene 10 (Geb) and scene 11 (Shu), the inscriptions of the scenes 15 and 16 are mainly destroyed.
54 Gasse 1984, 205, 8 (CB 12, 1-2).
55 Assmann 1983, 207, n. t; Quaegebeur 1991, 261-3.

56 Quaegebeur 1991, 262; Bács 1992.
57 Edfou III, 11. 3-4.
58 Quaegebeur 1991, 260, 264f.
59 Spellings such as  and  for the designation of the Ba of Osiris refer to the Ba's shape of a Benu-bird, cf. Junker 1913, 1, 61; El-Banna 1985, 165, Doc. 3 and fig. 1, 168.
60 Wild 1960, 49, 59f.; Zandee 1966, 27; Quaegebeur 1991, 260. For interchangeability of  and , see already *Wb* I, 411. 6 to 412. 10 and Wb I, 412. 9-12; further Parker, Leclant, Goyon 1979, pl. 40, A l. 8 and B l. 18; pl. 41, A l. 9-10 and B l. 20-1 (twice).
61 See n. 51.
62 Edfou IX, pl.23: 2nd register on the north and south walls.
63 Brugsch 1868; id. 1871, esp. 83; Wild 1960, 65f.; Brugsch 1968, 735-7; Assmann 1973, 73; Assmann 1983, 207; Voss 1994, 26-8.
64 As noted above, in this context Khepri is supplanted by Re in Graeco-Roman times.
65 On the analogy of the Ba text of the west side epithets of Re are expected.
66 On the analogy of the Ba text of the west side epithets of Shu and Geb are expected.
67 In the kiosk on the roof of the temple at Dendera the gods of 36 Egyptian nomes (as images of the 36 decans) are depicted as birds with human heads. Here the subject (decans in the sky) has influenced the outer appearance of the gods, see Goyon 1986; Dendara VIII, pl. 696-8.
68 Nash 1910; PM IV, 49; Iversen 1972, 152, no.1512.
69 Herodotus, Hist. II, 171; Gessler-Löhr 1983, 233-41.
70 See Chassinat 1968, 485f.; El-Sayed 1975, 208-13. Cf. the *ḥwt-ḥm3g* in the temple at Behbeit el-Hagar, Favard-Meeks 1991, 227-50, 367f.
71 Habachi 1943, 388f.; Müller 1954; Iversen 1968, 93-100 (fig. 51 shows the obelisk at Urbino); Habachi 1977, 101f.
72 Cf. Habachi 1943: 387-89: El-Sayed 1975, 24f., n. (d); id. 1982, 12 (Doc. 468), 32 (Doc. 467b), 118 (Doc. 291), 124 (Doc. 508, 267b), 325 (Doc. 291), 391 (Doc.420), 413 (Doc.467b), 609 (Doc. 984).
73 Sauneron 1958, 278; De Wit 1958-1962, 90; *id.* 1968, 46.
74 Edfou VII, 118. 11-12: *pr(t) r pt jn b3.(sn) n bḥdt ꜥnḫ.sn ḥnꜥ ꜥnḫw tḫn.tw ḫ3t.sn ḫnt j3t nṯrjt ḏsr.tw st.sn m jgrt*. For *bḥdt* as a name of the Sacred Distict at Edfu see Kurth 1994a.
75 In the 2nd century AD Athenagoras quotes this passage from Herodotus (Hist. II, 170), cf. Athenagoras, *Supplicatio pro Christianis*, XXIX c.
76 RE I A 1920, 1758f.; El-Sayed 1975, 208-13; LÄ V, 355 (s. v. "Saïs").
77 For literature see below. The only exception to this rule is the tomb of Osiris in the northeastern sector of Karnak temple. There is as yet no evidence that this tomb was ever associated with other divine burials. The author is indebted to S. Marchand, F. Leclère and L. Coulon for the opportunity to consult their manuscript '"Catacombes" osiriennes de Ptolémée IV à Karnak', then forthcoming in Karnak X.
78 Cf. the passages Strabo, Geogr. Lib. XVII, 803 = Jones 1982: 73f. ("... Philae which is situated above Syenê and Elephantine ..."); 806 = Jones 1982, 85 ("From Heliupolis, then, one comes to the Nile above the Delta.").
79 Lloyd 1988: 207 ("It should be noted, that the 'Οσιριδος 'ασυλον of Str. ... could not possibly have had anything to do with this building [i. e. the *ḥwt-bît*; annotation by the author] since his geographical information is incompatible with a Saite location").
80 For the architectural elements of the Sacred District of Behedet at Edfu see Kurth 1994c: 94f.
81 It was only during the reign of Nectanebo I that the Osirian complex - including the tomb of Osiris - at Karnak temple became part of the temenos by the erection of a new enclosure wall, see S.Marchand, Fr.Leclère and L.Coulon, in Karnak X (forthcoming).
82 Gutbub 1973 (Index): 13 - 14, s. v. "Nécropole divine".
83 Sauneron 1958; id. 1959, 28f.; id. 1962, 32f., 319-22, 334-7.
84 Chassinat 1966, 37, 61f., 71f., 91f., 227-30; id. 1968, 618-21. In Dendera the *štjt ḥrjt* is identified with one of the chapels on the roof of the temple of Hathor, see Chassinat 1966, 37, 227; id. 1968,

619; Beinlich 1984, 276-83. For references of the mysteries to these chapels see Cauville 1988 and Leitz 1989, 53f., n. 106.

85 In this connection a text from the temple of Apet at Karnak should be mentioned because it states that Amun-Re is buried both in the temple of Apet and at Djeme, cf. De Wit 1958 - 1962: 91; id. 1968: 44, 125, n. (52), 147.

86 It should be assumed that they rested in the proximity of the *ḥwt-ḥm3g*.

87 This subterranean tomb is described in the mysteries of Osiris (col. 80 - 81), see Chassinat 1968, 625-32.

88 *d3t št3(t) pw n m33 s(j) rmṯ nb*. Cf. also Esna no.196, 9.

89 For the Sacred District at Behedet see Kurth 1994b, 194f.; for Esna see Sauneron 1958; id. 1959, 28f.; id. 1983, 18-29. According to Papyrus Jumilhac the divine necropolis in the 18th Upper Egyptian nome covered an enormous area, see Vandier, 1961, 139, 245, n. (1008).

90 The best attested offering for the deceased gods is a combination of burning incense and a libation, cf. the list in Cauville 1987 (Catalogue), 56f., s.v. "dieux morts d'Edfou", and Edfou VIII, 118. 6-7. In the setting of very important festivities extensive offerings are made, cf. Edfou V, 131, 6-8.

91 See p.134.

92 See pp.132-3.

Bibliography

Alföldy, G 1990. *Der Obelisk auf dem Petersplatz in Rom. Ein historisches Monument der Antike.* Sitzungsberichte der Heidelberger Akademie der Wissenschaften, Philologisch-historische Klasse Jahrgang 1990, Bericht 2, Heidelberg.

Assmann, J 1973. *Das Grab des Basa (Nr. 389) in der thebanischen Nekropole.* Archäologische Veröffentlichungen 6. Mainz, Philipp von Zabern.

Assmann, J 1983. *Sonnenhymnen in thebanischen Gräbern.*THEBEN 1. Mainz, Philipp von Zabern.

Bács, T 1992. Amun-Re-Harakhti in the Late Ramesside Royal Tombs. In *Studia Aegyptiaca* 14, Budapest, 43-53.

El-Banna, E 1985. A propos du double phénix. In *Bulletin de l'Institut Français d'Archéologie Orientale* 85, 164-71.

Barguet, P 1950. L'obélisque de Saint-Jean-de-Lateran dans le temple de Ramsès II à Karnak. In *Annales du Service des Antiquités d'Egypte* 50, 269-80.

Barguet, P 1962. *Le temple d'Amon-Rê à Karnak. Essai d'exégèse.* Recherches d'Archéologie, de Philologie et d'Histoire 21. Cairo, Institut Français d'Archéologie Orientale.

Barta, W 1973. *Untersuchungen zum Götterkreis der Neunheit.* Münchner Ägyptologische Studien 28. Munich, Deutscher Kunstverlag.

Beinlich, H 1984. *Die "Osirisreliquien". Zum Motiv der Körperzerteilung in der altägyptischen Religion.* Ägyptologische Abhandlungen 42. Wiesbaden, Otto Harrassowitz.

Bierbrier, M (ed.) 1993. *Hieroglyphic Texts From Egyptian Stelae etc., Part 12.* London, British Museum Press.

Bourriau, J 1988. *Pharaohs and Mortals. Egyptian Art in the Middle Kingdom.* Cambridge University Press.

Brugsch, H 1868. Ueber die vier Elemente in altägyptischen Inschriften. In *Zeitschrift für Ägyptische Sprache und Altertumskunde* 6, 122-7.

Brugsch, H 1871. 𓊽𓊽𓏏𓊖 oder Mendes. In *Zeitschrift für Ägyptische Sprache und Altertumskunde* 9, 81-5.

Brugsch, H 1968. *Thesaurus Inscriptionum Aegyptiacarum.* Graz (reprint).

Burchardt, M 1910. Ein saitischer Statuensockel in Stockholm. In *Zeitschrift für Ägyptische Sprache und Altertumskunde* 47, 111-5.

Cauville, S 1987. *Essai sur la théologie du temple d'Horus à Edfou.* Bibliothèque d'Etude 102.1-2. Cairo, Institut Français d'Archéologie Orientale.

Cauville, S 1988. Les mystères d'Osiris à Dendera. - Interprétation des chapelles osiriennes. In *Bulletin de la Société Française d'Egyptologie* 112, 23-36.

Chaaban, M 1926. Rapport sur une mission à l'obélisque d'Abguîg (Fayoum). In *Annales du Service des Antiquités d'Egypte* 26, 105-8.
Chassinat, E 1916-1917. La mise à mort rituelle d'Apis. In *Recueil de Travaux* 38, 33-60.
Chassinat, E 1966-1968. *Le mystère d'Osiris au mois de Khoïak* I (1966), II (1968). Cairo, Institut Français d'Archéologie Orientale.
Daressy, G 1914. Graffiti de la Montagne Rouge. In *Annales du Service des Antiquités d'Egypte* 13, 43-47.
Daumas, F 1969. *Dendara et le temple d'Hathor. Notice sommaire.* Recherches d'Archéologie, de Philologie et d'Histoire 29. Cairo, Institut Français d'Archéologie Orientale.
De Wit, C 1957. Les génies des quatre vents au temple d'Opet. In *Chronique d'Egypte* 32, 25-39.
De Wit, C 1958-1962. *Les inscriptions du temple d'Opet à Karnak I - II.* Bibliotheca Aegyptiaca 11-12. Brussels, Fondation Egyptologique Reine Elisabethe.
De Wit, C 1968. *Les inscriptions du Temple d'Opet à Karnak III: Traduction intégrale des textes rituels — Essai d'interprétation.* Bibliotheca Aegyptiaca 13. Brussels, Fondation Egyptologique Reine Elisabethe.
Desroches-Noblecourt, C 1963. *Tut-ench-Amun.* Frankfurt, Berlin.
Engelbach, R 1929a. Evidence for the Use of a Mason's Pick in Ancient Egypt. In *Annales du Service des Antiquités d'Egypte* 29, 19-24.
Engelbach, R 1929b. The Direction of the Inscriptions on Obelisks. In *Annales du Service des Antiquités d'Egypte* 29, 25-30.
Favard-Meeks, C 1991. *Le temple de Behbeit el-Hagara. Essai de reconstruction et d'interprétation.* Studien zur Altägyptischen Kultur Beiheft 6. Hamburg.
Gasse, A 1984. La litanie des douze noms de Rê-Horakhty. In *Bulletin de l'Institut Français d'Archéologie Orientale* 84, 189-227.
Geßler-Löhr, B 1983. *Die heiligen Seen ägyptischer Tempel. Ein Beitrag zur Deutung sakraler Baukunst im Alten Ägypten.* Hildesheimer Ägyptologische Beiträge 21, Gerstenberg.
Goyon, J-C 1985. *Les dieux-gardiens et la genèse des temples (d'après les textes égyptiens de l'époque gréco - romaine). Les soixante d'Edfou et les soixante-dix-sept dieux de Pharbaetos.* Bibliothèque d'Etude 93.1-2. Cairo, Institut Français d'Archéologie Orientale.
Goyon, J-C 1986. Le feu nouveau du jour de l'an à Dendara at Karnak. In *Hommages à François Daumas* II, Montpellier, Publications de la Recherche, 331-44.
Grenier, J-C 1980. *Tôd: les inscriptions du temple ptolémaïque et romain, I: La salle hypostyle, textes N°s 1-172.* Fouilles de l'Institut Français d'Archéologie Orientale 18.1. Cairo, Institut Français d'Archéologie Orientale.
Gwyn Griffiths, J 1972. The Symbolism of Red in Egyptian Religion. In *Ex orbe religionum: studia Geo Widengren,* 81-90.
Gutbub, A 1973. *Textes fondamentaux de la théologie de Kôm Ombo.* Bibliothèque d'Etude 47.1-2. Cairo, Institut Français d'Archéologie Orientale.
Gutbub, A 1977. Die vier Winde im Tempel von Kom Ombo (Oberägypten). Bemerkungen zur Darstellung der Winde im Ägypten der griechisch-römischen Zeit. In O Keel, *Jahwe-Visionen und Siegelkunst. Eine neue Deutung der Majestätsschilderungen in Jes6, Ez1 und 10 und Sach4,* Stuttgarter Bibel-Studien 84/85, Stuttgart, 328-53.
Habachi, L 1943. Sais and its Monuments. In *Annales du Service des Antiquités d'Egypte* 42, 369-416.
Habachi, L 1977. *The Obelisks of Egypt. Skyscrapers of the Past.* New York, Charles Scribner's Sons.
Hamid Zayed, Abd el- 1964. A Free-standing Stela of the XIXth Dynasty. In *Revue d'Egyptologie* 16, 193-208.
Herbin, F-R 1982. Un hymne à la lune croissante. In *Bulletin de l'Institut Français d'Archéologie Orientale* 82, 237-82.
Hölbl, G 1994. *Geschichte des Ptolemäerreiches. Politik, Ideologie und religiöse Kultur von Alexander dem Großen bis zur römischen Eroberung.* Darmstadt.
Hornung, E 1971. *Der Eine und die Vielen, Ägyptische Gottesvorstellungen.* Darmstadt, Wissenschaftliche Buchgesellschaft.
Hugonot, J-C 1989. *Le jardin dans l'Egypte ancienne.* Europäische Hochschulschriften, Serie 38:

Archäologie, Band 27. Frankfurt, Bern, New York, Paris.
Iversen, E 1968. *Obelisks in Exile. I: The Obelisks of Rome.* Copenhagen, G E C Gad.
Iversen, E 1972. *Obelisks in Exile. II: The Obelisks of Istanbul and England.* Copenhagen, G E C Gad.
Jéquier, G 1935. *La pyramide d'Aba.* Fouilles à Saqqarah. Cairo, Institut Français d'Archéologie Orientale.
Jones, H 1982. *The Geography of Strabo VIII.* The Loeb Classical Library, London, W Heinemann.
Junker, H 1913. *Das Götterdekret über das Abaton.* Denkschriften der kaiserlichen Akademie der Wissenschaften in Wien, Philosophisch-Historische Klasse, LVI. Vienna.
Kaiser, W 1956. Zu den Sonnenheiligtümern der 5. Dynastie. In *Mitteilungen des Deutschen Archäologischen Instituts Abteilung Kairo* 14, 104-16.
Kees, H 1943. *Farbensymbolik in ägyptischen religiösen Texten,* NAWG, Philologisch-Historische Klasse, Jahrg. 1943, Nr. 11, Göttingen, 413-79.
Klein, R 1992. Review of Alföldy 1990. In *Gymnasium* 99, 275f.
Kurth, D 1983. *Die Dekoration der Säulen im Pronaos des Tempels von Edfu.* Göttinger Orientalische Forschungen IV. Reihe: Ägypten, Band 11, Wiesbaden.
Kurth, D 1989. Noch einmal zum "sdm.n.f" in den Tempeltexten der griechisch-römischen Zeit. In *Göttinger Miszellen* 113, 55-64.
Kurth, D 1990. *Zur Phonetik. In Inschriften des Tempels von Edfu.* Begleithefte 1, Wiesbaden 49-61.
Kurth, D 1994a. Die Reise der Hathor von Dendera nach Edfu. In Hildesheimer Ägyptologische Beiträge 37, Gerstenberg, 211-16.
Kurth, D 1994b. Zur Lage von Behedet, dem heiligen Bezirk von Edfu. In *Göttinger Miszellen* 142, 93-100.
Kurth, D 1994c. *Treffpunkt der Götter. Inschriften aus dem Tempel des Horus von Edfu.* Zürich, München.
Kurth, D 1994d. Das Lied von den vier Winden und seine angebliche pantomimische Darstellung. In *Essays in Egyptology in Honour of Hans Goedicke,* Baltimore, 135-46.
Leclant, J and J Yoyotte 1950. Les obélisques de Tanis (deuxième article), observations concernant la série des obélisques remployés. In *Kêmi* 11, 73 - 84.
Leclant, J and J Yoyotte 1957. Les obélisques de Tanis (troisième article), inventaire des obélisques remployés et des fragments d'obélisques de Tanis. In *Kêmi* 14, 43 - 80.
Lecuyot, G 1992. Un sanctuaire romain transformé en monastère: le Deir er-Roumi. In *Sesto Congresso Internazionale di Egittologia, Atti* I, Turin, 383-90.
Lecuyot, G and M Gabolde. Une "Douat" mystérieuse d'époque romaine au Deir er-Roumi. In C Eyre (ed.), *Seventh International Congress of Egyptologists, Abstracts of papers,* Oxford, 106f.
Lefebvre, G 1948. Sur l'obélisque du Lateran. In *Mélanges d'Archéologie et d'Histoire offerts à Charles Picard à l'occasion de son 65e anniversaire* II, Revue Archéologique 6e série, 32, Paris, 586-93.
Leitz, C 1989. Die obere und die untere Dat. In *Zeitschrift für Ägyptische Sprache und Altertumskunde* 116, 41-57.
Lloyd, A 1988. *Herodotus, Book II, Commentary 99-182.* Leiden, Brill.
Loeben, C and R Hillinger 1992. *Obelisken.* Landshut.
Loeben, C 1994. Nefertiti's pillars. In *Amarna Letters* 3, 1994 (forthcoming).
Mallet, D 1888. *Le culte de Neit à Saïs.* Paris, Ernest Leroux.
Mariette, A 1857. *Le sérapéum de Memphis.* Paris, Imprimerie Nationale.
Mariette, A 1880. *Catalogue général des monuments d'Abydos découverts pendants les fouilles de cette ville.* Paris.
Martin, K 1977. *Ein Garantsymbol des Lebens. Untersuchungen zu Ursprung und Geschichte der altägyptischen Obelisken bis zum Ende des Neuen Reiches.* Hildesheimer Ägyptologische Beiträge 3. Hildesheim.
Dimitri Meeks 1980. *Année lexicographique I (1977).* Paris.
Montet, P and G Georges Goyon 1935-1937. Les obélisques de Ramsès II. In *Kêmi* 5, 104-14.
Müller, H 1954. Der Obelisk von Urbino. In *Zeitschrift für Ägyptische Sprache und Altertumskunde* 79, 143-9.
Nash, W 1910. Notes on Some Egyptian Antiquities VIII. In *Proceedings of the Society for Biblical*

Archaeology 32, 193-4.
Pantalacci, L and C Traunecker. *Le temple d'el-Qalaa I.* Cairo, Institut Français d'Archéologie Orientale.
Parker, R, J Leclant and J-C Goyon 1979. *The Edifice of Taharqa by the Sacred Lake of Karnak.* Brown Egyptological Studies 8. Providence, Brown University Press.
Petrie, W M F 1888. *Tanis II.* London, Egypt Exploration Fund.
Petrie, W M F and E Mackay 1915. *Kafr Ammar and Shurafa.* London, Bernard Quaritch.
Piehl, K 1888. *Inscriptions hiéroglyphiques recueillies en Europe et en Egypte II: commentaire*, Leipzig, J C Hinrichs, 121-4, pl. 162-3.
PM II² = B Porter and R Moss, *Topographical Bibliography of Ancient Egyptian Hieroglyphic Texts, Reliefs, and Paintings. II, Theban Temples.* 2nd edition, 1972. Oxford, Clarendon Press
PM IV = B Porter and R Moss, *Topographical Bibliography of Ancient Egyptian Hieroglyphic Texts, Reliefs, and Paintings. IV, Lower and Middle Egypt (Delta and Cairo to Asyût).* 1934. Oxford, Clarendon Press.
Quaegebeur, J 1991. Les quatre dieux Min. In U Verhoeven and E Graefe (eds.), *Religion und Philosophie im Alten Ägypten (Festschrift Derchain)*, Orientalia Lovaniensia Analecta 39, Louvain, 253-68.
Ranke, H (no date). *Die ägyptischen Personennamen II.* Glückstadt.
Ranke, H 1935. *Die ägyptischen Personennamen I.* Glückstadt.
Redford, D 1989. *Akhenaten. The Heretic King.* Cairo.
Rochholz, M 1994. Sedfest, Sonnenheiligtum und Pyramidenbezirk. Zur Deutung der Grabanlangen der Könige der 5. und 6. Dynastie. In *Ägyptische Tempel - Struktur, Funktion und Programm (Akten der Ägyptologischen Tempeltagungen in Gosen 1990 und in Mainz 1992)*, Hildesheimer Ägyptologische Beiträge 37, 255-80.
Roullet, A 1972. *The Egyptian and Egyptianizing Monuments of Imperial Rome.* Etudes Préliminaires aux Religions Orientaux dans l'Empire Romain 20. Leiden, E J Brill.
El-Saghir, M 1991. Das Statuenversteck im Luxortempel. Antike Welt, 22. Jahrgang, Sondernummer 1991, Mainz.
Sauneron, S 1958. L'Abaton de la campagne d'Esna. In *Mitteilungen des Deutschen Archäologischen Instituts Abteilung Kairo* 16, 271-9.
Sauneron, S 1959. *Quatre campagnes à Esna. Esna I.* Cairo, Institut Français d'Archéologie Orientale.
Sauneron, S 1962. *Les fêtes religieuses d'Esna aux derniers siècles du paganisme. Esna V.* Cairo, Institut Français d'Archéologie Orientale.
Sauneron, S 1983. *Villes et légendes d'Egypte.* Bibliothèque d'Etude 90.2. Cairo, Institut Français d'Archéologie Orientale.
El-Sayed, R 1975. *Documents relatifs à Saïs et ses divinités.* Bibliothèque d'Etude 69. Cairo, Institut Français d'Archéologie Orientale.
El-Sayed, R 1982. *La déesse Neith de Saïs, I: Importance de son culte, II: Documentation.* Bibliothèque d'Etude 86.1-2, Cairo, Institut Français d'Archéologie Orientale.
Schenkel, W 1963. Die Farben in ägyptischer Kunst und Sprache. In *Zeitschrift für Ägyptische Sprache und Altertumskunde* 88, 131-47.
Sourouzian, H 1989. *Les monuments du roi Merenptah.* Sonderschriften des Deutschen Archäologischen Instituts Abteilung Kairo 22. Mainz, Philipp von Zabern.
Spiegelberg, W 1927. Die Falkenbezeichnung des Verstorbenen in der Spätzeit. In *Zeitschrift für Ägyptische Sprache und Altertumskunde* 62, 27-32.
Traunecker, C, F Le Saout and O Masson 1981. *La chapelle d'Achôris à Karnak II.* Recherche sur les grandes civilisations, Synthèse no.5, Paris.
Traunecker, C 1992. *Coptos. Hommes et dieux sur le parvis de Geb.* Orientalia Louvaniensia Analecta 43. Louvain.
Vandier, J 1961. *Le Papyrus Jumilhac.* Paris, Centre National de la Recherche Scientifique.
Voß, S 1994. *Die "Sonnenheiligtümer" in den thebanischen Totentempeln des Neuen Reiches.* Unpublished thesis, Heidelberg.
Wild, H 1960. Statue d'un noble mendésien du règne de Psamétik Ier aux Musées de Palerme et du Caire. In *Bulletin de l'Institut Français d'Archéologie Orientale* 60, 43-67.

Winter, E 1968. *Untersuchungen zu den ägyptischen Tempelreliefs der griechisch-römischen Zeit.* Österreichische Akademie der Wissenschaften, Philosophisch-Historische Klasse, Denkschriften 98, Vienna.
Yoyotte, J 1957. A propos de l'obélisque unique. In *Kêmi* XIV, 81-91.
Zabkar, L 1968. *A Study of the Ba Concept in Ancient Egyptian Texts.* Studies in Ancient Oriental Civilizations 34. Chicago.
Zandee, J 1966. *An Ancient Egyptian Crossword Puzzle.* Mededelingen en verhandelingen van het Vooraziatische-Egyptisch Genootschap "Ex Oriente Lux" 15, Leiden.

Addendum

In the main western necropolis at Marina el-Alamein (96 km west of Alexandria) funerary monuments[1] from the first century BC and first century AD have been excavated[2] of which at least the decoration of tomb T 12 is closely related to BM EA 1512. First, its pillar had been crowned by the statue of a falcon wearing the double crown,[3] a common motif in the funerary cult of the Roman Period.[4] In the second place, T 12 is a sepulchre: the pillar itself was erected on a pedestal which comprised two burial chambers[5] and served thus as a monumental tombstone. T 12 therefore supports the theory advanced above, that BM EA 1512 originates from a (divine) necropolis.

Addendum notes

1 I am indebted to Dr. Lorelei Corcoran for drawing these monuments to my attention.
2 Published by Wiktor A. Daszewski and Jaroslaw Dobrowolski in *Polish Archaeology in the Mediterranean* (in the following abbreviated as *PAM*) II, Polish Centre of Mediterranean Archaeology, Warsaw University, Warsaw 1991, 31-7, 44-7; *PAM* III (1992), 29-48; *PAM* IV (1993), 23-31; *PAM* V (1994), 21-39; *PAM* VI (1995), 28-36; *PAM* VII (1996), 40f.; *MDAIK* 46 (1990), 15-51.
3 *MDAIK* 46 (1990), 21, Tafel 11 a) and b); *PAM* VI (1995), 31; *PAM* VII (1996), 40 Fig. 1. A statue of a falcon or a lion might have crowned the other pillars and columns in the necropolis, see *MDAIK* 46 (1990), 27, 29; *PAM* VI (1995), 31.
4 Parlasca, *Mumienportraits*, pl. 34 (1), 35 (2), 36 (3); *MDAIK* 24 (1969), pl.XII b); *MDAIK* 26 (1970), pl. LXII b), LXVI b), LXVII b) and c); Evaristo Breccia, Le musée gréco-romain d'Alexandrie 1925-1931, Roma 1970, pl. XXIII (85); *MDAIK* 46 (1990), 21, n. 18; cf. Spiegelberg 1927.
5 The funerary monuments from Marina el-Alamein are unique in Egypt. The similarity with the funerary pillars from Xanthos in Lycia dating from the 6th to 4th cent. B.C. is striking, see Pierre Demargne, *Fouilles de Xanthos I: les piliers funéraires*, Paris 1958. The main differences are the location of the corpse, which was laid down in a chamber recessed in the top part of the pillar (only the pillar in the acropolis received two additional rock tombs below it, op. cit., fig. 19-21), and the decoration.

The present state of research into Graeco-Roman temples

Dieter Kurth

When Vivian Davies invited me to contribute a paper to this colloquium he asked me if I would like to give an overview of the present state of research into the temples of the Graeco-Roman Period. I accepted his suggestion at once, for the following reason: nowadays even the most ardent supporters of universality would have to confess that even Egyptology needs to specialize, if the subject is to advance. Yet if there is not to be a barren dispersal of knowledge, from time to time someone has to sum up the scattered results for the benefit of his colleagues.[1] And for that a colloquium presents a good opportunity.

As to degrees of specialization, I think that the temples of the Graeco-Roman Period, and particularly their inscriptions, are also developing into a special field of research, similar to Coptic or demotic. This is confirmed by the bibliographies of scholars, who were and still are successful in the field, such as Emile Chassinat, Fairman, Serge Sauneron, Adolphe Gutbub, Philippe Derchain, Erich Winter, Jean-Claude Goyon and Sylvie Cauville, because the bulk of their research deals with these temples, especially with their inscriptions.[2] Here I shall try to demonstrate that the subject necessarily requires a high level of commitment.

Compared with the great efforts made to study the inscriptions, the architecture of these temples has been neglected; this is due to causes that will be mentioned below. This paper concentrates upon the inscriptions, for lack of time; but I am aware that architecture and inscriptions of a temple are interdependent, to such an extent that, if we neglect any one of them, we cannot hope for a true understanding.

Egyptology belongs to the humanities, has but little practical value and therefore, on the whole, in most countries it develops independently, without a central direction; nevertheless the development possesses a certain inner logic. This observation is valid also for work on the temples of the Graeco-Roman Period. Here the course of research is influenced by two main factors. The first is the nature of the subject: large numbers of temples in remote locations, decorated with an enormous amount of coherent pictures and inscriptions, the inscriptions being written in a very complicated writing system. The second factor consists in the scholars themselves: each of them wants to prove that his method is superior to that of others, whether or not this is accepted by his colleagues.

Accordingly this paper is in three parts. The first contains a description of the subject. The second gives a picture of the present state of research in the area and also a view of current priorities, alongside a brief history of work. In the third part I offer some suggestions concerning priorities for future work.

Part One

More than a hundred temples of the period are known, all of them in Egyptian style. We find them in what we might perhaps call "Greater Egypt", from the Mediterranean coast to Nubia, and from the oases of the western desert to the Red Sea coast. In antiquity there must have been many more of them. This is clearly proved by the records of early travellers as well as by recent excavations.

The mammisi of Armant is a good example of a temple that has disappeared since the days of the early travellers; it was demolished by government order in the middle of the 19th century. On the evidence of this and other examples we may assume that still more temples have suffered the same fate, but remain unrecorded. Recent excavations have brought to light hitherto unknown temples, as for instance the temples of Birbiya (Mills 1983; 1985; 1986; 1990) and Ismant el-Kharab (contributions by Hope and Kaper in this volume) in the Dakhla oasis.

However, new temples are not only found in remote places like the oases, but also in the Nile valley, for example in the ancient town "Khirba" near El-Ma'abda (Markaz Abnoub, north of Asiut), where the scanty remains of a small Graeco-Roman temple have been found by Ursula Rössler and a mission of the University of Bonn (Leclant and Clère 1993, 223ff.). The visible remains of the town date from the third to the eighth centuries and they cover an area of about twelve hectares. There will probably never be a chance to excavate more than the tiniest fraction of the town. When the digging started nobody could anticipate finding a temple beneath the ruined houses, nor where it might be located. So there is a good chance that more temples will be unearthed; some, though, will probably never be discovered.

One must bear in mind, however, that the temples known to us so far vary greatly in their function, size and quality of decoration. During the Ptolemaic Period the Egyptians themselves distinguished between temples of the first, second and third rank. In order to obtain an impression of their variety one has to compare great temples (Edfu or Dendera) with temples of medium size (Kalabsha or Hibis) and smaller ones (Deir el-Medina or the temple of Alexander the Great in Bahriya oasis).[3]

Twenty-five years ago, Serge Sauneron reckoned that the complete publication of all the inscriptions of the Graeco-Roman temples would amount to some 10,000 pages (1972, 289 n.2). If one adds all the inscriptions of the recently discovered temples as well as those of the Graeco-Roman annexes to older buildings (for instance in the temple of Hatshepsut in Deir el-Bahari in Medinet Habu or in Karnak), I would imagine that they would fill 12,000 pages or even more.

One feature of Graeco-Roman temple inscriptions is well known: it is their difficult writing system. While the inscriptions in temples of earlier periods use some 750 hieroglyphic signs, those of Graeco-Roman times contain more than 7,000 different hieroglyphs.[4] The number of phonetic values borne by the hieroglyph is much increased; some have more than 30 values. It is therefore no surprise that, as Serge Sauneron showed, in the temple of Esna the phoneme "n" can be written with about 80 different hieroglyphs (1959, 51-52). This writing system is employed in all Graeco-Roman temples, but each temple has its own peculiarities.

As regards architecture, its study is hindered by the fact that the temples are in varying states of preservation. Thus, there are only a few pylons and enclosure walls constructed in stone, so that the material available for a comparative study is limited. This is, however, due partly to another factor, which is that Egyptian temples were constructed beginning with the inner parts so that in many cases, owing to the vicissitudes of history, the work was abandoned before the outer parts were completed.

Let me remark here that the study of architecture is also hindered by the predilection of scholars for the inscriptions. Many years ago Serge Sauneron put it in these terms ".....pour le malheur des recherches religieuses une tradition paresseuse, mais solidement enracinée, veut que l'on considère un temple de basse époque uniquement comme un "recueil" de textes intéressants" (1959, 143). This means that the walls of the temples are often regarded to be nothing but a kind of "writing paper". The articles of Jan Quaegebeur and Claude Traunecker in this volume show that modern Egyptology has begun to pay due attention to the architecture of the Graeco-Roman temples.

Another kind of source material has a major bearing on our subject: ostraca and papyri. These are written in demotic or Greek and many contain valuable information for the reconstruction of life in and around these temples. The problem is, however, that the enormous mass of ostraca and papyri is dispersed over many museums all over the world. The same is true of the hieratic papyri which can supply us with parallels for some of the inscriptions on the temple walls.

Part Two

If we consider both the enormous amount of sources and the philological difficulties, it goes without saying that anyone who wants to study the Graeco-Roman temples in a scholarly manner has to specialize, even within this tiny sector of Egyptology, and nowadays a high degree of specialization is normal.

By contrast, in the early days of Egyptology at the beginning of the nineteenth century, scholars could not afford to specialize in this way and I think that they were also not inclined to do so. For there were few of them, and when they confronted the temples they started by trying to establish the principal contents of the inscriptions. They soon learnt that these texts could yield most interesting information about Egyptian history, religion, literature, kingship, astronomy, geography and so on. Thus they started collecting and copying as many inscriptions as possible from the various temples, in order to take these treasures home to Europe, for further study. Heinrich Brugsch evidently regarded them as treasures, for he named one of his largest works *Thesaurus inscriptionum Aegyptiacarum.* In the six volumes of the Brugsch *Thesaurus* we find not only many inscriptions of the Graeco-Roman temples, but also contemporary texts in cursive writing. Facing the immense quantity of inscriptions Brugsch naturally had to make a selection, and he chose principally inscriptions concerning Egyptian history, religion, geography and astronomy. The figures of kings and deities were copied too, in simple hand drawings of his own.

Some other scholars made similar hand-copies of the representations and inscriptions, among them Ernst von Bergmann, Edouard Naville, Karl Piehl and Jacques de Rougé. Some of them had realized that for a better understanding of the inscriptions it was very important to assemble parallels. Johannes Dümichen for instance concentrated upon building inscriptions and geographical inscriptions.

It would be wrong not to mention Brugsch's *Dictionaire géographique de l'ancienne Egypte* (1879) or Simone Levi's *Vocabolario Geroglifico* (1887), which, while not restricted to the period under discussion, are largely based upon texts in Graeco-Roman temples. These works show that the scholars, who felt the need to compile dictionaries as tools for future research, included the inscriptions of the late temples. Nevertheless, most of the efforts of that period focused on an eclectic assembling of materials.

This Stone Age attitude of hunting and gathering was an unavoidable stage within the development of our subject, for it stimulated interest. The decline of this attitude began when the Marquis de Rochemonteix discovered that every temple formed a unit, was a world of its own, its ceiling representing the sky of the cosmos and its ground the earth (1894, 1-38). The logical consequence was the insight that every temple demanded a complete publication integrating its architecture, its inscriptions and its ritual scenes as well as other elements of its decoration. De Rochemonteix was the first person to undertake such an enterprise: In 1876 he began to copy the decoration of the temple of Edfu, following a strict plan and including inscriptions and representations. Through his publication of the temples of Edfu, Marquis de Rochemonteix had displayed what was an adequate way of providing scholars outside Egypt with the material they needed to study an Egyptian temple. His method was widely accepted and he was followed by others. In 1895 Jacques de Morgan published the first volume of the temples of Kom Ombo. In 1926 Otto Daum took the first steps towards preparing the temples of Philae for publication. The first volume of Emile Chassinat's *Temple de Dendara* appeared in 1934. Serge Sauneron began to copy the inscriptions of Esna in 1951. And, to give a recent example, in 1992 Christiane Zivie and her colleagues published the fourth volume of *Deir Chelouit*, a study of the architecture: the preceding three volumes contain the inscriptions.

The publications just mentioned as examples, as well as others which I have not mentioned, have many features in common. The copies of the texts are generally more reliable than earlier ones. This is my impression, although I am aware that the Marquis de Rochemonteix's first volume of the Edfu inscriptions, Auguste Mariette's edition of the Dendara texts and Jacques de Morgan's edition of the Kom Ombo texts do not satisfy the requirements of a solidly based philological work and need to be redone, but we should bear in mind that they represent the earliest attempts and that Emile Chassinat had not yet set his high standard of accuracy; moreover, the deficiency was seen and new editions have been undertaken by Emile Chassinat, François Daumas, Adolphe Gutbub and Sylvie Cauville. Another improvement in the later publications is that they indicate more exactly the position of each inscription; in the meantime it had been recognized that the contents of a text depend to a great extent upon its position within a temple. On the other hand these publications vary considerably in the methods they employ. So the texts in the volumes of Edfu, Dendera and Esna were printed in hieroglyphic type. Other publications, as for example those of el-Tod (Grenier 1980) and Deir

Chelouit, give hand-copies, whereas *Philä* and *Porte d'Evergète* (Sauneron 1983) give facsimiles. Another difference in method is that the inscriptions published in the two volumes of *Philä* have translations on the facing pages. Most other publications, however, have abstained from translating the texts.

Although publication of some of the largest temples has not yet been completed, since the end of the nineteenth century the quantity of published inscriptions has seemed to provide a basis for the next step, that is for the study of various topics. Some of these subjects had been treated before, while others were tackled for the first time. These studies are now so numerous, that I can only indicate some tendencies among them.

One of them was, and still is, to treat a single inscription and its parallels or to treat the decoration of a whole room of the temple. Recently, in her *Essai sur la théologie du Temple d' Horus à Edfou,* Sylvie Cauville has dealt with the theological system of an entire temple (1987).

Other scholars studied a particular theme and collected their sources from many temples or from all the inscriptions of one single temple. Thus Hermann Junker wrote an article on inscriptions that have a distinct touch of poetry (1906). Eberhard Otto collected texts showing how the concept of kingship has changed between earlier times and the Graeco-Roman Period (1964). Jean-Claude Goyon has made a thorough and profound inquiry into the guardian deities of the temple of Edfu (1985). Others have studied one of the numerous ritual scenes, for instance Marie-Louise Ryhiner in her work on the offering of lotus (1986), with the results of her searching through all the temples, tombs and papyri to find parallels. Maurice Alliot, in his monumental work *Le culte d'Horus à Edfou,* has put together all the texts that could help him to reconstruct religious life as it might have been in the temple of Edfu in ancient times.

Research in our field has advanced considerably thanks to several works on the system of temple decoration. Convinced that the decoration of the Graeco-Roman temples was governed by a set of rules, Philippe Derchain has coined the term "la grammaire du temple". Erich Winter has identified an outstanding example of such rules in his study on the "Randzeilen" or framing columns" of the ritual scenes, the structure and contents of which change according to the register to which a scene belongs (Winter 1968).

Other systematic studies provided us with the tools we urgently need for philological research. Herman Junker's doctoral thesis on the writing system in the temple of Dendara appeared in 1903. The same author's grammar of the Dendara texts was published in 1906, and this is the only grammar of Graeco-Roman temple inscriptions published so far. Fairman's studies of 1943 and 1945 on the phonetic values of the hieroglyphs were a breakthrough, because he proved beyond doubt that so-called "Ptolemaic" is "a logical system of writing" and not "a game without rules or method". Fairman's "consonantal principle" - after some fierce intellectual battles - had gained a victory over Etienne Drioton's "procédé acrophonique", a victory however, that lasted only until Serge Sauneron's publication of the Esna texts, for then it turned out that the two principles coexisted side by side (Sauneron 1982, 102 ff; Kurth 1983).

In 1979 Jean-Claude Grenier presented us with his *Index des citations,* an extremely useful book that helps to find among hundreds of scattered articles the one needed for the understanding of a certain passage in an inscription; unfortunately this concordance of secondary literature ends in the year 1974. Another important tool of Ptolemaic philology must be mentioned: this is the catalogue *Valeurs phonétiques des signes hiéroglyphiques d'Époque Gréco-Romaine,* the first volume of which appeared in 1988. This enterprise was started by François Daumas and collaborators and its aim has been to collect all the phonetic values of all hieroglyphic signs; the fourth and last volume has just appeared.

Finally, it should be pointed out that many Egyptological publications exploit for their own purposes the huge corpus of Graeco-Roman temple texts (eg the quotations from Edfu texts in Baum 1988, Aufrère 1991). Thus many results concerning the earlier periods depend in some way on conclusions derived from the late temple inscriptions. This is useful for the respective passages of Graeco-Roman temple texts, too, because they are enlightened by special knowledge from outside the temple. On the other side there is always a risk of misunderstanding these passages, especially when they are interpreted without their contexts.

Part Three

In this last section of my paper I will sketch out what I see as the priorities of future research into the Graeco-Roman temples. First, I should like to stress that nearly every study contributes to a better understanding of these temples, no matter what its subject may be, provided that its method and level of scholarship are adequate. I say this because the sum of all this work constitutes a kind of brainstorming; a wide range of ideas, questions and solutions has been stirred up and spread out among the community of Egyptologists, and as I have tried to show in the previous section our subject has for the most part advanced in logical stages.

And now (as a participant in that game I have this impression), it is time to take the next major step forward, which is to translate all the texts of each of the greater temples that have been published completely.[5]

More than eight years ago I myself started the Edfu-Projekt, the aim of which is to translate all the inscriptions in the temple of Edfu (see Kurth 1986). The project is generously supported by the Deutsche Forschungsgemeinschaft which has provided the project with the materials needed for this work and with four collaborators. Up to now a preliminary translation of the volumes Edfou V-VIII has been completed and large materials concerning grammar, vocabulary and formulae have been assembled. Edfou VIII is being prepared for publication.

Translating all the inscriptions of a single temple has several advantages. First, all the internal parallels will be found. Second, there is a wholesome compulsion to check every idea against the whole context, and here I must say that in the last eight years of wrestling with the inscriptions of Efdu many of my ready answers and quickly formed ideas have had to die, simply because in the course of work the corresponding parallels have come to light. The third advantage is that by means of an integral translation and with the help of extensive analytical indices on every significant topic all the information that would otherwise remain hidden and virtually undiscoverable within the immense mass of texts will be at hand.

However, as I have already mentioned, a complete and reliable publication is needed before such a work can start. Fortunately in recent years some new projects to publish temple-inscriptions have begun. For example Sylvie Cauville has resumed the edition of the Dendera-inscriptions and the publication of the Esna-texts will be continued by Jochen Hallof. There are, however, several temples whose publication has not even been begun.

The upper temple of Nadura in the Kharga Oasis is one of these. Its decorated interior walls can contribute supplementary information on Egyptian religion. One section of the north wall for example shows figures of the god Bes who is dancing and playing the tambourine before the goddess Mut of Karnak. This theme, of course belongs to the myth of the wrathful Eye-of-Re whose ire had to be quenched before she would return to Egypt. The figures and inscriptions, however have suffered extensive damage, and without shelter they will become ever more faint; moreover, one decorated block has recently been stolen (Kurth 1992).

These smaller temples should be published without delay because their inscriptions are important for the history of Egyptian religion. They will help to create a full picture of both the major and the minor cult-centres of Egypt. This new picture will be closer to the ancient reality since I feel that, because of the still incomplete and one-sided documentation, the importance of the major cult-centres has always been exaggerated.

As regards method I would like to emphasize five points:

1. The inscriptions and reliefs of the major temples of the Graeco-Roman period, such as Philae, should be published without translation, because philological work which requires that all the local and the more distant parallels be collected, is a separate undertaking. Later the results of this philological work will necessarily show that the published texts contain many mistakes which have their origin in the discrepancy between our physical and our intellectual eyes; so often, while trying to read a damaged inscription on a temple wall, our physical eye reads one hieroglyph A, but after comparison with parallels, after evaluation of secondary literature, and with a new idea in mind we can clearly discern a different hieroglyph. This latter point in turn carries with it the need for a final collation of the inscriptions and the correction of the translations. In my opinion four steps are required: a. copy on the spot; b. comparison and translation at home; c. collation on the spot; d. final correction at

home. Good photographs are indispensable but cannot alter the need for these four steps.
2. The inscriptions should more often be studied in their own right and not be misused as quarries for information about a variety of Egyptological questions and problems. This misuse brings a severe danger that the temple inscriptions will be misunderstood; like any historical source they should be interpreted in their own contexts before they are combined with other types of source material.
3. Further research into grammar and vocabulary is a desideratum and should be intensified, because in this field we are at the very beginning.
4. Texts and representations should be studied together.
5. Research into architecture should be increased and combined with research into reliefs and texts.

To sum up I would like to say that in view of the immense source material offered by the temples of the Graeco-Roman period, all the results we have achieved up till now are very preliminary. If we wish to reconstruct the religious life of the time, the official religion of the temples, popular religion and their mutual influence, as well as the function and significance of the temple in the social life of the community, much basic work has to be done and we need a lot of patience. The more we temper our curiosity and refrain from quick solutions and ready answers the better the results will be. Yet, of course, I am aware that here the utmost we can hope for will be a good compromise.

I would like to thank John Baines for correcting my English and for some useful suggestions.

Notes

1 This has been done by several authors in Sauneron 1972, especially vol.I, 45-46; 151-156; III, 229-77; 289-91.
2 Bearing in mind his excavations and his work on the Giza mastabas, Hermann Junker is of course an outstanding exception.
3 Half a century ago Ahmed Fakhry reported that in the temple of Alexander the Great many of the figures and inscriptions were "preserved undamaged" (1983, 99), but in 1992 I saw that nearly all of the decoration is irretrievably lost.
4 This number needs, however, needs to be qualified: far more than half of these "new" hieroglyphs are only variants (Hornung 1994, 179ff).
5 For the smaller temples there is of course no difficulty in treating each of them in all its aspects in one monograph, and to publish its inscriptions together with translations and commentary, as for example the excellent study by Traunecker (1992).

Bibliography

Alliot, M 1949-54. *Le culte d'Horus à Edfou.* Bibliothèque d'Etude 20. (2 vols.) Cairo, Institut Français d'Archéologie Orientale.
Brugsch, H 1879. *Dictionaire géographique de l'ancienne Egypte.*
Cauville, S 1987. *Essai sur la théologie du temple d'Horus à Edfou.* Bibliothèque d'Etude 102. Cairo, Institut Français d'Archéologie Orientale.
Daumas, F et al. 1988-95. *Valeurs phonétiques des signes hiéroglyphiques d'époque Gréco-Romaine.* (4 vols.). Montpellier, Publications de la Recherche, Université de Montpellier. A volume of addenda and corrigenda is planned to be published in about two years from now.
Fairman, H W 1943. Notes on the alphabetic signs empoyed in the hieroglyphic inscriptions of the temple of Edfu. In *Annales du Service des Antiquités d'Egypte* 43, 193-349.
Fairman, H W 1945. An introduction to the study of Ptolemaic signs and their values. In *Bulletin de l'Institut Français d'Archéologie Orientale* 43, 51-138.

l'Institut Français d'Archéologie Orientale 43, 51-138.
Fakhry, A 1983. *The oases of Egypt* 2. Cairo, the American University in Cairo Press.
Goyon, J-C 1985. *Les dieux-gardiens et la genèse des temples.* Bibliothèque d'Etude 93. Cairo, Institut Français d'Archéologie Orientale.
Grenier, J-C 1979. *Temples Ptolémaïques et Romains. Répertoire bibliographique. Index des citations 1955-1974 incluant l'index de citations de 1939 à 1954 réunies par N.Sauneron.* Bibliothèque d'Etude 75. Cairo, Institut Français d'Archéologie Orientale.
Grenier, J-C 1980. *Tôd* I. Cairo, Institut Français d'Archéologie Orientale.
Junker, H 1903. *Über das Schriftsystem im Tempel der Hathor in Dendera.* Berlin.
Junker, H 1906. *Grammatik der Denderatexte.* Leipzig, J C Hinrichs.
Kurth, D 1983. Die Lautwerte der Hieroglyphen in den Tempelinschriften der griechisch-römischen Zeit - zur Systematik ihrer Herleitungsprinzipien. In *Annales du Service des Antiquités d'Egypte* 69, 287-309.
Kurth, D 1986. Information über ein von der Deutschen Forschungsgemeinschaft gefördertes Projekt zur philologischen Gesamtbearbeitung der Inschriften des Tempels von Edfu. In *Göttinger Miszellen* 92, 93-94.
Kurth, D 1986. Antikenraub in den Oasen. In *Göttinger Miszellen* 130, 45-48.
Leclant, J and G Clère 1993. Fouilles et travaux en Egypte et au Soudan, 1991-1992. In *Orientalia N.S.* 62, 175-295, pl.6-57.
Levi, S 1887. *Vocabolario Geroglifico.*
Mills, A J 1983. The Dakhleh Oasis Project: report on the fifth season of survey, October 1982 - January 1983. In *Journal of the Society for the Study of Egyptian Antiquities* 13, 121-41.
Mills, A J 1985. The Dakhleh Oasis Project: a preliminary report on the field work of the 1985/1986 season. In *Journal of the Society for the Study of Egyptian Antiquities* 15, 105-13.
Mills, A J 1986. The Dakhleh Oasis Project: report on the 1986-1987 field season. In *Journal of the Society for the Study of Egyptian Antiquities* 16, 65-73.
Mills, A J 1990. The Dakhleh Oasis Project: report on the 1990-1991 field season. In *Journal of the Society for the Study of Egyptian Antiquities* 20, 11-16.
Otto, E 1964. *Gott und Mensch nach den ägyptischen Tempelinschriften der griechisch-römischen Zeit. Eine Untersuchung zur Phraseologie der Tempelinschriften.* Abhandlungen der Heidelberger Akademie der Wissenschaften, Philosophisch-historische Klasse, Jahrgang 1964 - 1.Abhandlung. Heidelberg, Carl Winter, Universitätsverlag.
Rochemonteix, M de 1894. *Oeuvres diverses publiées par G Maspero.* Paris, Ernest Leroux.
Ryhiner, M-L 1986. *L'offrande du lotus dans les temples égyptiens de l'époque tardive.* Rites Egyptiens VI. Brussels, Fondation Egyptologique Reine Elisabeth.
Sauneron, S 1959. *Esna I. Quatre Campagnes à Esna.* Cairo, Institut Français d'Archéologie Orientale.
Sauneron, S (ed.) 1972. *Textes et Langages de l'Egypte pharaonique. Cent cinquante années de recherche 1822-1972. Hommage à Jean-François Champollion.* (3 vols.) Bibliothèque d'Etude 64. Cairo, Institut Français d'Archéologie Orientale.
Sauneron, S 1982. *Esna VIII. L'Ecriture Figurative dans les textes d'Esna.* Cairo, Institut Français d'Archéologie Orientale.
Sauneron, S 1983. *La Porte Ptolémaïque de l'enceinte de Mout à Karnak.* Mémoires publiés par les membres de l'Institut Français d'Archéologie Orientale du Caire 107. Cairo, Institut Français d'Archéologie Orientale.
Traunecker, C 1992. *Coptos. Hommes et dieux sur le parvis de Geb.* Orientalia Lovaniensia Analecta 43. Louvain, Peeters.
Winter, E 1968. *Untersuchungen zu den ägyptischen Tempelreliefs der griechisch-römischen Zeit.* Österreichische Akademie der Wissenschaften, Philosophisch-historische Klasse, Denkschriften 98. Vienna, Österreichische Akademie der Wissenschaften in Wien.

Excavating the forgotten temple of Shenhur (Upper Egypt)

Jan Quaegebeur

Shenhur in Upper Egypt, to be distinguished from other places with the same name (Brugsch 1893, 19), is virtually unknown, both to Egyptologists and to non-specialists. One looks for it in vain in the well-known *Atlas of Ancient Egypt*, produced by Baines and Malek (1980). Yet, there are some maps, first of all the survey maps of Egypt (1/100.000, 1920 or 1934, 32/72 + 78) but also road-maps (e.g. Bartholomew: Egypt 1/1.000.000, 1991), and even tourist guides (Baedeker 1929, 240) where the place may be found.

The modern village of Shenhur is situated on the east side of the Nile, between Coptos and Thebes, more precisely 20 km south-east of Quft and 20 km north of Luxor (fig.1). Besides Coptos and Thebes, a third city is of importance, namely Qus, the nearest city at only 6 km north of Shenhur. Qus is another ancient site where one can visit the neglected remains of an important Ptolemaic temple (Baedeker 1929, 233). The fragmentary naos of Ptolemy II, lying there already when Napoleon's expedition passed at the end of the eighteenth century (Description de l'Egypte IV, pl. 1; Daressy 1917-18, 224-5), was deliberately damaged at the end of 1993 and subsequently brought by the Antiquities Organization to Dendara.

How do you reach Shenhur? Anyone who drives by car from Dendara to Luxor or from Luxor

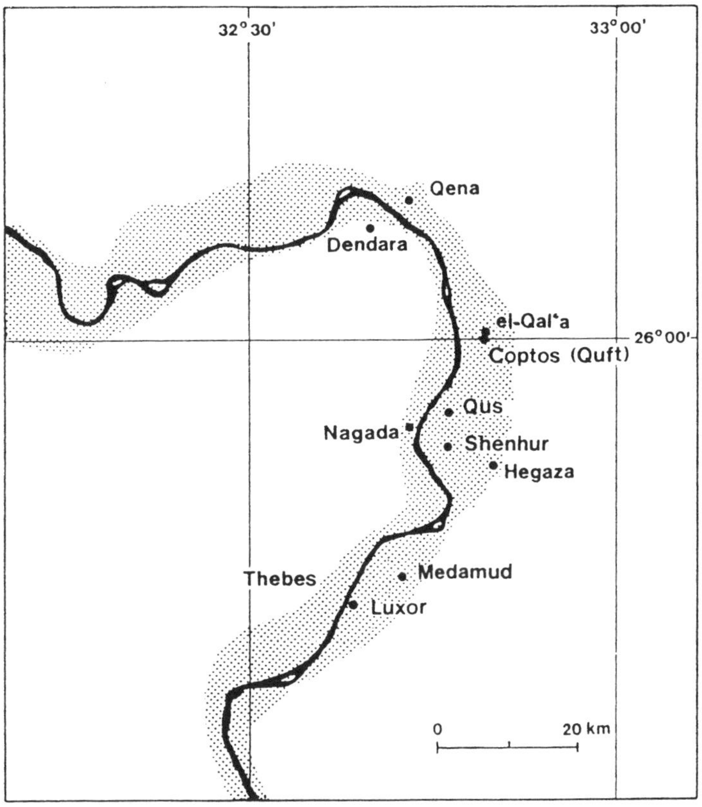

Fig.1 Location of Shenhur in the Coptite region.

to Dendara, two highlights on the tourist circuit, passes along the Shenhuria canal, named after the village Shenhur, which was once of some importance. As soon as one sees the sign-post on the road with the name el-Shenhuria written in Arabic, one has to cross the bridge over the canal and to drive carefully through the village to the mosque and the ancient temple (pl.43a: view from the south-west before starting the works). The name Shenhur transmits the ancient name, engraved several times in hieroglyphs on the walls of the temple; this was already recognized by Prisse d'Avennes, who discovered the site in the 1830s, some years after the decipherment of the Rosetta stone. On the rear wall, for example, we read *p3-š-n-ḥr*, normally translated as "The lake of Horus". The logo designed for the Shenhur project (fig.2) shows a simplified view of the temple ruins with the minaret of the Mamluk mosque and the tomb of the lokal sheikh, Abu Tayeb, in the background; the name of the place is added in hieroglyphs and in Arabic.

Fig.2 Logo of the Belgo-French archaeological expedition to Shenhur, showing the hieroglyphic and Arabic writings of the placename, over a schematic view of the temple and mosque.

The archaeological site consists of the temple, built and decorated under the Roman emperor Augustus and his successors, and of its immediate surroundings, an area of about 1.3 ha which is situated south-west of the present-day village. A recent view, taken from the top of the minaret (pl.43b), shows part of the area protected by the Egyptian Antiquities Organization.

The ancient name of this Shenhur seems not to occur in published hieroglyphic texts outside the Roman temple of Shenhur itself. A mention of *š-n-ḥr* in the temple of Esna (Sauneron 1969: 32 n° 425: reign of Vespasian), to which Dr. M.-T. Derchain-Urtel drew our attention, is not specific. The first attestation of the village however is in Greek and is a little older than the temple. Among a few Theban ostraca containing the place name Psenyris, there is one (O. Leiden F 1901/9.172), datable on palaeographical grounds to the late Ptolemaic period (end second/beginning first century BC), which mentions inhabitants of Psenyris (Bagnall 1980, 17 n° 32A); some other ostraca mentioning our Psenyris are Roman. According to a note published by G. Daressy (1926, 20), a block from a Ptolemaic door or gate was in 1889 brought from the village to the Cairo museum, where it is registered; its present location however is unknown. The early seventh century Coptic dossier of Bishop Pisentius of Coptos informs us that there was a village official at Pshenhôr and a monastery in the vicinity (Timm 1991, 2292-4). The name of Shenhur near Qus occurs also in medieval Arabic texts (Halm 1979, 75).

Shenhur temple became known to Egyptologists relatively late. None of the early travellers seems to have visited this place and the members of the Napoleonic expedition do not mention any monument there. The earliest information is provided by J.G. Wilkinson; in his *Topography of Thebes* (1835, 414), published 1835, we read: 'Shenhoor, on the east bank, a few miles south of Qoos, presents the extensive mounds of an ancient town'. In his book *Modern Egypt and Thebes* (1843, 132), he adds that 'M. Prisse found (there) a temple of Roman time, dedicated to Horus, with the name of the town in hieroglyphs, Sen-hor'. After Prisse d'Avennes, the temple was visited in 1839 by another French Egyptologist, Nestor L'Hôte, who made some drawings of parts of the temple; those valuable documents were not, however, published until 1963 (Vandier d'Abbadie 1963, 38-9; pl.xxv/2-xxvi). He copied some texts and scenes, and he made a good choice, since several of them have now disappeared, e.g. a hymn addressed to the emperor Claudius including a mention of Rome (pl.44a), to be added to de Wit's study (1961, 62-9). Only one block of the layer with the "bandeau de frise" of the eastern outer wall is left, and from the inscription only one fragment with the emperor's cartouche is preserved (pl.44b); the upper part of the block gives an idea of the decoration of the upper frieze (compare Kurth 1994).

The first published drawings of the temple were made during the royal German expedition of Lepsius and they date from 1843. In Lepsius's *Denkmäler* there is an engraving showing the lintel of the door to the sanctuary (only the scene furthest to the right showing Augustus offering to Thoth and Maat is now preserved), and two inscriptions from the inside of the sanctuary stating that the emperor Augustus built the temple for his mother The-Great-Goddess-Isis and for his mother Mut (Lepsius [no date], pl. 70; 1904, 258-60). After the time of the pioneers, too, visitors seem to have remained very rare. One of the exceptions, at the end of the nineteenth century, is the American Charles Edwin Wilbour. In his *Travels in Egypt* (1936, 524), he mentions a visit to Shenhur on 8 March 1889 and announces a second visit: 'next time I must carry a hatchet for the tamarisk bushes and a ladder and have a whole day or two', but he probably never returned. One of his notebooks containing a list of documents relating to different places mentions Shenhur. These documents, kept in the Brooklyn Museum together with the notebooks, are in fact copies of the drawings made by Nestor l'Hôte, except for a simple groundplan of the temple.

At the beginning of this century, in his *Guide to the Antiquities of Upper Egypt* (1910, 57-9), the British scholar Arthur Weigall made a thorough description of what was by that time visible of the temple; he further recorded that there were remains of a church.

In the following years, hardly anybody seems to have been interested in this place, but somebody must have prepared for the *Topographical Bibliography* of Porter and Moss (PM V, 120, 136; fig.3) the plan of what is there called the temple of Isis at Shenhur. After the second world-war, Charles Nims went to Shenhur in 1948 to take photographs of the partly preserved astronomical ceiling, already identified by the Frenchmen Legrain and Jéquier fifty years earlier. A drawing on the basis of Nims's photographs was reproduced by O. Neugebauer and R. Parker in the plates of their *Egyptian Astronomical Texts and Representations* (1969, 77; pl. 40A). It took until 1983, when Claude Traunecker's article on "Schanhur" appeared in the *Lexikon der Ägyptologie* (1983, 528-31), before it was realised that an Upper Egyptian temple remained to be excavated.

In August 1989, Claude Traunecker and the present writer visited the Shenhur temple and decided to join forces to clear the temple of its debris, at some places one metre and a half high, and to excavate its surroundings in the hope of locating the ancient village which functioned together with the temple. So the Belgian and French Archaeological Mission of Shenhur was created, a joint project of the universities of Leuven and of Lille. The main objectives were archaeological - to excavate the complete temple domain and the settlement - and epigraphical - to publish the inscriptions and decoration of this temple.

Before dealing with the archaeological activity started at the end of 1992, it has to be emphasized that the copies and drawings made by Nestor L'Hôte, Lepsius and others constitute an essential but completely neglected contribution to our knowledge of the temple, because what they saw has now partly disappeared. Moreover, we are well aware that the general appearance of the site has changed much in over hundred years. It is important to recognize that at some unknown date excavations or levelling works were carried out. When Nestor L'Hôte visited the temple more than hundred and fifty years ago, the temple was almost completely buried under the ruins of old houses (L'Hôte 1840, 88: 'presque entièrement enfoui sous les décombres de masures'). It is not clear at what time the eastern outer wall was exposed. This was probably some time ago and the whole wall with its three registers of twelve scenes each is now entirely visible. However the emperor Claudius, represented in front of dozens of Egyptian gods, has attracted no attention. The temple seems to have gone forgotten; no photograph of the site or the temple was ever published. Perhaps the quality of the reliefs and inscriptions, badly carved in a hard limestone and damaged by erosion and other factors, was not attractive enough for scholars for whom better preserved scenes and more easily legible hieroglyphs were available. Nevertheless, when one considers some of the details (pl.44c), one realizes that the quality is not too bad overall.

However, it cannot be said that noone was interested in the Shenhur temple. In the same period when work was started by the Belgian-French mission, Steven Snape of the University of Liverpool was preparing an expedition to Shenhur. When he noticed that good progress had already been made,

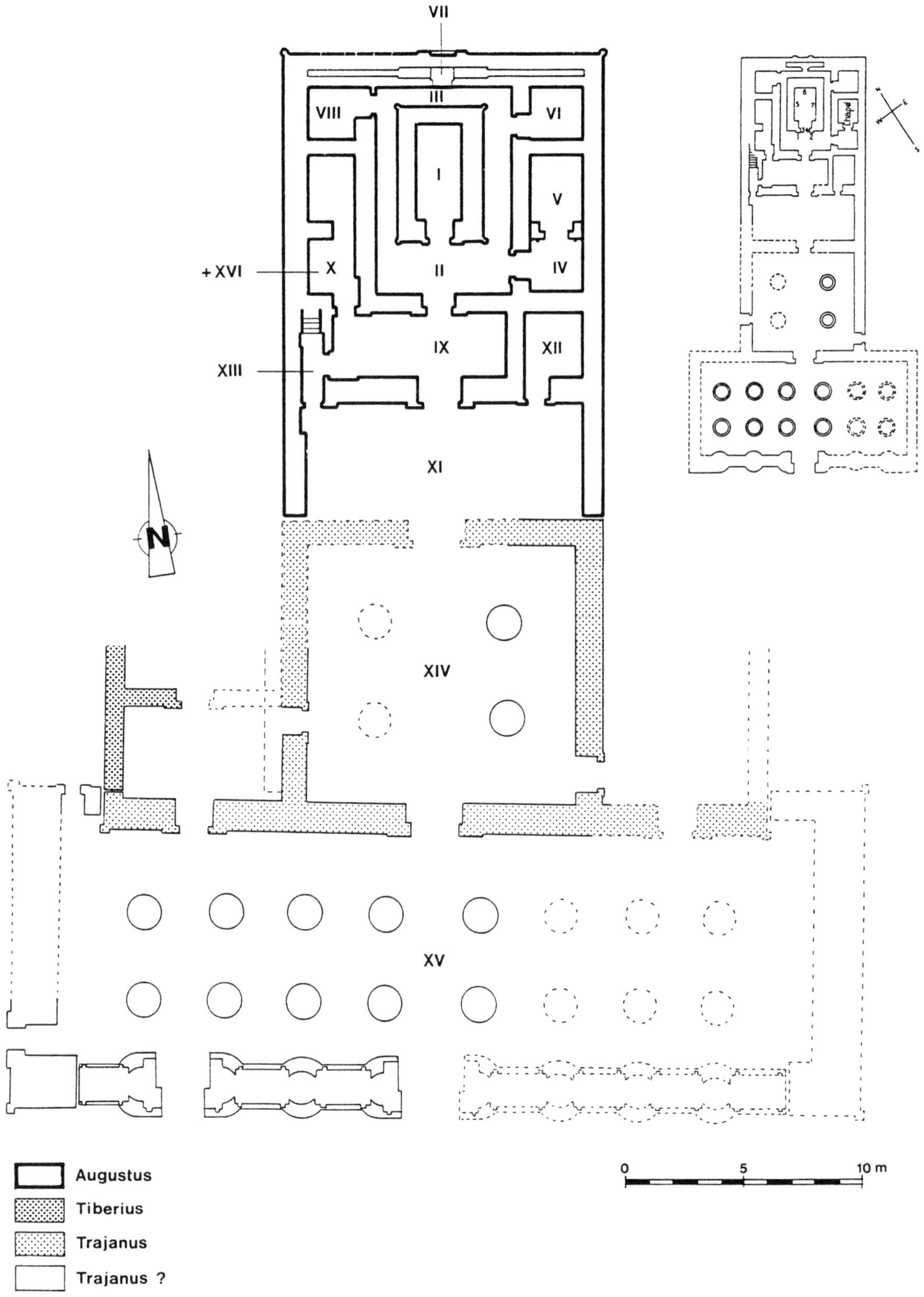

Fig.3 New plan of the temple at Shenhur, with (right) that given in PM.

he acted like a true English gentleman and withdrew his application. There was also some negative interest in the temple. The left (western) part of the façade of the sanctuary shows the Theban Mut being worshipped by the emperor Augustus. On the parallel scene to the right (east), the emperor Augustus was depicted offering to Isis of Coptos. This block with Isis, photographed in 1983 (pl.44d) but also in 1991, had disappeared by the time the excavations started.

Various aspects of the archaeological work, carried out by local workers and Quftis, will now be illustrated, but a complete chronological review of the excavations is not my intention. In addition, the building history of the temple, from Augustus to Trajan, and its decoration, revealing an original theology (see Quaegebeur and Traunecker 1994; Quaegebeur, forthcoming), and a trial dig outside the temple, which revealed a Coptic settlement from the sixth-seventh centuries with abundant ceramics, will not receive special attention here (Quaegebeur and Traunecker 1994; Roovers and Chartier-Raymond, forthcoming). Only the most important results of the first two campaigns will be presented, and the problems encountered outlined.

The new plan of the temple, including the excavated parts, when compared with the plan published in the *Topographical Bibliography* of PM V (fig. 3) and, eventually, also with that in the *Lexikon der Ägyptologie* (see also Arnold 1994, 225), reveals significant amendments. The pronaos (XV on the new plan) is much larger than supposed by Porter and Moss, and the exceptional width (28m), more than twice that of the square hypostyle hall (XIV), can now be explained by the discovery of a secondary chapel to the west of the hypostyle hall.

The temple complex was built in two or more phases. That there were at least two phases is evident from the different kinds of limestone used in the front and back parts of the temple. This fact explains the different state of preservation of the northern and southern part. The better preserved northern part, called the Augustan temple, is built in a very hard local limestone containing many shells and presumably extracted from the Hegaza quarries. The excavations started in the inner part of the Augustan temple. The sanctuary (I), the small vestibule (II), the corridor (III) (pl.42a-b), the side chapels and the chapel or niche in the back-wall (VII to VIII), as well as the wabet (V) have been excavated, but work in the wabet, where a crypt is to be cleared (see further), and in the small court of the New Year's festival (IV) is not yet finished. Other parts are not yet excavated: the staircase leading to the roof (XIII) and the room with a low ceiling to the east (X). Above this room is yet another room (XVI) which seems to have been a crypt, though the roof is not preserved. During the next campaign, the clearance of the front part of the Augustan temple is programmed: the rooms IX (called 'antichambre'), the 'magasin' XIII and the great vestibule (XI).

During the excavations, a variety of objects were found: Turkish pipe-bowls, perhaps from the eighteenth or nineteenth century, as well as fragments of the walls, and fragments of Roman concrete which probably covered the roof of the temple. We also encountered many traces of the reuse of the temple for habitation, after the cultic function of the temple had ceased; they may be dated by the pottery to the Coptic period (sixth and early seventh centuries). Everywhere the original floor was found intact.

In the sanctuary and in other parts of the Augustan temple, blocks which had fallen down and hindered the excavation had to be removed. Some could be replaced, e.g. two blocks were hoist up with a tackle and put back on the walls of the sanctuary by the specialized gang of rais Nahas of the Centre franco-égyptien de Karnak (pl.45c). Rais Amin from Quft and his assistant, placed at our disposal by the Egyptian Antiquities Organisation, were responsible for the restoration where needed. Most fallen blocks, including one ceiling block of more than three tonnes, were temporarily stored outside the temple (see pl.43b).

Another technical problem is the changing ground water table, caused by the pumping of water to irrigate the sugar-cane fields to the west of the site. Sometimes the water level is thirty centimetres higher than the pavement of the temple. Therefore, on the suggestion of Claude Traunecker, a protecting layer, fifty centimetres thick, of red bricks and gravel was put in place (see Traunecker 1981), while in the sanctuary a small cemented pit was also constructed which allows inspection of the raising of the water level (pl.42d).

Particulary interesting was the clearance of what seemed to be a kind of niche or chapel in the inner side of the back-wall, which could be closed by a door (see pl.45b). A bronze hinge is still in place. It turned out to be the entrance to two secret rooms in the thickness of the wall. On both sides, a moveable block gave access to the crypt: when this block, rolling on small wheels, was pushed forward, it opened an entrance between the two rails allowing a man to descend by three steps in the crypt (Traunecker 1994).

What are called the wabet (room V on Fig. 3) and the New Year's court (IV) were not recognized as such by Neugebauer and Parker, who thought that the preserved ceiling slab with its astronomical decoration, already mentioned, was a quarter of the ceiling of one long room (Neugebauer and Parker 1963: 77). The entrance to this room was blocked by fallen stones, which were removed with some difficulty. After excavation, the characteristic architecture of a wabet preceded by a court was clear: only one block of the ceiling of the wabet (V) is missing and the adjoining court (IV) is an open one. From the facsimile of the ceiling slab (Neugebauer and Parker 1963, pl. 40A), one recognizes a half scene with arms and legs of the goddess Nut, six signs of the zodiac (capricorn, sagittarius, scorpio, libra, virgo and leo), a crocodile headed figure representing the first arrow of Bastet (Rondeau 1989, 265), and some other figures, such as the well known Big Dipper, or Plough, and the planet Mercury (left beneath). During the work no trace of the second roofing block with the other part of the astronomical representation was found. However several architectural elements turned up, such as a block with a frieze of Hathor-heads, perhaps from the architrave over the entrance to the wabet. During the clearing of the wabet, reliefs from the reign of emperor Caligula appeared, revealing interesting scenes such as the goddess Nekhbet offering cloth to The-Great-Goddess and Nebet-ihy. Two short hymns were also uncovered (pl.46a; Traunecker, forthcoming).

Several collapsed blocks in the wabet sealed off the Coptic level. In the corner of the back wall, some pottery was found still *in situ* and, against the east wall, clearance revealed the entrance to another crypt, which we intend to clear out next season.

The Augustan temple, corresponding to the better preserved northern part, includes the great vestibule (XI), which, in the first phase, formed an entrance hall. It is not clear yet what the façade of the Augustan temple looked like; it may have been a 'templum in antis', with protruding side walls and columns in front. The later additions to the Augustan temple, built in a homogeneous white limestone, simply lean against the northern part (there are no cramps). If the front part of the temple, with the first and second hypostyle hall, is much less preserved, this is due, as we shall see, to lime-kiln working.

A trial dig was undertaken at the angle between the first (XV) and second (XIV) hypostyle hall, on a place considered to be outside the temple proper (fig.3). This turned out to be a good starting point because in one angle of the square a door jamb of Tiberius was discovered. The second door jamb was unfortunately missing. Just below surface level there were numerous small fragments of limestone and a thick layer of ashes from firing limestone. On one place, where the parallel door jamb is missing, one can see striking remains of lime-production and also lime which had hardened again (pl.46b).

Below this level there was a floor of several layers of red brick. People must have lived in this area, because there was a hearth and pottery was sunk into the floor. The ceramics in general and the many fragments of decorated pottery, sometimes containing Christian motives, point to the same period as the Coptic occupation of the inner part of the Augustan temple (see*supra*). The second door jamb of Tiberius must still have been in place at that time, for there is a hole in the brick floor where it had been (pl.46c). So the limestone blocs were taken away when the brick floor was already there. Further excavation showed that the door jamb with the name of Tiberius was in fact part of a chapel wall, with the main entrance from the south, that is from the pronaos or first hypostyle hall (XV). There was also an eastern entrance, from the second hypostyle hall (XIV), which has not yet been cleared. The southern entrance is decorated with two parallel scenes figuring Trajan in front of a goddess and a child-god. Between this register and the 'soubassement', which presents an offering procession, there is the 'bandeau inférieur' containing two elaborate cartouches of Trajan, who is here also designated by his epithet Dacicus. This 'bandeau' states that the emperor comes before Hor-udja and the divine mother of the latter, The-Great-Goddess. Therefore, it seems that this chapel is dedicated to Hor-udja and it may have functioned as a kind of mammisi (chapel celebrating the birth of the divine child).

During the continuation of the work to the west of the doorway of Trajan, we were in for another surprise: there was a torus (an additional rounded edging with a square basis) on the west corner (pl.46d). This had not been shaped round, indicating that part of the work was in an unfinished state. The same observation can be made for other places in the pronaos (XV). At about one meter above floor level this torus and the neighbouring wall are badly damaged, suggesting a periodical contact with water. That would explain the heightening of the floor by layers of red bricks in Coptic times. Next to the torus was another door jamb, preserved for only one layer of stone, giving us another door with a heightened threshold in the north-western corner of the first hypostyle hall (XV).

Looking at the plan (fig.3), we can try to understand the general evolution of the temple complex. It is not yet clear what the chapel of Hor-udja looked like in the time of Tiberius. Before the small hypostyle hall and the large pronaos (XIV and XV) were built, it was perhaps a free-standing construction. It seems that under Trajan, when the second hypostyle hall (XIV) was constructed, it incorporated the chapel in the new façade of the temple, by extending the western (and eastern ?) side wall of the chapel. The façade added to the western side wall of the chapel is not connected with cramps. What may have been an open court was thus turned into a first room, consisting of the door of Tiberius to the north, the side wall of the second hypostyle hall (XIV) to the east, the extended west wall of the chapel and a new door to the south. After the construction of the façade of the temple, which included at least one chapel on the west side, a pronaos (XV) was added to the temple, perhaps also under Trajan. Whether or not this reconstruction of events is correct will become clear in the forthcoming campaigns. The number of doors in this sector is certainly notable: besides the secondary cult axis, giving access to the chapel of Hor-udja, there are two other doors, one providing an entrance to the pronaos from the west, the other giving perhaps access to a south-north corridor along the west side of the temple.

Arriving at this point, we may formulate, by way of conclusion, some interesting perspectives that have been opened up by the Belgian and French project at Shenhur.

Further excavation of the main temple will surely yield some surprises. The continuation of clearance of the small hypostyle hall (XIV), for example, which was at least partly decorated, might provide the answers to several questions. What was the function of the western and northern side-doors of the pronaos? This can only be answered when one has some sense as to the limits of the temple domain. We have to look for the enclosure wall, we have to clear the court in front of the temple, and to excavate the western and eventually a small part of the eastern area to see if there are other secondary buildings. The rear wall too (pl.43b-c) deserves special attention. Until now only the main double scene has been studied (Quaegebeur and Traunecker 1994; Quaegebeur, forthcoming): it shows emperor Tiberius in front of the Theban (right) and Coptite (left) triad, to which, in each case, a local goddess is associated. In the middle of the back wall a false door may be seen. The holes for the two door-leaves are still recognizable in the lintel. Presumably some kind of cult-relief was put in the niche which could be closed and opened. To cover this place of popular cult, a kiosk in wood was constructed against the wall. One of the two beam holes to insert a beam is still visible above the door to the right. For this reason, there was no decoration above the false door. At some period this kiosk was enlarged to cover the entire length of the rear wall. The beam holes for the enlarged kiosk had destroyed part of the decoration. The excavations will show if any remains of the kiosk are left.

The identification of this place of prayer, confirmed by an inscription characterizing the god Tutu in the Coptite section as "the god who comes to the one who appeals to him" brings us to another aspect: theology and cult. The function and original theology of the temple have to be studied more closely; for this the texts are essential. We were not, however, yet able to engage fully in epigraphical work. We know, from the experience gained at el-Qalʿa, that we shall have to work at night with artificial light; until now the archaeological work has taken almost all our time and energy.

The theology and function of the temple may not be studied on their own; they have to be placed in a wider context. Shenhur is situated near the border of the fifth Upper Egyptian nome (the nome of Coptos) with the fourth or Theban nome. The principal goddesses of both places, Isis and Mut, and the main gods of these two cult centres were worshipped at Shenhur. In this temple, Haroeris of Qus is associated with the gods of Coptos; the crocodile god of Qus is also represented. Such data must be integrated into a larger inquiry into the links between Theban and Coptite cults in the Graeco-Roman period. We encounter the gods of Qus at Coptos (Traunecker 1992, 134-6 § 127-8) and the chapel of the Coptite Osiris is well known at Thebes (PM II², 20). Furthermore, Theban priests in charge of the cult of Osiris of Coptos are known (Fairman 1935). Private documents also show that Theban priests were in charge of cults from Qus. This can be illustrated by an unpublished situla in the British Museum (EA 38212) dedicated to a Theban priest who, among other titles, was prophet of Sobek of Qus (De Meulenaere 1960, 97, 102), and an interesting wooden stele from Ptolemaic Thebes (BM EA 8461), published by Morris Bierbrier (1987, 38-9, pl. 74-7), which mentions several cults from Qus, but no sure reference to a priest linked with "the lake of Horus" has yet been found.

The Shenhur temple, contemporary with the el-Qal'a temple (see the contribution by Claude Traunecker to this volume), should also be seen in its historical context: are these new temples a result of a deliberate policy by Augustus, who in southern and western frontier regions (i.e. in Nubia and in the oases of the western desert; see for the latter the paper of Olaf Kaper) seems to have given new encouragement to religious building activity?

Another perspective is the study of the connections between the temple domain and the Graeco-Roman settlement, which is almost certainly preserved under the Coptic buildings. All we have to date is one first century coin (AD 69) found in a disturbed context in a Coptic level .

A final interesting aspect is the fact that here it is possible to study the later, mainly Coptic, reuse of the temple buildings (at least during the sixth and early seventh centuries). The chronology of the progressive demolition of the temples at Shenhur has to be determined. The reasons are already clear: we have referred to the activities of lime-burners in the parts built of good quality limestone; the other parts suffered only from the phenomenon of stone robbing. The northern part was indeed exploited as a quarry by the locals in search of hard stone. We have already noted that the upper layers of the outer wall, seen by Nestor L'Hôte, have disappeared (see pl.43b-c, 44a-b). In the Mamluke minaret, blocks of the temple were used to built part of the staircase, and from a dilapidated stair to the west of the mosque comes a decorated block which does not fit the buildings unearthed to date.

Thus Shenhur offers an exceptional opportunity to investigate the rise, flourishing and ruin of an Upper Egyptian town and its temples during Greek, Roman, Coptic and early Islamic times.

Acknowledgements
In Belgium, the Shenhur project forms part of the programme on "Inter-University Poles of Attraction" (IPA 28) initiated by the Belgian State, Prime Minister's Office, Science Policy Programming. From the French side, it is integrated into the activities of the Unité de Recherches Archéologiques (URA 1275) of the CNRS, associated with the Institute of Papyrology and Egyptology of the University of Lille III directed by professor Dominique Valbelle.

Dr. R. Fazzini, keeper at The Brooklyn Museum, kindly gave me access to the Wilbour Notebooks, and generously sent me copies of the documents concerning Shenhur.

I would like to thank also Claude Traunecker, co-director of the Shenhur project, who commented on the first draft of this paper, P. Dils, who put at my disposal the text of his lecture on the Belgian-French mission to Shenhur, given at the Dutch Institute in Cairo on April 28, 1994, and Dr. Dorothy Thompson, who corrected my English.

Bibliography
Arnold, D 1994. *Lexikon der ägyptischen Baukunst.* Munich and Zurich, Artemis.
Baedeker 1929. *Baedeker's Egypt 1929* (re-edition London and New York 1985).
Baines, J and J Malek, 1980. Atlas of Ancient *Egypt.* Oxford.
Bagnall, R et al. 1980, *Greek Ostraka* (*CNMAL* 4). Zutphen.
Bierbrier, M 1987. *Hieroglyphic Texts from Egyptian Stelae etc.* 11. London, BM Publications.
Brugsch, H 1893. Möris-See. In *Zeitschrift für Ägyptische Sprache und Altertumskunde* 31, 17-31.
Daressy, G 1917-8. Deux naos de Qouss. In *Annales du Service des Antiquités d'Egypte* 17, 224-5.
Daressy, G 1926. Le voyage d'inspection de M. Grébaut en 1889. In *Annales du Service des Antiquités d'Egypte* 26, 1-22.

De Meulenaere, H 1960. Les monuments du culte des rois Nectanébo. In *Chronique d'Egypte* 92-107.
De Wit, C 1961. Une mention de Rome dans un texte hiéroglyphique du temps d'Auguste. In *Mélanges Mariette* (*Bibliotheque d'Etude* 32), Cairo, 62-9.
Fairman, H 1935. A Statue from the Karnak Cache. In *Journal of Egyptian Archaeology* 20, 1-4.
Halm, H 1979. *Ägypten nach den mamlukischen Leihensregistern* I (*Tübinger Atlas des Vorderen Orients*, Reihe B, 38/1). Wiesbaden, Dr. Ludwig Reichert.
Kurth, D 1994. Die Friese innerhalb der Tempeldekoration griechisch-römischer Zeit. In *Aspekte spätägyptischer Kultur. Festschrift für E. Winter* (*Aegyptiaca Treverensia* 7), Mainz, 191-201.
Lepsius, C R s.d. *Denkmäler aus Aegypten und Aethiopien* IV. Berlin, Nicolaische Buchhandlung.
Lepsius, C R 1904. *Denkmäler aus Aegypten und Aethiopien.Text* II. Leipzig, J C Hinrichs.
L'Hôte, N 1840. *Lettres écrites d'Egypte en 1838 et 1839.* Paris.
Neugebauer, O & R Parker, 1969. *Egyptian Astronomical Texts and Representations* III (*Brown Egyptological Studies* 6). Providence.
PM V = Porter, B & R Moss, 1937. *Topographical Bibliography* V. *Upper Egypt: Sites.* Oxford, Griffith Institute.
PM II = Porter, B & R Moss, 1972. *Topographical Bibliography* II. *Theban Temples.* 2nd edition. Oxford, Griffith Institute.
Quaegebeur, J and C Traunecker, 1994. Chenhour 1839-1993. Etat de la question et rapport des travaux de 1992 et de 1993. In *Cahiers de Recherches de l'Institut de Papyrologie et d'Egyptologie de Lille* 16, (in collaboration with Casseyas, C, Chartier-Raymond, M, Creemers, G, Dils, P and Roovers, I).
Quaegebeur, J, forthcoming. Le temple romain de Chenhour. Remarques sur l'histoire de sa construction et sur sa décoration. In D Kurth (ed.), *Systeme und Programme der ägyptischen Tempeldekoration.*
Rondeau, V, 1989. Une monographie bubastite. In *Bulletin de l'Institut Français d'Archéologie Orientale* 89, 249-70.
Roovers, I and M Chartier-Raymond, forthcoming. La céramique copte de Chenhour. In *Bulletin de liaison du Groupe international d'étude de la céramique égyptienne.*
Sauneron, S 1969. *Le temple d'Esna* IV/1. Cairo, Institut Français d'Archéologie Orientale.
Timm, S 1991. *Das christlich-koptische Ägypten in arabischer Zeit* (*Tübinger Atlas des Vorderen Orients*, Reihe B 41/5). Wiesbaden, Dr.Ludwig Reichert.
Traunecker, C 1981. La lutte contre la dégradation des grès à Karnak. In Grimal, N-C (ed.), *Prospection et sauvetage des antiquités de l'Egypte* (*Bibliotheque d'Etude* 88), Cairo, 57-70.
Traunecker, C 1983. Schanhur. In Helck, W, E Otto, and W Westendorf, *Lexikon der Ägyptologie* V, Wiesbaden, Otto Harrassowitz, 528-31.
Traunecker, C 1992. *Coptos. Hommes et dieux sur le parvis de Geb* (*Orientalia Lovaniensia Anlecta* 43). Leuven, Peeters.
Traunecker, C 1994. Cryptes connues et inconnues des temples tardifs. In *Bulletin de la Société Française d'Egyptologie* 129, 21-46.
Traunecker, C, forthcoming. Les ouabet de Chenhour et d'el-Qal'a: décoration et position. In D Kurth (ed.), *Systeme und Programme der ägyptischen Tempeldekoration.*
Vandier d'Abbadie, J 1963. *Nestor L'Hôte (1804-1842).* Leiden, E J Brill.
Weigall, A, 1910. *Guide to the Antiquities of Upper Egypt.* London (2nd. ed. 1913).
Wilbour, C 1936. *Wilbour's Travels in Egypt.* Brooklyn.
Wilkinson, J G 1835. *Topography of Thebes and General View of Egypt.* London, John Murray.
Wilkinson, J G 1843. *Modern Egypt and Thebes* II. London, John Murray.

Lessons from the Upper Egyptian temple of el-Qal'a

Claude Traunecker

I. Introduction

The traveller in Upper Egypt, eager to visit temples, is in a hurry to reach Thebes, its pylons and its obelisks. Thus, as soon as he has visited the temple of Hathor at Dendara, he rushes south the seventy kilometres or so to the ancient capital. Perhaps he will condescend to give a thought, but only a thought, to Coptos, hometown of the god Min and now called Qift. Besides, the guide will dissuade our traveller from paying such a disappointing and tiring visit.

A. A monument long known

However, hidden among the palmtrees of a little village north of Qift, is a small temple, rather well preserved, and covered with hieroglyphic inscriptions. Its name is el-Qal'a, which means 'the citadel' in Arabic (PM VI, 134). This small monument has been somewhat left to one side in archaeology. Its size, though modest, is not negligible (26 by 16 metres) and its walls still stand to a height of four metres.

Yet, despite its qualities, el-Qal'a was ignored by Egyptologists for almost two and a half centuries. Indeed, by an irony of history this temple was one of the first Egyptian temples to be described and surveyed by a European traveller, but one of the last to be copied and published.We are indebted to a young Englishman, Richard Pococke, for the discovery of the temple in 1738. An astonishing full-length portrait in the Museum of Fine Arts in Geneva, Switzerland, painted by Liotard in Istanbul the year of Pococke's visit at el-Qal'a, shows this young man, who held a thesis in theology and who was to become a bishop, dressed as a Turk. In his book published in 1743, Pococke presented a brief description of the temple, but also and most important, a map of the building (Pococke 1743, 88, pl. 27a). Thus, the el-Qal'a temple, despite its modern oblivion, was one of the first Egyptian temples the plan of which was presented to the curiosity of the European public.The French scholars of the *Description de l'Egypte* give only a report of the existence of the monument (Jollois and De Villiers 1821, 414). Champollion ignores it. A few fearless British travellers such as Hay and Wilkinson visited the temple at the beginning of the nineteenth century (Pantalacci and Traunecker 1990, 2, nn. 4-5), but they published nothing.

B. An illegible temple

We may ask ourselves: why this lack of interest in the el-Qal'a temple?

In May 1845, Richard Lepsius visits the temple. He makes a few copies of inscriptions, he reads some cartouches, among others those of the emperors Augustus and of Tiberius Claudius. However, the German follower of Champollion peremptorily concludes: "nirgends ist etwas fast zu lesen", ("there is virtually nowhere anything readable", Lepsius 1904, 256-7). Very few travellers mention the el-Qal'a temple. De Salle visited it in 1838 and described it briefly (De Salle 1840, 145-6). However most visitors who dared to venture into the region are satisfied with only a mention (Prokesch-Osten 1874, 343; Murray 1880, 447; Wilbour 1936 (March 1882), 149-50, 206-7). Exceptionally, in 1910, Weigall gives a relatively detailed description of the monument in his guide-book of Upper Egypt (Weigall 1913, 52). Thereafter the temple is no longer to be found in the general public publications.

The temple at el-Qal'a indeed has a peculiarity at once fortunate and terrible. The builders, who wanted to create an eternal work, renounced sandstone and fine limestone, which are fragile and especially recyclable materials. They chose instead a local stone: a poor macro-fossiliferous (Ostrea Reili) and coarse-grained limestone to be found at Hegaza (Dakhla formation) about 20 kms south-east of Coptos (Traunecker 1978, 302; Pantalacci and Traunecker 1990, 4). It is a hard, heterogeneous stone, difficult to work, but it has the considerable advantage of being a material of very poor quality rejected by lime-burners. Confronted by the hardness of this limestone, the builders renounced any attempt to polish the surfaces. As far as the engravers are concerned, they had the hardest time carving the hieroglyphic signs in the stone. That is why, when we face the shapeless scratches forming this epigraphy, it is difficult to distinguish the traces made by a quarry-man's pick from an intentional sign. In brief, the epigraphy of el-Qal'a is awful.

All these elements repelled the Egyptologists. Maspéro had the building partially cleared in 1883 (Reinach 1911, 196). But one must wait for 1910 and 1911 with the French excavations to have a first study. In 1911, Reinach published a detailed description of the monument with an excellent plan set by the architect Martineau (Reinach 1911, 193-237, pl.5). Reinach tried to read some cartouches, recognized the name of Tiberius-Claudius, and proposed the hypothesis that the temple was dedicated to Isis. But this attempt remained isolated and Lepsius' malediction concerning the impossible epigraphy of el-Qal'a continued to overshadow the monument.

At the instigation of Serge Sauneron I started work in 1975 on the publication of some monuments still visible at Coptos (Traunecker 1992, XV). This is how I first visited el-Qal'a, which gave me the material for the article in the *Lexikon der Ägyptologie* (identification of the temple with double axis: Traunecker 1983, 38-40). It was followed in 1982 by the first epigraphical campaigns carried out by Laure Pantalacci and myself (Pantalacci and Traunecker 1984-85, 1985). A first volume collecting all the texts and decorations of the two sanctuaries and of the offering room is already published (Pantalacci and Traunecker 1990). The second volume is being completed and concerns the mysterious corridor and its surrounding rooms. The following volumes will cover the remaining decoration of the temple and an architectural study completed by Françoise Traunecker. Between 1991 and 1993, the temple was cleared of its fallen blocks. A good number of these were installed back into place and some walls were reconstructed (Pantalacci and Traunecker 1993).

Before entering upon the content of the monument itself, I wish to say a few words on the way we warded off the malediction of Lepsius. Even preparatory work on photographs was impossible. Even if it is possible to identify the scenes and the elements of the decoration, it is impossible to distinguish the details of the texts, blurred by false shadows and the lack of scraping and rejointing of the walls. In no way could we make a facsimile, because of the imprecision of the engraving. We decided accordingly to use standardized copies with artificial light. Therefore we had to work at night, holding our lamps along the walls and multiplying our copies and collations.Typically, each scene has been copied twice and collated four times. The principle for the publication as we laid it down, lies in the legibility of the monument while giving the reader all the information about the iconography and the disposition of the scenes (Traunecker 1987; Pantalacci and Traunecker 1990, 14-15). We completed the editing with an index of all the known words or expressions.

II. Presentation of the monument

The temple of el-Qal'a is linked to the ruins of Coptos (Pantalacci and Traunecker 1984-85, 135; id. 1985, 202; id., 1). It stands 600 metres north of the temenos of Min and Isis. It was built at the border of the desert, which was then much closer to the Nile than nowadays. It is, in a way, an outlying temple, built at the border of a religious territory, as is for example the temple of Deir Shellouit (Zivie 1982, 1977, 1992), or the temple of Shenhur presented by my colleague, Jan Quaegebeur in a separate contribution to this colloquium (see *infra*).

The temple which was built during the reign of Augustus replaces an older one, made of bricks, according to two texts from the temple (Pantalacci and Traunecker 1990, n° 56, 82). The work of decoration was completed in three or four campaigns over the course of fifty to sixty years, and it covers all the walls. During the reign of Augustus, the inside walls of the two central and north sanctuaries were decorated. The decoration of the offering room was started under Caligula. The remaining parts of the temple, including the crypts, were decorated during the reign of Tiberius Claudius.

When we examine the plan of the edifice, the disposition at first seems classical (fig.1). In the rear part of the temple are found the chamber of worship, isolated from the rest of the temple by the mysterious corridor, and the side rooms with the usual "wabet" (Traunecker, forthcoming), an open-air court in front of a kind of liturgical platform used for the main local festivals including the New Year celebrations. In front of this stands an offering room, itself preceded by an intermediary room with side-rooms on the right and on the left a staircase. A large entry hall marks the façade of the temple. During our clearance work in the past few years, we discovered four crypts: one under the "wabet", one under the staircase, and two in the width of the front wall. All of them are decorated, which is highly unusual (Traunecker 1994, 22-3).

On closer examination, the el-Qal'a temple displays three specific features which make it unique:

1. The temple, built on the east bank, is oriented toward the east, that is, the desert.
2. The side room, north of the offering room is in fact a second sanctuary, reached through its own entrance. Thus, the temple of El-Qal'a is, like the temple of Kom Ombo, a dual temple with two cultual axis, but it is a unique example with two perpendicular axes.
3. All the walls were decorated, from the outside panels which were seen by everyone, to the dark and secret cubby-hole contrived in the temple foundations and the wall thickness. This is a rich decoration, but since it is a small size temple, its decoration is relatively easy to memorize. So we can say that the temple of el-Qal'a is a kind of an abstract for the architecture of the large temples like Dendara or Edfu. It is thus an exceptional place of observation for the scholar who is curious about the rules that governed temple decoration, a laboratory for the epigraphist of the Late Period temples, and, dare we say, a manoeuvring terrain for the explorers of the world of the wall deities.

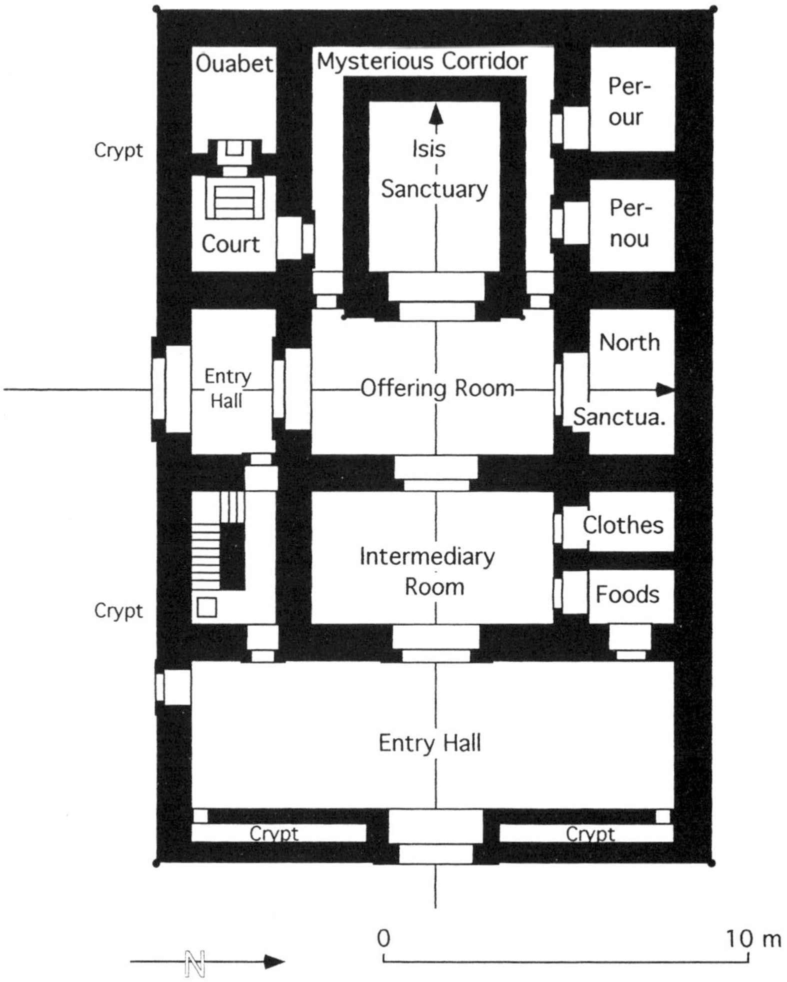

Fig.1 Plan of the temple of el-Qal'a.

III. The lessons of the temple of el-Qal'a

The purpose of this paper is to present, in brief, the contributions, the lessons which have emerged from the study of this monument, and go beyond. These lessons are of two kinds:
(1) theological processes and creation of new gods
(2) decoration principles as a theology

A.Theological processes: Principle of antonomasia

Who is the main deity of the temple of el-Qal'a ? According to the texts of the main sanctuary, it is "Isis, the Great, the Mother of Horus" (Pantalacci and Traunecker 1990, n°19). In the doorway, her title is also "The Great Goddess" (Pantalacci and Traunecker 1990, n°31). Later, during the decorative campaigns of Tiberius-Claudius, this title of Isis will become the name of a divine entity *per se* on wall decoration. She is then a goddess, represented and named on walls, and the recipient of rituals accomplished by the king. In other words, an epithet becomes a deity which in turn can be represented (fig.2).

This process of creation of a wall decoration deity can be called antonomasia. The antonomasia is a rhetorical process through which a person or a thing is designated by an epithet or an appellative. Thus a deity looses his or her usual name. The anonymity of the designation brings forward the function (such as the great goddess, mother of a divine child) at the detriment of the historical deity (such as Isis), who is the origin and the mythical reference. We shall see further how two deities, Isis and her antonomasia, The Great Goddess, share the walls of the temple of el-Qal'a during a decoration campaign under the Emperor Claudius. In some sequences, there is a new divine antonomasia : "the Venerable" (Shepset). This deity is drawn from the epithets of The Great Goddess. Relating to Isis, she is the result of a secondary antonomasia (fig.3). She serves as a companion to The Great Goddess, when in the symetrical scene, Isis is accompanied by her mother Nut (El-Qal'a II, n°209 and 212). This antonomastical process was particulary appreciated, so it seems, by the theologians of the Coptic region, who did not hesitate to apply it to Harpocrates, the divine infant.

1.*The Harpocrates of el-Qal'a, results of an antonomasian diastasis*

In the north sanctuary, a motherly deity is taking care of her divine child. This part of the temple, and thus the south-north axis, is devoted to the birth and childhood of this local divine child. During the "*Tempeltagung*" in Hamburg in June 1994, my colleague Laure Pantalacci, drew attention on the representation of the hippopotamus goddesses who protect the year, which decorates the reverse of the southern door. They are, among others, the signs of the mammisiac function of this axis (Pantalacci, forthcoming).

In the nursing scenes of the northern sanctuary, Isis generously offers her milk to a voracious child. It is indeed the ancient Isis filling her traditional role for Horus the Child, Harpocrates, who is well known all over Egypt despite his very likely Coptite origin (Meeks 1977, 1006; Traunecker 1992, § 289). Yet the theologians and decorators at el-Qal'a were not satisfied with this simple affirmation.

On the door lintel of the northern sanctuary, two scenes, which are laid out symmetrically to the axis, as they are supposed to be, show the king officiating in front of a seated goddess, followed by a Harpocrates and another goddess (Pantalacci and Traunecker 1990, 68). The two Harpocrates are different: the one on the left wears the crown of Amun (Pantalacci and Traunecker 1990, n°66), but the one on the right has the double crown (Pantalacci and Traunecker 1990, n°68). Here again, we have a process of the creation of a divine image by antonomasia. Both of them are Harpocrates, but the first, with his crown and titles is "the first of Amun" (Ballet 1982), in other words the heir of the paternal function, while the second is "the son of Isis and Osiris", that is, the biological and legitimate son. It is really a single deity such as is represented with both titles in a graffito in the Wady Hammamat (Couyat and Montet 1912, 74, pl.27).

Yet here, the antonomasia which created the divine image, operates by diastasis (separation). Likewise, the female protective deity is divided into two: on the left side, the Amonian Harpocrates is preceded by Isis, and on the right side, the Osirian Harpocrates is preceded by Nephthys (fig.4).

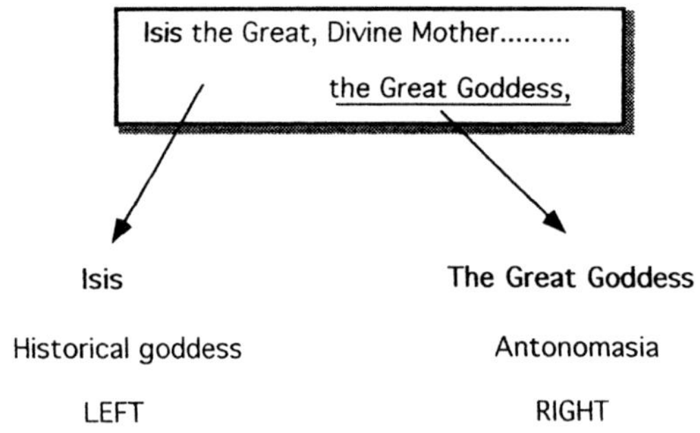

Fig.2. Principle of antonomasia.

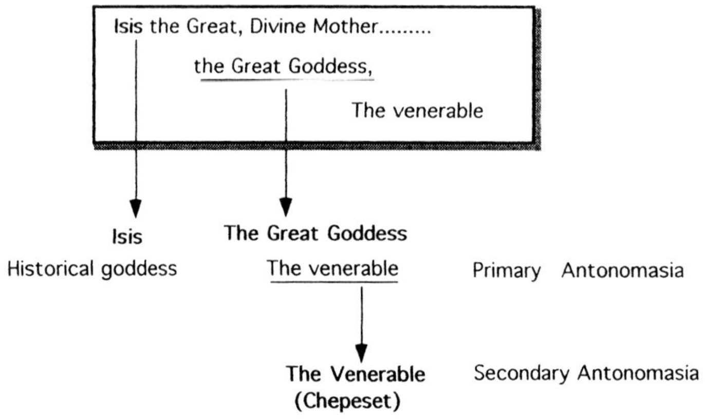

Fig.3 Primary and secondary antonomasia

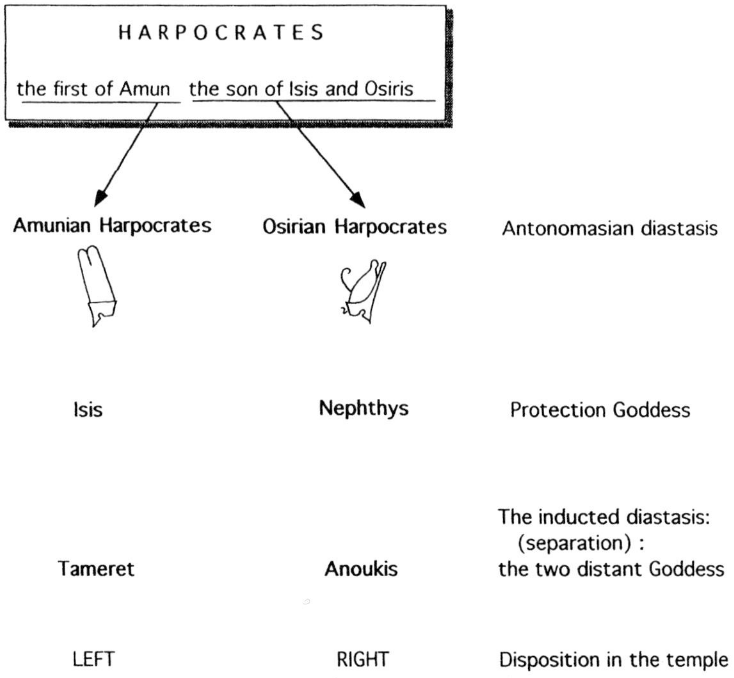

Fig. 4 The Harpocrates antonomasia (Augustus)

2. *The induced divisions: the two Distant Goddesses*

The kick-off for the game of the divine symmetries is given. The consequences in the decoration and the theological appearances are considerable. We found a few allusions, some of which clear, to the origin of these good goddesses, who protect the divine child (function of Isis-Nephthys). They are only the appeased, softened forms of wild and furious forces of the world not yet regulated (Derchain 1971, 23). In a few places in Egypt, a distant and dangerous goddess resides at the border of the desert in the aspect of a destructive lioness, and this goddess becomes a loving mother when she paces on the grass of the valley (Meeks 1980; Junker 1911). We have, for example, Sekhmet and Bastet in the Delta (Verhoeven and Derchain 1985, 75), Smitis and Nekhbet at Elkab (Derchain 1971, 12), Repit at Wanina (Petrie 1909; Verhoeven 1983) and Akhmim (Sourouzian 1983). At El-Qal'a, however, the diastasis of the antonomasia of the Harpocrates, followed by the similar process for the motherly deities, brings recourse to two distant goddesses. The doorway texts of the northern sanctuary of Augustus reveal their names: on the left, Tameret is associated to Isis, on the right, Anukis is linked to Nephthys.

B.Theology and decoration

1.*The different Harpocrates and the Distant Goddesses in the decorative apparatus of Tiberius Claudius*

When one last campaign of decoration started under Tiberius Claudius, "the Great Goddess", specific antonomasia of el-Qal'a, is assisted by the two Distant Goddesses, Tameret and Tairetperatoum, in other words, "the Eye of Pithom". This latter deity replaces Anukis in the Augustan theology at el-Qal'a. The dualist system of the Harpocrates is used again, and developed on the few walls still free of decoration like the so-called mysterious corridor.The left or southern side of the mysterious corridor is dedicated to Isis and the Amonian Harpocrates, and the other side to the Great Goddess which is the divine antonomasia of Isis and her Osirian Harpocrates, assisted by the two appeased Distant Goddesses (fig.5).

At the same time, it was then seen as necessary to distinguish this Osirian Harpocrates from his antonomasian doublet, with the adjunction of a new epithet: Hor-udja.

Two symmetrical scenes (external wall of the central sanctuary) (fig.6) show the Harpocrates in their own surrounding: in the south (Pantalacci and Traunecker 1990, n°125), the Harpocrates with Amonian feathers is accompanied by Min-Ra and Isis, the great Coptite Dyad, and in the north (Pantalacci and Traunecker 1990, n°130), Hor-udja the Child, is with Osiris Onnophris and Isis, "the Great Goddess, the Widow". The two Harpocrates allow the juxtaposition of a few mythical readings of the same entity, that is the divine child. The same system has been developed on the wabet walls (Traunecker forthcoming, fig.7; El Qal'a II, forthcoming, n°203, 206).

2.*Wall Theology*

The pure logic of these constructions and the beauty of the symmetry in the distribution of the representations is reassuring. Yet what precisely does it represent? Is it the expression of an independent religious thought established by theologians in search of absolute and who scrutinize transcendency in the silence of their studies ? Or rather, is it the result of theologians' meditations and efforts in front of walls they have to decorate? I think that it is the result of the encounter between a knowledge, that is ancestral deities with their epithets, and stimulating constraints, namely the walls to decorate. I proposed the term *wall theology* to designate these divine extrapolations.

3. *Divine polymorphism and unicity of liturgical action*

This multiplication through division of the deities on the walls of the temple has a second consequence for the decorative process. This is our second point. Let us take the decoration of the exterior walls of the central sanctuary.

The decorator's goal is clear. He wants to represent on the walls the principal acts of the daily worship, in eight panels with two register (fig.6).

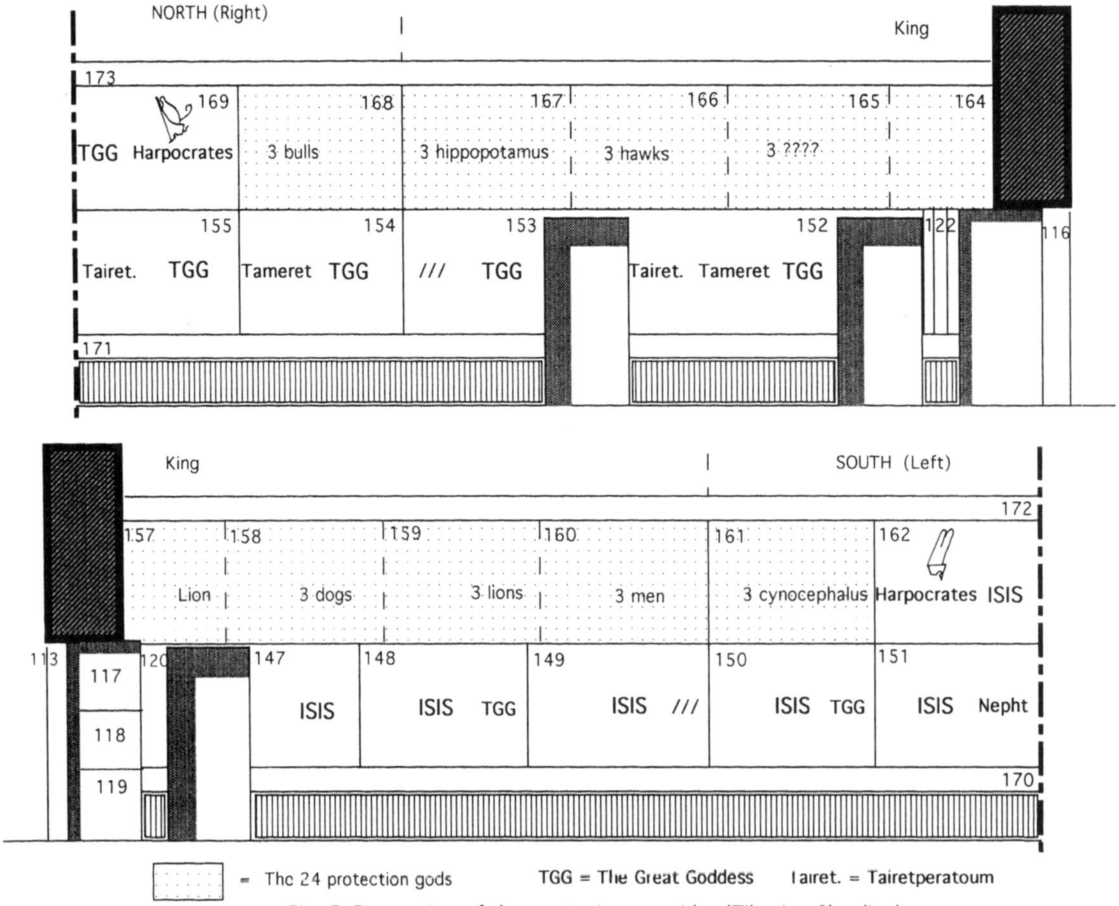

Fig. 5. Decoration of the mysterious corridor (Tiberius Claudius)

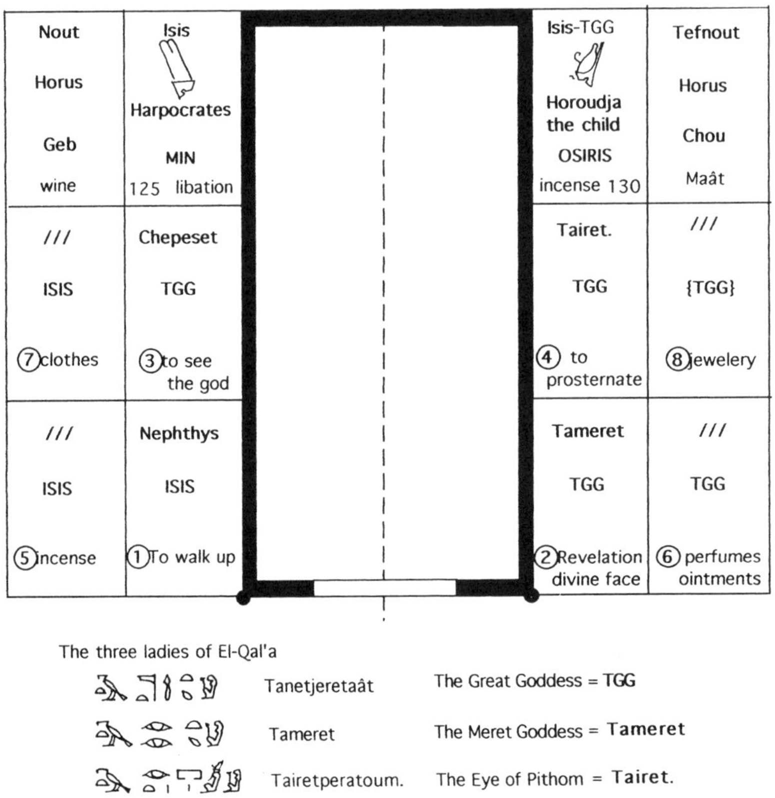

Fig. 6. Exterior walls of the central sanctuary (Tiberius Claudius)

The sequence is as follows : (1) to walk up towards the god; (2) revelation of the divine face; (3) to see the god; (4) to prostrate oneself; and then to make offerings of (5) incense, (6) perfumes and ointments, (7) clothing and (8) jewellery.

This is what I propose to name *action sequence* (Traunecker, forthcoming). It alternates on the two sides, the odd numbers on the south wall and the even numbers on the north side. If all was normal and logical, the recipient of these representations should be Isis of el-Qal'a, possibly with all her titles. Instead, the theologians preferred once more to present the developments through antonomasia of Isis and of the divine child, thus producing successions of divine images that I called *identity sequence*. On the south wall, Isis and Nephthys receive the odd number rituals. On the north wall, the Great Goddess and Tameret and Tairetperatum, the two distant goddesses, figure in the even rituals.

Thus we have the superposition of two composition grids: an action sequence and an identity sequence. In this case, the association of an offering with a deity is the contingent result of the interplay between two systems.

Another interesting example of this system is the composition of the decoration of the wabet (Traunecker, forthcoming). The action sequence includes the dressing ritual (ointment, various kinds of cloths, pectoral). The identity sequence shows on the left (or south) Isis, the Amonian Harpocrates, and on the right, the Great Goddess and the Osirian Harpocrates, Hor-udja.

4. *Scenes, catalogue of deities*

There is also another remarkable kind of wall representation. We have just seen that, for want of a priest to question, the analysis of the decoration alone allows us to delineate with some difficulty the composition of the pantheon of el-Qal'a. However a few scenes, true catalogues of deities, present together the whole pantheon in one or two rituals. They only exist in the crypts (Traunecker 1994, 40; Pantalacci and Traunecker 1993, 283). There, in the dimness of the secret chambers, Isis and Nephthys protecting Osiris, the Harpocrates and the three Ladies of el-Qal'a, side by side, in association with apotropaic deities not seen in the open temple, such as Tutu, keep watch.

IV. Conclusion

A. Destiny of an antonomasia: the Great Goddess at Shenhur

Must we conclude from this presentation of the theogenic procedures that only the cult statuettes in the two sanctuaries have a life outside the walls? Gods sometimes come down from the walls to live a new existence. Thus the Great Goddess, antonomasiac figure of the el-Qal'a Isis, is one of the divinities, of the contemporaneous Shenhur temple (Quaegebeur and Traunecker 1994; Quaegebeur forthcoming; id. *supra*).

Shenhur has the particuliarity of uniting two local theologies: on the rear wall of the temple and on the side panels of the sanctuary, two divine parties share the available space : on the left or west, the Theban gods, on the right or east the Coptite dieties. On the front wall the two main goddesses of these divine tutelary parties preside: on the left or west “Mut of the manifold appearances” (*ʿšꜣ ỉrw*) and on the right or east “the Great Goddess Isis”.

The deity which was adored in the secrecy of the sanctuary of Shenhur was, as at el-Qal'a, a local form of Isis, an antonomasia of the Coptite Isis, “the Great Goddess”, whom we already met at el-Qal'a. But in this complex system of theologies made of associations and symmetries, one cannot be satisfied with only one goddess. Thus, the Shenhur theologians created a local dyad through the association of the Great Goddess with a consort, “the Lady of Happiness” Nebetihy. In my opinion, this goddess is entirely manufactured and tailored. One scene of the lintel in the sanctuary shows the local dyad with the name of “Isis the Great Goddess” and “Nephthys Lady of Ihy”. It was indeed not astonishing to have recourse to Nephthys, the usual companion of Isis. Ihy, included in the Goddess' epithet, is a toponym (enclosure, stable: Wb I, 118,5) and it is not excluded that this Nephthys was a cultic reality in the Coptite region. Be that as it may, Nephthys, Lady of Ihy, is a matrix from which the theologians extract the goddess Nebetihy by antonomasia. However, the second term was likened through assonance to the word ihy, “happiness”, a term which concords well with birth theology. In short, we have two bipartitions (fig.7).

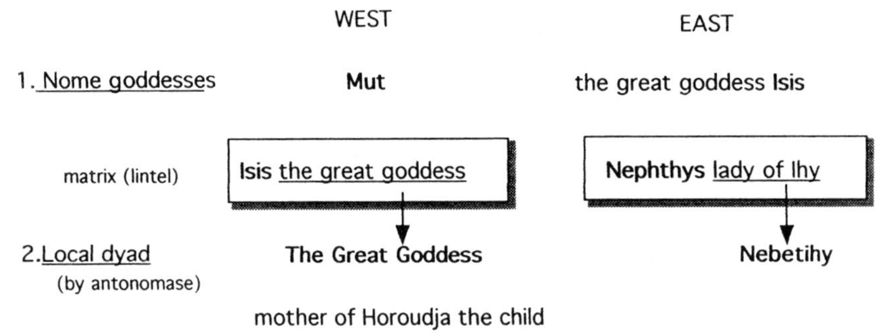

Fig.7. The antonomasian goddesses of Chenhour

1. The nome goddesses: Mut (west) facing the Coptite Isis (east)
2. The local dyad: the Great Goddess (west) and Nebetihy (east), local forms, issued through antonomasia from the divine matrix "Isis, the Great Goddess" and "Nephthys, Lady of Ihy" (Quaegebeur and Traunecker 1994, 205-7).

The Belgian and French Mission of Shenhur has recently discovered the remains of a chapel dating back to Trajan and possibly older (Tiberius ?), dedicated to the Great Goddess, Lady of the males and females, and to her son Hor-udja (Quaegebeur and Traunecker 1994, 180, 208). The Great Goddess and her offspring form here a kind of feminine counterpart to the procreative power of Min, the regional Great God. Twenty kilometres further south, the antonomasias of el-Qal'a became complete deities.

B. El-Qal'a, specific and renewed aspects of the temple in its functioning

Before closing this presentation let me indicate briefly what the study of el-Qal'a brings to the understanding of Roman Period liturgies. During the main festival at el-Qal'a, it was customary to present the Goddess and the Divine Child with beautiful flower bouquets. We know a hymn describing the variety and the scents of this offering in the door of the mammisi axis.

The study of the thresholds and of the axial doorposts allows the reconstruction of an apparatus made of low doors or gates set up in the passageways (Pantalacci and Traunecker 1990, 382, fig.3). It was then possible to keep the axial doors open, from the southern door to the northern sanctuary, in order to let the worshippers look at the cult statue while preventing any trespassing. The size of the crypts and comparison with other monuments such as the Opet Temple at Karnak lead us to believe that the el-Qal'a temple during these holidays rose from sleepiness (Traunecker 1994, 40-3). Coming from the centre of Coptos, a procession reached el-Qal'a. The crypts were opened, and the special liturgical utensils, which had remained undisturbed since the last holidays, were taken out.

At these festivals, the temple, which kept its sacral character through minimal liturgy during the intermediary periods, found again a new sacred life. A monument built for a specific liturgy, it received regularly and intermittently the worshipping Coptites with their fragrant bouquets, who had come to celebrate the birth of the divine child. He is the offspring of the meeting between the appeased feminine forces wandering the desert, rendered fertile at the entrance to the territory of Min, the procreator.

On the holiday when the birth of the divine child is celebrated, may we propose to see the temple of el-Qal'a then fully operating as a kind of a Christmas Eve Temple ?

Acknowledgement

I would like to thank my colleague Maryvonne Chartier-Raymond for the English version of this text.

Bibliography

Ballet, P 1982. Remarques sur Harpocrate amonien. In *Bulletin de l'Institut Français d'Archéologie Orientale*, 75-83.

Couyat, J and P Montet, 1912. *Les Inscriptions hiéroglyphiques et hiératiques du Ouâdi Hammâmât.* Mémoires publiés par les membres de l'Institut Français d'Archéologie Orientale du Caire 34. Cairo, Institut Français d'Archéologie Orientale.

Derchain, P 1971. *Elkab* I, *Les monuments religieux à l'entrée de l'ouady Hellal.* Brussels, Fondation Egyptologique Reine Elisabeth.

El Qal'a II, forthcoming. *Le temple d' el-Qal'a. Relevés des scènes et des textes II.* Cairo, Institut Français d'Archéologie Orientale.

Jollois, J-B and R De Villiers 1821. *Description de l'Egypte* III. Paris, édition Pancoucke.

Junker, H 1911. *Der Auszug der Hathor-Tefnout aus Nubien.* Abhandlungen der königlichen Preussischen Akademie der Wissenschaften, Philologisch-historische Klasse 1911 Anhang, Abhandlung 3. Berlin, Königliche Preussische Akademie der Wissenschaften.

Lepsius, R 1904. *Denkmäler aus Aegypten und Aethiopen. Text* II. Leipzig, J C Hinrichs.

Meeks, D 1977. Harpokrates. In Helck, W and W Westendorf (eds.), *Lexikon der Ägyptologie* II, Wiesbaden, Otto Harrassowitz, 1003-11.

Meeks, D 1980. Menhit. In Helck, W and W Westendorf (eds.), *Lexikon der Ägyptologie* IV, Wiesbaden, Otto Harrassowitz, 48-51.

Murray, J 1880. *Handbook for Travellers in Lower and Upper Egypt.* London.

Pantalacci, L and C Traunecker 1984-85. Premières observations sur le temple coptite d'el-Qal'a. In *Annales du Service des Antiquités d'Egypte* 70, 133-41.

Pantalacci, L and C Traunecker 1985. Le temple d'Isis à el-Qal'a près de Coptos. In S Schoske (ed.), *Akten des vierten internationalen Ägyptologen Kongresses, München 1985,* 3, 201-10.

Pantalacci, L and C Traunecker 1990. *Le temple d' el-Qal'a. Relevés des scènes et des textes. I.* Cairo, Institut Français d'Archéologie Orientale.

Pantalacci, L and C Traunecker 1993. Le temple d'el-Qal'a à Coptos: état des travaux. In *Bulletin de l'Institut Français d'Archéologie Orientale* 93, 379-390.

Pantalacci, L forthcoming. Compagnies de dieux-gardiens au temple d'el-Qal'a. In D Kurth (ed.), *Systeme und Programme der ägyptischen Tempeldekoration*.

Petrie, W M F 1909. *Athribis.* London, British School of Archaeology in Egypt, and Bernard Quaritch.

Pococke, R 1743. *Description of the East and Some Other Countries* I. London.

PM VI = B Porter and R Moss, *Topographical Bibliography of Ancient Egyptian Hieroglyphic Texts, Reliefs and Paintings. VI. Upper Egypt: Sites.* 1937. Oxford, Griffith Institute.

Prokesch-Osten, 1874. *Nilfahrt bis zu den zweiten Katarackten*, Leipzig.

Quaegebeur, J and C Traunecker 1994 (in collaboration with C Casseyas, M Chartier-Raymond, G Creemers, P Dils, P and I Roovers). Chenhour 1839-1993. Etat de la question et rapport des travaux de 1992 et de 1993. In *Cahier de Recherches de l'Institut de Papyrologie et d'Egyptologie de Lille* 16, 167-209.

Quaegebeur, J, forthcoming. Le temple romain de Chenhour. Remarques sur l'histoire de sa construction et sur sa decoration. In D Kurth (ed.), *Systeme und Programme der ägyptischen Tempeldekoration.*

Reinach, A 1911. Le temple d'el-Kala à Koptos. In *Annales du Service des Antiquités de l'Egypte* 11, 193-237.

Salle, E de 1840. *Pérégrinations en Orient, ou voyage pittoresque, historique et politique en Egypte, Nubie, Syrie, Turquie, Grèce en 1837-1839* I. Paris.

Sourouzian, H 1983. In *Mitteilungen des Deutschen Archäologischen Instituts Abteilung Kairo* 39, 220-3.

Traunecker, C 1978. Kalkstein. In Helck, W and W Westendorf (eds.), *Lexikon der Ägyptologie* III, Wiesbaden, Otto Harrassowitz, 302.

Traunecker, C 1983. El-Qal'a. In Helck, W and W Westendorf (eds.), *Lexikon der Ägyptologie* V, Wiesbaden, Otto Harrassowitz, 38-40.

Traunecker, C 1983. Schanhur. In Helck, W and W Westendorf (eds.), *Lexikon der Ägyptologie* V, Wiesbaden, Otto Harrassowitz, 528-31.
Traunecker, C 1987. Les techniques d'épigraphie de terrain: principes et pratique. In J Assmann, G Burkard, and W V Davies (eds.) *Problems and Priorities in Egyptian Archaeology,* London, 261-98.
Traunecker, C 1992. *Coptos. Hommes et dieux sur le parvis de Geb.* Orientalia Lovaniensia Analecta 43. Louvain, Peeters.
Traunecker, C 1994. Cryptes connues et inconnues des temples tardifs. In *Bulletin de la Société Française d'Egyptologie* 129, 21-45.
Traunecker, C forthcoming. Les ouabet des temples d'el-Qal'a et de Chenhour. Décoration, origine et évolution. In D Kurth (ed.), *Systeme und Programme der ägyptischen Tempeldekoration*.
Verhoeven, U and P Derchain 1985. *Le voyage de la déesse libyque.* Rites Egyptiens V. Brussels, Fondation Egyptologique Reine Elisabeth.
Verhoeven, U 1983. Repit. In Helck, W and W Westendorf (eds.), *Lexikon der Ägyptologie* V, Wiesbaden, Otto Harrassowitz, 236-42.
Weigall, A 1913. *A Guide to the Antiquities of Upper Egypt from Abydos to the Sudan Frontier.* London and New York, Macmillan (first ed. 1910).
Wilbour, C E 1936. J Capart (ed.), *Wilbour's Travels in Egypt, December 1880 to May 1891. Letters of Charles Edwin Wilbour.* Brooklyn Museum.
Wilkinson, J G 1835. *Topography of Thebes, and general view of Egypt.* London, John Murray.
Wilkinson, J G 1843. *Modern Egypt and Thebes* II. London, John Murray.
Zivie, C 1977. Trois campagnes épigraphiques au temple de Deir Chellouit. In *Bulletin de l'Institut Français d'Archéologie Orientale* 77, 151-61.
Zivie, C 1982. *Le temple de Deir Chelouit* I. Cairo, Institut Français d'Archéologie Orientale, VII-X.
Zivie, C 1992. *Le temple de Deir Chelouit* IV, *Etude architecturale.* Cairo, Institut Français d'Archéologie Orientale.

Slaughtering the crocodile at Edfu and Dendera

Penelope Wilson

The motif of the hippopotamus hunt in the marshes is well known in its different forms, from the hunt of King Den of the First Dynasty, through the Old, Middle and New Kingdom tomb representations of the hunt (Säve-Soderbergh 1953), to the mythological version in the Temple of Edfu dating to the Ptolemaic period (Blackman and Fairman 1935, 1942, 1943, 1944, 1944b; Drioton 1948; Fairman 1974). In the latter the emphasis is on the animal as a Sethian creature whose chase and destruction represent the end of chaos, the defeat of hostile forces and the assertion of the king's right to rule as a legitimate heir of ancestors who had also been successful in this ritual. Other temple scenes, particularly those of the Ptolemaic-Roman period, have this underlying symbolism in the temples. The killing of various Sethian or demonic beings - including the oryx, tortoise, Seth animal itself, Apopis serpent and foes of the king - also stress that the threats to the harmony of the cosmos and rule of Egypt have been removed (oryx, Derchain 1962; turtle, Gutbub 1979; Eye of Apopis, Borghouts 1973). Studies of these individual rites in particular, and indeed of other temple rituals, have stressed the antiquity of the rites and the ancient traditions upon which they were based and the ways in which they were re-written in later times (Egberts 1989). Often such rites also have a geographical bias and the later temples preserve the only hints of the rich panoply of early mythologies, albeit edited and codified in order to serve the cult of the specific god in whose temple the rites appear (Derchain 1962).

The scenes of the rite of slaying the crocodile, however, have seemingly no comparable older parallels or clear surviving mythology. They demonstrate an apparent contradiction in the Egyptian attitude to the crocodile which Egyptian texts are usually careful to avoid or to harmonise within the overall pattern of the whole system. They also show the way in which individual temples and therefore the 'House of Life' or scriptoria associated with them could present a different viewpoint from other temples elsewhere. It is also an interesting example of an anti-cult, which goes against the evident trend for the rest of Egypt and may even have been responsible for violent scenes at festivals.

Greek and Roman writers reported on the apparent contradictions they saw in the Egyptian attitude towards the crocodile (Hopfner 1913, 125-36). With its fierce nature and unnerving appearance, the animal excited comment in any case, but the way in which some sections of the Egyptian priesthood petted and revered the animal contrasted strongly with the way in which it was vilified and despised in some parts of Egypt. The account of Herodotus is the earliest (*Histories* Book II, 68-9) wherein he describes the animal and then comments upon the fact that at Thebes and around Lake Moeris the crocodile was especially sacred. It was adorned and fed on special food while alive, then embalmed and buried in sacred coffins when it died. But at Elephantine the crocodile was not regarded as sacred and was eaten. He also describes how the crocodile was hunted using a pork bait and when the creature was brought in on a harpoon line its eyes were smeared with mud so that the crocodile could be more easily killed. He writes too that when anyone was taken by a crocodile or drowned in the river, they were accorded special treatment and their bodies were dealt with by the priests of the Nile (Lloyd 1976, 1988, 307ff.).

Strabo also wrote about the hostility towards the crocodile, but stresses that, whereas other Egyptians knew of the bad qualities of the animal and yet still revered it, at Tentyra (Dendera) the people tracked and destroyed the crocodile in every possible way. They even went so far as to attack a crocodile displayed in Rome. He also notes that at Apollonospolis (*sic* Apollonopolis, Edfu) the people here also carried on war against crocodiles (*Geography*, XVII,1, 44 (C814) and XVII, 1, 47 (C817)). The hostility of the people of Dendera towards crocodiles was also noted by Seneca (*Naturales Quaestiones*, IVA, 2.12-15) and by Pliny the Elder (*Natural History*, XXVIII, 31). There is evidence from his Fifteenth Satire that Juvenal visited Egypt and it is probable that while he was there he picked up a story based on this aversion to crocodiles and turned it into the satire. The poem shows the lengths to which the Egyptians will go in their worship of strange and wonderful gods. He describes the smouldering hatred between the people of Tentyra and the people of Ombos because the people of Ombos revere the crocodile and the Tentyrites loathe it. During one of the festivals a riot breaks out between the two groups of people and it results in a man of Dendera falling to the enraged Ombites who tear him to pieces and eat him (Courtney 1980, 598). It it easy to allow Juvenal some poetic licence to exaggerate his story and embroider the details of what he had been told. However, it is clear that, in the first and second centuries AD, writers were able to point to the example of the people of Dendera to show that the worship of strange and dangerous animals in Egypt was not consistent and moreover could provoke violent local responses.

Similarly, Plutarch wrote that 'In Apollonopolis it is customary for everyone throughout the town to eat of a crocodile; and on one day, after hunting as many as they can and killing them, they throw them right opposite the temple; and they say that when Typhon (Seth) was running away from Horus, he changed into a crocodile, regarding all evil and harmful animals, plants and experiences as deeds, qualities and movements of Typhon' (*De Iside et Osiride*, 50; Gwyn-Griffiths 1970, 199 and 492 ff.). Aelian reported that the people of Dendera were the most skilled in dealing with the crocodile and that they had a rivalry with the people of Coptos who crucified hawks to annoy the Tentyrites. At Edfu, however, the crocodile was regarded as a form of Typhon, 'But the people of Apollinopolis, a district of Tentyra, net the Crocodiles, hang them up on persea-trees, flog them severely, mangling them with all the blows in the world, while the creatures whimper and shed tears; finally they cut them up and eat them' (*De Natura Animalium* X, 21 and 24).

The source of these stories may be the temples at Edfu and Dendera and the festival practices of the local populace. Whether travellers had been allowed to visit temples or had talked to the priests who lived and worked in them, or had observed local festivals and rites for themselves, they were informed about a local quirk which seemed odd enough to warrant comment. It is an almost impossible task to establish the origin and means of transmission of these stories. However, in the case of Edfu and Dendera the temple texts themselves survive to provide the Egyptian side of the story. The most striking detail from the outset is the fact that only at Dendera and Edfu are there scenes of crocodile slaying being performed as a ritual. Other Ptolemaic-Roman temples do not have such scenes, though admittedly it would be surprising if they did. Kom Ombo is a cult centre for the god Sobek and such scenes would be inappropriate for his temple; Esna has a cult for Neith who is a patroness of crocodiles and even at Philae the crocodile can be seen in a good light as the saviour of Osiris, whose mummy he is shown carrying on his back. Here, the cult celebrates the associations of the crocodile with the flood and its regenerative powers (Kákosy 1980; Kákosy 1963; Junker 1910, 41-5).

Comparison with the hippopotamus slaying scenes is not altogether spurious as at Edfu the crocodile and hippopotamus are regarded as the water creatures most associated with Seth and his host. The scenes of hippopotamus hunting in the marshes were part of the genre of tomb representations in Old Kingdom mastabas, probably in Middle Kingdom tombs and then in the New Kingdom 'pleasure trips' into the marshes (Säve-Soderbergh 1953). Unlike this corpus, crocodile slaying scenes occur rarely before the texts and ritual scenes at Edfu and Dendera.

There is an early example of a crocodile hunt, from a rock drawing. It shows men in papyrus boats sailing above a crocodile, with harpoons sticking into the animal (Capart 1905, 204 and fig.161). Images of the crocodile were common on predynastic palettes, white painted pottery and other vessels. Sometimes the animal is shown with a boat (Capart 1905, figs. 84, 105) and on a knife handle a hippopotamus stands on its hind legs holding the crocodile by the tail as if about to eat it (Capart 1905, 71, fig.36). Scenes showing the crocodile as a denizen of the water may represent the beginnings of the Sobek-crocodile cult, but also they seem to be a realistic reflection of the kind of dangers and everyday hazards to be encountered on the river. By facing the danger through drawings and paintings, people hoped to deal with their fears and use magic to control a real and fatal threat.

In the Old Kingdom, tomb scenes show the crocodile lurking in the marshes under boats either sailing there to catch birds, to fish, to hunt the hippopotamus, or to ford cattle through canals or river shallows. The crocodile is itself not hunted, however, though it can be attacked by the hippopotamus (Harpur 1987, figs. 68, 189-190, 192-193, 211). Crocodiles are rarely attested in the Middle and New Kingdom version of these marsh scenes (Tomb of Daga, end Dynasty XI, TT 103: Davies 1913, pl. XXXVIII.2, p.33-34 and pl. XXX, p.36 fragment 9). In these circumstances they do not seem to be aggressive towards humans and are not hunted. The threat they pose is relatively underplayed and the only acknowledgement of the crocodile by the boatmen is the gesture of magical protection they make to ward off the creature or the presence of a reciter of spells (Ritner 1993, 227-30). With the rise of crocodile cults all over Egypt during the Middle Kingdom the depiction of crocodile hunting seems not to be attested at this time. In Literary and Funerary Texts, however, the crocodile acts as an agent of fate, and a kind of random wild-card. It was not threatening in the way that hostile forces threaten to overturn the cosmos and bring about chaos and disaster, but if fate was against an individual then the crocodile, as a creature of the primeval waters and the underworld, might carry him away (Eyre 1976).

In the Harris Magical Papyrus, the crocodile is regarded as something more uncontrollable which required identification as a hostile force. The papyrus therefore contains spells against the animal to ward it off and keep people safe. In the papyrus the crocodile is identified with 'Mega, son of Seth' (Lange 1927, D II, 2-3). Though the relationship with Seth is not surprising, it is probably to be regarded in the light of the Sethification of 'dangerous' beings and animals and the rise of Horus and Isis as protectors of ordinary people against the dangers of everday life, including scorpions and crocodiles. In addition, it directly sets Mega son of Seth against Horus son of Osiris, equalising the contest for supremacy. The tradition of the child Horus hidden in the delta marshes from Seth, and triumphing over the creatures which threatened him as he grew up, is continued in the cippi of Horus dating from the Late Period onward.

Scenes of the spearing of crocodiles, comparable to those in the temples of Dendera and Edfu are not attested until the New Kingdom.

Chapter 31 of the Book of the Dead is 'Repulsing the crocodile which comes to carry away the magical spells from a man in the Underworld' and the vignettes for this show in the Eighteenth Dynasty a man holding a knife before three crocodiles (e.g. P. BM EA 10471, Book of the Dead of Nakht), or spearing the head of a crocodile with a *was*-sceptre (e.g. P. Louvre 3074 Naville 1886, pl.XLIV), or by the Saite period a man spearing one of four crocodiles in the head (Lepsius, Bl.16). From the Nineteenth Dynasty there was also a Chapter 32 with similar purpose, but different text to the earlier version (Budge 1985, cxvi-cxvii, 152-7). The spell is one of a series for dealing with different threats in the Underworld and the aim is to drive off dangerous creatures and keep the deceased safe.

The limestone votive stela of Pataweret, BM EA 1632, probably from Asyut (Bierbrier 1993, pl.83) dates to the Nineteeth to Twentieth Dynasty. It has three registers of which the top two show the standard of Wepwawet in procession and a libation offering to two jackal headed gods, both Anubis. In the lower register a jackal headed god spears a crocodile in the river apparently chasing a man swimming for his life in front of it. The brief text names the god as Wepwawet, 'the Rescuer (*p3 šdty*) of the Asyuti from the crocodile with every fish' and records the words of the swimmer as he swam, 'O Amun, the jackal (?) great of strength for the youth. May you cause that I reach it !' (that is the bank of the river). Sadek interprets this as a votive stela set up as a thank-offering to the local gods, because he had been saved from a crocodile while swimming in the river. It may be that this was an incident that happened in his youth, or it may be that it was his son who was saved by the god (Sadek 1988, 41-2). This unique and touching thank-offering is unparalleled and as such stands apart from the ritualised and formal slaughtering scenes of the cippi and temples.

The series of Constellation scenes and star-charts which depict a man spearing a crocodile begins with the scenes from the ceiling of the Tomb of Senenmut, dating to the reign of Hatshepsut, in the Eighteenth Dynasty (Neugebauer and Parker 1960, pl.24). A group of stars of the northern sky are seen as a crocodile, a crocodile tailed sphinx and a man standing before a crocodile with his hands raised as if holding a spear. The weapon however is not shown, either because it was lost or never drawn in the first place. If it was never drawn, this may be simply due to the fact that there were no stars which could be counted as the spear, or even to nullify the effect of the killing, with the crocodile still very much associated with Sobek and not Seth. The accompanying text is a corruption of the term *ḥtp-rdwy* known from subsequent versions of this scene. It is known as an epithet of Sobek, 'Restful of feet', perhaps because of the apparent immobility of the animal (Neugebauer and Parker 1969, 194 citing Gardiner 1957, 50 n.5).

The spearing scene occurs also in the Tomb of Rameses VI, on the ceilings in Hall E north and Corridor B east (Neugebauer and Parker 1964, pls. 2 and 5), in the Tomb of Rameses VII, on the vault of the ceiling of Hall B (Neugebauer and Parker 1964, pl. 7) and probably in the Tomb of Rameses IX on the ceiling of Corridor B (Neugebauer and Parker 1964, pls.8 and 15B). In these scenes the spear is shown in the hand of the man, stabbing into the underbelly of the crocodile.

Elsewhere, the spear disappears again, in the Tomb of Rameses VI on the ceiling of Corridor A and the ceiling of Hall E south (Neugebauer and Parker 1964, pls. 3, 4 and 1), in the Tomb of Ramesses VII on the ceiling of Hall B south (Neugebauer and Parker 1964, pl. 7), in the Tomb of Ramesses IX on the ceiling of Corridor B southern half (Neugebauer and Parker 1964, pls.8 and 15) and also on the sarcophagus of Nekhtnebef (Berlin 7: Neugebauer and Parker 1969, pl. 25). In the Tomb of Seti I on the ceiling of Hall K, the man again has no spear, but here his body is covered in stars and the crocodile is apparently called *srys3*, but it seems that this is a corrupt writing of the name of the lion constellation nearby (Neugebauer and Parker 1969, 193). This scene is also copied in the tomb of Tawosret (Neugebauer and Parker 1969, pl. 9).

The Constellation scenes provide the best evidence of an earlier genre of crocodile slaughtering scenes, but they are highly specialised in their nature and are used to explain a natural phenomenon, that is the stars, rather than deal with mythological and cult issues (list of the northern constellations in Neugebauer and Parker 1969, 183-94).

Magical Statues and Horus cippi provide unequivocal images of the destruction of crocodiles, among the other evils which could threaten man. The main image of the cippi is of Horus triumphant, standing upon the bodies of the crocodiles, brandishing the dead oryx and scorpions in his hands. But some areas of the stelae have scenes of the spearing of crocodiles, which can be directly related to both the stellar scenes and the temple ritual scenes. Cairo 9402 (JE 4751) shows a ram headed god, with solar disc spearing a crocodile in the back, as it turns its head back towards him. A hippopotamus goddess holding a knife stands beside them. Below, a double headed lioness goddess (Sakhmet) and Isis the Great of Magic stand upon the backs of crocodiles, holding their serpent wands over them. On the back of the stelae the ram headed god again spears a crocodile before a hippopotamus. The stela comes from Mit Rahineh (Daressy 1903, 3ff., pls.2-3). The dating of these objects is difficult and usually placed in the range 'Late Period-Ptolemaic', thus covering the Twenty-sixth Dynasty to the Roman Period (Seele 1947, 43-52). It is probable that the texts, and possibly the images, represent a codification of ancient myths and spells, some dating back to the Pyramid Texts, and this may have begun in earnest in the Third Intermediate Period (Bianchi 1989, Brooklyn 60.73 number 88).

A more dramatic image is shown on Cairo statue 9430 where a goddess in a chariot pulled by a winged griffin, and accompanied by Bes, shoots arrows at two crocodiles under her wheels (Daressy 1903, pl.11). The statue of Djedhor the Saviour (Cairo JE 4752) also has images showing Khnum, Horus upon his papyrus and Thoth spearing crocodiles. This magical statue is closely dated as the texts list the titles of Djedhor as chief guardian of the gates in the temple of Athribis in the time of Philip Arrhidaeus (Corteggiani 1987, number 113, 170-1; Jelínková-Reymond 1956). Similarly the famous Metternich Stela has scenes of crocodile slaughter and can be dated to the reign of Nectanebo II (Scott 1951, 201-17).

The scenes and texts of the magical stelae provide a context for the temple scenes, though the emphasis changes from one of more private devotion to the royal and divine cults. In the case of every day dangers the crocodile represented something to be destroyed and therefore could easily take his place with the Sethian creatures already established in the mythology of destruction. However, in the divine sphere too the crocodile already enjoyed a prominent role and up to this point the ambivalence towards the animal felt by the Egyptians mostly resolves itself as reverence rather than loathing leading to destruction. Fear is converted into active worship, perhaps in the hope that the terrible and fierce animal can be pacified and controlled, much in the same way that the lioness Sakhmet could be pacified and work for the good of men rather than their destruction, as is the point of the myth, 'The Destruction of Mankind'. The god Sobek may seem fierce, but he is a fertility god, a god of regeneration and a god who helps the sun-god in his journey through the night-world (Brunner-Traut 1980). He also enjoyed wide popularity throughout Egypt over a wide period of time particularly in the Fayum, around Lake Moeris, and at his cult centre at Kom Ombo. In the Late Period when crocodile mummies could be given as votive offerings the cult ranked alongside those of falcon and cat deities. Attempts to codify the widespread cults of Sobek were made in the Late Period, in the 'Book of the Fayum' (Lanzone 1896). Sobek was not the only crocodile god and the divine crocodile form was also represented for example by Khenty-Khety at Athribis, Senwi and Pnepheros. It may however be more useful to regard the crocodile god and the Seth-hostile crocodile as different entities, who both happen to have the form of the crocodile. At Edfu and Dendera the scenes of crocodile slaying are the overriding form of the animal and in order to avoid complications Sobek is not represented in the temple at all. In fact he is rarely mentioned at Edfu. In a geographical text, Sobek is said to be the god of the Fourth Lower Egyptian nome and his name is written with a crocodile sitting on top of a shrine (*Edfu* I 330,17). The lists of gods in the Hall of Offerings include 'Sobek, Lord of Pe' (*Edfu* XV 52, 17), and 'Sobek, Lod of Coptos' (*Edfu* XV 59,13), and possibly a 'Sobek, Sesi' (*Edfu* XV 49,14).

The lack of earlier material from Edfu, especially from the temple complexes makes it difficult to assess the anti-crocodile cult in the town. Its antiquity is not known, nor are any local Myths known which may have explained the aversion. In the temple of Horus of Behdet at Edfu, the rituals of slaying the crocodile fit easily into the Myth of Horus, his struggles against Seth for the kingship, and their destruction is symbolic of the victory of Horus (the king) over chaos and dangerous forces. The rituals form a complement to the slaying of other Sethian creatures on the temple's walls. However, at Dendera, the ritual is less easy to explain. The close links between Edfu and Dendera, with Hathor as the consort of Horus of Behdet, may be reason enough for the ritual to be adopted there. But there is the impression that the slaying of crocodiles had a longer tradition at Dendera and perhaps came from a local mythology. Originally, it seems that a town called *S3bt* was the chief town of the Denderite nome and its god was the crocodile god *iqr*. With the rise of Dendera and Hathor his cult was eclipsed but the nome-sign for Dendera could be written with a crocodile, sometimes with a feather on its head and sometimes with an arrow and later a knife in its head (Fischer 1968, 3-8, 13, 185-6). The slaying of the crocodile is not a natural ritual for the Hathor cult, but her role as the consort of Horus of Edfu and the emphasis on the protection of Osiris at Dendera enables the ritual to serve a purpose at Dendera too.

Translation of the Scenes at Edfu and Dendera

[1] Edfu, Exterior of Naos, east wall, first register (pl.47).
Edfu IX, pl. XCI, Ptolemy VIII.
The scene shows the king (left) striding out and stabbing his spear into the head of a crocodile which twists its head back towards him in its agony. The spear has a falcon-head terminal. Horus stands (right) holding out a khepesh sword in his right hand toward the king, and holding a harpoon surmounted by a falcon head in his left hand. The goddess Isis stands behind him, with her right hand raised and her left hand holding an *ankh*-sign. The king wears the *hemhemty*-crown.

Edfu IV 211,8-213,4

[211, 8 Title] Spearing (1) the crocodile
[211,9-212,4 Speech of King] Words spoken: 'I hold my harpoon ! I grasp my spear-shaft ! Heir of the Lord of Mesen am I ! I embark on my boat near Lake of Horus and I drive back the steps of all 'Those who are in the water'. [ ] the 'hidden ones', I cut to pieces 'Burning Mouths'. (As for) the Rehesu, I stab their bodies, I cut their old crocodiles and their young crocodiles, I slaughter their females and I smash their eggs. I have deflected the attack of the 'Images of Mega' against the 'Bird

with the Dappled Plumage'. I sever the gullet, it is stopped up and he does not go down to the high flood (2). His meat portions are for the children of the marsh-men and your crew. I am the son of Osiris.'
[212,5-6 Epithets of the King] (cartouche) Euergetes-excellent god, brave marsh-man, prowman in his warship, who cuts to pieces 'Burning Mouths' and 'Those who are in the water'.
[212,7-9 Second speech of the King] 'May the good god live ! Receive the harpoon and drive away the Qemau and 'Those who are in the water'. Horus True of Voice, he rushes out into battle, he takes to the river in his warship. Excellent harpooner, brave champion, Lord of the Flood, Son of Re (Ptolemy, living forever, beloved of Ptah).' *protection formulae*

[213, 3-4 Accolade of Horus] The King of Upper and Lower Egypt, the Falcon, Lord of the Harpoon, Wide Striding upon the Greedy One; the Falcon, Great of Might, who slaughters the Enemy; Wenty (or Horus Upon the Crocodile) who stabs the Failure; He who raises his arms to butcher Shenty; Horus Behedety, Lord of Mesen, the great god, The Bird with Dappled Plumage.
[212,10-13 Speech of Horus] Words spoken by Horus Behedety, the great god, Lord of the Sky, Lord of Mesen, who hunts the hippopotamus, who brings as booty the hidden one, who causes the aggressors to retreat, 'I give to you my strength to slaughter your enemies. How sweet is my knife making a massacre of them !' 'I cause my harpoon to be stuck firmly in the head of your foes. Hold fast, hold fast and do let let go !'

[212,14-213,2 Speech of Isis] Words spoken by Isis, the Great, who dwells in Wetjeset-Hor, god's mother of the Falcon of Gold, whose body is secret in its form of the warship, who raised her son to be a harpooner. 'I go down to your boat so that I might protect you, and that I might guard your limbs on the Lake of Horus. I make brave your arms hacking Henty to pieces, the enemy of your father Osiris.'

This text is followed by *sty-db*; then a water purification text. It is preceded by *dw3-nṯr*.

(1) Reading *sty* 'to shoot' (an arrow), 'to cast, throw' (a harpoon).
(2) Reading *sin ḥnggt ḏb3.tw n h3.tw.f ir ḥrt. ḥrt* is the word for 'flood' (Wb. III 144,2-4) written here with a sky determinative, perhaps as a pun on *ḥrt* 'heaven'.

[2] Edfu, Exterior of Naos, west wall, first register.
Edfu IX, pl. LXXXV, Ptolemy VIII.
The scene shown is the same as in [1], except in reverse, with the gods on the left and the king on the right. The harpoon which the king is using is clearly provided with two ropes, whereas it does not have them in [1].

Edfu IV 57,10-58,10

[57, 10 Title] Spearing the crocodile
[57,11-14 Speech of the King] Words spoken, 'The harpooner am I ! One who does what you like, killing the foe as a greeting for you. My arms are wide spread with your beautiful weapon, making a massacre of your enemy. I drive back their footsteps, slicing off their limbs. May your followers eat their flesh. I am the one who slaughters the enemy of your Majesty. I am the Sole One of your crew.'
[57, 15-16 Titles of the King] King of Upper and Lower Egypt (cartouche) Euergetes-excellent god, Son of Re (Ptolemy, living forever, beloved of Ptah) excellent god, harpooner, champion who brings an end by its wounds, who concentrates on making a massacre.
[57,16-58,2 Second speech of the King] May the good god live ! Wide of stride, who goes into battle watchfully. Hold fast, hold fast ! Mighty in his strength ! He who makes his foe to be non existent. Brave harpooner, the Lord of Mesen is not far from him, Lord of the knife (Ptolemy). *protection formulae behind him*

[58, 9-10 Accolade of Horus] King of Upper and Lower Egypt, brave in spearing, mighty in strength when striking the enemy, content at smiting, downhearted because of his bad deeds, who puts to death his enemies; the falcon great of strength, who lives by the knife (?); Horus Behedety, Lord of the sky, Lord of Mesen.
[58, 3-6 Speech of Horus] Words spoken by Horus Behedety, the great god, Bird with Dappled Plumage, perfect harpooner in Edfu; Horus of Gold, avenger of his father Osiris; who stabs Nehes in the Place of Stabbing (1), 'I give to you your foes as execration images beneath you, like Horus as Wenty. I make strong your arms, when striking your rebels and opponents. They go away at your attack.'

[58, 7-8 Titles and speech of Isis (?)] Words spoken by Isis (?), the Great god's Mother, mistress in Behdet, Khent-Iabet in Khent-Iabet, Shetat (2) her daughter (?) who protects her son,'I give to you your heart fixed firmly in its place, so that the enemy trembles through fear of you.'

Followed by *sm3-db* IV 58,12-59,12; then a purification with water. Preceded by *dw3-nṯr*.

(1) *st-wnp* is Edfu.
(2) Shetat is a vulture goddess, often identified with Nekhbet. She can also be the mother of Sobek, but here as a nurse of divine children she acts as the protectoress of Horus in the guise of Isis.

These two texts form a parallel pair, though the emphasis in the first is more specifically on the crocodile killing and the second is more vague about the enemy to be killed. The only word for crocodile used here is *iḥ* in the title, so that it may have been a standard 'enemy killing' text, borrowed to make the parallel to IV 210-212, and given the title *sty-iḥ* to show that it is a 'crocodile' text. It does contain a reference to Isis as Iabet in Khent-Iabet, to stress her delta connections and to also reinforce the role of Horus as a delta hunter and harpooner. The more 'Lower Egyptian' tone of this text matches the 'Upper Egyptian' nature of the first text with its emphasis on events in the Lake of Horus (the sacred lake at Edfu) and other sacred places at Edfu. In this way the two parts of Egypt are clearly represented (Labrique, 1992, 20-21).

[3] Edfu, Exterior of the Pronaos, east wall, first register
Edfu X, pl. CVII, Ptolemy X.
The scene shows an unanimated king (left) holding a falcon headed harpoon in the head of a tiny crocodile, which twists back towards the king. The king wears the *hemhemty*-crown. Horus stands to the right, holding a *was*-sceptre in his right hand and *ankh*-sign in his left.

Edfu IV 373,18-374,14

[373, 18 Title] Slaughtering the crocodile
[373,18-374, 5 Speech of the King] Words spoken, 'I receive the harpoon, I hold the shaft, I grasp the harpoon in my fist. I cut up the crocodile, I butcher Sety in front of your house, O Bird with Dappled Plumage. I trample Khefty and I put him on the slaughter block. Indeed I am Wenty !'
[374,6-10 Titles of the King] The King of Upper and Lower Egypt (cartouche) the god Philometor, the man of receiving the mooring post in the flood, who throws (the harpoon) at the enemy of his father. May the good god live ! Son of the Lord of Mesen, born of Isis, the perfect harpooner, sweet of deeds, One who holds firmly, the prowman in his warship. One who turns back the footsteps of the enemy who is in the flood, Lord of the harpoon, Son of Re (Ptolemy). *protection formulae behind him*

[374,13-14 Accolade of Horus] King of Upper and Lower Egypt, the harpooner, champion, the spearsman who raises his arm holding the harpoon. One who destroys the Heavy One, who brings as booty the hidden one, who makes the crocodiles retreat. Horus Wenty who stabs the enemy of his father; Horus Behedety, great god, Lord of the sky.
[374,11-374,13 Speech of Horus] Words spoken by Horus Behedety, the great god, Lord of the sky,

Lord of Mesen; Falcon of Gold son of Osiris, Lord of the harpoon, who makes the enemy fall, who strides upon the back of his opponents. 'I give to you your foes, hacked to pieces with the harpoon. Your enemies are burnt offerings.'

In the register above is a *wnp-nhs* scene. The crocodile scene abuts the door-jamb of the 'couloir de ronde', and there is an incense offering scene directly beside it.

[4] Edfu, First Hypostyle Hall (Pronaos), north wall, third register.
Edfu IX, pl.LXII, Ptolemy VIII.
The scene shows the king (left) not striding, holding a harpoon in an animal which has been defaced. He wears a side-lock and an *atef*-crown, with two disks and set upon ram horns. The god Horus (right) is seated on a throne, holding a *was*-sceptre in his right hand and *ankh*-sign in his left hand.

Edfu III 137,2-13
[137, 2 Title] Slaughtering the crocodile
[137, 3-4 Speech of the King] Words spoken, 'Mega is under the knife, Medy is under the blade. Your weapon is firmly stuck in the Bank Dweller.'
[137, 4-9 Titles of the King] The King of Upper and Lower Egypt (cartouche), Son of Re (Ptolemy), the excellent god, brave harpooner. He is like the one who created him, who protects his father by his strength. May the god live !, The child, son of Isis, living image of the Lord of Pe and Mesen. Brave harpooner destroying Henty; who holds the harpoon to repulse Khenty. Two Ladies Great of power, Lord of the Harpoon, Strong of arm with his weapons. *protection formulae behind him*

[137,12-13 Accolade of Horus] This noble god, image in [ ], the perfect harpooner in Edfu, who is equipped with the weapon. He is Mesen (? or Setty), the harpooner who repels an attacker. Mighty of power, he is powerful against the enemy, when he speeds in his warship.
[137, 10-12 Speech of Horus] Words spoken by Horus Behedety, great god, Bird with Dappled Plumage, brave harpooner, strong of arms, who speeds in his warship to slaughter his enemies. Indeed, he protects his father ! 'I give to you your opponents burning in the fire, your enemies roasted in the flame.'

Followed by *sm3-ˁ3pp,* then *sm3-m3-ḥḏ*, then a wedjat-offering. Preceded by *šms-ˁntyw*.

[5] Edfu, First Hypostyle Hall (Pronaos), front pilaster west, south wall, second register.
Edfu IX, pl. XLVIII, Ptolemy X.
The scene shows the king standing (left), stabbing his harpoon into a small crocodile. His face is defaced, but he is wearing the *hemhemty*-crown. Horus and Isis are seated on thrones (right): Horus holds a *was*-sceptre in his right hand and *ankh*-sign in his left; Isis raises her right hand and holds an *ankh*-sign in her left. This is one of four slaughtering scenes to deal with each aspect of Seth (turtle, snake, crocodile and hippopotamus).

Edfu III 3,16-4,9

[3,16-17 Title] I chop up Shenty. I place him upon the slaughter block. Sing praises O People of Mesen !
[3,18-4,4 Titles of the King] The King of Upper and Lower Egypt (cartouche) Son of Re (Ptolemy) [ ] slaughtering the crocodiles who are in the water, like Horus when he rushes out to battle. The King of Upper and Lower Egypt (cartouche) is upon his throne in the Great Place of the son of Isis, slaughtering Mega, hacking to pieces the Enemy, making a massacre of Those who are in the water. He is [Horus] son of Isis, in the prow of his warship (killing) his enemies. *protection formulae behind him*

[4,5-6 Speech of Horus] Words spoken by Horus Behedety, great god, Lord of the sky, Lord of Mesen, Bird with the dappled plumage, who comes from the horizon, image of Re, distinguished of births before the great name of every god. 'I give to you bravery like the son of Isis, I make strong your power like my Majesty.'

[4,7-9 Speech of Isis] Words spoken by Isis, the Great, god's mother foremost in Wetjeset-Hor; who protects her son in Khent-Iabet; Lady of Terror in the Ogdoad; God's mother [lost text] Horus the mighty, who puts to death and his mother Isis is his protection.

Followed (above) by a 'Slaying the Turtle' text *ḥmt m ḫbt*, then a 'massacring Apopis' text, then the cosmogonical texts.
Preceded by 'Consecrating everything entering the temple of his father.'

[6] Edfu, First Hypostyle Hall (Pronaos), east row of columns, third column, first register.
Edfu IX, pl. LXXVII, Ptolemy VIII.
The scene shows the king, standing (left) with his left foot resting on the tail of a crocodile. His left hand holds the sacred harpoon of Horus, while his right hand is sticking a plain harpoon into the back of the crocodile. The body of the beast is hatched to show its skin and it turns its head back towards the king. The king wears a *hemhemty*-crown. The god Khnum standing, (right) holds a *was*-sceptre in his right hand and *ankh*-sign in his left. He wears an *atef*-crown.

Edfu III 287, 6-11
[287,6-7 Title] Slaughtering the crocodile for his father Khnum, making god exult with his enemies.
[287, 8-9 Titles of the King] The King of Upper and Lower Egypt (cartouche), Son of Re, Lord of Crowns (Ptolemy), the excellent god, the perfect harpooner, like the son of Isis, when he spears the Greedy One with his harpoon. *protection formula*
[287,10-11 Speech of Khnum] Words spoken by Khnum, Lord of Semen-Hor, the great god [ ] -Wer, great of terror, Lord of Neferusy (1), 'I make firm your heart for you are my son; the enemy — may you hold him firmly !'

Sandwiched between a wensheb offering to Hathor and 'Opening the Mouth'.
Bibliography: Kurth 1983, 155-7.
This text is interesting in that Khnum is the recipient of the offering. As the guardian of the flood, he may be expected to be similar to the crocodile gods in this respect. However, in this case the assertion of Herodotus (above) that at Elephantine the crocodile was not revered, seems to be correct. Perhaps in the cataract area, where sailing could be hazardous, the crocodile was an ever present threat. The cult places named in this text are in various parts of Egypt: *smn-ḥr* is in the 21st Upper Egyptian nome (Montet 1961, 195), *ḥwt-wr* and *nfrw-sy* are in the 15th Lower Egyptian nome (Montet 1961, 151, 152). The slaughter of the crocodile and Khnum are also associated on the Statue of Djedhor the Saviour, in line 109 of the crocodile spell, 'Go away ! Go away, Enemy ! I am Khnum, Lord of Hut-Wer' (Jelínková-Reymond 1956, 48 and 54-5).

[7] Edfu, Pylon doorway, south face of jamb, second register.
Edfu XIV, pl.DCLXI, Ptolemy XII.
The scene shows the king standing, right, holding a harpoon in the back of a crocodile at his feet, with its head turned back towards him. The animal, area above it and lower body, legs and face of the king have been mutilated. The king wears the *hemhemty*-crown on his head. To the left are the gods Horus, who holds his staff in his left hand (or a harpoon) and a *khepesh*-sword in his right arm straight out to the king, and Hathor, who has an *ankh*-sign in her right hand and holds up her right hand in a gesture of reverence towards the king.

Edfu VIII 34, 5-35, 8
[34, 5 Title] Slaying the crocodile.
[34,5-11 Speech of the King] Words spoken, 'I receive the harpoon, I grasp the weapon, I hold the three-barbed harpoon in my fist. I cut the crocodiles to pieces [damaged text], I cut off his foreleg, I

tear out his heart [ ]; I make great his slaughter, I make heavy his massacre before the Bird with Dappled Plumage; enemies of [ ].'
[34,12-16 Titles of the King] The King of [Upper] and Lower Egypt (cartouche), son of Re (Ptolemy), Horus Wenty, who makes a slaughter of the rebellious, who repels the footsteps of those who are in the water. The good god [lost text] evening boat in order to perform (the ritual) of 'those who are in the net' at the festivals of the falcon of gold; who slays the enemies before the great of might, lord of valour, son of Re (Ptolemy). *protective formulae behind him*

[35,7-8 Accolade of Horus] King of Upper and Lower Egypt, falcon, champion, Sia-falcon (?) who makes great the gateway of [giving Maat], great of power, with the two blood-red eyes, he lives on drinking blood; Horus strong of arm, who stabs the foes of his father, Horus Behedety, great god, Lord of Heaven.
[35,1-3 Speech of Horus] Words of Horus Behedety, the great god, lord of heaven, Lord of Mesen, Bird with Dappled Plumage, who comes from the horizon; Horus of Gold, son of Osiris, perfect harpooner, exalted of front holding the harpoon, who strides upon the back of his enemy, 'I give to you bravery for your Majesty for your forearm, for the work (? unclear text).'

[35,4-6 Speech of Hathor] Words of Hathor of Iunet, Eye of Re, who lives in Behdet; Two Ladies Rekhyt, mistress of the goddesses; female falcon in Behdet, her protection is around her, god's mother of the bull, his god's mother, the arms of her majesty are protection around him, fire from the uraeus is against his enemies, 'I am with you, I am never far from you, I protect your Majesty at the flood.'

The scene is below a 'Seth in the fire' text and above a 'Presenting the Two Lands' text.
It is opposite a hippopotamus slaying text.

[8] Edfu, Court, east wall, second register.
Edfu X, pl. CXIX, Ptolemy X.
The scene shows the king standing, right, holding a harpoon out vertically in front of him in the head of a crocodile, upon which he stands. The crocodile has its head turned back towards him. This pose seems to be caused by the relative lack of space for the scenes on this wall. They are all mostly squashed together. The king wears the *hemhemty*-crown on his head. Horus sits at the left on his block-throne, holding *was*-sceptre in his left hand and *ankh*-sign in his right hand.

Edfu V 169, 4-169,13

[169, 4 Title] Slaughtering the crocodile.
[169,4-6 Speech of the King] Words spoken, 'I receive the harpoon, I cut to pieces 'He whose tongue is cut out', and make fall the crocodile enemy of your father Wenn-nefer, true of voice'.
[169,7-10 Titles of the King] King of Upper and Lower Egypt, Lord of the Two Lands (cartouche) son of Re, Lord of Appearances (Ptolemy) [text lost]. The son of Re (Ptolemy) is upon his throne before (?) the battleground [text lost] enemy, slaying Shenty [ ] in his middle. He is like Horus, the faithful of the gods, who avenges his father and mother. *short protection formula behind him*
[169, 11-14 Titles of Horus] Words spoken by Horus Behedety, the great god, Lord of the sky, great of justification, divine heir of the King of Upper and Lower Egypt, harpooner and champion in House of Horus the Strong, who turns away the crocodile attackers. The Lord of Wetjeset is powerful [text lost] Mighty one of the Mighty Ones, slashing the enemy, killing 'Failure', driving away 'Hot-Mouths' and those who are in the water. He is like Striker, who strikes down the enemy, who created himself, living divine flesh, of [text unclear].

Preceded by an 'offering the night barque' text and followed by a 'tying on the garland of reeds' text. The god's speech is not given here, suggesting this text has been shortened because of lack of space. This may be due to the fact that the festival texts are the important texts here, and the rituals on the court wall reflect those rituals which were carried out during the festival.

[9] Dendera, Rear Chamber, south-west (N), south wall, first register.
Dendara IV 12,13-13,6, pl.CCL and CCLV = Mariette, *Dendérah* II, 75b.
The King stands left, stabbing the crocodile under his left foot in the head. His spear has a falcon-head terminal. He wears a long tripartite wig and *hemhemty*-crown. Horus stands at the right holding a *was*-sceptre and *ankh*-sign.

[12,13 Title] Slaughtering the crocodile.
[12,13-15 Speech of the King] Words spoken, 'Mega is murdered before you, O Bird with Dappled Plumage and your harpoon is stuck firmly in Bank Dweller.'
[12,16-13,2 Titles of the King] King of Upper and Lower Egypt (cartouche empty) Son of Re (cartouche empty), the perfect harpooner, sweet of deeds, the champion like the son of Isis. May the perfect god live ! Brave champion, perfect harpooner, sweet of deeds, spearsman valiant at slaughtering Hentyu, who holds the harpoon tightly to drive back Khenty. Strong of power, great of might like the son of Isis, Lord of Valour, Son of Re (cartouche empty). *protection formula behind him*

[13, 4-6 Accolade of Horus] The King of Upper and Lower Egypt, the djerty-falcon, champion, fierce-faced against foes before him. He is the sole god, sweet of deeds, who rushes to repulse his rebels. Mighty god, great of strength, striking down his enemies, Horus Behedety, the great god, Lord of the sky.
[13, 3-4 Speech of Horus] Words spoken by Horus Behedety, the great god, Lord of the sky, Lord of Mesen, Bird with Dappled Plumage, who comes from the horizon, divine falcon, who strikes down foes (?), who makes a massacre of your enemies. 'I give you your opponents upon your butchers block; your enemies are roasted in the fire.'

Preceded by a myrrh offering text, and located at the end of the wall, so that nothing directly follows.

[10] Dendera, Rear Chamber, south-west (N), north wall, first register.
Dendara IV, 24,4-13, pl. CCLX = Mariette, *Dendérah* II, pl.75a.
The king stands at the right, stabbing the crocodile under his right foot with a spear with a falcon-head terminal. He wears the Double Crown. Horus stands at the left holding a *was*-sceptre and *ankh*-sign.

[24, 4 Title] Slaughtering the crocodile.
[24, 4-5 Speech of the King] Words spoken, [text lost] opposite you. I make content the hearts of the gods and goddesses.
[24, 6-9 Titles of the King] King of Upper and Lower Egypt (cartouche empty) Son of Re (cartouche empty), brave spearsman, strong of arms holding the harpoon. May the good god live ! Heir of the Great of True of Voice, living image of the falcon of gold. Perfect harpooner, destroying Henty, who grasps the harpoon to slaughter the enemies. Strong man who makes a massacre of the hippopotami and crocodiles who are in the water. Lord of valour, Son of Re (cartouche empty). *protection formula behind him*

[24, 10 Speech of Horus] Words spoken by Horus Behedety, the great god, Lord of heaven, Lord of Mesen, Lord of strength, Strong bull, who came from Isis, Lord of the harpoon, who fells the enemies, who strides upon the backs of his foes. 'I give to you might like the son of Isis. May your enemies fall under your feet.'
[24,12-13 Accolade of Horus] King of Upper and Lower Egypt, Mighty god, Lord of Might, Lord of Mesen, who makes joy, Great Djerty-falcon who cuts to pieces the Heavy One, strong of arm, who massacres the Greedy One, who makes sweet the heart of the mighty gods of Sunet (Egypt), Horus Behedety, the great god, Lord of heaven.

Preceded by a cloth offering text, and located at the end of the wall, so that nothing directly follows it. This text forms a pair with [9].

[11] Dendera, Hall of the New Year, east wall, second register.
Dendara IV, 194, 4-12, pl. CCCI.
The king, left, wears the *hemhemty*-crown upon a cap with the head-band around it. He strides forward and with his left foot upon the tail of the crocodile, he stabs his spear with falcon head terminal into the head of the crocodile as the animal turns its head back. Horus is seated right upon a throne on a dais. He wears the Double Crown and holds a *was*-sceptre.

[194,4 Title] Slaughtering the crocodile.
[194,4-5 Speech of the King] Words spoken, 'I have received the harpoon to drive away your foes, before your divine ba, Behedety.'
[194, 6-9 Titles of the King] King of Upper and Lower Egypt (cartouche empty) Son of Re (cartouche empty), perfect harpooner, strong of arms holding the harpoon, making a massacre of his enemies. The son of Re (cartouche empty) is upon his throne dais as the champion, watchful when bringing in the enemy, when driving away Shentyu, when cutting off the heads of the attackers. He is like the son of Isis, sweet of love, who throws (his harpoon) successfully at his enemies. *protection formula behind him*

[194,10 Titles of Horus] Words spoken by Horus Behedety, the great god, Lord of heaven, Bird with Dappled Plumage, who comes from the horizon. Perfect harpooner who slays the enemy of the Mighty gods, who raises up the hearts of [ ] the Ennead. The Lord of Mesen is shining in his place as the strong of arm, the great of might, cutting Khenty to pieces, destroying Henty, making the foes (into) execration images. He is the son of Osiris, Lord of the Great Green, trusted by the Ennead.

Preceded by *skr-ḥmꜣ* and followed by a *f3i-iḫt* offering.

[12] Dendera, East Crypt, west wall, second register.
Dendara V, 80, 2-81, 2, pl.CCCLXXXII and CCCLXXXV = Mariette, *Dendérah* III, pl. 81k
The king stands right wearing the Double Crown, spearing the crocodile before him. Horus stand left, holding an *ankh*-sign and *was*-sceptre.

[80, 2-4 Title] The Greedy One is massacred; the Winged Disc is safe and sound, his sanctuary is in joy [ ], the harpooner is joyful, the god and goddesses - their hearts are sweet.
[80, 5-8 Titles of the King] The King of Upper and Lower Egypt (cartouche empty), Son of Re (cartouche empty) heir of the great of True of Voice, brave man among the strong companions. He is like the one who created him. May the good god live ! Heir of the great of True of Voice, eldest son of Isis, strong champion. He is like the one who avenged his father, who has slain the Shentyu with his harpoon, who put to death the hippopotami and crocodiles in the water, lord of valour, the Son of Re (cartouche empty). *protection formula behind him*

[80,11-81,2 Accolade of Horus] The King of Upper and Lower Egypt, the falcon, the fighting ba, strong of arm, who strikes down the rebels, who puts to death and brings an end to the one who injured him, who makes a massacre of the Greedy Ones. The brave harpooner, high of brow holding the three barbed harpoon, Horus Behedety, the great god, Lord of the sky.
[80,9-11 Speech of Horus] Words spoken by Horus Behedety, the great god, Lord of the sky, Bird with Dappled Plumage, who comes from the horizon. The brave harpooner, strong of arm holding the trident. Fighting ba in the Great Ennead. 'I give to you might to slaughter your enemies, strength will be in your arms.'

Preceded by 'Green eye-paint for the right eye and kohl for the left eye' and followed by 'Offerings are offered with everything'.

[13] Dendera, South Crypt, north wall, second register.
Dendara VI, 25, 2-12, pl. CCCCLXXI = Mariette, *Dendérah* III, 50i.

The king stands right, with his spear with a falcon headed terminal in the back of the crocodile in front of him. He stands on its tail to keep it still. The king wears an *atef*-crown, upon ram's horns, surmounted by a solar disc. Horus stands to the left, wearing the Double Crown and holding the *was*-sceptre in his left hand and *ankh*-sign in his right hand.

[25, 2 Title] Slaughtering the crocodile.
[25, 2-4 Speech of the King] Words spoken, 'Mega is killed, Shenty is slain, Seizer is cut up, Henty is destroyed, your harpoon is united with the Bank Dweller.'
[25, 5-8 Titles of the King] The King of Upper and Lower Egypt (cartouche empty), Son of Re (cartouche empty), Horus Wenty, begotten of Horus son of Osiris, who came from Isis. May the good god live ! The child-ruler, valiant harpooner, destroying Henty, who holds the harpoon to repel Khenty. Champion (defeating) the 'Failure'. The harpooner, great of might, Lord of the harpoon, Lord of valour, Son of Re (cartouche empty). *protection formula behind him*

[25,11-12 Accolade of Horus] The King of Upper and Lower Egypt, Mighty god, Lord of Might, Lord of Mesen, who makes the djerty-falcon joyful. Great at cutting up Seizer, strong-armed at massacring the Greedy One, equipped with weapons. He is the net-man. Horus Behedety, the great god, Lord of heaven.
[25, 9-11 Speech of Horus] Words of Horus Behedety, the great god, Lord of heaven, Lord of Mesen. Strong bull who came from Isis, excellent avenger of his father Osiris. 'I make your enemies to be non-existent. I give to you strength from the son of Isis and your enemies fall beneath your feet.'

Preceded by a myrrh offering text and followed by 'offering incense for his Mistress'.

The crowns worn by the king in the ritual all suit the action and its significance. The *hemhemty*-crown is above all a martial crown, worn for war and destruction and by itself it can bring terror to the enemies of the king/Horus. The Double Crown stresses that the rite is concerned with the king's rightful claim to be ruler of the Two Lands. The *atef*-crown is the crown of Osiris and so lends an Osirian interpretation to the rite, again emphasising that the king is the rightful heir of his father Osiris.

[14] Geographical Texts.

The texts describing the customs and practices of the nomes include one text which is of interest in the context of an anti-crocodile cult. In the nome of the Heseb bull, the Eleventh nome of Lower Egypt, the following texts describe the vilification of the crocodile here. It is most likely that in fact the nome was the centre of a strong delta crocodile cult, but that the hostility of the Edfu and Dendera scribes caused them to change the text and emphasise the abomination of the animal. Usually because the nome has strong Sethian affinities the geographical descriptions pass over it in silence and refer to it as Shednu (Horbeit) (Montet 1957, 129-36; Beinlich 1984, 256-7).

Edfu I 332,18-333, 4
Heseb: The King comes, the son of Re, Lord of Appearances Ptolemy before you, Horus Behedety, great god, Lord of heaven. He brings the Heseb-nome, the town Heseb, with the djeser-limb (of Osiris), the left arm is whole and it is not injured. But the enemy is destroyed, his rituals do not exist. The Per-Mega is ruined. There is no priest (with enemy determinative), because no-one recalls his name, there is no temple chantress among the songstresses. The barque Neg-iter is burned, the canal of the Two Falcons is dry for the city, without its water. Per-ka (or ieh) is decayed, there is no sacred tree. Evil is established in its day and its night. On the third month of Akhet, day 18, the crocodile is killed on the Mound of the Hippopotamus. The name of its (sacred) snake is called Great Badness.

There are two almost identical texts at Dendera and Philae (117)
Dendera, Dümichen 1885, 37

'He comes to you Osiris, great god, Lord of Serqet (?), he is your son, greeting his father. He has overturned Heseb, he has made its lord into ashes and all its inhabitants are in the flames. He has overturned Per-Mega, he has destroyed the faithful of his enemies. He has put those who plot evil on the butchers block, those who commit wrongs shall be his bound sacrifices, his enemies are turned back from him. Busiris and Abydos, the nomes of Osiris, are in joy for Seth is non-existent.'

[15] The crocodile enemy at Dendera.
At Dendera there is a representation and description of the divine falcon. He is shown standing on a box, with a falcon-headed phallus, and crowned with the Double Crown and plumes. The lion Horus-Shu sits in front of him, a Nekhbet vulture spreads its wings behind him (both shown much smaller), and behind them stand a lioness faced Isis and vulture faced Nephthys. The text says that the phallus and feathers of the falcon are made of precious stones and his crown is made of gold. In the box or plinth upon which the falcon stands are two crocodiles, facing outward; the left has a knife and harpoon in his head and also in his back, the smaller on the right has a harpoon in his head and knife and harpoon in his back. Symbolically, these are all the defeated enemies of Horus (the king) in a Sethian guise, and represent the enemies of the king crushed under his feet (see *Dendara* IV, pl. CCLX and also in a slightly different guise CCL). Both of these scenes are the top register of a wall with a crocodile slaying ritual in the lowest register (for the interpretation of the scene, see Cauville 1984, 42 and fig.8).

[16] The crocodile enemy in the Myth of Horus at Edfu.
In the scenes accompanying the texts of the Myth of Horus and the Winged Disc, sometimes a crocodile is shown being speared from one of the Horus boats:
Enclosure Wall, inside, west wall, 2nd section, pl. CXLVI 2nd register: the king in a small boat leads Horus in his barque and both are shown spearing and harpooning a crocodile.
Enclosure Wall, inside, west wall, 3rd section, pl. CXLVII 2nd register: the king, then Horus, then the king or his son all in separate boats, each harpoon a crocodile.
Possibly in the central scene on this page, Horus also harpoons a crocodile, but the animal has been defaced and it could be a hippopotamus.

[17] In the library on the south wall, the king is shown spearing a crocodile; there seems to be no title for this scene, for it has only the names of the king and Horus.
Edfu IX, pl. LXXXII, E's.1g.
The king wears the *hemhemty*-crown, places his left foot on the tail of the crocodile and sticks his falcon headed spear into the head of the animal. Its head is turned back towards him.
Edfu III 349, 16-350, 4 He says, 'I am Iun(y) who casts [the harpoon], born of Isis of Wedjat.'
Horus Behdety is described as, 'Horus Behdety, the great god, Lord of Heaven, Lord of Mesen, who strikes down the hippopotamus, who brings as booty the Hidden One (*kꜣpw*).' He says, 'I give to you your foes in a great massacre.' This scene is back to back with a hippopotamus slaying scene.

[18] Among the books mentioned as being kept in the library is a book for driving off crocodiles. It occurs twice in a section devoted to success in hunting or destroying other animal foes:
Edfu III 347, 12 [Books of] 'Making Seth Fall, Driving Away the Crocodile' (*ẖsf msḥ*).... and *Edfu* III 348, 1 '[Books of] Hunting the Lion, Driving Away Crocodiles (*ẖsf msḥw*), the Prowsman (?), Driving Away Serpents'.
However, a book of the hippopotamus ritual is not directly mentioned by name in this list.

[19] During the Festival of Behdet, celebrated over a fourteen day period at Edfu, execration images of hippopotami and crocodiles are used in rituals.
Edfu V 133,8-134,1 'Words to be spoken: A hippopotamus made of red wax, make its face white with grains of sand, inscribed with the name of enemies as you wish. And also may you bring 6 meseh-crocodiles and 2 kapy-crocodiles: the throat of the right, with (its) throat of the left, right to right, left to left.' Other apotropaic rituals follow including the 'striking the eye (of Apopis)', the offering of the

hippopotamus cake, the trampling of fishes' and 'destruction of all the enemies of the king'. *Edfu* V 134,1ff. This method of positioning the crocodiles is demonstrated on the Horus cippi, where the crocodiles lie facing each other, neck to neck (the right side of one creature beside the right side of the other creature, and vice versa (Alliot 1954, 524).

Words used for 'crocodile' (see following table of hieroglyphic writings, pp.198-200)

3bwt-Mg. The execration models of crocodiles made to be destroyed in ritual ceremonies (see below for *Mg*).

3d 'Furious One', derived from *3d* 'to rage' and the nouns from it (Wb. I 24, 20-22 Angry One, but not referring to Seth). The term is used in the description of the fields of the Ninth Upper Egyptian nome (Panopolis), where the god is said to *ḫsf 3d* 'drive off the Furious One' (E IV 180,8). The reason for using the term in this context is probably not some local myth or belief, but that the word used for the 'field' of the Ninth Upper Egyptian nome is spelled *3dwt*, possibly close to the vocalisation of *3d*. Such word-plays or puns occur frequently in these texts. However, other non-punning words for various aspects of Seth are also used in this text, so it may not be so simple. This phrase also occurs at Edfu where *3d* refers to the hippopotamus, the other water based 'raging' form of Seth (E IV 58,13) and much earlier in the Eloquent Peasant B181 *ḫsf.n=ỉ 3d*.

ỉmyw-mw In an example from a tomb at Amarna *ỉmy-mw* is a general term for water creatures (Davies 1908, 15), but in the later temples the term specifically refers to Sethian aquatic animals (Wb. I 74, 7) and especially the hippopotamus and crocodile. It is used in harpoon offering texts, harpoon throwing texts, or killing Seth texts. It can be written with no determinative, one or other of the two animals or with both animals. Most often at Edfu the word has only the crocodile sign.

ỉḥ This is used in the title of the ritual *sty-ỉḥ* and as in epithets of Horus Behedety in the New Year Court. Here he destroys Seth, Apopis, the hippopotamus and *ỉḥ* the crocodile (E I 441,12) and makes the people of Mesen rejoice. The term derives from *ỉḥ* 'male bull' (Wb. I 119-120 Pyr.) and has been adapted to describe the fierce crocodile 'bull'.

ỉṯ 'One who Seizes', 'the Seizer', a term derived from the verb *ỉṯ* 'to seize' and referring to the natural ability of the crocodile to strike quickly and carry off its prey (D VI 25, 3.11).

ꜥfꜥ This is the later GR form (Wb. I 182, 13) of *ꜥfꜥ* 'be greedy' (Wb. I 182,12 NK) and *ꜥfꜥ* 'greedy one' (Wb. I 9,17 MK-NK). The term describes the voracious and greedy nature of the crocodile, perhaps in view of the natural habit of the animal to drag large prey down into the water, rather then chew off small pieces, and perhaps of raiding fishing nets. The word occurs in the same type of phrase, describing 'massacring the Greedy One with the harpoon', with alliteration of *'ayin* for extra powerful effect: *ꜥd ꜥfꜥ m ꜥbbt*, or similarly *ꜥbbt nt ꜥd ꜥfꜥw* 'harpoon of massacring the Greedy Ones' (E VI 239,1). In his aspect of Wenty, Horus is once described as *pḏ-nmtt ḥr ꜥfꜥ* 'Wide of stride upon the Greedy One' (E IV 213,3), an epithet repeated in a Nile-offering procession, where the context has perhaps defeated the scribe who spells the word very differently (E IV 45, 5).

wh-sp=f A phrase referring to Seth when he 'failed' in his contest against Horus to win the right to rule Egypt (Wb. I 339,15; Goyon 1985, 39,9). By contrast Horus/the king does not fail in throwing the harpoon or in any of his ritual and royal activities. The epithet can have general 'enemy' determinatives, as well as being specifically Seth, either in the full form or an abbreviated version *wh*.

Mg is first attested in the magical texts of the New Kingdom (Wb. II 164 (8-9)), where it refers specifically to the crocodile as a son of Seth (papyrus BM EA 10042 (8) rt.6, 4-9; Borghouts 1978,

86-7 (125)). Later, it refers to Seth himself as a crocodile (Sander-Hansen 1937, 34-5; Te Velde 1967, 150). At Edfu the term is a general word for Seth in various forms, as a hippopotamus, the Seth animal, or in a more general way without specific reference to the form (particularly in meat portion offerings on the outside of the Naos). *Mg* can also be written with the 'enemy' determinative. In crocodile slaying texts, however, *Mg* has its original meaning as the crocodile form of Seth. The derivation of the term may be from *Mg3* a Nubian soldier (Wb. II, 164,7-8) or 'skirmisher' (Caminos 1954, 53), itself probably a Nubian word (Säve-Soderbergh 1941, 143-44). In Dongolese Nubian, there is a root *mág* meaning 'to take wrongfully', 'to steal', with a host of derivative words and this may well be a remnant of an ancient Nubian term which became this Egyptian term for the crocodile form of Seth (Armbruster 1965, 135). In this way, Seth would be specifically aligned with one of the foreign menaces of Egyptian boundaries, especially if *Mg3* were indeed bandits or guerrillas threatening Egyptian interests, this would suit the chaotic nature of Seth himself. It is also possible that aside from crocodiles raised as cult animals in the Fayum and at Kom Ombo, the animals were quite rare in Upper Egypt and perceived to be more common in Nubia (for example on the Palestrina mosaic, a crocodile is shown at Philae, but not before Gullini 1956, Tav. XX). A form of *Mg3* is the crocodile genie at Athribis *Mg-ḫnt-ḫty* who is an aspect of the nome-god Horus-Khenty-Khety and drives away hostile forces (Vernus,1978, 415 n.2). According to a text at Edfu, the Eleventh Lower Egyptian Nome, to the north of the Athribis nome, has a shrine called *Pr-Mg3* (E I 333,2) which held the relic of Osiris. However this term was substituted for the real name of the shrine here to emphasise the 'Sethian' nature of the local cult (see above).

msḥ is the classical word for 'crocodile' (Wb. II 136,10-14 OK), but is not used very often in the context of crocodile slaughtering texts. It occurs twice in the Myth texts, which tend to use more 'classical' language and less poetical vocabulary: 'the crocodiles are driven away' (E VI 138, 8) and the 'crocodiles in the water are hunted down' (E VI 217,4). *msḥ* also occurs in the Festival Texts, again in a more straightforward narrative use. This kind of word usage is not echoed in the classical words for the hippopotamus, as *db* and *ḫ(3)b* continue to be found in hippopotamus slaughtering texts. The word *msḥ* apparently also continues in use in the spoken language to emerge eventually as Coptic *msah*. It is possible that *msḥ* was considered altogether too 'ordinary' and could not be used in the slaughter texts to describe a being who was both an embodiment of Seth and destined for destruction in the supernatural sphere. Perhaps, in this way, confusion over the identification of the crocodile god Sobek with the 'evil' crocodile might be avoided.

nmsw A term used at Dendera in one text, where the king cuts off the heads of *nmsw* D IV 194,8 (Wb. II 270 (2)). Its origins are not clear, but there is a term *nmsw* in P.Kahun Med. 1,7, which is an illness. The lack of other examples makes it difficult to know if both are derived from the same root.

r3-ḥs3w (Wb. II 398,5 GR *r3-ḥs3*). The term is used in various toponyms of the Fayum (Yoyotte 1961, 131-6) and as the name of the crocodile god in the Book of the Fayum (P. Fayum VIII,1 and II, 6) but at Edfu is used of the slain animal and where Horus Behedety, 'drives away *r3-ḥs3w* E V 56, 6. It literally means 'Mouth of terror', or 'Mouth of fierceness' (Wb. III 159 (15-17) and evokes the dread of the crocodile attack. The term can also be used of the lion (Wb. op. cit. 4).

ḥnt is known from the Book of the Dead, where it describes Seth and his allies at the Place of Purity, presumably about to be slaughtered (Lepsius, Chapter 145, 27). At Edfu this form of the crocodile is destroyed using the verb *ḥnt*, so that the alliteration and word-play *ḥnt ḥnt* has maximum effect. The determinative sign of the crocodile is also rendered powerless by an array of harpoons or knives. Other words are used in the alliteration: the crocodile is killed by the king's mace (*ḥḏ*) I 538,6; chopped up (*ḫnbb*) on the banks of the river (E VI 239,4, VII 173, 9); *ḥnt ḥms* (CD VI 25, 4). Only once is the use of the term extended, where it refers to the Apopis serpent *ḥnt* (E IV 305, 10). The term may derive from the verb *ḥnt* 'to be greedy' (Wb. III 121,12-13), describing an attribute of the crocodile. It also occurs in demotic (Erichsen, 1954, 315). However it is most likely to be an abbreviation of the name for the Fayum *r3-ḥnt* used from the Middle Kingdom and which could be written with a crocodile determinative (Wb. II 398, 3). This could mean 'Mouth of the canal', referring to the Fayum lake, and the crocodile determinative may have been added because it was a place associated with the animals. From this form the crocodile hieroglyph could be read as *ḫnt* both with reference to the animal and as a sign in other words such as *ṯḫnt* (Kurth 1989).

ḫʿw 'Bank Dweller'. The term also occurs in harpoon offering texts, where the weapon is said to be used for 'stabbing the crocodile' (VI 90,15); it sticks firmly into *ḫʿw* (CD IV 12,15), or unites with *ḫʿw* (CD VI 25, 4). The origin of the term is not clear, but it may be from the noun *ḫʿy* 'mound' and refer to the habit of the crocodile of basking on banks on the river's edge, from which it can plunge into the water. The term would therefore mean something like 'those of the mounds'. This seems to be more likely than the verb *ḫʿi* 'to appear', unless it refers to the sudden appearance of the animal out of the water as it attacks. A further consideration is that the crocodile could be considered to be a manifestation of the sun sinking into the primeval waters at night and rising from them in the morning. In such a context the verb *ḫʿi* would be most suitable for the crocodile (Brunner-Traut 1980, 795). Either etymology is possible, but what seems to be important in terms of the texts is that it alliterates with the word *ḥmt* 'harpoon' and the verbs used for 'to stab' in the Dendera texts, thus giving the actions more magical power and enabling them to be completely effective.

ḫb-snw The term occurs twice at Edfu in a harpoon text and in a slaughtering text. In each case *ḫb-snw* is the object of the verb *ḫbḫb*.The effect of the alliteration is further extended by the use of the word xmt for harpoon. The first part of the term is the verb *ḫbi* 'to annhilate, to destroy' (Wb. III 252, 6-14) and ultimately a more intense form of *ḫbi* 'to lessen', 'to divide'. *snw* is a Ptolemaic word for 'tongue' (Wb. IV 155,15) ultimately a metathesised form of old nz.t. Literally, *ḫb-snw* may mean 'one who divides the tongue' or 'one who cuts the tongue' and in a crocodile text at Dendera *snw* occurs alone: Horus, *ḥsḳ n.s snw.k* 'who cuts out your tongue for her (Isis)' (MD III 51n). It may be an allusion to a local Myth, not preserved otherwise, in which the tongue of the crocodile is cut out to be given to Isis for some purpose. In this case one might expect the epithet to be *ḫb-snw.f* 'he whose tongue is cut out. While the term may be no more than a poetical variant on other words for 'crocodile', it is more likely to have a deeper significance and symbolism.The teaching of Amenemope 22, 9-11 says, 'As for the crocodile, whose tongue is empty, his appearance is old' (Grumach 1972, 140-41; for the crocodile with no tongue see Brunner-Traut 1980, 792, n.22). In the Calendar of Lucky and Unlucky Days, on Day 22 of the second month of Akhet the advice is, 'Do not bathe on this day - it is the day of "Cutting the tongue of the enemy of Sobek, your (Neith) son" (Cairo 86637, recto XI, 8 and Bakir 1966, 21). Writers in antiquity stress the idea that the crocodile has no tongue and when crocodiles open their mouths wide, it does indeed appear as if the creature does not have a tongue (Aristotle, *Historia Animalium* II, X; ibid., Parts of Animals 660.b.15, 24-25, 28; Herodotus, *Histories* II, 68; Diodorus Siculus, I 35,5). The epithet reflects a commonly held belief in ancient times and emphasises the 'strangeness' of the crocodile. It may also imply that without its tongue the crocodile is unable to speak for itself and is damned when it comes to answer for its behaviour.

ḫft is a specialised form of the word *ḫfty* 'enemy'. It can refer to Seth as 'The Enemy' *par excellence* and in the crocodile slaughtering texts it is specifically Seth in his crocodile form.

ḫnt is one of the oldest terms attested for crocodile, occurring in literary texts of the Middle Kingdom (Wb. III 308,4). Gardiner suggested that it derived from *ḫnt* 'to sail south', a reference to the ability of the crocodile to swim swiftly upstream, against the current (Gardiner 1905, 29), and more recently Meeks has suggested that it comes directly from *ḫnt* 'front', referring to the crocodile lying on its front (Meeks 1976, 90). In the light of Eyre's remarks on crocodiles as agents of fate (Eyre 1976, 103-14), the term may even derive from *ḫnt* 'front' with the implication of 'future', giving the crocodile a role as a messenger of death (for example *Lebensmüde* 179; Hornung 1963, 120). Both examples in the crocodile slaughtering texts use the word in the same fully alliterative sentence, *ḫfʿ ḥmt r ḫt ḫnt* 'seizing the harpoon to kill the crocodile'. It seems that the underlying importance of the term is for its magical effect and that perhaps the earlier allusions to the role of the animal had been lost.

sty (?) This rare term seems to have been chosen as part of a paired-phrase and also to alliterate with the verb of which it is the object: *stf.ỉ sty* 'I cut up the crocodile before your house'. The term is also used of the Seth-serpent, in a harpoon offering text, where the king thrusts the weapon into *sty* (E III 138,6). In the case of the serpent, *sty* may refer to it 'shooting out' poison and so derive from the nuance of *sty* 'to shoot, throw' (Wb. IV 326-28). Such a meaning does not apply so easily to the crocodile, unless he is here 'one is is shot at', 'one who is thrown at' (by the harpoon). In a pun, *sty sty* (E V 56, 6), the writing may be a form of *sty* 'Seth' and this may ultimately be the origin of the term.

šnt A verb *šn* is used in 'The Discussion between a Man and his Ba', where it has been translated 'to be infested with crocodiles' (Faulkner 1962, 268), or less dramatically 'to be dangerous'. The noun *šn* 'crocodile' is not definitely attested until the Red and Black Chapel of Hatshepsut at Karnak, where Hatshepsut declares, *ỉnk šn ʿwn* 'I am a rapacious crocodile !' (Lacau and Chevrier 1977, 152 n.O, 150 line 10), but no more references are attested until Edfu where the term is more inimical still (Wb. IV 520, 6). However the definite existence of *šnt* in GR texts is more problematic in light of the following term *šntyw,* for which it may be a writing.

šnty The term is a specialised form of *šntyw* 'enemies' (Wb. IV 520, 3-5), deriving in turn from the verb *šnt* 'to quarrel' (both verbally and physically). It might be possible to ascribe a quarrelsome nature to the crocodile, but if it seems subjective now, it seems impossible to ascribe these sentiments to ancient minds. *šntyw* are clearly hostile foes and this is the light in which the crocodile is represented: in a harpoon text he is killed on the Island of Rage of Horus Behedety (E V 56, 6-7); Horus as the harpooner, takes up his harpoon and stabs *šnty* (E I 560,13); in the course of a hippopotamus killing, Horus also cuts off the forelegs of *šnty* (CD VIII 100,12); *šntyw* are slain with the harpoon (CD V 80,7); *šnty* is among animals sacrificed in the temple (E VI 13,4). What is striking about the word is the range of texts in which it occurs. It seems to be a useful and well-known alternative word for the crocodile, perhaps implying that it does after all say something about how the animal was regarded. Most interesting is a further text from the Eleventh Lower Egyptian nome which has a close connection with the crocodile, this time as *šntyw*: Horus is *ỉn-ḥpt,* who cuts off the heads of *šntyw* (E IV 30,6). It is possible that the earlier term *šn(t)* and *šntyw* have been conflated over time. However the examples seem to show a clear divergence in spelling and therefore two different words.

k3pw is first attested in the Instruction of Ptahhotep 9,3, where the crocodile is used in a metaphor for jealousy. The term derives from the verb *k3p* 'to hide, to cover' and probably suits the nature of the crocodile as an animal which can 'hide' in the mud, or remain camouflaged in undergrowth, all of which indicate its hidden, secretive and therefore dangerous nature. Nevertheless of all the terms used at Edfu for crocodile *k3pw* can be used in a more positive sense elsewhere, perhaps because it embodies a characteristic of the animal rather than simply condemning it outright as an 'enemy'. In parallel with *šn* (above), Hatshepsut declares, *ỉnk k3pw* (Lacau and Chevrier 1977, 152 n.0, 150 line 10). At Kom Ombo, it is one of the names for the crocodile god Sobek, 'the great crocodile who seizes with power' (KO I 17; 9, 2). At Edfu *k3pw* tends to be used in a set phrase, *k3pw* 'Striking at the hippopotamus, dragging out the crocodile' (referring to the harpooner throwing his harpoon and then pulling at the attached rope, to drag the harpooned animal toward him): E IV 246,8 (double-plume offering); invocation to Horus E III 350,3; M. 160,15; M. 94,3; a harpoon text E VII 293,1; in the city of Behdet E VI 4,3; festival text E V 133, 9. At Dendera, the term has a wider use: a knife wielding genie kills Seth in his forms of *k3pw* (MD IV 60b); or pieces of the crocodile are chopped up in a crocodile text (MD III 51n). The Edfu uses, in the one phrase do not suggest a wide-spread use for this term.

ḳmw is apparently used only once in GR texts and is not recorded by Wb. In this context, the king *šsp ʿbb ʿn-ʿʿ.wy ḳmw ỉmyw-mw* 'takes the harpoon and drives away the crocodiles which are in the water (or and those who are in the water)'. It may be a misspelling of *Mg* and alliteration does not help to decide upon the appropriate reading. If the alliteration of the sentence were to continue, then our word might read *ʿ3m,* the word for 'Asiatic' and therefore a suitable origin for a word for an enemy such as

Seth the crocodile. The reading *ḳmw* is however strengthened by a further example from a text describing the destruction of Seth, *km.ti* 'Seth is finished' (E III 188,7) - the donkey/Seth animal determinative and the context supplying the meaning.

ṯ3rw is known from earlier texts (Wb. V 233, 4-6) and derives from *ṯ3-r3* 'hot-mouth', referring originally to venomous serpents with their fiery-poison bites (Grumach 1972, 39). However, in the Book of the Dead the term usually has the 'enemy' determinative, rather than a snake. In this case the relevance of 'hot-mouth' could range from 'angry', to someone who 'rages', 'shouts' and 'swears' (cf. Allen 1974, 160). At Edfu, *ṯ3rw* is used for enemies in general written with the enemy determinative in a variety of contexts, and it is also used specifically for crocodiles, and for serpent enemies (E IV 159,17; E IV 2, 2; E IV 27, 6; *Esna* III no.265, 28). At Kom Ombo the word is a straightforward term for the crocodile (KO I 87, 25; possibly 82,7), where its qualities of 'burning mouth' are put to good use (Gutbub 1979, 394; cf. Goyon 1985, 87 n.3).

ṯsmm This term is often used in a phrase *ir ṯsmmw m ʿn-ʿʿ.wy* 'make the crocodiles retreat', which occurs in other contexts such as a double-plume presentation (E IV 246,8); and the phrase is one of the official epithets of Horus Behedety E II 19-20 (48). Unlike *k3pw* which has only its restricted use, *ṯsmm* has a wider use: in a harpoon offering, Horus slays *ṯsmmw* (E VII 132,6); in a hippopotamus text, *ṯsmmw* are cut up (E IV 58,13); the harpoon stabs *ṯsmmw* (E I 424,13). The origin of the term is unclear, but it may be a corruption of the word *tnm* 'to go against', 'to oppose' and so refer to 'opponents' (Wb. V 311, 2).

dp Among the official epithets of Horus he is 'Lord of Mesen, who pursues the hippopotamus and brings as booty *dep*' (E II 19-20, 47). The word has an earlier wide use as a word for the crocodile including Sobek himself (Wb. V 447, 13-16). It may be connected with the verb *dpi* 'to spit', which can range from the magical act of spitting on Apopis in P. Bremmer-Rhind 22, 2 to the Nun spewing out water to bring the inundation in KO I 62, 66. In this way Sobek could have been seen as the embodiment of the flood at Kom Ombo, spat out from Nun as an act of original creation. The term was then used further as a general term for the crocodile whatever its form.

Other terms for crocodiles used in Egyptian texts

ʿb Wb. I 174 (14) from the Amduat texts; *ḥr mri.t* Wb. II 110 (4) from *Lebensmüde* 75; *mḥw* 'drowned one' Wb.II 122 (20) used at Hibis Temple; *nti* Wb. II 355 (12) KO I 9, Nr.2 name for Sobek; *swi* Wb. IV 65 (13) wide use from Book of the Dead onwards; *sii* Wb. IV 415 (7) only used in the Old Kingdom; *šwi* Wb. IV 434 (8), possibly a later version of the last, used as a name of Sobek KO II 39, 579; *ṯ3.wi* Wb. V 341 (2) name of a young crocodile at Kom Ombo, KO I 59, 61, 39; 60, 62, 47.

Concluding remarks

The range of terms for the crocodile represents an accumulation of religious and secular vocabulary from three thousand years of language. The words show the different aspects of the crocodile, in this case, but this observation can be applied to other categories of object in the Ptolemaic and Roman temples. The wide ranging contexts which appear to provide some of the terms are misleading because of the comparatively small amount of surviving texts. However the reason for using all the words may not be simply that the writers or editors of the texts were indulging in intellectual games, or creating poetic allusions, to heighten the esoteric nature of the texts. Perhaps by using every term available for the crocodile, the texts would then cope with every form of the creature, so that none would escape to threaten the King and the cosmic harmony. The varying vocabulary shows the survival and perhaps increase in the power of naming names. It appears throughout Egyptian texts dealing with the afterlife and the divine sphere, and here is used to control a formidable and very dangerous creature in this world and the next.

Table of Spellings

ꜣbwt-Mg E IV 212,1-2

ꜣd E IV 180,8

ỉmyw-mw With crocodile determinative: E IV 211,10-1; E III 4,1; E VI 79,10; E VI 81,2; E IV 74,7; E IV 74,15-16; E IV 230,8.

With no determinative: E VII 238,11; E I 381,13; E IV 212,6; E IV 212,7.

With both hippopotamus and crocodile determinatives: E VI 239,5; E V 154,15; MD IV 24,8; D V 80,8.

With hippopotamus determinative: E VII 202,8; E VII 292,11; E IV 214,6.

ỉḥ E IV 57,10; E I 441,12.

ỉṯ D VI 25,3.11.

ꜥfꜥ E III 287,9; D IV 24,13; D VI 25,12; D IV 81,1; E III 69,18; E IV 343,13; E IV 13,10; E VI 239,1; E IV 213,3; Mam.E 94,6; E IV 45,5.

wḥ-sp=f E IV 213,3-4; E IV 180,8; D VI 25,7; cf. E V 169,13.

Mg E III 137,2; III 4,2; IV 212,1-2; D IV 12,13; D VI 25,2-3.

Referring to the hippopotamus: E IV 59,9.

With Seth animal determinative: E I 378,18.

With Enemy determinative: E IV 330,5.

Naos ritual texts: E IV 234,4; E IV 246,6; E IV 222,6; E IV 276,15; E IV 285,12; E IV 273,12.

E I 333,2.

msḥ E VI 138,8; E VI 217,4; [ ] E V 133,9.

nmsw D IV 194,8.

rꜣ-ḥsw E IV 211,12 ; //// E V 56,6.

ḥnt E III 137,7; E IV 213, 2; CD IV 12,17; *ḥnt ḥnt* : E I 564,6; E II 166,12; E IV 213,2; E V 56,1-2; E VIII 77,7; D IV 24,7; D IV 194,12.

Apopis: E IV 305,10.

ḫꜥw E IV 374,2; D VI 25,4.

ḫb-snw E VI 238,13; E V 169,5.

ḫft E IV 213,3; E IV 374,4; sim. E III 4,2; E V 169,6.

ḫnt E III 137,7-8; D VI 25,6; sim. D IV 13,1; D IV 194,12.

sty E IV 374,3; cf. E III 138,6; possibly E V 56,6.

šnt E III 3,16.

šnty E IV 213,4; D IV 194,8; D VI 25,3; E V 56, 6-7; E I 560,13; D VIII 100,12; D V 80,7; E VI 13,4; E IV 30,6.

k3pw E IV 211,11; E IV 212,12; E IV 374,13; E IV 246,8; E V 133,9; E III 350,3; M.160,15; M.94,3; MD IV 60b; MD III 51n.

ḳmw E IV 212,7.

t3rw E IV 211,11-12; E IV 212, 6; E V 169,13.

tšmm E IV 212, 12; E IV 374,14; E IV 343,14; E V 169,12; M. 160,15; E IV 246,8; E II 19-20 (48); E VII 132,6; E I 424,13; E VII 293,1.

Referring to the hippopotamus: E IV 58,13.

dp E II 19-20 (47).

Bibliography

Allen, T G 1974. *The Book of the Dead or Going Forth By Day.* Chicago.
Alliot, M 1954. *Le culte d'Horus à Edfou au temps de Ptolémées* II. Bibliothèque d'Etude 20.2. Cairo, Institut Français d'Archéologie Orientale.
Armbruster, C 1965. *Dongolese Nubian - A Lexicon.* Cambridge.
Bakir, Abd el-Mohsen 1966. *The Cairo Calendar No. 86637.* Cairo, General Organisation for Government Printing Offices.
Beinlich, H 1984. *Die "Osirisreliquien". Zum Motiv der Körperzergleiderung in der altägyptischen Religion.* Ägyptologische Abhandlungen 42. Wiesbaden, Otto Harrassowitz.
Bianchi, R 1989. *Ancient Egyptian Art in the Brooklyn Museum.* New York and London, The Brooklyn Museum and Thames and Hudson.
Bierbrier, M (ed.) 1993. *British Museum: Hieroglyphic Texts from Egyptian Stelae,* Part 12. London, British Museum Publications.
Blackman, A and H Fairman, 1935. The Myth of Horus at Edfu. Part I. In *Journal of Egyptian Archaeology* 21, 26-36.
Blackman, A and H Fairman, 1942. The Myth of Horus at Edfu. Part II. In *Journal of Egyptian Archaeology* 28, 32-8.
Blackman, A and H Fairman, 1943. The Myth of Horus at Edfu. Part III. In *Journal of Egyptian Archaeology* 29, 2-36.
Blackman, A and H Fairman, 1944. The Myth of Horus at Edfu. Part IV. In *Journal of Egyptian Archaeology* 30, 5-22.
Blackman, A and H Fairman, 1944b. The Myth of Horus at Edfu. Additions and Corrections. In *Journal of Egyptian Archaeology* 30, 79-80.
Borghouts, J 1973. The Evil Eye of Apopis. In *Journal of Egyptian Archaeology* 59, 114-50.
Borghouts, J 1978. *Ancient Egyptian Magical Texts.* Leiden, E J Brill.
Brunner-Traut, E 1980. Krokodil. In W Helck and W Westendorf (eds.), *Lexikon der Ägyptologie* III, Wiesbaden, Otto Harrassowitz, 791-801.
Budge, E W 1985. *The Book of the Dead,* with introduction by David Lorimer. London, Boston, Victoria, Henley-on-Thames.
Caminos, R 1954. *Late Egyptian Miscellanies.* Oxford.
Cauville, S 1984. *Edfou.* Bibliothèque Générale 6. Cairo, Institut Français d'Archéologie Orientale.
Corteggiani, J-P 1987. *The Egypt of the Pharaohs at the Cairo Museum.* London, Scala Publications.
Courteny, E 1980. *A Commentary on the Satires of Juvenal,* London.
Daressy, G 1903. *Catalogue général des antiquités égyptiennes du musée du Caire. Textes et dessins magiques, 9401-9449.* Cairo.
Davies, N de Garis 1908. *The Rock Tombs of El Amarna* Volume VI. London, Egypt Exploration Fund.
Davies, N de Garis 1913. *Five Theban Tombs.* London, Egypt Exploration Fund.
Derchain, P 1962. *Le sacrifice de l'oryx.* Rites égyptiens I. Brussels.
Drioton, E 1948. *Le texte dramatique d'Edfou.* Supplément aux Annales du Service des Antiquités de l'Egypte 11. Cairo, Institut Français d'Archéologie Orientale.
Dümichen, J 1885. *Geographische Inschriften Altägyptischer Denkmäler III.* Leipzig, J C Hinrichs.
Egberts, A 1989. Python or Worm ? Some Aspects of the Rite of Driving the Calves. In *Göttinger Miszellen* 111, 33-45.
Erichsen, W 1954. *Demotisches Glossar.* Copenhagen.
Eyre, C 1976. Fate, Crocodiles and the Judgement of the Dead. Some Mythological Allusions in Egyptian Literature. In *Studien zur Altägyptischen Kultur* 4, 103-14.
Fairman, H 1974. *The Triumph of Horus - An Ancient Egyptian Sacred Drama.* London.
Faulkner, R 1962. *A Concise Dictionary of Middle Egyptian.* Oxford University Press.
Fischer, H 1968. *Dendera in the Third Millennium B.C. down to the Theban domination of Upper Egypt.* New York.

Gardiner, A H 1905. Hymns to Amon from a Leiden Papyrus. In *Zeitschrift für Ägyptische Sprache* 42, 12-41.
Gauthier, H 1927. *Dictionnaire des noms géographiques contenus dans les textes hiéroglyphiques* IV. Cairo, Institut Français d'Archéologie Orientale.
Goyon, J-C 1985. *Les dieux-gardiens et la genèse des temples (d'après les textes égyptiens de l'époque gréco-romaine). Les soixante d'Edfou et les soixante-dix-sept dieux de Pharbaethos.* Bibliothèque d'Etude 93. Cairo, Institut Français d'Archéologie Orientale.
Grumach, I 1972. *Untersuchungen zur Lebeslehre des Amenope.* Münchner Ägyptologische Studien 23. Munich and Berlin, Deutscher Kunstverlag.
Gullini, G 1956. *I Mosaici di Palestrina.* Rome.
Gutbub, A 1979. La tortue - animal cosmique bénéfique à l'époque ptolémaique et romaine. In *Hommages à Serge Sauneron I*, Cairo, 391-435.
Gwyn-Griffiths, J 1970. *De Iside et Osiride.* University of Wales Press.
Harpur, Y 1987. *Decoration in Egyptian Tombs of the Old Kingdom.* London and New York, Kegan Paul International.
Hopfner, T 1913. *Der Tierkult der Alten Ägypter.* Denkschriften der Kaiserlichen Akademie der Wissenschaften in Wien, Philosophisch-historische Klasse, Abhandlung 57.2. Wien, A Hölder.
Hornung, E 1963. *Das Amduat. Die Schrift des Verborgenen Raumes.* II. Ägyptologische Abhandlungen 7. Wiesbaden, Otto Harrassowitz.
Jelínková-Reymond, E 1956. *Les inscriptions de la statue guérrisseuse de Djed-her le Sauveur.* Bibliothèque d'Etude 23. Cairo, Institut Français d'Archéologie Orientale.
Junker, H 1910. *Die Stundenwachen in den Osirismysterien nach den Inschriften von Dendera, Edfu und Philae.* Denkschriften der Kaiserlichen Akademie der Wissenschaften in Wien, Philosophisch-historische Klasse, Abhandlung 54. Wien, A Hölder.
Junker, H 1958. *Der Grosse Pylon des Tempels der Isis in Philä.* Österreichische Akademie der Wissenschaften, Philosophisch-historische Klasse, Denkschriften, Sonderband. Wien, Rudolf M Rohrer.
Kakosy, L 1963. Krokodil mit menschenkopf. *Zeitschrift für Ägyptische Sprache und Altertumskunde* 90, 67-74.
Kakosy, L 1980. Krokodilskulte. In W Helck and W Westendorf (eds.), *Lexikon der Ägyptologie* III, Wiesbaden, Otto Harrassowitz, 801-11.
Kurth, D 1983. *Die Dekoration der Saulen im Pronaos des Tempels von Edfu.* Göttinger Orientforschungen IV.11. Wiesbaden, Otto Harrassowitz.
Kurth, D 1989. Zu einem Wort in medizinischen Texten, *Göttinger Miszellen* 111, 81-3.
Lange, H 1927. *Der magische Papyrus Harris.* Det Kgl. Danske Videnskabernes Selskab, Historis-filologiske Meddelelser 24, 2. Copenhagen, Bianco Luno.
Lanzone, R 1896. *Les Papyrus du Lac Moeris.* Turin, Bocca Frères.
Lloyd, A 1976, 1988. *Herodotus Book II, Commentary.* Leiden, E J Brill.
Meeks, D 1976. Notes de lexicographie (§§2-4). In *Revue d'Égyptologie* 28, 87-96.
Montet, P 1957. *Géographie de l'Égypte ancienne* I. Paris, Imprimerie Nationale and Librairie C Klincksieck.
Montet, P 1961. *Géographie de l'Égypte ancienne* II. Paris, Librairie C Klincksieck.
Naville, E 1886. *Das Aegyptische Todtenbuch der XVIII. bis XX> Dynastie* I. Berlin, A Asher.
Neugebauer, O and R Parker, 1960. *Egyptian Astronomical Texts I. The Early Decans.* Providence, Rhode Island, and London. Brown University Press and Lund Humphries.
Neugebauer, O and R Parker, 1964. *Egyptian Astronomical Texts II. The Ramesside Star Clocks.* Providence, Rhode Island, and London. Brown University Press and Lund Humphries.
Neugebauer, O and R Parker, 1969. *Egyptian Astronomical Texts III. Decans, Planets, Constellations and Zodiacs.* Providence, Rhode Island, and London. Brown University Press and Lund Humphries.
Ritner, R 1993, *The Mechanics of Ancient Egyptian Magical Practice.* Studies in Ancient Oriental Civilizations 54. The University of Chicago.
Sadek, A 1988. *Popular religion in Egypt During the New Kingdom.* Hildesheimer Ägyptologische

Beiträge 27. Hildesheim, Gerstenberg Verlag.
Sander-Hansen, C 1937. *Die Religiosen Texte auf dem Sarg der Anchnesneferibre.* Copenhagen, Levin & Munksgaard, Ejnar Munksgaard.
Säve-Soderbergh, T 1941. *Ägypten und Nubien.* Lund, Håkan Ohlsson.
Säve-Soderbergh, T 1953. *On Egyptian Representations of Hippopotamus Hunting as a Religious Motive.* Uppsala, Appelberg.
Seele, K 1947. Horus on the Crocodiles. In *Journal for Near Eastern Studies* 6, 43-52.
Scott, N 1951. The Metternich Stela. In *Bulletin of the Metropolitan Museum of Art* New Series, 9, 201-17.
Te Velde, H 1967. *Seth, God of Confusion.* Leiden, E J Brill.
Vernus, P 1978. *Athribis - Textes et documents relatifs à la géographie, aux cultes et à l'histoire d'une ville du Delta égyptien à l'époque pharaonique.* Bibliothèque d'Etude 74. Cairo, Institut Français d'Archéologie Orientale.
Yoyotte, J 1961. Procession géographiques mentionnant le Fayoum et ses localités. In *Bulletin de l'Institut français d'Archéologie Orientale* 61, 79-138.

Abbreviations

Dendara
D
É. Chassinat, *Le Temple de Dendara.* Cairo. I, 1934; II, 1934; III, 1935; IV, 1935; V, two fasc., 1952 and 1947.
É. Chassinat and F. Daumas, *Le Temple de Dendara.* Cairo. VI, 1965; VII, 1972; VIII, two fasc. 1978.
F. Daumas. Cairo. *Le Temple de Dendara.* IX, two fasc. 1987.

MD I-IV
A. Mariette, *Dendérah - Description générale du grand temple de cette ville,* Tomes I-IV, 1870-1874, Paris.

Edfu
E
Marquis de Rochemonteix and É. Chassinat. *Le Temple d'Edfou,* I. Revised edition by S. Cauville and D. Devauchelle. Fasc. I, 1984; fasc. 2, 1984; fasc. 3, 1987; fasc. 4, 1987.
É. Chassinat. *Le Temple d'Edfou,* II. Revised edition by S. Cauville and D. Devauchelle. Fasc. 1, 1987; fasc. 2, 1990.
É. Chassinat, *Le Temple d'Edfou.* Cairo. III, 1928; IV, 1929; V, 1930; VI, 1931; VII, 1932; VIII, 1933; IX, 1929; X, two fasc. 1928 and 1960; XI, 1933; XII, 1934; XIII, 1934; XIV, 1934.
S. Cauville and D. Devauchelle. Cairo. *Le Temple d'Edfou,* XV, 1985.

Esna
S. Saunero. Cairo. *Le temple d'Esna,* III, 1968.

KO
J de Morgan et al., *Kom Ombos* Vienna. I, 1895; II, 1909.

A painting of the gods of Dakhla in the temple of Ismant el-Kharab

Olaf E Kaper

The number of temples in Egypt which were dedicated to Egyptian gods must have been enormous in antiquity: a recent list of those that survive in the archaeological record numbers 130 (Arnold 1992). However, several entries on this list comprise more than one temple, while the list remains incomplete in other respects. Notably, several Egyptian buildings from the Roman Period have been omitted, reflecting the general neglect of buildings from this period in the Egyptological literature. It has only been during the last few decades that the smaller temples from the Roman Period have begun to be studied in detail. The temples of Deir el-Shelwit, El-Qal'a and Shenhur in the Nile Valley are examples of this recent increase in interest. Smaller temples also remain in the Eastern Desert, such as those at Mons Claudianus and Berenike. In the Western Desert, recent discoveries include the shrine of Piyris at Ayn Labakha found by the Supreme Council of Antiquities, and a temple at Ayn Manawir located by the French Institute (IFAO), both situated in the Kharga Oasis. In recent years new temples have also been discovered in the Dakhla Oasis, and these will form the topic of the present paper. It is certainly no exaggeration to state that the end of the list is nowhere in sight. Egyptian and Greek papyri provide an accurate impression of the often dense spread of sanctuaries over the countryside, with temples in every town or sizeable village (e.g. Bowman 1986, 171ff.).

The Temples of the Dakhla Oasis

The Dakhleh Oasis Project, led by A J Mills, has been researching the oasis since 1978. During the archaeological survey of the oasis a total of twenty new temples were located. The Dakhla temples are mainly small in scale, in accordance with the size of the villages to which they belonged. The largest temple complex stood in the ancient (and modern) capital of the oasis, Mut. The enclosure wall of this temple measures 240 x 180 m (Mills 1981, 180-1, 187-8, pl.14), which can be compared with other preserved enclosure walls in Dakhla such as those at Ismant el-Kharab (*c.*150 x 170 m), Deir el-Haggar (78.5 x 41 m) and Ain el-Azizi (*c.*35 x 20 m).

The majority of the temples in the oasis were built entirely of mudbrick, and most conform to a design which seems characteristic for the temples in the Great Oasis (Dakhla and Kharga). The temples of this type have an elongated linear ground plan, with a succession of mostly vaulted chambers decorated with painted plaster (pl.VIa). Eight examples of this type were found by the Dakhleh Oasis Project, at site nos 31/435-K3-1, 31/435-B3-1, 31/435-M3-1 (two temples of this type), 31/435-N6-2 (three examples), 31/435-M4-1 (Mills 1983, 129-38). Comparable temples survive in the Kharga Oasis at the sites of Dush, el-Deir and Ayn Labakha (Naumann 1938, 12f), the latter still with traces of its original painted plaster decoration. This type of mudbrick architecture also had an influence upon the design of the stone temples at Ghuweita and Dush in Kharga which each received vaulted roofs over their sanctuaries.

A total of seven stone temples have been located in the Dakhla Oasis, at the sites of Deir Haggar, Amheida, Mut el-Kharab, Ain el-Azizi, Ismant el-Kharab (two stone temples) and Ain Birbiya. The latter two sites were selected for further study and excavation by the Dakhleh Oasis Project.

The temple complex of Ismant el-Kharab (ancient Kellis) has been under excavation since 1991 (pl.VIb). It comprises two small stone temples and a number of mudbrick shrines which were dedicated to the gods Tutu, Neith and the local goddess Tapsais. The relief decoration of the stone temples survives only in small fragments as the buildings have been quarried. By contrast, the large mudbrick Shrine I has preserved most of its original painted decoration complete. The latter consists of a sequence of two large chambers of which the inner chamber had a vaulted roof decorated with painted plaster in the manner of the mudbrick temples of the oases described above. The evidence uncovered at Kellis thus far dates the foundation of the Main Temple to about the period of Hadrian, even though there seem to be earlier remains on the site (Hope 1995).

The temple of Ain Birbiya (pl.VIc) was discovered in 1982 in the eastern part of the oasis buried up to its roof in sand and domestic remains (Mills 1983, 132-4; id. 1985, 109-13; id. 1986, 70-3; id. 1990, 14-6). Unfortunately, owing to the influence of irrigation waters, its state of preservation is very bad and a considerable conservation effort is required before its walls can slowly be uncovered. The temple is dedicated to the local god Amun-nakht and to Hathor. Its foundation seems to date to the (late) Ptolemaic Period because its earliest decoration, located on the outer gateway, dates to the reign of Octavian or early Augustus. The remainder of the temple was decorated at a later stage. The doorway inside the pronaos carries the name of Hadrian and another, as yet unidentified, emperor is depicted on the walls of the sanctuary.

The temple at Deir el-Haggar (pl.VIIa), which was dedicated to the Theban triad, has been known and visited since the early nineteenth century. The structure remained covered by its own debris until 1992 when the Dakhleh Oasis Project in collaboration with the Supreme Council of Antiquities started a programme of clearance and restoration in order to make the temple accessible to visitors. Its decoration dates to the reigns of Nero, Vespasian, Titus, Domitian and Hadrian. A description of the exposed parts of this temple was published by L Bull and H Winlock (Winlock 1936, 29-33, 65-77, pls.17-25).

The Paintings in Shrine I at Kellis

Shrine I is one of the subsidiary chapels within the temple complex at Ismant el-Kharab, which may have functioned as a mammisi. It is located to the south of the Main Temple, the orientation of which it shares. It is still being excavated at the time of writing (1994) and the observations presented here can therefore be only of a preliminary nature. The inner chamber of the shrine measures *c.* 12 x 5 m, and is still preserved intact up to *c.* 2.5 m which equals half of its presumed original height. At the rear end of the room, the preserved walls even reach a height of 3.5 m (pl.VIIb). Its vaulted roof collapsed in antiquity onto a layer of wind-blown sand and remained untouched until the present day (pl.VIIc). We thus have a unique opportunity to recover the entire decorative scheme of a mudbrick shrine.

The inner chamber of Shrine I had been entirely plastered and painted in two different artistic styles. The dado and the central band upon the vault were painted in the classical Roman style while the remaining surfaces were painted in the ancient Egyptian style of temple decoration. The scenes of the latter were divided into registers. The rear wall contained four registers, and the north and south walls each contained one register below the springing of the vault. Three more registers were added either side of the central panel of the vault which was painted in classical style. In the lowest registers of the shrine the paintings had been mutilated before the abandonment of the site, but in the upper registers they were virtually undamaged by human hands. The amount of information which the paintings contain will be most valuable for the study of artistic developments in Roman Egypt, as well as for our understanding of the cult of the god Tutu, to whom the shrine was dedicated.

The exact date of these paintings is still unknown because no king or emperor was represented within the scenes thus far reconstructed. The style of the paintings suggests an approximate date in the second century AD. It is hoped that future excavations in the shrine will yield more exact dating evidence. The fact that the king has been omitted from these traditional Pharaonic temple scenes argues in favour of a relatively late date of execution (cf. Hölbl 1989). A few unpublished scenes at the contemporary temples at Dush and Nadura in Kharga contain a limited number of similar examples which replace the king in his role as offering bearer with the depictions of deities. An explanation for this phenomenon may be found at Kellis when more of the decoration has been reconstructed.

When the vault of Shrine I collapsed, the mud bricks separated and the plaster decoration shattered into innumerable fragments. Before the original appearance of the shrine may be restored again on paper, these fragments are to be carefully excavated, conserved and reconstructed. The work on this gigantic jigsaw is likely to proceed slowly during the coming years. Fortunately, a part of the original decoration still adheres to the vaulting bricks, so that when these are lifted from the sand within the shrine, the loose fragments of plaster can be related to them during the reconstruction process.

To date, the results of the reconstruction work have been encouraging. It has been possible to reconstruct the original lay-out of all the scenes which have so far been excavated in the northwestern corner of the shrine. This section amounts to approximately one-third of the original Pharaonic style decoration of the shrine. In addition it has been possible to reconstruct on paper a complete section of the Pharaonic paintings, part of which is reproduced in the line drawing in fig.1. These paintings come from the collapsed northern side of the vault from the first register. The painting includes a section which is still preserved *in situ* upon the vault of the shrine (pl.VIIIa); it depicts the legs of the first goddess on the left in fig.1. Owing to their relatively accessible position in antiquity, the figures have all been vandalized. Despite this, a full reconstruction of the scene has been possible because the damaged divine figures are still identifiable by the details of the dress, and by the hieroglyphic legends which have generally survived intact.

The gods of Deir el-Haggar

The first register of the northern side of the vault has been found to include nineteen figures between the rear wall of the shrine (left in fig.2) and the doorway in the north wall. In the following discussion of these scenes, I will focus exclusively upon the deities represented. Neither the offerings presented to the gods nor the hieroglyphic legends, nor the artistic aspects of the paintings will be discussed here.

Within the first register, the figures have been arranged into groups of four or more deities who are shown receiving offerings from one or more gods facing them. The first group of gods at the rear end of the room (left in fig.1) contains Amun-Ra, Khons, Mut, Thoth and Nehmetaway:

The hieroglyphic writing for the name of Nehmetaway is unparalleled, but there can be no doubt as to the identity of the goddess. Between Mut and Thoth, the painting includes a vertical dividing line. The three gods to the right are well-known in Dakhla from the temple of Deir el-Haggar. For unknown reasons, the order of these deities is sometimes different in Dakhla from their appearance in the Theban temples which represent the same deities in the order Amun-Ra, Mut, Khons. At Deir el-Haggar, the alternative order Amun-Ra, Khons, Mut is found in some of the most prominent reliefs within the temple pronaos which date to the reign of Titus (pl.VIIIb).

The gods Thoth and Nehmetaway are depicted to the left of the dividing line. The veneration of these two deities at Deir el-Haggar is demonstrated by their depiction in several locations of the temple which are conventionally reserved for the main gods, such as the *soubassement* within the pronaos. In the sanctuary of the temple, Thoth and Nehmetaway appear upon the northern side wall, and Thoth has been included as a major deity within the astronomical ceiling of the sanctuary (Kaper 1995a). A number of *dipinti* painted upon the temenos wall show that Thoth and Amun-Ra were considered of equal importance in the eyes of the visitors to the temple. These *dipinti* date to the second century AD and were found during clearance work undertaken by the Dakhleh Oasis Project in 1993. Thoth probably held his position of prominence at Deir el-Haggar as a result of the popularity of the god in the western region of the whole oasis. Reused temple blocks which are found in the houses of the nearby village of El-Qasr attest to the former existence of a temple dedicated to Thoth in the vicinity (cf. Fakhry 1982, 40; Kaper 1992, 128-9). The most likely original location of this building was the Roman period town at Amheida (probably the ancient *Trimithis*), the ruins of which lie only three kilometres south of El-Qasr.

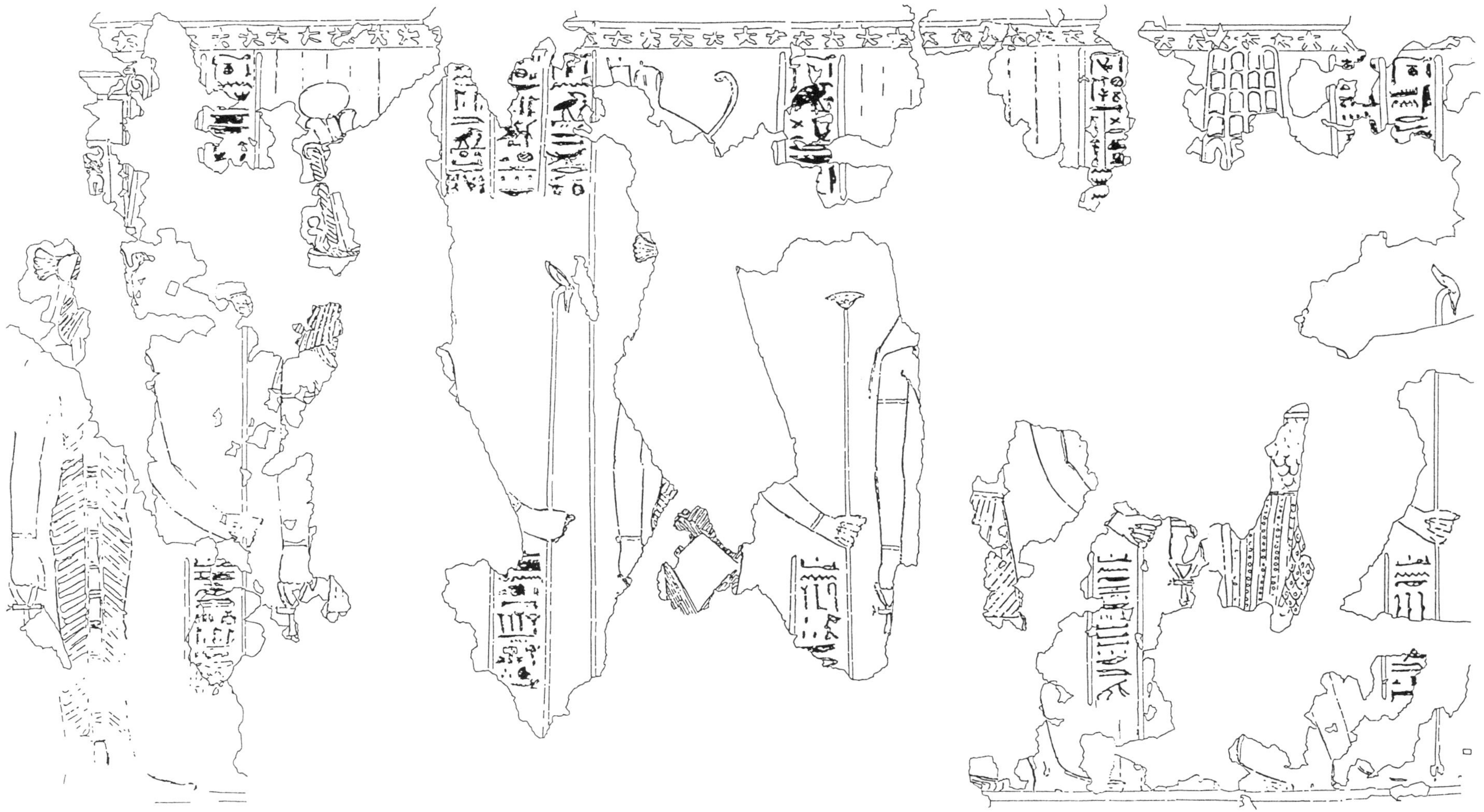

Fig.1 Reconstructed painting from the northern half of the vault of Shrine 1 at Ismant el-Kharab (Kellis). The deities are, from right to left, Amun-Ra, Khons, Mut, Thoth and Nehmetaway.

Osiris in Dakhla

In the middle section of the first register in Shrine I, the paintings contain a group of gods comprising Osiris, Harsiese, Isis and Nephthys: 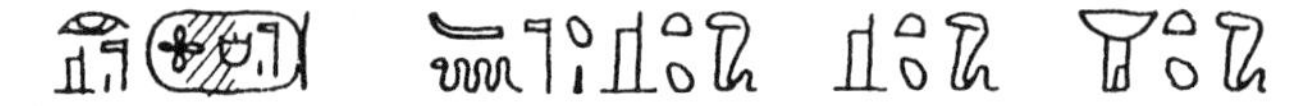

In the legends of this scene, Osiris is called "Lord of the Oasis" which indicates the local veneration of the god. Other gods who also receive this title in the temple inscriptions of the Dakhla oasis are Mut, Neith, Tapsais, Nephthys and Seth. The group of gods around Osiris is found again at Deir el-Haggar depicted upon the southern wall of the sanctuary (fig.3). In addition, the same group seems to have figured on the south wall of the sanctuary at Ain Birbiya, in the upper register, although only the last two deities of the group have been preserved there. In the tomb of Petosiris at el-Muzzawaka in Dakhla, the same group of gods occurs again (Fakhry 1982, 89, pl.29a). The appearance of Osiris in a tomb chapel is, of course, no cause for surprise, but it is rare to find in such a context the four gods in this precise order of appearance, and they are furthermore the only deities in this tomb provided with hieroglyphic legends (ibid., 90, pl.30f). The recurrence of this assembly of gods in Dakhla suggests that they were venerated as a group in one of the temples of the oasis.

A possible candidate for this hypothetical temple was found in 1980 in the western region of Dakhla (site no. 32/405-A2-1), in the form of a small temple which had a long history stretching back to the Pharaonic period (Mills 1981, 181-2, pl.8). It was built in mudbrick and it had been decorated with painted plaster. The excavations brought to light an elaborate statuette of Osiris inside the sanctuary. The figure measured 23.4 cm in height; it was made from two different kinds of unbaked clay which had originally been plastered and painted and its eyes were accentuated with stone inlays (ibid., pl.13a). This technique recalls the type of clay statues made in many temples in Egypt during the Osiris festivals of the month of Khoiak. According to the ritual prescriptions preserved in the temple at Dendera, a clay statue should be kept for one year inside the temple before its interment in the necropolis (cf. Cauville 1988, 31). The care with which the Dakhla statuette is made indicates its use as a ritual object. Even though the details of manufacture do not correspond closely to the prescriptions written on the walls of the temple at Dendera, it is known that these practices could vary locally, as is shown by the variety of this type of statue found at various sites in the Nile Valley (listed in Raven 1982, 18-25). The Osiris chapels in the temple of Hibis (cf. Osing 1986) demonstrate that the temples in the oases did not differ from those in the Nile Valley in their performance of the Osirian temple rituals. At Deir el-Haggar, the theme of the dismemberment of Osiris is mentioned in one of the *bandeau* inscriptions in the temple sanctuary (Kaper 1992, 127).

The order in which the Osirian gods appear in Dakhla may be a reflection of their Theban origin, since some temple reliefs from the Theban region depict the gods in the same order, i.e. Osiris, Harsiese, Isis, Nephthys (e.g. Traunecker 1980, 181-3, pl.48). A sandstone relief from Coptos dating to the reign of Domitian and now in the Egyptian Museum, Cairo (JdE 28918; v. Bissing 1914, 119 n.68) combines this group with the figure of Min-Ra, as on the southern sanctuary wall at Deir el-Haggar.

The gods of *ỉmrt*

The third section within the first register of the vault at Kellis comprises four gods bearing the names of Amun-nakht, Khnum, Isis and Hathor: 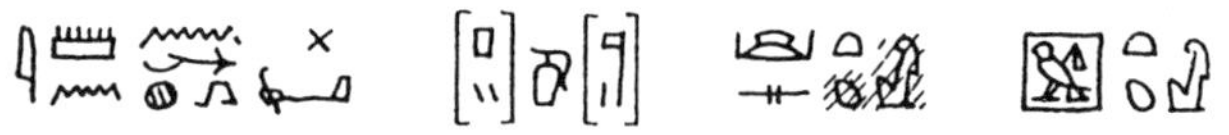

The legends with this scene assign the gods to the eastern end of Dakhla, to the region called *ỉmrt*. The inscriptions in the temple of Ain Birbiya confirm the location of *ỉmrt* (Kaper 1992, 122-4), as well as the names of two of the gods, Amun-nakht and Hathor.

Amun-nakht seems to be a god unique to the Dakhla oasis. The god bears characteristics of both Amun-Ra and Horus son of Osiris. The goddess Hathor is perhaps identified with Isis, the mother of the god. In the local mythology expressed in the inscriptions on the temple walls, Amun-nakht is said to run over the desert in pursuit of the enemies of his father Osiris. The iconography of Amun-

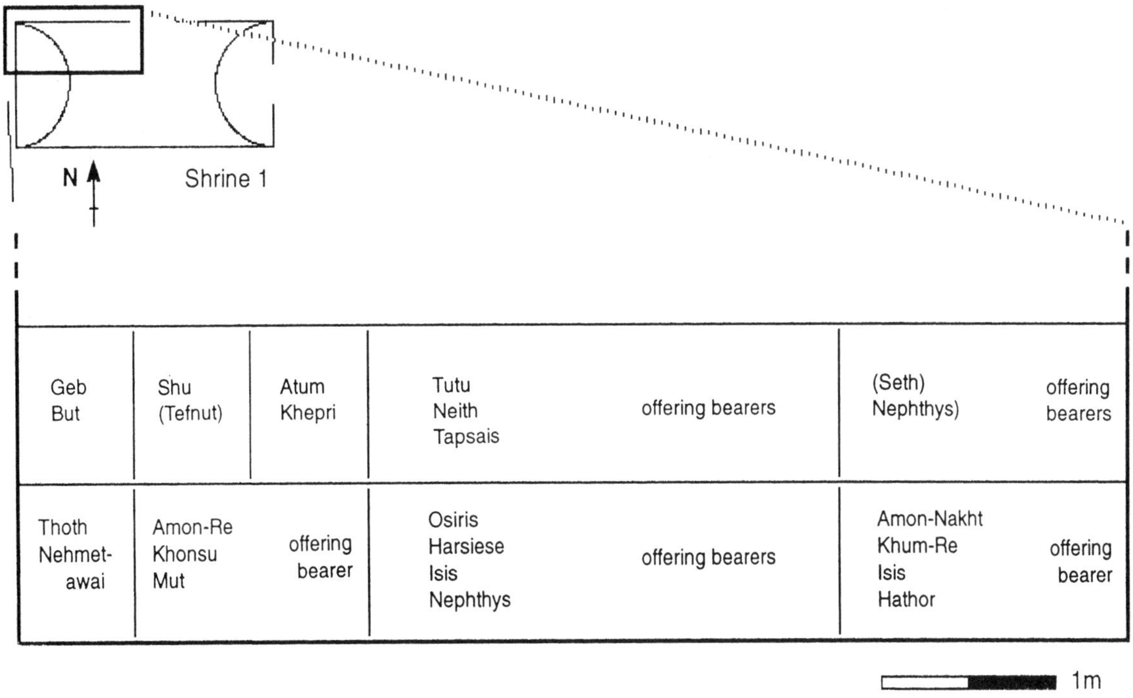

Fig.2 Schematic reconstruction of the northwest corner of Shrine I at Ismant el-Kharab (Kellis). The gods represented within the first two registers are indicated.

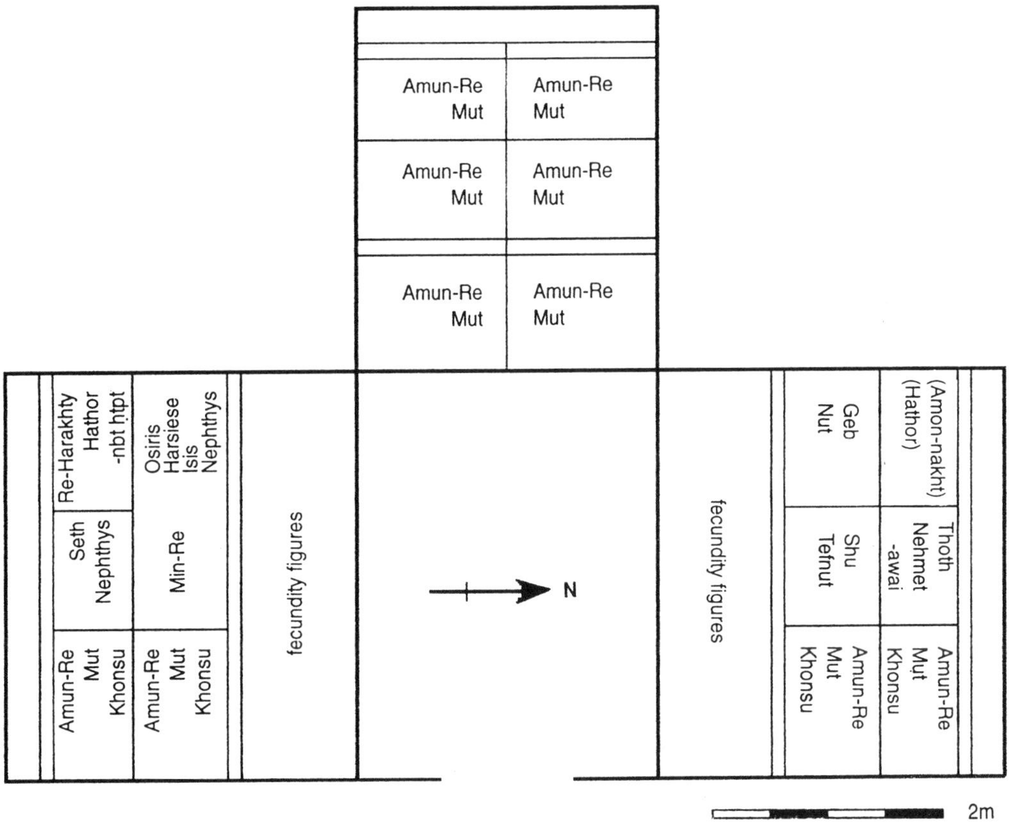

Fig.3 Schematic rendering of the decoration of the sanctuary of the temple of Deir el-Haggar . The gods represented upon the southern, western and northern walls are indicated.

nakht upon the gateway of the Ain Birbiya temple shows the god accordingly with a falcon's head and wings depicted in a running posture while spearing the figure of an enemy (cf. Mills 1985, pl.III.2). This same iconography has been copied in the painting at Kellis discussed here.

In the legends of the Kellis painting, the couple Khnum-Ra and Isis are associated with the same region, *ỉmrt*, although they are not mentioned on the preserved parts of the gateway at Ain Birbiya. In this case, the reliefs at Deir el-Haggar help to confirm the presence of a cult of Khnum-Ra in Dakhla as well as to explain the association of this god with Isis. In the reliefs upon two of the doorways at Deir el-Haggar, the goddess Isis is depicted together with Khnum-Ra in her manifestation as the star goddess Sothis (Sirius). In this form of hers, the relationship of the goddess with Khnum is well-known (e.g. Jaritz 1980, 29-30 n.185).

The Deir el-Haggar doorways contain images of Osiris and Khnum-Ra in parallel positions within the decoration. Both gods are designated in the inscriptions of the Dakhla temples as being responsible for the provision of water to the oasis. In fact, the role of these gods in Dakhla is similar to their role as expressed in Nile Valley inscriptions with regard to the inundation (Kaper 1995b). It is obvious that the supply of water to the oasis must have played an important part in local religious beliefs. The combined data from Deir el-Haggar and Kellis thus suggest that Khnum-Ra was venerated in the eastern part of Dakhla and Osiris in the western part.

The first register of the vault of Shrine I summarized

In general, the first register is the most important register upon a temple wall. Upon the vault in Shrine I, this register contains the principal deities of Dakhla: Amun-Ra, Thoth, Osiris, Amun-nakht and Khnum-Ra with their consorts and offspring. The gods appear on the vault in their correct, geographical order, that is to say the gods whose temples stand in the western part of Dakhla appear on the western end of the register, while those of the east are shown on the eastern end of the register. The temple reliefs at Deir el-Haggar confirm the prominence of these gods in the oasis, because the same figures are consistently depicted in major positions within the temple decoration.

Seth in Dakhla

After establishing that the first register of Shrine I depicts the major deities of the Dakhla oasis, we have to ask the question, where is Seth ? Seth was a major god in Dakhla from the Third Intermediate Period onwards, if not earlier, and his popularity persisted into the Roman Period (Osing 1985; Jacquet-Gordon 1991; Kaper 1995c). Various temple inscriptions in Dakhla leave no doubt about this fact. In the Nile Valley, Seth was considered to be the major god of *knmt* (Osing 1985, 229 n.2) which designates both Kharga and Dakhla together (Kaper 1992, 117-21). Nevertheless, in the Kharga temples Seth is found depicted only once - in the famous relief of the god at Hibis, the legend of which confirms that Seth was resident there (*ḥry-ỉb hbt*: Cruz-Uribe 1988, 147). From this lack of evidence from Kharga itself, it appears that the god may have been of greater prominence in the neighbouring Dakhla oasis.

A figure of Seth comparable to that of Hibis was depicted at Kellis upon the southern half of the vault of Shrine I, in the first register (Kaper 1995c, fig.2). Plaster fragments from the northern side of the vault, from the second register, preserve the remains of yet another figure of a similar nature which still awaits full reconstruction. The fragments show a set of wings and an inscription which includes the following phrase:

'He has slain Apophis in the prow of the bark (of Ra)'. The cosmic enemy Apophis is depicted as a serpent at the bottom of this scene, as in the Hibis relief. The legends that accompany the figure of Seth at Deir el-Haggar confirm the importance which was attached to the slaying of Apophis by the god (*sḫr ʿ3pp*: Osing 1985, 231, pl.37). The presence of Seth in the second register thus seems certain.

The temple of Seth was located at the site of Mut el-Kharab. The survey of this site by the Dakhleh Oasis Project showed that there had been a stone temple there of considerable antiquity, set within the largest known enclosure wall in the oasis. Two stelae from the Twenty-second and Twenty-fifth Dynasties, now in the Ashmolean Museum, Oxford (Gardiner 1933; Janssen 1968), which refer to an oracle of Seth, are claimed to have been found in this location.

The remaining gods within the second register

The presumed figure of Seth in the second register of Shrine I is followed by a goddess, whose figure has not yet been reconstructed but who should accordingly be identified as Nephthys. Then follow the gods of Kellis, namely Tutu, Neith and Tapsais:

The figure of Tutu has not yet been fully reconstructed either, but from the fragments it is clear that he was depicted in human from, similar to another representation of him on the southern half of the vault. The gods of Kellis are followed immediately by the gods of Heliopolis: Atum, Khepri, Shu, [Tefnut], Geb and Nut:

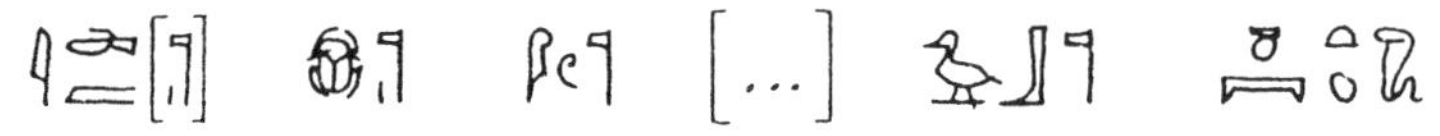

The name of Tefnut has not yet been found among the fragments, but it is clear that the figure corresponding to Tefnut in the series represented a goddess. The deities of Heliopolis are shown to be closely associated with the gods of Kellis, because the two groups of gods are nowhere interrupted by a dividing line, such as that which occurs between Mut and Thoth in the first register (fig.1).

The decorative scheme of the Deir el-Haggar wall reliefs

At this stage, it is instructive to examine the walls of the sanctuary in the temple at Deir el-Haggar (fig.3). The gods of this temple - Amun-Ra, Mut and Khons - appear in primary positions in both of the main registers upon the side walls of the sanctuary. They are followed by scenes which contain representations of the following gods: Seth and Nephthys, Thoth and Nehmetaway, the Osiris group together with Min-Ra, and the gods of Heliopolis. These are the same gods as occur in the Kellis paintings. In addition, they appear again upon some of the decorated doorways at Deir el-Haggar. The gateway throgh the temenos wall and the doorway leading into the hypostyle hall of the temple adhere to a decorative scheme of temple doorways which was originally developed for the Theban temples. Upon this type of doorway, the scenes at eye-level always depict the major gods of the temple while the remaining scenes upon the jambs depict the gods of the surrounding area (cf. in detail Kaper 1995d). The doorway into the hypostyle at Deir el-Haggar thus shows the gods Khnum-Ra and Sothis, Osiris and Isis, Atum and Hathor, Shu and Tefnut, Ptah and Sekhmet, Thoth and Nehmetaway, and Seth and Nephthys.

The Deir el-Haggar reliefs thus assist in the interpretation of the Kellis paintings.It appears from the above that the Dakhla temples do not depict gods from the Nile Valley; instead we find, almost exclusively, depictions of local deities from Dakhla itself. The major gods of the oasis were depicted upon the walls of the sanctuaries at Deir el-Haggar and Shrine I at Kellis and probably also at Ain Birbiya. Moreover, the same gods were depicted upon the jambs of temple doorways at Deir el-Haggar, Ain Birbiya and possibly Kellis. This situation is summarized in the table overleaf in which the various deities are related to the temples in which they are depicted upon either the sanctuary walls or the outer gateways.

	Deir el-Haggar	Kellis	Ain Birbiya
Osiris and Isis	x	x	x
Khnum-Ra and Isis-Sothis	x	x	
Seth and Nephthys	x	x	
Thoth and Nehmetaway	x	x	
Ra-Horakhty-Atum and Hathor *nbt-ḥtpt*	x	x	x
Shu and Tefnut	x	x	x
Geb and Nut	x	x	x
Amun-Ra and Mut	x	x	
Amun-nakht and Hathor	x?	x	x
Tutu, Neith and Tapsais		x	

The comparative lack of attestations of these gods at Ain Birbiya is mainly the result of our incomplete knowledge of this temple which is still largely buried. The gods of Ain Birbiya - Amun-nakht and Hathor - were represented in the sanctuary at Deir el-Haggar. The question mark with the corresponding entry reflects the fact that the identification of the gods is based solely upon their iconography, the legends having disappeared. Bull (in Winlock 1936, 73) identified the falcon-headed god in question as Mont, but the presence of Hathor in the same scene identifies him as Amun-nakht. The identity of Hathor is certain on the basis of her crown which is well attested at Ain Birbiya; it is composed of two tall feathers and a solar disc set within cow's horns.

The gods of Kellis are missing from the decoration in the other oasis temples. They were perhaps not considered important enough to be depicted within the Deir el-Haggar sanctuary, but it seems more likely that the cult at Kellis simply dated from a later period than the execution of the temple reliefs at Deir el-Haggar. It is noteworthy in this respect that the only relief in the latter temple which contains a depiction of Tutu - the astronomical ceiling from the sanctuary - can be dated to the second century AD (Kaper 1995a).

The deities Amun-Ra and Mut of Hibis as well as Ptah and Sekhmet appear to have been less important in Dakhla than the other gods mentioned here. This is suggested by the fact that even though Amenebis and Ptah were included within the doorway decoration at Ain Birbiya and Deir el-Haggar, they do not occur in the painted shrine at Kellis, nor on the side walls of the Deir el-Haggar sanctuary. The explanation for this distinction may lie in the location of the temples of these gods in the Kharga oasis instead of in Dakhla itself. Amun of Hibis (Amenebis) obviously originated in Kharga, while Ptah and Sekhmet are frequently found depicted on the temple walls in Hibis (cf. Cruz-Uribe 1988, 258-9 sub "Ptah", "Sekhmet"). From their less prominent position in Dakhla temple decoration, I conclude that Ptah and Sekhmet may have been venerated in a temple in Kharga. The frequent and close contacts between the two oases probably caused both Ptah and Amenebis with their consorts to be depicted in the Dakhla temples.

Geographical inventories of gods

Shrine I at Kellis can thus be shown to contain an inventory of the main gods of the Dakhla oasis. The same analysis may be applied to the sanctuary walls at Deir el-Haggar. The pronaos wall of the latter temple and the outer gate at Ain Birbiya are also comparable, even though these include the gods Amenebis and Ptah who were probably adopted from the temples in the Kharga oasis. We may add to this list the outer temenos gate at Deir el-Haggar and the sanctuary walls at Ain Birbiya which resemble the other inventories in many ways, even though their state of preservation is much inferior.

The major theme of temple decoration in the Dakhla oasis as a whole seems to have been an inventory of the local deities. This theme is contained in a cluster of temple scenes (a "Dekorationseinheit": Kurth 1994, 211) which can be compared with the inventories of gods contained in some temples outside the region, such as the decoration of the pronaos at Edfu and of the main sanctuary of the Hibis temple in Kharga. However, when compared to the extensive lists contained in the latter temples, the Dakhla temple decoration seems remarkably self-centred. The origin of Amun-Ra from Karnak is remembered in Deir el-Haggar, and the occasional images of Amenebis and even the gods of Dush (Kharga) are encountered in Shrine I at Kellis, but in general no temples from the Nile Valley are referred to in Dakhla temple decoration.

For parallels to such a provincial type of temple decoration, we may cite the New Kingdom temples in Nubia which are similarly self-centred. For these temples, Rolf Gundlach has introduced the term 'Kultlandschaft' to denote an area in which the temples of a specific area are strongly interrelated (Gundlach 1994, 70-1). The basis for his concept is the area which includes the temples at Ellesiya, Aniba and Qasr Ibrim, but the same concept may be applied, for instance, to the area around Coptos, for which see the contributions of Jan Quaegebeur and Claude Traunecker to this volume, and also to the totality of the Theban temples. The Theban temples were linked in a theological sense through relationships between their gods and by festival processions. The Festival of the Valley and the Opet festival are eloquent demonstrations of the latter.

That Theban temples were the model for the decoration of the temples in the Dakhla oasis is clear from the decoration upon the doorways in the temples (Kaper 1995d). Perhaps the emphasis on local gods in Dakhla temple decoration was likewise derived from a hypothetical festival in Dakhla in which all the gods of the region participated. An example of such a festival may also be found in the inscriptions at Esna. In the beginning of the month of Khoiak, all gods of the region of Esna, an area equalling roughly the size of Dakhla, were brought together in the town of Esna with the aim of regenerating the vegetation in the region (Sauneron 1962, 47-67). For the Dakhla oasis, we may perhaps reconstruct a comparable festival with visits by the statues of the gods to the various temples. This would then explain the repeated occurrences of the same gods on the gates and sanctuary walls of the temples throughout the oasis.

However, there may be another explanation for this phenomenon, one which I consider to be the more likely. When we compare the Dakhla temples to those in the Nile Valley and the Fayum, we find that the larger temples in the Valley, such as those of Dendera and Edfu, contain references to all cults throughout the Egyptian Nile Valley and the Delta. These temples are, in one sense, images of Egypt, and their respective gods are related in various ways to all other gods of the temples in the Nile Valley and Delta. The Fayum temples seem to be different again. Philippe Derchain has recently interpreted the Book of the Fayum, which dates from the Roman Period, as a manual of temple decoration (Derchain 1994, 42-50). The text refers exclusively to the cults of the Fayum and it describes a particular temple in this region as an image of the entire Fayum. According to Derchain, this description is confirmed by the reliefs in the destroyed pronaos of the temple at Tebtynis. By depicting the regional gods within the individual temples, the local gods were embedded within the theology of the region as a whole.

The latter situation may be compared to the Dakhla temples. The Dakhla oasis may be considered as a fundamentally self-contained region on a par with the Egyptian Nile Valley and the Fayum. Occasional references to the gods of Kharga and the Nile Valley in its temple decoration acknowledge the existence of the other regions, but these do not play an important role in the theology of the oasis. The role of Kharga seems to have been of more importance than that of the Nile Valley. By depicting the main gods of the Dakhla oasis upon the temple walls, the individual gods of the temples were shown in relation to the gods of the entire oasis region.

Conclusions

As a consequence of this interpretation of the Dakhla temples, the local cult topography ("Kulttopographie") of the oasis has emerged in considerable detail. The principal deities in Roman Dakhla appear to have been partly of local origin, such as Amun-nakht and Tapsais. On the other hand, the veneration in the oasis of Tutu proves the interaction of local beliefs with those of the Nile Valley, where Tutu had likewise become a popular god during the Roman period. The cults of Seth, Amun-Ra and Thoth follow a pattern which applies to the large oases of the Western Desert in general. In Bahriya and partly also in Siwa, these same gods held important positions in local religious beliefs (Giddy 1987, 102 n.52; Kuhlmann 1988, 50 ff.). The most surprising new information which the present study has yielded is the important position of the gods of Heliopolis and Memphis in the southern oasis. Even though the particular temples in which the cults of these gods were centred have not yet been located within the oasis, it is tempting to draw some historical conclusions from this information. The gods involved were of special importance in Egypt during the Ramesside period, and I would propose as a working hypothesis for future study that the cults of these gods were established in the southern oasis during this period. Contacts between the oases and the temple of Amun-Ra at Thebes can be traced back further to the Eighteenth Dynasty (Giddy 1987, 71-4, 154-5, Table VII), which may explain the primacy of the cult of Amun-Ra in the oases of the Western Desert.

It would be wrong to create the impression that local cults are all that is represented upon the Dakhla temple walls. For instance, only two registers in the decoration of the painted shrine at Kellis have been discussed here, while the remaining registers are filled with all the riches of Graeco-Roman temple decoration. The iconography of Shrine I compares favourably with the decorative schemes of the larger temples in the Nile Valley, and its further study promises to yield much new information during the years to come.

Acknowledgement
My debt to the Catholic University of Leuven for a scholarship during 1993 is gratefully acknowledged. Mr Nicholas Warner corrected my English.

Bibliography

Arnold, D 1992. *Die Tempel Ägyptens: Götterwohnungen, Kultstätten, Baudenkmäler.* Zurich, Artemis & Winkler.

Bowman, A 1986. *Egypt after the Pharaohs: 332 BC-AD 642 from Alexander to the Arab conquest.* London, British Museum Publications.

Cauville, S 1988. Les mystères d'Osiris à Dendera: Interprétation des chapelles osiriennes. In *Bulletin de la Société Française d'Egyptologie* 112, 23-36.

Cruz-Uribe, E 1988. *Hibis Temple Project: Translations, Commentary, Discussions and Sign List.* I. San Antonio, Texas, Van Siclen Books.

Derchain, P 1994. Review of H.Beinlich, *Das Buch vom Fayum.* In *Bibliotheca Orientalis* 51, 42-50.

Fakhry, A 1982. J Osing et al., *Denkmäler der Oase Dachla: aus dem Nachlass von Ahmed Fakhry.* Deutsches Archäologisches Institut Abteilung Kairo, Archäologische Veröffentlichungen 28. Mainz am Rhein, Philipp von Zabern.

Gardiner, A 1933. The Dakhleh Stela. In *Journal of Egyptian Archaeology* 19, 19-30.

Giddy, L L 1987. *Egyptian Oases: Bahariya, Dakhla, Farafra and Kharga during Pharaonic times.* Warminster, Aris & Phillips.

Gundlach, R 1994. Der Felstempel Thutmosis' III. bei Ellesija: Analyse des Dekorationsprogramms. In R Gundlach and M Rochholz (eds.), *Ägyptische Tempel - Struktur, Funktion und Programm (Akten der Ägyptologischen Tempeltagungen in Gosen 1990 und in Mainz 1992).* Hildesheimer Ägyptologische Beiträge 37, Gerstenberg Verlag, 69-87.

Hölbl, G 1989. Wer ist König in der Endphase der Ägyptischen Religion ? In S Schoske (ed.), *Akten des Vierten Internationalen Ägyptologenkongresses München 1985* 3, Hamburg, Helmut Buske Verlag, 261-68.

Hope, C 1995. Observations on the dating of the occupation at Ismant el-Kharab. In M Marlow (ed.), *Proceedings of the First International Symposium on the Dakhleh Oasis Durham 1994.* Oxford, Oxbow (forthcoming).

Jacquet-Gordon, H 1991. A Statue from Dakhla Oasis. In *Mitteilungen des Deutschen Archäologischen Instituts Abteilung Kairo* 47, 173-78.

Janssen, J J 1968. The smaller Dakhleh stela. In *Journal of Egyptian Archaeology* 54, 165-72.
Jaritz, H 1980. *Die Terrassen vor den Tempeln des Chnum und der Satet: Architektur und Deutung.* Deutsches Archäologisches Institut Abteilung Kairo, Archäologische Veröffentlichungen 32. Mainz am Rhein, Philipp von Zabern.
Kaper, O 1992. Egyptian toponyms of Dakhla Oasis. In *Bulletin de l'Institut Français d'Archéologie Orientale* 92, 117-32.
Kaper, O 1995a. The astronomical ceiling of Deir el-Haggar in the Dakhleh Oasis. In *Journal of Egyptian Archaeology* 81, forthcoming.
Kaper, O 1995b. Local perceptions of the fertility of the Dakhleh Oasis in the Roman Period. In M Marlow (ed.), *Acts of the 1994 Dakhleh Oasis Project conference.* Oxford, forthcoming.
Kaper, O 1995c. A votive statue from the Twenty-first Dynasty at Deir el-Haggar. In M Marlow (ed.), *Acts of the 1994 Dakhleh Oasis Project conference.* Oxford, forthcoming.
Kaper, O 1995d. Doorway decoration patterns in the Dakhleh Oasis. In D Kurth et al. (eds.), *Akten der Dritten Tempeltagung, Hamburg 1994.* Hamburg, Helmut Buske Verlag, forthcoming.
Kurth, D 1994. Die Reise der Hathor von Dendera nach Edfu. In R Gundlach and M Rochholz (eds.), *Ägyptische Tempel - Struktur, Funktion und Programm (Akten der Ägyptologischen Tempeltagungen in Gosen 1990 und in Mainz 1992).* Hildesheimer Ägyptologische Beiträge 37, Gerstenberg Verlag, 211-16.
Mills, A J 1981. The Dakhleh Oasis Project: report on the third season of survey, September - December 1980. In *Journal of the Society for the Study of Egyptian Antiquities* 11, 175-92.
Mills, A J 1983. The Dakhleh Oasis Project: report on the fifth season of survey, October 1982 - January 1983. In *Journal of the Society for the Study of Egyptian Antiquities* 13, 121-41.
Mills, A J 1985. The Dakhleh Oasis Project: a preliminary report on the field work of the 1985/1986 season. In *Journal of the Society for the Study of Egyptian Antiquities* 15, 105-13.
Mills, A J 1986. The Dakhleh Oasis Project: report on the 1986-1987 field season. In *Journal of the Society for the Study of Egyptian Antiquities* 16, 65-73.
Mills, A J 1990. The Dakhleh Oasis Project: report on the 1990-1991 field season. In *Journal of the Society for the Study of Egyptian Antiquities* 20, 11-16.
Naumann, R 1938. Bauwerke der Oase Khargeh. In *Mitteilungen des Deutschen Archäologischen Instituts Abteilung Kairo* 8, 1-16.
Osing, J 1985. Seth in Dachla und Charga. In *Mitteilungen des Deutschen Archäologischen Instituts Abteilung Kairo* 41, 229-33.
Osing, J 1986. Zu den Osiris-Räumen im Tempel von Hibis. In *Hommages à François Daumas* 2, Publication de la Recherche - Université de Montpellier, 511-16.
Raven, M 1982. Corn-mummies. In *Oudheidkundige Mededelingen uit het Rijksmuseum van Oudheden te Leiden* 63, 7-38.
Sauneron, S 1962. *Les fêtes religieuses d'Esna aux derniers siècles du paganisme.* Esna V. Cairo, Institut Français d'Archéologie Orientale.
Traunecker, C 1980. Chapelle Adossée. In *Cahiers de Karnak* VI (1973-1977), Cairo, Institut Français d'Archéologie Orientale, 167-96, pl.47-51.
Winlock, H 1936. *Ed Dakhleh Oasis: Journal of a Camel Trip Made in 1908.* New York, The Metropolitan Museum of Art.

Temples as symbols, guarantors, and participants in Egyptian civilization

John Baines

1 Context and terms of argument

The conventional scholarly and popular image of ancient Egyptian temples is as institutions that increasingly dominated their civilization, until in Roman times they and their institutional underpinnings remained as almost the sole carriers of its high culture. That vision is in keeping with the massive evidence from all times except the very latest (Frankfurter, in press), but it leaves questions open about the position of temples in earlier times. For the third millennium in particular, scholars tend to see kingship as the dominant institution in society. While the king's importance cannot be doubted, it is worth reviewing some aspects of that perception and asking how the institution of the divine cult temple was defined and how it endured. Naturally, even if there was tension between temple and king - church and state in older parlance - they need not be seen as fundamentally in opposition; rather, the relationship of the two should be explored and evaluated. Both kingship and temple were brought to life, sustained, and celebrated in the central high-cultural products of Egyptian civilization.

This essay studies aspects of the relationship between these three elements of temple, kingship, and the media through which both were projected, and rehearses some quite familiar topics. It is impossible to cover such a subject for Egypt as a whole. I focus upon the earliest and latest periods, taking an approach that is at one extreme among possible ones and exploring the preconditions, functions, and implications of temples as works of art - one aspect, if a vital one, among many. I attempt to draw out aspects that may have cross-cultural relevance.

Egyptian temples were functioning dwellings for deities, in addition to their religious status for their local communities, and their design and decoration reflect this fact. But at higher levels deities responded to more than just the provision of their material needs. As the supreme elements in the cosmos, their honour was worthy of the civilization's finest achievements. Those achievements, moreover, were not simply dedicated to them but also defined and expressed relationships between humanity and the divine world through humanity's protagonist, the king, as well as incorporating and celebrating the structure of the cosmos in themselves. The normative definition offered by temples and by the objects dedicated in them continued for millennia to be developed, refined, and extended.

That definition, which was central to religion and ultimately to Egyptian civilization, was formulated in terms we may extraneously characterize as artistic - extraneously insofar as the Egyptians did not have a verbally distinct category of 'art' (Baines 1994a). As a phenomenon, art seldom has a single function and should be seen rather as a way in which a culture or a civilization realizes and expresses itself. Temples and most offerings are works of art. Together with the linguistic and other performances occurring in them, temples were the core - but by no means the only - locus for architectural, visual, verbal and performance arts. The concentration of artistic endeavour around this centre is symptomatic of art's general significance. The hierarchy of meanings informing art in most, perhaps all, other domains was articulated in relation to the temple. The implications of these points mostly relate more strongly to the major state temples than - so far as we can tell - to the plethora of smaller foundations which existed throughout Egypt. This pattern is symptomatic of the inequality and centripetal focus of the civilization.

To approach temples from the perspective of their status as works of art is not entirely in keeping with tendencies in scholarship that have emphasized their practical significance on the one hand, and the almost unexamined or naive character that is often attributed to Egyptian monumental production on the other. How far is it correct to apply general art-historical or literary modes of analysis to the products of a civilization that may differ markedly from that of the West? This question has been complicated by the modern bias toward 'art for art's sake' and to the expectation that artistic development should signify values of change and individuality. In many respects, Egyptian art in general, and temples in particular, might seem to resist such a classification. Can one really say that the aesthetic is so vital for the meaning of temples? May the tendency to view things in this way not itself be ethnocentric and patronizing? Quite another point is whether one can validly focus on the artistic side and attend relatively little to the role of temples in peoples' religious lives; this will not be pursued here.

As an extreme illustration of how this artistic approach can nonetheless be more generally revealing, it may be worth considering the headings of the three sections in Wallace Stevens' crowning poem *Notes Toward a Supreme Fiction* (in Stevens 1953): 'It Must Be Abstract'; 'It Must Change'; 'It Must Give Pleasure'. While it may be acknowledged that temples are a 'supreme fiction' - an ultimate figurative or representational creation - as well as a supreme reality of Egyptian civilization, those proclaimed criteria might otherwise appear excessively remote from Egypt. Yet they can throw important features into relief, if a fourth criterion is added to them from a comparable source: to cite T. S. Eliot's *The Waste Land* (1922, Part 5, line 340), temples are 'fragments' that a civilization 'shores against [its] ruin'.

1.1 *It must be abstract*

It is not enough for the temple to have a crucial position in the culture. Ultimately, key features that characterize a culture or civilization, setting it apart from others and from what are not civilizations, can often be reduced to a relatively small number of often quite schematic elements. Egyptian civilization is strongly characterized, for example, by the general absence of a core narrative focus for its principal ideas. Instead of narrative, written compositions evince tabular presentation, fixed relations between such elements as deities - or relations that vary according to fixed schemas - and a love of lists (not so marked as in Mesopotamia). Outside texts, a limited range of architectural and artistic schemas is applicable in many contexts. Obvious examples in representational art are principles of register composition, of the rendering of the human form, and of the commensurability and incommensurability of different categories of material - that is, principles of decorum (Baines 1985, 277-305; 1990a; Podemann Sørensen 1989). In temple architecture, there is both a restricted repertory of building types - for example excluding the structural rather than decorative or symbolic application of the arch and vault - and a fundamental pattern of rising levels and reducing ground plans, as well as a small number of basic elements of vocabulary such as the torus moulding and cavetto cornice. Schemas for ground plans, and to a lesser extent elevations, occur across a wide range of contexts.

This primacy of schemas and patterns is an analogy for 'abstraction', even in a highly representational culture. Since any conventional cult temple exhibits most of the same schemas, these partake in the centripetal focus of Egyptian civilization, while also disseminating them down to all levels. The great disparity in size and significance between major and minor temples also embodies the high level of Egyptian inequality. The strong impress of the schemas on a potentially very diverse religion is markedly different from the variability and tendencies toward 'realism' of Western art. Schemas and patterns are essential symbols of Egyptian civilization.

1.2 *It must change*

Since more than one writer has championed the notion that Egyptian art - and thus monumental culture in general - was devised in the cause of 'invariance' (e.g. Davis 1989, 96-7; Assmann 1991a, 32–3), any insistence upon the centrality of change for temples might seem perverse. But a comparison of the third millennium temple of Satet at Elephantine (Dreyer 1986, pls. 1-4) with that of the second millennium (e.g. Kaiser et al. 1982, pls. 74-5), and still more with a major late temple such as that of Edfu (e.g. Cauville 1984), amply illustrates that change was of the essence in Egyptian culture as in others and that there was a progressive increase in the scale of major temple monuments. The temporal dimension is therefore vital, even if the pace of change was slower than it has been in more recent and more frenetic civilizations. Central cultural institutions existed in constant dialogue with the past (Baines 1989; Assmann 1992). The past they created was perhaps largely fictitious, but that did not make it any less important as a point of reference, and its fictitious character is probably shared by uses of the past in most cultures (e.g. Lowenthal 1985). Periods within a civilization define themselves by relating to a relatively distant past or by shorter-term continuity. The former strategy clothes radicalism in a conservative guise, while the latter tends to clothe conservatism in a rather more radical, in the sense of constantly but subtly changing, guise.

In processes of change, temples - here along with many other cultural manifestations - are essential participants in civilization; they became more central as other institutions withered in the first millennium BCE and later. If the dynamic and continuing developments of the Graeco-Roman Period are considered, and even if some forms crystallized rather early (see especially Winter 1968), the significance of change can be seen not to have ceased until near the end of the civilization, and in some senses perhaps not even then (see Frankfurter, in press; Fowden 1986, 13-31). What is clear for all periods is that change was not progressive but rather followed varying patterns and divided into major phases.

1.3 *It must give pleasure*

As in Stevens's poem, the most important principle for the present argument comes last. Central symbols of Egyptian civilization may have a schematic basis, but they are not bland or dour realizations. Rather, by their existence they enhance reality, enacting, celebrating, and enriching an ideal order; in this perspective one might say that Stevens's 'pleasure' puts the matter rather weakly, because so much is at stake. Symbols and enactments are 'performative' (e.g. Derchain 1989). In keeping with this celebratory character is the enormous expenditure of resources on these symbols, not to speak of the existence in the Egyptian language of at least thirty-seven that can be rendered 'to rejoice', the majority of them attested mainly from temples (list, no doubt partial: Erman and Grapow 1950, 55). In the broadest sense, aesthetic means are a primary medium for affirming the wholeness of civilization, of privileging its most important elements, and of binding deities, the dead, kings and people together. In the enactments and celebrations of ritual and festival, the aesthetic reaches out through performance beyond the temple, subsequently returning within the sacred enclosure without which the performance would not have meaning. These celebrations are perhaps the principal means by which the elite, centripetal religion of the temple speaks to the wider population (although caution is necessary there). The aesthetic celebrates the world of the divine and addresses deities in a fit manner, as well as demonstrating to people - so far as they can be aware of its presence - that that world is incomparably significant and splendid.

This principle must be taken together with the next one.

1.4 *Fragments shored against ruin*

Temples are visions of an ideal wholeness and perfection. Even if a supreme fiction may persuade the beholder otherwise - we cannot know how far they succeeded in doing so in Egypt - the world itself is not like that. Temples offer a foil to the world's imperfections, as well as a model toward which people can aspire and in which they can see some bulwark against the uncertainties and reversals of life - even though few have access to the world within the temple. The country outside the temple is a cosmos, but it is not so well demarcated and idealized as the figurative one of the temple. The temple reaches out from itself into the surrounding community both through the extension of its cosmic significance to cities (O'Connor in preparation) and through festivals and other integrative activities, but it more strongly demarcates itself and remains within its own limits. In a complex society such as Egypt, those who are principally affected by its model are the elite who appropriate the responsibility of realizing and enacting the temple's significance and protecting it against disorder, but that does not detract from its salience.

The most characteristic aspects the Egyptian temple presents to the world are exclusion and protection. The larger-scale but more imperfect order of the outside world both threatens and depends upon the greater but microcosmic order of the temple. In response, the temple presents on its outside a muted form of celebration that tends to emphasize the aggressive and protective. To the world, temples bespeak the fragility of order, whose endurance must be celebrated precisely because it is threatened. For so long as they are maintained, they are guarantors - in late times the self-proclaimed only ones - of civilization and order. That corollary of the fundamentally pessimistic and unstable Egyptian vision of the cosmos is a major reason for the importance of temples.

The fragility of the cosmos is also a fragility of civilization. In many periods, high-cultural artifacts cluster around temples, exhibiting a maximum of order and of aesthetic ideals. The fragility of civilizational traditions is exemplified most strongly in incompetent products such as some of the First Intermediate Period (e.g. Leclant and Clerc 1993, pl. 42 fig. 49, Balat); later there is a general tendency for works in temples - including the statuary dedicated there - to be of a higher evident standard of attainment than those in other areas (some scholars dispute this for the temples themselves; see also p. 1 here). The central traditions would imply that if the crudest forms of the First Intermediate Period had prevailed, Egyptian civilization and the Egyptian cosmos would not have survived - which could indeed have been so. The forms themselves, as well as the excellence with which they were realized, maintained the cosmos against encroaching disorder.

The points just evoked in relation to categories derived from poetry can be documented explicitly in Egyptian texts. Instead of doing that, however, I turn to the archaeological record for early times (2) and then, after an excursus on traditions and developments in intervening periods (3), to late temple decoration and inscription (4-5).

2 Temples and the formative period

The argument so far needs to be related to specific evidence and context, and the claimed cultural centrality of temples should be examined in relation to their general archaeological insignificance for the first half of dynastic history. The core group of monuments from the end of the predynastic period offers a point of departure. A model should be constructed for the aesthetic and monumental context within which that group emerged. It is most prudent to assume that gods and places in which they were worshipped formed part of the cosmos and society of predynastic Egyptians, and hence that developments toward forms known from dynastic times built upon conceptions that were already ancient (contrary to some arguments, e.g. Morenz 1960, 16-9).

2.1 *Early decoration: the temple context and representational art*

2.1.1 *The scale of temples*

The earliest preserved extensive decoration from Egypt is the wall painting in Tomb 100 at Hierakonpolis, dating roughly to Naqada IIc (Quibell and Green 1902, pls. 75-9). This contains in essence many of the conventions of developed Egyptian art, but in a different style and in mediocre execution. Such decoration implies the existence of comparable motifs and schemas in lost contexts from which traditions developed and in which compositions were realized to a higher aesthetic standard. Those contexts would be both stylistic–thematic, to be envisaged in terms of a growing thematic repertoire, and monumental, either supports on which pictorial material was executed or three-dimensional forms of representation. One should therefore model the artistic context as including decorated architectural environments and prestige materials such as ivory, as well as developments in statuary that might exist alongside, or in precedence to, relief and painting.

These hypothetical contexts originated long before there were large states. Writing, the essential element that completes the decorative and meaningful complex, can be seen in the next major preserved group of material. Writing's crucial role, and that of cultural symbols recorded in it, can be seen from finds in the royal Tomb U-j at Abydos, from Naqada IIIa2, significantly later than Tomb 100. The signs on small ivory tags from this tomb include two symbols of royalty, the throne and the *srḫ* 'palace facade/enclosure', as well as, significantly, the *pr-wr* or later regional shrine of Upper Egypt (Dreyer et al. 1993, pl. 7h-k). These signs imply a range of further contexts while contrasting with the less formal use of 'writing' on pottery, where one or two large signs were applied (Dreyer et al. 1993, pl. 8). This lack of systematic unity in writing styles and in the use of motifs suggests that

Tomb U-j should be placed earlier than the final development of the integrated system of representation visible on the palettes; the earlier difference between tag and pottery is not comparable with the slightly later distinction between hieroglyphic and cursive writing styles.

Temples can provide a broader context for these developments. Temple structures on a significant scale probably existed for at least a couple of centuries before the First Dynasty. They are implied by the *pr-wr* which, although always strongly associated with kingship, was a divine and not simply a royal building. Its form as a 'hieroglyph' in Tomb U-j, which is essentially the same as in later sources, is significant in being envisaged as made of perishable materials, unlike the *srḫ*, which is shown with the rectilinearity of brick. This distinction probably relates to the use of enclosures - for the palace in the case of the *srḫ* - and to the special role of the *pr-wr*, which was not a principal cult temple. This dichotomy of curved and perishable as against rectilinear and durable found its fullest and most paradoxical expression centuries later in the Step Pyramid complex at Saqqara.

More impressive evidence for the scale of cult temples is given by the three colossal statues of Min from Koptos, which are probably earlier than Tomb U-j, and may be the world's oldest known colossal statuary (Payne 1993, 13 nos. 1-4; dating: Dreyer 1995, with photographs). The wear on these pieces, which were about four metres high when complete, almost certainly derives from the attention of 'pilgrims' who wished to take away some of their hallowed substance, and demonstrates their long-lasting importance, but it may not help us to model their original setting, because it looks as if it took place when they were lying flat after their original use had ceased. Nonetheless, one may assume that they were in an outer area of the temple if, as in later times, worshippers did not have access to the sanctuary. The temple could have been constructed of mud brick or more perishable substances, with the colossal statues possibly forming its largest single element—as later in Egypt and in many other places, the outside is likely to have been on a larger scale than the buildings within (schematic reconstructions: Williams 1988, 50-1). On such an assumption, the temple would not have been very large, but it should not have been too insignificant in appearance if it was to avoid being swamped by the statues. The survival of three statues may suggest that the temple had more than one entrance, successive entrances along the same axis, or was flanked by two pairs of statues.

Koptos was an important place in a region of dense settlement, but it was never a very major centre. Accessible locations for such a structure have not been found at other sites, except perhaps at Hierakonpolis, so there is no need to seek special explanations for the prominence of Koptos in the record or to posit an exceptional status for the statues. Colossal representation could, however, have been particularly appropriate for Min, by analogy with the later exceptional public character of his iconography, as shown, for example, in his festival reliefs at Medinet Habu (Epigraphic Survey 1940, pls. 196-208. esp. 201-2) and by his image in Sety I's Hall of Barks at Abydos, where no other divine images are depicted (unpublished). In relation to temples, however, there is no evident reason why Min should have had a status that would require a larger structure than other deities. In addition to this evidence from Koptos, Hierakonpolis has produced significant material in the deposit deriving from the destroyed early temple (Adams 1974a, xii-xv; 1974b, 1-2; Dreyer 1986, 37-46), as well as in another early shrine found by the Hoffman expedition in the 1980s (R Friedman 1996), which Bruce Williams (1988, 47-50 with fig. 7) has related to the probable depiction of a shrine on the Narmer Macehead; David O'Connor (1992, 84-9) proposes a third temple, of the First Dynasty. Another site with an early, in this case modest temple is Elephantine (Dreyer 1986). Thus, whether or not other gods had colossal statues outside their cult places, significant temples or temple complexes could have been widespread in late predynastic times.

Various strands of evidence suggest that the furnishings of temples were at least as valuable as the structures themselves. This material includes rich finds at such sites as Hierakonpolis, the much later year names of the Palermo Stone; paradoxically, the absence of any cult images in precious and composite materials points in the same direction, because these can be confidently assumed to have existed. This does not, however, mean that the buildings were without ideological and artistic significance. They housed and interacted with the objects dedicated in them, while over the very long timespans of the Dynastic Period they seem to have become culturally at least as salient as those objects. In default of excavated evidence, one can do little more than posit early temples as a context, but the scale of an enclosure approached past the Min colossi would exceed any other building complex known for its period, although the unknown palaces of rulers could have been larger still. Such palaces are indirectly attested in Tomb U-j both by the tomb's architectural form and by the occurrence of the palace facade among hieroglyphs (Dreyer et al. 1993, pl. 7j). The factor of scale gives temples considerable importance as one of the great near-unknowns of early Egypt. It is no coincidence that they share this status with palaces and urban sites of any consequence. All will have been located primarily near the river, in places from which it is extremely difficult to recover evidence.

2.1.2 *Major representational works dedicated in temple complexes*

Probably rather later than the Min statues comes the sequence of relief-decorated palettes and maceheads ending with the Narmer Palette (cf. Baines 1995, 109-21; images: Asselberghs 1961; further references below). These in turn use motifs and compositional elements known as far back as Tomb 100, but gradually transform them into an integrated system. The palettes and maceheads for which an archaeological context is known were probably dedicated during Dynasty 0 in the principal temple at Hierakonpolis (conveniently: Dreyer 1986, 37-46).

From the Hunters' Palette and the Two Dog Palette to the Narmer Palette and Macehead, the relief-decorated works document the rapid evolution of essential compositional, representational and iconographic conventions. I suggest that they are best interpreted as also embodying developing conventions of decorum, and hence as relating to the largely unrepresented divine world. These categories of object disappear with the beginning of the First Dynasty, not to be replaced, and conventions that complement those of their decoration cannot be observed for a couple of centuries.

Deities are not themselves shown on the palettes and maceheads. The earliest preserved two-dimensional figures of deities in the forms familiar from later times date to the first two dynasties; some are essentially enlarged hieroglyphs rather than full representations (cf. Hornung 1982, 105-9 with fig. 10; Engelbach 1934). The distinctive feature of the indications of the divine world which can be read off the palettes is that they are either in marginal areas of the decoration or in an emblematic form that implies an underlying system whose centre would be in temple relief. Thus, the reliefs are most economically interpreted in relation to other, lost figurative material, to writing, and to the overall context of temples. Of these, the temple context is the most significant because it defines and circumscribes the rest, just as architecture generally supplies the overarching meaning for works of art. The pattern of what is preserved is full of gaps, but temples should be seen as its centre if it is to have coherent meaning.

It follows that the highest forms of representational art with the most portentous content were concentrated in temples. There will have been a progressive restriction from the rather more widespread use of pictorial representation on Decorated Ware pottery of Naqada II (cf. Finkenstaedt 1985) to its near-disappearance around the beginning of the First Dynasty, when it had been appropriated for divine, royal, and inner elite purposes. Representational art continued to be created, but mostly, it seems, in lost contexts - I suggest principally temples - and to have expanded very gradually from there. Much of it was on small mobile objects.

This significance of temples is indicated in inscriptions of the Early Dynastic Period, which include schematic representations of them (Baines 1991) as well as many mentions on the Palermo Stone (Schäfer 1902) and in much later texts that may preserve genuine information about quite early times (list of gods at Abydos: Baines 1988). All the evidence reviewed above suggests that temples were at least comparably important during Dynasty 0, and thus that they were central to the original phase of definition of Egyptian high culture and civilization.

2.1.3 *Conventions of the works and implications for later times*

The developing conventions of the palettes and maceheads are a mixture of the representational, the compositional and the iconographic. They provided the framework for most later developments, even if later style and content were radically different from what is known from the beginning or can be posited for then. The conventions are not the same thing as a style. Although the objects' style is distinctively 'Egyptian', it is far from the 'classical' style of the end of the Early Dynastic Period and the Old Kingdom.

The conventions govern: the representation of the human figure, as well as perhaps its proportions; the use of registers and base lines; relationships of scale; the combination and varying compatibility of different categories of material, such as full and emblematic representations or human and royal figures, in single scenes or larger compositions; the integration of pictorial, emblematic, and written forms; and much else besides. These conventions are largely inchoate or only implied on the Hunters' Palette and the Two Dog Palette (cf. Baines 1993), whereas all of them, as well as something of a repertory of themes that survived into later times, can be seen in operation on the Cities Palette, the Scorpion Macehead, and the Narmer Palette and Macehead.

The main registers of these reliefs show a variety of rituals, from the slaughter of enemies and inspection of a battlefield on the Narmer Palette to an apparently agricultural ceremony and a celebration involving women carried on litters on the Scorpion Macehead (cf. Gauthier and Midant-Reynes 1995). The top of the Narmer Palette probably signifies the sky, while the spreadeagled bodies of enemies below the bottom register line relate to the disordered realm. In between is the world that is ordered by royal action, made possible by and dedicated to the gods. This quasi-real world with human actors is one of two possible worlds; the other is the abstract world of temple relief, known from the Early Dynastic Period on, in which the gods and the king can interact directly. On the palettes, the world of outside action is brought into the temple and dedicated to the gods, but if it were depicted on an immovable surface, that would be an exterior, like the later smiting reliefs on the rocks of Maghara in Sinai (Gardiner *et al.* 1952, pls. 1-8) and smiting scenes in temples (not attested on exterior wall surfaces for the Old Kingdom).

In the palette reliefs, deities, among whom the most salient are the falcons presenting captive regions of the country to the king on the Narmer Palette and giving his catfish life on a contemporaneous ivory cylinder (Baines 1995, 151 fig. 3.6), are not shown as active integrated beings, but are rendered emblematic by scale, by zoomorphic representation, or by the addition of human limbs (Baines 1985, 41-63, 277-305). This treatment is appropriate to depictions on objects that have the marginal status because they are movable and could therefore be situated in contexts where deities would not be shown. Moreover, for a millennium deities were absent from scenes where human beings other than the king were present. In contrast, full representations of deities on fixed surfaces show direct interaction between king and god, including embracing and suckling. Such forms very often signify something different from what they superficially depict - for example, embraces often substitute in confined spaces for other forms of interaction - but their plain and unqualified character marks their centrality: the world they present is abstract and is the supreme analogy for royal-divine relations.

At least in some periods, the system of decorum probably included further terms within the religious sphere that were constituted on the one hand by cult images of deities and ceremonial forms of enactment of the cult, and on the other hand by images of the next world as embodied much later in the underworld books. Most evidence for the appearance of cult images dates from the Late and Graeco-Roman periods (see section 1 here) and suggests that they were far more bizarre and various in form than the sober schemas of temple relief. Neither of these areas, however, relates so directly to the alternations of full and emblematic, interior and marginal/exterior as does the typological pair of interior temple offering scene and exterior scene of royal victory or ritual. I therefore retain the assumption that the core of the system was temple relief.

Thus, the conventions seen on the palettes point to the crucial absent participants, the deities, whom they evoke as intervening in human - principally royal - affairs and as circumscribing and sustaining the cosmos. With the First Dynasty, this arena of divine, royal, and human interaction largely disappears from the preserved record. This invisibility could be a matter of chance, but it seems unlikely that objects such as the palettes and maceheads continued to be made. Erich Winter (1994) has proposed an interpretation, which more successfully integrates the evidence than almost any other suggestion, that palettes ceased to be made because the role of cosmetics from which they ultimately derived ceased to have the same fundamental importance as previously; this would place their ritual associations at the core of their significance. Two further possible explanations - from silence - for their disappearance are that as large-scale architecture and relief developed the focus of decoration shifted to walls, and that royal votive objects were generally in precious materials that were later removed or recycled. Indirect evidence for the latter possibility may be provided by the calcite baboon of Narmer (Priese *et al.* 1991, no. 8; Krauss 1994). The more modest limestone votive figure of the goddess Repút in a public form on a carrying chair, perhaps of the First Dynasty, implies a distinction between exterior and interior and thus fits with the system of decorum (Müller 1964, no. A31).

Two implications of the early objects should be discussed here. First, they represent worlds - they are explicitly cosmological - and yet were deposited in a location where the most restricted cosmology and representation of the world were current. They are thus rarefied tokens of the variety and imperfection of life in the world outside that were probably brought into the still more rarefied temple sanctuary. This distinction between the most sacred and restricted and the rather more general and mobile brings out the progressive refinement of an imperfect world within the perfected context of the temple. It is not appropriate to see early Egypt in general as a kind of pristine world that was witness to a later fall from grace, as has too often been done. Rather, the pristine world could be created or recreated inside the temple and could be aspired to, but not otherwise realized, outside the realm of ritual. In depositing objects of intermediate character such as the Narmer Palette, kings were consecrating the imperfect world and expressing its dedication in the cause of the more perfect one (compare Frandsen 1989).

The second implication is in the presence of human figures additional to the king on these pieces, both as ritual participants/royal servants and as defeated enemies. Human beings were almost entirely eliminated from reliefs in the central areas of later temples and these examples mark the greatest extent of human participation in central religious action. This pattern continued later broadly unchanged, with priests as the only human presence in rituals or processions shown within temples (principally their outer courts) and other human protagonists largely confined to emblematic forms and to battle scenes. Within these formalized conventions, human beings could not present or offer themselves to the deity except through the king, and they could not interact with the deity at all (in much later times these conventions changed in relation to non-royal non-temple monuments). This restriction is, however, an artistic and broadly symbolic convention rather than a statement of reality. It addresses the way in which the core of state and ideology were formulated and may tell us little about the performance of the cult of the gods and of human participation in religious action. Some late texts state or imply that the priest substitutes for the king, or that there is an alternation in role of priest and king, or that the king presents himself to the deity as a priest (Otto 1964, 67-74; Derchain forthcoming). Nonetheless, the convention that the king stands before the gods and other human beings do not is better seen as an embodiment of rules of decorum and a statement of how and through what styles of interaction the cosmic roles are distributed, rather than a depiction of any specific action and a statement of who was entitled to approach a god in reality and of delegation from the king to priests. Almost everywhere, it has proved far more difficult to identify real ritual sequences in temple reliefs than to study the symbolism of scenes and principles of their organization. This pattern of interpretation reflects real features of the material and of the status of temple relief as a supreme, meaningful fiction: it coheres as a system but does not directly describe anything.

The temples which do not fit these generalizations well are royal mortuary structures of the Old Kingdom. These have naturally tended to dominate discussion for their period, to the extent that a scholar has asserted that there was then no state construction of temples for the gods (Assmann 1991b, 113-15); but much in them is difficult to reconcile with long-term developments in divine cult temples. It seems better to see the latter, which certainly existed before and after the royal ones, as the primary phenomenon and to understand the royal temples as transformations of an underlying system devised for another purpose, rather than constituting the primary system (cf. Baines 1985, 68-75). I therefore suggest that the royal temples are offshoots from the more central divine tradition, to which fewer resources were devoted than in later, and probably earlier, periods (cf. O'Connor 1992).

2.2 *The Early Dynastic Period*

Evidence for Early Dynastic temples survives in texts and in the 'annals'. Works of art in relief and painting probably continued to be made through the couple of centuries from which no remains are preserved. Arguments for this reconstruction are the maintenance of comparable traditions into the next period from which material remains survive - the late Second and Third dynasties - and the continuity, development and elaborate character of compositional and technical skills. The pattern of development of stone vases and statuary from the period shows that artistic accomplishments were not simply transferable from one medium to another. A masterpiece such as the stela of King Wadj (e.g. Lange and Hirmer 1968, pl. 6) could not exist in a vacuum and implies that there was some corpus of reliefs, even if it was not extensive. More broadly, from the painting in Tomb 100 at Hierakonpolis on, representational and other works point to the existence of different media, such as ivory carving, in which material might be more expertly executed than in surviving evidence, while objects like the inlaid stone relief gaming discs from the tomb of Hemaka point to the existence of genres that are otherwise almost completely lost (Emery 1938, pl. 12; Lange and Hirmer 1968, pl. I). Among continuing genres, wall painting can be seen in such outliers as the painted patterning on exteriors of Early Dynastic tombs (e.g. Emery 1949-58, I pl. 50), and for the Third Dynasty in the tomb of Hezyre at Saqqara, which also produced the superb wooden reliefs that are tokens of an otherwise almost entirely lost medium (Wood 1978); wooden statuary, attested by the feet from two non-royal pieces of the First Dynasty (Emery 1949-58, III pl. 27), was no doubt also a significant genre, as later. All of these forms could have contributed to the furnishing and decor of temples. The fact that the only significant surviving evidence is in ivory (e.g. Adams 1974) and faience (Müller 1964, nos. A8-17; Dreyer 1986, pls. 11-28), objects in the latter being formally crude and prestigious for what they were made from, points to the importance of the materials used. Stone vessels, a major category of Early Dynastic object, are known mainly from funerary deposits (e.g. Lacau and Lauer 1961-5), but evidence from their inscriptions points to their being used also in temple cults (cf. Roth 1991, 145-95, esp. 192-3).

Thus, the decoration and furnishing of temple door surrounds, walls and spaces probably continued to develop in the Early Dynastic Period, perhaps in media ranging from metal and stone through wood to painting. Similar decoration was probably applied to smaller objects, on a scale comparable to that of the Narmer Palette, but perhaps different in both genre and subject matter. Evidence for this view comes from the end of the Second Dynasty, in a decorated lintel from Hierakonpolis that bears a relief fully within dynastic conventions (see p. 216), and in works of the reign of Djoser. The Step Pyramid complex at Saqqara seems to have had little relief decoration, although the underground panels are assured and complex works (cf. F Friedman 1995) and the large group of rough stones with *jmjwt*–Anubis motifs (Firth and Quibell 1935, pls. 86-7) exhibits developed iconographic conventions. More revealing, however, are the fragmentary miniature limestone reliefs of Djoser from Heliopolis (Turin, not fully published: W S Smith 1949, 133-7 figs. 49-53). These include figures of the king with his family and, more importantly, a group of deities represented in the pattern that was later typical for enneads depicted on doorways. They decorated the outside of a small shrine that could have contained a statuette, conceivably a cult image.

The small scale of these pieces might suggest that whole wall surfaces were not being painted or carved in relief at that date, and the other material I have cited could fit with such a possibility because it is all in the form of panels or door decoration. But as David O'Connor has remarked (personal communication), some of these works appear 'monumental' in conception and may relate to much larger lost pieces (additional material from Hierakonpolis: Alexanian 1995). Moreover, in later buildings doors were sometimes carved while walls were left blank, perhaps for subsequent decoration or for execution in less durable media. Such a reading would, however, ignore the central position in the decorative system of scenes showing the king interacting directly with deities, the absence of rules of decorum requiring more indirect formulations. In comparison, doors are marginal or liminal areas with restricted decorum and meaning (Baines 1985, 281). The principal wall scenes, which fill Graeco-Roman Period temples in their thousands, give a formalized, highly abstract framework for interaction between the divine and the human. They do not report directly on the cult, and the statues upon which the cult was performed often fell far outside the decorum of the reliefs, as can be seen in material in the temple of Hibis (Davies 1953, pls. 2-5; Sternberg-el Hotabi 1994 [interpretation problematic]), the naos of Saft el-Hinna (Roeder 1914:CG 70021), and in the crypts and some other rooms at Dendara (Chassinat 1934, 1947-52; Chassinat and Daumas 1965: most distinctively marked by indications of material).

The formalized scenes constitute the core of Egyptian iconography. They may have evolved from the end of predynastic times through the first two dynasties to reach something like a 'classical' form around the end of the Early Dynastic Period. How widely they were carved or painted on temple walls cannot be known. As David O'Connor (1992) has noted in discussing Barry Kemp's ideas on early temples (1989, 65-83; Kemp's reply, 1995, 41-2, does not address all issues), the available material all comes from sites that are likely to have been exceptional. I would add to O'Connor's body of evidence the reliefs in royal funerary temples - the best known evidence from the Old Kingdom, which points to the underlying decorative system of temples to the cult of the gods.

Thus, in contrast with the dominance in the record of non-royal and royal tombs and the latter's associated cult structures primarily around the capital, the divine cult temple should be seen as the essential defining element in the way the elite presented the coherence of the cosmos and celebrated it through artistic representation. As a discreet and discrete, but adapting and enduring core, the temple was a supreme participant and guarantor in defining civilization. Primarily in its architectural and environmental aspects it was also a symbol. To return to Wallace Stevens's criteria, it was abstract - that is, rule-bound and formalized in its central features - changing, and profoundly aesthetic.

The architectural model of the temple inherited from late predynastic times was predicated on the distinction and demarcation of the 'sacred' inside and 'secular' outside. Such a distinction, whose simplest manifestations are in such forms as enclosures or compounds containing one or many buildings, need not be restricted to elite contexts, and in its most basic forms applies to almost any dwelling. Temple versions are comparable but are either on a larger scale than domestic forms or are more complex and highly charged symbolically, as also tends to be true of temples in comparison with palaces. Despite this commonality of basic structures and symbolism, an elite rather than divine reading of temple architecture may not be appropriate. Unlike pictorial decoration, temples and palaces could speak to the population as a whole, either through a dominating presence, as is probable for early palaces, or through their pervasive but relatively modest presence in the settled environment. Even minor temples, however, appear to have had a pole with pendent cloth as a signal of divine presence of essentially the same form as the hieroglyph for 'god' (Baines 1990b): they too relied for their significance on demarcation and presented an abstract 'supreme fiction' in a local context. The abstract sign both generalized the temple's significance, by subordinating it to an overarching category, and characteristically excluded all but a select few from participating in the divine presence or even seeing specific symbols of most deities. Compared to the situation of the Naqada II period, this was a severe restriction in the availability of divine symbols.

Outside the period considered so far, the system of architecture and decoration has a significant outlier in Old Kingdom nonroyal tombs. These include little directly religious decoration and no figures of the king. The Horus, Nebty and Golden Horus names, the most evidently divine kingly titles, are also absent (e.g. Helck 1972, 11). The tombs did, however, have restrictive features of their own. Among their inscriptions are frequent curse formulae addressed to those who might enter the tomb in a state of impurity. Hermann Junker connected this factor of purity with the absence of representations of the king, extrapolating that superior levels of purity were required for kings and deities to be representation (Junker 1955, 132-3; cf. Wolf 1957, 685 n. 70:2). While this is likely enough in itself, it seems best to understand the tomb decoration more broadly as being intrinsically incompatible with the royal and the divine—that is, to see this decoration as integrated with the cosmography of architecture and decoration in general, including that of temples. The insistence on purity in tombs is paralleled by a stronger insistence in temples, where everyone who entered was enjoined to 'purify four times' (perhaps not attested in temple relief before the New Kingdom). As in almost any culture, purity was a reinforcing marker of the demarcations of the sacred and the significant. Spaces that lacked the requisite significance and purity - that is, almost any spaces - could not be the symbols and guarantors of central traditions and values.

Temples were thus the crucial guardians of a 'great tradition'. Since they were spread throughout the country, they brought the tradition everywhere and sustained its vitality (here I follow O'Connor, 1992, rather than Kemp, 1989), in some sense making the cosmos a living reality through the presence of so many sanctified microcosms. Yet this maintenance of the tradition was within the temple structures, which were themselves inside enclosures. The temples therefore reinforced the message that the great tradition was the concern of the elite and only marginally of the whole people - although they must also have carried to the wider society the conviction that the tradition's continuance was an enterprise in the interests of all. As indicated earlier (p. 218), such a message could well have had substance, but since history cannot be relived according a different scenario, such an idea cannot be tested.

3 Transition

Many themes of this essay could be exemplified for any period in antiquity; from the second millennium I cite just two aspects.

First, temples evolved within the tradition and the limiting conventions set in early times. Development was conscious and deliberate and had a strong historical sense. Whereas Luxor is still a place where temples form a significant element in the landscape, we find it difficult to comprehend their prevalence in antiquity, especially since no major temple is preserved in anything like its ancient form north of Abydos, which itself is in the southernmost third of the country. On present evidence, a distinctive development of the New Kingdom was the integration of temples into cosmically elaborated cities, inscribing a meaning that their structure and decoration had always had into the environment on a much grander and more socially inclusive scale (O'Connor, in preparation; for the reign of Amenhotpe III, see Kozloff and Bryan 1992, 82-104, 100-11). Here too, however, an older tendency may have increased in significance, since indirect evidence points at least to the pervasive presence of temples in earlier periods (Baines 1988). This theme has been little explored for later periods. For the Graeco-Roman Period, interconnections between groups of sanctuaries around a nome metropolis, well known for Dendara (Daumas 1969) and Esna (Sauneron 1959, 29-31), as well as the regional integration of Edfu with Dendara (e.g. Alliot 1954, 441-560; Cauville 1988) and the relations between Philae and Lower Nubia (e.g. Winter 1976b, 4-6), exhibit similar phenomena at least in ritual.

For the New Kingdom we can discern patterns of development in which particular structures relate to earlier ones nearby. The best known case is perhaps the virtual copy of the classic White Chapel of Senwosret I at Karnak that was executed under Amenhotpe I, about four hundred years later (Björkman 1971, 58-9, 134 no. 10:J). Less certain but in some ways more significant, examples can be cited from same period, when the temple of Hatshepsut at Deir el-Bahri in particular was decorated with much archaic and archaizing material (e.g. Assmann 1969, 122-49, 159-64; Graefe 1995). Each major period seems to have legitimized itself to a great extent in terms of its predecessor (Baines 1989). The case of Hatshepsut is significant because the material extends to the inscriptions memorializing the hymns of the solar cult and thus demonstrates that the use of the past encompassed the total high-cultural context of the reliefs, from the visual arts to aspects that were, at least in theory, performance-oriented.

It is difficult to evaluate these developments in context because such a small proportion of ancient temples is preserved, a problem that is intensified by the general tendency for temples to conform to a small number of basic types. Apart from some special-purpose forms, these can be reduced to the pair of axial temples, generally oriented at right angles to the Nile, and transverse temples, which sit parallel to the Nile and more specifically at right angles to the axis of the nearby principal temple. (Very small numbers of basic forms are of course found in other traditions, as with churches and mosques.) The transverse temple is characterized by an open, often peripteral structure, typically with pillars rather than columns, and appears designed for temporary occupation. The axial temple is closed on the outside, generally has columns rather than pillars, and is designed for continuous, permanent occupation. In addition to this simple overall typology and such features as the flagpoles which descended from the markers of divinity mentioned above, there is evidence that key texts, in particular, were disseminated in temples throughout the country. These encompassed both major rituals and the general literary stream of tradition, which is attested for the Late Period from Elephantine (Burkard and Fischer-Elfert 1994) to Saqqara (H S Smith and Tait 1983), and probably as far as Tanis (Griffith and Petrie 1889; the texts on carbonized papyri recently found at Tanis are not yet identified). It is therefore risky to say that any parallel we happen to identify in temples across different periods demonstrates a dependence of the later on the earlier. It is generally better to assume that the different examples belonged to a common tradition, or in some cases relate to a common archetype. To create a plausible picture of the interplay of tradition it is necessary to argue from silence, because the selection preserved is affected by chance factors. The principal, and important, exception to this stricture is in some Late Period temple and other decoration that appears to depend on known exemplars and traditions (e.g. Macadam 1955, 63-6). This dependence is confirmed in some cases by traces of copying on the older monuments (e.g. Baines 1973). We can envisage a landscape of the mid first millennium BCE in which many of the great temples and other monuments of the past, including the major pyramid complexes, were partly ruined and could serve either as source material for the creators of the temples of the day and their texts (e.g. M. Smith 1977; Baines 1994b) - or as quarries from which to construct those temples. In this landscape, at least in the south, preserved Late Period temples are much smaller than their New Kingdom predecessors, often consisting of additions to earlier structures or complexes. Appearances may, however, be misleading, because Memphite and Delta temples, which were in the country's most creative region, were probably the most important projects of the time and are hardly accessible. The surviving material in the deep south may have been seen even in its day as residing in a cultural backwater. That is the impression one gains to some extent from nonroyal tombs of the 7th-4th centuries, among which those in the north are far more innovative, although less opulent, than those in Thebes (L Leahy 1988).

While available evidence is skewed as described, temples appear to have been at least as important in the Late Period as earlier, if not more so, in view of the general decline in the scale and number of funerary monuments. In the next section I present arguments for the position of temples that apply both to Late and to Graeco-Roman temples. An architectural feature that points in the same direction is the appearance of major nonroyal tombs in the form of temples, a development made possible, among other factors, by the slowly loosening rules of decorum. The classic example is the tomb of Petosiris at Tuna el-Gebel (Lefebvre 1923-4), which was not as unique in its time as it now appears, since there was at least one comparable structure at Tuna (Gabra 1941, 11-37), apart from other sites (block noticed on site at Tod).

4 The Graeco-Roman Period

Whereas developments of the Dynastic Period are generally seen as lying within accepted Egyptian artistic canons, art historians outside the francophone world have tended almost to ignore the enormous legacy, from the largest to the smallest temples, of the Graeco-Roman Period. The standard textbook by a leading art historian, Cyril Aldred's *Egyptian Art* (1980, 240), speaks of their style of decoration as 'deplorable'. Statuary of the period, almost all of which was set up in temples, is accepted as belonging within Egyptian traditions and extending them creatively (Bothmer 1960; Bianchi 1988, 55-80), while the temples have often been seen as largely debased creations, even if it is acknowledged that they are within native Egyptian tradition rather than a hybrid that might be diminished by inconsistency or lack of coherence. Although different artistic genres often display different levels of execution and may diverge strongly in style, such a radical dichotomy between statuary and the architecture and reliefs of the buildings which housed it is hardly plausible and would be rare in almost any culture. The essential difficulty - which cannot be mitigated in this essay - is that the temples have hardly been studied from an art-historical perspective. Emile Chassinat (1934, vi-vii) remarked when completing the publication of 468 plates of the temple of Edfu (with only a selection of the reliefs) that he was presenting to art historians a vast, well dated and exactly localized corpus that had barely been studied. The principal response to that challenge is Eleni Vassilika's very valuable *Ptolemaic Philae* (1989). Otherwise, the remark is almost as valid now as then.

This dismissal especially of relief decoration contrasts with the interest accorded to the textual matter in these temples, which mixes the traditional with the novel, and in total constitutes a multiple of what is known from earlier times. The texts and their vastly expanded writing system have attracted much philological attention, although generally from a small group of scholars. These accidents essentially of twentieth century scholarship, together with a tendency (from which this essay is not exempt) to show more interest in early forms than in later ones, contributes to the neglect of the temples' artistic aspects. In artistic terms, these temples exemplify strongly both the principles of my title and Wallace Stevens' precepts.

The significance of temples for the Late and Graeco-Roman periods can be seen from the pattern of their construction, which relates also to political history. The late eighth and seventh century revival associated with the Nubian unifiers Shabaka and Taharqa (on dating, see A. Leahy 1992) continued throughout the Twenty-sixth Dynasty. All these rulers built small extensions and additions to temple complexes in many places, especially the Theban area (Leclant 1965). In their homeland the Nubians created new complexes in the Napata area (Griffith 1922; Dunham 1970) and, for example, at Kawa (Macadam 1955). Twenty-sixth Dynasty kings also evidently built much, from which little survives, at Sais and elsewhere in the Delta (el-Sayed, 1975, presents some raw material). Both the Persian conqueror Cambyses and his later successor Darius I presented themselves as favouring the temples. Cambyses was celebrated by Udjahorresne as saving the temple of Sais (Baines 1996, with refs.), and Darius decorated the temple of Hibis in el-Kharga Oasis, which had probably been constructed in the late 26th Dynasty (Cruz-Uribe 1986, 164-5; 1987, 225-30). During the country's renewed independence in the fourth century, Egyptian kings took up temple building roughly where the Twenty-Sixth Dynasty had left off, as well as starting some grandiose projects, such as the temple of Isis at Behbeit el-Hagar, which was uniquely constructed entirely in hard stone (Favard-Meeks 1991).

The Ptolemaic Period (305-30) brought a complete and continuing renewal, both in temples constructed and in style. Almost all surviving buildings of the time are in the far south, and this bias brings familiar problems of interpretation. Their significance, however, can be seen almost anywhere. In cases where the state extended its territory or incorporated it more fully, as in the oases and Lower Nubia, where there were phases of annexation in mid-Ptolemaic times and under Augustus, evidence for building is particularly extensive in relation to what went before and to the probably very low levels of local population. The outstanding exceptions to the pattern of new construction are Thebes and, on a lesser scale, Abydos (Memphis is another possibility, but cannot easily be evaluated because it is poorly preserved). Within Thebes, Graeco-Roman work is confined to relatively small additions to existing structures, the demarcation of the sacred area of Karnak with new monumental gateways, and the construction of quite modest new temples, such as those of the goddess Opet at Karnak (de Wit 1958-68) or Deir el-Medina for Hathor (PM II,[2] 401-7), Qasr el-Aguz for Thoth (Mallet 1909), and Deir el-Shelwit for Isis (Zivie and Hanafi 1982-6) on the West Bank. A comparison of this activity with larger projects elsewhere suggests that a general aim of the policy - no doubt negotiated in complex fashion among central government and local, primarily elite interest, may have been to create a more uniform provision of temples through the country and across different cults, as against the inherited focus on a smaller number of major centres, at least in the Nile Valley. The enormous ancient temples of Thebes were kept in use and refurbished selectively, but not replaced. Perhaps only the smallest local shrines, particularly those of Hellenistic character, will have been due largely to local initiative.

A further indication of the importance of temples throughout the Nile Valley is their ongoing reconstruction. At Philae, where the temples were excavated one course below ground level when they were moved to Agilkia, so that some archaeological conclusions can be drawn (Haeny 1985), and at Edfu and Dendara, the Graeco-Roman structures were built upon earlier ones. The earlier temples at Philae dated to the Late Period, while further work around the turn of the era led to the resiting of a 'kiosk' of Nectanebo I (380-361; Haeny 1985, 204-6, 223-7; Vassilika 1989, 22-5), a piece of reverence for the past known also from the rebuilding of a comparable structure of Amenhotpe II at Karnak, about 1200 years earlier (van Siclen 1990). In the case of Edfu, the pavement of the current forecourt, completed in the first century BCE, incorporated very fine blocks of Ptolemy I (305-282), principally from a doorway that could have stood in or in front of the earlier Ptolemaic temple (unpublished, but laid out in the forecourt for the visitor to see). Building texts (Kurth 1994a, 26, 70, with refs.) state that construction of the main extant temple began in the reign of Ptolemy III Euergetes I (246-221), and the blocks of Ptolemy I might have come from somewhere in that temple's predecessor, which would then have stood for only about sixty years. Alternatively, the doorway could have stood in an outside area that was replaced only later. The change in axis from the Ramessid temple (cf. Murnane and Yurco 1992) must have been accomplished when the initial Ptolemaic complex was laid out, because a temple on the axis of the surviving Ramessid pylon would have been too small and should have left remains to the west of the complex, where no finds are reported.

At Dendara it is possible to observe on site Thirtieth Dynasty and Ptolemaic blocks incorporated as fill into the foundation courses of the main temple of Hathor and the temple of Isis to its south (cf. Cauville 1992). The enlargement of the Hathor temple enclosure begun in Roman times, itself reusing Ptolemaic blocks, cut through the existing Thirtieth Dynasty and Ptolemaic birth house and so led to the construction in the second century CE of a replacement on a larger scale than any of its predecessors (Daumas 1958, 102-17). The most striking discarding of a recent structure is at Kalabsha in Lower Nubia, where a gateway from early in the reign of Augustus (30 BCE–14 CE) was incorporated later in the same reign into the foundations of new the principal temple of Mandulis. The gateway, which is interesting ideologically for the detailed Roman involvement in its texts (Winter n.d.) as well as being architecturally imposing, now stands reerected in the Ägyptisches Museum in Berlin (Berlin 1989, no. 69).

These reuses are examples of the intensity of effort which went into temples of the Graeco-Roman Period. (The following presentation cannot be documented in detail; it relies upon surveying general patterns of dates of construction and decoration in the temples. Schloz, 1994, comes to partly divergent conclusions; see also Hölbl 1994, *passim.*) Phases of work on the temples fall into broad patterns which can be compared with the period's history (see in general Bowman 1996). Relatively few large monuments are known from the first two Ptolemies, although signs of their activity are found throughout the country. This lack is no doubt due to their having been built over by their successors, but where later constructions can be compared with earlier, they are generally larger. This trend in construction has a parallel in the New Kingdom, when large-scale building did not get underway until a generation or two after the Hyksos were expelled, and then continued in a rising pattern (cf. Hornung 1971, esp. 56-8). The kings from whose reigns there is most evidence are Ptolemies VIII Euergetes II (principally 145-116) and XII Neos Dionysos (80-58, 55-51). These kings ruled in troubled times when there were several native Egyptian rebellions in the Thebaid and periodic violent dissensions in the ruling house, while the loss of foreign territory and the rise of Rome increasingly constrained policy and reduced revenues (see in general Thompson 1994). During the following reign of Cleopatra VII Philopator (51-30), much of Upper Egypt seems to have been scarcely under the control of central government, but her name nevertheless appears on a number of monuments, sometimes together with her son by Julius Caesar, Ptolemy XV Caesarion. Thus, the construction and decoration of major provincial temples, on a scale never before seen, lasted through periods of strife and relative decline, and even reached a peak precisely when the regions in which they are preserved were in administrative disarray. (Nineteenth century publications add a number of significant temples to those presently extant, conveniently gathered by Arnold, 1992.)

The pattern of royal involvement in construction is exemplified to the fullest for the reign of Augustus, from which more temples bear a royal cartouche than from any other. Through the temple policy implemented by his prefects and officials Augustus evidently sought to win over the native population to his conquest, as well as marking the reannexation of northern Lower Nubia by building throughout the area, presumably in the wake of the war with Meroe (e.g. Adams 1977, 338-42). The Roman Period is also characterized by large numbers of smaller temples and by the pervasive extension of temple culture to remote regions, such as the oases of Kharga and Dakhla. A final peak of construction, not on the level of that of Augustus, was reached in the reigns of Trajan (98-117) and Hadrian (117-138). During the Roman Period, unlike the Ptolemaic, years of prosperity parallel intensity of building fairly closely.

It seems beyond question that the Ptolemies and Roman emperors attached great importance to these undertakings - which are their principal surviving monuments in Egypt. Yet these rulers knew little of the meaning of what was built in Egypt and they could not read the inscriptions set up in the temples; few emperors visited Egypt. This policy was surely stimulated by the native elite, whose life and values focused around the temples, no doubt partly in default of a role in civil affairs comparable with that of earlier times. Some of the negotiation between local government officials and the temples can be seen in monuments of *strategoi* of the Dendara nome from the early years CE, which show them using both Greek and Demotic and contributing actively to the furnishing of the temple - but not personally to its construction (Shore 1979; Bowman and Rathbone 1992, 107–8; La'da 1994). As the only temple to have a dedicatory inscription carved in its masonry in Greek (34 CE, almost invisible to the naked eye), Dendara shows government, or at least official, involvement in another way too (Daumas 1969, 31, citing Letronne).

It is unlikely that the initiative for temple construction originated with the rulers themselves. They adopted a traditional role, but they did not do so in a passive way. The earliest extant monument of a Ptolemaic ruler, the Satrap Stela from before Ptolemy I assumed the title of king, presents him as the active protector and restorer of a temple's endowments in the wake of Persian expropriation (*Urk.* II, 11-22; translation: Bresciani 1990, 637-41). Details of the inscriptions, such as the patterns of epithets in titularies (Winter n.d.) and the meticulous naming and occasional erasure of titularies of current Roman emperors (e.g. Sauneron 1952a), demonstrate close central control of what was done. But central involvement in construction and decoration does not prove that the policies were personal ones of the king or emperor. The decision to build a temple and to undertake a project of a particular size must have had royal sanction and was presumably the result of long negotiation among the native elite and central officials. In principle, the cost of construction was met centrally, because endowments appear only to have covered the maintenance of the cult and did not expand greatly (Meeks 1972, 131-5). The nature of the projects was such that they had to be planned for execution over decades (about 180 years from start to finish in the case of Edfu: Kurth 1994a, 26-9), and the royal names inscribed in any particular area of a temple reflected who the living ruler was rather than a deliberate gift for that part of the decoration (hardly any of which mentions specific historical events, unlike such texts as the Ptolemaic sacerdotal decrees). One should therefore posit institutions that mediated between local aspirations and central largesse and smoothed the flow of work, while acceding over long periods to the tendency to increase it. Preserved temples are only a fraction of those which existed and the whole apparatus of construction and control must have been very large, so much so that kings - as against their officials - are unlikely to have concerned themselves with its detail more than occasionally. Their acceptance of this apparatus and its expansion is nonetheless eloquent testimony to the temples' significance for the state as a whole.

Development in temple design, style and ideology was almost wholly in native Egyptian terms. Ongoing stylistic changes to relief figures (as well as some representational details), in which sunk relief in particular became more plastic and three-dimensional, could be seen as relating to the Hellenistic environment, but this is uncertain because they had forerunners in Egypt as far back as the Twenty-fifth Dynasty. The evolution of a generally lighter colour palette similarly has Hellenistic analogues but could be internally driven. In these changes, the role of the king as depicted in the temples perhaps naturally became almost abstract. As shown by Philippe Derchain (1962; in press), within the temples the presentation of the king was as strongly idealized as it ever had been; yet in some ways he was presented as secondary and legitimized as a priest as much as for himself (Otto 1964; Winter 1976a). More generally, in relation to my initial categories, essential aspects of the temples were the requirement that they give pleasure - an idea endlessly repeated in perorations on the joy of the gods and of the people at the completion of the temples and the celebration of associated festivals - and the darker underlying belief that temples are fragments shored against a culture's ruins.

This last point is best seen in two texts, one from the Ptolemaic temple milieu and the other, the Hermetic *Asclepius*, preserved in Latin and partly in Coptic, and dating to Roman times (§§ 24-7: Copenhaver 1992, 81-4, with refs.; see also Fowden 1986). The Ptolemaic Papyrus Jumilhac, which is something like a cult handbook from the 18th Upper Egyptian nome, includes a discourse on the importance of maintaining the cults of the gods, couched partly in terms of its opposite - the destruction of the world of Egypt that would follow if the cult were not maintained (Vandier 1961, xvii, 14-xviii, 21; cf. Derchain 1990). The eschatological notions visible here were so powerful that they were carried over into the early Egyptian Christian *Apocalypse of Elijah* (Frankfurter 1994). What is striking about the passage in P Jumilhac in relation to the current argument - and particularly since it emanates from a cult context - is that it makes no mention of the king (nor does the *Asclepius*). This absence cannot be explained by responding that many hymns to deities also do not mention the king, because their setting guaranteed that they were royal; these discursive texts could mention him but do not. The king - that is, the state - in principle provided the resources for building the temples and was the linchpin of the artistic system, but outside the pictorial context he seems to have been conceptually dispensable. One of the latest preserved temples, at Ismant el-Kharab in Dakhla Oasis, which may be roughly contemporary with the *Asclepius*, takes the next logical step and omits figures of the king (Kaper, this volume), but it is stylistically quite far from 'classical' forms and may well not fit their categories, so we cannot say that the king really could be removed from the decorative organization of indigenous temples. (Dakhla also contains two of the most thoroughly Graeco-Egyptian nonroyal tombs, dating to the first centuries CE: Fakhry et al. 1982, pls. 20-45.)

The Graeco-Roman temples were not simply structures decorated throughout that contained a great wealth of furnishings now lost or recycled (e.g. Insley Green 1987) and witnessed elaborate daily rituals in their interiors as well as witnessing periodic performances that involved a larger proportion of the local population. They were also general repositories of native Egyptian culture. While this function can be seen only indirectly in the principal surviving temples - mainly from the 'library catalogues' inscribed on the walls of some rooms (Grimm 1989) - it is clear both from the sites of North Saqqara (Smith and Tait 1983) and Elephantine (Burkard and Fischer-Elfert 1994) and from small temples in the Fayyum, especially Tebtunis (Tait 1977; Frandsen 1991, cf. 'Einleitung' by Karl-Theodor Zauzich, pp. 1-11). These have produced an unparalleled collection of literary texts in almost all genres that demonstrate the vitality and inventiveness of broader high-cultural traditions, even in small centres that, in the case of the Fayyum, had little ancient tradition behind them (the same may have been true of Dakhla Oasis). Texts newly composed in the period, such as the biography of the Memphite high priest's wife Taimhotep (e.g. Lichtheim 1980, 59-65), also confirm that ancient literary traditions were maintained, comprehended and exploited.

Temples were the site of constant creative thought that cannot be reduced to the purely textual. Their decorative and architectural schemas brought forth new possibilities of their own. These aspects can be seen in major temples, such as Kom Ombo, and in minor local ones, such as the temple of the reign of Augustus at el-Qal'a on the outskirts of Koptos - the place which is the point of departure for studying temples. The double temple of Kom Ombo was dedicated to Sobek and Haroeris and exhibits an architectural doubling of almost all its elements that results in an almost uniquely complex ground plan for a structure with a unitary conception (e.g. Gutbub 1973, plan; PM VI, 178, 180). In this period temples were frequently dedicated to triads of whom the principal deity formed the centre, as was the case also at Kom Ombo. The triad of Sobek looks normal, consisting of himself, Hathor and Khons, but that of Haroeris, whose cult may have been secondary in this region, is exceptional. His counterpart goddess is Tsenetnofret 'The Good Sister/Spouse' and the youthful god is Pnebtawy 'The Lord of the Two Lands' (Gutbub 1973, xv–xvii; these names look like Late Egyptian rather than a subsequent linguistic phase, and the deities themselves could have existed long before this temple was built). The name Pnebtawy alludes to the kingly role and iconography of all youthful gods in this period (I know of no specific study of this topic).

Thus, in the continuation and elaboration of traditions, new deities were devised to fill roles and their names reflected the characteristics of those roles, making the device transparent. This does not imply that there was no belief in the system. Belief in a deity whose essence is reduced to a role and who has no individual characteristics may be difficult for an outsider to comprehend, in contrast with figures that have 'personalities' - but perhaps not necessarily more difficult than comprehending monotheism. A salient feature of Egyptian deities is in any case that their roles and persons are variable, so that this is an extreme example of the prominence of role, analogous with personification (Guglielmi 1982; Baines 1985; in general Hornung 1982). Here again, one encounters the abstraction of 'supreme fictions'. Some effects of this tendency on the king have been noted above; another is in frequent cases where royal names, which were necessary for relief compositions and inscription bands, had a blank cartouche because the identity of a particular king was unknown or irrelevant. The treatment of these 'anonymous' deities is in some respects comparable.

At el-Qal'a such forms are more pronounced and very inventive (Traunecker, this volume; Pantalacci and Traunecker 1990, 1993). In one case the later decoration ceases to name the principal deity, Isis, and calls her simply 'The Great Goddess'. Other deities are effectively split into aspects and distributed on either side of the two temple axes. These combinations then alternate across the axes to produce interwoven compositions in which a coherent sequence of actions is shared among a range of different, abstract identities. Neither at Kom Ombo nor at el-Qal'a should this abstraction of deities be taken as a sign of decline in the system's vitality. To do so would be wrongly to use hindsight from the perspective of the middle and late Roman Empire and the rise of Christianity in Egypt; too often studies of the period have been vitiated by this teleological vision.

Two points should be stressed here. First, more than early Koptos, Roman Period el-Qal'a was a minor sanctuary on the periphery of a city that was not central to the country or its traditions. The temple also appears to have been used only seasonally, and thus to have been among the less significant of its area. Yet the intellectual vitality and 'blessed rage for order' of its decoration is remarkable (phrase: Wallace Stevens, *The Idea of Order at Key West*, 1936, last stanza - perhaps not coincidentally the title of two theological books and a doctoral dissertation: Tracy 1975; Argyros 1991; Bell 1972). How much greater was probably the vitality, and the cultural importance, of a centre such as Roman Akhmim (Panopolis), some way to the north, which had major temples of this period (Sauneron 1952b; al-Masri 1983) and in which private stelae continued to be dedicated at least into the time of Hadrian (Otto 1954, no. 75; imaginative study: Derchain 1987), in the centuries before it became the homeland of the Christian abbot Shenoute. Into the middle of the fourth centuries, prominent individuals with Egyptian names were active in literary traditions and in the local cults (e.g. Willis 1979) and people from there had a wider impact (Fowden 1986, 120, 173–4). Further north, Asyut (Lykopolis) was the regional centre from which the philosopher Plotinus emerged (Reemes in press). Greek and Egyptian cultures did not coexist without mutual influence, and the emergence in this region of these protagonists of other belief systems - as well as its significance for Manicheism and Gnosticism - was surely connected with its importance as an Egyptian religious centre. Because of continuing habitation, however, very little archaeological evidence survives from sites in this area.

Second, and crucially here, the temple material is no less 'artistic' for being primarily verbal. The temples are total works of art, not only of architecture and relief; the term *Gesamtkunstwerke* may be remote from Egypt, but it reminds us additionally that they were stages for highly aesthetic ritual performances that included music and dance. The verbal aspect is illustrated by the major temple of Edfu, in a feature discovered by Erich Winter (1968, part 1 for what follows). The four registers of decoration that structured most Graeco-Roman temple walls were organized principally through framing columns of inscription at the edge of each scene, the content of which related to the principal deity shown or to the king, according to the side on which they were situated. In an overall pattern, their verbal formulation down the four registers coalesced into a monumental proclamation of the king's titulary and thus affirmed the presence of the invariable protagonist on a superhuman scale and in a form not tied to human figures. The specific content relating to any particular scene was adapted within this rigid verbal schema, rather as a sonnet cycle has to work within constraints of form and decorum to express its meaning. Deity and style of offering, a well as iconography, were chosen separately in an elaborate counterpoint to be fitted within the verbal schema, which organized rather than dominated the visual aspect (cf. Vassilika 1989, 8-11). This schema, which crystallized under Ptolemy VIII Euergetes II (145-116), goes back to New Kingdom forerunners which express the idea of the temple as cosmos, its everlasting duration, and the notion of celebration (Baines 1994b). All these features will have resonated to the designers who maintained and elaborated the tradition, to the learned members of the priesthood went who through the temple, and most importantly for the intent of the structure to the vast range of deities who were associated with it. As the Renaissance man who walked through a villa might sense the ideal proportions of the spheres in the design ratios of the rooms (Wittkower 1962, 101-54, esp. 142), so a learned Egyptian or Egyptian deity could experience at many levels of design the temple's royal and cosmic harmony and joyous affirmation of order against chaos.

Winter's discovery raises another issue for the interpretation of the 'great tradition'. He has suggested (1968, 58-9) that Edfu, the temple that we can study which was in full course of decoration under Ptolemy VIII, was where the synthesis of this feature coalesced and from which it was diffused. The difficulty with this reconstruction is that Ptolemaic Edfu was a provincial place in the far south of a country ruled from Alexandria, even though it contained an extraordinary temple. It seems more likely that the schema was devised further north, in a region from which nothing comparable survives. In studying forerunners of Winter's formula, however, I identified almost exclusively material in the Theban area (Baines 1994b), and this might after all suggest a southern point of dissemination.

But the limited survival of evidence must be recalled here, as well as the vast amount of traditional religious knowledge transmitted in the temples through manuscript sources rather than through study of the monuments themselves. Since in the Late Period people went and copied reliefs on standing monuments (e.g. Otto 1954, 122-4; Baines 1973; 1992, 254, with refs.), the designers probably relied first of all on their libraries or 'houses of life', which are almost entirely lost. One should therefore leave open the possibility of diffusion from the north, as against assuming that native Egyptian high culture was cut off from the general centre of intellectual life in Memphis and the Delta, as the Edfu hypothesis would rather imply. That vision would also run counter to the pattern of biographical texts, which have been found more widely spread across the country than temple reliefs.

5 Conclusion: Graeco-Roman temples and the significance of temples

I have focused on preconditions for the decoration of temples of the Graeco-Roman Period and on their general cultural importance. In view of the vast investment in their construction and decoration, as well as their architectural sophistication and the presence of an explicit symbolism that at times almost provides a critical commentary on their nature and function, it would seem absurd to deny them the status of premier works of art, as some scholars have done.

Many of these temples display a high standard of execution. Evaluation of their style is a personal matter and will not lead to a consensus. Preserved works may not be the greatest of their day, sited as they are deep in the provinces. Parts of some are incompetent in execution (cf. Sauneron 1975, v), while the largely lost works of the early Ptolemaic Period are of a standard of craftsmanship seldom seen later, in a style more akin to those of earlier times and especially of the fourth century BCE (e.g. material excavated from the forecourt at Edfu and now visible there; temple of Isis at Behbeit el-Hagar: Favard-Meeks 1991). Their strongly developing style emphasizes the three-dimensionality of figures. Within this tendency, striking examples of surface treatment can be found, both at a small scale, as with details of plumage on cult figures of *ba* birds (Chassinat and Daumas 1947-42, pls.337-8) and a falcon (in limestone and not sandstone: ibid., pl.435; Cauville 1990, 59) in crypts at Dendara, and at a larger scale with the development of royal kilts into encapsulated smiting scenes (e.g. Vandersleyen et al. 1975, pl. 324). On the enclosure walls at Kom Ombo, a colossal figure of the king exhibits a rendering of the stretched toes of a foot on tiptoe that exploits the almost three-dimensional scale to create a new schematic form (no published photograph). In the temples, colours and the use of colour were (almost all of it has gone) innovative and displayed a lighter palette, as well as a complex, proliferating symbolism that cannot easily be paralleled from earlier. An example among many is the occurrence of the forms of both the white and the red crowns coloured blue (Kom Ombo, forecourt; Edfu, birth house): these cannot be dismissed as chance aberrations and surely display a symbolism comparable to the frequent cases where the offerings named in scenes are different from those depicted but complementary with them.

The point at issue here is not finally any superficial elegance or attractiveness - or even complexity and stylistic inventiveness - of these temples, any more than it is at issue for the colossi of Min from Koptos. With their presence, the colossi give authority to the idea of the temple and set a framework for its developing artistic significance. The distinctive and overwhelming strength of the Graeco-Roman temples is in their conceptual design and iconography. Their frieze decoration, to take one element, is incomparably rich and varied (Kurth 1994b addresses only a part of this), while their cosmography is remarkably intricate. They are creations addressed primarily to the gods, but also to the knowledgeable circle who had access to them, no doubt including access to the designs as they were being elaborated and to the scaffolding from which the carving and painting were executed. The scale of the decoration is generally not large, especially in interiors, allowing a huge amount of content to be incorporated but not proclaiming that content at a distance. Except by virtue of their overall dimensions, their broad architectural features, and some exterior reliefs, the temples do not speak to a large audience, and this recherché quality is one of their principal characteristics, seen most evidently in the vastly elaborated script in which very few can have been literate.

An instance of this ambivalence in respect of audience is the great outer court on the island of Philae, which dates in its current form to the reign of Augustus and could have been influenced by public spaces outside native Egypt (although it had some sort of predecessor on the site). While an obvious source of inspiration would be in public spaces in the Hellenistic world, there are points of comparison with the layout of Musawwarat el-Sufra and its Great Enclosure in the Sudan (e.g. W Adams 1977, 318-21, pl. XIIIa; Hintze and Hintze 1967, pls. 104-8). The court was evidently accessible to visitors, who came to Philae from great distances, including the Sudan. This unfinished complex may be indicative of what were the limits of Egyptian temple design, and of the dialectic of public and accessible as against consecrated and restricted.

The partial insulation of Graeco-Roman Period temples from the society of the period is visible in their cultivation of complexity in seeming oblivion of audience - something that can be paralleled in works of art of many civilizations and exemplifies the social and indeed cosmological ambivalence of high-cultural products even when they penetrate to small-scale, local monuments, as they did in Egypt (cf. Baines and Yoffee, in press). It has an evident correlate in the availability of funds provided by central government or local elites (or a combination of the two) which built them and may have tempered the obligations of temple personnel toward local populations, perhaps finally contributing, together with many other factors, to the demise of the temples as institutions (for all these questions, see Frankfurter, in press). The general political and administrative development of the Roman Period, which favoured Hellenized elites over native ones (Bowman and Rathbone 1992), must have played a part in this process. Here, the increased evidence from the 3rd century on of elite participation in Hellenistic/Roman building projects may form part of the background to the cessation of building on native temples after about 250 CE (Bowman 1992). For this interpretation to be valid, it must be assumed at the least that local elites tended to channel central benefactions in particular directions - which is likely to be true in any case. Perhaps it was a combination of elite Hellenization and reduction in central and local funds that resulted in there being hardly any further construction in native temples, even though such native institutions as the Buchis Bull in Armant survived with their hieroglyphic inscriptions well into the mid fourth century (Grenier 1983).

Yet some of the strongest evidence for the importance of the native temples comes from the latest period - probably the 4th–6th centuries CE - and takes the form of the mutilation of their figures, something they underwent to a greater extent than earlier temples that were standing and accessible at the time (I know of no detailed study; these remarks are based on general observation). This mutilation, which was mostly of the exposed flesh parts of publicly visible figures (inner areas were often attacked less), formed part of the deconsecration of the temples with the rise of Christianity. Many temples had churches built near them or within their complexes. Mutilation should be related to this proximity, to the enduring power of the temples of the old religion and of the sacred spaces where they were located. It is remarkable both in the amount of resources devoted to desecration, which must have involved erecting scaffolding over large areas, and in the knowledge and care involved in singling out the flesh for attack. At Philae again, where the cult was the last to be closed down, around 535 (e.g. Winter 1980, 1026), the mutilation of the colossal relief figures of Isis, the king, and some deities on the main pylon was particularly severe, in this case extending over the entire clothed body (Junker 1958, pl. II, for some reason done only to the west massif on the front, but to the entire width on the back: Lange and Hirmer 1968, pl. 269).

Thus, down to the end, after the latest dated hieroglyphic and even demotic inscription (394 and 452 respectively, both at Philae), this temple, no doubt together with its surrounding complex, was the leading participant in, and protagonist of, the ancient civilization, attracting visitors from far away in Nubia as well as from the surrounding area. Native Egyptian civilization had by then been pushed to the margins of the country and to support from the kingdoms of the post-Meroitic Ballana Culture in Lower Nubia. At that date as earlier, iconography of human and divine figures dominated the decoration and provided the focus of interest and concern, although they were integrated into the enriching cosmological textual schemas discussed above; it was therefore these figures that also suffered as the living residues of the cult itself were suppressed.

The figures and their architectural envelope also impressed across the cultural divide to the early Christian world, as well as being the focus of renewed interest in the revival of Egyptian forms and ultimately of ancient Egypt itself in the eighteenth and nineteenth centuries. Early Egyptologists approached this material more directly than their successors. Much of the content of the present essay is contained in essence in the studies of Maxence de Rochemonteix (1885), who spent a year living in the temple of Edfu during the 1870s (Maspero 1894, xxv-xxvi). Scholars took a century to regain his appreciation of the significance of Graeco-Roman temples. They may continue to underestimate the importance of early ones. I suggest that in the origins and formulation of Egyptian civilization, the temples were central participants. In acting as symbols and guarantors, they and the kingship formed the centres around which the complexity of civilization was embodied in a legitimate material and symbolic order. They looked to core schemas and meanings that were abstract, that repeatedly changed and were renewed through innovation and by reference to proximate and distant past models, and that created persuasive and pleasurable affirmations of order, which they maintained against the perpetual and ultimately inescapable threat of dissolution.

Note

This essay arises from my concluding remarks at the British Museum colloquium, which sought to complement the papers with additional considerations as well as addressing their topics directly. I develop an argument from a specific perspective rather than a commentary on the papers, which are not available to me in their final forms. The first main section carries forward discussions in Baines (1985, 41-62, 68-75; 1995, 108-21) and relates to Baines and Yoffee (in press). I do not document the general points reviewed in the first section because that would add little; the rest of the text is only lightly referenced. Essential information about most Egyptian temples is presented effectively by Arnold (1992). I have been able to incorporate little from the numerous recent conferences on temples.

I am grateful to audiences at the Institute of Fine Arts, New York, and at Emory University, Atlanta, for stimulating discussion of an intermediate version, to Vivian Davies for the invitation to the original colloquium, to David Frankfurter and Alan Bowman for comments on drafts, to Dana Reemes for making an article available before publication, and to Heinz-Josef Thissen and Ghislaine Widmer for help with references.

Bibliography

Adams, B 1974a. *Ancient Hierakonpolis.* Warminster, Aris & Phillips.

Adams, B1974b. *Ancient Hierakonpolis: supplement.* Warminster, Aris & Phillips.

Adams, W 1977. *Nubia: corridor to Africa.* London, Allen Lane.

Aldred, C 1980. *Egyptian art in the days of the pharaohs 3100–320 BC.* London, Thames & Hudson.

Alexanian, N 1995. The relief-decoration of King Khasekhemui from the so-called Fort at Hierakonpolis. In C Eyre (ed.), *Seventh International Congress of Egyptology, Cambridge, 3–9 September 1995: abstracts of papers*, 3. Oxford, Oxbow.

Alliot, M 1954. *Le culte d'Horus à Edfou au temps des Ptolémées*, fasc. 2. Bibliothèque d'Etude 20. Cairo, Institut Français d'Archéologie Orientale.

Argyros, A 1991. *A blessed rage for order: deconstruction, evolution, and chaos.* Ann Arbor, University of Michigan Press.

Arnold, D 1992. *Die Tempel Ägyptens: Götterwohnungen, Kultstätten, Baudenkmäler.* Zurich, Artemis & Winkler.

Asselberghs, H 1961. *Chaos en beheersing: documenten uit het aeneolitisch Egypte.* Documenta et Monumenta Orientis Antiqui 8. Leiden, E. J. Brill.

Assmann, J 1969. *Liturgische Lieder an den Sonnengott: Studien zur altägyptischen Hymnik* I. Münchner Ägyptologische Studien 19. Berlin, Bruno Hessling.

Assmann, J 1991a. *Stein und Zeit: Mensch und Gesellschaft im alten Ägypten.* Munich, Wilhelm Fink.

Assmann, J 1991b. Das ägyptische Prozessionsfest. In *Das Fest und das Heilige: religiöse Kontrapunkte zur Alltagswelt*, Jan Assmann and Theo Sundermeier (eds.), 105–22. Studien zum Verstehen Fremder Religionen 1. Gütersloh, Gerd Mohn.

Assmann, J 1992. *Das kulturelle Gedächtnis: Schrift, Erinnerung und politische Identität in frühen Hochkulturen.* Munich, C. H. Beck.
Baines, J 1973. The destruction of the pyramid temple of Sahure'. In *Göttinger Miszellen* 4, 9–14.
Baines, J 1985. *Fecundity figures: Egyptian personification and the iconology of a genre.* Warminster, Aris & Phillips; Chicago, Bolchazy Carducci.
Baines, J 1988. An Abydos list of gods and an Old Kingdom use of texts. In J Baines et al. (eds.), *Pyramid studies and other essays presented to I. E. S. Edwards,* 124–33. Occasional Publications 7. London, Egypt Exploration Society.
Baines, J 1989. Ancient Egyptian concepts and uses of the past: 3rd to 2nd millennium BC evidence. In R Layton (ed.), *Who needs the past? Indigenous values and archaeology,* 131–49. One World Archaeology. London, Unwin Hyman.
Baines, J 1990a. Restricted knowledge, hierarchy, and decorum: modern perceptions and ancient institutions. In *Journal of the American Research Center in Egypt* 27,1–23.
Baines, J 1990b. Trône et dieu: aspects du symbolisme royal et divin des temps archaïques. In *Bulletin de la Société Française d'Egyptologie* 118, 5–37.
Baines, J 1991. On the symbolic context of the principal hieroglyph for "god". In U Verhoeven and E Graefe (eds.), *Religion und Philosophie im alten Ägypten: Festgabe für Philippe Derchain zu seinem 65. Geburtstag am 24. Juli 1991,* 29–46. OLA 39.
Baines, J 1992. Merit by proxy: the biographies of the dwarf Djeho and his patron Tjaiharpta. In *Journal of Egyptian Archaeology* 78, 241–57.
Baines, J 1993. Symbolic aspects of canine figures on early monuments. In *Archéo-Nil* 3, 57–74.
Baines, J 1994a. On the status and purposes of ancient Egyptian art. In *Cambridge Archaeological Journal* 4, 69–95.
Baines, J 1994b. King, temple, and cosmos: an earlier model for framing columns in temple scenes of the Graeco-Roman Period. In Minas and Zeidler 1994, 26–33.
Baines, J 1995. Origins of Egyptian kingship. In David O'Connor and David P. Silverman (eds.), *Ancient Egyptian kingship,* Probleme der Ägyptologie 9, Leiden, E J Brill, 95–156.
Baines, J 1996. On the composition and inscription of the Vatican statue of Udjahorresne. In P Der Manuelian (ed.), *Studies in honor of William Kelly Simpson,* Boston, Department of Egyptian Art, Museum of Fine Arts, I, 83-92.
Baines, J , and N Yoffee, in press. Order, legitimacy, and wealth in ancient Egypt and Mesopotamia. In G Feinman and J Marcus (eds.), *Archaic states: a comparative perspective.* Santa Fe, SAR Press.
Bell, R 1972. "The blessed rage for order": studies in autobiography from Bunyan to Boswell. PhD dissertation, Harvard University.
Berlin 1989. *Ägyptisches Museum Berlin.* Berlin, Ägyptisches Museum SMPK.
Bianchi, R 1988. *Cleopatra's Egypt: age of the Ptolemies.* Exhibition catalogue, The Brooklyn Museum.
Björkman, G 1971. *Kings at Karnak: a study of the treatment of the monuments of royal predecessors in the early New Kingdom.* Boreas 2. Stockholm, Almqvist and Wiksell.
Bowman, A 1992. Public buildings in Roman Egypt. In *Journal of Roman Archaeology* 5, 495–503.
Bowman, A 1996. *Egypt after the pharaohs 332 BC-AD 642: from Alexander to the Arab conquest.* 2nd edition. London, British Museum Publications.
Bowman, A , and D Rathbone 1992. Cities and administration in Roman Egypt. In *Journal of Roman Studies* 82, 107–27.
Bresciani, E 1990. *Letteratura e poesia dell'antico Egitto.* 2nd edition. I Millenni. Turin, Giulio Einaudi.
Burkard, G, and H-W Fischer-Elfert 1994. *Ägyptische Handschriften* 4, Erich Lüddeckens (ed.). Verzeichnis der Orientalischen Handschriften in Deutschland 19.4. Stuttgart, Franz Steiner.
Cauville, S 1984. *Edfou.* Les Guides Archéologiques de l'Institut Français du Caire. Bibliothèque Générale 6. Cairo, Institut Français d'Archéologie Orientale.
Cauville, S 1988. Le panthéon d'Edfou à Dendera. In *Bulletin de l'Institut Français d'Archéologie Orientale au Caire* 88, 7–23.
Cauville, S 1990. *Le temple de Dendera: guide archéologique.* Les Guides Archéologiques de l'Institut

Français du Caire. Bibliothèque Générale 12. Cairo, Institut Français d'Archéologie Orientale.
Cauville, S 1992. Le temple d'Isis à Dendera. In *Bulletin de la Société Française d'Egyptologie* 123, 31–48.
Chassinat, E 1934. *Le temple d'Edfou* XIV. Mémoires publiés par les membres de la Mission Archéologique au Caire 31. Cairo, Institut Français d'Archéologie Orientale.
Chassinat, E 1935. *Le temple de Dendara* III. Cairo, Institut Français d'Archéologie Orientale.
Chassinat, E, and F Daumas 1947–52. *Le temple de Dendara* V. Cairo, Institut Français d'Archéologie Orientale.
Chassinat, E, and F Daumas 1965. *Le temple de Dendara* VI. Cairo, Institut Français d'Archéologie Orientale.
Copenhaver, B 1992. *Hermetica.* Cambridge, Cambridge University Press.
Cruz-Uribe, E 1986. The Hibis Temple Project: 1984–85 field season, preliminary report. In *Journal of the American Research Center in Egypt* 23, 157–66.
Cruz-Uribe, E 1987. Hibis Temple Project: preliminary report, 1985–1986 and summer 1986 field seasons. In *Varia Aegyptiaca* 3, 215–30.
Daumas, F 1958. *Les mammisis des temples égyptiens.* Annales de l'Université de Lyon III: Lettres 32. Paris, Les Belles Lettres.
Daumas, F 1969. *Dendara et le temple d'Hathor: notice sommaire.* Institut Français d'Archéologie Orientale au Caire, Recherches d'Archéologie, de Philologie et d'Histoire 29. Cairo, Institut Français d'Archéologie Orientale.
Davis, W 1989. *The Canonical Tradition in Ancient Egyptian Art.* Cambridge, Cambridge University Press.
Derchain, P 1962. Le rôle du roi d'Egypte dans le maintien de l'ordre cosmique. In L de Heusch et al., *Le pouvoir et le sacré*, 61–73. Annales du Centre d'Etude des Religions 1. Université Libre de Bruxelles, Institut de Sociologie. Brussels.
Derchain, P 1987. *Le dernier obélisque.* Brussels, Fondation Egyptologique Reine Elisabeth.
Derchain, P 1989. A propos de performativité: pensers anciens et articles récents. In *Göttinger Miszellen* 110, 13–18.
Derchain, P 1990. L'auteur du Papyrus Jumilhac. In *Revue d'Egyptologie* 41, 9–30.
Derchain, P, in press. La différence abolie: dieu et pharaon dans les scènes rituelles ptolémaïques. In R Gundlach and C Raedler (eds.), *Selbstverständnis und Relaität: Akten des Sympsosiums zur ägyptischen Königsideologie, Mainz 15.-17.6.1995.* Ägypten und Altes Testament 36. Wiesbaden, Harrassowitz.
Dreyer, G 1986. *Elephantine VIII: Der Tempel der Satet, die Funde der Frühzeit und des Alten Reiches.* Deutsches Archäologisches Institut Abteilung Kairo, Archäologische Veröffentlichungen 39. Mainz am Rhein, Philipp von Zabern.
Dreyer, G 1995. Die Datierung der Min-Statuen aus Koptos. In *Kunst des Alten Reiches: Symposium im Deutschen Archäologischen Institut Kairo am 29. und 30. Oktober 1991*, 49–56. Deutsches Archäologisches Institut Abteilung Kairo, Sonderschrift 28. Mainz am Rhein, Philipp von Zabern.
Dreyer, G et al. 1993. Umm el-Qaab: Nachuntersuchungen im frühzeitlichen Königsfriedhof, 5./6. Vorbericht. In *Mitteilungen des Deutschen Archäologischen Instituts Abteilung Kairo* 49, 23–62.
Dunham, D 1970. *The Barkal temples.* Boston, Museum of Fine Arts.
Emery, W 1938. *The tomb of Hemaka.* Excavations at Saqqara. Cairo, Government Press.
Emery, W 1949–58. *Great tombs of the First Dynasty.* 3 vols. Service des Antiquités de l'Egypte, Excavations at Saqqara. Cairo: Government Press/London, Egypt Exploration Society.
Engelbach, R 1934. A foundation scene of the Second Dynasty. In *Journal of Egyptian Archaeology* 20, 183–4.
Epigraphic Survey, the 1940. *Festival scenes of Ramses III.* Medinet Habu IV. Oriental Institute Publications 51. Chicago, University of Chicago Press.
Erman, A, and H Grapow 1950. *Wörterbuch der ägyptischen Sprache* VI *Deutsch–ägyptisches Wörterverzeichnis.* Berlin, Akademie-Verlag; Leipzig, J C Hinrichs.
Fakhry, A et al. 1982. *Denkmäler der Oase Dachle, aus dem Nachlass bearbeitet von* Jürgen Osing et al. Deutsches Archäologisches Institut Abteilung Kairo, Archäologische Veröffentlichungen 28. Mainz

am Rhein, Philipp von Zabern.
Finkenstaedt, E 1985. On the life-span of Decorated Ware of the Gerzean period. In *Zeitschrift für Ägyptische Sprache und Altertumskunde* 112, 17–19.
Firth, C, and J Quibell 1935. *The Step Pyramid.* 2 vols. Service des Antiquités de l'Egypte, Excavations at Saqqara. Cairo, Institut Français d'Archéologie Orientale.
Fowden, G 1986. *The Egyptian Hermes: a historical approach to the late pagan mind.* Cambridge, Cambridge University Press. 2nd ed. Princeton, Princeton University Press 1993.
Frandsen, P 1989. Trade and cult. In G Englund (ed.), *The religion of the ancient Egyptians: cognitive structures and popular expressions*, Boreas 20. Stockholm, Almqvist & Wiksell, 95–108.
Frandsen, P (ed.) 1991. *Demotic texts from the collection. The Carlsberg Papyri* 1. Carsten Niebuhr Institute Publications 15. Copenhagen, Museum Tusculanum Press.
Frankfurter, D T 1994. The cult of the martyrs in Egypt before Constantine: the evidence of the Coptic Apocalypse of Elijah. In *Vigiliae Christianae* 48, 25–47.
Frankfurter, D, in press. *The armor of Horus: persistence and transformation in religion in Roman Egypt.* Princeton, Princeton University Press.
Frandsen, P forthcoming. *The armor of Horus: persistence and transformation in Egyptian religion of the Roman period.* Princeton, Princeton University Press.
Friedman, F 1995. The underground relief panels of King Djoser at the Step Pyramid complex. In *Journal of the American Research Center in Egypt* 32, 1–42.
Friedman, R 1996. The ceremonial centre at Hierakonpolis Locality HK29A. In J Spencer (ed.), *Aspects of early Egypt*, 16–35. London, British Museum Press.
Gabra, S et al. 1941. *Rapport sur les fouilles d'Hermoupolis ouest (Touna el-Gebel).* Université Fouad Ier. Cairo, Institut Français d'Archéologie Orientale.
Gardiner, A et al. 1952. *The inscriptions of Sinai* I: *Introduction and plates.* London, Egypt Exploration Society
Gauthier, P, and B Midant-Reynes 1995. La tête de massue du roi Scorpion. In *Archéo-Nil* 5, 87–127.
Graefe, E 1995. Das Stundenritual in thebanischen Gräbern der Spätzeit (über den Stand der Arbeit an der Edition). In Jan Assmann et al. (eds.), *Thebanische Beamtennekropolen: neue Perspektiven archäologischer Forschung; Internationales Symposion Heidelberg 9.–13.6.1993*, 85–93. Studien zur Archäologie und Geschichte Altägyptens 12. Heidelberg, Heidelberger Orientverlag.
Grenier, J-C 1983. La stèle du dernier Taureau Bouchis (Caire JE 31901 = Stèle *Bucheum* 20) Ermant—4 novembre 340. In *Bulletin de l'Institut Français d'Archéologie Orientale au Caire* 83, 197–208.
Griffith, F 1922. Oxford excavations in Nubia - *continued.* In *Liverpool Annals of Archaeology and Anthropology* 9, 67–124.
Griffith, F, and W M F Petrie 1889. *Two hieroglyphic papyri from Tanis.* Egypt Exploration Fund, Extra Memoir. London, Trübner.
Grimm, A 1989. Altägyptische Tempelliteratur: zur Gliederung und Funktion der Bücherkataloge von Edfu und et-Tôd. In S Schoske (ed.), *Akten des vierten Internationalen Ägyptologenkongresses München 1985* 3, Studien zur Altägyptischen Kultur, Beiheft 3, 159–69.
Guglielmi, W 1982. Personifikation. In W Helck and W Westendorf (eds.), *Lexikon der Ägyptologie* IV, Wiesbaden, Otto Harrassowitz, 978–87.
Gutbub, A 1973. *Textes fondamentaux de la théologie de Kom Ombo.* 2 vols. Bibliothèque d'Etude 47. Cairo, Institut Français d'Archéologie Orientale.
Haeny G 1985. A short architectural history of Philae. In *Bulletin de l'Institut Français d'Archéologie Orientale au Caire* 85, 197–233.
Helck, W 1972. Zur Frage der Entstehung der ägyptischen "Literatur". In *Wiener Zeitschrift für die Kunde des Morgenlandes* 63/64, 6–26.
Hintze, F, and U Hintze 1967. *Alte Kulturen im Sudan.* Munich, Callwey.
Hölbl, G 1994. *Geschichte des Ptolemäerreiches: Politik, Ideologie und religiöse Kultur von Alexander dem Grossen bis zur römischen Eroberung.* Darmstadt, Wissenschaftliche Buchgesellschaft.
Hoffman, M 1986. *The predynastic of Hierakonpolis: An interim report to the National Endowment for the Humanities on Predynastic Research at Hierakonpolis.*
Hornung, E 1971. Politische Planung und Realität im alten Ägypten. In *Saeculum* 22, 48-58.

Hornung, E 1982. *Conceptions of god in ancient Egypt: the one and the many.* Trans. John Baines. Ithaca, Cornell University Press; London, Routledge 1983.
Insley Green, C 1987. *The temple furniture from the sacred animal necropolis at North Saqqâra 1964–1976.* Egypt Exploration Society, Memoir 53. London, Egypt Exploration Society.
Junker, H 1955. *Gîza* XII. Österreichische Akademie der Wissenschaften, Philosophisch-historische Klasse, Denkschriften, 75.2. Vienna, Rudolf M. Rohrer.
Junker, H 1958. *Der grosse Pylon des Tempels der Isis in Philä.* Österreichische Akademie der Wissenschaften, Philosophisch-historische Klasse, Denkschriften, Sonderband. Vienna, Rudolf M. Rohrer.
Kaiser, W et al. 1982. Stadt und Tempel von Elephantine: Neunter/Zehnter Grabungsbericht. In *Mitteilungen des Deutschen Archäologischen Instituts Abteilung Kairo* 39, 271–344.
Kemp, B 1989. *Ancient Egypt: anatomy of a civilization.* London, Routledge.
Kemp, B 1995. How religious were the ancient Egyptians? In *Cambridge Archaeological Journal* 5, 25–54.
Kozloff, A, B Bryan and L Berman 1992. *Egypt's Dazzling Sun: Amenhotep III and his world.* Exhibition catalogue. Cleveland, Cleveland Museum of Art; Indiana University Press.
Krauss, R 1994. Bemerkungen zum Narmer-Pavian (Berlin 22607) und seiner Inschrift. In *Mitteilungen des Deutschen Archäologischen Instituts Abteilung Kairo* 50, 223–30.
Kurth, D 1994a. *Treffpunkt der Götter: Inschriften aus dem Tempel des Horus von Edfu.* Zurich and Munich, Artemis.
Kurth, D 1994b. Die Friese innerhalb der Tempeldekoration griechisch-römischer Zeit. In Minas and Zeidler 1994, 191–201.
Lacau, P and J-P Lauer 1961–5. *La Pyramide à Degrés* IV–V. Service des Antiquités de l'Egypte, Fouilles à Saqqarah. Cairo, Institut Français d'Archéologie Orientale.
La'da, C 1994. One stone: two messages (CG 50044). In A Bülow-Jacobsen (ed.), *Proceedings of the 20th International Congress of Papyrologists, Copenhagen 23–29 August 1992*, 160–64. Copenhagen, Museum Tusculanum Press.
Lange, K, and M Hirmer 1968. *Egypt: architecture, sculpture, painting in three thousand years.* Trans. R. H. Boothroyd et al. 4th ed. London & New York, Phaidon.
Leahy, A 1992. Royal iconography and dynastic change 750–525 BC: the blue and cap crowns. In *Journal of Egyptian Archaeology* 78, 223–40.
Leahy, L 1988. *Private tomb reliefs of the Late Period from Lower Egypt.* Doctoral dissertation, University of Oxford.
Leclant, J 1965. *Recherches sur les monuments thébains de la XXVe dynastie dite éthiopienne.* 2 vols. Bibliothèque d'Etude 36. Cairo, Institut Français d'Archéologie Orientale.
Leclant, J, and G Clerc 1993. Fouilles et travaux en Egypte et au Soudan, 1991–1992. In *Orientalia* 62, 175–295.
Lichtheim, M 1980. *Ancient Egyptian literature: a book of readings* III: *The Late Period.* Berkeley etc., University of California Press.
Lefebvre, G 1923–4. *Le tombeau de Petosiris.* 3 vols. Service des Antiquités de l'Egypte. Cairo, Institut Français d'Archéologie Orientale.
Lowenthal, D 1985. *The past is a foreign country.* Cambridge, Cambridge University Press.
Macadam, M 1955. *The temples of Kawa* II: *History and archaeology of the site.* Oxford University Excavations in Nubia. 2 vols., text and plates. London, Geoffrey Cumberlege, Oxford University Press, for Griffith Institute, Oxford.
Mallet, D 1909. *Le Kasr el-Agoûz.* Mémoires publiés par les membres de l'Institut Françcais d'Archéologie Orientale 11.
Maspero, G 1894. Notice sur la vie de M. de Rochemonteix. In Rochemonteix, *Œuvres diverses* i–xxxix. Bibliothèque Egyptologique 3. Paris, Leroux.
Masri, Y 1983. Preliminary report on the excavations in Akhmim by the Egyptian Antiquities Organization. In *Annales du Service des Antiquités de l'Egypte* 69, 7–13.
Meeks, D 1972. *Le grand Texte des donations au temple d'Edfou.* Bibliothèque d'Etude 59. Cairo, Institut Français d'Archéologie Orientale.

Meeks-Favard, C 1991. *Le temple de Behbeit el-Hagara: essai de reconstitution et d'interprétation.* Studien zur Altägyptischen Kultur, Beiheft 6.
Minas, M, and J Zeidler (eds.) 1994. *Aspekte spätägyptischer Kultur: Festschrift Erich Winter zum 65. Geburtstag.* Aegyptiaca Treverensia 7. Mainz, Philipp von Zabern.
Morenz, S 1960. *Ägyptische Religion.* Die Religionen der Menschheit 8. Stuttgart, W. Kohlhammer. Trans. A Keep, *Egyptian religion.* London, Methuen 1973.
Müller, H 1964. *Ägyptische Kunstwerke, Kleinfunde und Glas in the Sammlung E. und M. Kofler-Truniger, Luzern.* Münchner Ägyptologische Studien 5. Berlin, Bruno Hessling.
Murnane, W, and F Yurco 1992. Once again the date of the New Kingdom pylon at Edfu. In R Friedman and B Adams (eds.), *The Followers of Horus: studies dedicated to Michael Allen Hoffman,* Egyptian Studies Association Publication 2, Oxbow Monograph 20, Oxford, Oxbow, 337–46.
O'Connor, D 1992. The status of early Egyptian temples: an alternative theory. In B Adams and R Friedman (eds.), *The Followers of Horus: studies in ancient Egypt dedicated to Michael Allen Hoffman,* 83–98. Oxford, Oxbow Books.
O'Connor, D in preparation. *City and cosmos in Ancient Egypt.* London, Athlone.
Otto, E 1954. *Die biographischen Inschriften der ägyptischen Spätzeit: ihre geistesgeschichtliche und literarische Bedeutung.* Problem der Ägyptologie 2. Leiden, Brill.
Otto, E 1964. *Gott und Mensch nach den ägyptischen Tempelinschriften der griechisch-römischen Zeit: Eine Untersuchung zur Phraseologie der Tempelinschriften.* Abhandlungen der Heidelberger Akademie der Wissenschaften 1964.1. Heidelberg, Carl Winter, Universitätsverlag.
Pantalacci, L and C Traunecker 1990. *Le temple d'el-Qal'a* I: *Relevés des scènes et des textes ... 1 à 112.* Cairo, Institut Français d'Archéologie Orientale.
Pantalacci, L and C Traunecker1993. Le temple d'el-Qal'a à Coptos: état des travaux. In *Bulletin de l'Institut Français d'Archéologie Orientale au Caire* 93, 379–90.
Payne, J 1993. *Catalogue of the predynastic Egyptian collection in the Ashmolean Museum.* Oxford, Clarendon Press.
Podemann Sørensen, J 1989. Divine access: the so-called democratization of funerary literature as a socio-cultural process. In G Englund (ed.), *The religion of the ancient Egyptians: cognitive structures and popular expressions,* Boreas 20. Stockholm, Almqvist & Wiksell, 109–25.
Priese, K-H et al. 1991. *Ägyptisches Museum.* Staatliche Museen zu Berlin, Preussischer Kulturbesitz. Mainz, Philipp von Zabern.
Quibell, J, and F Green 1902. *Hierakonpolis* II. Egyptian Research Account Memoir 5. London, Bernard Quaritch.
Reemes, D in press. The name "Plotinus". In *Lingua Aegyptia* 5.
Rochemonteix, M de 1885. Le temple égyptien. In *Revue Internationale de l'Enseignement* 7:2:19–38. Reprinted in *Œuvres diverses* 1–38. Bibliothèque Egyptologique 3, 1894. Paris, Leroux.
Roeder, G 1914. *Naos.* Catalogue Générale des Antiquités Égyptiennes du Musée du Caire Nr.70001-70050. Leipzig, Breitkopf & Härtel.
Roth, A 1991. *Egyptian phyles in the Old Kingdom: the evolution of a system of social organization.* Studies in Ancient Oriental Civilizations 48.
Sauneron, S 1952a. Les querelles impériales vues à travers les scènes du temple d'Esné. In *Bulletin de l'Institut Français d'Archéologie Orientale du Caire* 51, 111–21.
Sauneron, S 1952b. Le temple d'Akhmîm décrit par Ibn Jobair. In *Bulletin de l'Institut Français d'Archéologie Orientale au Caire* 51, 125–35.
Sauneron, S 1959. *Quatre campagnes à Esna.* Esna 1. Cairo, Institut Français d'Archéologie Orientale.
Sauneron, S 1975. *Le temple d'Esna Nos 473–546.* Esna VI:1. Cairo, Institut Français d'Archéologie Orientale.
Sayed, R el- 1975. *Documents relatifs à Saïs et ses divinités.* Bibliothèque d'Etude 69. Cairo, Institut Français d'Archéologie Orientale.
Schäfer, H 1902. *Ein Bruchstück altägyptischer Annalen.* Aus dem Anhang zu den Abhandlungen der Königlichen Preussischen Akademie der Wissenschaften zu Berlin. Berlin, Königliche Akademie der Wissenschaften.
Schloz, S 1994. Das Tempelbauprogramm der Ptolemäer: die Darstellung eines Rekonstruktionsprob-

lems. In R Gundlach and M Rochholz (eds.), *Ägyptische Tempel—Struktur, Funktion und Programm (Akten der ägyptologischen Tempeltagungen in Gosen 1990 und in Mainz 1992)*, Hildesheimer Ägyptologischer Beiträge 37, Hildesheim, Gerstenberg, 281–6.
Shore, A 1979. Votive objects from Dendera of the Graeco-Roman period. In J Ruffle et al. (eds.), *Glimpses of ancient Egypt: studies in honour of H. W. Fairman*, Warminster, Aris and Phillips, 138–60.
Smith, H, and W J Tait 1983. *Saqqara Demotic papyri* I. Texts from Excavations 7. London, Egypt Exploration Society.
Smith, M 1977. A new version of a well-known Egyptian hymn. In *Enchoria* 7, 115–49.
Smith, W S 1949. *A history of Egyptian sculpture and painting in the Old Kingdom*. 2nd edition. London, Oxford University Press for Museum of Fine Arts Boston.
Sternberg-el Hotabi, H 1994. Die 'Götterliste' des Sanktuars im Hibis-Tempel von El-Chargeh: Überlegungen zur Tradierung und Kodifizierung religiösen und kulttopographischen Gedankengutes. In Minas and Zeidler 1994, 239–54.
Stevens, W 1936. *Ideas of order*. New York, Alfred A. Knopf.
Stevens, W 1953. *Selected poems*. London, Faber & Faber.
Tait, W J 1977. *Papyri from Tebtunis in Egyptian and Greek (P. Tebt. Tait)*. Texts from Excavations 3. London, Egypt Exploration Society.
Thompson, D 1994. Egypt, 146–31 B.C. In J A Crook et al. (eds.), *Cambridge Ancient History* IX: *The last age of the Roman Republic, 146–31 B.C.*, 310–26. Cambridge, Cambridge University Press.
Tracy, D 1975. *Blessed rage for order: the new pluralism in theology*. New York, Seabury Press.
Van Siclen, C 1990. Preliminary report on epigraphic work done in the edifice of Amenhotep II, seasons of 1988–89 and 1989–90. In *Varia Aegyptiaca* 6, 75–90.
Vandersleyen, C et al. 1975. *Das alte Ägypten*. Propyläen Kunstgeschichte 15. Berlin, Propyläen.
Vandier, J [1961]. *Le Papyrus Jumilhac*. [Paris], Centre National de la Recherche Scientifique.
Vassilika, E 1989. *Ptolemaic Philae*. Orientalia Lovaniensia Analecta 34. Leuven, Peeters.
Williams, B 1988. Narmer and the Coptos colossi. In *Journal of the American Research Center in Egypt* 25, 35–59.
Willis, W 1979. The letter of Ammon of Panopolis to his mother. In *Actes du XVe Congrès International de Papyrologie* II: *Papyrus inédits*, Papyrological Bruxellensia 17, Brussels, Fondation Egyptologique Reine Elisabeth, 98–115.
Winter, E 1968. *Untersuchungen zu den ägyptischen Tempelreliefs der griechisch-römischen Zeit*. Österreichische Akademie der Wissenschaften, Philosophisch-historische Klasse, Denkschriften 98. Vienna, Hermann Böhlaus Nachfolger.
Winter, E 1976a. Der Herrscherkult in den ägyptischen Ptolemäertempeln. In H Maehler and V M Strocka (eds.), *Das ptolemäische Ägypten: Akten des internationalen Symposions 27.–29. September 1976 in Berlin*, Mainz, Philipp von Zabern, 147–60.
Winter, E 1976b. Die Tempel von Philae und das Problem ihrer Rettung. In *Antike Welt* 7.3, 3–15.
Winter, E 1980. Philae. In W Helck and W Westendorf (eds.), *Lexikon der Ägyptologie* IV, Wiesbaden, Otto Harrassowitz, 1022–7.
Winter, E n.d. Lecture on the gateway of Augustus from Kalabsha, in the Ägyptisches Museum Berlin, delivered at University College, London.
Winter, E 1994. Wer steht hinter Narmer? In M Bietak et al. (eds.), *Zwischen den beiden Ewigkeiten: Festschrift Gertrud Thausing*, Vienna, Institut für Ägyptologie der Universität, 279–90.
Wit, C de 1958–71. *Le temple d'Opet, à Karnak*. 3 vols. Bibliotheca Aegyptiaca 11–13. Brussels, Fondation Égyptologique Reine Élisabeth.
Wittkower, R 1962. *Architectural principles in the age of humanism*. 3rd edition. London, Alec Tiranti.
Wolf, W 1957. *Die Kunst Ägyptens: Gestalt und Geschichte*. Stuttgart, W Kohlhammer.
Wood, W 1978. A reconstruction of the reliefs of Hesy-re. In *Journal of the American Research Center in Egypt* 15, 9–24.
Zivie, C, with Y Hamed Hanafi 1981–6. *Le temple de Deir Chelouit*. 3 vols. Cairo, Institut Français d'Archéologie Orientale.

ERRATUM

THE TEMPLE IN ANCIENT EGYPT
New Discoveries and Recent Research
Edited by Stephen Quirke

ISBN 0-7141-0993-2

The publishers regret that Plates 39d and 44d have been incorrectly printed. They are reproduced in their entirety below.

Plate 39d. Bronze falcons on boxes found in caches at Hepnebes. The boxes, in some cases closed by a sliding panel, were designed to receive a papyrus or mummified fauna.

Plate 44d. Scene with Isis on the façade of the sanctuary at Shenhur, now lost.

THE PLATES

a. Valley temple of Snofru at Dahshur.

b. Northern pyramid of Snofru at Dahshur. Excavation at the East Side. Area of the Pyramid Temple.

a. Northern pyramid of Snofru at Dahshur. Walls and foundations of the pyramid temple.

b. Northern pyramid of Snofru at Dahshur. Pyramid temple, walls reinforced.

a. Northern pyramid of Snofru at Dahshur. Pyramidion.

b. Northern pyramid of Snofru at Dahshur. Relief fragment from the pyramid temple.

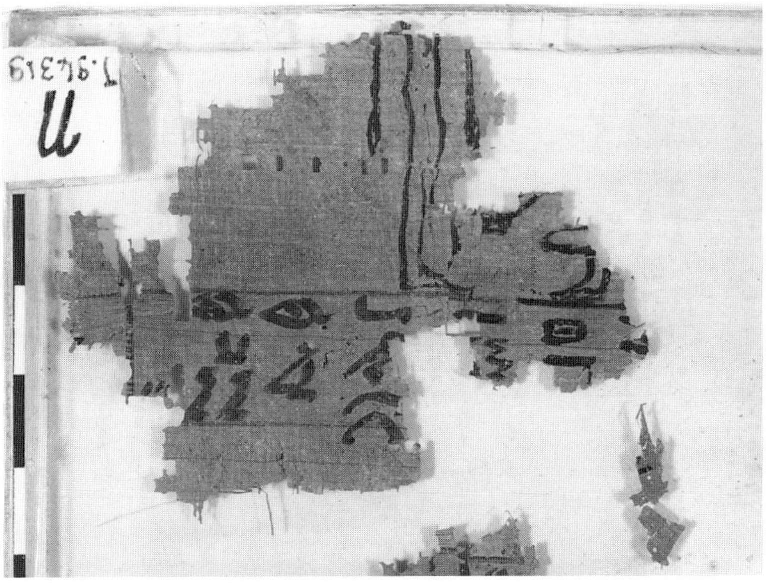

Papyrus fragments from the temple of queen Khentkaus at Abusir:

a. *above* Standing figure of a queen with 'eyebrows and eyes of k33-stone'.

b. *left* Standing queen (*below*); description of shrine with figures of lapis and gold (*above*).

c. Faience fragments from the temple of Khentkaus at Abusir, including a throned queen.

a. Hathor in the arbor with the deities who govern the days of the year advancing, led by *akhet* I,1 and *peret* III,1. Line drawing after Leitz 1989, 21.

b–e. Clepsydra of Amenhotep III, Cairo Temp. no. 2/12/26/17.

b.

c.

d.

e.

a. Thutmose III adoring the gods governing the day and night hours, with the solar bark in the centre of the lunette. Line drawing after Ricke 1939.

b. Amenhotep III in the solar bark towed like the sun-god during the first *sed*, as depicted in the tomb-chapel of Kheruef, TT 192. Line drawing after the Epigraphic Survey 1980.

W 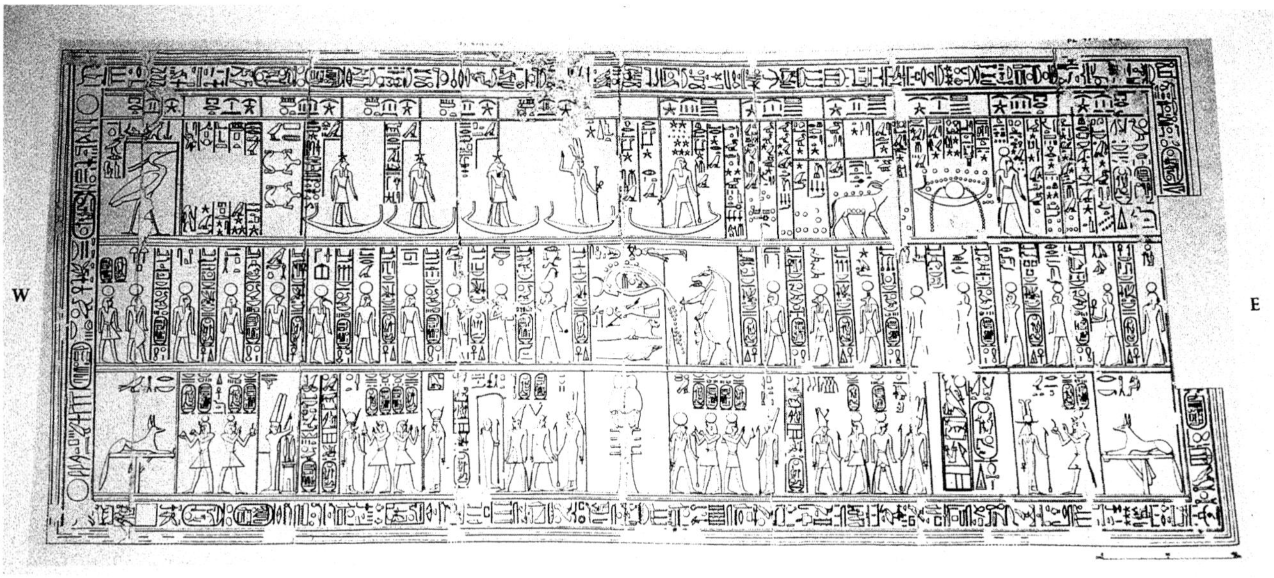 E

a. Astronomical ceiling of Ramses II, from the Ramesseum. After Neugebauer and Parker 1969, pl. 5.

b. Detail of the astronomical ceiling of Senenmut from TT 353, showing the crocodile-lion sphinx deity.

a. Head from Cat. 1 of the king wearing sun disc, Cairo JE 54477.

b. Cat. 2: Recarved dyad of the king with Ptah Tatenen, from Memphis, Cairo CG 554.

Cat. 5: Statue of Ptah, Medinet Habu.

a. *above left* Cat 6: Two colossal seated royal figures, Kom el Heitan.

b. *above right* Base with nome procession, Medinet Habu, possibly for one of the colossi, Cat. 6.

c. Cat. 7: Base of statue of Osiris the Great Saw, lord of the *sed*, Medinet Habu.

Cat. 9: Mummiform god, from Sheikh Abada, Cairo Temp. no. 7/3/45/2.

Cat. 10: Mummiform god, from Sheikh Abada, Cairo JE 89616.

a. Cat. 16: Face of an unidentified god, from the temple of Merenptah, BM EA 69053.

b. Cat. 17: Unidentified god, Kom el Heitan.

Cat. 24: Nephthys statue from Herakleopolis, Louvre E 25389.

a. Cat. 25: Base of statue of Maat, from Thebes, BM EA 91.

b. Cat. 26: Base of statue of Weret-Hekaw, Cairo N127.

a. *above* Cat. 27: Goddess, perhaps Isis, from Coptos, Turin 694.

b. *below* Cat. 28: Unidentified goddess, Marseilles 206.

a.

a–b. Cat. 29: Statue of king with Asbet, (a) front and (b) inscribed back.

b.

Cat. 30: Serpent of Hor-Khent-Khety, from Athribis, Cairo Temp. no. 30/10/26/9.

Cat. 32: Statue of Thoth, from Sheikh Abada, Cairo Temp. no. 7/3/45/1.

a. *above* Cat. 33: Base of statue of Khnum, Medinet Habu.

b. *below* Cat. 35: Statue of a ram-headed god, from Karnak, Cairo CG 38500.

a.

a–b. Cat. 36: Soul of Nekhen, from Karnak, Cairo JE 41211, now in Beni Suef Museum.

b.

a. *above* Cat. 38: Base of statue of Horus Maa-kheru, Dendera (photograph Robert Morkot).

b. Cat. 39: Falcon-headed god, from Sheikh Abada, Cairo JE 89615. Profile view showing rounded shoulders and slightly bulging paunch characteristic of statuary of Amenhotep III.

Cat. 40: Falcon-headed god, originally with sun disc atop head, from Tanis, Cairo JE 37485.

a. *above* Cat. 41: Falcon deity, Cairo, no registration number.

b. Cat. 42: Falcon-headed god, from Rome, Munich WÄF 22.

a.

b.

a–b. Cat. 46: Soul of Nekhen, from Karnak, Cairo JE 41210, now in Beni Suef Museum.

a. Cat. 47: Anubis enthroned, Copenhagen Ny Carlsberg Glyptothek AEIN 33.

b. Cat. 48: Jackal-headed god, from Tanis, Cairo CG 38517.

a.

a–b. Head from Cat. 49: recumbent jackal deity, BM EA 64400.

b.

a.

a–b. Cat. 50: Jackal head, Smith College 1970.19.

b.

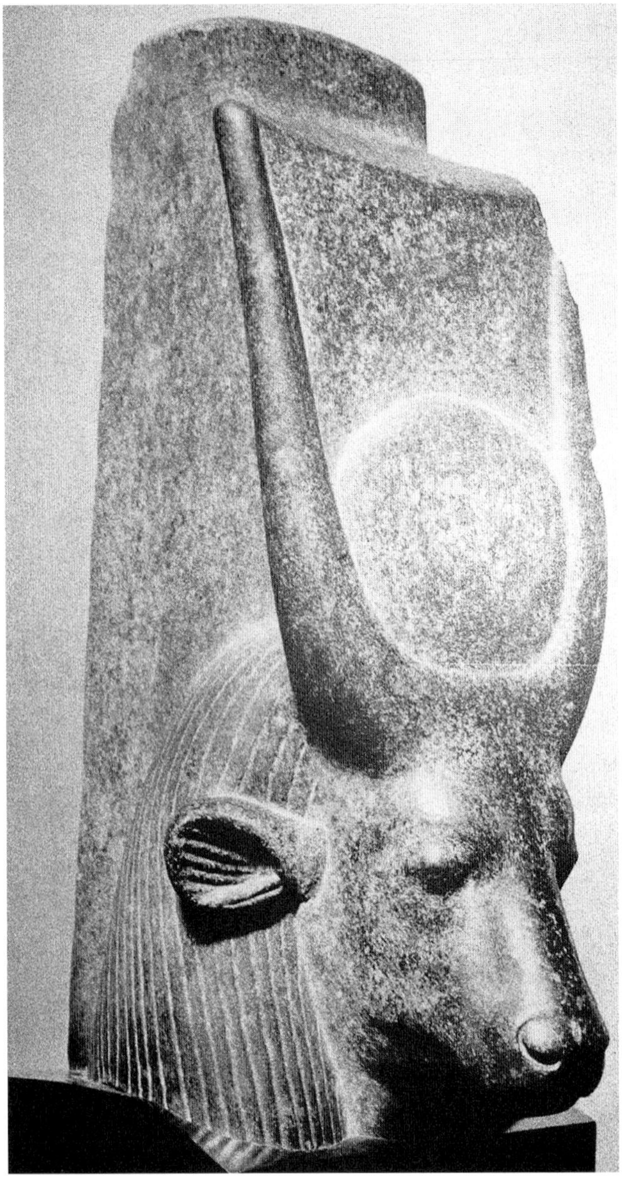

a. Cat. 51: Cow-headed goddess, from Thebes, MMA 19.2.5.

b. *above* Cat. 52: Bull-headed god, Vatican Museum 22808.

c. *left* Cat. 53: Base of statue of Bastet, Cairo, no registration number.

Traces of the doubling of the processional way, Serabit el-Khadim.

a.

a–b. The northern and main entrances at Serabit el-Khadim (a) before and (b) after consolidation.

b.

The portico of the Hathor speos, Serabit el-Khadim.

a. General view of the temple at Behbeit el-Hagara, showing one of the heaps of blocks.

b. The fragmentary evidence of an alleged *dromos* of Nectanebo II.

c. The left wing of the entrance façade.

d. One of the few blocks of the right wing. In the dedicatory inscription Berenice II (whose name is mentioned on another block) is said to have made monuments for her mother and to have renewed her house. *below* The top of the third register where Osiris is described as the "Great 'Prince' in the Chapel of the Prince".

a. A view of the columned hall and staircase at Behbeit el-Hagara.

b. The many blocks of the staircase.

c. From the columned hall, a view of the left wing of the façade of the Isis sanctuary.

d. The lintel of the entrance to the Isis sanctuary.

a. The first register of the south wall of the Isis sanctuary. The block shows the king censing the bark of Isis.

b. From the northern corridor, the king introducing a Nile procession to 'Isis the great, divine mother, mistress of Hebyt, Eye of Rê, mistress of the sky, queen of all the gods'. The block marks the north-east corner of the Isis sanctuary.

c. From the Chapel of the 'Prince', the first register of the axial wall. On each side of the axis Osiris is offered, on the left, the *Wesekh*-collar and, on the right, the '*Wedja*-pectoral for protection'. In the following offering scene, Nut receiving milk is called 'the one who gave birth to the gods and who saves her son Osiris in the Chapel of the Prince'. Photo Fauvel, Guide Bleu.

d. From the Chapel of Osiris-*Res-wedja*, the Nile procession reaching the central inscribed panel, then half buried.

a. Blocks from the High House. This chapel gathers together many different gods. They have the specific function of protecting Osiris' body variously described (remains, body, flesh, statue). On the block in the background the jackal-headed god is a compound figure of Anubis and Harsiesis.

b–c. Blocks from the Chapel of Osiris-*Hemag*,
(b) one representation of Osiris as found on all the fragments of this chapel. In this chapel the type of offering is not always indicated; see the king on the right.
(c) A very fragmentary example of the top register belonging to the series of seated divinities which probably ran continuously around the room.

d. A block ascribed to the hypothetical 'Divine (place)'.

a. Anubieion: painted mud-statue group of Bes and female companion on the east wall of one of the 'Bes-chambers'.

b. Sacred Animal Necropolis precinct at Hepnebes: brick entrance ramp and west gate from the west, with central temple on the terrace beyond.

c. Hepnebes: miniature double-stairway in central temple courtyard (fig. 4a), with kiosk, second pylon and sanctuary beyond.

d. Hepnebes: sanctuary of central temple (fig. 4, shrine a), looking west from the cliff above.

a. Hepnebes: stairway and gate (fig. 4d), north of central temple, with entrance to a tomb re-used for cow burials in the background.

b. Hepnebes: in the foreground, the sacred way and stairway (fig. 4b) in the Baboon complex from the south, with central temple courtyard and stairway (figs. 4a and 4d).

c. Hepnebes: Baboon complex from the west. From left to right: stairway, gate and brick chapel (fig. 4b); chapel with ornamental façade; gate (fig. 4c) with *dromos* and entrance to Baboon catacomb.

d. Hepnebes: Baboon chapel with ornamental façade, gate (fig. 4c), *dromos* and entrance to Baboon catacomb.

a. Hepnebes: the western portion of the main temple precinct during excavation, where caches of dedicatory figurines were found below the removed terrace pavement.

b. *above right* Bronze altars and offering- or incense-stands, found in Cache 9 from Gallery 16 of the Falcon catacomb, Hepnebes.

c. *right* Bronze statuette of Harpokrates wearing ram-horns and *hemhemet*-crown, with dedicatory inscription on the base; from Hepnebes.

d. Bronze falcons on boxes found in caches at Hepnebes. The boxes, in some cases closed by a sliding panel, were designed to receive a papyrus or mummified fauna.

a. The west side of BM EA 1512.

b. The east side of BM EA 1512.

a. The north side of BM EA 1512.

b. The south side of BM EA 1512.

a.

b.

a–c. The remains of the crowning falcon on the top of the 'gabled-roof' of BM EA 1512, (a) from the south side, (b) from the south-east corner, and (c) from the east side.

c.

a. View of Shenhur temple and the mosque from the south-west (P. Dils, October 1991).

b. General view of Shenhur temple from the minaret (P. Dils, June 1994).

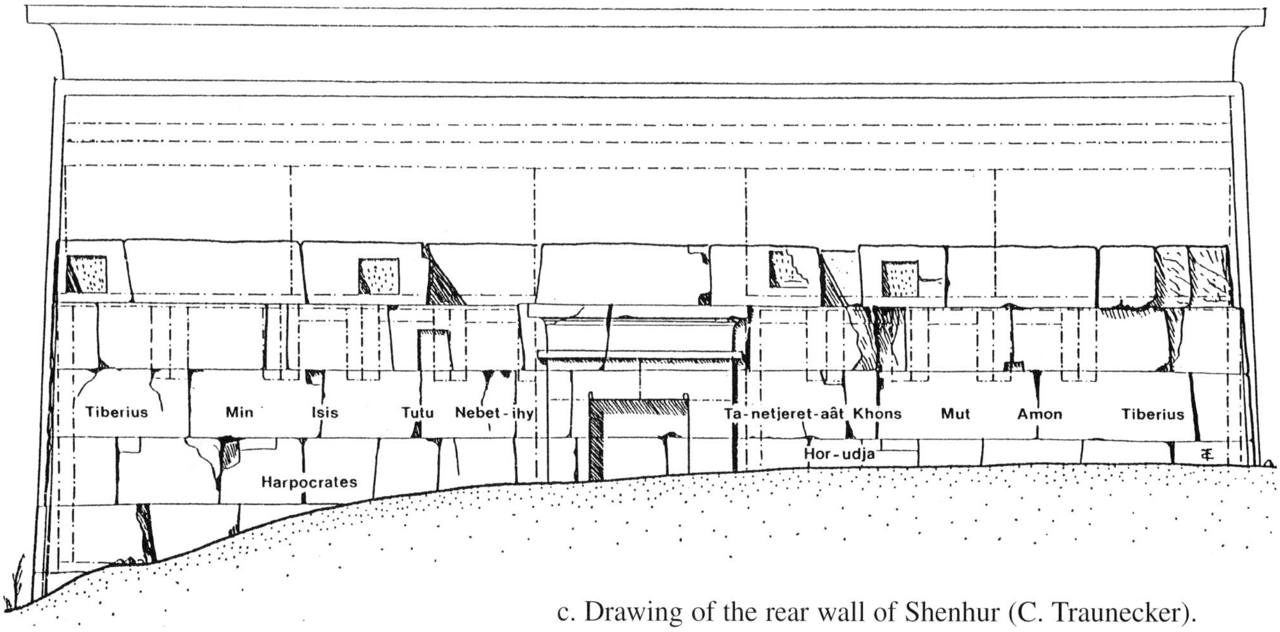

c. Drawing of the rear wall of Shenhur (C. Traunecker).

a. Hymn addressed to Claudius, copied by Nestor L'Hôte at Shenhur (1839).

b. Block of the 'bandeau de frise' on the eastern outer wall of Shenhur temple.

c. *left* Detail from the eastern outer wall of Shenhur temple showing the emperor Claudius.

d. *right* Scene with Isis on the façade of the sanctuary at Shenhur, now lost.

a. North part of the corridor at Shenhur before the excavation.

b. North part of the corridor at Shenhur after the excavation with entrance to the crypts.

c. Shenhur ceiling block tackled up.

d. View of Shenhur sanctuary during protection work.

a. View of the wabet at Shenhur.

b. *below* Remains of lime production at Shenhur.

c. *right* Shenhur: rick floor with hole where the wall is lacking.

d. West corner of the chapel of Hor-udja at Shenhur.

'Slaying the Crocodile', Temple of Edfu, exterior of Naos, Edfu IV, 211,8-213,4 (photograph by S.R. Snape).

a. Golden quartzite lintel of Senusret III, BM EA 145.

b. White quartzite lintel of Senusret III, BM EA 74753.

a. View of the mortuary temple of Amenhotep III at Kom el Heitan, from the south-west, showing cat. 55 in the mud.

c. Fragments of mortuary temple statuary in red and black granitic stones, calcite and quartzite, on the surface at Kom el Heitan.

b. View of the mortuary temple of Amenhotep III, taken from Qurnet Murai to the west.

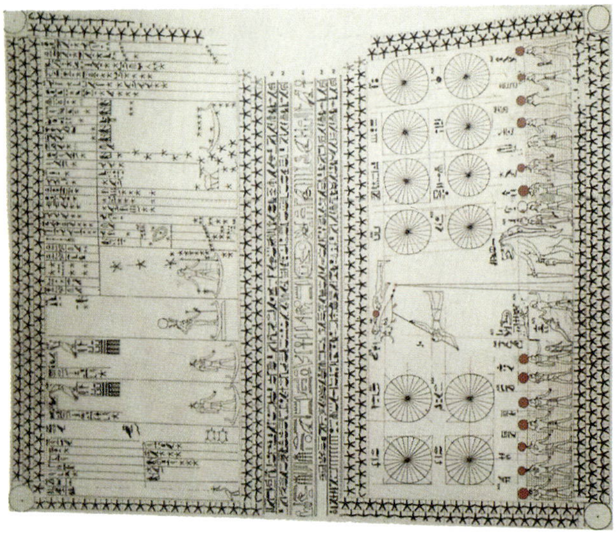

d. Astronomical ceiling of Senenmut from TT 353, showing four circles representing the pillars of heaven and enclosures of star bands. After Dorman 1991, pl. 85.

a. Statue of Sakhmet, MMA 15.8.2.

b. Cat. 1: King with sun disc, with a goddess, at Medinet Habu.

a. Cat 4: Sakhmet, Amenhotep III, Amen and Amenet, at Kom el Heitan.

b. *below* Cat. 9: Seated mummiform god from Sheikh Abada; detail of head.
c. *right* Cat. 12: Unidentified god, University of Chicago Oriental Institute 10607.

d. Cat. 13: Unidentified god, De Young Museum 5466.

a. Cat. 31: King with sun disc, with a moon god, at Medinet Habu.

b. Cat. 39: Falcon god from Sheikh Abada, Cairo JE 89615

c. Cat. 54: Khepri as a scarab, Karnak.

d. Cat. 55: Crocodile-lion sphinx, Kom el Heitan.

a. A well-preserved example of a mudbrick temple in the eastern end of Dakhla (site no. 31/435–K3–1). The total length of the building is *c.* 30m.

c. The buried temple of Ain Birbiya in the eastern end of the Dakhla Oasis, as seen from the east, showing the outer gateway of Augustus.

b. *below* Overview of the remains of the stone temple of Tutu at Ismant el-Kharab, facing west, taken during the excavations.

a. The temple of Deir el-Haggar after the completion of clearance works in 1995. View from the north-east.

b. View taken during the excavations in 1995 of the western half of Shrine I at Ismant el-Kharab.

c. A section of the southern wall and vault of Shrine I at Ismant el-Kharab with the collapsed part of the vault lying *in situ* below.

a. The only section which did not collapse from the northern side of the vault of Shrine I, with the legs and arm of the figure of the goddess Nehmetaway, included in the reconstruction in fig. 1.

b. The gods of Deir el-Haggar: Amun-Ra, Khons and Mut, as depicted in the newly uncovered pronaos of Titus at Deir el-Haggar.